MARKET EFFICIENT CYCLE THEORY

www.royalcollins.com

MARKET EFFICIENT CYCLE THEORY

Construction, Empirical Study, and Application

By SONG YUCHEN

Translated by ZHANG CHAOHUI

Books Beyond Boundaries

ROYAL COLLINS

Market Efficient Cycle Theory: Construction, Empirical Study, and Application

By Song Yuchen
Translated by Zhang Chaohui

First published in 2024 by Royal Collins Publishing Group Inc.
Groupe Publication Royal Collins Inc.
BKM Royalcollins Publishers Private Limited

Headquarters: 550-555 boul. René-Lévesque O Montréal (Québec) H2Z1B1 Canada
India office: 805 Hemkunt House, 8th Floor, Rajendra Place, New Delhi 110 008

Arranged by China Renmin University Press

This book is sponsored by the Academic Translation Program of Jilin University.

ISBN: 978-1-4878-1244-7

To find out more about our publications, please visit www.royalcollins.com.

Contents

Preface

This book attempts to challenge major fundamental theoretical issues in finance; the research significance is self-evident. After more than years of dedicated research, I have tried to construct a new financial theory system based on questioning the research paradigm of modern Western finance, attempting to achieve breakthroughs in the study of financial theory. I am willing to discuss with colleagues in the industry and hope to make theoretical progress.

Firstly, there are contradictions and divergences in the modern Western finance research paradigm. There are apparent theoretical differences in modern Western finance, focusing on standard and behavioral finance research paradigms. The research paradigm of traditional finance proposes "rational people" and "risk-free arbitrage," while the research paradigm of behavioral finance suggests "bounded rationality" and "limited arbitrage." The emergence of such disagreements and their continued lack of resolution make us speculate from two aspects: these contradictions and conflicts cannot be resolved. On the other hand, the financial theory community has yet to find a breakthrough to solve the contradictions and differences between the two.

Secondly, the stagnation of the development of modern Western financial theory. A review of the development history of modern Western economic theory found that the golden period of financial growth was from the 1950s to the 1980s. Representative research achievements mainly include mean-variance models, capital asset pricing models, arbitrage pricing models, option pricing models, efficient market hypothesis, and various modified research results based on these theories and models. The financial view of this era did not deviate from the assumption of rational people. The pseudo truth of "bounded rationality" in behavioral finance, which attempts to explain the anomalies of standard finance theory based on the assumption of rational people from a psychological perspective, seems refreshing to the financial community. Its "bounded rationality" ideology has confused the logic of economic research. There is no difference between "bounded rationality" and "irrational." Negating the rational person hypothesis in behavioral finance has led financial analysis to deviate from the scientific track. The overthrow of the sensible person hypothesis is a pseudoscience, which not only overturns the theoretical foundation of finance but also overturns the basic assumptions of economics. The stagnation point of finance lies in negating the rational person hypothesis.

The main research content of this book can be summarized as follows:

(1) Propose and construct the theoretical ideas of the market efficient cycle and average rationality

The most significant innovation, in theory, is the attempt to construct a new theoretical system of finance based on questioning the research paradigm of modern Western finance. a) Construct market efficient cycle theory and resolve financial theoretical disagreements. The market efficient cycle theory is proposed and constructed by revising the efficient market hypothesis, the cornerstone of the contemporary Western economic approach. The fatal flaw of the efficient market hypothesis is to test the validity of time points, which means that securities prices reflect all information promptly and accurately at any given time point. This idealized constraint leaves the theory with significant flaws and significantly undermines its application value. The market is not effective at every point in time; it is only effective from a specific period; that is, there is an effective cycle. The so-called market efficiency cycle refers to the existence of a sufficiently long period that allows securities prices to reflect all information within that period fully, and the market is called an efficiency market. If we replace the "time point efficiency" of the efficient market hypothesis with "effective cycle (or period efficiency)," that is, there exists an effective cycle in the securities market. In theory, the large number of anomalies revealed by empirical research in behavioral finance only negates "point effectiveness" and does not negate "period effectiveness." If the "market efficiency" of the efficient market hypothesis is defined as the "effective cycle," it will solve the vast contradiction and divergence in this theory. The market efficient cycle theory can solve the controversies and disagreements in financial theory. b) Propose the idea of average rationality. It is not the "rational person" of standard finance, nor the "bounded rationality" of behavioral finance, but the "average rationality." The most significant limitation of behavioral finance theory is that it abandons the assumption of rational people, cannot form a unified and mature theoretical system, and provides rigorous explanations for various phenomena in the financial market. Investors should be neither rational people in standard finance nor bounded rational people in behavioral finance and should have reasonable characteristics on average, that is, average rationality. In response to the two hypotheses of "rational people" and "risk-free arbitrage" proposed by standard finance, behavioral finance offers "bounded rationality" and "limited arbitrage." We suggest two theoretical categories: "average rationality" and "long-term risk-free arbitrage."

(2) The application value of average rationality and market efficient cycle theory
From the applied perspective, we also propose the following innovative ideas: The market efficient cycle theory can scientifically explain the price discovery function of the capital market. The empirical method we use to test the relationship between average rationality and the mean effective cycle of the market is the mean reversion feature test. The mean is the intrinsic value of security, and returning to inherent value is the price discovery process. The market has the function of automatically correcting price deviation from intrinsic value; that is, when the securities price is higher or lower than intrinsic value, it will automatically update its pricing deviation. From a long-term perspective, stock prices that deviate from intrinsic value will return to their inherent value, playing the primary function of price discovery in the capital market. The market efficient cycle theory has crucial practical application value in scientifically explaining the price discovery function of the capital market. The market-effective cycle can provide a scientific basis for government behavior in the capital market. From the perspective of government regulation, the goal of government regulation of the capital market is to shorten the adequate period as much as possible. The shorter the effective period, the healthier the market, and the stronger the reaction function of the capital market to economic growth. The theory of the market efficient cycle has crucial practical application value in providing a scientific basis for government behavior in the capital market. The market efficiency cycle theory can deduce the matching process between the capital market and economic growth. The deviation between the securities price index reflecting changes in the capital market and the GDP growth rate reflecting changes in economic growth is only a temporary phenomenon, and the two must match each other for a sufficiently long period. The deviation between capital market trends and economic growth during a specific period is a normal phenomenon, and many empirical studies have shown that its main reason is the selection bias of sample intervals. The key to our research on this issue is not to test whether the two deviate but to determine which period they match. The shorter the matching period, the better the reflection effect of the capital market on economic growth. The longer the matching cycle, the worse the capital market's response to economic growth. The matching cycle theory between capital markets and economic growth has crucial practical application value for observing macroeconomic trends. The market efficient cycle is used to distinguish and analyze macro and micro insider trading, and how to promote the efficiency of information reflection in the stock market is studied. The market practical cycle theory can scientifically reveal the formation mechanism of systemic financial risks.

Since the existence of market-effective cycles is inevitable, mean reversion is unavoidable, but the time and speed of mean reversion are both stochastic. Rapid degeneration can lead to a sharp drop in securities prices in the short term and directly manifest as a financial crisis. The market efficient cycle theory has crucial practical application value in scientifically revealing the formation mechanism of systemic financial risks. The market-effective cycle theory can provide a scientific basis for long-term investment strategies. In the long run, the deviation of securities prices from their intrinsic value is only temporary. Within a certain period, the market will correct the pricing deviation caused by its short-term randomness; correcting its own pricing deviation and price discovery are inherent attributes of the market economy. Buying a security at a significant discount below its intrinsic value and selling it at a price equivalent to or higher than its inherent value after the security price rises, thereby obtaining excess profits. A long-term, rational, and investment-oriented approach is necessary for successful investment.

The writing process of this book needs to thank my graduate students for providing data and empirical support!

After nearly ten years of research, I have written this book and am willing to communicate and learn from colleagues in the financial industry! This study aims to challenge major fundamental theoretical issues in finance, and the significance of the research is self-evident. However, the degree of rigor our exploration can achieve still needs to be confirmed, and it is not in vain to break the ice. Based on questioning the research paradigm of modern Western finance, we attempt to construct a new financial theoretical system and achieve breakthroughs in the research of financial theory. We are willing to discuss this with industry colleagues and hope to progress academically. Science and exploration are always on the way, and we will not do it perfectly. As long as we strive and go, there should be scientific value.

SONG YUCHEN
Tuesday, September 19, 2023

CHAPTER 1

Historical Evolution of Financial Investment Theory

Investment is an important form of financial activity. To study financial theory from the perspective of investment, we call it financial investment theory. Research on the characteristics of future securities trends is an eternal topic of financial investment theory. Studying financial theory from the perspective of investment is nothing more than predicting the trend of securities to achieve the goal of improving profits. When the unpredictable trend of securities becomes common sense, portfolio investment becomes the inevitable, helpless, scientific, and even revolutionary choice and has milestone significance. Therefore, under the theoretical framework of portfolio investment, financial investment theory takes the allocation and selection of financial assets as the research object. Realizing the optimal allocation of asset risk and proceeds under uncertainty has become the research theme of current financial investment theory.

From the perspective of financial investment, we divide modern financial investment theory into three stages: traditional investment theory, including technical analysis, basic analysis, and so on; portfolio investment theory, including portfolio investment theory based on efficient market hypothesis (EMH), capital asset pricing model (CAPM), arbitrage pricing theory (APT), option pricing theory (OPT), etc; behavioral financial investment theory, including expected utility theory (EUT), behavioral asset pricing model (BAPM), behavioral portfolio theory (BPT), and so on. With the development of finance, investment theory is also undergoing its own evolution process; investment theory plays a vital role in the development of finance.

1.1 Traditional Investment Theory

The main representatives of traditional financial investment theory are random walk theory, technical analysis theory, and basic analysis theory. These theories occupied an important position in the securities investment industry from the early 20th century to the 1940s. Both technical analysis and basic analysis had an important impact at that time and swept the world. Random walk theory still occupies an important position in the later theoretical research and empirical analysis of the efficient market hypothesis. The birth time of random walk theory was almost synchronous with technical analysis methods, and it also has a great impact on modern financial investment theory.

1.1.1 Random Walk Theory

In 1900, Bachelier's doctoral thesis, *Speculation Theory,* at the Sorbonne University in France made the earliest exploration of the change law of stock price. Bachelier used a variety of mathematical methods to prove that the change in securities price can hardly be predicted by mathematical methods. Each transaction price at a specific time point reflects the different views of the buyer and the seller. The buyer believes that the price will rise, and the seller believes that the price will fall. Therefore, neither buyer nor seller has the advantage of price information. Their probability of winning or losing accounts for 50%, respectively, and "their mathematical expectation is equal to zero." Bachelier believes that at any time, the probability of a price rise is equal to that of a price fall. But no one knows when the market will change and in what direction. There is always a 50% rise probability and a 50% fall probability in the securities market. Bachelier's contribution to investment theory is mainly reflected in that he was the first to introduce probability analysis into the prediction of stock returns and summarized the concept of stochastic process. These have been widely used in various investment theories in the future. Bachelier's view that the stock price cannot be predicted and the market has reflected various events in the past, present, and future coincides with the efficient market hypothesis born more than half a century later. The historical status of his theory should be self-evident. Random walk theory holds that the fluctuation of securities price is random and has no law. It can also be seen from the long-term price trend chart that the opportunities for price fluctuation are almost equal, and it is impossible to find an invariable law.

Random walk theory holds that the price trend is affected by many factors. The same information has different effects on stock price; perhaps an insignificant event may also have a great impact on the market. In the early efficient market model, short-term randomness (that is, the trend of securities can not be predicted) can prove the effectiveness of the market. The information obtained from the "full reflection" of one market price of a security is assumed to be the independent distribution of continuous price changes (or continuous period returns), constituting a random walk model. It is most suitable to consider the random walk model as a special case of general expected return or "fair game" model. The "fair game" model only shows that the market equilibrium conditions can be specified by expected return, and there is little involved in the stochastic process of generating return. When the environment changes, such as the change in investor preference, the emergence of new information, or the emergence of new equilibrium, the income distribution set by the random walk model still repeats itself. Therefore, in terms of supporting the test of the model, the random walk model (in fact, the test of "fair game" nature) is stronger than that of other simple independent hypotheses. The random walk model was first stated and verified by Bachelier in 1900. He proposed that the "fundamental principle" of price behavior is speculation, and the expected profit should be zero for speculators. This should be regarded as a "fair game" and fundamentally a martingale. Bachelier's contribution to investment theory is mainly reflected in: first, he introduced probability theory into the prediction of stock returns. He developed the concept of random process from the derived prediction equation, which has been widely used in various investment theories in the future. Second, Bachelier's view that stock prices cannot be predicted and the market has reflected various events in the past, present, and future actually coincides with the efficient market theory put forward by scholars in the 1960s. In 1954, when Paul A. Samuelson, a famous economist and statistical mathematician, was looking up materials in the Chicago Library, he accidentally turned to a pamphlet on speculation and investment published by Bachelier in 1914. At that time, Samuelson was studying the theory of market behavior and building his own evaluation model. He accidentally found a copy of Bachellier's doctoral thesis in the MIT library. Samuelson immediately agreed with Bachellier's views and the theoretical value of his works and commented that "Bachellier has his own unique ideas, very unique," so he widely shared the theory with his economic peers. In Samuelson's early analysis of speculation, we can clearly see the influence of Bachelier on him. So far, the market stochastic theory, which has been obliterated for half a century, has really entered the eyes of the world. Samuelson, the Nobel Laureate in economics, found the value of Bachelier's theory, but this is half a century after the theory appeared. Bachelier's theory and method of analyzing the financial market with random probability has very super era value in academia. However, as an inventor, he failed in his life, and his theory was almost annihilated by history. Why? Truth takes another step forward and becomes a fallacy. Bachelier's tragedy is also a tragedy of history. As Benoit Mandelbrot, the pioneer of differential geometry, said in 1966, no one can properly classify Bachelier's findings, and no existing tools can apply his findings; therefore, his research has been ignored for 60 years.

Random walk theory tells us the randomness of stock price trends. However, some readers will raise objections. Aren't there a lot of correct predictions in reality? In fact, random events must be predicted correctly; otherwise, they are not random events; they are inevitable events. In real transactions, taking stock commentators as an example, if most of their predictions are correct (such as 60% or higher), their views and investment suggestions on the stock market are of great guiding significance. On the contrary, if most of his predictions are wrong (such as 60% or higher), this prediction also has important guiding significance, but it operates in the opposite direction of his prediction. In reality, if the prediction of stock commentators is about 50% correct and about 50% wrong, the prediction of stock commentators is meaningless. According to the random walk theory, the prediction of stock commentators is the same as coin tossing over a long time. The probability of being correct and wrong once is 50%, and the probability of being correct twice in a row is 50% square, 25%, and so on. The probability of continuous correctness and continuous error will become smaller and smaller. If a lucky person makes a correct judgment continuously, he will become an investor, stock god, and other famous people. The best way to become a well-known person is never to judge the trends of the securities market in the future, so as to maintain honor. Otherwise, you may become the biggest loser. This is the interpretation of random walk. Kendall and Hill (1953) investigated the weekly variation characteristics of the British industrial stock price index, New York cotton, and Chicago wheat spot prices in the 19th century in their paper on price time series. Through a series of correlation analyses, they believe that the price series is like a drunk, and the stock price sequence is like walking randomly. The price of the next week is the price of the previous week plus a random number. Roberts (1959) analyzed the trend of the stock market on the basis of the price independence hypothesis and the identically distributed hypothesis. It is concluded that the fluctuation of stock price conforms to Brownian motion, and there is some uncertainty law in price change, which is a completely random phenomenon. In fact, there are many empirical studies on the random walk of securities trend, and the practice of securities investment also proves that the random walk theory has high historical value.

1.1.2 Technical Analysis Theory

Technical analysis refers to the sum of the methods that take the market trading behavior as the research object, judge the market trend, and follow the periodic changes of the trend to make securities trading decisions. Technical analysis includes three assumptions: first, market behavior is inclusive and digests everything. All changes in securities prices are a comprehensive reflection of various factors that determine their prices. Various factors affecting prices include fundamentals, political factors, psychological factors, etc.; that is, price changes reflect the relationship between supply and demand, which determines price changes. Second, prices evolve in a trending manner. The formed trend usually continues to evolve along the existing trend. As an economic phenomenon, the stock market must follow certain economic laws. The stock price of technical analysis is the balance point of supply and demand between trading parties, which is a dynamic balance. The change of stock price always tends to balance the supply and demand. After reaching the balance, new factors will break the balance. The stock price changes and reaches a new balance. The process of stock price change is the supply-demand relationship change between the trading parties. Third, history will repeat itself. Technical analysis and market behavior have a certain relationship with human psychology. The price form shows people's psychology of being optimistic or bearish about a market through specific charts. Human nature is quite fixed and will produce established reactions under similar circumstances. Studying the phenomena of past market turning points can help us judge the main market turning points.

The technical analysis method is based on the traditional securities investment theory, takes the stock price as the main research object, takes the prediction of the stock price fluctuation trend as the main purpose, and starts with the historical chart of the stock price change to analyze the fluctuation law of the stock market. Technical analysis holds that market behavior is inclusive and digests everything, and stock price fluctuations can be analyzed and predicted quantitatively, such as Dow theory, Gann theory, and wave theory.

1. Dow Theory

Dow theory is known as the originator of all market technology research. Its formation has experienced decades. In 1902, after the death of Charles Dow, Hamilton inherited the theory of Dow, organized and summarized it in writing comments on the stock market, and became the technical analysis theory we see today. The so-called "Dow Theory" is generally the common research achievement of Charles Dow, Hamilton, and others. Charles Dow was born in New England in 1851. He is the founder of the Dow Jones financial company and the *Wall Street Journal*. He founded the Dow Jones Industrial Index in 1895. Dow theory reached its peak in the 1930s, and the *Wall Street Journal* wrote a daily stock market editorial based on Dow theory. On October 23, 1929, the *Wall Street Journal* published an article, "The Turn of the Tide," correctly pointing out that the "bull market" has ended and the era of "bear market" has come. This article is a prediction based on the Dow theory. Immediately after this prediction, there was a terrible stock market crash, followed by the well-known Great Depression from 1929 to 1933. The stock market plummeted continuously, and the Dow theory gained a great reputation.

In Robert Rhea's book *Dow Theory*, he discusses three extremely important assumptions and five theorems in Dow theory and summarizes the essence of Dow theory.

Three hypotheses of Dow theory: Hypothesis 1: manipulation—the daily and weekly fluctuations of indexes or securities may be artificially operated, and the secondary reactions may also be limited in this regard, for example, the common adjustment trend, but the primary trend will not be artificially operated. Hypothesis 2: the market index will reflect every piece of information—all the hopes, disappointments, and knowledge of every market person who knows about financial affairs will be reflected in the daily closing price fluctuation of the index. Therefore, the market index will always properly anticipate the impact of future events. Hypothesis 3: Dow theory is an objective analysis theory—successful use of it to assist speculation or investment requires in-depth research and objective judgment. When it is used subjectively, it will make mistakes and make losses.

Five theorems of Dow theory: Theorem 1: the change in stock index has three trends in any market. Short-term trend, lasting for several days to several weeks; medium-term trend, lasting for several weeks to several months; long-term trend, lasting for months to years. In any market, these three trends must exist at the same time. Long-term trends are the most important and are most easily identified, classified, and understood. Medium-term and short-term trends are subordinate to long-term trends. Only by understanding their position in the long-term trend can we fully understand them and benefit from them. The medium-term trend is secondary to investors, but it is the main consideration of speculators. It may or may not be in the same direction as the long-term trend. If the medium-term trend deviates seriously from the long-term trend, it is regarded as a secondary turn-back trend or correction. Theorem 2: main trend (bear or bull market). The main trend represents the basic trend of the whole, which is usually called a bull or bear market. The duration may be less than one year or even several years. Correctly judging the direction of the main trend is the most important factor for the success of speculation. There is no known method to predict the duration of major trends. Understanding the long-term trend (main trend) is the minimum condition for successful speculation or investment. Theorem 3: primary bear markets. The main bear market is a long-term downward trend mixed with an important rebound. It comes from various adverse economic factors. This trend will not end until the stock price fully reflects the worst possible situation. The bear market will go through three main stages: in the first stage, market participants no longer expect stocks to maintain excessively inflated prices; the second stage of selling pressure is to reflect the economic situation and the decline of enterprise surplus; the third stage is the disappointing selling pressure from the stocks with good performance. No matter what the value is, many people are eager to cash in at least part of the stocks. Theorem 4: primary bull markets. The main bull market is an overall upward trend mixed with a secondary turnaround trend. During this period, due to the improvement of the economic situation and the prosperity of speculation, the demand for investment and speculation increased, which pushed up the stock price. The bull market has three stages: the first stage is to restore people's confidence in the future's prosperity; in the second stage, stocks react to the known improvement of corporate earnings; in the third stage, the speculative boom turns hot, and the stock price rises obviously. The stock price rise at this stage is based on expectation and hope. Theorem 5: secondary reactions. For the discussion here, the second reaction is the important downward trend in the bull market or an important upward trend in the bear market, which usually lasts from three weeks to several months; during this period, the turn-back amplitude is 33% to 66% of the main trend amplitude after the end of the previous secondary reaction. The second reaction is often mistaken for the change of the main trend, because the initial trend of the bull market may be only the second reaction of the bear market, and the opposite will happen after the top of the bull market.

2. Gann Theory

Gann theory holds that there are also natural rules in the stock market like in the universe, the price operation trend of the market is not messy, and it can be predicted by mathematical methods. Its essence is to establish a strict trading order in the seemingly disordered market. He established Gann time rule, Gann price rule, Gann line, etc. It can be used to find out when the price will call back and to what level. Gann theory focuses on the study of market measurement. Through the comprehensive application of mathematics, geometry, religion, and astronomy, Gann established his own unique analysis method and market measurement theory. Because his analysis method has very high accuracy, sometimes even to an incredible degree, many researchers of Gann theory pay great attention to Gann's market measurement system. However, in addition to the market measurement system, Gann has also established a complete set of operating systems. When the market measurement system makes mistakes, the operating system will remedy them in time. When evaluating his theory, Gann believes that the theory can achieve very high accuracy by using the market measurement system and the operating system together to complement each other.

Gann warned investors to carefully study the market before investing, because you may make wrong trading decisions completely opposite to the market, and you must learn how to deal with these mistakes. A successful investor does not make mistakes, because in the face of the ever-changing and uncertain market in the securities market, anyone may make mistakes, even serious mistakes. But the key to success or failure is that winners know how to deal with mistakes and don't make them expand; the losers' hesitation and indecision lead to more mistakes and cause greater losses. Gann's analysis is worth learning from. For example, Gann believes that there are three reasons that can cause investors to suffer heavy losses: (1) Overbuying and selling on limited capital. In other words, the operation is too frequent. High operating skills are required for short-term and ultra-short-term in the market. Before investors do not master these operating skills, too much emphasis on the short-term will often lead to big losses. (2) Investors did not set a stop loss point to control losses. Many investors suffered huge losses just because they did not set an appropriate stop loss point. As a result, they allowed their mistakes to develop indefinitely and suffered more and more losses. Therefore, learning how to set a stop loss point to control risk is one of the basic skills that investors must learn. Some investors, even some market veterans, set stop loss points but did not resolutely implement them in actual operation. As a result, they suffered huge losses due to a lapse of thought. (3) Lack of market knowledge is the most important reason for losses in market trading. Some investors do not pay attention to learning market knowledge, but take it for granted or subjectively think that the market will not distinguish the authenticity of the news. As a result, they are misled and suffer huge losses. Some other investors only rely on the knowledge learned from books to guide practice and indiscriminately apply it, resulting in huge losses. Gann emphasizes the market's knowledge and practical experience. This kind of market knowledge often takes quite a long time to really understand the market's roiling.

However, many things are incomprehensible and even religious. In fact, it is an unexplainable chance and coincidence. For example, Gann's sixth trading rule is as follows: (1) If the trend is upward, when there is an adjustment of 5 to 7 points in the market, it can be absorbed when it is low. Generally, the market adjustment will not exceed 9 to 10 points. (2) If the trend is downward, when the market rebounds from 5 to 7 points, you can take advantage of the high to sell short. (3) In some cases, the rebound or adjustment of 10 to 12 points is also an opportunity to enter the market. (4) If the market rebounds from the top or bottom or adjusts the 18 to 21-point level, investors should be careful because the market may have a short-term reversal. Gann specifically listed that the important turning time of each month in a year is often unable to explain its scientificity. It is reasonable that Gann himself does not know why. The reason why so many predictions have been fulfilled, as far as I'm concerned, is that he has many theoretical methods and many opportunities to fulfill them. It is said that when Gann died in 1955, he only left a legacy of $100,000. Some people said that he did not make money in stock trading. His son said that his father could not make a living by trading, but only by selling teaching materials. Maybe Gann's income from selling books in his life was far more than $100,000. Can you think that part of his income from selling books has also been lost in investment, but how could great Gann tell the world this?

3. Wave Theory

Ralph Nelson Elliott, an American Securities analyst, found and proposed a set of market analysis methods and refined 13 types of markets. These types appear repeatedly in the market, but the time interval and amplitude are not necessarily recurring. Later, he found that these structural patterns could be connected to form larger patterns of the same type, and put forward a series of authoritative deductive rules to explain the behavior of the market, with special emphasis on the predictive value of the fluctuation principle. This is the famous Elliott wave theory, also known as wave theory.

The basic points of wave theory are: (1) A complete cycle includes eight waves, five rises, and three falls. (2) Waves can be merged into higher-level waves or subdivided into lower-level waves. (3) The wave following the mainstream can be divided into five small waves at the lower level. (4) Among the waves 1, 3, and 5, the third wave cannot be the shortest wave. (5) If any one of the three push waves becomes an extension wave, the running time and amplitude of the other two waves will be consistent. (6) Adjustment waves usually run in the form of three waves. (7) The golden ratio theory and singular number combination are the databases of wave theory. (8) The frequent recall rates were 0.382, 0.5, and 0.618. (9) The bottom of the fourth wave may not be lower than the top of the first wave. (10) Eliot's wave theory includes three parts: type, ratio, and time. Its importance is in order of ranking. Eliot's wave theory mainly reflects the psychology of the masses. He himself believed that the more market participants, the higher the accuracy.

Four basic characteristics: (1) The rise and fall of the stock index will alternate. (2) Push wave and adjustment wave are the two most basic types of price fluctuation. Push waves (i.e., waves consistent with the trend of the market) can be divided into five small waves, generally represented by wave 1, wave 2, wave 3, wave 4, and wave 5. Adjustment waves can also be divided into three small waves, usually represented by wave A, wave B, and wave C. (3) After the above eight waves (five up and three down), one cycle is completed, and the trend will enter the next eight wave cycle. (4) The length of time will not change the shape of the wave, because the market will still develop according to its basic pattern. Waves can be elongated or narrowed, but their basic form remains unchanged. Wave theory can be summarized as "eight waves cycle" in one sentence. Wave theory, golden section, and strange numbers are the essence of wave theory.

4. Summary of Technical Analysis

The evaluation of technical analysis theory should be explained from two aspects: first, from the perspective of investment history, so far, there is no sufficient empirical evidence to prove the effect of the above analysis methods in the world, but there are many cases of speculative failure of investors who believe in these methods. Second, it can be seen from the historical data that even the inventors of these methods have no evidence of great success in their investment. Dow theory, Gann theory, and wave theory, their inventors themselves did not achieve great success in investment, and even ended in investment failure. For example, Gann theory seems to have very abundant reason to explain the bottom and top of the past, but the effect of predicting the future is extremely limited. Fundamentally speaking, through the comprehensive application of mathematics, geometry, religion, and astronomy, we have reason to believe that we can choose the method that can explain the past trend in the interpretation of the past trend, but we don't know which method to choose in the prediction of the future. The answer seems to be yes to whether there is a great chance of using different theories, such as geometry and astronomy, to predict past trends. For another example, wave theory has so many strange numbers and so many possibilities of coincidence in its predictions that its application must be extremely limited.

1.1.3 The Basic Analysis Theory

The basic analysis method takes the enterprise value as the main research object through a detailed analysis of the macroeconomic situation, industry development prospects, and enterprise operation conditions that determine the internal value of the enterprise and affect the stock price, so as to roughly calculate the long-term investment value and safety margin of the listed company, and compare it with the current stock price to form corresponding investment suggestions, the basic analysis starts with various basic factors that determine the value of stocks.

The following will mainly introduce the main contents of the basic analysis theory and the dividend discount model (Chen 2008) under this theoretical framework.

1. Basic Analysis Theory

No matter how random the stock price fluctuates, in the long run, it is its intrinsic value that determines the stock price. The so-called measurement method of intrinsic value is to look at the basic factors such as asset value per share, price-earnings ratio, price-to-book ratio, dividend payout ratio, growth prospect of the company, and so on. To study the basic analysis, we should start with Graham and Fisher. Graham, an investor, is known as the ancestor of basic analysis. In 1934, Graham published the epoch-making book *Security Analysis*, which established his immortal position as a master of securities analysis.

Graham's *Security Analysis* deals with an area that has not been touched upon by him so far. He believes that "investment is a kind of behavior that can be expected to guarantee the principal and obtain satisfactory returns through careful analysis and research. The behavior that does not meet these conditions is called speculation. "Investment" and "speculation" are both basic forms of trading activities in the securities market. The most basic difference or core between the two lies in whether they can obtain safe income. Graham's definition of investment is different. He emphatically pointed out that the safety guarantee especially emphasized by "investment" cannot be based on false market information, unfounded assumptions, the dissemination of internal gossip, or even full gambling; the security of "investment" must depend on whether the investment object has real internal value or there is a space for value change, but to accurately grasp this key point or achieve "marginal security," only through the use of objective standard can we make a detailed analysis of the information we can grasp. Graham believes that for securities regarded as an investment, the capital must have a certain degree of security and a satisfactory rate of return. Of course, the so-called security does not mean absolute security, but that the investment should not lose capital under reasonable conditions. In case of extremely unusual or unexpected emergencies, it will also turn safer bonds into waste paper in an instant. Satisfactory returns include not only dividend or interest income, but also price appreciation. Graham points out that the so-called "satisfaction" is a subjective word; as long as the investor does it wisely and within the limits of the definition of investment, the investment return can be any amount, even if it is very low; it can be called "satisfactory." The key to judging whether a person is an investor or a speculator lies in his motivation.

In the book *Security Analysis*, Graham pointed out that there are three reasons for the sharp decline of the stock market: first, the manipulation of stocks by trading brokers and investment institutions. In order to control the rise and fall of a certain stock, brokers will release some news every day to tell customers how wise it would be to buy or sell a certain stock, so that customers blindly enter the trap they set. Second, the financial policy of lending to stock buyers. In the 1920s, speculators in the stock market could obtain loans from banks to buy stocks. From 1921 to 1929, their loans for buying stocks increased from $1 billion to $8.5 billion. Because the loan is supported by the stock market price, everything will fall like a domino once the stock market plummets. Until the United States promulgated *The Securities Act of 1932*, it effectively protected individual investors from being cheated by brokers, and the situation of buying securities by deposits began to decrease gradually. Third, excessive optimism. This reason is the most fundamental of the three reasons and can not be controlled by legislation.

Graham's safety margin theory is based on some specific assumptions. Graham believes that the unreasonable price of stocks is largely due to human's fear and greed. When extremely optimistic, greed makes the stock price higher than its internal value, thus forming an overestimated market; when extremely pessimistic, fear makes the stock price lower than its intrinsic value and then forms an undervalued market. Investors profit from the correction of an inefficient market. Investors must be rational when facing the stock market. At the same time, Graham reminded investors not to focus on the market price, but on the enterprises behind the stocks, because the market is a mixture of rationality and sensibility, and its performance is often wrong. The secret of investment is to invest when the price is far lower than the intrinsic value, wait for the market to correct its mistakes, and when the market corrects its mistakes, this is when the investors make profits.

Invest according to the intrinsic value of the company, not according to the fluctuation of the market. Stocks represent part of the ownership of the company and should not be proof of daily price changes. The stock market is a "voting machine" in the short term and a "weighing machine" in the long term. To buy a stock with a high margin of safety, an investor should keep a price difference between the price he is willing to pay and the price he estimates, i.e., a large price difference, which is the so-called margin of safety. The greater the margin of safety, the lower the risk of investment and the greater the expected return.

While Graham was writing *Security Analysis*, Philip Fisher put forward Fisher's theory, which believes that there are two factors that can increase the internal value of the company: one is the development prospect of the company, and the other is the management ability of the company. Investors must fully investigate the company before investing in the company. Fisher believes that when judging whether the company has development prospects, it is not necessary to pay too much attention to the annual growth rate of the company's sales in one or two years, but should be judged from its operating conditions for many years; at the same time, we should also examine whether the company is committed to maintaining its low cost, making profits grow synchronously with sales growth, and the company's future growth ability without requiring equity financing. When examining the management ability of the company, we should pay attention to whether the managers have a feasible policy to subordinate the short-term interests to the long-term interests, whether the management personnel are honest and upright and can handle the working relationship with employees well, and the reason why the company distinguishes the business or management characteristics of other companies in the same industry. Fisher's theory advocates buying stocks that can increase their long-term intrinsic value.

2. Dividend Discount Model

When investors buy stocks, they usually expect to obtain two kinds of cash flows: dividends during the period of holding stocks and the expected stock price at the end of the period of holding stocks. Because the expected price of the stock at the end of the holding period is determined by the expected dividend of the stock in the future, the general model of stock pricing is the dividend discount model, also known as the capitalization method of income. This method holds that the intrinsic value of any asset depends on the expected future cash flow income from holding the asset. Since the future cash flow depends on the expectations of investors, and its value is in the form of future value, it is necessary to discount the future cash flow to its present value at a discount rate. So, there is a discount rate model for the intrinsic value of stocks:

$$E(V_0) = \frac{E(D_1)}{1+r_s} + \frac{E(D_2)}{(1+r_s)^2} + \cdots + \frac{E(D_t)}{(1+r_s)^t} + \cdots = \sum_{t=1}^{\infty} \frac{E(D_t)}{(1+r_s)^t} \qquad (1\text{-}1)$$

$E(V_0)$ represents the current intrinsic value of the stock, $E(D_t)$ represents the expected cash flow at the end of the year $t-1$, and r_s represents the rate of return on investment. If we use the investor's expected rate of return $E(r)$ to replace r_s, the above equation can be written as:

$$E(V_0) = \sum_{t=1}^{\infty} \frac{E(D_t)}{(1+E(r))^t} \qquad (1\text{-}2)$$

If we consider the expected value of the stock in year t, then:

$$E(V_t) = \sum_{i=t+1}^{\infty} \frac{E(D_i)}{(1+E(r))^{i-t}} \qquad (1\text{-}3)$$

$E(V_t)$ represents the expected value of stocks at the end of year t.

In most cases, investors always observe the changes in the market at all times. Once the stock price rises, they sell their stocks to realize the return on stock capital. At this time, investors become short-term investors. Suppose an investor buys a stock at the price of $E\left(V_0\right)$ when $t=0$, and sells it at the expected price $E\left(V_t\right)$ when $t=T$, then:

$$E\left(V_0\right) = \sum_{t=1}^{T} \frac{E\left(D_t\right)}{(1 + E(r))^t} + \frac{E\left(V_t\right)}{(1 + E(r))^T}$$

$$= \sum_{t=1}^{T} \frac{E\left(D_t\right)}{(1 + E(r))^t} + \frac{1}{(1 + E(r))^T} \sum_{i=T+1}^{\infty} \frac{E\left(D_i\right)}{(1 + E(r))^{i-T}}$$

$$= \sum_{t=1}^{T} \frac{E\left(D_t\right)}{(1 + E(r))^t} + \sum_{i=T+1}^{\infty} \frac{E\left(D_i\right)}{(1 + E(r))^i}$$

$$= \sum_{i=1}^{\infty} \frac{E\left(D_t\right)}{(1 + E(r))^t} \tag{1-4}$$

Equation 1-4 shows that whether the investors facing the market are long-term investors or short-term investors, the decisions of stock value are the same. In other words, the decision of stock value does not change with the length of investors' holding period.

Since it is unrealistic to expect cash dividends indefinitely, people have constructed several different forms of dividend discount models according to different assumptions about future growth rates, mainly including the Gordon model, the stable growth stock pricing model, the two-stage growth model, the three-stage growth model, the H model, and so on.

(1) Gordon model

The stocks that are expected to pay the same dividend every year are called zero-growth stocks. The investors who hold such stocks expect to get a constant dividend every year in the future, that is, $E(D) = E\left(D_1\right) = E\left(D_2\right) = \cdots$, the pricing model of zero growth stocks:

$$E\left(V_0\right) = \sum_{t=1}^{\infty} \frac{E(D)}{(1 + E(r))^t} = \frac{E(D)}{E(r)} \tag{1-5}$$

That is, the current value of the stock completely depends on the expected dividend or bonus of the stock and the expected rate of return on investment.

(2) Stable growth stock pricing model

If the company is operating well, its profits will continue to increase, which will obviously affect the stock price. We especially consider that the expected dividend or bonus of the company changes at a certain constant growth rate. Such stocks are called stable growth stocks. The dividend of these companies is expected to grow at a certain stable rate for a long time. What is its pricing model?

If the dividend or bonus of the latest period D_0 has been paid, the expected dividend or bonus at the end of any period t is:

$$E(D_t) = [1 + E(g)] \cdot E(D_{t-1}) = \cdots = [1 + E(g)]^t \cdot D_0 \tag{1-6}$$

Where, $E(g)$ represents the stable growth rate of expected dividends or bonuses, which is substituted into the basic pricing model, including:

$$E(V_0) = \sum_{t=1}^{\infty} \frac{E(D_t)}{[1+E(r)]^t} = \sum_{t=1}^{\infty} \frac{[1+E(g)]^t D_0}{[1+E(r)]^t}$$

$$= D_0 \sum_{t=1}^{\infty} \left(\frac{1+E(g)}{1+E(r)} \right)^t = D_0 \frac{\frac{1+E(g)}{1+E(r)}}{1 - \frac{1+E(g)}{1+E(r)}}$$

$$= D_0 \frac{1+E(g)}{E(g)-E(r)} = \frac{E(D_1)}{E(r)-E(g)} \quad \text{and } E(g) < E(r) \tag{1-7}$$

Note that Equation 1-7 do not converge in time $E(g) > E(r)$, and Equation 1-7 are called the Gordon pricing model. For stocks with general growth, if the expected growth rate of the company's earnings relative to the previous period is expressed in $E(g_t)$, then:

$$E(D_t) = [1 + E(g_t)] \cdot E(D_{t-1})$$

$$= [1 + E(g_t)] \cdot [1 + E(g_{t-1})] E(D_{t-2})$$

$$\cdots \cdots$$

$$= [1 + E(g_t)] \cdot [1 + E(g_{t-1})] \cdots \cdots [1 + E(g_1)] \cdot E(D_0) \tag{1-8}$$

Then, there is a general growth stock pricing model:

$$E(V_0) = \sum_{t=1}^{\infty} \frac{[1 + E(g_1)] \cdot [1 + E(g_2)] \cdots \cdots [1 + E(g_t)] \cdot D_0}{[1 + E(r_1)] \cdot [1 + E(r_2)] \cdots \cdots [1 + E(r_t)]} \tag{1-9}$$

Where, $E(r_t)$ refers to the expected return on investment in year t.

(3) Two-stage growth stock pricing model

Obviously, it is unrealistic for the company's earnings to increase at the same expected growth rate. Therefore, assuming that the expected dividend of the company increases or decreases at the same rate $E\left(g_1\right)$ from now to period T, and changes at the same rate $E\left(g_2\right)$ after period T, the stock pricing model is the modified Gordon model:

$$
\begin{aligned}
E\left(V_0\right) &= \sum_{t=1}^{\infty} \frac{E\left(D_t\right)}{(1+E(r))^t} \\
&= \sum_{t=1}^{T} \frac{\left(1+E\left(g_1\right)\right)^t D_0}{(1+E(r))^t} + \sum_{t=T+1}^{\infty} \frac{\left(1+E\left(g_2\right)\right)^{t-T} E\left(D_T\right)}{(1+E(r))^t} \\
&= \sum_{t=1}^{T} \frac{\left(1+E\left(g_1\right)\right)^t D_0}{(1+E(r))^t} + \sum_{t=T+1}^{\infty} \frac{\left(1+E\left(g_2\right)\right)^{t-T} \left(1+E\left(g_1\right)\right)^T D_0}{(1+E(r))^t} \\
&= D_0 \left\{ \sum_{t=1}^{T} \left(\frac{1+E\left(g_1\right)}{(1+E(r))}\right)^t + \left(\frac{\left(1+E\left(g_1\right)\right)}{1+E\left(g_2\right)}\right)^T \sum_{t=T+1}^{\infty} \left(\frac{1+E\left(g_2\right)}{1+E(r)}\right)^t \right\}
\end{aligned} \tag{1-10}
$$

Similarly, we can derive a stock pricing model with different expected dividend growth rates in different periods.

(4) Three-stage growth stock pricing model

The three-stage growth model divides dividend growth into three different stages. In the first stage (the term is T_1), the dividend growth rate is a constant $E\left(g_1\right)$. The second stage (the term is $T_1 + 1$ to T_2) is the turning point of dividend growth. The dividend growth rate changes from $E\left(g_1\right)$ to $E\left(g_2\right)$ in a linear way, which $E\left(g_2\right)$ is the dividend growth rate of the third stage. If $E\left(g_1\right) > E\left(g_2\right)$, it will show a decreasing dividend growth rate during the transition period. On the contrary, it shows an increasing dividend growth rate. In the third stage (the term is from T_2 later to forever), the dividend growth rate is also a constant $E\left(g_2\right)$, which is the normal long-term growth rate of the company. The three stages of dividend growth can be shown in Figure 1-1.

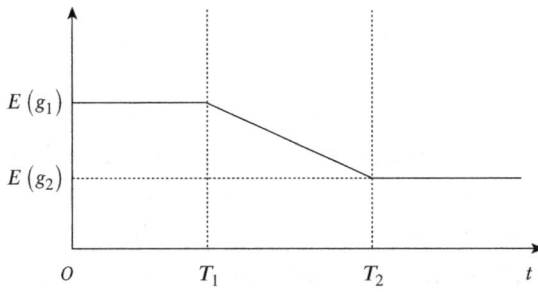

Figure 1-1 Three-Stage Growth Model

The dividend growth rate at any point during the turning period $E\left(g_t\right)$ can be expressed in Equation 1-11:

$$E\left(g_t\right) = E\left(g_1\right) - \left[E\left(g_1\right) - E\left(g_2\right)\right] \cdot \frac{t - T_1}{T_2 - T_1}, E\left(g_1\right) > E\left(g_2\right) \qquad (1\text{-}11)$$

The calculation equation of the three-stage growth model is:

$$E\left(V_0\right) = \sum_{t=1}^{T_1} \frac{D_0\left(1 + E\left(g_1\right)\right)^t}{\left(1 + E(r)\right)^t} + \sum_{t=T_1+1}^{T_2} \frac{E\left(D_{t-1}\right)\left(1 + E\left(g_t\right)\right)}{\left(1 + E(r)\right)^t} + \sum_{t=T_2+1}^{\infty} \frac{E\left(D_{T_2}\right)\left(1 + E\left(g_2\right)\right)^{t-T_2}}{\left(1 + E(r)\right)^t}$$

$$= D_0 \sum_{t=1}^{\pi} \left(\frac{1 + E\left(g_1\right)}{1 + E(r)}\right)^t + \sum_{t=T_1+1}^{T_2} \frac{E\left(D_{t-1}\right)\left(1 + E\left(g_t\right)\right)}{\left(1 + E(r)\right)^t} + \frac{E\left(D_{T_2}\right)\left(1 + E\left(g_2\right)\right)}{\left(1 + E(r)\right)^{T_2}\left(E(r) - E\left(g_2\right)\right)}$$

$$(1\text{-}12)$$

The three items in Equation 1-12 correspond to the three growth stages of dividends, respectively.

(5) H model

The assumption of the H model is that the initial growth rate of dividends is $E\left(g_1\right)$, and then decreases (or increases) to $E\left(g_2\right)$ in a linear way, assuming that its duration is *2H*, but $E\left(g_2\right)$ is a long-term normal dividend growth rate. In the process of dividend decreasing or increasing, the dividend growth rate at the point *H* is just the average of the initial growth rate $E\left(g_1\right)$ and the constant growth rate $E\left(g_2\right)$. When $E\left(g_1\right)$ is greater than $E\left(g_2\right)$, the dividend growth rate before *2H* decreases. When $t = H$, we get:

$$E(g_H) = \frac{1}{2}[E(g_1) + E(g_2)] \qquad (1\text{-}13)$$

Under the H model, the intrinsic value of the stock can be expressed as Equation 1-14, as shown in Figure 1-2.

$$E(V_0) = \frac{D_0}{E(r) - E(g_2)}\{1 + E(g_2) + H \cdot [E(g_1) - E(g_2)]\} \qquad (1\text{-}14)$$

Graham said: "The difficulty is that in order to get the stock value that Williams said, people must make some important assumptions, including the trajectory of future interest rate changes, the growth rate of corporate profits, and the final value of the stock when growth stops. One may ask, compared with those precise mathematical methods based on them, whether these necessary and random assumptions have too large differences. This conservatism is not included in the author's equation. However, if more advanced arithmetic can persuade investors to take a wise attitude, I would like to vote loudly for this more advanced arithmetic."

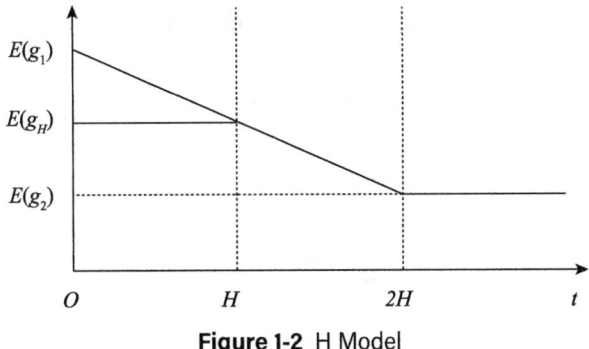

Figure 1-2 H Model

1.2 Portfolio Investment Theory

Technical analysis was popular in the 1920s and 1930s, and the technical analysis methods represented by Dow theory were widely used. However, the actual situation of stock trading was that technical analysis failed repeatedly. A highly expected investment strategy has led to the ruin of many people, and people are increasingly suspicious of technical analysis methods. Therefore, the basic analysis means represented by Graham came into being under this background and became the mainstream of stock market analysis means, as well as an important analysis tool to replace technical analysis means. However, in the 1940s, basic analysis also came to the end of history. Investors still had great difficulty or uncertainty in grasping the fundamentals, which could not change the fate of only a few people making money in the stock market. In fact, even the top decision-maker of a company cannot fully grasp the future of a company's fundamentals, because competitors are uncertain. Basic analysis still does not have the ability to defeat the stock market. How to defeat the stock market and become a successful investor has become the absolute luxury of the world. Under the historical background that both technical analysis and basic analysis were invalid, Markowitz's portfolio investment theory was born in 1952 and gradually became an important trading method to overcome the stock market risk. From the historical perspective of financial investment, portfolio investment is not only a revolution in the history of financial investment theory, but also a helpless choice. From a previous perspective, the technical analysis and basic analysis methods with great influence have been popular and mainstream in the development history of financial investment theories for less than 20 years, while Markowitz portfolio investment theory has become mainstream and occupies an important position for more than 60 years, and the portfolio investment theory has been widely accepted by major funds, institutional investors, and even small and medium-sized investors in the world, we cannot but say that this is a revolution. From the latter point of view, the portfolio is a helpless choice when it is impossible to choose the best stock, because the best investment is to choose the stock with the largest rise. Therefore, Buffett, who has always opposed portfolio investment, said that "diversified investment is a protection for ignorance." However, if we do not choose portfolio investment, so far, we have not found an effective way to overcome the stock market risk and replace portfolio investment.

Standard finance is based on the assumption of a rational person. Modern standard finance theory originated in the 1950s, developed in the 1960s, matured in the 1970s, and finally became the mainstream theory. In 1952, Markowitz published *Portfolio Selection*, which became the beginning of modern standard financial theory. In 1970, Fama published an article entitled "Efficient Capital Markets: A Review of Theory and Empirical Work" and proposed the efficient market hypothesis (EMH). The market was endowed with three different efficiencies, namely, weak efficient market, semi-strong efficient market, and strong efficient market. Sharpe (1964), Lintner (1965), and Mossin (1966) constructed a statistically verifiable CAPM model to describe the price mechanism of the capital market, arguing that coefficient β (Greek) singly determines the risk, and investors are required to get a risk premium because they bear this risk. EMH and CAPM are endogenous and consistent and are interrelated in a sense; that is, the latter provides a set of methods to test the former. This combination opens the door to the effectiveness of the hypothesis and pricing model. Through this door, a large number of studies have tested the validity of the hypothesis and model. The subsequent development includes Ross's (1976) arbitrage pricing model (APT) and Scholes's (1972) option pricing model (OPM), etc. In the mid-1970s, the standard financial theory based on the efficient market hypothesis (EMH) and capital market pricing theory, and modern portfolio theory established its position in the financial and economic field. Generally speaking, modern classical financial theory has three key conceptual assumptions: rational investors, efficient markets, and random walk.

1.2.1 Measurement of Expected Return and Risks

Expected return is an indicator to measure the future return of investment varieties, and variance or standard deviation is an indicator to measure risk. Let's introduce it in three aspects.

1. Earnings and Risks of Individual Security

In the securities investment theory, the expected rate of return is equal to the sum of the product of the results of various returns and their probabilities, and the risk is the uncertainty of the expected return. In the case of certainty, the rate of return is the best basis for making investment decisions. In the case of uncertainty, it is not necessarily equal to the expected rate of return to judge the quality of securities and make investment decisions only by relying on the expected rate of return. It may be higher or lower than the expected rate of return. The greater the gap between them, the greater the possibility of not realizing the expected rate of return and the greater the investment risk. In this way, the volatility of the actual rate of return of investment products around the rate of return becomes the second indicator to judge the quality of securities, namely the risk indicator.

Expected rate of return: the expected value of future rate of return, which can be recorded as:

$$E(R) = p_1 R_1 + p_2 R_2 + \cdots + p_n R_n = \sum_{i-1}^{n} p_i R_i \tag{1-15}$$

Where, $E(R)$ represents the expected rate of return, p_i represents the probability of occurrence of the ith situation, and R_i represents various possible rates of return, $i = 1, 2, 3, ..., n$.

$$\sigma^2 = \sum_{i=1}^{n} p_i \left[R_i - E(R) \right]^2 \tag{1-16}$$

Where, σ^2 is variance, σ is the standard deviation, and variance and standard deviation are indicators of risk.

2. Earnings and Risks of the Two Securities

The expected returns of two securities investment portfolios can be expressed by the weighted average of the expected returns of the two investment products included. The risk is determined by the risk of each security (i.e., standard deviation), their respective weights, and the degree of correlation between the two. The degree of correlation can be expressed by statistical covariance or correlation coefficient. Expected return of two securities portfolios is:

$$E(R_p) = w_1 E(R_1) + w_2 E(R_2) \tag{1-17}$$

Where, $E(R_p)$ represents the expected rate of return of the portfolio, w_1 and w_2 represent the proportion of the two securities respectively, R_1 and R_2 represent expected yield of the first and second securities.

Variance of portfolio is:

$$\sigma_p^2 = w_1^2 \sigma_1^2 + w_2^2 \sigma_2^2 + 2 w_1 w_2 \sigma_{1,2} = w_1^2 \sigma_1^2 + w_2^2 \sigma_2^2 + 2 w_1 w_2 \rho_{1,2} \sigma_1 \sigma_2 \tag{1-18}$$

Where, σ_p^2 represents the variance of the combination, $\sigma_{1,2}$ is the covariance, and $p_{1,2}$ is the correlation coefficient.

3. Earnings and Risks of Multiple Securities

The expected rate of return of multiple portfolios can be expressed by the weighted average of the expected rate of return of various investment products. The risk measurement of investment portfolios is a complicated problem. This is because, first, the opportunities for choice have been greatly increased. Investors can not only choose among a variety of investment products, but also invest their funds in these kinds of securities in different ways. Each collocation mode is a kind of investment portfolio and an opportunity for choice. Second, more importantly, unlike the expected return, the risk of a portfolio is not equal to the weighted average of the risks of a single investment in the portfolio. In many cases, the former is less than the latter. The risk of a portfolio depends not only on the risks of its various investment products, but also on their weights and correlation coefficients.

$$E(R_p) = \sum_{i=1}^{n} w_i E(R_i) \tag{1-19}$$

$$\sigma_p^2 = E[R_p - E(R_p)] = E\{\sum_{i=1}^{n} w_i [R_i - E(R_i)]\}^2 = \sum_{i=1}^{n} \sum_{j=1}^{n} w_i w_j \sigma_{ij} \tag{1-20}$$

Where, $E(R_p)$ represents the expected return of the portfolio, w_i respectively represents the proportion of each security, $i = 1, 2, 3, ..., n$, σ_p^2 represents the variance of the portfolio.

1.2.2 Capital Asset Pricing Model

Capital asset pricing model (CAPM) is an asset pricing model developed by American scholars Sharpe (1964), Lintner (1965), and Mossin (1966) on the basis of Markowitz's portfolio theory. It is the pillar of modern financial market price theory. The capital asset pricing model is developed on the basis of portfolio theory and has become a mature theoretical asset pricing theory. It mainly studies the relationship between the expected rate of return of assets and risky assets in the securities market, as well as the formation of equilibrium prices.

1. Basic Assumptions of Capital Asset Pricing Model

(1) All investors plan their investment portfolio in the same single investment period.
(2) Investors choose an investment portfolio according to the mean and variance of the rate of return.
(3) Investors pursue the maximization of expected utility. Therefore, when faced with two choices with the same conditions, they will choose the one with a higher expected rate of return.
(4) Investors are risk averse, so when faced with two choices with the same other conditions, they will choose the one with the smaller standard deviation.

(5) There are a large number of investors who are price receivers.

(6) Investors can borrow and lend without restriction at risk-free interest rates.

(7) There is no tax burden, no transaction cost, and no incomplete market.

(8) Investors have the same expectation for the mean, variance, and covariance of securities return, which means that all investors have the same opinion on securities evaluation and economic situation. In this way, the probability distribution expectation of investors on the return rate of securities is consistent.

From the perspective of risk and return ratio, when reviewing the risk degree of an asset, what matters is not the risk of the asset itself, but its covariance with the market portfolio. Assets with high risks do not mean that their expected returns are correspondingly high, while assets with low risks do not necessarily have low returns. The expected return level of a single asset should depend on its covariance with the market portfolio.

2. Securities Market Line (SML)

The securities market line describes the relationship between the risk and return of a single security (or an invalid portfolio). It shows that the income of a single security consists of two parts, namely, risk-free interest rate and the return obtained by taking the systematic risk, and only the marginal contribution to market risk can obtain the corresponding income or return.

SML reflects the linear relationship between the covariance of a single asset or invalid portfolio and the market portfolio and the expected return of the single security or invalid portfolio at the time of market equilibrium. Among them, β_i is called the beta coefficient of security i, which is another way to express the covariance of asset i and market portfolio: $E(r_i) = r_f + \beta_i \cdot [E(r_M) - r_f]$, as shown in Figure 1-3.

Figure 1-3 shows the securities market line, namely the capital asset pricing model (CAPM). When $\beta_i = 0$, the securities investment belongs to risk-free investment. When

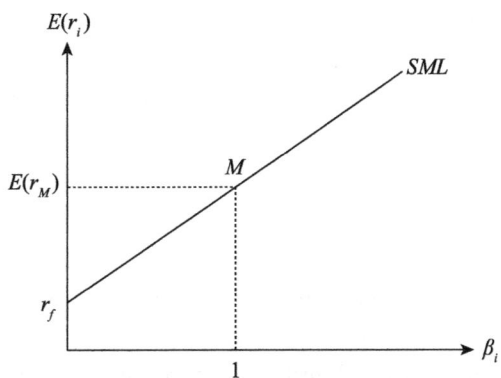

Figure 1-3 Securities Market Line (SML)

$\beta_i=1$, the return of the security is exactly equal to the market return $E\left(R_M\right)$. If the yield of the selected securities is above the securities market line, that is, the yield obtained is higher than the equilibrium yield, indicating that the securities value is undervalued. If the yield of the selected securities is below the line of the securities market, that is, the yield obtained is lower than the equilibrium yield, indicating that the value of the securities is overvalued.

1.2.3 Arbitrage Pricing Theory (APT)

In the process of using the CAPM model to build the asset portfolio, it is necessary to estimate the expected return, variance, and covariance of each stock in the asset portfolio. If the asset portfolio contains a large number of stocks, such as 60 stocks, the covariance needs to be calculated as many as 1,770. In addition to the mean and variance, 1,890 estimates need to be estimated, which can be said to be a huge workload when computer technology is not mature. In order to simplify the research of portfolio analysis, the arbitrage pricing theory (APT), founded by Stephen A. Ross in 1976, provides another asset pricing model.

Arbitrage pricing theory believes that arbitrage behavior is a decisive factor in the formation of modern efficient markets (i.e., market equilibrium prices). If the market does not reach equilibrium, there will be no arbitrage opportunities in the market. We know that there is a linear relationship between the return of all securities predicted by CAPM and the return of the market portfolio, the only common factor. APT has expanded this conclusion. This model is based on the multi-factor model of yield formation and uses the concept of arbitrage to define equilibrium. If the return rate of the market portfolio is taken as the only factor, the risk-return relationship derived by APT is identical to CAPM. Therefore, CAPM can be regarded as a special case of APT.

1. APT's Assumption Basis

(1) The capital market is completely competitive and frictionless.
(2) Investors are risk-averse and unsatisfied. When there are arbitrage opportunities, they will construct arbitrage portfolios to increase their wealth, so as to maximize utility.
(3) All investors have the same expectations. The yield of any security i follows the factor model:

$$R_i = E(\bar{R}_i) + b_{i1}F_1 + b_{i2}F_2 + \cdots + b_{ik}F_k + \varepsilon_i \tag{1-21}$$

Where, R_i represents the actual return rate of security i, which is a random variable;
$E(\bar{R}_i)$ represents expected yield of security i;
F_k represents the index of the kth influencing factor;
b_{ik} represent the sensitivity of security i's return to factor k;

ε_i represents the random error affecting the yield of security i, and $E(\varepsilon_i) = 0$.

(4) The securities variety n in the market must far exceed the number k of influencing factors in the model.

(5) The error term ε_i is used to measure the non-systematic risk part of the securities i return. It is independent of all influencing factors and the error term of other securities other than securities i.

The above factor model shows that, except for the influence of non-factor risk, all securities or securities portfolios with common risk factor sensitivity should have the same expected yield; otherwise, arbitrage opportunities will occur. At this time, investors will take advantage of these opportunities to gain income until the arbitrage opportunities disappear, so that the expected yield of all assets reaches an equilibrium state, which is the essential logic of the APT Model.

2. Arbitrage Portfolio

If security meets the following conditions: no additional investment is required, the sensitivity to risk factors is zero, and the expected rate of return is positive, it is called an arbitrage portfolio. In mathematical language:

(1) No additional investment is required. If x_i represents the change in the amount of securities i held by investors or the change in the proportion of arbitrage portfolio investment, that is:

$$x_1 + x_2 + \cdots x_n = 0 \tag{1-22}$$

(2) The sensitivity to risk factors is zero. In other words, it does not bear factor risk, that is:

$$x_1 b_{1i} + x_2 b_{2i} + \cdots + x_n b_{ni} = 0 \quad i = 1, 2 \cdots, k \quad (n > k) \tag{1-23}$$

Strictly speaking, in addition to factor risk equal to zero, the non-factor risk of the arbitrage portfolio should also be equal to zero. In fact, the non-factor risk of the arbitrage portfolio is usually greater than zero, but according to the law of large numbers, it can be inferred that when the number of securities n included in the arbitrage portfolio is large enough, the non-factor risk of the arbitrage portfolio will tend to zero, that is, the non-system risk can be eliminated through decentralization.

(3) The expected rate of return is positive, that is:

$$x_1 r_1 + x_2 r_2 + \cdots + x_n r_n > 0 \tag{1-24}$$

3. Arbitrage Pricing Theoretical Model

According to the basic principle of the arbitrage pricing model, if the securities market is in an equilibrium state, then the expected rate of return of the securities portfolio that does not require additional investment and has no factor risk must be zero, that is, if Equations 1-22 and 1-23 are met, there must be:

$$x_1 r_1 + x_2 r_2 + \cdots + x_n r_n = 0 \tag{1-25}$$

According to *Farkas* lemma, the expected return rate of asset i $E(\bar{R}_i)$ must be a linear combination of constant vector $(\lambda_0, \lambda_1, \lambda_2 \cdots, \lambda_k)$ and sensitivity vector $(b_{i1}, b_{i2} \cdots, b_{ik})$ in Equation 1-21, that is:

$$E(\bar{R}_i) = \lambda_0 + \lambda_1 b_{i1} + \cdots + \lambda_k b_{ik}, i = 1, 2, \cdots, n. \tag{1-26}$$

Furthermore, if there is an asset portfolio that has unit sensitivity only to the kth factor, but has zero sensitivity to other risk factors, making the expected return of the asset portfolio to be $\bar{\delta}_i$, then $\lambda_k = \bar{\delta}_k - R_f$, it can be regarded as the "risk premium" of kth common risk factors, λ_0 is equivalent to the risk-free rate of return, that is, $\lambda_0 = R_f$. Therefore, Equation 1-26 can be re-expressed as:

$$E(\bar{R}_i) = R_f + (\bar{\delta}_1 - R_f) b_{i1} + \cdots + (\bar{\delta}_k - R_f) b_{ik} \tag{1-27}$$

This is the general expression of arbitrage pricing theory. The arbitrage pricing theory is different from the single factor market risk determinism in the capital asset pricing theory. It believes that the systematic risk of securities is determined by k common factors that exist universally. Each security has different reaction coefficients and sensitivities to these k common factors, which leads to different returns between different securities.

1.3 Behavioral Financial Investment Theory

Behavioral finance is a research method and theoretical system that combines psychology, behavioral theory, and financial analysis. It analyzes the influence of people's psychology, emotions, and behavior on people's financial decisions, financial product pricing, and financial market trends. Behavioral finance theory is formed under the background of challenges and doubts to modern financial theory. It brings human psychology and behavior into the financial research framework. Behavioral finance theory emphasizes the research on human individual and group behavior, which has facilitated the transformation of traditional research methods to a life-centered nonlinear complex paradigm, making it possible to resolve the differences between financial investment theory and investment practice. Behavioral finance theory deeply reflects on the modern financial theory in the original rational framework, explains the market behavior from the human perspective, and fully considers the role of psychological factors of market participants, providing a new perspective for people to understand the financial market.

1.3.1 Basic Theory of Behavioral Finance—Expectancy Theory

1. Expected Utility Theory

Expectancy theory is an important theoretical basis of behavioral finance. Through experimental comparison, Kahneman and Tversky (1979) found that most investors are not completely rational but limited rational, and their behavior is not always risk avoidance. Expectancy theory holds that the utility function of investors to income is a concave function, while the utility function to loss is a convex function. Investors are extremely risk-averse when investment losses occur. When investment profits, with the increase in income, the speed of satisfaction slows down, and the marginal utility decreases. Expectancy theory is a representative theory in behavioral finance research. Kahneman and Tversky (1979) summarized it into the following three effects:

(1) The certainty effect refers to the fact that decision-makers tend to give greater weight to the deterministic results and are willing to rely on the deterministic results for investment decisions compared with the results with only possibility, while they usually give lower weight to the possible results. Due to the influence of the certainty effect, decision-makers will show a risk aversion tendency to certain positive rewards. If the dividend of one stock is small but the result is certain, while the dividend of the other stock is large but the result is uncertain, most stockbrokers will tend to buy stocks with small dividends, but is certain to get dividends, and no one will take risks to buy stocks with large dividends but only with the possibility of getting dividends. This negates the assumption of the subjective expected utility theory model, that is, the decision-maker always chooses the scheme with the greatest benefit.

(2) The reflection effect refers to the fact that when facing the prospect of possible loss, people tend to pursue risks; when facing the prospect of profit, people tend to avoid risks. People focus on the wealth change relative to a reference point rather than the expected return value of the final wealth. Individuals have a tendency of risk preference when facing losses and a tendency of risk aversion when facing profits, which is also inconsistent with the expected utility theory.

(3) The isolation effect refers to the fact that people often temporarily eliminate the same factors in swap expectations when analyzing and evaluating different expectations to be selected. But usually, a group of expectations can be decomposed into the same and different factors in more than one way. The diversity of such decomposition

methods will lead to the inconsistency of people's preferences and choices, which is the separation effect. Individuals will have different decomposition methods and different choices because of different problem description methods, which is the so-called framework dependency phenomenon.

2. Main Contents of Expected Utility Theory
The so-called expectation is the result of various risks. The choice of expectation follows a special psychological process and law, rather than the axioms assumed by the expected utility theory. The expectation defined by Kahneman and Tversky (1979) is an uncertain event.

(1) Personal risk decision-making process
Expectancy theory believes that when individuals make choices under risk conditions, they will go through two stages: the editing stage and the evaluation stage. Editing is to simplify and recode different expectations. The editing stage mainly includes coding, merging, splitting, and canceling. Evaluation is to assume that the decision-maker evaluates every expectation edited and then selects the highest value expectation.

(2) Value function
The value function is the utility expressed by the expected utility theory. Its difference from the standard utility function is that it is no longer a function of wealth, but a function of profit or loss. As shown in Figure 1-4:

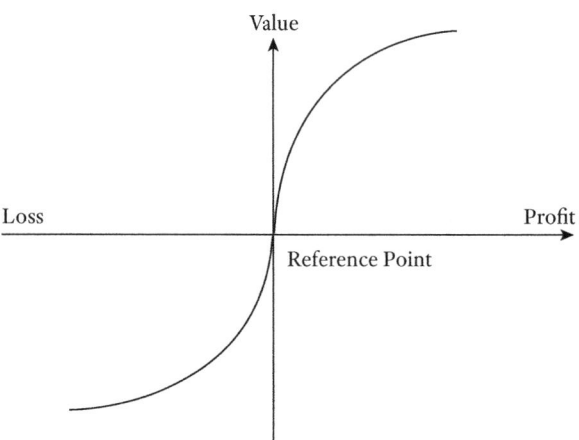

Figure 1-4 Value Function

The value function proposed by Kahneman and Tversky (1979) has the following four important characteristics: 1) The value function is defined as the gain and loss relative to a certain reference point, rather than the ending wealth or consumption that the general traditional theory attaches importance to. The decision of reference point is usually based on the current wealth level, but sometimes, it is not necessarily the case. The reference point may have different considerations due to investors' different expectations of future wealth positions. For example, an investor who is not reconciled to the loss may accept the gamble that he would not have accepted. 2) The value function is defined by the degree of deviation from the reference point. The reflection character deviates from the return and loss of the reference point, which is called the reflection effect. 3) It is a concave function in the face of profit and a convex function in the face of loss, which means that investors are risk averse when they are in the income state, and the utility increased by each unit of income is lower than that brought by the previous unit. In the loss state, investors are risk preference, and the lost utility of each additional unit of loss is lower than that of the previous unit. 4) The slope of the value function is steeper when it is in the loss state than when it is in the income state; that is, the marginal loss of investors is more sensitive than the marginal income when they are in the corresponding income and loss state. The marginal pain of losing a unit is greater than that of acquiring a unit of marginal profit; that is, individuals tend to avoid loss. Thaler (1980) calls this situation the Endowment Effect.

1.3.2 Main Theoretical Models of Behavioral Finance

1. Noise Trading Model (DSSW)

The noise trading model established by De Long, Summers, and Waldman (1990) consists of noise traders and arbitrageurs. Noise traders refer to investors who form a wrong idea about the future return of risky assets. They choose securities portfolios according to the wrong idea. Correspondingly, the optimal strategy of the arbitrageurs is to use this error of the noise traders to push the securities price back to a level consistent with the basic value of the securities, but this does not mean that they can completely do this. In the DSSW model, there are two types of investors: rational traders and noise traders. Noise traders mistakenly believe that they have special information about the future price of risky assets. Their confidence in this special information may be false signals from technical analysis methods, brokers, or other consulting institutions. Their irrationality lies in their belief that these signals contain valuable information and serve as the basis for investment decisions. As a response to the noise traders' behavior, the optimal strategy of rational investors should be to use these irrational ideas of noise traders as opportunities to earn profits. They will buy when noise traders drive down prices and sell at the opposite time. This strategy is called the Contrarian Trading Strategy. This reverse trading strategy will make the asset price tend to its fundamental value in some cases, but it can not always achieve this effect. In other words, the role of arbitrage strategy of rational investors in the return of assets to their fundamental value should not be exaggerated because, in many cases, the function of arbitrage is limited.

The basic model they proposed is a Stripped-Down Overlapping Generations Model (Samuelson 1958) composed of actors living in two periods. The model assumes that there is no consumption in the first period, and labor supply and inheritance factors are not considered. Therefore, all the resources used by actors to invest are exogenous variables. The only decision they have to make is how to choose their asset portfolio when they are young. This economy includes two types of assets that pay exactly the same dividend income. One is Risk Free Asset s, which pay a fixed actual dividend income r each period. The supply of such assets is fully elastic, which means that in two periods, one unit of such assets can be created at any time, and one unit of assets can be freely converted to one unit of consumer goods. If the consumption of each period is taken as the value scale, the price of risk-free assets is always 1; therefore, the return r paid to asset s is the risk-free rate of return. The other asset is Risk Asset u, which also obtains the same fixed real income r as asset s. However, the supply of u is not completely elastic, but the quantity is fixed and standardized to 1 unit. In period t, the price of asset u is expressed as p_t. If the price of each asset is exactly equal to the net present value calculated according to the future dividend income, then asset s and asset u can be completely replaced, and the transfer price in each period is exactly the same. But it cannot be understood that the price is determined in this way when noise traders exist. What we are discussing is a model in which the investor mentality is interrelated, and the arbitrageur's risk tolerance is limited.

Suppose there are two kinds of actors: rational expectation arbitrageurs (denoted by a) and noise traders (denoted by n). If the share of noise traders in this model is u, then the share of arbitrageurs is 1-u, and there is no difference between investors of the same type. Suppose that the average values of the two types of investors' assumptions about the price distribution of risky asset u in the t+1 period have been given in advance, and what they do when they are young is to select the portfolio according to the principle of maximizing the expected utility. The young arbitrageur's wrong valuation of the expected price of risk assets in period t is a normal random variable ρ_t with independent distribution:

$$\rho_t \sim N(\rho^*, \sigma_\rho^2) \tag{1-28}$$

The average wrong valuation ρ^* is used to measure the average bullish sentiment of noise traders. σ_ρ^2 is the variance of the noise traders' wrong valuation of the expected return of each unit of risky assets. Given the dividend in the next period, if ρ_{t+1} variance in that period and their mean value of the wrong estimate of the price distribution of u in the next period ρ_t are higher than the true value, noise traders can maximize their expected utility. The utility of each person is expressed by the stable absolute risk avoidance function of his wealth when he is old:

$$U = -e^{-2\gamma w} \tag{1-29}$$

Here γ is the absolute risk avoidance coefficient, w is the wealth owned in old age. Assuming that their ideas remain unchanged, they will decide the combination ratio of u and s when they are young. When they get old, they will turn their s into consumer goods and sell u to the next generation of young people at the price of p_{t+1}, and they will consume all their wealth.

It is assumed that the return on holding each unit of risk assets follows a normal distribution. When the expected value is maximized, the demand for risk assets is in direct proportion to the expected return assumed and in inverse proportion to the variance of the expected return assumed. The number of risk assets u owned by the arbitrageur is λ_t^α, the risk assets owned by the noise trader are λ_t^n, at the time of period t, the price of rational expectation u at period $t+1$ is $_t p_{t+1}$, then:

$$_t\sigma_{p_{t+1}}^2 = E_t\left\{[p_{t+1} - E_t(P_{t+1})]^2\right\} \tag{1-30}$$

Where, $_t\sigma_{p_{t+1}}^2$ is the variance of the advance period. The sum of the purchase quantity of risk assets λ_t^n and λ_t^α is a function of the expected price and variance of its current price, as well as the error valuation of noise traders ρ_t. Here, arbitrageurs and noise traders are allowed to have negative demand for risky assets; that is, they can sell short if they want. The specific demand function expression is:

$$\lambda_t^i = \frac{r + _t p_{t+1} - (1+r)p_t}{2\gamma(_t\sigma_{t+1})}$$

$$\lambda_t^n = \frac{r + _t p_{t+1} - (1+r)p_t}{2\gamma(_t\sigma_{t+1}^2)} + \frac{\rho_t}{2\gamma(_t\sigma_{t+1}^2)} \tag{1-31}$$

Pricing function: In order to calculate the equilibrium price, we can consider the elderly holding securities to sell and the young as demanders as a whole, that is:

$$p_t = \frac{1}{1+r}\left[r + _t p_{t+1} - 2\gamma(_t\sigma_{p_{t+1}}^2) + \mu\rho_t\right] \tag{1-32}$$

Equation 1-31 shows that the price of risk assets in period t is a function of the noise traders' wrong valuation ρ_t in that period, the technical coefficient r and behavior coefficient of the model γ, and the potential difference of the price distribution $_t p_{t+1}$ in the first period ahead. Since only the stable equilibrium is considered, that is, the unconditional distribution p_{t+1} is equal to the distribution of p_t, the price distribution of asset u generated in a period ahead of time is eliminated from the Equation 1-32 by recursive method to obtain the following equation:

$$p_t = 1 + \frac{\mu_t(\rho_t - \rho^*)}{1+r} + \frac{\mu_t \rho^*}{r} + \frac{(2\gamma)}{r}(_t\sigma_{p_{t+1}}^2) \qquad (1\text{-}33)$$

In Equation 1-33, only the second term is variable, because γ, ρ^* and r are all constant, and the variance of the next period of p_t is only a simple stable function of the constant variance of ρ_t this generation of noise traders' wrong valuation:

$$_t\sigma_{p_{t+1}}^2 = \sigma_{p_{t+1}}^2 = \frac{\mu^2 \sigma_\rho^2}{(1+r)^2} \qquad (1\text{-}34)$$

The final price form of μ depends on exogenous variables and noise traders as public information's wrong valuation of the present and future, namely:

$$p_t = 1 + \frac{\mu_t(\rho_t - \rho^*)}{1+r} + \frac{\mu_t \rho^*}{r} - (2\gamma)\frac{\mu_t^2 \sigma_\rho^2}{r(1+r)^2} \qquad (1\text{-}35)$$

The last three items of Equation 1-35 represent the impact of noise traders on the price form of asset u. As the distribution of ρ_t gradually converges to 0, the equilibrium price function p_t will also converge to the basic price 1. The second item represents the price fluctuation of risk asset u caused by the change. If the majority of noise traders in a generation are optimistic about the future market, they will push the price of u up. When the majority of people are pessimistic about the future market, the price of u will fall. If their opinion is just moderate, $\rho_t = \rho^*$, it is zero. The third item indicates the deviation degree from p_t and the basic value when the average value of the noise traders' wrong valuation is not zero. If noise traders are generally bullish, this price pressure effect will push the price of risky assets to the level it should have. Compared with the general situation, optimistic noise traders bear a larger share of price risk. The last item is the core of the model. The arbitrageur will not hold risk assets unless the noise maker is compensated for the risk caused by the decline in the price of risk assets due to his bearish outlook on the future. In period t, even though noise traders and sophisticated investors know that the price of asset u has deviated, no one is willing to hold more chips at this time because of p_{t+1} uncertainty. At the marginal level, the gain from increasing the position of the asset that everyone believes has a price deviation (different investors believe that the price deviation direction is different) is just offset by the additional price risk. In this way, noise traders have created space for their own operations: the psychological uncertainty of noise traders in the next period makes the asset u, which is essentially risk-free, become full of risks, and thus, the price decreases and the income increases. Although noise traders and arbitrage traders often hold securities portfolios with the same basic risk level, the above phenomenon will still occur. From the perspective of the economy as a whole, there is actually no risk.

2. Investor Mentality Model

Behavioral finance has two theoretical foundations: one is limited arbitrage, and the other is investor psychology analysis. From the first theoretical basis, traditional finance believes that arbitrage plays a key role in realizing market effectiveness. That is to say, even if there are irrational investors who make the price of securities deviate from the basic value, they will encounter rational arbitrageurs who will eliminate the influence of the former on the price and return the price of securities to the basic value. However, behavioral finance believes that due to the lack of complete substitutes for securities, Noise Trader Risk, time, investors, and other factors, arbitrage, which appears to be almost perfect on the surface, actually plays a very limited role, greatly reducing its key role in achieving market effectiveness. In this regard, behavioral financiers put forward the DSSW model to explain. From the second theoretical basis, although limited arbitrage explains why the market will be in an inefficient state under the interference of noise traders, it cannot tell us what specific form this inefficiency takes. Therefore, it is necessary to establish the second theoretical basis of behavioral finance: investor mentality analysis. In view of the two main types of anomalies in the securities market, namely, overreaction and underreaction, behavioral financiers, based on psychology, put forward some investor behavior models to explain the phenomena of overreaction and underreaction. The most important three models are the BSV model, the DHS model, and the HS model.

BSV model (Barberis, Shleffer, and Vishny 1998) believes that there are two kinds of wrong paradigms when deciding on investment: One is representative bias, that is, investors pay too much attention to the change mode of recent data, but not enough attention to the overall characteristics of these data, which leads to the under-reaction of stock prices to changes in earnings. The other is conservatism. Investors can't modify their prediction models according to the changed conditions in time, which leads to over-reaction of stock prices. The BSV model starts from these two deviations and explains how the investor decision-making model leads to the deviation of the market price change of securities from the efficient market hypothesis.

DHS model (Daniel, Hirsheifer, and Subramanyam 1998) divides investors into two categories: with information and without information. Investors without information have no judgment bias, while investors with information have overconfidence and biased serf-contribution. Overconfidence leads investors to exaggerate the accuracy of their judgment on stock value. The biased self-attribution makes them underestimate the public signals about the stock value. As public information finally overcomes behavioral biases, overreaction to personal information and underreaction to public information will lead to short-term continuity and long-term reversal of stock returns. Therefore, Fama (1998) believes that although the DHS model and BSV model are based on different behavioral premises, their conclusions are similar.

HS model (Hong and Stein 1999), also known as the unified theoretical model. The difference between the unified theoretical model and the BSV and DHS model is that it focuses on the mechanism of different actors rather than the cognitive bias of actors. The model divides actors into two categories: "news observer" and "momentum trader." Observers make predictions based on information about future value, which is limited to completely independent of current or past prices; "Momentum traders" are completely dependent on past price changes, and their limitation is that their predictions must be simple functions of past price history. Under the above assumptions, the model attributes underreaction and overreaction to the gradual diffusion of basic value information, excluding other needs for investor emotional stimulation and liquidity trading. The model believes that "momentum traders" tried to take advantage of this by hedging strategies because of the initial tendency of "observing informants" to underreact to private information, and the result of doing so just went to the other extreme—overreaction.

3. Behavioral Asset Pricing Model

The behavioral asset pricing model (BAPM) was proposed by Shefrin and Statman (1994). This model integrates information traders, noise traders, and their interactions in the market into the asset pricing framework and proposes the concept of behavioral beta. On the one hand, BAPM accepts the effectiveness of the market in the sense that it cannot defeat the market. On the other hand, the rejection of market efficiency from a rational perspective has profound implications for the future development of financial research. Schefflin and Statman proposed the behavioral portfolio theory (BPT) in 2000, drawing on Markowitz's modern portfolio theory (MPT). This theory breaks the limitations of modern portfolio theory: the limitations of rational people, investors who are risk averse, and the limitations of risk measurement, and is closer to the actual investment behavior of investors. It has aroused widespread concern in the financial sector.

The behavioral asset pricing model is an extension of the standard financial capital asset pricing model. In the behavioral asset pricing model, investors are divided into information traders and noise traders. Information traders are defined as rational traders. They support the capital asset pricing model of standard financial theory and have a mean-variance preference. Noise traders usually jump out of the capital asset pricing model, are easy to make cognitive mistakes, and there is no strict mean-variance preference. When information traders occupy the main body of transactions, the market is efficient, while when the latter occupies the main body of transactions, the market is inefficient. In the behavioral asset pricing model, the expected return of securities is determined by their behavioral beta, and the behavioral asset portfolio artificially increases the proportion of growth stocks compared with the market portfolio. Therefore, in the behavioral asset pricing model, the problem of the capital market portfolio still exists, but the mean-variance effective portfolio will change over time. In addition, the behavioral asset pricing model also conducts a comprehensive study on the distribution of market portfolio returns, risk premium, term structure, option pricing, and other issues in the presence of noise traders. In the behavioral asset pricing model, because it considers both the characteristics of value performance and the characteristics of utilitarianism, on the one hand, it accepts the market effectiveness in the sense that it cannot defeat the market, and on the other hand, it rejects the market effectiveness in the sense of rationalism.

The behavioral asset pricing model typically reflects the basic concept of behavioral finance, the long-term and substantial existence of irrational traders, and it describes the asset pricing method under the interaction between rational traders and irrational traders. In this model, rational traders, namely information traders, follow the CAPM model and are market actors with good cognition, professional skills, and mean-variance preferences that are preset in traditional theories. However, irrational traders, namely noise traders, do not have the knowledge reserves and behavior patterns that investors in an ideal state should have. They do not have a mean-variance preference and often deviate from the capital asset pricing model. Therefore, in the behavioral asset pricing model, unlike the capital asset pricing model β, the coefficient is related to the behavior; such behavior β is related to the tangent of the effective portfolio of mean-variance, not to the market portfolio. It can be seen that the behavioral asset pricing model accepts market efficiency to a certain extent and also pursues the limited rationality and limited arbitrage pursued by behavioral finance.

1.3.3 Transaction Strategy of Behavioral Finance

1. Positive Feedback Trading

Positive feedback trading refers to the existence of various deviations, such as cognitive deviation and emotional deviation of investors, which ultimately leads to pricing deviation of different assets, and asset pricing deviation will in turn affect the process of investors' understanding and judgment of such assets. Using the feedback mechanism to formulate trading strategies is a positive feedback trading strategy. According to the efficient market hypothesis, the positive feedback trading behavior is irrational. For the widespread phenomenon of positive feedback strategies, behavioral finance gives the following explanations. First of all, it takes a period of time for market participants to fully digest new information, and it takes a period of time for market prices to fully reflect all information, so traders can take advantage of this period to make profits. Secondly, investors' psychological expectations. Feedback occurs because the past price rise has generated the expectation of further price rise, or because the price rise has increased the confidence of investors, and the continuous price rise will stimulate the optimism of investors. Thirdly, the continuous rise or fall of the price will sometimes lead to a large number of investors buying or selling, which may be attributed to the herding behavior of investors and finally lead to price deviation. Finally, arbitrageurs may hype wildly after holding assets in heavy positions and stimulate noise traders to trade through various means, affecting people's expectations of prices. Positive feedback trading behavior may form a price foam. There are many price foam in history, including the tulip boom in Holland in the 17th century, the foam in the South China Sea in the 18th century, the foam in Mississippi, the first railway boom in Britain, and the foam in the American stock market in the 1920s.

De Long, Shliefer, Summers, and Waldmann (1990) proposed to explain the behavior of noise traders with positive feedback trading in the stock market and constructed an asset pricing model, which is called the four-stage DSSW model for short. The model divides investors into positive feedback traders, rational speculative traders, and negative traders and assumes that the sum of the latter two types of investors is constant, describing the trading behavior of various traders in different periods of stock price changes (period 0, period 1, period 2, and period 3). The empirical research on positive feedback trading behavior and abnormal stock price volatility mainly focuses on the correlation between institutional investors' behavior and stock price changes. After Sentana and Wadhwani (1992) investigated the hourly trading data in October 1987 and the daily trading data in 1885–1988 in the US stock market, they found that when the stock price fluctuated slightly, the stock returns showed positive autocorrelation in a short period of time, but when the volatility was quite large, it showed negative autocorrelation. The greater the volatility, the more obvious the performance. The research conducted by Koutmos (1997) on the stock markets of six major industrialized countries (Australia, Belgium, Germany, Italy, Japan, and the United Kingdom) shows that for short-term stock returns, positive feedback trading behavior is an important factor affecting stock returns. Nofsinger and Sais (1999) found that institutional investors adopted more positive feedback trading strategies than individual investors.

2. Time Diversification

Time diversification includes two aspects: one is that the risk of stock investment decreases with the increase of the investment period. One suggestion is that young people should allocate a high proportion of stocks in their portfolios and gradually reduce this proportion as they grow older. Fisher and Statman (1999) explained and analyzed the time decentralization strategy from four aspects of behavioral finance: expectation theory, cognitive error, self-control, and regret aversion. The expectation theory shows that the utility function curve of investors is convex and concave in the income and loss regions, respectively, so investors are risk averse in the income region and loss averse in the loss region. The holding rule in the time decentralization strategy can reduce the regret brought by the book loss. Because the book loss is different from the actual loss, it still retains the hope of the actual balance of payments. However, when the term expires, this hope may be dashed. At this time, it is most valuable to use option tools to extend the term. The time decentralization strategy shifts investors' attention from their fear of short-term losses to their expectation of pride in long-term returns. At the same time, it is an effective tool to avoid regret when combined with option instruments. Fisher and Statman (1999) vividly likened the time decentralization strategy to "glasses," which may wrongly correct the vision of a normal person, but it may also correct the vision of amblyopia.

3. Dollar-Cost Averaging Strategy

The dollar-cost averaging strategy ignores the market timing, which can help investors avoid investing too much when the stock market is rising and too little when the stock market is falling. The dollar-cost averaging strategy is to invest a fixed amount in each period, that is, the average of the total investment, regardless of market fluctuations. The dollar-cost averaging strategy has the following advantages: encouraging investors to stick to their investment plans, eliminating investors' unnecessary worries about the normal fluctuation of the market, and enabling investors to continuously invest in the market so as not to miss favorable investment opportunities. Although the dollar-cost averaging strategy eliminates the speculation on the timing of investment, it does not provide a certain guarantee of profitability, nor can it avoid loss when the market is generally low.

4. Short Term Momentum Trading Strategy and Long-Term Contrarian Trading Strategy

De Bondt and Thaler (1985, 1987) initially proposed the reverse trading strategy. They classified the company's stocks according to the stock price performance and formed a winner's portfolio from the companies with the highest cumulative stock returns in the first three years and a loser's portfolio from the companies with the lowest cumulative returns in the same period. Then, they compared the loser's portfolio with the winner's portfolio in the five years after the construction between 1933 and 1985 and found that the loser's portfolio showed high returns after the formation period. The winner's portfolio shows a lower return. The resulting reversal strategy believes that buying the past loser portfolio and selling the past winner portfolio can obtain an extraordinary return of about 8% per year (De Bondt and Thaler 1985). Jegadeesh and Titman (1993, 2001) put forward Momentum Strategy. They found that the price trend of individual stocks in the past 3–12 months tends to show the same trend in the next six months through their investigation of the earnings of the US stock market. The resulting momentum trading strategy believes that buying stocks with high yield in the earlier period and selling stocks with low yield in the same period in the earlier period can obtain extraordinary returns. Rouwenhorst (1998, 1999) selected the stock markets of 12 European countries from 1980 to 1995 as the sample objects. By studying the returns of diversified portfolios in the international market, it was found that the monthly return of the past winner portfolio was about 1% higher than that of the loser portfolio. From this, it was concluded that the momentum trading strategy is also applicable to the international market. The behavioral model believes that insufficient reaction leads to short-term continuity of stock returns, and overreaction leads to long-term reversals. HS (Hong and Stein 1997) proposed a market model of "news observer" and "momentum trader" with two types of bounded rational actors. Both types of bounded rational investors can only "process" a subset of all public information. Message observers make predictions based on the signals they privately observe about the basic situation in the future. Their limitation is that they cannot make predictions based on current and past price information. Momentum traders, on the contrary, can make predictions based on past price changes, but their predictions are simple functions of past prices. The HS model attributes underreaction and overreaction to the gradual diffusion of messages. Information is gradually diffused among investors, and the price has insufficient reaction in the short term, which means momentum traders can profit from chasing up and killing down.

CHAPTER 2

Dual Differences between Modern Financial Investment Theory and Investment Practice

From the development history of finance, finance has experienced a historical evolution from traditional finance, standard finance, to behavioral finance. The key difference between traditional finance and standard finance is reflected in the analytical paradigm. Traditional finance emphasizes institutional analysis and more qualitative analysis; standard finance emphasizes mathematical analysis or quantitative research. The research, which was from quality to quantity, is a revolutionary leap in finance development. Standard finance is based on the efficient market hypothesis, capital asset pricing model, arbitrage pricing model, and option pricing theory; behavioral finance brings human psychology and behavior into the research framework of finance, which is a great impetus to the development of modern finance.

From the development of financial investment theory and investment practice in recent decades, we find that there are clearly two serious differences. Theoretically, the standard finance based on the efficient market hypothesis has been widely questioned by the theories represented by behavioral finance; from the perspective of the application of theory to financial practice, the great success of great practitioners represented by Buffett and Peter Lynch is not the application of the existing so-called mature financial theory. We call the differences in financial theory, financial investment theory, and financial investment practice double differences. The research of this book starts from here.

2.1 An Overview of the Dual Differences between Modern Financial Investment Theory and Investment Practice

The development of any theory cannot be absolutely perfect, and the financial investment theory must be no exception. Since the birth of financial theory as an independent theory, disputes and differences have accompanied the development of this theory. Behavioral finance presents a severe challenge to standard finance by using a large number of empirical research results, which shows that the standard finance theory based on the efficient market hypothesis is at least an imperfect theory. The constraint of the efficient market hypothesis itself is the rational person hypothesis. Behavioral finance believes that investors are not completely rational but limited rationality. Under the assumption of bounded rationality, behavioral finance negates the standard finance theory through a large number of empirical studies and fundamentally determines the theoretical cornerstone of the standard finance-market efficiency hypothesis. However, after overthrowing the standard financial theory, behavioral finance has not established a complete and independent theoretical system, and its application value is far inferior to the standard financial theory denied. Perhaps behavioral finance theory is just a passer-by in the history of financial theory.

From the perspective of the application of theory to practice, the great practitioners represented by Buffett achieved great success, but they did not use the existing so-called mature financial investment theory. These practitioners even opposed the standard financial theory based on the efficient market hypothesis. This influential theory did not successfully guide investment practice. The limitations of the capital asset pricing model and arbitrage pricing model in empirical research limit the application value of standard finance. At the same time, from the perspective of behavioral finance, we cannot find a theoretical basis to explain their great success, which is rare in various scientific research and applications. The research of standard financial theory based on the rational human hypothesis has great limitations. This also shows that there is still a huge development space for the research of financial investment theory from another angle. In a general sense, the core issue of financial investment theory research must be inseparable from asset pricing and then the prediction of the future trend of an asset price. Even if the asset price cannot be accurately priced, it should clearly reveal the fundamental reason for the inability to price accurately.

2.2 Theoretical Divergence of Modern Financial Investment Theory

Standard finance emphasizes mathematical analysis or quantitative research. From qualitative research to quantitative research, it is a revolutionary leap in the development of financial investment theory. Standard finance is based on the efficient market hypothesis, capital asset pricing model, arbitrage pricing model, and option pricing theory. It is a science based on quantitative economics. It mainly uses quantitative analysis methods to study financial problems, especially for the pricing of complex financial products and dynamic market equilibrium. Standard finance emphasizes mathematical analysis or quantitative research. From qualitative to quantitative research is a revolutionary leap in the development of financial investment theory. Standard finance is based on the efficient market hypothesis, capital asset pricing model, arbitrage pricing model, and option pricing theory. It is a science based on quantitative economics. It mainly uses quantitative analysis methods to study financial problems, especially for the pricing of complex financial products and dynamic market equilibrium. Its symbol is Harry M. Markowitz's *Portfolio Selection* in 1952 and *Portfolio Selection: Efficient Diversification of Investments* in 1959, which is recognized as the opening work of modern portfolio theory (MPT) and also marks the birth of standard financial theory. Markowitz also won the Nobel Prize in economics in 1990, which is the best proof of its theoretical value.

In terms of the development process of standard finance itself, it was founded in the 1950s, developed in the 1960s, matured in the 1970s, and finally became the mainstream finance theory. Following Markowitz, Eugene F. Fama published *Efficient Capital Markets: A Review of Theory and Empirical Work* in 1970, which systematically summarized the previous EMH research and put forward a complete theoretical framework of the efficient market hypothesis. The efficient market hypothesis (EMH) was first proposed by Samuelson (1965) and Fama (1965) and comprehensively elaborated by Fama. The core content of the hypothesis is that the securities price can always fully reflect the available information. The so-called efficient market means that the market is composed of a large number of rational investors. Based on the fully flowing information in the market, these investors make judgments on the future market value of securities and compete with each other to maximize their own interests. The core content of the efficient market hypothesis is that securities prices can always fully reflect the available information. Based on different responses to information sets, market efficiency is divided into three levels: weak form efficiency, semi-strong form efficiency, and strong form efficiency. The implied premise and conclusion of this theory can be summarized as that the relevant information in the securities market is equal to each investor, and each investor can make rational investment decisions in time according to the information he has. Then, no investor can obtain extraordinary income, and the securities market is effective. Since all information is reflected in the price, the market follows a random walk, and the daily price has nothing to do with the activities of the previous day. EMH obviously assumes that all investors will respond immediately to new information, so the future has nothing to do with the past or present.

Sharpe (1964), Lintner (1965), and Mossin (1966) constructed the capital asset pricing model (CAPM) model to describe the price mechanism of the capital market. EMH and CAPM are consistent and interrelated, and the latter provides a set of methods to test the former. This combination opened the door to testing the effectiveness of the market through empirical methods. Subsequently, a large number of empirical studies have tested the efficient market hypothesis and provided strong support for the theory. Then there are Ross's arbitrage pricing model (APT) and Scholes's (1972) option pricing model (OPT), etc. In the mid-1970s, the standard financial theory based on the efficient market hypothesis (EMH), capital market pricing theory, and modern portfolio theory established its position in the field of the financial economy. To sum up, all the research done by standard financial theory is based on two assumptions: rational man and risk-free arbitrage.

2.2.1 Efficient Market Hypothesis

In 1964, Osborne put forward the random walk theory. He believed that the change in stock price is similar to the molecular "Brownian motion" in chemistry, which has the characteristics of a "random walk," that is, the path of its change is unpredictable. In 1970, Fama also believed that the stock price return series did not have "memory" statistically, so investors could not predict its future trend according to historical prices. This conclusion inevitably frustrates many people who are doing stock price analysis. They try their best to study the accounting statements and future prospects of each company to determine its value and try to make correct financial decisions on this basis. Is the stock price really so random that there is no law of economics in the financial market?

Samuelson believes that the financial market does not operate according to the economic law. On the contrary, it is an efficient market formed according to the role of the economic law.

In 1965, Fama published an article, "Random Walks in Stock Market Prices," in the *Financial Analysts Journal*. In this article, he first mentioned the concept of an "efficient market." He believed that an efficient market is a market in which there are a large number of rational investors pursuing maximum interests. They actively participate in the competition, everyone tries to predict the future market price of a single stock, and everyone can easily obtain the currently important information. In an efficient market, the competition among many smart investors leads to a situation where at any time, the market price of a single stock reflects what has happened and has not yet happened, but what the market expects to happen.

In 1970, Fama formally put forward the efficient markets hypothesis, which defined the efficient market as a market where the price completely reflects all available information in a securities market.

There are two signs to measure whether the securities market has external efficiency: first, whether the price can change freely according to relevant information; second, whether the relevant information of securities can be fully disclosed and evenly distributed so that each investor can get the same amount and quality of information at the same time. According to this assumption, investors will make rapid and effective use of possible information when buying and selling stocks. All known factors affecting the stock price have been reflected in the stock price. Therefore, according to this theory, the technical analysis of stocks is invalid. First, everyone in the market is a rational economic man. The companies represented by each stock in the financial market are under the strict supervision of these rational people. They conduct basic analysis every day, evaluate the company's stock price based on the company's future profitability, and convert the future value into today's present value, carefully tradeoff between risk and benefit. Second, the stock price reflects the balance between the supply and demand of these rational people. The number of people who want to buy is just the number of people who want to sell. That is, the people who think the stock price is overvalued and the people who think the stock price is undervalued are equal. If someone finds that the two are not equal, that is, it is possible to arbitrage, they will immediately use the method of buying or selling stocks to make the stock price change rapidly until the two are equal. Third, the stock price can also fully reflect all available information about the asset. That is, the information is effective. When the information changes, the stock price will change accordingly. When good news or bad news just came out, the stock price began to change. When it was well known, the stock price had also risen or fallen to the appropriate price.

The efficient market hypothesis actually means that there is no free lunch and nothing in the world. In a normal and efficient market, everyone should not expect to make unexpected profits. Therefore, it is not wise for us to take time to see whether there is money on the road. It is useless for us to bother to analyze the value of stocks. It will waste our minds.

Of course, the efficient market hypothesis is only a theoretical hypothesis. In fact, not everyone is always rational, nor is information effective at every point in time.

Based on the analysis method of Samuelson (1965) and Roberts (1967), Fama (1970) formally put forward the efficient market hypothesis and divided the market efficiency into the following three types:

The first type is weak form of efficiency market. In the weak efficient market, the stock price has reflected all the information that can be obtained from the market trading data, including, for example, the past stock price history and trading volume. Therefore, the technical analysis is invalid. The test method includes sequence autocorrelation analysis. If the stock return has time autocorrelation, that is, the previous return can affect the current return, the technical analysis is useful, and the weak efficiency cannot be established. It also includes run tests and filter rules.

The second type is the semi-strong form of efficiency market. In the semi-strong efficient market, securities prices fully reflect all public information, including financial statements published by the company and historical price information. Therefore, technical analysis and basic analysis are invalid. The test method uses the event test method, that is, to test whether there is a rapid response to the change in stock price when events related to the fundamentals of the company occur. If it can respond quickly, investors cannot obtain excess profits through new information, the basic analysis fails, and the semi-strong type is valid.

The third type is the strong form of efficiency market. In the strong efficient market, the securities price fully reflects all information, including public and insider information. Therefore, the technical analysis and basic analysis are invalid. The test method is to test the investment performance evaluation of the fund or insiders. If the investment performance of the evaluated person is indeed better than the market average, strong efficiency cannot be established.

The efficient market hypothesis is based on three gradually relaxed assumptions. Firstly, investors are considered rational, so they can make a reasonable value evaluation of securities; secondly, to some extent, some investors are not rational, but for the reason that the securities trading between them is random, their irrationality will offset each other, so the securities price will not be affected; finally, in some cases, irrational investors will make the same mistake, but they will encounter rational arbitragers in the market, which will eliminate the impact of the former on the price.

In Fama's landmark empirical analysis of stock price, he defined "efficient market" for the first time and concluded that stock price follows a random walk. Samuelson (1965) provided formal economic parameters for the "efficient market" for the first time, and his contribution was summarized in the title of his article "The Proof of Correctly Expecting Random Price Fluctuation," he focused on the concept of martingale rather than a random walk. Fama and Blume (1966) concluded that sequence correlation might be as effective as the Alexander filtering rule in measuring the direction and dependence of price changes. Mandelbrot (1966) proved that in a competitive market, when the investors are rational and risk-neutral, and the return is unpredictable, the securities price follows a martingale. Jensen (1968) evaluated the performance of mutual funds and concluded: "On average, these funds are obviously not good enough in their trading activities, so that they can't even recover their brokerage fees." Fama (1970) defined an efficient market in this way: the price in a market can always "fully reflect" the available information, which is called "efficiency." He was also the first person to consider the "joint hypothesis problem." Scholes (1972) studied the impact of the secondary issue price and believed that the market is effective except for some signs of price drift after events. Grossman (1976) described such a model: "An efficient system of price information perfectly summarizes all kinds of information." Osborne (1977) published *The Stock Market and Finance from a Physicist's Viewpoint*, where he discussed market decisions, random walks, statistical methods, and sequence analysis of stock market data. Ball (1978) reflected the excess return consistent with the announcement of the company's revenue. Jensen (1968) pointed out that "I believe there is no economic proposition in economics with more solid empirical evidence than the efficient market hypothesis." He defined efficiency as: "If it is impossible to obtain excess returns through available information in the market, the market is effective." Lucas (1972) established a theoretical model of reasonable agency, which shows that martingale property does not need to be held under the condition of risk aversion. Through a theoretical model, Radner (1979) shows that when rational equilibrium expectation exists, it can reveal its initial information to all traders. Dimson (1979) commented on the problem of risk measurement (evaluation test) when stocks are traded frequently. Harrison and Kreps (1979) published *Martingales and Arbitrage in Multiperiod Securities Markets*. Shiller (1979) showed that the volatility of long-term interest rates is greater than predicted.

2.2.2 Challenges of Efficient Market Hypothesis

In the development of standard finance theory, many empirical studies have drawn many "unsolved mysteries." Scholars believe that standard finance ignores the research on the actual decision-making behavior of investors. Through a large number of empirical studies, they revealed many anomalies that violated the efficient market hypothesis, such as the "January effect," "weekend effect," "equity risk premium problem," "herding effect," and "Arles paradox." The traditional assumption of "rational man" can no longer explain the economic life and behavior of real people, and the expected utility theory has also been questioned. Behavioral finance began to become the mainstream of the development of financial theory. They fundamentally denied the theoretical assumptions of standard finance through various anomalies revealed by a large number of empirical studies. Behavioral finance applies the achievements of behavioral science, psychology, and cognitive science to the financial market. "Limited rationality" and "limited arbitrage" are its two pillars. Through experimental comparison, Kahneman and Tversky (1979) found that most investors are not standard financial investors but behavioral investors, and their behavior is not always rational and risk-averse. Representative models of behavioral finance mainly include the BSV model (Barberism, Shleffer, and Vishny 1998), the DHS model (Daniel, Hirsheifer, and Subramanyam 1998), and the HS model (Hong and Stein 1999). BSV model believes that there are selective deviations and conservative deviations in people's investment decision-making. The model explains that the investment decision-making process eventually leads to the deviation of the market price from the efficient market from these two deviations. The DHS model divides investors into those who have information and those who do not. Investors without information do not have judgment bias, and investors with information have overconfidence and biased self-attribution. Fama (1998) believes that although the DHS and BSV models are based on different behavioral premises, their conclusions are similar. The HS model is also known as the unified theoretical model. It divides the actors into "observer" and "momentum trader." The "observer" forecasts according to the information about future value obtained, while the "momentum trader" completely depends on past price changes. The model believes that at first, due to the tendency of "observing informants" under-react to private information, the "momentum traders" try to make use of this through a hedging strategy, and the result of this just goes to overreaction. It can be said that behavioral finance overthrows the theoretical system constructed by standard finance. However, behavioral finance has not established a theoretical system that can replace the status of standard finance, and its application value even lags behind standard finance. The difference between efficient market hypothesis and behavioral finance is whether the market is effective or not. Their theoretical views are diametrically opposite. At least one of the two theories is imperfect or has serious mistakes. On October 8, 2002, the Nobel Prize in Economics was awarded to Daniel Kahneman and Vernon L. Smith, representatives of behavioral finance. They integrated the research results of psychology with finance, especially in people's judgment and decision-making under uncertainty. This is strong evidence that behavioral finance has reached its peak.

From the perspective of the empirical challenges faced by EMH, the three gradually relaxed hypotheses of EMH theory build three lines of defense when facing the challenges of behavioral finance. The first line of defense, assuming that investors are rational, they can determine the basic value of each security. When the information that determines the securities price changes, investors can respond quickly, timely, and accurately, so that the securities price can be adjusted to the corresponding level with the change of new information. It is impossible for behavioral finance to assume that ordinary investors are completely rational people. Many investors often make investment decisions based on "noise" rather than relevant information. They are easily influenced by the market atmosphere, often trade, and frequently change their portfolio. The second line of defense, the efficient market hypothesis, assumes that in many cases, although investors are not completely rational. However, the trading behavior of irrational investors in the stock market is random. When this type of investor exists in large numbers, and each investor's trading strategies are independent, their trading behaviors are likely to offset each other. Although the trading volume between irrational investors is large, the securities price can remain around the basic value. Behavioral finance believes that people do not just occasionally deviate from rationality, but often have the same behavior. The transactions between them are not completely random, with roughly the same trading directions. Everyone is likely to buy or sell the same stocks, such as the pursuit of market hot spots. The third line of defense is that even if the trading strategies of investors are relevant, the conclusion that the market is effective can still be established. If the price of a security has exceeded the basic value due to the interrelated rush purchase of non-deep or irrational investors, the arbitrager will sell this high-priced stock and buy other securities with a similar nature for risk hedging.

If such replaceable security can be found and the arbitrager can buy and sell it, the overvalued security price will return to the basic value.

The premise of the efficient market hypothesis is that investors can correctly interpret all kinds of investment information. This hypothesis actually assumes that investors are rational people. The rational man is the basis for the establishment and development of traditional financial theory. It means that investors take the maximization of utility as the goal in decision-making and can correctly process the known information, while behavioral finance calls out a challenge of the EMH's rational man hypothesis. Behavioral finance theory holds that people will not achieve complete rationality. In addition to being driven by interests, individual behavior will also be affected by their own flexible preferences, personality psychological characteristics, values, beliefs, and other psychological factors. Investors are not all rational. The market cannot be completely dominated by rational investors. Irrational investors can continue to exist and have an impact on the formation of securities market prices. It is for this reason that various anomalies appear in the market, specifically as follows:

(1) Scale effect. The change in stock price is closely related to the scale of the company represented by the stock. The stocks of small companies are easier to obtain higher returns than those of larger companies.

(2) Time effect. The return of stocks on Monday is obviously negative, and the return on Friday is significantly higher than that on other trading days of the week. Therefore, a stock trading at some specific time can obtain an excess return.

(3) Reverse investment strategy. It is found that the degree of concern of a stock (measured by the ratio of stock market value to its book value; the higher the ratio, the higher the degree of concern) also affects the change of stock price. The concerned stocks often have a lower rate of return, while the less concerned stocks can always obtain a higher return on investment. Therefore, Investors can adopt the strategy of reverse investment to obtain an excess return.

(4) The mystery of closed-end funds. The number of units issued by closed-end funds is fixed, and these fund units can be transferred and traded in the securities market. It is found that the representative transfer price of each closed-end fund unit is not equal to the average market value of assets held by each fund. Although closed-end funds sometimes transfer at a price higher than the value of net assets, they are usually transferred at a discount of 10%–20% lower than the value. After considering the agency cost, liquidity, capital gains tax payable, and other factors, it still cannot explain the sharp discount of closed-end funds.

(5) The mystery of asset premium. Asset premium refers to the difference between the historical average return of the stock market and the historical average return of the bond or treasury bond market. Asset premium refers to the higher historical average return of stocks relative to bonds.

Table 2-1 Summary of the Birth of Behavioral Finance and Its Challenges to Standard Finance after 1980

Year	Event
1980	Grossman and Stiglitz (1980) show that it is impossible for the market to be completely effective. Because the information is expensive, the price cannot perfectly reflect the available information; otherwise, those investors who spend a lot of resources on obtaining and analyzing the price will not be compensated. A reasonable market equilibrium model must leave some incentives for information collectors (security analysis).
1981	LeRoy and Porter (1981) show that the stock market is "excessive volatility," and they refuse market efficiency. Stiglitz (1981) shows that even if there is an obvious competitive and "efficient" market, the resource allocation may not be Pareto optimal. Shiller's (1981) research shows that the stock price fluctuation is too large, which means that the dividend change is reasonable, that is, excessive fluctuation.
1982	Milgrom and Stokey (1982) show that in some cases, the private information received cannot be an incentive to create transactions. Tirole's (1982) research shows that when investors are in the equilibrium state of rational expectation, their share of securities mainly depends on their risk preference. People's different expectations of future returns of securities (i.e., inconsistent expectations on which speculation depends) are an important factor in securities trading.
1984	Roll (1984) examined the impact of American orange juice futures price and weather and found excessive volatility.
1985	De Bondt and Thaler (1985) discovered the stock market overreaction and proved the inefficiency of a large number of weak form markets. This paper has become the symbol of behavioral finance.
1986	Marsh and Merton (1986) analyzed Shiller's method of analyzing variance constraints and concluded that this method could not be used to test the hypothesis of stock market rationality. They also highlighted the practical consequences of rejecting the efficient market hypothesis. Fischer Black (1986) introduced the concept of "noise traders," which refers to those who only rely on information for trading, and showed that noise traders are necessary for the existence of a circulation market. Summers (1986) discussed that many statistical tests of market efficiency are of little significance for discriminating against reasonable forms of low efficiency. French and Roll (1986) found that asset prices are more volatile in foreign exchange trading time than in non-trading time. They inferred that this is due to transactions in the private information market to produce their own news.
1988	Fama and French (1988) found a negative autocorrelation of the returns of stock portfolios over a year. Lo and MacKinlay (1988) strongly rejected the random walk hypothesis of weekly stock market return by using the variance ratio test. Poterba and Summers (1988) show that stock returns are positively correlated in the short-term market and negatively correlated in the long-term market. Conrad and Kaul (1988) characterized the random behavior of the expected return of a common stock.

(Continued)

Year	Event
1989	Cutler, Poterba, and Summers (1989) found that information cannot fully explain market movements.
	Eun and Shim (1989) found that there is a lot of interdependence between national stock markets, and the results are consistent in the international stock market with effective information.
	Ball (1989) discussed the regulation of stock market efficiency.
	Guimaraes, Kingsman, and Taylor (1989) edited the book *A Reappraisal of the Efficiency of Financial Markets*.
	Shiller (1989) published *Market Volatility*, a book on the sources of volatility that challenge the efficient market hypothesis.
	LeRoy (1989) published his research paper "Efficient Capital Markets and Martingales." He clearly showed that the intuitive concept of market efficiency and the transition between martingale is not direct.
1990	Laffont and Maskin (1990) show that if there is imperfect competition, the efficient market hypothesis is likely to fail.
	Lehmann (1990) found a reversal in weekly safety returns and rejected the efficient market hypothesis.
	Jegadeesh (1990) studied the strong evidence of the predictable behavior of safe return and rejected the random walk hypothesis.
1991	Kim, Nelson, and Startz (1991) reexamined the empirical research on mean regression behavior of stock price and found that mean regression was a phenomenon before World War II.
	Matthew Jackson (1991) defined the model of the price formation process, indicating that if the agent is not the price recipient, there may be a balance between fully revealing the price and expensive information collection.
	Fama (1991) wrote the second of his three review papers. Instead of weak form testing, the first category covers the more general regional testing of the predictability of test returns.
1992	Chopra, Lakonishok, and Ritter (1992) found that the stock market overreacted.
	Belkat and Hodrick (1992) were predictable components that characterize excess returns in the stock and foreign exchange markets.
	Bernstein (1992) published the book *Capital Ideas Evolving*, which is devoted to studying the history and stock price anecdotes about shaping modern finance.
	Malkiel (1992) wrote an article in *The New Palgrave Dictionary of Money and Finance—Efficient Market Hypothesis*.
1993	Jegadeesh and Titman (1993) found that significant abnormal returns were achieved through the trading strategy of buying former winners and selling former losers.
	Richardson showed that the estimation model of sequence correlation and its scale observed in previous studies should be estimated under the independent null hypothesis.
1994	Huang and Stoll (1994) provided new evidence on market microstructure and stock return prediction.
	Metcalfan and Malkiel (1994) found that the stock portfolio selected by experts did not consistently beat the market.
	Lakonishok, Shleifer, and Vishny provided evidence that value strategies produce higher returns because they take advantage of the ideal behavior of typical investors rather than because they are fundamentally risky. (See Lakonishok, Shleifer, and Vishny 1994)

(Continued)

Year	Event
1995	Haugen published *The New Finance: The Case against Efficient Markets. Overreaction* (causing price shocks) can lead to long-term reversals (when the market realizes its past mistakes). (See Haugen 1995)
1996	Campbell, Lo, and MacKinlay (1996) published their creative book on empirical finance, *The Econometrics of Financial Markets*.
	Chan, Jagadeesh, and Lakonishok observed the momentum strategy. Their research results showed that the market could only gradually reflect new information.
1997	Arthur et al. (1997) put forward asset pricing theory by creating an artificial stock market with heterogeneous agents and endogenous expectations.
	Andrew Lo (1997) edited two volumes that collected the most influential articles on the efficient market hypothesis.
	Chan, Gup, and Pan (1997) concluded that the global stock market is weak in efficiency.
	Dow and Gorton (1997) discussed the relationship between stock market efficiency and economic benefits.
1998	Dimson and Mussavian (1998) gave a brief history of market efficiency.
	In the third of the three reviews, Fama (1998) concluded that the challenge of the efficiency market comes from abnormal long-term returns.
1999	Lo and MacKinlay (1999) published *A Non-Random Walk Down Wall Street*.
	Haugen (1999) published the second edition of his book, giving examples of inefficient markets, which are positioned as an efficient market model with an extreme spectrum of possible states.
	Bernstein (1999) criticized the efficient market hypothesis and claimed that the marginal income of investors' information exceeded the marginal cost.
	Farmer and Lo (1999) published a good but brief review article.
2000	Shleifer (2000) published *Inefficient Markets: An Introduction to Behavioral Finance*, which questioned the hypothesis of investor rationality and perfect arbitrage.
	Beechey, Vickery, and Gruen (2000) published research papers on the efficient market hypothesis.
	Shiller (2000) published the first edition of *Irrational Exuberance*, which challenged the efficient market hypothesis and showed that the market could not be explained by the historical movement of corporate profits or dividends.
2001	Fama became the first researcher elected to the American Financial Association. An excellent historical review document, since Bachelier (1900) tried to evaluate how statistical models capture empirical laws through speculative price data, Andreou, Pittis, and Spanos (2001) tracked the development of various models proposed by them.
	Rubinstein (2001) reexamined some of the most serious historical data against market rationality and concluded that the market is rational.
	Shafer and Vovk (2001) published *Probability and Finance: It's Only a Game!* To show how probability theory is based on game theory and then applied to finance.
2002	Lewellen and Shanken (2002) concluded that parameter uncertainty is important for characterizing and testing market efficiency.

(Continued)

Year	Event
2003	Malkiel (2003) examined the merits of the efficient market hypothesis and concluded that the stock market is more effective but less predictable than recent academic papers. Schwert (2003) showed that when anomalies occur, practitioners rely on documents to implement strategic plans, and then the anomalies weaken or disappear. In other words, the research results make the market more efficient.
2004	Timmermann and Granger (2004) discussed the efficient market hypothesis from the perspective of modern forecasting methods.
2005	Malkiel (2005) shows that professional investment managers do not exceed the index benchmark and provides evidence that prices in the large market seem to reflect all available information.
2006	Blakey (2006) observed the causes and consequences of some random price behaviors. T'oth and Kert'esz (2006) found evidence of improving efficiency in the New York Stock Exchange.
2008	McCauley, Bassler, and Gunaratne (2008) show that martingale stochastic processes are independent of production and generally non-stationary increments. This explains why martingales show a simple average and two-point correlation level for Markov proof that the topology of arbitrary martingale Wiener processes is not equivalent. Lo (2008) wrote an article, "Efficient Market Hypothesis for The New Palgrave Dictionary of Economics."

Note: This part draws lessons from Martin Sewell, History of the Efficient Market Hypothesis, Department of Computer Science University College London, August 2008 (amended September 2008).

Since the 1960s and 1970s, the empirical test of EMH has mainly been based on two ideas: first, the stock price can always fully reflect the changes in available information. That is, the information reflection is immediate and accurate. "Instant" requires information to be transmitted quickly from the initial information source, investors to the price. It is measured according to the time of price adjustment. There is no unified standard for measurement. The shorter the time of price adjustment to the information, the more in line with the requirements. Second, the securities price is always equal to its basic value. When the information affecting the basic value of securities does not change, the securities price should remain unchanged. Instant and accuracy are the fatal defects of efficient market theory. What it emphasizes is that the market is effective at any time point, which requires the market to be absolutely effective at any time point. Behavioral finance just grasps this point and reveals various anomalies in the securities market through a large number of empirical tests. Questioning the empirical test of effective market theory mainly includes irrational bubbles in the Shiller-Summers model (see Shiller 1981), overreaction (see De Bondt and Thaler 1985), inadequate response (see Jegadeesh and Titman 1993), E/P ratio prediction ability, and time anomalies (see De Bondt and Thaler 1985), the research on arbitrage substitutes (see Roll 1988) and the research conclusions on the change of stock price without fundamental change (see Harris and Gurel 1986; Shleifer 1986), they all questioned the efficient market theory. Although Fama (1991,

1998) attributed the above phenomena to bad models and accidental phenomena and even gave the Fama-French three-factor model (Fama and French 1992, 1993, 1996) to explain that the existence of some anomalies is a joint test problem, the impact of behavioral finance is expanding, at least indicating that the financial circles do not accept this explanation. The empirical study of Ding Zhiguo and Su Zhi (2005) also found that the reflection of securities prices on information changes is not timely and accurate, there is value deviation, and the market will not reach effectiveness in the sense of Fama.

Therefore, the core of the divergence between the efficient market hypothesis and behavioral finance is whether the market is effective. The biggest limitation of behavioral finance theory is that it has not formed a unified and mature theoretical system and cannot give a consistent explanation of various phenomena in the capital market. The reason why the classical standard financial theory can become the mainstream financial theory and receive extensive attention and praise is that it uses simple mathematical equations to establish a unified theory to solve various financial problems in the financial market. Behavioral finance theory is not mature and perfect in the construction of a model. Most research remains in the qualitative description and historical observation of visions and people's psychological deviation. How to combine them with mathematical models remains to be further studied.

2.3 Differences between Modern Financial Investment Theory and Financial Investment Practice

From the development of financial investment theory, there is another obvious contradiction. The great successful practitioners represented by Buffett and Peter Lynch did not use financial investment theory, especially the standard financial theory, with their wealth growth. They even despised these theories. We cannot help saying that this is a very humorous problem. The theory is a summary of practice and a guide to practice. The gap between theory and practice is so large. Buffett's success seems to be a mockery of modern finance, or Buffett's success is accidental.

The following is Buffett's evaluation of the efficient market hypothesis and standard finance on different occasions:

Buffett once told investors: "To succeed in investment, you don't need to study what is β value, efficient markets, modern portfolio theory, option pricing or emerging markets; in fact, you'd better know nothing about these theories." "If the market is always effective, I can only make a living by begging." Peter Lynch believes that "the stock market theory in academia has no real value. The courses learned at Wharton Business School should have helped you invest successfully, but in my opinion, it can only lead to your investment failure," "Many strange phenomena in the stock market I saw let me begin to doubt those academic theories that think the market is rational. So far, no one has become a successful practitioner by relying on the hypothesis of efficient market theory.

Buffett believes that "advocates of efficient market theory never seem to be interested in evidence inconsistent with their theory. It is clear that people who are unwilling to renounce their beliefs and uncover the mystery do not exist only among theologians." He believes that the main reasons the efficient market theory is vulnerable are: first, investors are not always rational; second, investors cannot correctly analyze the information; third, performance leverage emphasizes short-term performance, which makes it impossible to beat the market in the long run. Buffett believes that the efficient market hypothesis does not provide any successful assumptions for investors who comprehensively analyze the available information and thus occupy a competitive advantage. He also pointed out that "the view that the market is effective is correct, but it is wrong to conclude that the market is effective forever. The difference between the two assumptions is like day and night."

Buffett's strategic investment concept is sublimated from actual combat, and at the same time, it guides his investment behavior in practice. The core of the concept is the long-term investment and holding of enterprises and enterprise stocks with real value (excellent performance). This strategic investment concept, close to zero risk, is to fully understand and grasp the market, stay away from the market, and then overcome the market. When Buffett invests, he pays more attention to the company itself than the stock price. When choosing enterprises to invest in, Buffett abides by the same investment strategy: whether the internal value of the enterprise is conducive to long-term investment, whether the market price of the enterprise is lower than the market value, whether the business of the enterprise is conducive to understanding and mastering, whether the operation of the enterprise is stable and has development prospects, and whether the management of the enterprise is rational, honest and talented. This is the strategic investment principle that Buffett adheres to, namely, enterprise principle, operation principle, financial principle, and market principle.

The two hypotheses of the basic analysis school represented by Buffett are: the value of the stock determines its price, and the stock price fluctuates around the value. Therefore, the value becomes the yardstick to measure whether the price is reasonable or not. Such a definition should be very consistent with the investment philosophy advocated by Graham in securities analysis. Buffett has also repeatedly stressed the importance of the stock value ratio to price.

The basic analysis corresponds to a semi-strong form efficiency market. If the market can fully reflect all public information, the basic analysis is invalid, but Buffett emphasizes that the basic analysis has achieved great success. Buffett denied the effectiveness of the market with successful investment examples.

Buffett often emphasizes: "Fear when others are greedy, greed when others are afraid." In fact, this is that the market overreacts to bad news during the downturn, making the stock price lower than the decline corresponding to bad news; on the contrary, when the market is rising, it overreacts to the good, which makes the stock price higher than the rise corresponding to the good. This negates the efficient market hypothesis by using information response bias, that is, overreaction and under-reaction. Graham believes that: "The unreasonable price of stocks is largely due to human fear and greed. When extremely optimistic, greed makes the stock price higher than its intrinsic value, thus forming an overvalued market; when extremely pessimistic, fear makes the stock price lower than its intrinsic value, thus forming an undervalued market. It is in the correction of inefficient markets that investors profit." The above successful investment examples and the efficient market hypothesis are contradictory phenomena coexisting in the same era, and the conflict between theory and practice is obvious.

In his long-term investment practice, Buffett has found another way to study the modern securities investment theory, collect and analyze the information of the securities market, understand the requirements of investor behavior and psychological quality, choose investment varieties, and grasp investment opportunities. In addition, his critical reverse thinking and investment behavior have formed his unique strategic investment concept.

Buffett's unique theory and modern securities investment theory (such as diversified securities investment theory, simplified securities investment analysis model, and efficient market theory) have had a wide impact on the research of investors, securities investment analysts, and the investment industry. In addition to paying attention to the actual securities market, Buffett also paid close attention to the evolution of securities investment theories and found the fatal weaknesses of these theories, so as to find the investment method to obtain the gap in the high-yield market (or given by the fatal weaknesses of those theories). At the same time, Buffett also formed his own unique strategic investment theory, for example, Buffett's near-zero venture capital theory. Buffett's "near zero risk" investment theory or market risk aversion investment theory is mainly based on the recent stock price fluctuation of the non-stock market. He pays more attention to the enterprise itself than the stock price. The basic point of his theory is that as long as the general trend of society and the market is to develop in a good way, on this premise, choose the way of long-term investment. Long-term investment mainly focuses on the selected specific enterprises. The development prospects of these enterprises and the satisfaction with the economic situation in recent years (mainly the continuous annual rate of return) are good. They are blue-chip enterprises, so they can make a centralized and long-term investment, which will reduce the risk and obtain better income, that is, close to zero-risk investment. Buffett's near zero-risk strategic investment concept urges him to purposefully focus his attention on several selective companies in his investment strategy, and study them as closely as possible, grasp their internal value, look for opportunities, focus on the investment portfolio, and hold it for a long time, so as to obtain better investment return.

Buffett opposes and criticizes the diversified portfolio theory. He believes that "diversification only protects ignorance. If you want the market to have no bad effect on you, you should own every kind of stock, which is a perfect strategy for those who do not know how to analyze the situation of enterprises." In many ways, modern investment theory protects investors who do not know and understand how to evaluate enterprises, but these investors also do not get satisfactory returns.

These are enough to prove that successful investors are not the application of the so-called mature investment theory or even negative. At least the difference between financial investment theory and practice is obvious.

CHAPTER 3

Construction of Market Efficient Cycle Theory and Explanation of Double Divergence

Through the previous theoretical analysis, we explain the dual differences between modern financial investment theory and investment practice, that is, the theoretical differences between standard and behavioral finance based on effective market hypothesis and the differences between modern financial investment theory and financial investment practice. The core of the theoretical divergence between standard finance and behavioral finance lies in whether the market is effective. The empirical research results of behavioral finance clearly reveal various abnormal phenomena and deny the market effectiveness from a certain angle. If you deny the market effectiveness, you almost completely deny the standard finance theory, including the theoretical system and model design. This is the focus problem of financial investment theory in recent decades. An efficient market hypothesis is the cornerstone of standard finance; the core of the divergence between modern financial investment theory and practice is that there is no evidence that successful investors represented by Buffett and Peter Lynch are the application of ready-made investment theory, which is an incredible phenomenon in the field of financial investment. In fact, the ultimate root of this dual divergence is the market response to information; that is, the existence of information reflection deviation is the main reason for the dual divergence between financial investment theory and practice. Therefore, we take the information response deviation as the research starting point for theoretical analysis. The ultimate goal is to construct the market efficient cycle theory, and we also try to explain the dual differences between financial investment theory and practice.

3.1 Construction of Market Efficient Cycle Theory

The starting point of constructing market efficient cycle theory must be an efficient market hypothesis. Our research should start from this hypothesis. The fatal defect of the efficient market hypothesis is to test the validity of the time point. That is, the securities price can reflect all information immediately and accurately at any time point. This idealized constraint not only greatly reduces its application value but also causes the theory to have great defects. The response of the market to information will never be effective at any time point. It must go through a process. That is, the securities price can only reflect its internal value from the perspective of the average in a certain period. The definition of science should not be "time point effective" but "period effective."

The so-called market efficient cycle theory is that there must be a long enough time cycle to make the securities price fully reflect all the information in that time period, and the market is an effective market.

If the "time point efficiency" of the efficient market hypothesis is replaced by "effective period (or period efficiency)," that is, there is an effective period in the securities market. Theoretically, a large number of anomalies revealed by the empirical research of behavioral finance only deny the validity of time points, not the validity of time periods. If the market efficiency of the efficient market hypothesis is defined as the effective cycle, this great difference, in theory, will be solved. From the perspective of financial practice, the successful practitioners represented by Buffett and Peter Lynch just make use of the invalid time point for buying an operation and then use the effective cycle; that is, after returning to the internal value, they sell the operation to obtain profits.

On the issue of explaining the dual differences between financial investment theory and practice, we put forward the market efficient cycle theory, which cannot only explain the differences between standard finance and behavioral finance but also explain the differences between financial theory and financial investment practice. The essential difference between market efficient cycle theory and efficient market hypothesis is mainly reflected in the definition of an efficient market, that is, whether it is time point efficiency or period efficiency. The theory of the market efficient cycle holds that the market is effective in a period of time; that is, the average price of the market in a certain period of time fully reflects all the information that determines the securities price; the efficient market hypothesis holds that the securities market is effective at each time point, that is, it fully reflects all the information that determines the securities price at each time point. Market efficient cycle means that the response of the securities market to information is a process, not a rapid realization. Whether the market is effective or not, the efficient market hypothesis and the market efficient cycle theory have exactly the same views. They both believe that the market is effective.

3.1.1 Theoretical Basis of Information Response Deviation

The direct reason why the market cannot reach the effective time point is the deviation of investors' information reflection, which makes it impossible for the market to fully reflect all information at all times. The reaction of securities prices to information cannot be completely accurate. There is almost always a deviation in the reaction of securities prices to information at every time point. Even for the same information, the market may have three reaction results: overreaction, normal reaction, and under-reaction. Both overreaction and under-reaction are reflected in the reaction deviation of the stock market to information, that is, information response bias. Overreaction refers to the phenomenon that the change in stock price exceeds the expected reasonable level caused by an event. Its market performance is as follows: after the event, the stock price changes sharply beyond the expected level, followed by a reverse correction, and the stock price returns to its due price; under-reaction refers to the phenomenon that the change of stock price caused by an event is lower than the expected reasonable level. Its market performance is that the stock price rises or falls slowly after the event, and the stock price finally changes to its due price.

Theoretically, the uncertainty of stock price is determined by the cognitive deviation of investors. Due to the cognitive deviation of investors, the investment behavior and its consequences—stock prices must have strong uncertainty. In fact, because the stock market's response to information cannot be completely accurate, the stock market cannot fully reflect the direction and strength of information in many cases. Behavioral finance analyzes the internal mechanism of stock price specificity from the perspective of cognitive psychology and uses the behavioral finance model to explain the causes of information response deviation in the stock market. Among them, the most representative include the BSV model, DHS model, and HS model. BSV model believes that overreaction and under-reaction are caused by representativeness deviation and conservatism deviation. One is representative bias. Investors pay too much attention to the change mode of recent data but do not pay enough attention to the overall characteristics of these data. When the stock price or profit information changes, investors believe that these changes are lasting, and then the same trend will continue, so the stock price overreacts; the other is conservation bias, in which investors cannot timely correct the increased prediction model according to the changed situation. Based on these two deviations, the BSV model explains how the investor decision-making model leads to the change in market price and deviates from the efficient market hypothesis. Overreaction and under-reaction are two situations in which investors respond to market information. When investors are involved in investment behavior related to statistics in the process of investment decision-making, people's psychology will distort the process of reasoning.

The typicality of events will lead to overreaction. The typicality of events means that people usually classify things quickly, and the human brain usually classifies some things with the same characteristics on the surface but different contents. When the typicality of events helps people organize and handle a large number of data and information, it will cause investors to overreact to some old information; anchoring will cause an insufficient response. Anchoring deviation is often manifested as anchoring the stock price in the stock market. Conservative deviation leads to insufficient response because it cannot correct its own prediction according to the changed situation in time. Underreaction and overreaction will lead to the deviation of the stock price from the efficient market hypothesis. DHS model believes that overconfidence and biased self-attribution lead to overreaction and under-reaction. In the DHS model, investors are divided into informational investors and uninformative investors. The market price is determined by those with information. Those without information are not easy to make mistakes, while those with information are easy to make two kinds of mistakes. One is overconfidence. Overconfidence is when investors believe too much in their judgment, overestimate their chances of success, attribute success to their abilities, and underestimate the role of luck and opportunities. Behavioral finance finds that overconfidence is a typical and common cognitive bias and plays an important role in the process of investment decision-making; the second is self-attribution. Overconfidence makes them exaggerate the accuracy of stock private information, and self-attribution reduces the value of public information, especially when private information conflicts with public information. Overreaction to private information and insufficient response to public information are prone to the reversal of long-term benefits. DHS model explains the short-term continuity and long-term correction of stock returns. HS model attributed overreaction and under-reaction to the gradual diffusion of basic value information. The initial "news observer" had an insufficient response to personal information, and the "momentum trader" tried to use an arbitrage strategy, resulting in overreaction and under-reaction. Different from the BSV and DHS models, the HS model divides investors into two categories: news observers and momentum traders. When forecasting the stock price, the news observer does not consider the current or past price at all but trades according to the information about the future value of the stock he obtained; momentum traders base their forecasts on a simple function based on past historical prices. At the same time, the model assumes that private information is gradually diffused in message observation. HS model believes that at first, the news observer did not respond enough to private information, and momentum traders tried to use this to arbitrage, but the result just led to the overreaction of stock price. HS model focuses on the mechanism of different actors rather than the cognitive bias of actors. In this model, under-reaction and overreaction are attributed to the gradual diffusion of basic value information, excluding other needs for investors' emotional stimulation and liquidity trading. It is believed that initially, due to the tendency of "news observers" to under-react to private information, the "momentum traders" try to take advantage of this through hedging strategy, and the result of doing so just goes to the other extreme—overreaction.

Not only in theory, but a large number of empirical research results also prove that the response deviation of the stock market to information is a common phenomenon. The above behavioral finance theories not only deny the efficient market theory but also explain the inevitability of stock market failure and the necessity of government behavior.

3.1.2 *Macro Information Response Deviation and Micro Information Response Deviation*

Information is the driving force of stock price fluctuation. We divide it into macro information and micro information according to the influence range of information on the stock market. Among them, macro information refers to the information that affects all stocks in the whole stock market and leads to systemic risk; micro information refers to the information that affects the stock price of a stock or an industry and leads to non-systematic risk. We believe that there is a strict difference between the test methods of macro information response deviation and micro information response deviation. Compared with the deviation of macro information response, if there is an overreaction, the government's policy strength should be small or coordinate control measures in the opposite direction; if there is an insufficient response, the government's policy should be stronger or cooperate with continuous and stronger regulation and control measures. Compared with the deviation of micro information response, the government is generally difficult to regulate. It does not need to be regulated, because in a huge stock market, the government should never regulate and control the overreaction of some stocks and the under-reaction of others, which can be solved by the market itself and will be solved by the market mechanism. In general, the deviation of micro information response does not constitute a macroeconomic risk. From a macro perspective, for the same policy information, the market may have three reaction results, namely overreaction, normal response, and insufficient response. The deviation of the stock index's response to macro policy information puts forward higher requirements for government behavior in regulating the stock market.

The empirical analysis method of information response deviation is essentially to study whether the securities price exceeds (higher or lower) the level of rational expectation. If it does not exceed the level of rational expectation, it is a normal response; otherwise, there will be response deviation. De Bondt and Thaler (1985) developed the event analysis method, that is, to construct a "loser portfolio" and a "winner portfolio" to test whether there is reverse correction between the two portfolios. In essence, they compare the "loser portfolio" and "winner portfolio" and test the future income of the constructed sample "loser portfolio" and "winner portfolio." If the future income of the former is significantly greater than that of the latter, it comes to the conclusion of overreaction. If the income of the former is significantly less than that of the latter, it comes to the conclusion of under-reaction. If it is not significant, it is considered as a normal response, and there is no information response deviation. When there is an overreaction in the stock market, it should have the following characteristics: after the stock market price changes sharply under the influence of an event, it should make a reverse correction to its price in the subsequent time. The result of reverse correction makes the abnormal return of the stocks of the companies with better expectations appear negative, and the abnormal return of the stocks of the companies with worse expectations appear positive, so as to promote them to return to a reasonable level. According to the research results of De Bondt and Thaler, the "winner portfolio" has a low future rate of return during the sample period, and the "loser portfolio" has a high future rate of return, which is statistically significant, indicating the prevalence of market overreaction.

Event analysis is a milestone empirical method to test the information response deviation of the stock market, so it has been widely recognized by the securities theory circle. However, we believe that the event research method is only an empirical method to test the response deviation of micro information. If there is a reverse correction phenomenon, it reveals the overreaction of the "loser portfolio" to previous bad information, and the overreaction of the "winner portfolio" to previous good information cannot reveal the response characteristics of macro information. Because the whole market reacts to good and bad information together, it is impossible to test according to the later income of the "loser portfolio" and "winner portfolio," and the policy information acts on all stocks at the same time. There is a severe misunderstanding of China's securities theory circle. The main reason is that there is no distinction between micro and macro information. In essence, the event analysis method compares the late returns of the "loser portfolio" and "winner portfolio" to obtain the information response deviation of the two portfolios. In contrast, the response of the stock index to policy information (including good and bad) cannot be directly compared and analyzed by looking for an object. Fung and Lam (2004) empirically tested the Hong Kong stock market by comparing the stock index futures with the spot market and came to the conclusion that the market has overreaction. However, China's Shanghai and Shenzhen stock markets did not launch stock index futures until 2012. This empirical analysis method is obviously not suitable for empirical research on China's stock market. To test the response deviation of macro information is to see whether the stock price index is inertial or reverse after the release of macro information. If it belongs to the former, it is under-reaction, and the latter is an overreaction. Here, we use the mean regression theory to make an empirical analysis of China's stock market, because the mean regression shows that the stock market has a reverse correction, that is, overreaction; if it is mean avoidance, that is, trend characteristics or inertia characteristics, it belongs to insufficient response.

There are many empirical studies on the micro information response deviation of the stock market by using the event analysis method. For example, the research results of De Bondt and Thaler (1987) show that from January 1926 to December 1982, the average cumulative excess return of "loser portfolio" is 24.26% higher than that of "winner portfolio" in the next 3–5 years, indicating that there is an obvious overreaction phenomenon in the American stock market, but it cannot fully explain that in the portfolio test period, the "loser portfolio" obtains positive excess return every month. Vermanelen and Verstringe (1986) used the same method to test the Belgian stock market, Alonso and Rubio (1990) tested the stock markets of the United States and Spain, Costa (1994) used the data of the Brazilian stock market from 1986 to 1993, Liu Yuzhen, Liu Weiqi, and Xie Zhengneng (1990) used the data of Taiwan stock market from 1982 to 1989, Liu Li and Chen Xingzhu (2001) reached the conclusion of long-term overreaction with the data of China stock market from 1993 to 2000. Unlike the above views, Jegadeesh and Titman (1993) discovered the "inertia strategy," which can use historical information to obtain returns that exceed the market average. The so-called "inertia strategy" refers to the trading strategy of buying stocks with rising prices in the previous 3–12 months (winner portfolio) and selling stocks with falling prices in the previous 3–12 months (loser portfolio). Using this strategy to test the American stock market from 1965 to 1989, it is found that there is a significant positive abnormal return in the holding period of the next 3–12 months. For example, based on the yield of the past six months, buying a winner portfolio and selling a loser portfolio can achieve an average annual abnormal return of 12.01% in the next six months. In the next six months, the holding period can achieve an average annual abnormal return of 12.01%, indicating that the market has an insufficient response to information.

However, there are also some opposite empirical results. For example, Kryzanowski and Zhang (1992) found that the Canadian stock market has not overreacted for a long time. Mitchell and Ricardo (1998) tested the emerging stock markets in Asia and Latin America and found that the empirical data of mature stock markets (such as the United States and Japan) support the overreaction hypothesis and uncertain information hypothesis, while the response patterns of emerging stock markets are not consistent, some statistics are not significant, and some do not support it at all. In addition, some scholars also tested the short-term overreaction phenomenon. Lehman (1990) tested the short-term overreaction phenomenon in weeks. The cumulative excess return of the "loser portfolio" exceeded that of the "winner portfolio" by 1.21%–1.79%. The research using daily income data to test short-term overreaction includes the research conclusions of French, Schwert, and Stambaugh (1987) and Bowman and Iverson (1998) which supported the phenomenon of short-term overreaction. In further research, some scholars proposed to use the cumulative abnormal return (CAR) as the division index of the formation period. However, CAR cannot represent the real income, but there is also a deviation in the income of a single period due to the calculation error. Therefore, other indicators or corrections are adopted for the measurement of income. Conrad and Kaul (1993) used Buy and Hold Return to replace CAR, but their conclusions didn't support the overreaction theory, and attributed the findings of De Bondt and Thaler to the role of bid-ask effect, while Conrad and Kaul's conclusions were caused by their statistical methods, they confused cross-sectional data patterns with time series average inversion patterns. Domestic scholars Zhang Renji, Zhu Pingfang, and Wang Huaifang (1998) tested 48 listed companies in Shanghai Stock Exchange, and the conclusion rejected the hypothesis of overreaction in the Shanghai stock market. Shen Yifeng and Wu Shilong (1999) used the same method to divide "winner portfolio" and "loser portfolio" according to the after-tax profit margin of net assets. The empirical analysis of the Shanghai stock market also reached the same conclusion. That is, they did not support the overreaction hypothesis. These conclusions have important guiding significance for investors to formulate investment strategies, but they cannot study and judge whether there is response deviation in the government's macro information, nor can they become the basis for the government to formulate policies. At the same time, they did not distinguish between macro information and micro information, which would inevitably affect the robustness of the research conclusion. The main problem of the above research was directly using the micro information response deviation test method to test the macro information, which made severe mistakes.

The research on the micro information overreaction of the securities market helps guide investors in choosing the correct investment strategy. In contrast, the research on the macro information overreaction of the securities market helps to provide a theoretical basis for the government's macro-control of the securities market so that the government can formulate appropriate policies to promote the healthy development of the securities market. For the research on macro information overreaction, the event analysis method described above cannot be used because the impact of macro information on all stocks in the stock market is in the same direction and cannot be compared. Fung and Lam (2004) empirically tested the Hong Kong stock market by comparing the stock index futures with the spot market and concluded that there is an overreaction in the Hong Kong stock market. Wang Chunfeng et al. (2003) directly tested the deviation of macro information response by using the event analysis method. He issued the notice on *The Allotment of Shares of Listed Companies in 1996* on January 27, 1996; editorial on "Correct Understanding of the Current Stock Market" in *People's Daily* on December 16, 1996; the promulgation and implementation of *Securities Law of the People's Republic of China* on July 1, 1999; the insurance funds entered the market and placed new shares to investors in the secondary market (two favorable policies for short) announced on April 14, 2000. The results showed that there is evidence of reverse correction in the "loser portfolio" and "winner portfolio," which leads to the conclusion that China's securities market overreacts to policy information. The reverse correction of "loser combination" and "winner combination" occurs at the same time.

Is it an overreaction to the government's good information or an overreaction to the bad information? Generally speaking, the same measure taken by the government to regulate the stock market cannot be both good and bad. Song Ling and Zhang Ling (2002) used the samples of China's securities market and selected the editorial published by *People's Daily* on May 21, 1999, as the central event to empirically test whether China's securities market is overreacting. The results showed that the overall development of China's securities market in recent years tends to be standardized and effective, and there is no overreaction in the securities market. Cao Honghui (2002) took the reduction of state-owned shares in China's securities market as the central event to empirically test the overreaction of the market. He set February 2, 2001, to June 12, 2001, as the portfolio formation stage and June 12, 2001, to October 31, 2001, as the portfolio test stage. According to the ranking order of return on net assets at the end of 2000, the top 50 stocks in the Shanghai and Shenzhen stock markets were composed of the "winner portfolio," the last 50 stocks formed the "loser portfolio," which led to the conclusion that there is an overreaction in Shanghai stock market and no overreaction in Shenzhen stock market. Then, is the reduction of state-owned shares good or bad for the securities market, bad for the loser portfolio, and good for the winner portfolio? Obviously, the above research angle has made at least one mistake. That is, the selection of the quantitative analysis method is inappropriate. The problem is to use the method to test the micro information response deviation to test the macro information response deviation. Therefore, the research on the micro information response deviation of the stock market is helpful in guiding investors to choose the correct investment strategy. The research on the macro information response deviation of the stock market is not only helpful to guide investors to choose the correct long-term investment strategy, but also helpful to provide the theoretical basis for the government's macro-control of the stock market, so that the government can formulate appropriate policies to promote the healthy development of the stock market.

In short, from the above research results, the market's response to information is not and cannot achieve complete accuracy, and the existence of information reflection deviation is inevitable. However, when we turn the research perspective from "time point" to "period," we will find that the efficient market theory becomes truly scientific and practical.

3.2 Explanation of the Divergence between Standard Finance and Behavioral Finance by Market Efficient Cycle Theory

The core of the efficient market hypothesis is a rational expectation and perfect arbitrage. An effective market must fully reflect all information. Its basic requirement is that the securities price reflect the information immediately and accurately. What "immediate" and "accuracy" require is that the market is effective at every time point. Such a market is not realistic. The fatal defect of the efficient market hypothesis is to test the time point efficiency. Behavioral finance just catches the flaw of the efficient market hypothesis and questions it. In fact, a large number of anomalies in empirical research just show that the market does not have time point efficiency but cannot deny the period efficiency. That is, the market has an effective cycle. Market efficiency is a time cycle, not a time point. The absolute efficiency of the market at a certain time point is accidental, and the non-efficiency of the time point is the normal of the market. Gao Hongzhen and Lin Jiayong (2005) believed that the transmission of market information and price response is conditional and takes time. In the real securities market, due to the incomplete rationality of investors, the transmission of information and price response will not be complete in an instant. If the time point validity of the efficient market hypothesis is replaced by the period validity, that is, there is an effective cycle in the securities market. Theoretically, whether the time point validity is denied by a large number of anomalies revealed by the empirical research of behavioral finance, but it does not deny the period validity. If the market efficiency of the efficient market hypothesis is defined as period efficiency or effective cycle, the great difference, in theory, will be solved.

Therefore, we propose the following important innovative categories:

(1) Effective mean value. Under a market mechanism, the mean value itself is the internal value of securities, and the mean value reflects the market's recognition of the securities' price within a certain length of time. Objectively speaking, at a certain time point, the change of securities price has strong randomness, while the mean has strong stability characteristics. The mean has the effect of ironing out the random fluctuation of securities prices, but it does not completely eliminate the randomness. The longer the time period of mean selection, the better the stability effect will be.

(2) Long-term rationality. Investors' behavior may be irrational at a certain time point, but over a long time period, this irrational behavior will be corrected, and the corrected behavior will not be properly realized at any time point. There will also be deviation, and the securities price may be higher or lower than the internal value of the securities, but in the long run, securities deviating from intrinsic value will return to their intrinsic value, that is, mean return. Regression to mean value is an inevitable phenomenon, but it has randomness in regression time and space.

(3) Average rationality. This should be studied from both horizontal and vertical angles. Horizontally, every individual can be irrational, but the possibility of a group's irrationality will become smaller and smaller and will tend to be rational on average; vertically, an individual can be irrational at a certain time point, but it will tend to be rational on average over a long period of time. Therefore, the possibility of realizing average rationality is far greater than that of an individual at a specific time point.

In view of the two assumptions of "rational man" and "risk-free arbitrage" put forward by standard finance, behavioral finance puts forward "limited rationality" and "limited arbitrage." In contrast, the market efficient cycle theory we build puts forward two categories of "long-term rationality" and "long-term risk-free arbitrage (i.e., mean regression)."

There must be an effective period in the market, not a time point; that is, the market is effective in a certain period of time. A large number of anomalies revealed by the empirical research of behavioral finance only deny the validity of time points, not the validity of time periods. We find that market efficient cycle theory can scientifically solve the huge differences between standard finance and behavioral finance. The market efficient cycle theory accepts not only the efficient market hypothesis of standard finance but also the "abnormal phenomena" of behavioral finance. These abnormal phenomena only occur in a specific time period or even at a certain time point, and they do not deny the market efficient cycle. For a long enough period, the market must be effective, but the length of the effective cycle is uncertain. The shorter the effective period, the more fully the market responds to information and the stronger the market function; otherwise, the worse. From another perspective, there is an effective cycle in the market in a certain period of time, and it is also a normal phenomenon that the market is invalid at each time point. Since there is an effective cycle, it is inevitable that the securities price will automatically correct the information reflection deviation under the action of the market mechanism. That is, the securities market price slowly returns to the internal value, and the deviation from the internal value has a tendency to return to the internal value, that is, the mean return of the rate of return. However, deviation does not mean immediate regression, and it may continue to show trend characteristics along the direction of deviation in a specific period of time. The longer the return time cycle, the longer the market efficient cycle and the worse the market effectiveness. In the long run, rational expectation and arbitrage may correct the ineffectiveness of the time point and form a market efficient cycle.

3.3 Explanation of Buffett's Successful Investment Practice by Market Efficient Cycle Theory

In the long run, the stock price will return to its internal value. The process of returning to the internal value is the process of mean reversion. The mean value is the internal value of the stock from a time period. From the perspective of the market efficient cycle, the stock mean value is the reflection of the information that determines the stock price in a time period. The mean regression cycle is the market efficient cycle.

The stock price is too high. That is, if the bubble is too large, it most likely results in a sharp fall in a market crash or a slow fall. If the stock price is too low or the negative bubble is too large, the most likely result is a rapid rise or a slow rise. If there is no time length constraint, mean regression is inevitable. The great practitioner of using this theory and method for investment is Warren Buffett. He believes that "the most basic strategy of value investing is to make use of the deviation between stock price and enterprise value, buy stocks at a discount price quite lower than the intrinsic value of stocks, and sell them at a price equal to or higher than the intrinsic value after the stock price rises, so as to obtain excess profits." However, mean regression does not mean that stock returns are fully predictable. In fact, investment guru Buffett only knows whether stocks are undervalued or overvalued. He does not know when they rise and fall. In fact, the mean value is the intrinsic value of the stock. In the long run, the function of the market to find the price is undeniable. The deviation of the stock price from the intrinsic value is only a temporary phenomenon. Within a certain length of time, the market will be bound to correct the pricing deviation caused by its short-term randomness. Correcting its own pricing deviation and discovering price are the internal attributes of the market economy.

The theory that explains the success of Buffett's investment behavior should be the market efficient cycle theory. In other words, the basis for Buffett's success is to buy stocks below the intrinsic value and then sell them equal to or above the intrinsic value. The reason for his almost inevitable success is that the market must be effective and will not be distorted forever. If the market is effective at each time point, the securities price fully reflects all information at each time point, and there will be no basis for investors' investment behavior. There will be no investors' investment behavior in the world, only speculation. Buffett believes that the market has never been effective. People will overestimate or underestimate stocks because they don't know. His job is to find those good stocks that are undervalued, buy them, and hold them for a long time. Sooner or later, everyone will find the value of the stock, and then the demand will increase, the price will rise, and his investment will increase. In the long run, the market will return to internal value, which shows that an individual can be irrational, but in the long run, the overall market behavior will tend to be rational. In fact, we can find the answer from the market efficient cycle theory.

The market efficient cycle theory holds that the market can be ineffective at a certain time point, but in the long run, the market must be effective. That is, there must be a return to internal value. Therefore, Buffett made use of the market efficient cycle theory based on "time point invalidity" and "period validity" to achieve success in investment practice. In addition, the theoretical basis of the "safety margin" proposed by Benjamin Graham is also the market efficient cycle theory. He believes that "the safety margin is the degree to which the value is undervalued compared with the price. When the stock price is lower than the intrinsic value, there is a safety margin, which exists only when the value is undervalued." Graham's definition of safety margin: "safety margin is the degree to which value is undervalued compared with price. When the stock price is lower than the intrinsic value, there is a safety margin, and there is a safety margin only when the value is undervalued."

Buffett opposes and criticizes the diversified portfolio theory. He believes that "diversification can only protect ignorance. If you want the market to have no bad effect on you, you should own every kind of stock, which is a perfect strategy for those who do not know and understand how to analyze the enterprise situation." Standard finance takes the efficient market hypothesis as the cornerstone, portfolio investment as the best investment strategy, and rational human as a hypothesis. In fact, portfolio investment is aimed at overcoming non-systematic risks, and there is nothing to do in terms of systematic risks. Therefore, the performance of fund managers is highly correlated with the quality of the market. The market efficient cycle theory is aimed at both non-systematic risk and systematic risk. From the perspective of overcoming non-systematic risks, following the investment strategy of an effective cycle, and taking the mean value of securities as the investment basis; from the perspective of overcoming non-systematic risks, following the investment strategy of an effective cycle and taking the mean value of the whole securities market as the investment basis; this is the application value of market efficient cycle theory.

CHAPTER 4

The Empirical Study of Market Efficient Cycle Theory

The theory of market efficient cycle has scientifically solved the double divergence between financial investment theory and investment practice. What we need to do now is conduct an empirical test on the market efficient cycle theory and use empirical research methods to prove that the market does have an effective cycle. In our opinion, if the market yield tends to approach the intrinsic value, showing a mean reversion feature, then the market has an effective period. The period of returning to the intrinsic value is the market effective period. Within an effective period, the securities price fully reflects all the information that determines the securities value.

4.1 Empirical Analysis Path of Market Efficient Cycle Theory

The method used to test the market efficient cycle should choose the mean regression theory and its empirical research method. If the market has an effective period, it must be characterized by mean reversion; that is, both overreaction and underreaction will achieve market effectiveness through reverse correction. Conversely, if there is mean reversion, the market has an effective cycle. Therefore, we chose the mean value regression theory as the theoretical basis and chose the quantitative method of mean value regression for empirical research. This method can be used to test whether the stock price index has significant reverse correction after the information release causes the stock price to rise or fall. That is, choose different time periods to analyze whether the stock price index has mean reversion or trend characteristics. The former is the "Reverse Effect," in which the stock index has an excessive response to information, and the latter is the "Inertia Effect" or "Momentum Effect," in which the stock index has an insufficient response to information.

Mean reversion refers to the trend that no matter whether the stock price is higher or lower than the value center (or the mean), it will return to the value center with a high probability. In the case of mean reversion, it can be concluded that there is reverse correction, and the market is overreacting.

The mean reversion theory has had a great impact in recent years, especially in developed countries, which has attracted the attention of many scholars. It is a new milestone and historic leap in securities investment theory and also a breakthrough in the theory of predictable stock prices. Fama and French (1988) and Poterba and Summers (1988) conducted an empirical study on the New York stock market in the United States and reached the conclusion that the stock price showed a long-term mean regression feature for the first time. Mean reversion theory plays an important role in the securities investment theory in developed countries. There are many research results and related literature, but there are very few studies in this field in China at present. The mean reversion theory believes that stock returns are not unpredictable. In the long run, they should show negative autocorrelation, that is, a trend of regression to the mean. Dimitrios and Richard (1999) examined the stock markets of seven Southeast Asian countries or regions and found a large amount of evidence of mean reversion. Balvers and Gilliland (2000) conducted an empirical study on the stock market data of 18 representative countries from 1969 to 1996. The results showed that there was a very obvious mean regression feature. Gropp's (2004) empirical analysis of AMEX, NYSE, and NASDAQ also found evidence of significant mean reversion. Chaudhuri and Wu (2003) used ANST-GARCH (Asymmetric Nonlinear Smooth-Transition GARCH) model to conduct an empirical test on 17 developing countries and regions such as Brazil and Argentina. It is found that there is no obvious evidence of mean reversion in these emerging markets.

However, many scholars have found evidence against mean reversion, that is, there is no overreaction. Lo and MacKinlay (1989), Richardson and Stock (1989), and Richardson (1993) all believed that the number of samples for empirical tests such as Fama was limited, and there was a small sample deviation. According to the research of Kim, Nelson, and Startz (1991), Fama and French also ignored the difference in stock price changes before and after World War II. Their empirical research found that there was no mean reversion of stock returns in the New York market after World War II. This conclusion was also proved by the empirical research of McQueen (1992). Mills (2002) conducted an empirical test on the Financial Times Actuaries (FTA) of the United Kingdom. The result was that Mills rejected the mean reversion hypothesis and reached the conclusion of Mean Aversion; that is, the stock price was positively correlated with the return rate for a long time, and the market was under-responsive.

From the theory of market effective period, we can draw the following inferences: from the perspective of a single security, the security price should fluctuate randomly around its intrinsic value, but the long-term average value must be equal to its intrinsic value. From the perspective of the whole market, the rate of return on securities investment formed by the fluctuation of securities prices must fluctuate randomly around the fundamentals of the economic growth of the whole country, but in the long run, the rate of return on the stock price index representing the fluctuation of the stock market must be consistent with the GDP growth rate representing the economic development index of the whole country. Empirical research on the theory of market efficient cycle is conducted from the latter perspective; that is, the empirical test is conducted from the perspective of the matching cycle of the stock market and macro-economy.

4.2 Empirical Test and Conclusion

4.2.1 Selection of Research Methods

1. Theoretical Framework

Unlike the previous studies on the lead-lag relationship between futures and spot markets, we will test the price discovery ability of the stock market under the framework of the mean reversion theory. As we mentioned earlier, the process of stock market price discovery is the process of stock price fluctuation around its intrinsic value, and the long-term average value of the security price itself is the intrinsic value of the security, which reflects the recognition of the market for the security price within a certain period of time. At a certain time point, the change of security price has strong randomness, while the mean value has the function of smoothing the random fluctuation of price. If the stock market has the ability of price discovery, then if the stock price is higher than its intrinsic value, the market's own force will drive the price down gradually. If the stock price is lower than its intrinsic value, the market's own force will raise the price. In the long run, the trend of stock prices is characterized by mean reversion.

We believe that the test of stock market price discovery ability can be transformed into the test of average regression of stock market returns. If there is a significant negative correlation between the current and late stock returns, it indicates that the stock market is characterized by mean reversion, which further indicates that the market has an effective cycle. On the contrary, if there is no significant negative correlation between the current and lag returns of stocks, then the stock market shows a trend rather than a mean reversion, and there is no market efficient cycle.

2. Selection of Research Methods

The basic principle of the mean regression test is to test the process of stock price fluctuation around its intrinsic value, that is, the correlation between current and delayed stock price. The early testing methods for mean regression were mainly autocorrelation tests and variance ratio tests. Both of these testing methods assumed that stock prices fluctuated around their basic values and had linear characteristics, so the testing model was mainly a linear model. In reality, the fluctuation of stock price generally does not strictly follow the process of linear fluctuation. At the micro level, the response time, size, and direction of each individual investor to information shocks cannot be completely consistent. At the macro level, there are obvious differences in the effect of government regulatory policies on the stock market, which lead to the nonlinear process of stock price fluctuations.

In the late 1970s, many scholars were clearly aware of the limitations of linear time series models in practical applications and began to study nonlinear time series models. The Markov switching regime model (MSR) proposed by Hamilton (1989) is a milestone. After that, the threshold autoregression model (TAR) and smooth transition autoregressive model (STAR) appeared. These three models are all used to describe different forms of mechanism-switching behavior in the process of time series fluctuation. The difference is that the Markov switching regime model (MSR) assumes that the process of mechanism transformation is determined by exogenous unobservable Markov chains. The threshold autoregression model (TAR) will determine the endogenous variables of mechanism change and can be observed. Both of them assume that the process of mechanism transformation is jumping and discrete. The smooth transition autoregressive model (STAR) smoothes the transformation between the two mechanisms. Since the transformation of the stock price volatility mechanism is a continuous and gradual change process, the STAR model chosen here is closer to reality.

Monoyios and Sarno (2002) used the STAR model to test the Standard & Poor's 500 Index (S&P 500 Index) in the United States and the FTSE 100 Index in the United Kingdom since 1987. The results showed that the two indexes showed significant nonlinear mean regression during this period. Boswijk, Hommes, and Manzan (2007) discussed whether the US stock market can reasonably reflect the intrinsic value of the stock and used the STAR model to simulate the deviation path of the stock to its basic value. The results showed that the dynamic process of stock price deviation from its basic price presented a nonlinear adjustment process; that is, there was a nonlinear mean regression of stock price in this interval. Jorge et al. (2005) used the STAR model to analyze the Ibex-35 Index. The conclusion showed that the index had an asymmetric mean regression characteristic, indicating that the stock market had the function of price discovery. Lim and Liew (2007) adopted the nonlinear unit root test method proposed by Kapetanios et al. (2003) in the STAR model. They believed that the stock returns of Bangkok, Hong Kong (China), South Korea, Kuala Lumpur, Japan, Singapore, and

Taiwan (China) had a nonlinear mean regression phenomenon between 1986 and 2003. Chen and Kim (2011) used the static nonlinear unit root test to test the stock prices of emerging Asian countries and found that the stock prices of these countries showed a nonlinear mean regression trend.

STAR model of two mechanisms is most widely used in time series analysis, and its general expression is shown in Equation 4-1.

$$y_t = \beta_1 x_t + \beta_2 x_t G(s_t; \gamma, c) + \varepsilon_t \tag{4-1}$$

Where, $x_t = (y_{t-1}, \cdots, y_{t-p})'$ is the independent variable vector, p is the lagging order, β_1 and β_2 are the parameter vectors of the independent variables. The distribution function $G(s_t; \gamma, c)$ is the weight, s_t is the transformation variable, and parameter γ determines the smoothness of the function, and the parameter c is the threshold value between the two mechanisms. When $G(s_t; \gamma, c) = 1 - exp\left(-\gamma (s_t - c)^2\right) (\gamma > 0)$, it is an exponential smooth transfer model (ESTAR). Empirical research shows that the ESTAR model is more suitable for analyzing the nonlinear movement of stock prices in time series. The purpose of this paper is to study whether the stock price has the characteristics of mean reversion, that is, whether there is a correlation between the current stock return rate and the lag stock return rate. Therefore, Equation 4-1 is written as the ESTAR model:

$$y_t = \beta_1 y_{t-p} + \beta_2 y_{t-p}\{1 - exp(-\gamma y_{t-d}^2)\} + \varepsilon_t \tag{4-2}$$

From Equation 4-2, we can see that the parameters to be tested are β_1, β_2 and γ. The original assumptions are: $H_0^1 : \beta_1 = 0$, $H_0^2 : \beta_2 = 0$ and $H_0^3 : \gamma = 0$, and the alternative assumptions are $H_1^1 : \beta_1 \neq 0$, $H_1^2 : \beta_2 \neq 0$ and $H_1^3 : \gamma \neq 0$. It should be pointed out that, in the case of the original hypothesis $H_0^3 : \gamma = 0$, γ is not defined, and it is not feasible to directly test the original hypothesis. In order to overcome this problem, Kapetanios et al. (2003) re-parameterized Equation 4-2 through first-order Taylor approximation expansion, and obtained the auxiliary regression as shown in Equation 4-3.

$$y_t = \delta_1 y_{t-p} + \delta_2 y_{t-p} y_{t-d}^2 + e_t \tag{4-3}$$

In this way, our original hypothesis is transformed into: $H_0^1 : \delta_1 = 0$, $H_0^2 : \delta_2 = 0$, and the alternative hypothesis is transformed into: $H_1^1 : \delta_1 \neq 0$, $H_1^2 : \delta_2 \neq 0$. According to the above, the feature of mean value regression is that the stock index return in the current period is significantly negatively correlated with the stock index return in the lag period. Therefore, the existence of the mean value regression feature can only be proved when the estimation result of parameter δ_1 and δ_2 is negative and the significance is not zero.[1]

---

[1] If parameters exist δ_1 and δ_2, one is significantly positive and the other is significantly negative, it is impossible to judge whether there is mean value regression, and we will not list this situation as a mean value regression feature.

4.2.2 Empirical Test

1. Variable Selection and Data Processing

Here, we will test the price discovery ability of stock markets in China, the United States, the United Kingdom, Germany, and Japan, respectively. The stock price index will select the most representative comprehensive indexes in these countries, including the Shanghai Composite Index in China, the Dow Jones Industrial Index, the NASDAQ Index and the S&P 500 Index in the United States, the FTSE 100 Index in the United Kingdom, the DAX Index in Germany and the Nikkei 225 Index in Japan. Among these indexes, the Shanghai Composite Index was officially released in July 1991 because it was the latest one to be launched. Therefore, the yield of each index from December 1991 to December 2013 is taken as the test object. The current closing price of the stock index is p_t, and the closing price of the lagged period is p_{t-1}. The equation of the stock index yield y_t calculated with continuous compound interest is shown in Equation 4-4.

$$y_t = ln_{p_t} - ln_{p_{t-1}} \tag{4-4}$$

2. Data Stability Test

In order to test the stability of the data, we conducted an ADF test on the seven stock index yield series respectively, and the results are shown in Table 4-1. For convenience, $y_t^i\,(i=1,2,3,4,5,6,7)$ is used to represent the monthly returns of the Shanghai Composite Index, US Dow Jones Industrial Index, NASDAQ Index, S&P 500 Index, UK FTSE 100 Index, Germany DAX Index, and Nikkei 225 Index, respectively:

Table 4-1 Stability Test Results of Return Rate of Each Index

Variable	y_t^1	y_t^2	y_t^3	y_t^4	y_t^5	y_t^6	y_t^7
t	−17.2515	−15.7709	−14.7221	−14.8101	−15.6774	−15.4020	−14.6000
p	0.0000	0.0000	0.0000	0.0000	0.0000	0.0000	0.0000

The critical values of ADF test t statistics are −3.455, −2.872, and −2.573 at the significant levels of 1%, 5%, and 10%, respectively. It can be seen from Table 4-1 that the absolute value of the test result is greater than the critical value, so it can be considered that the seven-time series is stable.

3. KSS Test Empirical Results

In order to facilitate the comparative analysis, the delay parameter d is set as 1 with reference to Kapetanios et al. (2003). Since we use monthly data, the unit of the regression cycle is the month. Take the lag order p as 1, 2, 3, 6, 9, 12, 24, and 48, respectively, where

1, 2, and 3 hours represent the short-term lag, 6, 9, and 12 represent the medium-term lag, and 24 and 48 represent the long-term lag. Equation 4-3 can be rewritten as

$$y_t^i = \delta_1^i y_{t-p}^i + \delta_2^i y_{t-p}^i y_{t-1}^i{}^2 + e_t \tag{4-5}$$

Substitute the monthly yield data of seven groups of indexes into Equation 4-5 for nonlinear regression analysis, and the empirical results are shown in Table 4-2.

Table 4-2 KSS Inspection Results

Lag Order	1	2	3	6	9	12	24	48
δ_1^1	−0.0653	0.0641	−0.0182	−0.0456	0.1744	0.0188	−0.1173	−0.0689
	0.4346	0.3207	0.7918	0.5021	0.0062	0.7745	0.0192	0.1662
δ_2^1	0.0081	−0.0841	0.2146	−1.3511	0.1992	−1.7491	−1.1330	0.8797
	0.9558	0.8514	0.7996	0.8476	0.7360	0.0514	0.1798	0.6987
δ_1^2	0.1311	0.0812	0.2067	−0.0089	0.0013	0.0384	−0.0299	0.0368
	0.1362	0.2810	0.0099	0.9068	0.9867	0.5879	0.7007	0.6510
δ_2^2	−11.4747	−36.1947	−56.3881	−19.1259	−3.9378	60.7551	41.8892	−5.6990
	0.1664	0.0302	0.0069	0.3198	0.8262	0.0053	0.0509	0.4421
δ_1^3	0.0919	0.1223	0.0120	0.0275	0.0838	−0.0144	0.0010	−0.0458
	0.3023	0.1148	0.8782	0.7237	0.2561	0.8449	0.9893	0.5652
δ_2^3	0.5720	−13.1239	2.7931	4.5911	−11.5980	−3.4098	−3.2411	1.0104
	0.8520	0.0110	0.5844	0.3277	0.0462	0.4485	0.6041	0.9236
δ_1^4	0.0843	0.0113	0.2278	0.0061	−0.0241	0.0407	0.0089	−0.0052
	0.3055	0.8781	0.0043	0.4444	0.7495	0.5687	0.9110	0.9500
δ_2^4	2.3188	−4.2937	−39.1717	−36.8133	8.8736	30.9827	2.0531	−21.2948
	0.7318	0.7197	0.0399	0.0409	0.6627	0.0964	0.9209	0.3124
δ_1^5	−0.1151	0.0239	0.0737	0.0433	−0.0278	0.1304	0.0080	0.0065
	0.2376	0.7531	0.3286	0.5610	0.6954	0.0749	0.9158	0.9345
δ_2^5	26.2005	−25.0506	−38.3156	−32.7073	13.8538	−28.7874	−26.6835	6.6574
	0.0430	0.1712	0.0539	0.1305	0.4705	0.2344	0.3298	0.7644
δ_1^6	0.1758	0.0788	0.1254	0.1123	−0.0199	0.1086	0.0031	0.0364
	0.0342	0.2938	0.0657	0.1223	0.7881	0.1209	0.9659	0.6348
δ_2^6	−5.5034	−9.0381	−11.4045	−12.8408	−3.9584	3.3663	11.8710	−2.0971
	0.0379	0.2703	0.0071	0.0890	0.6976	0.6895	0.2823	0.7752
δ_1^7	0.0933	−0.0050	0.1167	−0.0267	−0.0450	−0.0137	−0.0664	−0.0953
	0.2361	0.9403	0.1186	0.7181	0.5400	0.8449	0.4302	0.261I
δ_2^7	0.5482	0.0133	−7.3946	−20.4497	29.5156	4.0165	12.6667	24.7038
	0.8689	0.9981	0.4846	0.0841	0.0122	0.6950	0.4475	0.1714

Note: The first line in the table is the coefficient, and the second line is the corresponding p value.

From the results in Table 4-2, we can summarize the average regression of the monthly return rate of each index at the significant level of 10%, as shown in Table 4-3.

Table 4-3 Regression Lag Cycle of Average Return Rate of Each Index

National Stock Index	Lag Period of Mean Regression
SSE Composite Index	12 months (δ_2^1 significantly negative), 24 months (δ_1^1 significantly negative)
US DowJones Industrial Index	2 months (δ_2^2 significantly negative)
US NASDAQ Index	2 months (δ_2^3 significantly negative)
US S&P 500 Index	6 months (δ_2^4 significantly negative)
FTSE 100	3 months (δ_2^5 significantly negative)
Germany DAX Index	6 months (δ_2^6 significantly negative)
Japan Nikkei 225 Index	6 months (δ_2^7 significantly negative)

According to the empirical results in Table 4-3, compared with the Dow Jones Index, NASDAQ Index, S&P 500 Index, FTSE 100 Index, DAX Index, and Nikkei 225 Index, China's Shanghai Composite Index has a longer average regression cycle, and most of them show nonlinear mean regression characteristics.

Based on the above empirical research results, we draw the following conclusions:

Our research only proves that the stock market has an effective period. The deviation of the yield from the mean can be regarded as a non-persistent phenomenon. It can be quickly or slowly regressed, or it can not be regressed temporarily. It is not that the yield deviates from the mean must return to the mean. In a specific period of time, it may also run in the direction of more serious deviation from the mean. Still, the probability is getting smaller and smaller, and the probability of regression is getting larger and larger. The period of regression is random. However, the longer the time period is, the better the stability of regression is.

Market efficient cycle theory has made great progress in resolving the debate between the efficient market hypothesis and behavioral finance theory, which should be a beneficial exploration and even a great attempt to enrich and develop modern financial investment theory. Great progress has also been made in resolving the differences between financial investment theory and practice. Market efficient cycle theory can explain the investment behavior of successful practitioners represented by Buffett.

The mean reversion theory actually negates the market time point effectiveness. It shows not only that the market time point effectiveness is accidental but also that the market efficient cycle exists. Securities prices are only slowly adjusting information, and the study of market effectiveness must examine long-term returns. Many researchers put forward that market inefficiency, especially the insufficient or excessive response to information, is actually an involuntary recognition that time point effectiveness is an accidental phenomenon. Our research focus should turn to the study of the market efficient cycle, rather than the endless debate around time point effectiveness.

It further shows that it is inevitable for the market to have an effective period, but the length of the cycle is random. The essence of market effectiveness is all the information that the securities price reaction determines its change. The shorter the effective cycle, the healthier the market. The government's regulation of securities should be based on shortening the effective cycle of the market, and investors' long-term investment behavior should be based on the mean value.

CHAPTER 5

Research on the Price Discovery Function of the Stock Market Based on the Market Efficient Cycle Theory

The mean is the intrinsic value of the stock, which is also suitable for the pricing of other commodities. Statisticians have long given the best explanation, calling the mean value mathematical expectation, and Markowitz defined the mean value of security returns as the expected rate of return. The process of price discovery is the process of mean value pricing, and the process of price discovery is the process of mean reversion. This theory is basically consistent with the idea of no-arbitrage pricing. No arbitrage pricing principle: it is very convenient and fast to implement arbitrage in the financial market. The convenience of such arbitrage also makes the existence of arbitrage opportunities in the financial market always temporary, because once there are arbitrage opportunities, investors will quickly implement arbitrage and make the market return to the equilibrium without arbitrage opportunities. Therefore, no arbitrage equilibrium is used to price financial products. The reasonable price of financial products in the market is the price that makes the market free of risk arbitrage opportunities, which is the principle of no-arbitrage pricing. No arbitrage price can be reflected in that the random components of price fluctuations around the intrinsic value are ironed out, and the mean value is the intrinsic value of the stock.

5.1 Overview of Price Discovery Function

The process of returning to internal value is the process of price discovery. Price discovery is the basic function of the stock market; that is, through the adjustment mechanism of the stock market itself, when the price deviates from the intrinsic value, the stock price returns to the intrinsic value. The market has the function of automatically correcting the price deviation from the intrinsic value; that is, when the stock price is higher or lower than the intrinsic value, it will automatically correct its pricing deviation. Only when the stock price reflects its intrinsic value can the stock market truly play its role in effectively raising funds and optimizing the allocation of resources, so that the stock price reflects the intrinsic value of listed companies. Thus, the entire stock market reflects the changes in the macro-economy. Schroeder et al. (1997) believed that price discovery refers to the process in which the buyers and sellers reach a transaction price for the quality and quantity of a commodity at a given time and trading place. This process is due to the large number of participants in stock trading, that buyers and sellers compete in an open competitive market with high transparency, centralized trading, and free quotation. When the stock price is high and forms a bubble, rational arbitrageurs will eventually play a role in restraining the rise of the stock price and reducing the degree of the bubble by selling stocks. When the stock price is low and forms a negative bubble, rational arbitrageurs will eventually push the stock price up and return the stock price to its intrinsic value by buying stocks. At a certain point in time, the stock price may be higher or lower than its intrinsic value, with strong randomness. However, from a sufficiently long period of time, the stock price has the characteristics of mean reversion, that is, "it refers to the trend that whether the securities price is higher or lower than the value center (or the mean), it will return to the value center with a high probability." In other words, in the short term, the stock price may be higher or lower than the intrinsic value of the stock or even far from its intrinsic value. For a long time, the stock price deviating from the intrinsic value will return to its intrinsic value, giving play to the basic function of price discovery of the stock market.

Scheiber and Schwartz (1986) described price discovery as a process of effectively incorporating new information into asset prices. Price discovery refers to the dynamic process in which a certain quantity and quality of products reach a transaction equilibrium price at a certain time and place due to the interaction between supply and demand in the market. In a market, new information generated randomly will be reflected on the price of assets through the relationship between supply and demand and trading behavior, and this process realizes price discovery. In this process, there are many stock trading participants, and buyers and sellers simultaneously conduct centralized trading and free bidding in a highly transparent, open, and competitive market. If the price discovery can quickly and accurately reflect the information, then the efficient market described by Fama will be presented. That is to say, price discovery is a process of finding an equilibrium price. One of the characteristics of the efficient market is that it can quickly and accurately reflect new information, so the stock price of the efficient market will quickly adjust to a balanced position. However, the reality is that prices often deviate from their equilibrium position. When the stock price is higher than the intrinsic value of the stock, the rational arbitrageur will sell the stock to gain profits, and such behavior will reduce the stock price. When the stock price is lower than the intrinsic value of the stock, the rational arbitrageurs will promote the stock price to rise and return to the intrinsic value by buying the stock. As an important topic in the research of market microstructure, price discovery discusses the speed at which market prices respond to new information. The price discovery function is a key function of the stock market. Nowadays, in the environment of constantly introducing new financial derivatives, the price discovery function is more used in the financial derivatives market, such as the relationship between stock index futures and the stock market. Garbade and Silber (1983) took the dominant market and the micro market as the research object, applied the relationship between the leading market and the backward market in price discovery, and found that market information would be preferentially reflected in the price by the dominant market. Then, the micro market was pulled to follow up and reflect the market information. The market reflecting the leading speed of information is the leading market with the price discovery function. Luo, Sun, and Mweene (2005) proposed some characteristics of the process of price discovery: first, price discovery is a dynamic process. Second, different markets respond to information at different speeds. It has a stronger price discovery function for markets with faster information response.

In previous studies, most people believed that the price discovery function is one of the two main functions of the futures market. Therefore, when they study the price discovery problem, they often associate it with the futures market and believe that the price discovery function is unique to the futures market. In fact, the price discovery function is not limited to the futures market, and it is a function that every market should have. If the market is completely efficient, the price will respond to sudden information shocks and reach a new equilibrium state in time. Therefore, the stock market also has the function of price discovery, which is one of its common and important functions. Price discovery is different from price determination, which mainly considers the value of the subject matter itself. In contrast, price discovery emphasizes a dynamic process, that is, how the market finds information and constantly adjusts to the real price. This kind of adjustment is not achieved overnight, but is formed by countless investors through countless bids in countless trading hours. Every transaction of investors is based on the interpretation of new market information, which may come from the prediction of macro-economy, the development prospects of listed companies, or the introduction of a certain policy. The complex information combination and analysis enable investors to have their own psychological expectations for stock prices. However, the integrated analysis of information by each individual investor is limited, and the prediction of stock price may not be correct. Some investors expect too much, while others expect too little. Therefore, every bid is a trial and error process. Numerous investors and countless trading behaviors can offset errors and finally form a reasonable and stable price, which is the market discovery price that can reflect the stock's own situation. Therefore, the market with a price discovery function often has four elements: the first is a large number of trading participants, the second is a huge trading volume, the third is that traders are familiar with the commodity market, and the fourth is that trading transparency is high. The stock market meets the above four conditions, so it also has the function of price discovery.

On October 24, 2012, the overseas edition of the *People's Daily* published an article, "Why Are Stocks 'High Quality and Low Price' Everywhere." The article said that Guo Shuqing, chairman of China Securities Regulatory Commission, believed that the main problem in China's capital market was the imbalance of the share price structure, and the problems of speculation and poor performance were serious. The average P/E ratio of new shares issued in 2011 was 48 times, while the annual average P/E ratio of Shanghai and Shenzhen stock markets was only 17.76 times. The problem of high quality and low price was prominent, and the stock price could not objectively reflect the intrinsic value of the stock. At least the price discovery function of China's stock market has not been well developed, and the market's maturity is still limited. Under the condition of a market economy, the stock market realizes the basic function of price discovery through spontaneous regulation. If the stock price deviates from its intrinsic value for a long time, it shows that the market does not have the function of price discovery, and it is impossible to call it a perfect stock market.

The lack of a price discovery function in China's stock market is mainly reflected in a series of distortions and even confusion. The stock price cannot reflect the internal value of listed companies well. The low price is not low, and the high price is not high. There is no such phenomenon as the coexistence of stocks with a price of several hundred yuan and less than one yuan in mature stock markets in Europe and America, and speculation in low, new, and ST stocks is prevalent. Garbage shares rise to heaven. The stock market did not reflect China's macroeconomic situation well in most of the time periods and even showed a serious deviation. A single stock price cannot reflect the fundamental changes of the listed company, so the stock market has not become a "barometer" reflecting China's macroeconomic growth. A large number of empirical studies have shown that the stock market deviates from economic growth. Liang Qi and Teng Jianzhou (2005) found a relationship between economic growth and stock market development in the model system by using cointegration vector analysis under the constraint of over-identification conditions. Weak exogenous tests showed that there was no causal relationship between stock market development and economic growth. The empirical research of Wu Zhiwen and Zhou Jianjun (2005) believed that there has been a comprehensive but not partial deviation between the Chinese stock market and the macro-economy. The stock market was neither a barometer of the state-owned economy nor a barometer of the non-state-owned economy. The objective existence of the deviation between the stock market and the economy cannot be questioned. Sun Xiaochong et al. (2005) started with the internal operating efficiency of China's stock market and analyzed the relationship between China's listed companies and the national economy, as well as the relationship between stock prices and company performance. The research results showed that China's stock index was separated from China's economic fundamentals to a certain extent. Du Jiang and Shen Shaobo (2010) used trend analysis, cointegration analysis, and causality test methods to empirically test whether there was a deviation between China's stock market and the real economy. The research results showed that there was a deviation between China's stock market and the real economy. These facts show that China's stock market has not fully played the function of price discovery. Overall, China's stock market has not effectively reflected the fundamentals of rapid and stable growth of China's macro-economy in recent years.

5.2 Research Literature on Price Discovery Function

For the research on the price discovery function of the securities market, there is a lot of research literature from different research angles and using different quantitative research methods. As for the literature on price discovery function, the early research of foreign scholars mainly focused on the correlation between spot and futures markets. Because futures markets have information about future spots, they can give priority to reaction and then transmit the information to the spot market, so most of the conclusions are that futures are ahead of the spot. These studies generally believe that the futures market has a leading position in price discovery because of its advantageous market structure of high leverage and low cost.

Chen et al. (1991) used the bivariate GARCH model to study the changes and volatility of prices between the spot and index futures of the S&P 500. The research period was from 1984 to 1989, and the data were daily data. The conclusions were as follows: (1) The intraday price volatility of the two markets was obviously stable and predictable. (2) After the information was generated, the price volatility between the two markets was obviously dependent, but the degree of dependence would gradually decrease in the next period. (3) After excluding some market factors, the above phenomenon still held. The previous literature showed that the intraday futures price was significantly higher than the spot price; that is, the futures market was the price-leading market. This paper was verified by the dependence of price volatility, which not only accorded with the earlier literature, but also strengthened the credibility of this phenomenon. Wahab and Lashgari (1993) used the error correction model, Granger causality test, and vector autoregression model to analyze the relationship between S&P 500 and futures price and the relationship between FTSE Index spot price and futures price. The sample period was from January 4, 1988, to May 30, 1992. The results showed that (1) there was a cointegration relationship between the futures and spot of the two indexes; (2) the early price had only a weak impact on the current price, which meant that the early price forecasting ability is not significant; (3) the phenomenon of spot leading futures was more obvious than that of futures leading spot; and (4) the error correction model took long-term and short-term effects into account in the model, so it had better prediction ability than the vectorial autoregression model. Iihara, Kato, and Tokunaga (1996) used the GMM model to study the data of Japan's Nikkei 225 Stock Index (TSE) and futures (OSE) every five minutes to explore whether the market's response to new information will be affected when the market boom and trading system change. They divided the market into three periods for analysis, namely bull market, early bear market, and late bear market. The data samples were taken from March 1989 to January 1991. The results showed that the futures returns were significantly ahead of the spot returns for the whole period. Still, in the late bear market, the effect of the returns leading was not as obvious as in the bull market and the early bear market. Moreover, strict control measures will reduce the liquidity of futures, slow down their response to new information, and thus reduce the price discovery function of futures. Chu, Hsieh, and Xie (1999) discussed the price discovery capabilities of the three markets of the S&P 500, including the spot index, futures, and SPDRs. SPDRs, the first ETF fund in the United States, were launched on January 29, 1993, and the tracking index was the S&P 500. The sample period was from January 29, 1993, to December 31, 1999, with 5-minute price data. The research method was cointegration analysis and vector error correction model (VECM). The results showed that the price discovery function of the futures market was better than that of the other two markets, while the SPDRs were better than that of the spot market. Its conclusion pointed out that there were two reasons for this result: first, S&P 500 futures and SPDRs had lower transaction costs. Second, S&P 500 futures provided higher financial leverage than SPDRs. Turkington and Walsh (1999) used the VECM method to explore the ability of price discovery in Australia's futures and spot markets. The data period was from January 3 to December 21, 1995. In previous empirical studies in Europe and America, the futures market was often the leading spot market, while the author took Australia (SPI) futures contracts and index spot (AOI) as the research object. The reason was the particularity of the Australian market; that is, the spot market was the open outcry of the futures market, which was contrary to most of the European and American markets. The empirical results were as follows: (1) If the information impact came from the spot market, it will be reflected in the spot market first, and the response will be completed within 5 to 15 minutes. It took about one hour to reflect the futures market. (2) If the information came from the futures market, the futures market will respond within 15 minutes. The spot market also needs to be adjusted in about one hour. (3) No market was leading or lagging behind, but which market first obtained new information was the most important factor. Frino and West (2003) compared the leading and lagging relationship of price discovery ability of the same underlying assets with different transaction costs under different futures exchanges. The sample adopted is that Nikkei 225 Stock Index futures were simultaneously traded in three exchanges (SIMEX, OSE, and CME), of which the trading volume of CME was too small to be representative. The transaction cost of OSE was the highest after comparing futures contracts in detail. The research period was 1 minute of price data from August 10, 1998, to September 18, 1998. The research method was to establish ARMA (p, q) models (Index-OSE, Index-SIMEX, and OSE-SIMEX, respectively) and compare the lag period coefficient to judge the relationship between leading and lagging. The results showed that SIMEX Nikkei 225 Stock Index futures with low transaction costs led the OSE market in terms of returns, and its price discovery ability was better, indicating that investors preferred the market with low transaction costs.

There is a lot of research literature on the price discovery function of the securities market in China from different research angles and using different quantitative research methods. It is often concluded that the stock index futures market plays a leading role in information response and price discovery as a leading market. Cai Chuijun and Li Cunxiu (2004) used the VECM-BI-EGARCH model to make an empirical analysis of the information transmission of Taiwan stock index futures, studied the price discovery function through the lead-lag relationship between the futures market and the spot market, and explained the connotation of futures price volatility with the persistence, asymmetry, and spillover of return volatility. The data samples were the opening and closing prices of the Taiwan Weighted Stock Index from January 2, 2001, to December 31, 2002, as well as the data every five minutes and daily and overnight data. The results showed that the price leadership effect of the futures overnight returns was the most obvious. The futures returns fluctuated continuously every five minutes, within the day and overnight, and the bad news and unexpected large deviation news of the futures market would have an impact on the futures returns, causing asymmetric fluctuations. Xiao Hui, Bao Jianping, and Wu Chongfeng (2006) studied the price discovery function of five representative stock indexes and stock index futures in the United States, Britain, Japan, and Hong Kong (China), using two methods: impulse response and general factor analysis. The results showed that the futures market was in the leading position in price discovery, and with the development of the futures market, its price discovery function was more obvious. He Chengying, Zhang Longbin, and Chen Wei (2011) used a vector error correction model and impulse response function to analyze 1-minute high-frequency data and discussed the price discovery ability of Shanghai and Shenzhen 300 stock index futures. The target was the reaction speed of stock index futures and spot to new information and the integration ratio of new information. The results showed that the stock index futures market reflected new information faster than the spot market, and the price discovery ability of the CSI 300 Index futures market was stronger than that of the index spot market. Fang Kuangnan and Cai Zhenzhong (2012) used the cointegration test, error correction model, and impulse response function to analyze 5-minute high-frequency data and studied the price discovery function of Shanghai and Shenzhen 300 stock index futures in China. The results showed that the contribution of price discovery in China's stock index futures market was relatively large. Su Zhi and Chen Yanglong (2012), in order to explore the price discovery efficiency of stock index futures, compared the dynamic correlation between representative stock index futures and spot price series in China and abroad, used the Morlet wavelet time-frequency cross-correlation analysis method to test, and the results showed that within the range of low-frequency long period and high-frequency short period, the CSI 300 Index and stock index futures had the characteristics of long-term high correlation and cooperative fluctuation, there was also a phenomenon of mutual interlacing guidance between the two, so the price discovery efficiency of China's stock index futures market was low. There is still a big gap compared with the mature markets in Europe and America.

At present, the test methods for the market price discovery function are basically empirical tests that compare the spot and futures markets. This test method should be based on price rationality. Generally speaking, if the two prices are consistent, there are two possibilities: rational price and irrational price. If the two prices tested are inconsistent, at least one price is irrational. The method of spot and futures comparison is used to empirically test the price discovery function. We believe that this method has some limitations in its scientific nature. At least one of the two parties to the comparison can only be compared at a reasonable price. If it cannot be proved that at least one of them is reasonable, this method has great limitations. Here, we use the mean reversion principle to test the price discovery function of the stock market.

5.3 Empirical Study on the Price Discovery Function of the Stock Market

5.3.1 Smooth Transition Autoregressive Model

There are three kinds of switching regime models for studying nonlinear time series, which are the Markov switching model (MSR), threshold autoregressive model (TAR), and smooth transition autoregressive model (STAR). However, the case where the former two are applicable is that the transition mechanism jumps suddenly, is discrete, and has no continuity. But in real life, the process of many mechanism transitions is continuous and gradually changing, not discrete jumping. For example, the transition from depression to prosperity in the economic cycle is a process of gradual recovery, not a sudden jump. Therefore, in the time series switching regime model, STAR is more consistent with the process of describing the gradual change of economic conditions, which describes the continuous smooth transition process between the two extreme mechanisms.

STAR model can simulate the continuous smooth conversion process between several reversion mechanisms, but the Univariate STAR model is commonly used to investigate the smooth conversion process between two mechanisms. A simple description of the univariate smooth transition model is the weighted average of two Linear AR Processes. The model's expression is shown in Equations 5-1 and 5-2.

$$y_t = \phi_1' x_t \left[1 - G\left(s_t; \gamma, c\right)\right] + \phi_2' x_t G\left(s_t; \gamma, c\right) + \varepsilon_t \tag{5-1}$$

Or

$$y_t = \phi_1' x_t + \left(\phi_2 - \phi_1\right)' x_t G\left(s_t; \gamma, c\right) + \varepsilon_t \tag{5-2}$$

$x_t = \left(y_{t-1}, \ldots, y_{t-p}\right)'$ is the independent variable vector. ϕ_1' and ϕ_2' are the coefficient of the independent variable, $G\left(s_t; \gamma, c\right)$ is the transformation function, and is also the weight in the weighted average. It describes the transition process of the mechanism. s_t is a convert variable, it can be either a lagging endogenous variable or an exogenous variable. The parameter γ determines the smoothness of the transition function, and the parameter c is the threshold value between the two mechanisms.

Next, the transition function $G\left(s_t; \gamma, c\right)$ in STAR is described. There are two forms of transition function, namely, Logistic Smooth Transaction Auto Regression (LSTAR) and Exponential Smooth Transaction Auto Regression (ESTAR).

The expression of the distribution function is shown in Equations 5-3 and 5-4.

In LSTAR model:

$$G\left(s_t; \gamma, c\right) = \frac{1}{1 + exp\left[-\gamma\left(s_t - c\right)\right]}, \quad \gamma > 0 \tag{5-3}$$

The function $G\left(s_t; \gamma, c\right)$ increases monotonically from 0 to 1 as the transition variable s_t increases. The smaller γ is, the smoother the switching regime process is.

In the model ESTAR:

$$G\left(s_t; \gamma, c\right) = 1 - exp\left[-\gamma\left(s_t - c\right)^2\right], \quad \gamma > 0 \tag{5-4}$$

Exponential function is more suitable for studying the case of obvious inflection points in time series. Here, we mainly study the mean reversion characteristics of stock market returns, that is, the correlation between the current period and the lag period. Therefore, we make the following transition to the STAR model. Equation 5-5 can be obtained from the deformation of Equation 5-2.

$$\Delta y_t = \sum_{j=1}^{p} \beta_j y_{t-j} + \sum_{j=1}^{p} \beta_j^* y_{t-j} G\left(y_{t-d}; \gamma, c\right) + \varepsilon_t \tag{5-5}$$

Take the CSI 300 as an example, y_t is the current CSI 300, y_{t-j} is the CSI 300 lagged j period, and Δy_t is the current index minus the lagged 1 period index. The transition variable s_t takes y_{t-d}, d as the delay parameter.

The standard estimation steps of STAR are as follows:

First, determine an appropriate p-order linear autoregressive model. After testing the stationarity of the sequence, the p-order autoregression model is established, and the appropriate lag order is determined according to the corresponding values of AIC and SC criteria. Generally, the lag order p is between 1 and 6.

Secondly, the model is tested for linearity. Test the null hypothesis and alternative hypothesis. If the null hypothesis is rejected, it indicates that the nonlinear process conforms to the STAR form.

Thirdly, the coefficient constraints of the LSTAR function and ESTAR function are tested respectively, and the appropriate transition variable s_t and transition function $G\left(s_t; \gamma, c\right)$ are selected according to the test results.

Finally, each determined transition variable and transition function are brought into the model to estimate each parameter of the STAR model.

5.3.2 Empirical Analysis

Here, we take the CSI 300, Shanghai Composite Index, Shenzhen Composite Index, GEM Index, and SME Board Index as representatives to conduct a mean reversion test to study whether China's stock market has the function of price discovery. The sample data of the CSI 300, GEM Index, and Shenzhen SME Board Index are from the index release date to December 2013, which are October 2005 to December 2013, June 2010 to December 2013, and June 2005 to December 2013, respectively. In order to exclude the impact of the non-tradable shares reform on stock returns, the Shanghai Composite Index and Shenzhen Composite Index select the data after the non-tradable shares reform as samples. The sample data period is from January 2006 to December 2013.

1. Test of Stationary Time Series

Here, we use the ADF unit root test method to test the time series. The unit root test is conducted on the monthly return time series of the CSI 300, the Shanghai Composite Index, the Shenzhen Composite Index, the GEM Index, and the Shenzhen SME Board Index, respectively. The results show that the ADF statistics are significantly less than the critical values under the confidence levels of 1%, 5%, and 10%, and the P value is 0.0000. Therefore, the sample data of the CSI 300, Shanghai Composite Index, Shenzhen Composite Index, GEM Index, and SZSE SME Composite Index are stable time series. The test results are shown in Table 5-1.

Table 5-1 ADF Test Results of Monthly Yield Series of Each Index

Share Index	ADF Test t Statistic	p Value
CSI 300	9.0466	0.0000
Shanghai Composite Index	6.4190	0.0000
Shenzhen Composite Index	6.6728	0.0000
GEM Index	5.6462	0.0000
SZSE SME Composite Index	7.0790	0.0000

Note: The critical values of t statistics at 1%, 5%, and 10% significance levels are −3.50, −2.89, and −2.58, respectively.

It can be seen from the results in Table 5-1 that the absolute value of the ADF test value of the return rate series of each index is greater than the critical value at each significant level, indicating that the return rate series of each index is stable.

2. **Mean Reversion Test**

According to the estimation steps of the STAR model, the CSI 300, Shanghai Composite Index, Shenzhen Composite Index, GEM Index, and the SZSE SME Composite Index are tested by means of mean reversion.

(1) Determine the j-order autoregressive model

Establish the *j*-order autoregressive model for the stable yield time series and select the appropriate lag order according to AIC and SC criteria. Generally, the lag order *j* is between 1 and 6. Autoregressive models of order 1 to 6 are established respectively, and the AIC and SC test results are shown in Table 5-2.

Table 5-2 Lag Order Table of Autoregressive Model

Lag Order		1	2	3	4	5	6
CSI 300	AIC	−1.7896	−1.7965	−1.7830	−1.8345	−1.8039	−1.8350
	SC	−1.7640	−1.7450	−1.7054	−1.7303	−1.6729	−1.6767
Shanghai Composite Index	AIC	−2.4492	−2.3821	−2.3491	−2.3919	−2.3427	−2.3173
	SC	−2.1610	−2.1409	−2.1389	−2.2057	−2.1744	−2.2291
Shenzhen Composite Index	AIC	−2.1610	−2.1409	−2.1389	−2.2057	−2.1744	−2.2291
	SC	−2.1339	−2.0864	−2.0566	−2.0954	−2.0355	−2.0614
GEM Index	AIC	−2.4059	−2.4013	−2.4375	−2.4124	−2.4169	−2.3300
	SC	−2.3641	−2.3169	−2.3096	−2.2400	−2.1992	−2.0661
SZSE SME Composite Index	AIC	−2.2134	−2.1993	−2.1709	−2.1920	−2.1653	−2.1571
	SC	−2.1875	−2.1472	−2.0922	−2.0865	−2.0326	−1.9968

From the results in Table 5-2, it can be seen that the CSI 300 gets the minimum value of AIC when $p=6$ and the minimum value of SC when $p=1$. When the values corresponding to the AIC criterion and SC criterion are different, we usually take the results corresponding to the SC criterion as the selection criteria. Therefore, the first-order lag is selected as the lag order of the model. Similarly, the Shanghai Composite Index, Shenzhen Composite Index, GEM Index, and SZSE SME Composite Index take the SC criterion as the standard and also select one order lag as the lag order of the model. Therefore, Equation 5-5 of the model is rewritten as Equation 5-6:

$$\Delta y_t = \beta_1 y_{t-1} + \beta_2 y_{t-1} G\left(y_{t-d}; \gamma, c\right) + \varepsilon_t \tag{5-6}$$

(2) Linear test of model
First, the model is tested for linearity. If there is nonlinearity, the appropriate delay parameter d is determined. Since the meaning of parameter γ is not defined in Equation 5-6, the linearity test is performed after transition. The auxiliary regression is obtained by expanding the first-order Taylor formula of the transition function at $\gamma = 0$.

For the LSTAR model, the form of auxiliary regression is shown in Equation 5-7.

$$\Delta y_t = \phi_1 y_{t-1} + \phi_2 y_{t-1} y_{t-d} + w_t \tag{5-7}$$

For the ESTAR model, the form of auxiliary regression is shown in Equation 5-8.

$$\Delta y_t = \phi_1 y_{t-1} + \phi_2 y_{t-1} y_{t-d} + \phi_3 y_{t-1} y_{t-d}^2 + w_t \tag{5-8}$$

Comparing Equations 5-7 and 5-8, we can see that Equation 5-8 contains Equation 5-7, so the linearity test of Equation 5-7 is required. The original assumption is: H_0: $\phi_2 = \phi_3 = 0$. If the original assumption is rejected, it is nonlinear. d takes 1 to 7 respectively for Wald inspection, and the test results are shown in Table 5-3.

Table 5-3 Wald Test Results

Delay Parameter d	1	2	3	4	5	6	7
CSI 300	3.6249	3.9530	5.8910	7.2842	12.5399	15.1410	11.5864
	(0.0302)	(0.0223)	(0.0038)	(0.0011)	(0.0000)	(0.0001)	(0.0000)
Shanghai Composite Index	5.3589	8.1606	10.0183	13.7059	17.3428	15.5561	19.0081
	(0.0063)	(0.0006)	(0.0001)	(0.0001)	(0.0000)	(0.0000)	(0.0000)
Shenzhen Composite Index	8.5107	10.5181	11.8302	18.6531	13.5189	16.2673	17.7615
	(0.0004)	(0.0002)	(0.0001)	(0.0000)	(0.0001)	(0.0000)	(0.0000)

(Continued)

Delay Parameter d	1	2	3	4	5	6	7
GEM Index	0.3785	0.2603	0.8930	2.3261	2.3872	2.5346	4.6742
	(0.6874)	(0.7722)	(0.4183)	(0.1126)	(0.1071)	(0.0946)	(0.0166)
SZSE SME Composite Index	7.0554	7.4461	7.5132	10.4191	11.6712	9.8129	10.1783
	(0.0014)	(0.0010)	(0.0009)	(0.0001)	(0.0000)	(0.0001)	(0.0001)

Note: The corresponding p value is shown in brackets in Table 5-3.

According to the test results in Table 5-3, the nonlinear alternative hypothesis is accepted at the 5% confidence level. The smooth transition variable is determined by the delay parameter corresponding to the minimum p value. The smooth transition variable of the CSI 300 is y_{t-5}, the smooth transition variable of the Shanghai Composite Index is y_{t-5}, the smooth transition variable of the Shenzhen Composite Index is y_{t-4}, the smooth transition variable of the GEM Index is y_{t-7}, and the smooth transition variable of the SZSE SME Composite Index is y_{t-5}.

(3) Select transition function form

If $\phi_3 \neq 0$ in Equation 5-8, the ESTAR model is used as the distribution function; otherwise, the LSTAR model is used as the distribution function. Set the original assumption as $H_0 : \phi_3 = 0$, and conduct the Wald test again.

Table 5-4 Constraint Test Results

	CSI 300	Shanghai Composite Index	Shenzhen Composite Index	GEM Index	SZSE SME Composite Index
F-Statistic	4.4937	1.1562	6.7228	3.3898	5.0503
	(0.0366)	(0.2852)	(0.0111)	(0.0494)	(0.0270)
Chi-Square Statistic	4.4937	1.1562	6.7228	3.3898	5.0503
	(0.0340)	(0.2823)	(0.0095)	(0.0456)	(0.0246)

Note: The corresponding p value is shown in brackets in Table 5-4.

The test results are shown in Table 5-4. At the 5% confidence level, the corresponding p value of the CSI 300, Shenzhen Composite Index, GEM Index, and SZSE SME Composite Index is less than 0.05, rejecting the original hypothesis, while the corresponding p value of the Shanghai Composite Index is greater than 0.05, accepting the original hypothesis. According to the above results, the ESTAR model is used for the distribution function of the CSI 300, Shenzhen Composite Index, GEM Index, and SZSE SME Composite Index, and the LSTAR model is used for the distribution function of the Shanghai Composite Index.

(4) Empirical results

Through the above steps, the model to be estimated is preliminarily determined, as shown in Equations 5-9 to 5-13.

CSI 300:

$$\Delta y_t = \beta_1 y_{t-1} + \beta_2 y_{t-1} \left(1 - exp\left(-\gamma y_{t-5}^2\right)\right), \gamma > 0 \qquad (5\text{-}9)$$

Shanghai Composite Index:

$$\Delta y_t = \beta_1 y_{t-1} + \beta_2 y_{t-1} \left(\frac{1}{1 + exp\left(-\gamma y_{t-5}\right)}\right), \gamma > 0 \qquad (5\text{-}10)$$

Shenzhen Composite Index:

$$\Delta y_t = \beta_1 y_{t-1} + \beta_2 y_{t-1} \left(1 - exp\left(-\gamma y_{t-4}^2\right)\right), \gamma > 0 \qquad (5\text{-}11)$$

GEM Index:

$$\Delta y_t = \beta_1 y_{t-1} + \beta_2 y_{t-1} \left(1 - exp\left(-\gamma y_{t-7}^2\right)\right), \gamma > 0 \qquad (5\text{-}12)$$

SZSE SME Composite Index:

$$\Delta y_t = \beta_1 y_{t-1} + \beta_2 y_{t-1} \left(1 - exp\left(-\gamma y_{t-5}^2\right)\right), \gamma > 0 \qquad (5\text{-}13)$$

Use the extensive least squares method to estimate Equation 5-9 to Equation 5-13, and the results are shown in Table 5-5.

Table 5-5 Nonlinear Least Squares Estimation Results

Parameters to Be Estimated	β_1	β_2	γ
	0.0287	0.0004	0.0001
Equation (9)	(0.1901)	(0.0000)	(0.0000)
	(0.8496)	(0.9980)	(0.9978)
	0.0247	0.0029	−0.0356
Equation (10)	(0.9663)	(0.2286)	(−0.7757)
	(0.3365)	(0.8197)	(0.4518)
	0.0377	0.0189	−0.0228
Equation (11)	(0.9061)	(0.1612)	(−0.3231)
	(0.3673)	(0.8723)	(0.7474)

(Continued)

Parameters to Be Estimated	β_1	β_2	γ
	0.0631	−12.8638	0.0001
Equation (12)	(0.3708)	(−0.0008)	(0.0008)
	(0.7132)	(0.9993)	(0.9993)
	0.0109	0.0000	−0.0858
Equation (13)	(1.9365)	(0.1948)	(−1.3497)
	(0.0558)	(0.8459)	(0.1804)

Note: The first line of the estimated results of each equation in Table 5-5 is the estimated value of the parameter to be estimated, the first bracket below is the corresponding *t*-test value, and the second bracket is the corresponding *p*-value.

It can be seen from the results in Table 5-5 that at the 5% confidence level, the three parameters in Equations 5-9, 5-10, 5-11, 5-12, and 5-13 are not significant. There is no inevitable relationship between the price of the lag period and the price of the current period, which does not have the characteristics of mean reversion.

5.3.3 Conclusion

Through the empirical analysis of the nonlinear STAR, the results show that the CSI 300, Shanghai Composite Index, Shenzhen Composite Index, GEM Index, and SZSE SME Composite Index all show the feature of mean aversion within the sample interval, which indicates that the current Chinese stock market lacks the function of price discovery. The lack of the price discovery function directly determines the effective play of the resource optimization allocation function and the reflection function.

The imperfect function of market price discovery mainly stems from the imperfect market mechanism. From a worldwide perspective, China's stock market is almost the only market established from top to bottom, and the issuance and listing of shares are controlled by the government administrative departments. The primary stock market dominated by government departments directly affects the opening price of the secondary market and even the subsequent stock price trend, affects the income level of investors, and ultimately affects the healthy development of the stock market. By 2014, the number of listed companies in China's stock market had reached more than 2,500. It took more than 20 years to complete the hundreds-year journey in developed countries in Europe and America. The rapid development and remarkable achievements shocked the world. In the process of China's stock market from scratch, government behavior plays an irreplaceable role. This process can be summarized as the process of establishing the stock market driven by the government supervision department. It can be believed that without the government's administrative means, there will be no successful debut of China's stock market and the gradual process of maturity. However, in general, the degree of marketization is not high. With the new share issuance system of government approval and examination, the degree of marketization of the primary IPO market is extremely limited, and the degree of marketization of the secondary market, which is nicknamed "policy market," driven by policies is also limited. If we want to make the stock market give full play to its own functions, we must carry out market-oriented reform, effectively improve the operating efficiency of the stock market, improve the macro environment of the domestic stock market, and give full play to the role of the market mechanism. Only by successfully implementing the market-oriented reform of China's stock market can the basic function of stock market price discovery be fully exerted.

5.4 Countermeasures for Perfecting the Price Discovery Function of China's Stock Market

If the stock market is dominated by rational investors, the stock market will return the stock price to its intrinsic value under the influence of the supply and demand power of rational investors. This process is the mean reversion process mentioned above, which is also the realization process of the price discovery ability of the stock market. If the process of mean reversion is fast and the mean reversion cycle is short, it proves that the stock market has a high degree of information tolerance; that is, it is more efficient to accept information shocks, absorb shock fluctuations, and correct price deviations. It is a flexible market with good price discovery capabilities. If the process of mean reversion is slow and the mean reversion cycle is long, it proves that the response speed of the stock market's information tolerance to information is slow, the space to absorb shocks is small, the efficiency in correcting price deviation is low, and then the price discovery ability of the stock market is problematic. The mean reversion cycle of China's stock market is longer than that of the United States, the United Kingdom, Japan, and India, which means that the price discovery ability in China's stock market is relatively poor, and it cannot flexibly and effectively deal with information interference from outside, non-enterprise economic fundamentals.

5.4.1 Reasons for the Lack of Price Discovery Ability in China's Stock Market
To sum up, the main reason for the lack of price discovery function in China's stock market is the low degree of marketization, especially the strong administrative color of the primary market, which does not enable the market mechanism to play its basic regulatory role.

First, China's stock market has a large irrational component and is too speculative. The premise of the price discovery process is that rational investors occupy a dominant position in the stock market. The supply and demand relationship formed by rational investors forms the "invisible hand" of the stock market, thus providing the power source for the stock price to return to the mean. First of all, China's individual investors do not account for a small number of stock market investments, and most of them are not good at rational analysis and mainly rely on obtaining "news" to make buying and selling decisions. Secondly, the stock market has a very high turnover rate. The majority of investors are actually speculators rather than investors, and most of the stock investors are short-term investors who only focus on whether the stock price reaches the psychological level in the short term. Before buying and selling stocks, they even don't analyze the development of the company. Few people hold stocks in the mentality of shareholders and participate in dividends. Thirdly, the number of rational institutional investors is small. Only about 10% of China's stock market transactions are institutional investors, and the proportion of retail exchanges is as high as 90%. The sources and channels of information, the ability to analyze information, and the judgment of future trends of retail investors are generally immature, and personal investment sentiment has a great impact on investment decisions. The irrational sentiment in the stock market is pervasive, causing the stock price to wander randomly and deviate from the average. In general, the irrational factors in China's stock market can not be underestimated. The volatility and frequent ups and downs of the stock prices of listed companies are the direct manifestations of the irrational stock market.

Second, the division of the primary and secondary stock markets. In the stock market of developed countries, the primary issue market and secondary issue market are highly marketized, and the pricing process is completely determined by the bidding of both suppliers in the market. However, there is a serious artificial segmentation between the primary market and the secondary market in China's stock market. The primary stock market is mainly about the IPO process of enterprises. The pricing of IPOs in China's stock market is not strictly determined by the roadshow contracted by foreign investment banks but is mainly controlled by the government regulatory authorities. However, the secondary market is a trading market where the price is determined by the supply and demand relationship composed of many investors. In contrast, the primary market has more characteristics of a planned economy, and the degree of marketization of the secondary market is far higher than that of the primary market. Although the purpose of China's shareholding reform is to establish a modern enterprise system, in practice, many companies are following the model of state-owned enterprises, and the direct purpose of issuing shares is to "capture money." The government priced the IPO too high, exceeding its intrinsic value. In the secondary market, the supply and demand relationship caused the stock price to fall back. The malaise of the secondary market directly affected the smooth IPO of the primary market. At this time, the government took the initiative to prop up the falling stock price with policies, which is the so-called "policy market." It is precisely because of this "policy market" that the price discovery function of the secondary market is constantly destroyed.

5.4.2 *The General Assumption of Improving the Price Discovery Function of the Stock Market*

If we want to give full play to the function of stock market price discovery, we must make full use of the role of market mechanism, and we must carry out market-oriented reform to make full use of the role of market mechanism. There is no doubt that market-oriented reform is the institutional guarantee for the price discovery function and the only way for the healthy development of China's stock market. The general direction of capital market reform is to promote marketization step by step. Only by getting rid of the "policy market" can the stock market become mature. In the market-oriented reform of China's stock market, we should recognize the root cause of the lack of price discovery function in China's stock market. China's stock market was born under the planned economic system, and the government led the process from its establishment to its growth. From the approval system to the audit system, from pricing to inquiry, we cannot really get rid of the dominance of government behavior. Jia Li (2006) believed that among more than 100 securities markets in the world, China's stock market is the only one that has been established from top to bottom and is the only single-level stock market. At the same time, it is also the only market in which the government administrative department controls the size of stock issuance and listing. This is totally different from the stock market formed by the spontaneous trading under the wutong tree in New York and the coffee shop in London. The establishment of the stock market in New York and London is a spontaneous bottom-up market, and the market mechanism has played a leading role from the beginning.

It has only taken less than 20 years since the emergence and development of China's stock market and almost completed the development of the stock market in Western developed countries for more than 200 years. This is a brilliant reform achievement. Compared with the stock markets in many Western countries, there is not much difference in the organizational structure of the market, the efficiency of the trading clearing system, and even the size of the market. The growth and development of China's stock market are important achievements in China's economic transformation from a planned system to a market system. The experience of capital market reform and development is also an important part of China's successful experience in economic reform. China's stock market is not a natural product of China's economic development but an imported product that spans the stage of social and economic development. It is not a stock market rooted in a mature market economy system and fully following the laws of market economy, but a market based on the transition economy from a socialist planned economy to a market economy.

Only by successfully implementing the market-oriented reform of China's stock market can the basic function of price discovery be fully exerted. Excessive government intervention will inhibit the role of the market mechanism and destroy the basic function of stock market price discovery. The overall direction of reform is to reduce the intervention of the regulatory authorities. Only when the stock price reflects its intrinsic value can the function of resource optimization and reflection be fully exerted. With the deepening of the marketization of China's stock market and the gradual improvement of the market mechanism, the value measurement system and price discovery function of the stock market will gradually mature.

5.4.3 IPO Marketization Reform and Improvement of Price Discovery Function

The construction of the IPO system is the core issue of the construction of the whole stock market system and also the focus of the market-oriented reform of China's stock market. IPO marketization is the ultimate goal of China's stock market system construction, and the main problem of non-marketization behavior lies in the primary market. Since the establishment of the stock market, the construction of the IPO system has never stopped. The issuance system of the stock market has gone through two stages: the examination and approval system and the approval system. The pricing of new shares has gone through four stages: the fixed issue price pricing method, the fixed price-earnings ratio pricing method, the price-earnings ratio interval pricing method, and the inquiry system. The non-market equilibrium pricing method is mainly carried out with the participation of government regulators or a small number of market entities. The issuance of new shares did not follow the rules of the market mechanism. This paper analyzes and studies the possible risks faced by the marketization reform in combination with the marketization evolution process of China's IPO model and puts forward corresponding countermeasures in order to maximize the fairness and justice of all agents in the stock market, avoid turning the marketization reform into a distribution process led by the regulatory authorities at the expense of the interests of vulnerable groups, and further ensure the stable and healthy development of the stock market.

1. The Process of IPO Marketization Reform in China's Stock Market

The overall direction of IPO system reform is to move towards marketization gradually. It mainly includes the marketization of new share issuance quota, new share issuance pricing, refinancing, listing and delisting, etc. Since the establishment of the Shanghai Stock Exchange in December 1990, the issuance of shares has gone through quota management, index management, channel system, recommendation system, and inquiry system. The IPO pricing model has mainly gone through three stages: fixed price (1990–1995), fixed price-earnings ratio (1996–2003), and inquiry system (2004 to date). From the perspective of institutional change itself, the inquiry of new shares is an important measure in the market-oriented reform of the issuance system and a leap forward to marketization. It weakens the administrative intervention in the issuance price and greatly promotes the marketization of the stock market. Next, we will take IPO pricing as the main line for analysis.

(1) Fixed price issuance and par value issuance of new shares under the examination and approval system

The evolution of the IPO system can be traced back to 1984. Feilo Acoustics was the first stock issued in China, and the stock was issued at par at that time. In 1985, Yanzhong Industry and Aishi Electronics issued shares of 5 million yuan and 400,000 yuan, respectively. In 1987, Vacuum Electronics and Feilo Shares issued shares of 10 million yuan and 2.1 million yuan, respectively. Yuyuan Shopping Center issued 1,291,000 yuan in 1988, and Shenhua Industrial issued 460,000 yuan. In February 1992, Vacuum Electronics issued its first B share. The initial stock market was not optimistic. Shenzhen Shenfa was issued in 1987, and later, Vanke, Jintian, Yuanye, and other stocks, without exception, encountered unexpected indifference in investment subscription. However, soon after, these stocks created a wealth myth that rose dozens or even hundreds of times. The significance of these wealth myths is not in the stocks themselves, nor even in discussing whether these stocks are worth the money. In a country that knows very little about stocks, the rise of these stocks and their huge wealth effect have far exceeded the significance of these stocks themselves, which can no longer be measured by the stock investment value itself, but should be evaluated from the historical perspective of China's capital market and even China's economic development. These events together determined the successful opening of the Shanghai and Shenzhen Stock Exchanges in 1990 and 1991. Later, with the spread of the rag-to-riches myth, the entire stock market also showed a trend of rapid growth and a gratifying situation. As a result, the issue of stocks at a premium and the problem of oversupply were born. The IPO issuance quota and IPO pricing became the two important factors dominating the Chinese stock market.

This stage is the birth stage of the stock market, and China's stock market started with only dozens of listed companies. By 2000, the number of listed companies had reached nearly 1,000, and it took about ten years for the developed countries in Europe and America to complete the journey of hundreds of years. In the process of China's stock market from scratch, government behavior plays an irreplaceable role. This process can be summarized as the process of establishing the stock market driven by the government regulatory authorities. It can be believed that without the government's administrative means, there would be no successful debut of China's stock market and gradual maturity process.

(2) Fixed P/E pricing method and premium issuance of new shares under the examination and approval system

From 1990 to 2000, the IPO adopted the administrative examination and approval system. The number of listed companies is basically allocated according to the administrative subordination. The internal subscription before 1992, the sudden wealth effect of the direct listing mode of internal employee shares, still plays a huge role in promoting the development of China's stock market. Later, as the subscribers became more and more enthusiastic, the form of issuing a lottery subscription form was adopted. In 1993, it adopted the forms of full prepayment, proportional allotment, refund of the balance, and transfer of the balance. The pricing method determines the issue price according to the P/E ratio, which is basically distributed between 15 and 20 times. The P/E ratio is adjusted according to the size of the IPO company's equity. The issue price is lower for large IPOs and higher for small IPOs. In 2001, IPO was reformed from the examination and approval system to the approval system, which is more market-oriented than the examination and approval system and is an important step towards marketization. China's *Securities Law* clearly stipulates that "public issuance of securities must meet the conditions prescribed by laws and administrative regulations, and be reported to the securities regulatory authority under the State Council or the department authorized by the State Council for approval according to law. Without approval according to law, no unit or individual may publicly issue securities." This provision has changed the original examination and approval system of government allocation of listing quotas and established the IPO system of securities issuance approval system. Zhou Xiaohua, Zhao Weike, and Liu Xing (2006) used the IPO data of Shanghai and Shenzhen markets from 1995 to 1999 and from 2001 to 2005 to make a comparative study of the IPO pricing efficiency under the two issuance systems and concluded that the IPO pricing efficiency under the approval system has improved. The IPO pricing tends to be reasonable, which shows that the approval system has made progress towards marketization. The issuance method is online pricing issuance and online bidding issuance, and the pricing of new shares is still a fixed price-earnings ratio. At this stage, the myth that new shares are invincible has been staged repeatedly. It is not uncommon for the opening price of the secondary market to be dozens of percentage points higher than the issuance price of the primary market or even double. As a result, the government regulatory department began to pay more attention to the issue of speculation under the idea of promoting market-oriented construction. It adopted the inquiry system for pricing in 2004, which also made the pricing method further move towards marketization. Before July 1, 1999, the IPO pricing was determined by the issuer and the underwriter through consultation and reported to the CSRC for approval. The CSRC controlled the issue price by the upper limit of the price-earnings ratio. All new shares were issued to public investors. From 1999 to the first half of 2001, the price-earnings ratio control of the issuance was gradually relaxed, and the inquiry mechanism began to be tried. In terms of the selling method, legal person placement was introduced, and the pilot market value placement was started. From the second half of 2001 to 2004, the regulatory authorities strictly controlled the P/E ratio of the issuance again, and the market value placement was fully implemented. At this stage, the issuance quota and pricing power were completely controlled by the government supervision department. The top-down stock market led by the government could not be managed and operated by administrative means forever. The idea of market-oriented reform was gradually put on the agenda.

(3) Inquiry system under approval system
The examination and approval system for stock issuance was changed to the approval system, changing how government departments determine the planned quota, select and recommend listed enterprises, and approve stock issuance, and establishing the principle that the lead underwriter recommends companies to be listed according to market needs, the CSRC conducts preliminary compliance review, and the issuance review committee independently reviews and votes. On March 17, 2001, China's stock issuance approval system was officially launched.

The so-called inquiry system is that when pricing stocks, investment banks and listed companies determine a range of issuance prices according to the fundamental situation and market demand. According to the feedback of investors in the market, the issue price is determined according to the price level acceptable to most investors. After the establishment of the inquiry system, both the IPO issuance method and the pricing method of the stock market have made a big step towards marketization, which is a decisive step in the marketization process of China's stock market. On August 20, 2010, the China Securities Regulatory Commission issued the *Guiding Opinions on Deepening the Reform of the New Share Issuance System*, which was mainly improved from the aspects of the restrictive mechanism of quotation application and placement, expanding the scope of inquiry objects, and enhancing the transparency of pricing information. The issuance of new shares in 2004 followed the inquiry system, and the regulatory authorities no longer approved the price of new shares. In 2006, after the division between the old and the new, the market value allocation was canceled, and the combination of offline inquiry allocation and online fund subscription was introduced. Since 2009, the market-oriented reform of the new share issuance system with the main content of "marketization of new share issuance pricing" and "marketization of new share issuance rhythm" is essentially to let the primary market remove the administrative process and restore the market. This round of reform has achieved certain results and achieved the expected results. However, new problems immediately emerged. The most important was the phenomenon of "three highs" of new shares, namely, "high issue price," "high issue P/E ratio," and "ultra-high raised funds." The securities regulatory authorities had to take various measures to curb the excessive speculation in the market. The regulatory authority blamed the "three highs" on the small amount of stock supply and increased the supply of new shares as much as possible. The first batch of 28 companies listed on the GEM at the same time was out of this consideration, which directly promoted the acceleration of the expansion pace, accompanied by the continuous decline of the stock market. In order to control the speculation, measures such as the limit on the rise and fall of new shares on the first day of listing and the ladder suspension system were also implemented, and the "three highs" problem was curbed to a certain extent. However, many market participants attributed the decline of the stock market to the direct result of market expansion, which put the regulatory authorities in a dilemma.

The CSRC has continuously introduced measures to govern the capital market. The purpose of the delisting system and the reform of the new share issuance system is to deter investors from speculating in stocks with poor performance and new stocks, guide investors to choose high-quality listed companies, and promote the concept of long-term investment and value investment. The leadership of the CSRC has made several statements directly against the problem of high-quality and low prices in China's stock market for many years and believes that blue chips have investment value. The fundamental way to solve the stock market is to remove the shadow of the planned economy and transition to marketization. What cannot be avoided in this process is that it will bring about many expected and unexpected problems. For example, the implementation of the inquiry system in IPO has not cured the "three highs" problem of new share issuance through this systematic reform that has always been marching towards marketization but has become more and more serious. The ST company was specially dealt with to punish its poor performance and warn investors. Instead, the ST stock became more and more popular and became the most speculative "opportunity" in recent years, which has been repeatedly prohibited.

2. Possible Risks of IPO Marketization Reform

The general direction of IPO marketization reform is to reduce the intervention of regulatory authorities and strengthen the spontaneous regulation of the internal mechanism of the market. Since the establishment of the Shanghai Stock Exchange in December 1990, China's stock issuance system has been continuously reformed. As a whole, it has gone through two stages: the examination and approval system and the approval system. This means that in the process of transition to marketization, we will inevitably encounter problems that other countries' stock markets do not encounter and face risks that other countries' stock markets do not face. Marketization reform is a direction, but it is not totally successful to achieve marketization. The market mechanism is imperfect, and problems such as market failure also exist for a long time. As the marketization reform of China's stock market is carried out from top to bottom, the following risks may be faced in a certain period of time after gradually liberalizing the issuance quota and issuance pricing power.

(1) Stock market expansion spurs supply surge, and marketization reform may trigger a market downturn

As we all know, the introduction of market-oriented reform measures will certainly reduce the approval process of the government supervision department, thus greatly reducing the threshold for listing, and the direct consequence is the rapid listing of a large number of enterprises. For a long time, listing for the direct purpose of circulating money has become an inertial mode of thinking in the stock market. As the regulatory authorities formed a large number of enterprises to be listed in the audit process, the decentralization process of market-oriented reform is likely to be the process of releasing a large number of IPOs. In 2012, more and more companies to be listed lined up for review have become the best proof. A sudden large-scale listing will inevitably lead to a serious oversupply of stocks and a shortage of funds. The stock market will fall sharply, and in serious cases, the stock market will collapse. The existence of large-scale companies to be listed means that if the government regulatory authorities do not control them well, they will return to the old path of the "policy market." For example, in 2012, the stock market was in a serious downturn, and the Shanghai Composite Index was declining. Many industry insiders suggested suspending the issuance of new shares to boost market confidence. In fact, the suspension of new shares was a typical administrative regulation, which did not conform to the direction of market-oriented reform and was a historic setback. Since the implementation of the new policy of governing the market by the CSRC, the mechanism of China's stock market has been improved to a great extent, and the market-oriented reform has made obvious progress. In this case, it seemed that it was not appropriate to let the market decide the pace of new share issuance. However, although the regulatory authorities did not make a clear announcement, it can be seen from the fact that the IPO has been suspended after the review of the IPO applications of two enterprises by the Issuance Examination Committee of the CSRC on October 10, 2012. This suspension of IPO has led to the rapid rise of the stock market. The securities regulatory authorities are unwilling to give up the results of market-oriented reform and to see the continuous decline of the stock market. This measure is both helpless and contains a good intention to get rid of the "policy market."

The contradiction between the market-oriented reform and the downturn of the stock market is like a child being held by adults. When adults let go, there will be certain risks. The birth of China's stock market is led by the government, which is an inevitable choice of history. Under the government's leadership, the phenomenon of shell resource shortage and even high value will inevitably be formed. The direction of market-oriented reform is gradually changing from government-led to market-led. The slow trend of shell resource value to zero is the symbol of successful market-oriented reform. However, in the process of market-oriented reform, it is bound to experience serious pain; that is, through market behavior to rectify or even punish the non-market-oriented behavior of investors and listed companies, the market can be rational and can gradually have the characteristics of marketization and become mature. After the market-oriented reform, from the investors' perspective, junk stocks may become immortal stocks (stocks with a price below 1 yuan), and blue chip stocks can be truly discovered. In the era dominated by the regulatory authorities, shell resources are more valuable than performance, which is why there are speculation behaviors of fowls and dogs turning immortals and full of countless restructuring imagination, and the government regulatory authorities have repeatedly prohibited them. From the perspective of listed companies, the shares of the original shareholders may be higher or lower than the original subscription price after the listing. It is difficult to have a wealth creation process of more than ten, dozens, or even hundreds of times. The reason for the rapid wealth creation is the result of the high value of the listing qualification itself (i.e., shell resources).

(2) The contradiction between the "three highs" of listing and market-oriented reform
The so-called "three highs" refer to "high issue price, high P/E ratio, and high fund-raising amount." The premise of market-oriented pricing is to have a standardized and mature capital market. The IPO inquiry system is an effective pricing method widely used in mature markets. However, due to the immaturity of the stock market environment in China, the implementation effect is not ideal. The phenomenon of high-price issuance, which damages the interests of investors to capture money, occurs frequently. Cen Jian (2011) believed that the "three highs" phenomenon of new share issuance had very serious consequences on the market, which caused great pressure on the capital side of the market, fundamentally violated the reform goal of optimizing market resource allocation, caused a great waste of market resources, and also became a channel for many large shareholders to cash out at a high price and underwriters to seek illegitimate interests by unscrupulous means.

The way to realize the marketization of new share issuance will not be smooth. Since the adoption of the inquiry system, the securities regulatory authorities have stopped pricing, but this has led to the "three highs" phenomenon. The prevalence of speculation in China's stock market will inevitably lead to a high issue price, which will be accompanied by a high P/E ratio of new shares. The issuing price of new shares has been controlled by the lead underwriter and institutions for a long time. Driven by interests, the sponsor institution will definitely raise the issuing price and the listing price. In addition, the excessive raising can also obtain more commissions and underwriting fees. They will do everything possible to promote the "three highs" of new share issuance. In order to compete for chips, inquiry agencies will also try their best to raise prices, which has played a role in fueling the huge amount of over-raised funds. In order to curb the "three highs" phenomenon, the government regulatory authorities increased the scale of listing, resulting in the stock market falling. In 2006, 70 new shares were issued, of which 33% were issued with a P/E ratio of 10–20 times, 61% were issued with a P/E ratio of 20–30 times, and 6% were issued with a P/E ratio of more than 30 times. In 2007, 118 new shares were issued, of which 2% were issued with a P/E ratio of 10–20 times, 88% were issued with a P/E ratio of 20–30 times, and 10% were issued with a P/E ratio of more than 30 times. Since the resumption of IPO in June 2009, the level of the P/E ratio of the A-share market has also been constantly raised. The arithmetic average P/E ratio of 99 listed new shares in 2009 was 51.5 times, much higher than the P/E ratio of 26.7 times in

2008, an increase of 93%. From 2010 to 2011, the average P/E ratio of new share issuance was 59.49 times for the GEM, 48.53 times for the SME board, and 37.55 times for the Shanghai main board. In 2012, due to the continuous downturn of the stock market, the issue price-earnings ratio declined to a certain extent, and the "three highs" problem of new shares also converged. The average P/E ratio of A-share IPO continued to fall, from 47.6 times in 2011 to 30.2 times in 2012. The main reason for this phenomenon was not the effect of regulation but the downturn of the stock market. The first day of IPO breaking often occurred. Of the 154 newly listed enterprises in 2011, 41 broke on the first day, accounting for 26.6%. This should be a normal phenomenon, and it should also be a normal phenomenon in a relatively perfect securities market. On November 30, 2013, the CSRC issued the *Opinions on Further Promoting the Reform of the IPO System*, saying that it would no longer implement the "25% rule" and would solve the problems of high pricing and "money trapping" of new shares from three aspects, including promoting the stock issuance. In the two years from 2013 to 2014, the IPO market stopped for a second, and the phenomenon of multiple consecutive trading limit boards became "normal."

The formation of price is the core mechanism of resource allocation, and the reform of the pricing mechanism will determine the success or failure of IPO issuance mechanism reform. The biggest problem with the current pricing mechanism is that the initiative is in the hands of large shareholders, which is bound to tend to the interests of large shareholders too much. In contrast, the interests of small and medium-sized shareholders are difficult to reflect. This unfair interest distribution mechanism hurts the Chinese stock market. In order to curb the "three highs" problem, the CSRC decided to open the lock-up period for offline placement of shares so that an offline to online call-back mechanism should be established for those new shares that institutions were not optimistic about. This was undoubtedly to encourage those privileged placement institutions to earn faster and more stable income, which was a setback for the reform of the new share issuance system. Over consideration of the interests of institutional investors will aggravate the manipulation of the new share issuance price by these institutions.

(3) Investor losses erode confidence in China's market reform
In the process of market-oriented reform, it is bound to bring pain. Any reform is a process of redistributing and adjusting interests and moving towards fairness. The marketization reform of China's stock market is also bound to have this experience. If this pain can be successfully passed through and out of the shadow, it is the best choice and the best result. If investors lose confidence in the stock market or lead to the collapse of the stock market in this intense pain, it will become a necessary countermeasure to clean up the mess with government actions. At that time, China's stock market will return to the starting point of the original reform characterized by government leadership, that is, return to the "policy market," and all efforts and attempts made for the reform

will inevitably be wasted. Since the reform of the new share issuance system in 2009, the regulatory authorities have made great efforts to realize the marketization of the issuance quota and pricing. However, the continuous decline of the stock market has made it impossible to stabilize the stock market by stopping the issuance of new shares, which was a commonly used positive countermeasure in the past. To curb the decline of the stock market, the government regulatory authorities are in a dilemma. Without the "policy market," the stock market fell continuously, and the policy rescue turned into a "policy market." The financial verification started on January 8, 2013, and scared off some IPO companies that were waiting in line. Under the pressure of the financial verification storm, some IPO companies that were waiting in line announced their withdrawal. The original intention of the regulatory authorities was to control the rhythm of new share issuance, which was a negation of the previous review and listing.

The number of new shares issued has always been an important factor affecting the rise and fall of stocks. It seems that the market-oriented reform of IPO always affects the trend of China's stock market, while the performance of listed companies, as the fundamental factor determining the trend of stock prices, always looks pale. The market-oriented reform has made investors bear the risk of stock decline, and the regulatory authorities have repeatedly interpreted the cycle of the "policy market" in frustration. "Suspension of new share issuance" has become a direct means of regulating China's stock market. In fact, it is the investment value of stocks, rather than the rhythm of new stock issuance, that determines the trend of the stock market. Since the birth of China's stock market, there have been seven IPO pauses: the first was from November 1, 1994, to January 24, 1995; the second was from April 11, 1995, to June 29, 1995; the third was from July 1, 1995, to October 10, 1995; the fourth was from September 10, 2001, to November 29, 2001; the fifth was from September 9, 2004, to February 3, 2005; the sixth was from June 7, 2005, to June 19, 2006; the seventh time was from September 25, 2008, to June 18, 2009. We notice that, except for the fourth suspension of IPO, the effect was not very significant; the other times stopped the decline to varying degrees and even directly led to a bull market.

(4) Stock market dysfunctions: price discovery, valuation, and fund-raising challenges
On October 24, 2012, the overseas edition of the *People's Daily* published an article entitled "Why Are Stocks 'High Quality and Low Price' Everywhere." The article said that Guo Shuqing, the then chairman of the CSRC, believed that the main problem in China's capital market was the imbalance of the current share price structure. The average price-earnings ratio of new shares issued in 2011 was 48 times, while the annual average price-earnings ratio of Shanghai and Shenzhen markets was only 17.76 times. The problem of high quality and low price emerged, and the stock price could not objectively reflect the intrinsic value of the stock. In 2012, the average P/E ratio of stocks in the secondary market was only 12 times, while the P/E ratio of new stock issuance was more

than 30 times. On the one hand, it shows that the rational degree of market investors is extremely limited. On the other hand, it is also the result of market speculation for many years. There are serious problems in the market investment concept, which has become the main obstacle to the healthy development of China's stock market and the success of the system construction. The strange phenomenon of valuation inversion in the primary and secondary markets was extremely significant in 2011 and 2012, when the stock market was sluggish. In 2011, Xinyan shares with the highest P/E ratio were issued more than 150 times, and five shares with a P/E ratio of more than 100 times were issued throughout the year. In the same period, the P/E ratio of blue chip stocks in the secondary stock market was declining, which was nearly ten times the historical low by the end of 2012. Zhu Hongjun and Qian Youwen (2008) selected A-share IPO samples from 1992 to 2008 and tested them after controlling other factors, such as the market atmosphere. The actual results did not conform to the "pricing efficiency view" but basically conformed to the "rent distribution view." The government's regulation of stock supply tends to cause artificial demand exceeding supply, which leads to a higher price that the market can accept for the shares of "approved to issue" companies than in the fully competitive market. The higher price is the "rent" in regulatory economics. The irrational speculation behavior was far greater than the rational investment behavior. The market financing function has been artificially amplified by the speculation behavior. The stock market has become a place for grabbing money, which directly destroyed the resource allocation function and the price discovery function. Tu Renmeng (2012) believed that the long-term functional orientation and system design of China's stock market were biased towards financiers, which played an important role in solving the capital problem of state-owned enterprises and promoting the rapid development of China's economy. However, listed companies had a prominent effect of valuing financing over returns to encircle money, and the efficiency of market resource allocation was low. The stock market has become a place for a few people to make money, which has seriously damaged the interests of ordinary investors.

3. Countermeasure Analysis
Yi Xianrong (2007) believed that the basic system of China's stock market was not well prepared, which caused it to face many obstacles in its sustainable development. The establishment and improvement of the basic system is the key to the sustainable and healthy development of China's securities market. From the perspective of the construction of the stock issuance system, neither the registration system nor the approval system can be perfect. As an important part of the whole capital market operation, the IPO system must be reformed and improved in the continuous development of the capital market. Throughout the evolution of the new share issuance system in China's stock market for more than 20 years, from the examination and approval system that ended in 2001 to the approval system that is being used, the starting point of reform measures is to establish

a securities issuance system model based on the principles of openness, fairness, and justice. Qian Kangning and Jiang Jianrong (2012) believed that the formation and change of the stock issuance system was not only a reflection of the inherent requirements of a country or region's securities market development, but also an extension of its political, economic, and legal systems. The approval system represented by the United Kingdom and Germany and the registration system represented by the United States and Japan are the two issuance systems adopted by the current mature stock market. The follow-up reform of China's IPO system should adopt a gradual approach, following the principle of stability and development, efficiency and fairness, continue to marketize and rationalize the issuance scale and pricing mechanism, simultaneously develop risk prevention and innovation of the new share issuance system, and gradually shift to the registration system in stages to promote the coordinated and healthy development of the primary market and the secondary market. Fu Yan and Deng Zixin (2012) believed that although the registration system with a high degree of marketization is the goal of the reform of the new share issuance system in China's stock market, the success and progress control of the reform of the new share issuance system in China's stock market depend on whether the supporting legal system and environment are perfect. The two kinds of issuance review systems, with their own advantages and disadvantages, are neither one nor the other in the actual operation of the securities market, and there is no absolute difference between progress and backwardness. The registration system pursues market autonomy, recognizes that the issuance right of securities belongs to the scope of corporate autonomy rather than being granted by the state, emphasizes market efficiency and freedom, and fully respects the regulatory role of the invisible hand of the market in resource allocation. The approval system advocates government intervention, emphasizes market fairness and order, and fully reflects the participation of administrative power in securities issuance. It will not be smooth on the path of IPO marketization reform in China's stock market, and we will certainly encounter problems and difficulties of one kind or another. We propose the following countermeasures for the above analysis of risk problems.

(1) The mode of separating stock issuance from listing can be tried
Follow the steps of issuing and listing marketization, and the two marketizations together form a complete marketization model. After a company to be listed issues new shares, the uncertainty of whether it can be listed will enable investors to choose new shares rationally, which can not only enable companies with growth potential to receive direct financing support, but also will not increase the pressure on the secondary market, while preventing the occurrence of money encirclement. Issuing and listing at the same time is the direct motive force for the listing of stocks and becoming a money trap. Because the listing is a monopoly resource, at least to a certain extent, the resultant force of various factors has led to the smooth conduct of the above market as the carrier of money

circling. Generally speaking, the purpose of listing is to solve the liquidity problem of stocks, which cannot return the principal. A significant feature of China's stock market is that the direct purpose of listing is to raise funds. Companies are likely to take money circling as the motivation for listing. After the issuance and listing are separated, the enterprise shares can be issued as long as they meet the conditions, realizing the full marketization of the issuance and being selected by the market investors. After the issuance, it is not necessarily listed for trading, enabling investors to invest in the primary market selectively. Zeng Yang (2012) believed that in China's securities legal system, there has been no clear provision on whether stocks should or must be listed after public issuance. However, China's securities market rules and practices have gradually made "all companies must be listed after public issuance" a "common sense understanding." The unity of issuance and listing has actually formed the procedural convention that the condition of listing was issuance in China, leading to the dependence of investment risks on government departments in the capital market, which was the root of the formation of the "policy market" in China's stock market.

The newly issued shares do not necessarily need to be listed and circulated. The issuance of shares is just a means of raising funds, and the listing and circulation are to solve the liquidity. Stock issuance and stock listing were originally two separate and independent processes. Listing and issuance can be carried out separately and independently in time or in combination and consecutively in time. The separation of issuance and listing can eliminate the false prosperity of the issuance market and restore the risks that should exist in the primary market.

(2) Expand the scope of inquiry
The establishment of an inquiry system is an important step towards marketization. The participation of many professional institutional investors in pricing will certainly reduce the subjectivity and arbitrariness of new share pricing and also make the behavior of investors, sponsors, and other participants more market-oriented, considering the interests of issuers and investors in a certain sense. However, the result of implementing the inquiry system in recent years is that the regulatory authorities still have a great influence or even a decisive role in the price of new shares and have not fully played the basic function of the inquiry system in the market-oriented reform. Zhang Zheng and Ouyang Shan (2012) believed that the inquiry system was not perfect; investors did not bid according to their true intentions, and there was a phenomenon of low reporting and high buying, high reporting, and low buying or not buying, which made inquiry in many cases a mere formality and difficult to reflect the true value of the stock. Pricing is an indispensable part of the numerous documents of issuance review and listing recommendation. The underwriting instructions of the sponsor must include the type, quantity, amount, and issuing price of the underwritten shares. Through the supervision of the qualification of the inquiry object and the quotation behavior, and in combination

with the window guidance of the inquiry process, the regulatory department has implemented factual control over the inquiry behavior.

At present, the imperfection of the inquiry system is obvious. The decline of most new shares after listing indicates that the new shares are priced too high, far exceeding their intrinsic value. The original shareholders of the listing got rich overnight, and the myth of getting rich overnight can be found everywhere in the GEM and SME boards. As a universal phenomenon, it must not conform to logic. The market environment and thinking inertia have become a persistent disease. The successful issuance of the new shares depends on the acceptance of investors. How do we make investors accept them? There is only one reason, and that is the profit-making effect. The huge difference between the primary market and the secondary market is the profit-making effect. The high issue price has to win the lot, which not only helps the purchasers in the primary market but also the performance of underwriters. Bubble and non-market pricing behavior have become the biggest problem in China's stock market, and the secondary market has become the norm of losing more and earning less, which inevitably seriously reduces the investment value of China's stock market and its attractiveness to investors. Investors like Buffett hardly emerge in the secondary market, and becoming a major shareholder of a listed company through a power intermediary and successfully listing is almost the only way to achieve wealth. These no longer require research ability and rational judgment of the market. The power or qualification of the listing is rational, and the capital game has become a legal pyramid-selling activity in a certain sense.

In 2009, China's new share issuance approval system experienced a major change, which was the market-oriented reform plan of issuance pricing. From administrative pricing to inquiry by issuers and intermediaries themselves, it can be said that the reform in 2009 made a big step towards marketization in pricing. In the process of government administrative pricing, pricing by specifying the P/E ratio has played a very important role in the transition to marketization. Expanding the scope of inquiry and involving more subjects can not only implement the inquiry system, but also more effectively promote the marketization process of China's stock market.

(3) Enhancing pricing and listing amid a stock market downturn for market stability
The release of pricing liberalization and listing when the stock market rises will cause the stock market to experience a long period of huge downward pressure, increase the risk of stock market decline, and increase the risk of macroeconomic fluctuations. It is better to carry out system reform when the stock market is depressed and cooperate with some stability measures, which will reduce the risks to the stock market and macroeconomic. This can draw rich experience from the major historical event of the non-tradable shares reform. As an institutional reform to promote the reform and opening up and stable development of the capital market, the stock market is almost bound to fall. The reason is that the cost of state-owned shares and corporate shares is greatly different from that of

public shares, which is undoubtedly a huge pressure on China's stock market, where only public shares are traded. Every institutional decision made by the securities regulatory authorities on state-owned shares and corporate shares has become a huge force to push the market down. On January 31, 2004, the State Council issued *Several Opinions of the State Council on Promoting the Reform and Opening up and Stable Development of the Capital Market*, which clearly proposed to actively and steadily solve the problem of non-tradable shares. On April 29, 2005, the CSRC issued the *Notice on Issues Related to the Pilot of the Share Trading Reform of Listed Companies*, marking the official launch of the share trading reform. After this institutional change, an insurmountable gap has become an opportunity for China's stock market to exit the largest bull market. After this "bad," China's stock market has gone out of the largest bull market in history. The resolution to the split share structure problem has taken a decisive step for the marketization reform of China's stock market and laid a good foundation for the institutionalization of the next step of the marketization idea of the stock market. It can be said that it is a great success in the history of the development of China's stock market. The market has accepted the solution to the split share structure problem. As long as the problems are handled properly, they should not be big problems. The reform of the new share issuance system inevitably has an impact on the market, and some important countermeasures that will have a greater impact on the market should be introduced when the stock market is depressed. On the one hand, from the perspective of its intrinsic value, the stock market has limited falling space and less impact, reducing the chances of sharp falls. On the other hand, the effect of some favorable policies is also obvious. The favorable policies in the downturn will form an effective force to stabilize the market with the advantages of stock market valuation. The market timing of the share trading scheme is very worthy of reference.

(4) Establish a reserve board to mitigate the impact of IPO on the market
The so-called reserve board is to let the companies to be listed apply for IPO to the CSRC and, at the same time, regulate their behavior according to the management system of listed companies. The implementation of the reserve board system can delay the over-centralized IPO problem in the process of marketization and can test the applicant company through continuous information disclosure. Regularly disclosing information, including annual reports, semi-annual reports, quarterly reports, major information disclosure reports, etc. The information published must meet the requirements of authenticity, accuracy, integrity, and timeliness. Enterprises have an urgent desire for IPO, which mainly lies in the strong demonstration effect of circling money. Under the incentive of this effect, many enterprises will have the internal impulse to cobble together investment projects and apply for IPO, whether they need funds or not. After the establishment of the reserve board, through continuous information disclosure, the market and regulatory authorities can be provided with convenient conditions, which can

make the preparation before listing more scientific and orderly. After the establishment of the reserve board system, due to the supervision of the whole market, it will be very difficult for enterprises to cheat. After their possible fraud is exposed, because they have not yet issued shares publicly, it will do much less harm to the market.

The implementation of the reserve board system can not only delay the IPO of overly concentrated enterprises, but also test the advantages and disadvantages of the applicant companies through this continuous information disclosure, which can enable some enterprises to automatically choose whether to apply for IPO according to their own conditions. On the reserve board, let these enterprises first accept the real test according to the requirements of listed companies, so that they can truly feel the pressure the market brings on enterprise operations. It is an unprecedented idea to establish a reserve board in the A-share market, which seems to exceed the existing institutional arrangements of the stock market. However, in the market-oriented Chinese stock market, we must maintain fairness in the face of pain, and this innovation has a strong application value.

In a word, the new round of new share issuance system reform is a huge leap and progress from the administrative control of new share issuance to the market-oriented reform. It is precisely because the opening of the new share issuance quota and pricing mechanism touches the deep-seated problems in the stock market system, which will inevitably cause many problems. At the beginning of the opening up, the issuance of a high P/E ratio and high premium was very serious. This must be a problem in the development process, and the market will eventually make a choice. When the stocks issued at a high price break one after another, the issue of high price will be corrected naturally. However, this process shocks the stock market and makes investors bear great risks. However, market investors will gradually become rational after a certain pain, and the stock price will return to its intrinsic value. To sum up, the basis of the price discovery function is that the market mechanism plays a leading role.

CHAPTER 6

Game Analysis of Government Behavior in Stock Market Based on Market Efficient Cycle Theory

The goal of the government's regulation of the stock market is to shorten the effective period of the market, improve the efficiency of the market's response to information, and ultimately enable the stock market to better reflect the changes in the national macroeconomy. Fundamentally speaking, the stock market will not be effective in the sense of Fama and will not reflect the entire macroeconomic changes at every time point. The stock market will also fail like other markets. The government's important function is to rectify market failure and promote market efficiency. The government's regulation of the stock market is actually the game process of various actors, including the government, investors, listed companies, and financial intermediaries. Since market behavior is not optimal and market failure is a normal phenomenon, government regulation has become an important guarantee and driving factor for the healthy development of the stock market.

There are many debates on government behavior in the stock market in the theoretical circle. The more important thing is not the qualitative affirmation or negation of government behavior but the quantitative determination of how to reasonably position government behavior in the stock market. Rational government behavior is an important factor in forming a healthy stock market development. As the rule setter, sometimes the government also participates in market regulation and even directly participates in market transactions. The particularity of its status is obvious. In the face of these unavoidable facts, we believe that government behavior is one of the important factors determining the effectiveness of the stock market. Throughout the development history of the world stock market for nearly a hundred years, whether developed or developing countries, the history of the stock market has left a deep mark on the government's behavior.

This part mainly reviews the theoretical and empirical studies on the stock market failure and government behavior at home and abroad. First of all, it introduces the specific performance of the stock market failure and the causes of the failure and forms a general understanding of the development process and research context of the theory and empirical research of the stock market failure and government behavior. Secondly, it summarizes the government's corrective actions to the stock market failure and the relevant results of the performance and causes of the government failure. Thirdly, it makes a game analysis of the stock market actors, including the government, and studies the conditions for forming the game equilibrium.

6.1 Overview of Government Behaviors

The failure of the stock market is the direct reason for the implementation of government behaviors. The government is the only subject to correct the failure of the stock market, which is determined by the special status of the government. The means of implementing government behaviors include supervision and regulation of the stock market. The symbol of the healthy development of the stock market is to make it match with economic growth and make the stock market one of the important factors to promote economic growth, which is an important reason for the establishment, existence, and development of the stock market. How to position government behavior in the stock market is an important theoretical and practical problem. China's stock market was born in the process of transition from a planned economy to a market economy. It unconsciously had a more obvious color of planned economy, which is different from the growth of stock markets in developed countries. In many pieces of literature on China's stock market in the field of securities investment theory, there are more positive attitudes toward government behavior in the stock market and fewer negative attitudes. In my opinion, government behavior is an important guarantee factor for the healthy development of the stock market. The positioning of government behavior in the stock market should be neither absent nor offside but reasonable. Non-management theorists and investors have raised many doubts about the government's policies. The evaluation of the government's behavior in the stock market must be based on rigorous theoretical demonstration and a large number of empirical studies; otherwise, any evaluation is not rigorous. So far, the research on the government function of the stock market has not formed a systematic theory, and the existing literature is relatively scattered analysis and research from different angles.

The stock market cannot achieve absolute efficiency; there must be market failure, and the government is the only subject to correct market failure. Efficient market theory is the most influential theory in securities investment theory. Its birth is a new milestone in securities investment theory and has a profound impact on the research of the entire securities investment. Fama (1970) comprehensively and systematically elaborated the efficient market hypothesis (EMH). The so-called efficient market means that the stock price can always fully reflect all information, and the stock price is equal to its "intrinsic value," that is, the discount value of the expected future cash flow. In recent years, many financial theories represented by behavioral finance have questioned the efficient market theory. Many theoretical and empirical research results show that the market is not completely effective. In recent years, the influential behavioral finance has made use of a large number of empirical analysis methods to draw the conclusion that the market is not effective. The limited rationality of investors is the main reason for the failure of the stock market. The only subject to correct the market failure is the government. Since the government's behavior does not achieve absolute rationality, sometimes the market failure will be reduced or even eliminated in the correction process, but sometimes the market may become worse. The government has provided us with broad research space on the behavioral choice of correcting the stock market failure.

By the end of 2014, there were more than 2,500 A-share companies listed in Shanghai and Shenzhen Stock Exchanges, with a total market value of 33 trillion yuan, accounting for more than 50% of GDP. Although there is still a certain gap compared with developed countries, they already have a considerable scale. If we exclude the fact that the stock market has been too sluggish in recent years, this proportion will increase, which shows that the stock market is increasingly relevant to the entire national economy. The role of China's stock market in economic development has become increasingly prominent. A healthy stock market cannot be separated from the rational regulation of the government. Standardized government behavior is of great significance to the healthy development of the stock market and even to the growth of the entire national economy. Of course, what we study here is not only for the Chinese stock market, but also for the behavior norms of the government in the stock market in a general sense, and also for the government behavior in the stock market of some developed countries, because no matter how mature the stock market of developed countries is, it will not be completely effective, and there are problems of market failure and government correction in any stock market. At the same time, it can provide a reference for the government's behavior in China's stock market.

From the history of the development of the stock market, no stock market can fully rely on the inherent laws of the market itself to become mature and perfect, and they are all affected or even controlled by government behaviors to varying degrees. There is a lot of research literature on government behavior in the stock market at home and abroad. We think that the problem should be classified into two types: first, whether the government should intervene in the stock market, and second, how the government intervenes in the stock market. There are few absolute negative views on government behavior, and most of the debates focus on how to implement government behavior, that is, how to position government behavior. In recent years, China's stock market has been dubbed as a "policy market." Although there are both positive and negative comments, at least the participation of the government behavior has become an indisputable fact.

In the modern market economy, it is not only the economic operation that determines the prosperity of the stock market. The stock market acts as a "barometer" to reflect and predict the operation of the national economy. More importantly, the stable development of the stock market has become a booster of economic development. In a certain sense, the stock market has become an important factor affecting economic development. Studies have shown that the sustained growth of the US economy in the 1990s had a strong correlation with the bull market of the US stock market. This study is different from some traditional views that the macro-economy determines the trend of the stock market, and the stock market depends on economic fundamentals. Now, it seems that the relationship between the stock market and the macro-economy has developed from one-way reflection to two-way interaction. The prosperity and stability of the stock market can promote the healthy development of the economy. The stability of the stock market plays an important role in the security of the economy. The international financial crisis in recent years has given us important inspiration. The security of the stock market is related to the security of the financial system, and the safe operation of the financial system is related to the security of the economy and then to the security of the country and society. The government of any country or region pays more attention to the operation of the stock market. When the stock market is overheated, the government can use appropriate means to regulate the stock market and cool down the overheated stock market. When the stock market is excessively depressed, the government can also use appropriate means to promote the rise of stock prices, which is common in the stock market of Western developed countries where the government regulates the stock market and even supports and rescues the market. When the stock market is abnormal, the government will generally take extraordinary measures to intervene in the stock market forcibly and directly. For example, during the Asian financial crisis, the Hong Kong SAR government directly intervened in the Hong Kong stock market from August 14, 1998, invested nearly 100 billion Hong Kong dollars in two weeks to protect the market, directly fought with international speculators in the spot and futures markets for ten consecutive trading days at the same time, successfully held the Hang Seng Index from its lowest point in five years on August 13 to 7,829.74 on August 28, an increase of 17.55%, effectively maintaining the stability of the Hong Kong stock market, it has also maintained the stability of Hong Kong's economy in a deeper sense. In real economic life, neither a pure market economy nor complete government intervention exist. In the financial market, market mechanisms and government intervention often work at the same time. When the price distortion and unfair distribution caused by market failure are enough to lead to the collapse of the market mechanism, government intervention is indispensable. When the Southeast Asian financial crisis occurred, the intervention decision of the Hong Kong SAR government was very effective in resisting the financial crisis, avoiding the collapse of the financial system that may have been caused by the sharp decline of the stock market and foreign exchange market, and restoring the confidence of Hong Kong people and other investors.

In fact, Hong Kong is not the first case in which the government has chosen to intervene directly in the financial market in the overall interests of the country or the region. The Central Banks of the seven Western countries have jointly intervened in the foreign exchange market more than once. After the Asian financial crisis in 1997, governments continued to take strict monitoring measures to restore the financial system. In addition, international organizations such as the International Monetary Fund and Western countries have also actively offered suggestions, rescue plans, and even direct financial assistance to help the countries concerned get out of the predicament as soon as possible. International organizations such as the International Monetary Fund and Western countries have provided Mexico, Thailand, and South Korea with 30 billion and 50 billion dollars to support and save the market. Objectively speaking, without the support and intervention of international organizations and Western countries, it was difficult for these countries to get out of the crisis as soon as possible. This also shows from another perspective that government regulation of the stock market is not limited to one country. Still, there is also the possibility of several countries' governments jointly regulating the market. With the formation of the trend of globalization, liberalization, and economic integration of the stock market, this feature will become increasingly obvious. After the September 11 attacks in the United States, all relevant departments of the United States federal government stepped forward to actively intervene in the market in various ways, which enabled the stock market to resolve the crisis. It should be recognized that government intervention in the stock market will inevitably bring negative effects to the market. These need to be explored in theory and practice to minimize the negative impact. Zhou Zhengqing, member of the Standing Committee of the National People's Congress, vice chairman of the Finance and Economic Committee of the National People's Congress, and former chairman of the CSRC, pointed out pointedly that it is the common practice of many governments in the world to implement active intervention policies in the securities market, and that the view that denying government intervention in the market and allowing the market to develop naturally is incorrect.

China's stock market has a history of more than 20 years, from its birth to the present. Due to the unique historical stage of domestic and international economic development in which China is located, the path we have taken from the establishment of the stock market to the present is significantly different from that of developed countries. Regardless of the evaluation of the government behavior in the stock market, it is now certain that it is wrong to completely deny the positive significance of the government behavior in the stock market. Because the market reaches an absolute effective state, that is, the Pareto optimal efficiency in economics is impossible. In other words, there is room for Pareto improvement as long as it is not the optimal efficiency. This space is completed by the government, which is to correct the failure of the stock market. The theoretical background of this problem is the macro-control advocated by the macroeconomic theory represented by Keynes. The greatness of Keynesianism has been proved by the practice of economic growth in developed countries after World War II. Its birth was the product of the Great Depression in the 1930s, and government regulation is the core content of Keynesianism. However, Keynes's theory unconsciously needs to take rational government behavior as the premise. In fact, government behavior cannot be absolutely rational. In the process of implementing government behavior in the stock market, there will also be government failure. The public choice theory represented by Buchanan has become an important theoretical reference for studying this problem.

Therefore, we define the following basic concepts: stock market failure, government failure, and stock market government behavior.

(1) Stock market failure. Our definition of stock market failure is the deviation of the stock market's response to information; that is, the market is not effective at any time. It can be seen from the previous analysis that the existence of the market efficient cycle is inevitable, but the market efficient cycle is too long, that is, if the stock price cannot fully reflect the various information that determines its price for a long period of time, it will destroy the resource allocation function and financing function of the stock market, and will not play its role as a "barometer" of the national economy. The effective market is the realm that economists dream of. The market is not absolutely effective or absolutely invalid, but between the two. As long as the market does not reach absolute efficiency, there will be market failure to different degrees, and as long as there is market failure, there will be room for government behavior.

(2) Government failure. When carrying out macro-control on the stock market, we should take the rational behavior of the government as the prerequisite. But in fact, because of insufficient information, information asymmetry, the stock market's deviation in reflecting information, and the rent-seeking behavior of government decision-makers, the government, like investors, has limited rationality. The specific performance of government failure is the government's supervision and regulation behavior. On the one hand, the government's behavior does not correct the stock market failure; that is, it doesn't alleviate the degree of market failure. On the other hand, government behavior not only fails to rectify market failure, but also

makes the market failure even more serious sometimes, both of which constitute government failure. The government's intervention policy may be temporary, utilitarian, changeable, and uncertain due to the lack of continuity and stability. The government often intervenes in the operation of the stock market according to the policy needs and often makes a highly subjective evaluation of the market. Excessive government intervention is very unfavorable to the stable development of the securities market, because in an environment with strong government intervention, the market has a large systematic risk. Obviously, the main body of market activities can not fully rely on the fundamentals of the economy and enterprises to invest. The interaction between government intervention and market feedback must be considered. The game between investors and the government plays a very important role in investment decisions.

(3) Stock market government behavior. Macro-control must be based on the rationality of government behavior. In fact, government regulation sometimes promotes the improvement of social welfare, but sometimes it will not, even make the market worse, that is, government failure. Because of the random walk characteristic of stock price, rational government behavior becomes more and more difficult. In a general sense, it is difficult for the government to grasp the response of stock prices to information before the introduction of regulatory measures on the stock market, which will increase the difficulty of government regulation on the stock market. In many cases, the stock market cannot fully reflect the direction and strength of policy information, which is a major problem of ideal government behavior. In China's stock market, which has experienced more than 20 years of development, different subjects of market activities have different views on the market due to their own interests. As one of the main bodies of stock market activities, how should the government play its due role?

The issue of the efficiency of the stock market has been debated for a long time, but one thing is certain: the market has failure problems to varying degrees before it reaches the "time point efficiency" (that is, absolute efficiency), which provides an alternative space for government intervention. Before the market reaches the "time point efficiency," any government action to promote market efficiency is beneficial, which is called Pareto improvement. Since the birth of macroeconomics (Keynes 1936), government behavior has become an indispensable factor in promoting the effective operation of the market and the smooth operation of the economy. The Keynesian government behavior unconsciously has a hypothesis that the government behavior is correct and effective. However, it is not only the market that is out of order, but also the public choice theory (see Buchanan 1979) that believes that government policies are out of order. The positioning of government behavior is a major theoretical and practical problem.

Here, we analyze the government behavior in the stock market based on the macro-control theory and the public choice theory. The macro-control theory believes that government behavior is conducive to correcting market failure, and the public choice theory believes that government behavior will also fail.

First, when the market fails, government intervention can restrain or at least reduce the degree of failure. Under the condition of a market economy, state intervention is the basic requirement of organized economic activities. The only occasion where the state has reason to intervene is when there is market failure. When there is market failure, it is necessary to investigate whether government intervention is beneficial to the economy. If economic behavior produces such a result, that is, the result of competition is inefficient, then it is necessary for the state to intervene or control the state of inefficiency. The basic functions of the stock market are to raise funds, allocate resources, reflect, and adjust. These functions must require that the stock price fully reflect all relevant information on the stock market. Only when the stock price fully reflects all the information can the market raise funds reasonably, promote the effective allocation of resources, accurately reflect the development of the national economy, and become an effective tool for the government to conduct macro-control. The stock price fully reflects all information, which is Fama's definition of an efficient market. The practice of world economic development has proved that the stock market plays an increasingly important role in the national economy. A developed and perfect stock market provides convenient financing conditions for joint-stock companies, which is an important factor in promoting economic growth. The continuous prosperity of the American economy during the Clinton period was the period when the Dow Index continued to rise. At the same time, in recent years, many countries have experienced huge economic fluctuations. Economic collapse suddenly occurred when market prices, interest rates, and various economic entities were fairly stable. The fundamental reason for this economic phenomenon did not come from the field familiar with traditional economics but from the financial market, with the stock market as the main body. The stock market, which was seen as dependent on economic entities in the past, has changed its subordinate position and has become the leading role in the operation of the leading economy. Regulating the stock market has become an important part of today's government's economic regulation.

Second, government behavior will promote market efficiency, but government behavior will also fail. Market failure is a direct reason for the government to intervene in the market by administrative, legal, and economic means. As long as government behaviors can promote the effectiveness of the market, it is meaningful to promote the improvement of social welfare. When the government intervenes in the market, due to the characteristics or limitations of the market itself and policies, sometimes it will not improve the market effectiveness, but also make the market more ineffective; that is, the decline of social welfare is farther from Pareto optimal efficiency, which belongs to the category of government failure. The correction subject of market failure is the government, which is based on the macroeconomic theory. The correction of government failure is also the government, which is based on the public choice theory.

The government behavior in the stock market can be divided into supervision and regulation. Government supervision aims to establish a fair, just, and open stock market and provide a market environment with equal opportunities for all stock market actors (investors, fundraisers, securities intermediaries, etc.). Therefore, the government should supervise all kinds of acts that undermine market fairness. The regulation of the stock market can be divided into indirect regulation and direct regulation. Indirect regulation refers to the behavior of the government using various policy tools or through the psychological impact on the main body of market activities to affect the stock market indirectly. Direct regulation refers to the behavior of the government using funds to participate in stock market transactions and affect the stock price to change according to the government's goals. The relationship between the government and the stock market is essentially the relationship between the government's behavior and the market mechanism, which essentially belongs to the economic theory of government intervention in the market.

6.1.1 Efficient Market Hypothesis and Stock Market Failure

The ideal state of the stock market should be to promote the optimal allocation of social resources on the basis of effectively raising funds and ultimately make it an important factor that reflects and promotes economic growth. The practice of economic development shows that the role of the stock market as a direct financing channel in economic development is self-evident. The ideal goal of economists is to make it become a market where enterprises can make accurate investment and financing decisions, and prices can provide accurate signals that reflect various information about listed companies. Under the assumption that securities prices fully reflect all relevant information at any time, investors can choose from these stocks that represent the company's ownership. If the price fully reflects all relevant information, this is the efficient market theory or efficient market hypothesis. The concise and clear EMH reflects the rational result of competition equilibrium. The establishment of EMH ensures the applicability of financial theory and is also the basis of classical financial economics. For more mature capital markets, the empirical test of the efficient market hypothesis is still controversial in the short term, but it is true in the long term. Behavioral finance explains some short-term "market failure" phenomena in the capital market through people's "irrational" behavior and investor sentiment.

Empirical evidence before the 1970s shows that there is no important evidence against weak and semi-strong efficient markets, and the only evidence against efficient market theory appears in limited strong efficient market tests. From a large number of empirical test results, we can see that the evidence against strong efficiency is the most sufficient, and the market is difficult to achieve strong efficiency. This shows that insider trading and information asymmetry are universal. Generally speaking, weak and semi-strong markets are pure market efficiency problems. Only the constraints of strong efficient markets are closely related to government behaviors. Only government behaviors can eliminate or reduce information asymmetry and insider trading.

The weak test of the efficient market hypothesis is the most abundant, and its results also have strong support. The semi-strong test also supports the efficient market hypothesis. In the strong test, two types of deviations were observed. First of all, Osborne (1966) believed that professional investors in major stock exchanges had a way to understand the restrictions that had not yet been implemented and used this information to obtain trading profits. This raises the question of whether the market-making function of professional investors can be implemented by other mechanisms without such monopoly methods. Secondly, Scholes (1972) found that insiders usually mastered the monopoly method of company-related information. As long as the market was not strong-form efficiency, the market would fail to some extent. Only when the market was strong-form efficiency could it be truly effective.

6.1.2 Performance of Stock Market Failure

Generally speaking, the failure of the stock market is that the stock price cannot effectively reflect all kinds of information. Specifically, it should include the following.

First, the deviation between the stock market and economic growth is one of the manifestations of stock market failure. The main indicators reflecting the development of the stock market, namely, the stock price index and the national economic growth indicator GDP, should match each other. There are no more than two conclusions in a large amount of domestic and foreign literature on the correlation between the stock price index and GDP. One is that the stock market has a strong correlation with economic growth, and the other is that the stock market deviates from economic growth. In fact, it is impossible for the stock market to deviate from economic growth for a long time. If the above result occurs, it will mean that investors have been irrational for a long time, and arbitrage behavior does not exist, which must be contradictory to reality. In the long run, there must be a strong correlation between the two. The conclusion that deviates is that different time periods have been chosen. The shorter the matching cycle between the stock market and economic growth, the more effective the stock market is, and the less market failure is.

Second, information asymmetry and insider trading: the second performance of stock market failure. Information asymmetry refers to the fact that both parties in the market do not have the same amount and quality of information about the object or content to be traded. Asymmetric information is the main reason for abnormal fluctuations in stock prices. It will undermine the basic principles of openness, fairness, and justice and cause moral hazard and adverse selection problems in the stock market.

Moral hazard refers to the behavior in which one party of the market transaction cannot observe the information controlled by the other party, and the latter intentionally fails to report the situation or fabricates false information to deceive others. Adverse selection refers to the situation in which inferior products drive out high-quality products when one party cannot observe the important characteristics of the other party in the market transaction. Information asymmetry is directly manifested as insider trading. Only in the case of information asymmetry can insider trading occur, and information asymmetry and insider trading can easily lead to the failure of the stock market.

Third, the stock market's response deviation to information: the third performance of the stock market failure. The stock market's reaction bias to information includes overreaction and underreaction. Overreaction refers to the phenomenon in which an event causes the change in stock price to exceed the expected reasonable level. Its market performance is that after the event, the stock price changes dramatically beyond the expected level, and then reverse correction occurs, and the stock price returns to its due price. Underreaction refers to the phenomenon that the change in stock price caused by an event is lower than the expected reasonable level. Its market performance is that the stock price rises or falls slowly after the event, and the stock price changes to its due price level. The information reaction deviation of the stock market often exists, but the degree is different; that is, the market reaction to information is sufficient is an accidental phenomenon. The deviation of the stock price's reaction to information will lead to the stock price not accurately reflecting the information that determines its price, thus leading to the failure of the stock market.

6.1.3 *Market Failure and Government Correction*

Franz (1993) believed that "the market is fragile, and if left unchecked, it will tend to be unfair and inefficient, and public regulation is just a cost-free, effective and benevolent response to the needs of social justice and efficiency." Regulation is a response of the government to the public's request to correct the unfair, inefficient, or little efficient practices of some social individuals and organizations. The public interest theory discusses the reasons for the existence of supervision and the possible scope of supervision from the causes and consequences of market failure. Through supervision, the price distortion caused by market failure can be eliminated, thus making up for the efficiency loss of the market mechanism in the process of resource allocation. Government intervention is an unusual management means, and a special measure is taken when the stock market fluctuates abnormally.

Government intervention in the stock market is mainly based on the following reasons: (1) Managing emergencies. Under the reality that China's market system structure is far from being straightened out, in order to eliminate or reduce the impact of various new situations and problems on the stock market, the government needs to strengthen the management of emergencies to achieve the normal development of the stock market. (2) Maintain market stability and curb excessive speculation. Since its birth, the Chinese stock market has always been filled with a strong atmosphere of speculation. The ups and downs and the prevalence of banker behavior have kept the market in a disorderly state. In order to curb these speculations, when "speculation in the stock market prevails," the government takes strong policies and regulatory measures to intervene in the market, which helps to stabilize the volatility of stock prices. (3) Ensure the implementation of the plan. China's stock market has a very clear task: to support the reform of state-owned enterprises and raise funds for their development. To ensure the realization of the above strategic objectives, China's stock market has adopted a special market structure: the primary stock issuance market and the secondary stock circulation market. The primary issue is that the market implements a planned system. Its plans are formulated according to the process of state-owned enterprise reform and the needs of national economic development. Government intervention helps to implement these plans. The secondary market should provide a circulation place for stocks issued in the primary market, and its importance is also obvious. Without a healthy development of the secondary market, there will be no smooth issuance of the primary market. Therefore, whenever the Chinese stock market is in a downturn, the government will often introduce favorable policies for regulation, and there is no doubt about the positive role of these policies. Although it is an ideal goal to move towards marketization, no market can fully achieve this goal. Even the stock markets of developed countries with a hundred years of history are the same. The difference lies in the scope, frequency, and means of regulation.

Taking the September 11 attacks in the United States as an example, the US government has taken many policy measures to intervene in the stock market. First, when the September 11 attacks occurred, the US Securities Regulatory Commission announced a series of emergency measures. In addition to announcing the temporary suspension of the stock market, it also relaxed the restrictions on company repurchases, allowing listed companies to access the market with funds. Some restrictive measures have been adopted to protect the interests of investors. The suspension of the delisting rule that the stock price continued to be less than one dollar has enabled about 660 companies to escape the "death penalty." It also injected huge funds into the financial market and provided credit lines. Second, the Federal Reserve also responded immediately. The Federal Reserve announced a 0.5 percentage point cut in interest rates, bringing the federal funds rate to its lowest level in 39 years. It also injected about 80 billion dollars into the financial market. The Federal Reserve's two major measures were aimed at helping the market restore its liquidity. In addition, President Bush also proposed a package plan to stimulate the economy. Stimulated and affected by a series of positive stock market intervention policies, investor confidence began to stabilize, thus avoiding the "stock market disaster" and the possible economic recession and making the US stock market out of the initial crisis after the September 11 attacks and began to stabilize and rise gradually.

The institutional change in China's securities market is mainly driven by the government. As a product designed by the government during the transition from a planned economy to a market economy, the securities market has the strong feature of the "policy market." The reasons for the formation of a "policy market" are as follows: (1) The congenital defects of equity division. Because the design of China's stock market overemphasizes the financing function of the market, it has congenital institutional defects. Due to the weak constraints of shareholders on listed companies, low financing costs, and scarce listing quotas, administrative quota allocation must be adopted. At the same time, because most listed companies and securities institutions are state-owned, the continuous market downturn will damage the country's interests. Therefore, the government is strongly motivated to intervene in the stock market. The solution to the problems of market segmentation and share splitting must be promoted by the government supervision department. It is difficult to maintain fairness and justice by the market mechanism. (2) In the process of standardization, marketization, and internationalization of emerging markets, the government plays a major role in institutional innovation. In mature markets, innovation and change are more driven by market participants. (3) In emerging markets, especially in the early stage of development, due to the immature investment concept, false listing, false information disclosure, price manipulation, and insider trading are relatively serious, and the regulatory authorities must intensify their efforts to crack down. (4) At a specific stage, the government, as the maker and implementer of macro policies, sometimes takes the stock market as a means to implement policy intentions. Policy guidance is formed through leaders' speeches, media opinions, and temporary policy measures to guide the stock market to meet its expected policy objectives. Policy intervention is often very utilitarian.

For example, when the stock market is depressed, the government often takes various ways to rescue the market. When the stock market rises too much, policy measures are often taken to suppress the stock market. From February 1993 to July 1994, due to the continuous downturn of Shenzhen and Shanghai stock markets, on July 30, 1994, the government introduced the "three major market rescue policies" of suspending the issuance and listing of new shares, strictly controlling the scale of share allotment of listed companies, and taking measures to expand the scope of capital entering the market, resulting in a sharp rise in the stock market. In 1996, the stock market rose too much. Since October, the securities management department has successively introduced measures to curb the overheating of the stock market. On December 16, the *People's Daily* published a special commentator article, pointing out that China's stock market had a high P/E ratio and excessive speculation. As a result, excessive speculation in the stock market has been curbed promptly, which played an important role in preventing the stock market bubble caused by excessive speculation. In May 1999, the government tried to expand domestic demand and stimulate economic growth by giving play to the wealth effect of the stock market. On June 15, the *People's Daily* published a special commentator's article, pointing out that the stock market rise was a "normal recovery rise." Since then, the stock market has entered a two-year bull market stage. During the falling stage of the stock market from 2001 to 2005, the government used policies to regulate the market many times, and government intervention stabilized the stock market to a certain extent. From 2005 to 2007, China's stock market emerged from the largest bull market in history, mainly due to the downturn of the stock market before 2005, and the government has taken some positive measures. First of all, the CSRC has taken a series of emergency measures. For example, in order to emphasize the protection of the interests of investors, it was announced in 2005 to relax the restrictions on listed companies buying back public shares, allowing fund companies to use their own funds for fund investment, attracting insurance funds to the market, and approving banks to establish fund companies to expand capital access to the stock market. Secondly, the Central Bank also positively responded to the continued downturn in the stock market at that time. It implied that they would help the market gradually recover its liquidity, give some securities companies low-interest loans, and inject huge amounts of money into securities companies. Third, other government departments also actively cooperated, such as reducing dividend tax. Of course, what was more important is that on January 31, 2004, the Chinese government launched the *Several Opinions on Promoting the Reform and Opening Up and Stable Development of the Capital Market* to stimulate and revitalize the Chinese stock market, referred to as the "Nine Policies of State Department." Specific contents include the following: First, fully understand the importance of vigorously developing the capital market. Second, the guiding ideology and task of promoting the reform and opening up and stable development of the capital market. Third, relevant policies should be improved to promote the stable development of the capital market. Fourth, improve the capital market system and enrich securities investment varieties. Fifth, further improve the quality of listed companies and promote the standardized operation of listed companies. Sixth, promote the standardized development of capital market intermediary service institutions and improve their professional level. Seventh, strengthen the construction of the legal system and integrity and improve the level of capital market supervision. Eighth, strengthen coordination and cooperation to prevent and defuse market risks. Ninth, earnestly summarize the experience and actively and steadily promote opening up. This is a landmark programmatic document for regulating the stock market and plays an important role in the future long-term development of the stock market.

Reviewing the development of China's stock market, we will find that many policies with far-reaching impact have been introduced when the stock market was very low and very high. In 2007, the stock market soared, and the government introduced a series of regulatory measures to curb the overheating of the stock market. From 6,124 points in June 2007 to 1,664 points on October 28, 2008, the Shanghai Composite Index fell by more than 70%. Faced with the continuous downturn of the stock market, the government has launched a combination of "market rescue." First, it announced the unilateral imposition of stamp duty; second, Huijin Company temporarily acted as a stabilization fund and repurchased the shares of Bank of China, China Construction Bank, and ICBC from now on; third, the SASAC expressed its support for the actions of central enterprises to increase their holdings and buy back the shares of listed companies they held according to their own development needs. In order to cooperate with SASAC, on September 21, 2008, the CSRC issued the *Supplementary Provisions on Share Repurchase by Listed Companies through Centralized Competitive Trading (Draft for Comments)*. According to the Provisions, listed companies need not wait for the administrative permission of the regulatory authorities to repurchase their own shares. These measures are important measures the government takes to maintain the stability and healthy development of the stock market.

The basic principles of government intervention are as follows: (1) The government should be the maker of the game rules of the stock market, and the basic requirement of the rules is to promote the improvement of market effectiveness. (2) The government should formulate clear policies and regulations and follow the principles of openness and fairness, so that investors, listed companies, financial intermediaries, and other actors can accurately understand the available opportunities and understand whether their decisions will produce rational results. At the same time, in order to make the results of the rules well known to people, these rules should not be changed frequently, but should have certain stability. (3) Government intervention should not be aimed at regulating market fluctuations or some parameters of the market, but should be aimed at cultivating the rationality of the market and allowing the market mechanism to fully play its role. (4) The government should reduce short-term behavior and take into account the expectations of investors and other actors when formulating policies. The ultimate goal of these positive measures is to realize the healthy development of the stock market and make it a tool for China's economic growth.

6.2   Research Status of Government Behavior in the Stock Market

The development of China's stock market and the establishment and improvement of the system largely reflect the leading role of government behavior in the development of the stock market. Compared with the stock market in developed countries, the government's behavior in China has a more obvious impact on the operation and development of the stock market. The government behavior in the operation of China's stock market is still not mature and perfect, so it is of great practical value to deeply study and improve the government behavior in China's stock market.

6.2.1 Theoretical Background of Government Behavior in the Stock Market

From the perspective of economics, demonstrating the position and role of the government in the stock market will help us grasp the key factors in the complicated analysis and seek their internal meaning when analyzing the government's policies. Looking back on the history of economics, there have always been two different views on the relationship between government and the market. One is based on Adam Smith's laissez-faire, David Ricardo, Marshall, Hayek, and others, and Friedman's monetarism, which fundamentally negated the necessity and effectiveness of state intervention. The other view is the Keynesian theory of government intervention, which was later inherited and developed by Samuelson, forming the neo-classical comprehensive school theory, and the modern theory of state intervention represented by Stiglitz in the contemporary era. Stiglitz believes that the basic feature of the modern market economy is relatively obvious government intervention. The collapse of the bubble of the new economy in the United States, especially after the emergence of some big corporate scandals, the US regulatory authorities did not play the role of government intervention, which is an important reason for the recession of the US economy.

The debate on whether the government should intervene in the stock market has not subsided in Western economic circles. We analyze the government's positioning in the stock market from the perspective of welfare economics. Welfare economics starts from the effective allocation of production resources and the distribution of national income among social members to analyze the conditions required for a country to achieve maximum socio-economic welfare and the policy measures that the country should take to improve social welfare. Therefore, welfare economics should not only point out the results of an economic state or an economic policy measure, but also tell whether its impact on social welfare is good or bad, whether it is to improve or reduce social welfare. In the literature of welfare economics, the optimal allocation of production resources is called the "efficiency" standard for testing social welfare, and the average distribution trend of national income is called the "fairness" standard. Hobson (1858–1940), a British bourgeois reformist, proposed at the beginning of the 20th century that the central task of economics was to improve the welfare of human society. The state should take various measures to improve the welfare of all members of the social organization as an organism. In order to achieve the maximum social welfare, Hobson advocated that the state must carry out government intervention rather than the traditional "laissez-faire." Pigou, a representative of the British Cambridge School who had a significant impact on bourgeois economics, proposed that private evaluation in economic action should be separated from social evaluation, and the phenomenon of differences between private interests and social interests should be collectively referred to as "external effects." If a person's consumption or production activities enable other members of society to gain benefits without paying a price, it is said to provide "external economy," otherwise it is said to provide "external diseconomy."

The basic views of welfare economics confirm the necessity of government intervention in the economy, and the stock market is no exception. As a place for enterprise financing and redistribution of social wealth, the stock market should naturally follow the principle of maximum social welfare.

First, listed companies obtain a large amount of funds through stock market financing and then use or consume a large amount of social resources through investment. If the government does not intervene in its production and operation activities and does not control the effective use of resources, it will inevitably affect the optimal allocation of social production resources, and social welfare will show a weakening trend. If the government does not control the violations that damage the operating mechanism of the stock market, it will inevitably damage the interests of other members of the society, thus producing the "external diseconomy" effect. This is true not only for enterprises, but also for other investors and intermediaries in the stock market.

Second, from the perspective of information economics, it analyzes the government's positioning in the stock market. A perfectly competitive market implies a premise that all parties in the market have the information they need to make correct decisions. However, in real economic life, there is no perfectly competitive market. When one side of the market cannot observe the actions of the other side or cannot obtain the complete information of the other side, "asymmetric information" appears, and "immoral behavior" will occur under incomplete information or asymmetric information, making the party at the information disadvantage in the "adverse selection" position. The value of information has been fully reflected in the stock market. The adequacy, timeliness, and accuracy of information acquisition directly affect the interests of investors. However, there is information asymmetry in the stock market itself, and insiders are always on the information advantage side. In order to protect small and medium-sized investors from the information disadvantage of the stock market, all countries regard information disclosure as the primary principle of the stock market. In order to ensure information disclosure, there must be mandatory government measures to regulate the behavior of information disclosure through the formulation of a series of laws and regulations, reduce or eliminate the market disorder caused by "information asymmetry," and protect the interests of small and medium-sized investors. On September 2, 1993, China promulgated the *Interim Measures for the Prohibition of Securities Fraud*, which provided for the prohibition and punishment of market manipulation, insider trading, and customer fraud. However, in practice, the events that damage the interests of small and medium-sized investors due to information asymmetry are still common. This is mainly because there are various hidden ways to make profits by using information advantages. The government should strengthen the investigation and punishment of these illegal phenomena and make up for the corners that laws and regulations cannot reach temporarily through system construction and relevant supporting policies.

Third, from the perspective of rent-seeking, it analyzes the government's positioning in the stock market. Rent-seeking was first proposed in the article "The Political Economy of Rent-Seeking Society," published by American scholar Anno Kruger in 1974. Rent-seeking can be regarded as an effort to obtain monopoly status and rent by the privilege permitted by the government. The rent here refers to the surplus that the income obtained by the resource owner exceeds its opportunity cost. In the case of government intervention in the stock market, "rent-seeking" may occur. For example, under the stock issuance examination and approval system, some enterprises, in order to obtain low-cost financing opportunities in the stock market, will buy government officials by bribery and other means to obtain scarce listing qualifications. In a series of cases of low-quality listed companies investigated and dealt with in China's stock market in recent years, there are serious rent-seeking phenomena. To put an end to rent-seeking, we must reform China's stock issuance system and implement the issuance registration system.

The debate on the position and role of the government in the stock market has never stopped. The main views can be summarized into two categories: one tends to emphasize the government's intervention and supervision of the stock market; that is, the government should comprehensively use fiscal and financial policies and industrial policies to guide the stock market to serve the national economy, optimize resource allocation, and use appropriate intervention measures to control the pace of stock market development, reduce its negative impact on other sectors of the national economy and other markets, and mitigate the impact of emergencies on the stock market. Another view tends to weaken the government's intervention in the stock market, prevent the government's inappropriate policies from adversely affecting the stock market, and reverse the current "policy market" phenomenon. This view believes that the operation and development of the stock market has its own laws. The government should focus on the construction of laws and regulations on the stock market, try to reduce the intervention in the stock market, let the participants of the stock market spontaneously adapt to the market rules under the influence of the market rules, and gradually develop and mature under the control of "an invisible hand."

6.2.2 Different Views on Government Behavior in the Stock Market

The main views on the position and role of the government in the stock market can be summarized into two categories: the first category tends to emphasize the supervision and regulation of the government on the stock market. The government's supervision is to create a market environment with equal opportunities for all participants in the stock market, promote fair competition, and thus promote economic growth. It mainly uses legal, administrative, and other means to implement government behaviors. The government's regulation behavior can be divided into direct and indirect regulation.

Direct regulation means that the government directly participates in stock trading to control the rise and fall of stock prices, so as to achieve the regulation goal. Indirect regulation is a government behavior in which the government uses various economic levers to exert indirect influence on the stock market to achieve the purpose of regulation. In the past 20 years since the birth of China's stock market, there has been no record of using direct regulation means. The second kind of view tends to deny the government's intervention in the stock market, prevent the adverse impact of government policies on the stock market, and reverse the current "policy market" phenomenon in China. This view believes that the operation and development of the stock market has its own laws. The government should try to reduce the intervention in the stock market, so that the participants can spontaneously adapt to the market laws. We believe that government behavior is an important factor in ensuring the healthy development of the stock market. It is an indisputable fact that the market is invalid, that is, the existence of market failure. The government is the only subject to correct the stock market failure based on the profound background of macroeconomic theory. The efficient market is the highest realm that economists have always dreamed of. A large number of theoretical and empirical studies have shown that the stock market cannot be absolutely efficient or absolutely ineffective but is somewhere between the two. We call the ineffective part stock market failure. The effectiveness of the market is measured by the reaction of stock prices to information. As long as there is no absolute effectiveness, there will be market failure and room for the government to act. Government behavior is to promote the effectiveness of the market. However, government behaviors do not always promote market efficiency and sometimes make the market more ineffective, that is government failure.

There are many discussions about government behavior in the stock market in the domestic and foreign theoretical circles. Su et al. (2002) conducted an empirical study on the intervention behavior of the Hong Kong SAR government in 1998. They believed that government behavior not only changed the downward trend of the stock market, but also reduced the degree of price volatility. The government played an important role in the healthy development of the stock market. Domestic scholars Zou Haoping, Tang Limin, and Yuan Guoliang (2000) used the game analysis method to build a dynamic game model with incomplete information between the government and investors. After conducting empirical research on the multiple interventions of China's stock market policies, they affirmed the positive role of several major policies in China's stock market. Lukequn (2002) advocated that in the future development of the stock market, we should try our best to avoid big ups and downs. As an important part of the macroeconomic system, it is necessary for the government to bring the stock market into the perspective of macro-control and carry out necessary macro-control on the stock market. Zeng Xin (2003) believed that the goal of the government's decision-making is to maintain the stable and healthy development of the stock market. From past experience, the government is fully capable and necessary to adjust the stock market to the track consistent with the development of the national economy. On the one hand, it prevents the stock market from overheating; on the other hand, it also prevents the stock market from being too sluggish. The policy intervention in China's stock market has effectively changed the investors' collective expectations and the event's outcome. Different from the above views, Wang Chunfeng (2003) concluded that the operation of the policy cycle directly determines the operation of the stock market cycle through empirical research on China's stock market. He used the ARCH model to study the relationship between China's stock market volatility and policy. He believed that policy intervention was the direct reason for driving the huge changes in China's stock market volatility.

The government's macro-control or intervention policies on the stock market have also been strongly rejected by some economists. In 1998, the Hong Kong government of China used funds to intervene in the Hong Kong stock market during the crisis, which was criticized by many economists and Wall Street market people. Friedman criticized: "This is the beginning of the end of the free economic system. It is absolutely the worst method and the worst information to the world." Miller said frankly: "It is a big mistake to intervene in the stock market and futures market, which will eventually hurt Hong Kong (China), which is totally against the principle of the free economy." As for the intervention of the Chinese government in the mainland stock market, the voices of opposition are endless. For example, "The government is the referee and should not play football"; "The securities regulatory authority should not be responsible for the rise and fall of the stock market, nor should it support or rescue the market from the position of the owner of state-owned assets." Since 1993, China's stock market management authorities have repeatedly "rescued the market" and "supported the market." Some people blame government intervention as the cause of the ups and downs of the stock market.

There are also a lot of empirical research results on the evaluation of government behavior in China's stock market. Through empirical research, Lü Jihong and Zhao Zhenquan (2000) believe that China's stock market is greatly affected by policies. Several large abnormal fluctuations in the market are caused by government policies, and the role of policies in stabilizing the market in the short term is very limited. Qiao Guiming and Zhan Yubo (2002) conducted a game analysis on the behavior of the government and investors and concluded that it is irrational to guide the trend of the stock index through policies. They believed that government intervention in the stock market should be reduced as much as possible. Zhang Rui (2003) believed that the government's intervention in the stock market disturbed the normal expectations of the market, and the market suddenly increased uncertainty, which increased the systematic risk of the stock market. Qi Guanghua (2003) analyzed from the perspectives of ideological rigidity, cognitive limitations, temporary policies replacing laws and regulations, multiple conflicts of interest, etc. He believed that China's stock market policies were volatile, leading to policy failures in the supervision of China's stock market. By comparing the Chinese and American stock markets, Wu Ge and Liao Jun (2003) believed that the "failure" in the American stock market was a market failure and that the "failure" in the Chinese stock market was not a market failure but a government failure. They basically denied the government policy of the Chinese stock market. Li Yuankui (2005) believed that due to various reasons, the government's involvement in China's securities market was too deep, and the future orientation of the government behavior was to withdraw moderately, so he denied the government intervention in the stock market.

Wang Guogang (2002) distinguished stock market regulation from stock market control and believed that the stock market can only be regulated, not controlled, because stock market control has neither clear goals nor policy means to control. He believes that the so-called theory of stock market control is wrong. Wu Jinglian (2001) distinguished the government's market rescue from supporting the market and the regulation of the stock market and advocated that the government should only regulate the market, regardless of rescuing or supporting the market. Wu Xiaoqiu (1995) divided the government control of the stock market into two levels: the first level is to mediate the structure and institutional framework of the stock market and the long-term development of the stock market. The second level is to mediate the abnormal operation of the stock market and the short-term fluctuation of the stock market. The former is mainly carried out through policy guidance and legal constraints, including the improvement of securities market laws and regulations, unified and efficient supervision, and overall planning for the development of the securities market. The latter focuses on controlling the short-term fluctuation of the stock market and preventing the stock index from soaring and plummeting. Zhao Wenguang and Qi Jianhong (2003) distinguished between "policy market" and "market market," believing that the stock market where markets dominate is a "market market." The stock market driven by government forces is a "policy market," and the regulation and control of the stock market is a "policy market." Shen Xiaoping (2004) believed that the focus of stock market supervision was to improve the market mechanism and the stock market's effectiveness. On the basis of ensuring the truthfulness, accuracy, integrity, and timeliness of information disclosure, imposing legal sanctions on securities fraud, misleading and false statements, and standardizing the behavior mode of market subjects, so as to ensure the openness, fairness, impartiality, and credibility of the market, and overcome the problem of "market failure" caused by asymmetric information distribution, establishing a strong and effective market is the starting point of stock market supervision. The regulation of the stock market often involves making laws, regulations, administrative orders, and other ways to directly restrict market participants, while the control of the stock market often needs to take market-oriented measures to make up for and correct market defects. The regulation of the stock market is a long-term and continuous process, which means that the regulation of the stock market should be constantly carried out. The control of the stock market is timely and needs to be implemented when the stock market reaches a certain critical point, which is often manifested as an intermittent operation process with short-term characteristics.

Zhou Zhengqing (2003) has repeatedly said that in order to maintain and stabilize the development of the securities market in China, we must take the stock market as an important object of the government's macro-control and timely adjust the stock market's sharp rise and fall and irrational excessive fluctuations. Wang Kaiguo (2002) believed that there was no effective market regulation means in China, so we should further improve the market-oriented regulation means and enhance the government's regulation ability. Xie Baisan (2003) believed that the stock market should not be "left to its own devices, let it develop and do nothing." Instead, the government should regulate the stock market with its power. Xu Hongyuan (2002) believed that the government must intervene if the stock market falls by more than 10% in one month. If the stock market falls by 30% in three months, it is a stock disaster, and stronger policies need to be adopted. Han Zhiguo (2003) believed that China's current stock market policy was generally a relatively negative policy, which, to a considerable extent, caused the tendency of the stock market to be increasingly marginalized. Therefore, the direction and strength of the stock market policy should be comprehensively adjusted. He Qiang (2003) believed that "the direct administrative intervention of the government on the stock market will gradually fade, but regular regulatory regulation through market means with plans and steps will exist for a long time."

At the same time, there are also many views that the government should reduce its intervention in the stock market. Zhou Xiaochuan (2002) believed that in the process of stock market operation, the market should be allowed to adjust what the market mechanism can. Deregulation is an inevitable trend, and the regulatory approach should consider gradually changing from a "positive list" to a "negative list." The government is the referee and should not play football. In an emergency, the government can handle it specially, but it needs to take decisive action and take certain risks. Cheng Siwei (2003) also believed that the securities regulatory authority should not be responsible for the rise and fall of the stock market, nor should it support or rescue the market from the position of the owner of state-owned assets. Under extremely special or necessary circumstances, the securities regulatory authority should require the government to intervene in the market appropriately according to legal procedures. Wu Jinglian (2001) said, "Since 1993, China's stock market management authorities have repeatedly 'rescued' and 'supported' the market, but the results were not good. Such actions not only did not really support the stock market, but on the contrary, led to huge fluctuations in the stock price, and missed the opportunity to guide the healthy development of the stock market again and again." "The government's support of the market and the state-owned enterprises' encirclement of money are policies that harm the country and reflect the people, and must be stopped." Yi Xianrong (2004) believed that "the government is only the maker and executor of the market game rules, and only the watchman of the market rules, not the rapid expansion of the government's, bureaucratic and administrative unrestricted power, so that the autonomy and innovation spirit of the market parties are suppressed, and the wealth of the vulnerable people in the market is plundered." Wang Guogang (2004) also believed, "In the stock market, the focus of administrative supervision should have been to ensure the operation order of the stock market by cracking down on illegal acts, but what happened in practice was that government departments directly used administrative mechanisms to manage various affairs in the stock market, which really hurt investors' rights and interests at a deeper level. Therefore, deepening the reform of the capital market operation mechanism, replacing the planning mechanism with the market mechanism, is the fundamental way to safeguard investors' rights and interests effectively."

1. **The Main Reasons for Supporting the Government's Macro-Control of the Stock Market**
(1) Through the regulation and control of the stock market, the stock price fluctuation is affected, so as to make the society approach the Pareto optimal state and improve the social welfare. Scholars in favor of this view believe that the stock market is a frictional market, and investors may not be able to obtain key information as the basis for investment decisions, or may not be able to produce a truly balanced price because of the defects in the trading system, which objectively requires the government to intervene in the price formation process properly. In particular, due to the tendency of investors to overreact and pursue the rise and sell the fall, appropriate measures must be taken to stabilize the stock price so that it does not deviate too much from the reasonable price. Shiller (1981) and others found that the volatility of the stock market often exceeded the range that basic factors can explain through empirical research, so they also agreed with the government to take measures to stabilize the stock price.
(2) The government's regulation of the stock market can optimize the efficiency of resource allocation. Wan Ming (2002) believed that China's stock market is a typical emerging market, and its development is very immature. In such a market, simply relying on the strength of the stock market itself is not enough to maintain the effective operation of the stock market, and the function of optimizing resource allocation that the stock market has will not be effectively played.
(3) Government regulation can reduce the internal friction of resources in the stock market, accelerate the pace of maturity of the stock market, and thus reduce the risk caused by the immature stock market. Wan Ming (2002) believed that the development history of China's stock market, which has only been more than ten years since its establishment, is far from that of the developed market, whether it is the construction of the legal system and the improvement of the operating mechanism or the improvement of the quality of the market subjects. In the

process of changing the market from imperfect to perfect, from underdeveloped to developed, government intervention will reduce the internal friction of market resources to a certain extent, thus promoting the market to grow and mature faster. Zhao Wenguang (2003) believed that an important prerequisite for the government not to intervene in the market is "to ensure the stability of property rights," and there is always a variable about the fate of the property rights of the state-owned shares and corporate shares accounting for two-thirds of the listed companies in China. Therefore, the premise of the government not to intervene theory is not tenable at this stage in China.

(4) Moderate government intervention is conducive to reducing the impact of stock market fluctuations on the national economy, which is conducive to the sustainable and healthy development of the national economy. Like other markets, the stock market has some defects in its regulatory function, such as short-term, hysteresis, and uncertainty of regulatory results. These defects cause an imbalance of capital supply and demand in the stock market. While causing stock market volatility, they also affect the imbalance in the total amount of capital and macrostructure, causing fluctuations in the national economy and exacerbating the overheating or supercooling of the economy. The government can carry out necessary intervention in the stock market through appropriate stock market regulation and control policies to reduce the volatility of the stock market and avoid the resulting economic instability. Li Zhilin (2002) put forward that "although stability cannot solve everything in China, stability is the overriding task. When necessary, it is very important to use policies to correct the stock market."

2. The Main Reasons against the Government's Macro-Control of the Stock Market

(1) The government's intervention in the stock market has disturbed the normal expectation of the market, which has made the uncertainty of the market suddenly increase, and it was more difficult to establish the consensus expectation of the market, which has increased the systematic risk of the securities market (Zhang Rui 2003).

(2) In fact, the government's regulation behavior vaguely indicates to the market subjects that the government undertakes a certain degree of implicit insurance for the top management, which makes the risk and income in the top management unmatched, the market price signal distorted, and the normal price formation mechanism distorted, which may damage the price discovery function and resource allocation function of the stock market.

(3) The government intervenes in the issuance, listing, and circulation of stocks through administrative mechanisms and administrative means. The time lag in the introduction and transmission of policies to intervene in the stock market is very easy to induce corruption, rent-seeking, information arbitrage, profiteering, and other illegal acts, which seriously damage the interests of small and medium-sized

investors, undermine market rules, and undermine the principle of market fairness and integrity.

(4) The stock market regulation may also make the government lose its authority. Once people find that the government will yield under pressure, whether reasonable or not, investors will bargain with the government, which will affect the government's authority in exercising policies.

In addition, there is another view that there is nothing wrong with the action of policy intervention in the direction of the stock market; the key is what skills to use and how to intervene. Chen Dongqi (1999) believed that the US government intervention is more effective. In addition to a mature market economy environment and the government's economic functions being less and more sophisticated, another important reason is that the market parameter "regulates the economy by means of the market economy." Its effectiveness is shown in that it generally does not interrupt the market operation, or break the competition rules, but plays a corrective role. Tan Weimin (2001) and Wu Weimin (2002) believed that it would be acceptable if soft intervention was carried out in a market-oriented way to make the market run naturally on the track that the management hoped. If it appears in a stiff face and uses the emergency brake to make the stock market a "policy market," it would be undesirable.

Shen Xiaoping (2004) believed that whether to regulate the stock market reflects an essential government problem; that is, there is an optimal behavior boundary between the government and the market. Due to the different characteristics of the market itself and its development degree, the required government behavior patterns are different in different industries and markets. First, the externalities and volatility of the market are different. Generally speaking, the greater the externality, the stronger the volatility, and the more effective the government is, the greater the role of the government. Secondly, different levels of market development also require different government behaviors. In the case of an imperfect market foundation and immature market development, the market's ability to self-rectify and repair in the operation process is also worse, and the government's position in it is more important. In the mature market, the market has already had the ability of self-repair, and the function of the government should be weakened. Therefore, in different markets and at different development stages of the same market, there should be different government behavior patterns, and there is no absolute and unified boundary of optimal government behavior.

Some scholars represented by Rosenstein-Rodan believe that market development is a slow process for developing countries. The development idea of trying to promote a country's economic development solely by relying on the development of market mechanisms is not only infeasible, but also "market forces always favor countries with strong economic strength." When considering this, it is ridiculous. Therefore, for developing countries, the government should intervene in the market more actively, especially to study more deeply how the government can effectively intervene in the market, so as to get rid of the old way of centralized government control of the economy in the past. Fan Gang (1998) also believed that governments in developing countries should or can play an "extra role" in the process of economic growth and economic transformation than governments in general, especially those in developed countries. Chen Dongqi (1999) believed that, from the perspective of teleology, it is acceptable for the governments of developing countries to "play a more important role," because to narrow the gap between the developing market and the mature market, we should not only deal with the problems of development speed, structural adjustment and institutional transition, but also overcome many functional defects caused by the congenital deficiencies of the market. Under the dual objectives, it is bound to take a longer time and a greater cost to let the market evolve spontaneously. After the government's role is properly played, the time of market evolution can be shortened, and the cost can be reduced. Therefore, it is not appropriate to accuse the Chinese government of having deeply intervened in the stock market, which should be an inevitable choice in the process of institutional evolution. Without government intervention, the stock market would have to pay a higher cost today. The research results of Xu Junhua et al. (2001) show that since 1997, the frequency of policy intervention has increased, but the extent of abnormal market volatility caused by it has decreased significantly. The stock market's response to policy intervention and earnings volatility has weakened, indicating that the degree of marketization of China's stock market is improving, the securities market is more standardized and market-oriented, institutional investors are more rational, and the efficiency of the market is improving, The management is more cautious in using policies to regulate the market and pays more attention to the market's own laws.

6.2.3 Brief Review

Because the conditions of a "perfect competition market" are not fully met in real economic life, there is objectively a phenomenon of "market failure" in the stock market. Under such circumstances, the Pareto optimal state cannot be achieved through laissez-faire policies, and the government can take measures to alleviate the low efficiency of the stock market caused by laissez-faire. Because the view that the government does not intervene in the stock market does not meet the conditions in theory at first, the important premise of this theory is market clearing. Second, any capital can freely enter and exit the stock market. Third, the stock price fully reflects the market information. Fourth, the stock market has a considerable scale, and the relationship between supply and demand is roughly balanced. On this basis, it will automatically achieve balanced economic development through a laissez-faire market mechanism. However, there is still no country in the world that really meets such conditions. The defects of market mechanisms in regulating economic activities (market failure) have been proved to exist objectively in theory. Stiglitz, the winner of the Nobel Prize in Economics in 2001, put forward the theory of information asymmetry, which pointed out the shortcomings and defects in the market system and clearly proposed that the government should play a strong role in the market system if it wants to reduce the impact of information asymmetry on the economy.

In the modern economy, the government mainly performs four economic functions: establishing laws, formulating macroeconomic stability policies, affecting the allocation of resources to improve economic efficiency, and establishing programs that affect income distribution. The government's intervention in the stock market should be considered from the following aspects.

First, appropriate government intervention in the stock market is the common choice of all countries in the world. The stock market plays an important role in a country's national economy, and the stock market crisis causes many economic crises. At the end of the 1920s, the United States government advocated laissez-faire economic policies, leading to a comprehensive economic crisis. This lesson is profound. After the crisis, Western countries generally began to attach importance to the role of the government in intervening and regulating the stock market. Although the debate continues, the outbreak of the Southeast Asian financial crisis, for example, once again proves that the government is indispensable in intervening and regulating the stock market, especially when there is a crisis or crisis precursor in the stock market, the role of the government will be more obvious. For example, the Japanese stock market fell all the way in 2001 and fell below 12,000 points on March 12. The spokesman of the Japanese government said that the three-party coalition regime and the government set up a special working group within a week to rescue the increasingly critical stock market. When the stock market fell to 11,000 points, the government came forward to ask for support to keep the stock market stable. It can be seen that the implementation of the intervention policy on the stock market is the consensus of all countries in the world. Its purpose is to protect the interests of investors and the long-term healthy operation of the stock market and avoid a larger crisis caused by excessive stock market volatility.

Second, government intervention can optimize the efficiency of resource allocation. Under the premise that the development of China's stock market is not yet mature, simply relying on the strength of the stock market itself is not enough to maintain the effective operation of the stock market. For example, in the early 1990s, due to the imbalance between the supply and demand of the stock market, there was a degraded allocation of resources on the issue of share allotment. The worse the company is, the more it will allocate shares on a large scale to maintain its operation. If the government did not issue appropriate policies to regulate the share allotment promptly, the function of the stock market to optimize the allocation of resources would be seriously damaged. In addition, the government should coordinate the development of all sectors of society and optimize the industrial structure from the overall perspective. The government guides the investment of social funds by formulating industrial policies, optimizes the efficiency of resource allocation, promotes the development of pillar industries, environmental protection industries, and high-tech industries, and improves the scientific and technological progress and social welfare of the whole society. These goals cannot be achieved without the government's regulation and guidance.

Third, government intervention can reduce risks caused by an immature stock market. The history of China's stock market development is only more than 20 years. The construction of the legal system, the improvement of the operating mechanism, and the improvement of the quality of the market subjects are far from meeting the requirements of a mature stock market. In cultivating market maturity, government intervention will reduce the internal consumption of resources and accelerate the pace of market maturity. It can be seen from some cases in 2001 that a small number of interest groups, driven by the interest mechanism and taking advantage of the vacuum of government supervision, have committed some events that harm the interests of small and medium-sized investors and the healthy development of the stock market. If the government had not investigated and dealt with a large number of illegal funds and illegal acts of listed companies, many deep problems would not have been exposed, and the crisis in the stock market would grow. Now, there is a view that the government can only intervene in the stock market when there is a crisis, and the government should try not to intervene in the stock market at other times. This view actually denies that there is a process of accumulation of risks in the stock market. The practice has proved that intervention is most effective only when risks have not reached a critical state. Moreover, it is also very difficult to grasp and quantify the "critical value" of risks. The government's understanding of risks from the overall perspective and investors' understanding of risks from their own interests are also biased. Therefore, risk control is a continuous process. At the same time, the government should also improve its ability to grasp the nature of risk and the level of risk monitoring, try to reduce the severe impact on the stock market, and prevent the weakening and destruction of its own operating mechanism.

To sum up the above aspects, we can draw the conclusion that the behavior and economic activities of each person and interest group affect the interests of others, as well as the interests of future people. The government is independent of the stakeholders of the stock market. It is most acceptable for all parties in the market to intervene and regulate the stock market in a detached position. In order to prevent the occurrence of "external diseconomy," it is inevitable for the government to intervene and regulate the stock market. Still, in different periods and development stages, the way and intensity of its intervention and regulation are different. It is reasonable to think that the development process of the capital market itself is a process of constantly escaping from government regulation, interference, and supervision, and the development of the entire capitalist market economy has not escaped from the shadow of government regulation. The market develops in a cycle of regulation and anti-regulation, and the government always lags behind the market, which is the market development process. However, today's information and communication means make the government not necessarily lag behind the market in many aspects. Therefore, we should not be confused by some dogma. The origin and development of China's stock market are dominated by the government. Some laws and problems are shared with other countries' stock markets, and some are unique to China. This is an unchangeable historical fact. It is impossible to expect the government to adopt a laissez-faire and liberal attitude towards the stock market. Still, the role and positioning of the government in the stock market need to be constantly adjusted according to different stages of development. If the stock market is more standardized, the market subjects have more conscious and law-abiding market behavior, and the indirect regulation means are more effective for the stock market regulation, the administrative means and interference will inevitably be reduced; otherwise, it is impossible. Therefore, the government's positioning in the stock market is adjusted according to the development and perfection of the market itself and should not be judged by the theoretical value of a dogma.

6.3 Government Failure in the Stock Market

6.3.1 Reasons for Government Failure

The ineffectiveness of government intervention, that is, government failure, is the irrational behavior of the government in the process of stock market supervision and regulation. The modern public choice theory represented by Buchanan believes that the first reason for the ineffectiveness of government intervention is due to the moral hazard and opportunistic tendency of government officials, as well as the limited rationality of government officials. Therefore, a good government's behavior is limited rationality at most. Therefore, the government is not better than the individual investors, and the decision-making behavior will not be more rational. Moreover, the government's intervention behavior is made after the market behavior occurs, often slower than the market, leaving sufficient decision-making time for individual investors. The second reason for the ineffectiveness of government intervention is that investors can generate "adaptive expectations" for government behavior according to the changes in the stock market and relevant information and take countermeasures in advance, resulting in the ineffectiveness of government intervention or failure to achieve the expected purpose. For example, in order to crack down on speculation in the stock market, the government will formulate policies based on the immediate information of the stock market. Still, investors can predict the government's behavior in advance and adjust the stock structure in advance. When the government's policies are issued, they will take the opportunity to carry out short operations and suppress the stock market, resulting in a stock market crash or even failure to rise. As a result, the government's policies create conditions for "forerunners" to manipulate the market; the policy of cracking down on speculators has made speculators successful and caused great harm to ordinary investors. The third reason for the ineffectiveness of government intervention is that the government and investors have different expectations of the stock market under different interests. The government plays two roles in the stock market, both as the supervisor of the stock market and as the holder of state-owned shares, and becomes the largest shareholder of listed companies. As a regulator, the government hopes that the stock market will develop healthily and steadily. Therefore, the government will send out good news when the stock market is depressed and bad news when the stock market is crazy, so as to keep the stock index running in the box. The stock price movement of China's stock market reflects the above behavioral characteristics to a considerable extent. At the same time, as the largest shareholder of listed companies, in order to maintain and increase the value of state-owned assets, the government may use its influence on the board of directors to propose dividend policies in favor of itself (such as no dividend or less dividend), force small and medium-sized shareholders to reinvest in the company, and damage the interests of small and medium-sized investors. Investors (whether small and medium-sized investors or institutional investors) have only one goal: maximizing their investment returns and minimizing investment risks. Therefore, driven by their respective interests, the government and investors will have completely different expectations of the stock market's volatility.

Just as there are different types and causes of market defects and market failures, there are also different manifestations, types, and causes of government failures, which is the most basic problem that the theory of government failure should discuss. There are various manifestations of government failure, which can be summarized as the basic types such as public decision-making mistakes, inefficiency and waste of bureaucracy in providing public goods, internality and government expansion, rent-seeking, and corruption.

First, public policy is invalid. According to the theory of public choice, the basic means for the government to intervene in economic life is to formulate and implement public policies and use policies, regulations, and administrative means to make up for market defects and correct market failures. Public decision-making is the decision-making made by the state or government departments for producing and supplying public goods and for the intervention of economic operations in society. First of all, public policy is a complex process. Due to various difficulties, obstacles, and constraints, it is difficult for the government to formulate and implement a good and reasonable public policy, leading to the failure of public policy. The main reasons for public decision-making mistakes or policy failures are the complexity and difficulties of the public decision-making process itself and the defects of the existing public decision-making system and methods. Specifically, there is no so-called public interest as the goal of the government's public policy in society. It is inherently difficult to add individual preferences or interests to collective preferences. It is generally impossible to deduce the order of social choice that meets certain rational conditions from the order of individual choice under certain social conditions. Simple addition is not enough to arrange a consistent common order in personal preferences, which are also classified according to different standards. Secondly, in public decision-making, there is actually no process of making choices based on public interests, but only a "contracting" process between various special interests. Democracy based on the majority principle is a universal decision-making system adopted by modern countries. It is a great progress and more reasonable decision-making system compared with autocracy or despotism. However, this democratic system is far from perfect or even quite undemocratic. Both direct democracy and indirect (representative) democracy have their inherent defects: the inherent problems of the former include the periodic cycle or voting paradox and whether preference display is true; the inherent problem of the latter is that the elected representatives pursue the maximization of their own interests because of their "economic man" characteristics, rather than the maximization of voters or public interests, while voters are difficult to implement effective supervision on them. The existing voting rules or voting methods (such as unanimous approval, majority, considerable majority, absolute majority, two-thirds majority) are far from perfect. The majority principle cannot be completely democratic, and it will impose the majority on the minority. The decision-making cost of the principle of consensus is too high, and it is easy to delay the opportunity. Even decisions made according to the majority principle may not necessarily reflect the preferences of most people. So far, there is no voting system that can communicate individuals and collectives in a satisfactory way, so there is no perfect democratic politics. Thirdly, incomplete information, deviation from the public decision-making agenda, and voter's "myopia effect, deposition cost, precedent" restrict rational decision-making. For example, the acquisition of decision-making information always requires costs, and the information that voters and politicians have is limited, so many public policies are actually made under the condition of incomplete information, which easily leads to decision-making mistakes. For another example, the "short-sighted effect" of politicians and voters is also a reason for the failure of public decision-making. Because of the policy effect's complexity, most voters find it difficult to predict its impact on the future, so they focus on the recent impact or current interests. However, because politicians or officials are affected by the election cycle or tenure, their time discount rate is higher than the social time discount rate, and the result is usually a clear disconnect between the short-term behavior and long-term interests of politicians or officials. In order to show their achievements and seek re-election or promotion, they will cater to the shortsightedness of voters and formulate some policies that will do more harm than good in the long run. This phenomenon is called "myopia inherent in the political process." Finally, there are obstacles to policy implementation. The effective implementation of policies depends on various factors or conditions. Idealized policies, implementing agencies, target groups, and the environment are the factors involved in the process of policy implementation. Specifically, the formation, type, scope, and degree of support of the policy, and the impression of the society on the policy; the methods and skills of the executing agency and personnel, the competent leadership, and the ability and confidence of the execution; the organization or institutionalization degree of the target group, the acceptance of leadership and previous policy experience; differences political, economic and cultural environments in society. These are all factors that need to be considered and identified to influence the success or failure of policy implementation. Any of these factors or the coordination between them may lead to the failure of the policy. For example, in the game of policy implementation, due to the difference between the central and local interests, local governments may bargain with the central government to obtain more benefits from the central government, which leads to the phenomenon of "there are policies above and countermeasures below."

Second, bureaucracy is inefficient and wasteful in providing public goods. In order to make up for market defects and correct market failures, public organizations, especially government agencies, will perform the functions of public goods providers, that is, directly provide public goods that may be insufficient in the market and perform the roles of market order maintainer, external effect eliminator, and control natural monopoly, external effect, information asymmetry, etc. However, due to the nature of public institutions, especially government institutions, and the characteristics of the relationship between supply and demand of public goods, it is difficult for them to provide public goods efficiently, especially the phenomenon of excess public goods and increased costs. The main reasons for the inefficiency of public institutions in providing public goods, especially the bureaucracy, are as follows: Firstly, the difficulties in the evaluation or assessment of public goods. Bureaucratic institutions provide public goods in pursuit of social benefits rather than economic benefits. The measurement of social benefits lacks accurate standards and feasible estimation methods and technologies. At the same time, it is difficult, even impossible, to reasonably determine the amount of demand for a certain type of public goods, the size of government institutions providing public goods, and the evaluation of the performance of these institutions. It can be said that there is no equation that can explain the necessity and minimum limit of the output of government activities. Secondly, public institutions, especially government departments, monopolize the supply of public goods and lack a competitive mechanism. Public institutions do not face direct competition in providing public goods. Even if they operate inefficiently, they can still survive, resulting in "low efficiency." That is, because there is no competitor, the bureaucracy may over-invest, produce more public goods than the society needs, and improperly expand institutions, increase employees, raise salaries and fees, resulting in a lot of waste.

Third, government agencies and officials lack the motivation to pursue profits. First of all, private enterprise managers have the motivation to reduce costs and pursue profits. Their enterprises have innovative incentive mechanisms, government agencies have no such mechanisms, and their officials have no profit motivation. Because bureaucrats cannot take profits for themselves, and the cost and benefit of public goods are difficult to measure, the goal of bureaucrats is not to maximize profits, but to maximize the size of institutions and personnel, so as to increase their promotion opportunities and expand their sphere of influence. Perhaps some public sectors are as efficient as private enterprises, but there is another kind of waste. That is, the public sector that provides public goods has an inherent tendency to overproduce public goods. This "excess" product or service is ultimately a social waste at the cost of huge social costs. Secondly, there are defects in the supervision mechanism. The behaviors of government officials must be subject to political supervision by legislators, citizens, or voters. However, the existing supervision mechanism is imperfect, especially the asymmetry and incompleteness of supervision information, which makes the supervision of officials meaningless. Government officials generally work in an asymmetric information environment. Legislators and voters lack enough necessary information to supervise the activities of public institutions and their officials effectively. Officials (supervised) have more information about public goods and services than supervisors (legislators and voters), especially costs and prices. In this way, the supervisor may be manipulated by the supervisor, who may formulate and implement some public policies that are conducive to their own interests and damage the public interest.

Fourth, rent-seeking and corruption. Rent-seeking and corruption are other basic types of government failure. Modern rent-seeking theory believes that all activities that make great profits by using administrative power can be called rent-seeking activities. Rent generally refers to the differential income formed by government intervention or administrative management of the market (that is, the differential price that exceeds the opportunity cost). All administrative management systems in the market economy will create such differential income, that is, rent. The characteristic of rent-seeking activities is to use various legal or illegal means (such as lobbying, relationship building, etc.) to obtain the privilege of owning rent. Rent-seeking activities lead to government corruption, because they distort the allocation of resources or make ineffective allocation of resources. As a non-productive activity, rent-seeking does not add any new products or new wealth, but changes the property right relationship of production factors and puts a greater part of social wealth into private pockets. Rent-seeking leads to different government departments and officials competing for power and profit, affecting the government's reputation and increasing the cost of integrity. It hinders the formulation and implementation of public policies, reduces the efficiency of administrative operation, and even endangers the stability of the regime. Rent-seeking and corruption are traps for economic development, political stability, and cultural progress. Once falling into this trap, society will be in a state of inefficiency, stagnation, or even disorder. Public choice scholars generally attribute the rent to the government's intervention in the free market economy. Under the market system, only the government can create an unequal competitive environment and maintain the rent owned by some people through administrative and legal means. Buchanan believes that as long as the government's behaviors are limited to private contracts that protect individual rights, persons, and property and implement voluntary bargaining, the market process will dominate economic behavior and ensure that any economic rent will disappear due to competitive entry.

In a word, through the analysis of the manifestations, types, and root causes of government failure, we draw the basic conclusion that market defects or market failures are not sufficient conditions for transferring problems to the government. If the market does not solve problems well, the government may not solve them well, or even make things worse. As the American economist Wolff said, "An appropriate non-market mechanism for enterprises to avoid non-market defects is no better than the prospect of creating a complete and appropriate market to overcome market defects. In other words, where the "invisible hand" of the market cannot turn private bad behavior into behavior in the public interest, it may be difficult to construct a visible hand to achieve this goal.

6.3.2 Standardization of Government Behavior

In China's stock market, government behavior is ubiquitous, and normative and rational government behavior is conducive to the healthy development of the stock market. Fundamentally speaking, rational government regulation and supervision is the basic premise to achieve optimal government behavior. Therefore, we should start from the following aspects.

First, policy formulation should be scientific and transparent. Over the past 20 years, the government's supervision of the stock market has gone from being absent and offside to returning to its original position. The practice has proved that the "policy market" sometimes distorts the internal operating rules of the stock market, artificially increasing or changing the operating direction and fluctuation space of the stock market. Policy plays an absolute leading role among the main factors that determine the stock market, which affects the changes in fundamentals, technology, and capital. If this situation does not change, the development of China's stock market will be difficult to meet the inherent requirements of the modern market economy, and it will be difficult to assume the strategic task of promoting the transition of China's economic system to the market economy. The CSRC has taken measures to change this situation, announcing that it will no longer take the regulation of the stock price index as the goal and will give top priority to protecting the interests of investors, especially small and medium-sized investors, which reflects the comprehensive adjustment of the government's regulatory policies. With the further deepening of China's reform and opening up and the gradual improvement of the market economy, the government will focus on the improvement and innovation of the stock market system to improve the efficiency of the stock market operation. At the same time, in policy formulation, more attention will be paid to the experts' opinions. In some areas, expert committees will be formed to vote on the choice of certain policies, so as to make policy formulation more scientific. So far, the CSRC has proposed that China considers establishing a "no objection letter" system to strengthen the transparency and predictability of policies, which indicates that the government will no longer intervene in the specific affairs that should be undertaken by intermediaries, investors, and issuers. The main function of regulators will turn to formulating standards and rules, promoting the improvement of laws and policy systems, and thus maintaining a fair, transparent, efficient, and orderly market.

Second, the market mechanism will play a leading role, and government regulation will play a guaranteed role. The core of the institutional innovation of China's stock market is to take the road of marketization. Because the stock market of our country was created and developed in the gap between the planned economy and the market economy, in this process, it is inevitable to make compromises in one way or another for the acquisition and continuation of the right to life, so the administrative mechanism not only survived in the stock market of our country, but also appears quite strong, which is prominently reflected in the administrative departments through administrative levels and administrative means, controlling the whole process from stock issuance to listing, from initial financing to refinancing, the competition mechanism of the stock market has been greatly weakened, and the marketization mechanism of resource allocation has been distorted to varying degrees. It can be said that China's stock market is the fastest growing market in the world, but also the market with the largest administrative power and the highest degree of distortion. In recent years, China's securities market regulatory authorities have done a lot of work in reducing administrative functions and enlarging market functions. Competition mechanisms have been introduced into the primary and secondary stock markets. The market decides who can enter, who can develop, and who should be eliminated. The improvement of these systems will be the main task of China's stock market in the future.

Third, government behaviors that do not follow the rules of the stock market will gradually decrease, and China's stock market will usher in an era of comprehensive integration with international practices in the future. The stock market is an investment place with common laws and common language. Its advantages and disadvantages, strengths and weaknesses, mainly come from its inherent nature and unique laws. Due to the continuous conflict and compromise between the planned economy and market economy, traditional thinking, and modern ideas, China's stock market has deviated from the operation track of the modern market economy to a considerable extent in the whole process of the emergence and development of China's stock market. This is reflected not only in the large-scale intervention of administrative power and mechanism in the stock market, but also in the characterization of China's stock market, the universal implementation of class shares, and the focus on serving the reform of state-owned enterprises. In recent years, a series of legislation and system construction issued by China's securities regulatory authorities have shown respect for the market operation rules and also indicated the main trend of changes in the government's regulatory means in the future.

Fourth, a new regulatory pattern is taking shape. Since the second half of 2001, the management has successively introduced a number of regulatory policies for the stock market. Several characteristics of the new regulatory pattern can be seen from the regulatory policies that have been issued: (1) The focus of supervision has shifted from approval-type supervision to market order supervision. For example, 2002 was designated by the regulators as the year of corporate governance of listed companies. (2) Frontline supervision will be entrusted with heavy responsibilities. The frontline regulatory responsibilities of the exchange and other institutions will be strengthened, strengthening the regulatory power and channels. (3) The means of supervision are dynamic and institutionalized. (4) Supervision will be more standardized. The management will further clarify the standards of punishment and the scope of supervision by formulating laws and regulations that adapt to the standardization of the securities market, strengthen the legal constraints on the participants in the stock market, increase the penalties for fraud, insider trading, major concealment, and other illegal acts, and substantially introduce criminal punishment and civil litigation systems. In 2002, China's courts introduced the civil compensation system for securities disputes, which undoubtedly played an important role in restricting illegal acts that disrupt the market order. From the above analysis, we can see that both the emphasis on moderate government intervention and the opposition to excessive government intervention are for long-term healthy stock market development.

Due to historical reasons, our government has intervened too much in the development of the stock market in the past, which has caused some negative effects. However, from the perspective of the whole development process of the stock market, the way and strength of government intervention and regulation of the stock market have changed greatly, which is actually a sign of the gradual maturity of the stock market. Rationally, the debate over government intervention and regulation of the stock market in China over the years has objectively achieved good effects, prompting the government to improve the means of supervision, improve the scientific and transparent nature of supervision and policy, and also improve the efficiency of supervision, which is what is urgently needed in the development of an emerging stock market.

6.3.3 Application of Public Choice Theory in Stock Market
The research on government failure and its theoretical achievements have changed the situation that modern Western social sciences, especially economics and politics, focus on the study of market defects while ignoring government failure in the study

of the relationship between government and market, making government failure become one of the focuses of Western scholars. As far as the subject of supervision is concerned, supervision can be divided into government supervision and private supervision. However, most economists believe that the subject of supervision should be the government, and supervision is mainly a government behavior (Zhao Xijun 2000). In view of the low efficiency caused by too loose regulation, on the one hand, it is necessary to put forward higher requirements for the regulatory authorities to enhance their sense of responsibility and regulatory capacity; on the other hand, it is necessary to design appropriate incentive mechanisms to ensure the timeliness and effectiveness of regulatory intervention. In view of the over-strict supervision, economists such as Llewellyn proposed establishing a competitive regulatory agency to make the regulatory authorities tend to restrain their own oversupervision tendency internally and dynamically (Liu Yufei 1999). In view of the current situation of the stock market, domestic scholars have put forward various methods to deal with the situation of loose supervision. Xia Wanjun (2004) believed that increasing the punishment of investors' illegal acts is an effective way to conduct securities supervision in the short term. In the long run, we should strengthen the contact and cooperation between the CSRC, the CIRC, the CBRC, and other regulatory authorities, reduce the cost of supervision, and thus improve the efficiency of supervision. Chen Ling (2004), Zhao Xisan (2004), and others emphasized that the independence of regulators should be guaranteed by the system, and the rent-setting and rent-seeking behaviors of regulators should be reduced, so as to improve regulatory efficiency. You Daming, Zhou Wei, and others (2002) proposed to implement effective internal control mechanisms and external supervision mechanisms for regulatory authorities, avoid collusion between regulators and interest groups, improve the quality and transparency of regulatory services, and ensure the efficiency of supervision.

6.3.4 Brief Review

Government intervention in the stock market is inevitable, but we should pay attention to the following issues.

First, government intervention may weaken the law of market operation. It is undeniable that both the stock market and other markets have their own inherent operating rules. The development process of the stock market is the process of constantly discovering and following its rules. In this process, government intervention may destroy the operation law of the market itself. Although some local interests may be obtained in the short term, the long-term interests of the market may be sacrificed in the long run. "The power of administration is too strong, the market mechanism is too weak, the disclosure of information is too gray, and the orientation of supervision is too chaotic," which is the basic summary of Han Zhiguo, a famous economist and director of Beijing Banghe

Wealth Research Institute, on the existing drawbacks of China's stock market. For more than 20 years, China's stock market has been dominated by administrative forces. An effective market mechanism has not yet been formed, and the role of the market mechanism has not been fully played, leading to chaos in the market. As a result, the resource allocation function of the stock market has been greatly weakened. All kinds of abnormal phenomena in the current market are more or less related to this. Therefore, when the government intervenes in the stock market, it should strengthen its understanding of the operating rules of the stock market, fully listen to the opinions of all sectors of society, and constantly revise its own behavior in practice. The CSRC's extensive solicitation of opinions from all walks of life on the reduction of state-owned shares reflects that the government has begun institutional innovation in respect of market rules and improving the efficiency of policies and supervision.

Second, improper government intervention may weaken the function of optimal allocation of resources. If the administrative choice mechanism excludes or replaces the market choice mechanism, it will lead to a serious lack of competition mechanism in the stock market. Since the establishment of China's stock market, the issuance and listing of the market have been restricted by administrative mechanisms, forming a mechanism of stock issuance and listing dominated by administrative power. This administrative listing selection system, on the one hand, has formed the dependence of listed companies and intermediaries on administrative power, leading to listed companies and intermediaries being responsible for administrative power rather than for the market and investors and even causing a "rent-seeking phenomenon." On the other hand, in order to protect local interests and departmental interests, the administrative department, from the perspective of guaranteeing the listing quota and listing indicators, connived at or even participated in the fraud of listed companies and intermediaries, thus forming a relatively widespread effect of "packaging" and "fraud" in the stock market. The financial fraud of listed companies is closely related to the issuance and listing system implemented in previous years. If we do not solve the administrative leading problem of China's stock market from the system and then introduce the competition mechanism into the market in an all-round way, it will only take stopgap measures, and it will be impossible to solve the problem fundamentally. China's stock issuance has now changed from a simple administrative examination and approval system to an approval system, which is important progress. However, it still has not gotten rid of the way of administrative choice, and the competition mechanism in stock issuance and listing is still unable to form. Moreover, the problem of functional dislocation between the stock market regulatory authority and the stock exchange has not been solved. Under the condition that the national stock regulatory authority still carries out the approval of stock issuance and reissue, the market regulatory system is difficult to form and fully play its role. Therefore, the government should try its best to speed up the reform and innovation of the system and establish an efficient stock market system that is compatible with the socialist market economic system as soon as possible, starting from the principle of maximizing the efficiency of stock market resource allocation and the principle of protecting the interests of small and medium-sized investors.

Third, government intervention cannot replace the mature process of market players. Although the government, out of goodwill, hopes to make the market subject develop more rationally and maturely through intervention and supervision, this may not be the case. For example, the special commentator article in the *People's Daily* was published in 1996 to give investors a risk education lesson. The negative effect is that investors are more dependent on the government. When they suffer losses, they either blame the government for failing to protect investors or expect the government to support the market. In the face of a new market, its participants cannot enhance their ability to resist risks without being tested by wind and rain. The reason why the stock markets of Western developed countries are mature today is that they have been subjected to countless cruel tests. Through the competition and testing of the market, eliminating a number of listed companies, securities companies, and investors is actually the optimal allocation of resources. It can be said that if the governments at all levels did not protect some junk stocks, there would be no serious loss of a group of listed companies today. Sometimes, because the government frequently intervenes in the stock market, investors are used to speculating about the government's intentions and neglect to grasp the operating rules of the stock market itself, which is not conducive to the cultivation of rational investors in the market. It is precisely because China's stock market has always been characterized by a typical "policy market," and government regulation has always been the most important force to determine the trend of stock prices, which has led to the tight and lax investigation and punishment of illegal acts of intermediaries. For example, from 1996 to the first half of 1997, the policy orientation was "short selling," and more than ten "gold medals" of the regulatory authorities were all aimed at suppressing stock prices. After the Asian financial crisis broke out in 1997, the policy orientation was to "do more," and the various measures taken by the regulatory authorities were mostly to promote the rise of stock prices. For more than three years, there was almost no investigation and punishment of market violations and illegal acts, and there were scenes of song and dance everywhere. The stocks rose and fell at the same time, and the price discovery function of the market was found to be invalid, even "the poorer, the more glorious." No matter how large the loss was, as long as it touched the edge of "asset restructuring," the stock price would immediately "rise." The "banker" behavior was objectively connived, and it seemed that in the market, as long as it was consistent with the national policy orientation and not too deviant, it would not be investigated. Listed companies were keen on making themes to match the market trend of stock prices. The phenomenon that listed companies hit the net at the beginning of 2000 is clear proof. In such a market pattern, listed companies do not focus on improving their own quality, investors do not focus on the analysis and grasp of the intrinsic value of stocks, regulatory authorities do not specialize in maintaining market order, and the role orientation and function grasp of the whole market are in serious confusion. In such a market atmosphere, it is impossible to talk about improving the efficiency of resource allocation. It can be seen from this that strengthening the cultivation of participants in the stock market and standardizing their behavior can fundamentally maintain the healthy operation of the stock market. Governments at all levels should devote considerable energy to improving the quality of listed companies and intermediary institutions, creating a good development environment for the stock market, which is also a critical factor for improving investors' confidence.

Fourth, the dual identity of the government makes the intervention unfair. Compared with the developed stock markets in the world, China's stock market is a little different; that is, our government is a dual participant in the stock market. On the one hand, as the maker of the game rules of the stock market, the government should participate in the stock market as an all-round supervisor. On the other hand, the government, as the representative of the overwhelming majority of state-owned shares in China's stock market, also participates as a major shareholder. It is easy to see from the history of the development of China's stock market that the government often takes the stock market as a means to solve the difficulties of state-owned enterprises, and its policies are obviously beneficial to state-owned enterprises and state-owned assets, which is discrimination against non-state-owned listed companies.

Fifth, the government should enhance transparency and science in policy formulation. In this regard, the most typical are the state-owned and corporate shares. If there is still some basis for the existence of state-owned shares and corporate shares before the formal implementation of the *Company Law* on July 1, 1994, it is illegal to continue the definition of state-owned shares, corporate shares, and individual shares and continue to adopt the incremental listing method when the *Company Law* officially takes effect and formally abolishes the distinction between state-owned shares and corporate shares. At the same time, such important measures as the reduction of state-owned shares, which are related to the overall situation of the stock market, must be transparent in the decision-making process. But the initial reduction plan of state-owned shares was a "secret operation," which itself is a copy of the "administrative mechanism" in the stock market, and it is impossible not to harm the market and investors. What's stranger is that although we know that the unreasonable ownership structure is the main source of the failure of the governance structure of listed companies in China, we are "reducing" and "increasing" while trying to solve the problem of the construction of the governance structure of listed companies, while replicating the unreasonable corporate governance structure. What kind of value orientation should the stock market supervision follow? It is really a question that cannot be avoided and should be seriously considered. Therefore, the government should develop a scientific and reasonable policy formulation system and can learn from the Western hearing system, widely solicit opinions from all sectors of society, avoid "black box operation" or "gray box operation," and enhance the scientificity and transparency of policy formulation.

6.4 Game Analysis of Government Behavior in Stock Market

The game behavior of the stock market mainly occurs among investors, who spontaneously form equilibrium under the role of the internal mechanism of the market. However, pure equilibrium is only a special case, while disequilibrium is the normal state of the market. The government's participation plays an irreplaceable role in promoting the market to move towards equilibrium and realizing Pareto efficiency. Therefore, the stock market has become a game arena for governments, listed companies, investors, and other parties to participate. In order to maximize their own effectiveness, all parties must observe the behavior strategies of other parties to formulate their own action strategies. The behavior among the above subjects is a game behavior, and the parties involved in the stock market game should include the government, listed companies, investors, and other subjects. In general, the purpose of the government's policy decisions is to achieve certain policy objectives, which are characterized by diversification. That is, it is not only to provide financing places for listed companies, but also to help the whole society optimize the allocation of resources and reflect and adjust the entire macroeconomy. The purpose of listed companies' financing decisions is to obtain reasonable financing capital, that is, more favorable funds than other financing methods, to promote the development and growth of the company. The main purpose of investors is to make money. On the surface, because the stock price explains everything, the main body of the game is mainly the government and investors. Investors care about the price, and all means of government regulation are ultimately reflected in the price. In the absence of government regulation, the stock market price is formed by the game between investors (including institutional investors and institutional investors, institutional investors and small and medium-sized investors, small and medium-sized investors, etc.). Whether the stock price positioning is scientific or not is the core issue that determines the function of the stock market. Therefore, the study of government behavior in the stock market mainly focuses on the game equilibrium between the government and investors.

6.4.1 Literature Review of Using Game Theory to Study the Stock Market

1. Brief Overview of Game Theory

Game theory studies the interaction of each rational decision-making individual and the equilibrium of decision-making. Neumann and Morgenstern (1944) systematically introduced game theory into economic research and analysis for the first time. In the

1950s, the non-cooperative game began to emerge. Nash (1950) clearly proposed the "Nash Equilibrium," which laid the cornerstone of modern non-cooperative games. Selten (1965) introduced dynamic analysis into game theory for the first time and proposed "Subgame Perfect Nash Equilibrium," which was an important improvement of Nash equilibrium based on the sequence of players' game actions. Harsanyi (1968) also introduced the incompleteness of information into the game analysis and proposed "Static Games of Incomplete Information," that is, in the economic game, participants did not know the type and payment function of other participants, and all participants acted at the same time, The famous Harsanyi transformation further transforms this game into a "complete but imperfect information dynamic game involving simultaneous actions."

With the deepening of game theory research, economists also bring the research on dynamic games with incomplete information into the research field of game theory. In real economic life, the game between participants is more about mutual observation and reasoning under incomplete and asymmetric information. First, we start with the transcendental beliefs about other participants' types. After observing the strategies of the first movers, we successively revise the type probability judgments of the first movers to form the posterior beliefs and then take the most appropriate action strategies. At the same time, the forerunners should also speculate and analyze the possible strategic actions taken by the latecomers after observing their own actions and choosing their own optimal economic decisions, that is, forming a second-order belief about the participants. Thus, Fudenberg and Tirole (1991) further developed the Dynamic Games of Incomplete Information game theory and formed their basic equilibrium concept, "Perfect Baysian-Nash Equilibrium." Game theory has gradually evolved into a powerful methodology for analyzing economic decision-making behavior. Economic game theory highlights the hypothesis of a rational person, breaks through the definite state of complete information, and puts a rational person in an economic atmosphere of uncertainty and incomplete or asymmetric information for analysis, thus greatly enhancing the ability to explain economic phenomena. Economic game theory turns the focus of economic analysis to the interaction between decision-makers, analyzing economic problems more dynamic. The core issue of economic game analysis is game equilibrium. It emphasizes the interaction and influence between decision-makers, analyzes the actions between decision-makers, and selects action strategies to make economic activities reach a relatively balanced state. In real economic life, rational and irrational behaviors coexist. Economic game theory undoubtedly provides a powerful methodology to analyze the contradiction between individual and collective decision-making. The research paradigm of economic game theory is that under given constraints, given the strategy space, information type, and utility function of the participants, the decision makers pursue their own utility maximization through their optimal choices and finally achieve game equilibrium.

2. Equilibrium Game Theory of Asset Pricing in Stock Market

(1) Equilibrium game of rational expected price

Demsetz (1968) first analyzed the decision mechanism of the transaction price of securities. He believed that there were two supply curves and demand curves at specific time points in the securities market. The price of securities depended on the traders' real buying and selling actions rather than just their desire to trade. Due to the intervention of time, the securities price contains an implicit transaction cost (the price paid for spot transactions). This hidden transaction cost will lead to two "equilibrium prices" in the securities market, which further explains the function and source of the market maker trading system and discusses the relationship between the securities price and the number of traders and trading volume. Radner (1979) also pointed out that, under the condition of asymmetric information, to analyze the equilibrium state of securities prices, we should give a detailed description of the trading mechanism rather than the usual general equilibrium analysis. Grossman and Stiglitz (1980) systematically criticized the price formation mechanism of Wallace's general equilibrium theory under the condition of asymmetric information, introduced information asymmetry into the study of asset pricing, defined the concept of non-strategic expected equilibrium, and assumed that each market participant could know the price from the market, but could not affect the market price, so we can combine asymmetric information with competitive analysis.

Lucas (1972) established a two-stage trading model of the securities market with rational expectation equilibrium: traders enter the market with different private information y^j (exogenous) and finally form a balanced securities price $P^*(y)$. Rational traders can infer other information $y\left(y = y^1, y^2, \ldots y^m\right)$ from $P^*(y)$ realized value $P^*(y) = P$. This rational expectation equilibrium is a random equilibrium under information dispersion. The equilibrium price $P^*(y)$ requires: If all traders choose the demand to maximize their expected utility at the price P, and the formation of the equilibrium price has taken advantage of the private information of traders y^j (information contained in the price P), then given any information y, when $P^*(y) = P$, all markets are in a clear state.

Grossman (1978) also used the "sufficient statistic" method to describe the reaction of equilibrium price to security information. $t(y)$ is a sufficient statistic of y, which means that when a trader calculates expected utility, the overall information y is equivalent to $t(y)$ which is known:

$$E\left[U^i(\bullet)\middle|\tilde{y} = y\right] = E\left[U^i(\bullet)\middle|t\left(\tilde{y}\right) = t(y)\right] \qquad (6\text{-}1)$$

Radner (1972) proved that there is a general one-to-one correspondence between the equilibrium price and the signal in the perfectly competitive securities market where the signal set is finite and short selling is not allowed. Allen (1982) carried out research on Radner. If the signal dimension is smaller than the number of securities, the equilibrium price can generally and completely reveal information. According to Madrigal and Smith (1995), in a finite-dimensional space, as long as traders' utility functions are strictly restricted, there is still an equilibrium price that fully reveals rational expectations in an incomplete market. When the supply of securities is fixed, the condition for its allocation to be Pareto optimal is that all traders' utility functions meet:

$$\frac{\partial U^i\left(W^i, S^i\right)}{\partial W^i} = \left[g^i\left(a_i, s^i\right) + bw_i\right]^{-1/b} \tag{6-2}$$

Among them: w_i represents wealth, $g(\bullet)$ represents function, and a and b are constants.

Grossman (1976) proved the existence of a rational expected price $P^*(y)$ under the condition of pure exchange economy and pointed out that a rational expected price is a self-fulfilling equilibrium process. When all the transaction-identified prices are generated by $P^*(y)$, the market behavior just makes the market clear at $P^*(y)$.

(2) Competitive equilibrium with incomplete information

The explanation of rational expectation equilibrium to the securities market is not complete. In order to further analyze the equilibrium condition under asymmetric information and information dispersion, many scholars further deepen the game model. They divided investors into informed and uninformed and introduced noise traders to investigate the game behaviors of various traders and their effects on security prices. Grossman and Stiglitz (1980) established a famous single-risk asset, a two-period rational expectations model with noise. Under certain conditions, the paper explained the influence of factors such as traders' risk preference, posterior belief, information accuracy, number of informed traders, and proportion of total trading volume on the validity of security price information. Assuming that traders all have rational expectations, they are divided into the informed I and the uninformed U, whose utility functions are as follows: $U(\widetilde{W}) = -e^{-\alpha \widetilde{w}}$. Initially hold $\widetilde{M}$ unit risk-free securities and X_i unit of risk securities, $\bar{r}$ and r_0 are the ending earnings of risk securities and risk-free securities, respectively.

And $\widetilde{r} = \widetilde{\theta} + \widetilde{\varepsilon}$, where, $\widetilde{\theta}$ is an observable variable, $\widetilde{\varepsilon}$ is a random disturbance term.

Informed traders have observed $\widetilde{\theta} = \theta$ at the beginning and form their own posterior belief about $\bar{r}$, $E(\bar{r}|\theta) = \theta$, $Var(\frac{r}{\theta}) = Var\widetilde{\varepsilon} \equiv \sigma_\varepsilon^2$. Uninformed traders can only infer information from the equilibrium price and make their own decisions.

Traders maximize expected utility within their budget constraints. Expected utility is related to the difference between income and conditions. $E[U(\widetilde{W})|\theta]$ maximizes the demand function of risky securities by the informed.

$$X_1(P, \theta) = \frac{\theta - r_0 P}{a\sigma_\varepsilon^2} \tag{6-3}$$

It is assumed that the per capita supply of risky securities x is a random variable, which is the noise source introduced by the model, so that the uninformed cannot infer private information from the price. The equilibrium price is a function of (θ, x). Let $P^*(\theta, x)$ be the rational expectation function owned by the uninformed, maximize $E[U(\tilde{W})|P^*(\theta, x)]$, and obtain the demand function of the uninformed risky securities:

$$X_u(P, P^*) = \frac{E\left[\frac{\bar{r}}{P^*(\theta,x)} = P\right] - r_0 P}{\alpha Var\left[\bar{r}\middle|P^*(\theta, x) = P\right]} \tag{6-4}$$

Let λ be the proportion of informed traders, then the equilibrium price of rational expectations can be denoted as $P^*(\theta, \lambda)$, and the market random equilibrium condition is:

$$\lambda X_1(P, \theta) + (1 - \lambda) X_u(P, P^*) = x \tag{6-5}$$

The random form of x is caused by the behavior of noise traders. The decision of noise trading is based on irrational emotion or some other sudden factors rather than expected utility maximization. The trading result of noise trading has a random impact on rational traders and increases the uncertainty factor of the securities market.

Suppose a rational trader has a prior belief $(\tilde{\theta}, \tilde{\varepsilon}, x)$ and obtains an equilibrium price under market equilibrium conditions:

$$P^*_\lambda(\theta, x) = \frac{\left(\frac{\lambda}{ab_\varepsilon^2}\theta + \frac{1-\lambda}{aVar(\bar{r}+P^*_\lambda)}E\left(\bar{r}\middle|P^*_\lambda\right) - x\right)}{r_0\left(\frac{\lambda}{a\sigma_\varepsilon^2} + \frac{1-\lambda}{aVar(\bar{r}|P^*_\lambda)}\right)} \tag{6-6}$$

Where: $\frac{\lambda}{\sigma_\varepsilon^2} + \frac{1-\lambda}{Var(\bar{r}|P^*_\lambda)}$ is the overall view of information accuracy of $\bar{r}$ formed by the market, and $P^*_\lambda(\theta, x)$ is the equilibrium price. After observing $P^*_\lambda(\theta, x) = P$, an uninformed trader cannot separate the effects of θ and x on the price and thus cannot infer the information θ of the informed trader. Therefore, a statistic $w_\lambda(\theta, x)$ is introduced:

$$w_\lambda(\theta, x) = \begin{cases} \theta - \frac{a\sigma_\varepsilon^2(x-Ex)}{\lambda} & (\lambda > 0) \\ \lambda & (\lambda < 0) \end{cases} \tag{6-7}$$

Then, the equilibrium price of securities becomes:

$$P^*_\lambda(\theta, x) = \frac{\left(\frac{\lambda}{ab_\varepsilon^2}w_\lambda + \frac{1-\lambda}{aVar(\bar{r}+P^*_\lambda)}E\left(\bar{r}\middle|P^*_\lambda\right) - Ex\right)}{r_0\left(\frac{\lambda}{a\sigma_\varepsilon^2} + \frac{1-\lambda}{aVar(\bar{v}|P^*_\lambda)}\right)} \tag{6-8}$$

So $P_\lambda^*(\theta,x)$ is a linear function of $w_\lambda(\theta,x)$. And $E(\bar{r}|P_\lambda^*)=E(\bar{r}|w_\lambda)$, $Var(\bar{v}|P_\lambda^*)\equiv Var(\bar{r}|w_\lambda)$, further verifies the equilibrium price:

$$P_\lambda^*(\theta,x)=\frac{\left(\frac{\lambda}{ab_\varepsilon^2}w_\lambda+\frac{1-\lambda}{aVar(\bar{r}|w_\lambda)}E\left(\bar{r}|w_\lambda\right)-E(x)\right)}{r_0\left(\frac{\lambda}{a\sigma_\varepsilon^2}+\frac{1-\lambda}{aVar(\bar{v}|w_\lambda)}\right)} \tag{6-9}$$

For any (θ,x) is the equilibrium price, and the conditional expected variance satisfies:

$$E\left[\bar{r}|w_\lambda\right]=E\left(\tilde{\theta}\right)+\frac{\sigma_\theta^2}{Var(w_\lambda)}\left[w_\lambda-E\left(\tilde{\theta}\right)\right] \tag{6-10}$$

$$Var\left(\bar{r}|w_\lambda\right)=\sigma_\theta^2+\sigma_\varepsilon^2-\frac{\sigma_\theta^2}{Var(w_\lambda)} \tag{6-11}$$

$$Var(w_\lambda)=\sigma_\theta^2+\left(\frac{a\sigma_\varepsilon^2}{\lambda}\right)^2Var(x) \tag{6-12}$$

When uninformed traders observe $P_\lambda^*(\theta,x)=P$, they can know $w_\lambda(\theta,x)$, but traders still cannot accurately get information θ, $w_\lambda(\theta,x)$ has noise $-a\sigma_\varepsilon^2[x-E(x)]/\lambda$, whose variance is $(a\sigma_\varepsilon^2/\lambda)Var(x)$, and $Var(x)$ measures the uncertainty of security supply. This model illustrates the influence of traders' preferences, beliefs, and information θ on security price $P_\lambda^*(\theta,x)$, and describes the role of preference and belief in information transmission.

6.4.2 Game Analysis between Government and Investors

The stock price level is the core measure that comprehensively reflects the state of the stock market. Reasonable stock prices can not only overcome the market bubble and avoid financial turmoil and even financial crisis, but also avoid the excessive downturn of the stock market, which will reduce or even lose the basic function of raising funds. In fact, there are many games between the government and the stock market, that is, between the government and investors, between the government and listed companies, between institutional investors and small and medium-sized investors, and between institutional investors. The main activities of the stock market include listed companies, investors (speculators), securities companies, and the government. The government behavior in the stock market is mainly a game between the government and investors, and all the information in the stock market is ultimately reflected by the stock price.

In analyzing this problem, we make the following assumptions: First, suppose that the players in the policy effect game are government (G) and investor (I). The government plays a dominant role in the policy effect signal game, and its relevant policies can reverse the market or strengthen the trend of market rise and fall. However, since the government needs investors to change their action strategies after the policy is issued, the stock price index will fluctuate to achieve the policy effect. Therefore, whether the policy effect can be achieved depends on the degree of investors' identification with the policy. The role of investors here is to change the level of stock prices by buying and selling stocks, so that the government can get information about whether or not to introduce policies and how aggressive they will be. Therefore, the relationship between the government and investors is a game. Second, assume that the interests of all types of investors are the same when playing the game with the government. Although there are fierce conflicts of interest among actual investors, especially between institutional investors and small and medium investors, the introduction of policies has a consistent impact on the utility function of various investors. Therefore, in the analysis of the policy effect of the game, do not consider the competition between investors. The decision-making goal of the investors is to make as much profit as possible by buying, selling, and holding the stock. In our stock market, most investors hope to make capital gains from the short-term stock price upswing. Third, the government's decision-making goals are complex and phased. The government should maximize benefits, which is mainly reflected in maintaining the stability and development of the stock market. Of course, due to the institutional characteristics of ideology, bureaucratic system, and legal environment, the regulation and control of the stock market by government policies may also conflict with the social objective function. Therefore, the current decision-making objectives of the Chinese government in the stock market include helping state-owned enterprises raise funds to get out of trouble, which is determined by the economic system transformation. To protect the interests of investors and maintain the stock market and social stability, the government takes actions such as strengthening market supervision (which may cause the market to fall) and market rescue (which stimulates the stock price to rise).

The action sequence of each participant in the dynamic game of incomplete information of government effect is as follows: under a certain market level, the government observes the market trend, makes a judgment on the level of the market according to the needs of its utility function, and then decides whether to issue and what kind of policies to issue. Investors adjust their investment strategies according to policies, ultimately affecting market trends. Based on this, the government judges the degree of investor's reaction to the policy and decides the next policy adjustment strategy. In this cycle, the government's policy objectives are finally achieved. Under the premise of rational policy, the stock market will develop in a healthy way.

1. The Pluralistic Characteristics of Government Objectives

Different subjects in the stock market have different behavioral goals, but they are all for the maximization of their own interests. The goal of listed companies is to maximize their own interests by raising funds. The goal of investors is to maximize their own interests by gaining more returns. The goal of securities companies is to make use of the liquidity of the market to gain more commission income and maximize their own interests. The government's behavioral goals have diversified characteristics: (1) promote the economic growth of the whole society; (2) avoid excessive volatility in the stock market, maintain its liquidity, and promote its stable and healthy development; (3) get stamp duty and other income; and (4) avoid excessively high stock prices resulting in bubbles and excessively low stock prices causing the stock market to reduce or lose its financing function. The two main concerns of the government are short-term volatility and the absolute level of stock prices. When short-term stock prices fluctuate excessively, it will cause excessive speculation and other problems, which will destroy the efficiency of the stock market. When the absolute price of a stock is too high or too low, that is, when the price of a stock is seriously out of line with its intrinsic value, the stock market is out of a healthy range. In both cases, the government behavior will play a positive corrective role, bringing the stock market back to the rational range.

2. Government and Investor Utility Function

Utility function of government:

$$U_G = \beta^t \sum \lambda_t \left[T\left(P, Q, r\right) - f\left(I_t, \overline{I}\right) - g\left(B_t, B_t^*\right) + \varepsilon_t \right] \tag{6-13}$$

Where, $T\left(P, Q, r\right) = P_t Q_t r_t$ and P_t represent the stock price of period t, Q_t represents the trading volume of period t, and r_t represents the stamp tax rate of period t, this index reflects the stamp tax revenue of the government from the stock market, and $\partial U_G / \partial T > 0$ indicates that the more stamp tax revenue, the more utility of the government. $f(I_t, \overline{I}) = [(I_t - \overline{I})/\overline{I}]^2$, I_t represents the stock price index in period t, $\overline{I}$ represents the short-term mean value of the stock price index, which actually reflects the short-term fluctuation range of stock prices, and $\partial U_G / \partial f < 0$ indicates that the greater the short-term fluctuation of stock prices, the lower the utility of the government. $g\left(B_t, B_t^*\right) = [(B_t - B_t^*)/B_t^*]^2$, B_t represents the market P/E ratio in the t period, B_t^* represents the reasonable P/E ratio, which reflects the distance between the actual P/E ratio and the mean P/E ratio (reasonable P/E ratio), that is, the difference between the actual price and the real value of the stock. Moreover, $\partial U_G / \partial g < 0$ indicates that the further the stock price deviates from its intrinsic value in the long term, the smaller the utility of the government. $\varepsilon \in (-\alpha, \alpha)$ is the fluctuation range of the stock price index tolerated by the government and is also the functional optimization range of the stock market, including the fluctuation range tolerable in the short term and the deviation degree of valuation tolerable in the long term. $0 < \lambda_t < 1$ reflects the government's concern about the stock market, which represents the importance of the stock market in the whole macroeconomic operation under the premise of rational government behavior. β^t is the discount rate of period t, and the above equation can be written as:

$$U_G = \beta^t \sum \lambda_t \left[\left(P_t Q_t r_t - \frac{I_t - \overline{I}}{\overline{I}} \right)^2 - \left(\frac{B_t - B_t^*}{B_t^*} \right)^2 + \varepsilon_t \right] \qquad (6\text{-}14)$$

Therefore, the utility function of the government is determined by the range of short-term stock price volatility, the difference between the actual price and the real value of the stock and the government's stamp duty revenue.

Investor's utility function:

$$U_I = \beta^t \left[(P_t - P_0) \cdot Q + \sum D_t \right] \qquad (6\text{-}15)$$

Where, P_t represents the stock price in period t, P_0 represents the purchase price, Q represents the trading volume, and $\sum D_t$ represents the dividend payout amount.

Order: $\Delta P = |P_t - P_0|$

When $P_t > P_0$, $U_I = \beta^t \left[\Delta P \cdot Q + \sum D_t \right]$

When $P_t < P_0$, $U_I = \beta^t \left[-\Delta P \cdot Q + \sum D_t \right]$

3. Analysis of the Game Process between Government and Investors

If the market investor makes a choice, he thinks the stock price is high with probability p and low with probability $1-p$. In the process of a dynamic game, investor judges the current market level according to the policy type and then adjust their investment strategy. According to game theory, investors follow Bayes' rule when adjusting investment strategy. The design of related variables with Bayesian inference is as follows: Set policy type $S_i (i = 0, 1, 2)$ issued by the government, where S_1 represents positive policy, S_2 represents negative policy, S_0 represents no policy. The judgment type made by investors on the market level is $W_j (j = 1, 2)$, where W_1 represents high market level and W_2 represents low market level. Let investors make a prior judgment on market conditions as $P(W_j)$, and $P(W_1) = p$, $P(W_2) = 1 - p$, when market conditions are W_j, the conditional probability of government issuing policy S_i is $P(S_i|W_j)$, and investors make a posteriori judgment on market conditions W_j made by policy type S_i is $P(W_j|S_i)$. Investors will then revise their posterior probabilities according to Bayes' law to judge the current market level.

Suppose $P(W_j|S_i)$ is the posterior judgment made by investors on the stock market after observing policy information, $P(W_1|S_i) = q$ is the probability that investors believe the stock market will rise, and $P(W_2|S_i) = 1 - q$ is the probability that investors believe the stock market will fall. Then, the expected utility function of investors is:

$$\begin{aligned} E(U_i) &= P(W_1|S_i) \cdot U_1(W_1) + P(W_2|S_i) \cdot U_1(W_2) \\ &= q \cdot \beta^t \cdot \left(\Delta P \cdot Q + \sum D_t \right) + (1 - q) \cdot \beta^t \cdot \left(-\Delta P \cdot Q + \sum D_t \right) \\ &= \beta^t \cdot \left[(2q - 1)\Delta P \cdot Q + \sum D_t \right] \end{aligned} \qquad (6\text{-}16)$$

Due to the large fluctuation range of China's stock market, investors' preference for capital gains far exceeds their preference for stock cash bonuses. Whether institutional investors or small and medium investors, the pursuit of capital gains is very important in the game process. What the government should use in the game process with investors is mainly the influence on capital gains rather than the influence on stock dividends. In this way, we can ignore the impact of dividends, which is indeed the case. On the one hand, the dividend ratio of listed companies in China's stock market is very low, which is mostly due to the catering to the relevant regulations of the government. On the other hand, the dividends of listed companies in China's stock market are also extremely unstable. Of course, this is also due to the unstable performance of listed companies. Some people even believe that there are no real blue chips in China's stock market. So, let's ignore $\sum D_t$. Equation 6-16 can be rewritten as:

$$E(U_i) = \beta^t \left[(2q-1)\Delta P \cdot Q \right] \tag{6-17}$$

Since $\Delta P = 0$ is a fluke, $E(U_i)$ is determined only by q. When $0 \leq q < 0.5$, $E(U_i) < 0$, investors choose to sell the stock. When $0.5 < q \leq 1$, $E(U_i) > 0$, investors choose to buy stocks. When $q=0.5$, investors have no choice.

The closer q is to 0, the more likely the government will take a policy to suppress the stock market. When $q=0$, the possibility of the government taking such a measure is certain. The closer the q value is to 1, the more likely it is that the government will adopt policies to encourage the rise of the stock market. When $q=1$, the possibility of the government taking such measures is certain.

4. The Equilibrium and Disequilibrium Analysis of the Game between the Government and Investors

The game is actually a dynamic and infinite repetition of the equilibrium game process. In the long run, there will be a cooperative balance between the government and investors, in which the government does not intervene, and investors invest rationally. The starting point of our analysis is the natural state of the stock market. If the volatility range of the stock price index tolerated by the government of $\varepsilon \in (-\alpha, \alpha)$ is also the functional optimization range of the stock market, there will be no policies to regulate the stock market. When the stock price deviates further, the more likely it is to introduce regulatory policies. In this game process, investors gradually evolve from irrational to rational.

We study the game process between the government and investors from the high and low stock market prices. If the market is in the ideal range $\varepsilon \in (-\alpha, \alpha)$ of the government, that is, the stock price is in a moderate equilibrium state, the game between the government and investors will not occur in the market, and the market is already in an equilibrium state.

When the price of the stock market is low or high, the government can choose to introduce good or bad policies for regulation, or it can not introduce policies for regulation and use the inherent function of the market mechanism to form an equilibrium state automatically. This is not only possible but also better than the government's direct intervention in many cases. Generally speaking, the government should intervene directly only when the market mechanism fails completely. Before the game equilibrium is formed, let's make the following statement:

(1) $P(S_1|W_2) = P_{11}$ represents the probability that the government will introduce favorable policies under the condition that the market stock price is low.
(2) $P(S_2|W_1) = P_{22}$ represents the probability that the government will introduce negative policies when the market stock price is high.
(3) $P(S_0|W_2) = 1 - P_{11}$ represents the probability that the government will not introduce favorable policies when the market stock price is low.
(4) $P(S_0|W_1) = 1 - P_{22}$ represents the probability that the government will not issue negative policies under the condition of high stock prices in the market.
(5) $P(S_1|W_1) = 0$ indicates that the probability of positive results is zero when the stock price is high.
(6) $P(S_2|W_2) = 0$ indicates that the probability of negative results is zero when the stock price is low.

The game tree graph is described as follows:

(1) "high" and "low" indicate that the stock price is high or low.
(2) "Buy" and "sell" represent the difference between the trading volume of investors in the stock market. If the selling energy minus the buying energy is positive, it is defined as selling; that is, the stock price falls. If the energy to sell minus the energy to buy is negative, it is defined as buying, and the price of the stock goes up. No matter how much regulation and control policies the government adopts, buyers and sellers coexist in the stock market, but the different forces of buying and selling lead to the rise or fall of the stock price; that is, the strong buying power will make the stock price rise, while the strong selling power will make the stock price fall. In fact, under the condition that the information is impossible to be completely symmetrical, investors are divided into the informed, uninformed, and noise traders, so as to investigate the game behavior of various traders and its impact on security prices.
(3) "Nothing" means that the government does not introduce measures to regulate the stock market.

(4) The main body of the game is the government (G) and the investor (I). All kinds of investors have the same interests in the game, and investors aim at maximizing investment returns.

(5) The government is seen as a rational economic man, namely: $P(S_1|W_1) = 0$ or $P(S_2|W_2) = 0$.

(6) We divide the government's policies to regulate the stock market into positive and negative. When the stock price is high or low, the government can either choose to regulate the stock market in a negative or positive way, or it can keep silent and let the market adjust itself.

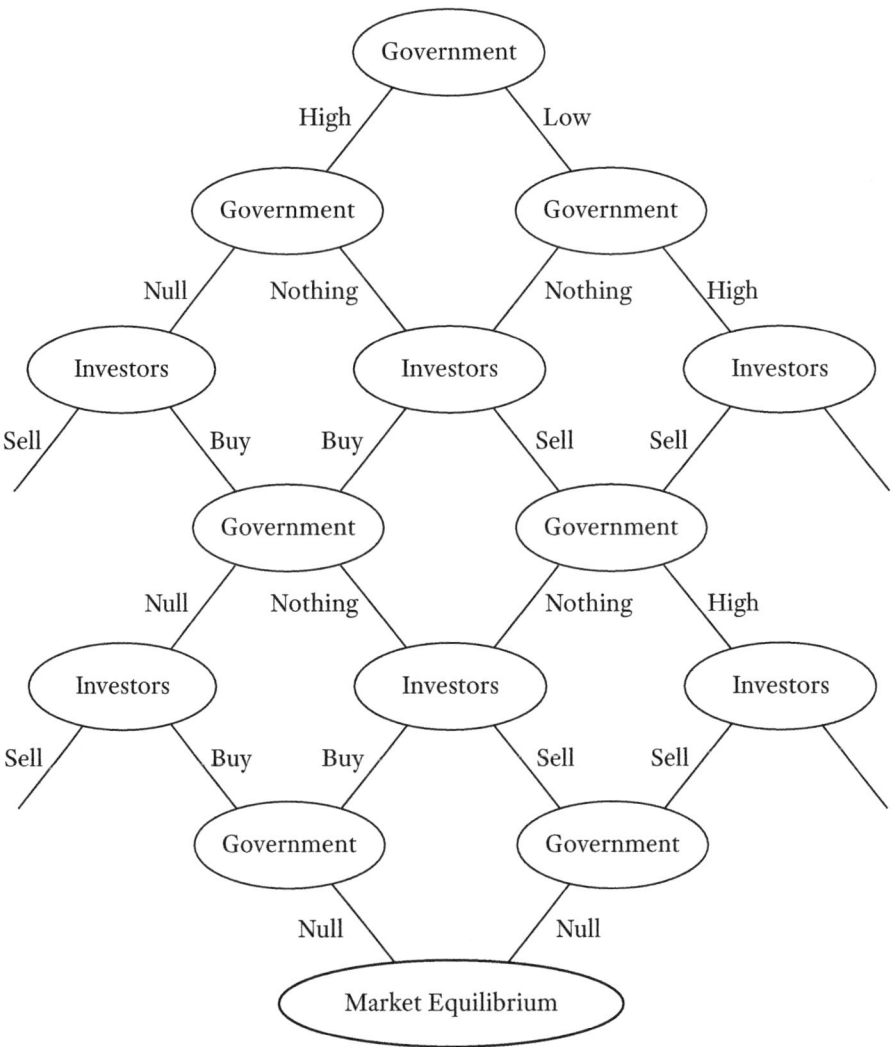

Figure 6-1 Game Tree between Government and Investors

In the first case, the market stock price is low, and the dynamic repeated game process between the government and investors.

When the stock price is low, the government chooses to issue favorable policies to make the stock price rise or not to issue policies and let the stock market adjust itself. In other words, when the stock price is low, there are two situations: the government takes regulatory measures and does not take regulatory measures.

(1) When favorable policies are introduced, the government intends to enhance investors' confidence in the market so that stock prices can rise; that is, the government chooses $P(S_1|W_2) = P_{11}$, and P_{11} is the probability that the government chooses favorable policies when the market prices are low. Investors have two choices. One is to buy stocks. In this case, investors believe that the probability $q = P(S_1|W_2) = 1$ of the stock market rising and the stock price rising is also in line with the government's policy intention. The government does not need to introduce continuous favorable policies for regulation and control, and investors can obtain the following benefits: $E(U_i) = \beta^t \cdot [(2q-1)\Delta P \cdot Q] = \beta^t \cdot \Delta P \cdot Q$. The other is that investors sell stocks, making stock prices continue to fall, which conflicts with the government's policy intention, and the government will introduce favorable measures for regulation. After the second favorable policy, the government intended to raise stock prices, and investors still faced two options: buying and selling stocks. Buying would be consistent with the government's policy intentions, and the market would move closer to the desired range of stock prices. If investors choose to sell, the government will continue introducing positive measures. This repeated game makes the market finally reach the ideal equilibrium state.

(2) In the absence of favorable policies, the government chooses $P(S_0|W_2) = 1 - P_{11}$. The government's original intention is to spontaneously return to the intrinsic value through the function of the internal market mechanism without government intervention, that is, the stock price rises. At this time, investors will also face two choices after the research and analysis of the market, that is, buy and sell. If the investor's behavior is to choose to buy, it is consistent with the government's intention, and the government does not need to introduce favorable policies for regulation. If investors choose to sell, the stock price will continue to fall, and the government should consider introducing favorable measures for adjustment or using the market's internal mechanism for spontaneous adjustment. After the introduction of good measures, investors will still have two choices, that is, buy or sell, so repeated game. In the absence of favorable policies, if an investor buys stocks, it can be regarded as the probability $q = P(S_1|W_2) = 1$ that the investor thinks the stock market will rise and the stock price will rise, which is also in line with the government's policy intention, so the government does not need to introduce favorable policies continuously for regulation and control. The returns to the investor are as follows:

$$E(U_i) = \beta^t \cdot [(2q-1)\Delta P \cdot Q] = \beta^t \cdot \Delta P \cdot Q \qquad (6\text{-}18)$$

In the second case, the market stock price is high, and the dynamic game process between the government and investors is repeated.

When the stock price is high, the government should choose to issue negative policies to make the stock price fall to restrain excessive speculation or choose not to issue policies and let the stock market adjust itself; that is, when the stock price is high, there are two situations: the government takes regulatory measures and does not take regulatory measures.

(1) In the case of negative policies, the government intends to curb excessive speculation and reduce stock price bubbles. That is, when the market price is high, the government chooses $P(S_2|W_1) = P_{22}$, P_{22} is the probability of the government choosing negative policies. Investors are faced with two choices: one is to sell, which makes the stock price fall. This situation is in line with the government's policy intention, and the government does not need to take negative measures continuously to curb the excessively high stock price, so investors can avoid losses by selling. In the stock market, where short selling is allowed, the investor gains by short selling. The posterior judgment of the investor on the market is: $1 - q = P(S_2|W_1) = 1$, the investor's return is $-E(U_i) = -\beta^t \cdot [(2q-1)\Delta P \cdot Q] = \beta^t \cdot \Delta P \cdot Q$. The other is to buy, so that stock prices continue to rise, which is in conflict with the government's policy intention, the government will continuously introduce negative measures to control. After the second negative policy, the government's policy intended to drive stock prices down, and investors were still faced with two options: buying and selling stocks. If it is to sell, it will be consistent with the government's policy intention, and the market will move closer to the desired range of stock prices. If investors choose to buy, the government will introduce successive negative measures. This repeated game makes the market finally reach the ideal equilibrium state.

(2) In the absence of negative policies, that is, the government chooses $P(S_0|W_1) = 1 - P_{22}$. The government's original intention is to spontaneously return to the intrinsic value through the internal mechanism of the market without government intervention, so as to reduce or eliminate stock market bubbles. At this time, investors will also face two choices after the research and analysis of the market, that is, buy and sell. If the investor's behavior is to sell, it is consistent with the government's intention, and the government does not need to introduce negative policies for regulation. If investors choose to buy, the stock price will continue to rise, and the government should consider taking negative measures to adjust or continue to use the internal mechanism of the market for spontaneous adjustment. In this case, investors will still have two choices after the government takes negative measures: buy or sell, so repeated game.

In the process of such repeated games, investors will gradually mature and be rational under the behavior of a rational government. When the market stock price is low or high, rational arbitrageurs will automatically make buying and selling transactions. Because rational arbitrageurs will predict that the government will introduce good or bad policies to regulate the market, they may trade ahead of the policies and finally make the market automatically achieve the ideal equilibrium state. At this time, the market is already in a state without government regulation, and the equilibrium will naturally form, which is the wonderful equilibrium of the stock market pursued by the government and also a sign that the stock market has entered a virtuous cycle and a healthy development.

But from another point of view, there will be insufficient or overreaction of the market when the government introduces good or bad policies. Under the condition that the stock market is not sufficiently responsive to information, the government should introduce more vigorous regulation policies continuously or at one time. Under the condition that the stock market overreacts to information, the government should make preparations for the corresponding negative or positive policies with less strength after the introduction of positive or negative policies, so as to avoid the phenomenon of price booms and busts. However, this will make the stock market form a game equilibrium time period and space period to extend or expand. However, the government can take advantage of its special status of regulating the economy and gradually cultivate a healthy concept conducive to the development of the stock market. The establishment of this concept of investors will naturally form a healthy stock market. Otherwise, the stock market will fall into a vicious cycle of decline—good—boom—bad—slump, which will not only affect the healthy development of the stock market, but also challenge the authority of the government.

6.4.3 *Analysis of Public Choice to Reduce Government Failure*

According to the research of Hu Jinyan (2002), the development practices of the stock markets all over the world show that the implementation of national macro policies will have a certain impact on the price trend of the stock market, but different markets have different sensitivity and reaction degrees to the policies, which is the so-called "policy effect" of the stock market. Theoretically speaking, we can summarize the effect of stock market policy into four basic forms: The first manifestation is "no policy effect," that is when the national macro policies are promulgated, the stock market not only has no expected price reaction before the promulgation of the policies, but also does regular random fluctuations along the original running track after the promulgation of the policies, and the market hardly reacts to the macro policies. The second manifestation is "insufficient policy response," that is, when a national macro policy is promulgated, the stock price index not only reacts up or down quickly on the policy release day, but also has an expected reaction even before the policy announcement day, and continues to rise or fall after the policy announcement. This situation shows that the stock price index's response to the macro policy is inadequate before and on the policy promulgation date, resulting in a delayed effect after the policy promulgation date. The third manifestation is "policy overreaction," that is, when the national macro policy is promulgated, the stock price index will react up or down quickly on the policy announcement date. Sometimes, there is an expected reaction before the policy announcement date, but the stock price index will decline or rise in the opposite direction after the policy announcement. This situation shows that there is an overreaction of the stock price index to macro policies before and on the promulgation date, and thus, the reverse correction occurs after the promulgation date. The fourth manifestation is "adequate policy response." In other words, when the national macro policy is promulgated, the stock price index quickly rises or falls on the policy announcement date but quickly returns to normal random fluctuations after the policy announcement. This indicates that the stock market has digested the information about the macro policy in time, so that the stock price index has been fully reflected.

In addition to the first case, the stock market in the other three cases has a "policy effect" on macro policies. However, the existence of a policy effect in the stock market does not necessarily mean that the stock market has "policy efficiency." According to the "efficient market hypothesis" proposed by Fama (1965) and other scholars, in the financial market, the word "efficiency" has a special meaning different from "Pareto efficiency." It means that in the financial market, if all the latest information can be fully digested by the market at every moment and reflected in the price of financial products, Then the market's response to information is "efficient," and the market is efficient. According to this definition, a stock market with "policy effect" on macro policies is "efficient" only in the fourth case above, namely "adequate policy response." That is to say, only when the stock market reacts quickly after the introduction of macro policies and puts the price response in place within a short period of time, can there be "policy efficiency." Neither "insufficient policy response" nor "excessive policy response" has complete policy efficiency. Seen from the actual performance of China's stock market in recent years, most of the time, it is overreacting to policies; that is, favorable policies often cause excessive increases, while negative policies often cause excessive declines.

Government measures to improve market efficiency can be taken from the following aspects:

First, help develop more institutional investors and provide retail investors with the necessary investment knowledge. In financial analysis, institutional investors are usually regarded as the representatives of rational investors. Compared with retail investors, institutional investors have stronger information sources, investment techniques, and psychological qualities and can avoid blindly chasing gains and dumping losses. At the same time, retail investors should be widely inculcated in investment concepts and investment techniques, so as to cultivate the behavior of investment rather than speculation in the Chinese stock market.

Second, speed up the primary stock market marketization process. Our country has always used fixed prices in the past; that is, the lead underwriters determine an issue price according to the result of valuation and the expectation of investors' demand. This fixed-price method is relatively simple but inefficient, and the scope for government intervention is large. Drawing on the IPO pricing experience of foreign countries, the China Securities Regulatory Commission launched the IPO inquiry mechanism on December 7, 2004. The IPO price was not determined in advance. Instead, the lead underwriter first determined the IPO price range, held a roadshow and promotion meeting, corrected the IPO price repeatedly according to the demand and demand price information, and finally determined the IPO price. The move, a key step toward market-based IPO pricing, should continue to reduce the government's power in securities issuance and transfer IPO pricing power to the market. On the other hand, we will gradually solve the problem of listing state-owned and legal shares, continue to implement the allocation and reduction of state-owned shares, reduce the proportion of state-owned shares to legal shares, and inject market forces. On March 21, 2014, the China Securities Regulatory Commission issued the preferred stock pilot management measures, which are of great significance to the marketization of China's primary stock issuance.

Third, reduce the trading cost of the stock market and improve the stock market supervision system. The development of price discovery ability needs to be realized through the buying and selling behavior of the stock market. The high transaction cost will affect the equilibrium price of the supply and demand balance, so that it cannot accurately reflect the real value of the enterprise. Therefore, we should strengthen the construction of the stock market, reduce transaction costs, reduce barriers to information transmission, and achieve high efficiency, high transparency, and high fairness. In addition, we will improve legal supervision and crack down on non-market behaviors such as insider information and artificial market price support.

6.5 Stock Market Government Risk and Its Prevention

Risk refers to the uncertainty or volatility of the future outcome. Here, we define risk as the loss of the corresponding subject's interest. The risk is relative to different subjects, such as investors, listed companies, securities brokers, and the government. When we analyze stock market risk, we always stand in investors' perspective. In fact, the same kind of risk is not a risk for all the participants, and different participants in the stock market take different risks. As one of the main bodies of stock market activities, the government mainly faces the following risks:

Short-term volatility risk. That is, in a relatively short period of time, there is a risk that stock prices will rise and fall sharply. The government does not want to see short-term drastic fluctuations, which may cause financial market volatility and even social unrest. This is a risk for the government, but it may not necessarily be a risk for investors, listed companies, and securities intermediaries. It may even be an opportunity for securities brokers, because sharp fluctuations are generally accompanied by increased trading volume and commission income.

Stock price deviation from intrinsic value risk, that is long-term risk. It is the risk that the stock price deviates too far from the intrinsic value. There are two situations in which the stock price deviates from the intrinsic value. First, it is too high, forming a bubble in the stock market. The second is too low, also known as a negative bubble. The former will increase the systemic risk of the stock market, which easily causes the stock crash and national economy turbulence, and the governments of various countries attach great importance to the stock market bubble. The latter will reduce the stock market or even lose the financing function. This risk is also a risk for investors and listed companies.

Fair trading risk, namely regulatory risk. Creating a fair, just, and open trading environment is the common goal pursued by all governments. Without fair trading, fraud and insider trading may occur in the market, which is very unfavorable to the healthy development of the stock market and one of the main manifestations of the government's stock market risk.

In this part, the stock market government risks of the above are classified and analyzed respectively for short-term risk, long-term risk, and market supervision behavior.

6.5.1 Short-Term Stock Price Fluctuation Risk and Government Behavior

Short-term volatility of the stock market is that the stock price rises and falls sharply in a short period of time, which is a phenomenon that all governments do not want to see. It is detrimental to economic stability and even social stability. The government should use various means to reduce the occurrence of this phenomenon. In China's stock market, the government's supervision and control behavior has not eliminated or reduced short-term fluctuations, but caused some short-term fluctuations due to the government's supervision and control behavior. When a policy or measure that has a great impact on the stock market is announced, it often causes a violent shock in the stock market, which is the immature performance of both the stock market investors and the government's control measures.

When the government announces information that has a great impact on the stock price, it will generally cause abnormal stock price fluctuations, which is the common dilemma faced by the government behavior in the stock market of all countries. We find that most of the time, government regulation and control measures have caused abnormal fluctuations in the stock market, which is the negative impact of government behavior on the stock market and contrary to the government's goal of stock market behavior. The government should further improve the means of supervision and control and avoid the introduction of strong measures as far as possible, so that the market can run smoothly. For example, in May 1997, when the government introduced several measures in succession rather than at one time, excessive speculation in the stock market was curtailed and did not cause a stock market crash. However, due to the randomness of the trend of stock prices and the sensitivity of the response to information, it is difficult for the stock market to reflect the direction and strength of the government's policies completely, which is also difficult for the government to regulate and supervise the stock market. A large number of empirical studies show that the stock market has both overreaction and underreaction to information, and the government must take this information reaction characteristic into account when regulating the stock market. Before introducing a regulation policy, the government cannot fully grasp the degree of market reaction to the policy. The same policy published at different times and occasions will produce different market reactions. This is a significant feature of the stock market, which is different from other market types. Regulating the stock market is not only a tool, but also an art.

The government behavior caused abnormal short-term fluctuations in the stock market. When the stock market rises and falls, the government uses negative and favorable policies to regulate the stock market. In several abnormal fluctuations in the downturn of the stock market (such as the August 1994 "market rescue," May 1996 to encourage investors to invest in the stock market, 1999 "5.19," 2001 "6.24," and the first half of 2006), the government has correctly corrected the stock market continued to be depressed, forming a reversal trend. Several unusual fluctuations during the stock market boom (e.g., February 1993, December 1996, May 1997, etc.) have been accurately curtailed the over speculations by the government. All these are enough to prove that the government behavior in China's stock market promotes the healthy development of the stock market, at least in the general direction. However, government regulation and control measures have often caused abnormal fluctuations in the stock market, which is the negative influence of government behaviors on the stock market. In fact, reducing or even eliminating short-term abnormal fluctuations is one of the government's behavioral goals in the stock market. However, in many cases, it backfires. Due to the sensitivity of stock prices to information, short-term abnormal fluctuations eventually happen. Therefore, the means of the supervision and control of government management departments should be further improved.

6.5.2   Risk of Stock Price Deviation from Intrinsic Value and Government Behavior

Deviation from intrinsic value indicates problems in market effectiveness. The government's monitoring of the market mainly starts from whether there are positive or negative bubbles in the market. Government behavior aims to correct these deviations from a long-term perspective.

1.   Distribution Characteristics of the P/E Ratio in Chinese Stock Market

Stock price deviation from intrinsic value can cause stock market failure. On the one hand, if the stock price is higher than the intrinsic value, too much will produce a stock market bubble, directly increasing the risk of the stock market. On the other hand, if the stock price is too much lower than its intrinsic value, the stock market will lose its financing function, which will destroy the resource allocation function of the stock market. This section selects the price-earnings ratio to analyze the risk of stock price deviation from intrinsic value. The P/E ratio is an indicator to determine the level of stock price from the profitability perspective. When the P/E ratio is too high, the stock price has exceeded its value. When the P/E ratio is too low, the stock price is below its value. Foreign theories on P/E ratio research have been relatively perfect. Benjamin Graham, the founder of modern securities analysis theory, first made a formal expression on the P/E ratio in his book Security Analysis. Based on his decades of experience in stock market investment, he believed that the P/E ratio of good stocks in general is about 15 times, and the P/E ratio of high-growth stocks can be higher, between 25 and 40 times. Fama and French et al. (1992) believe that there is a negative correlation between the P/E ratio and the stock yield. However, Fuller, Hubert, and Levinson et al. (1993) found that stocks with high P/E ratios had higher returns than those with low P/E ratios. Blanchard and Watson (1982), based on the rational expectation model of stock price, studied the P/E ratio of the stock market with probabilistic statistical methods. West (1998) discussed the inadequacy of stock price determination based on traditional models and proposed a "non-standardized" approach to price determination. Allen and Gorton (1993) believed that the P/E ratio of stock price originated from the spontaneous behavior of the market itself.

Many domestic scholars have studied the P/E ratio of China's stock market. Many scholars have published their own views or studied it from different perspectives. Wu Mingli (2001) analyzed that the P/E ratio of different stocks in China's stock market varies greatly, and it is not appropriate for insiders to use a simple average as the actual P/E ratio. Compared with the NASDAQ stock market, the bubble level of China's stock market is still acceptable. Li Honggang and Fu Qian (2002) estimated that the reasonable price-earnings ratio of China's stock market was between 8 and 24 based on the basic model of asset pricing and Chinese data. Therefore, they believed that the actual price-earnings ratio of China's stock market was high most of the time. Han Bing and Yan Bing (2004) believed that the P/E ratio is a dynamic indicator, which always changes from low to high and then from high to low. The current P/E ratio is the P/E ratio corresponding to the market interest rate and is in line with the basic national conditions of China.

2. Comparative Analysis of Theoretical P/E Ratio and Actual P/E Ratio of Chinese Stock Market

The "reasonable P/E ratio" is a quantifiable indicator. In the modern stock market, we calculate it by the stock price. According to capital asset pricing theory, the average return of the stock market should be equal to the risk-free interest rate plus the total risk-reward of the market. For the mature stock market, the reasonable P/E ratio should be the inverse of the average market return level, the theoretical P/E ratio. The one-year bank rate is usually regarded as the average yield level of the market.

From the experience of developed countries, the actual P/E ratio of the stock market is always smaller than the theoretical P/E ratio, and the difference between the two (i.e., the actual P/E ratio minus the theoretical P/E ratio) is the risk premium. Chinese stock market has also shown this feature since 1999. To accurately reflect the degree of risk premium, we introduce the risk premium rate:

$$\text{Risk premium rate} = \frac{\text{Actual P/E ratio} - \text{Theoretical P/E ratio}}{\text{Theoretical P/E ratio}} \quad (6\text{-}19)$$

At present, there is no unified opinion on how to quantify this index. The best choice here is to make a vertical and horizontal comparison. From the vertical point of view, it is compared with the development of China's stock market in recent years. It is compared with the developed countries' stock markets from a horizontal perspective.

From the historical changes in the P/E ratio of China's A-share market, the P/E ratio of China's stock market in 2013 has been at a low level for more than ten years, and the P/E ratio dropped rapidly after 2008 due to the continuous decline of the market. The highest risk premium for the Shanghai and Shenzhen stock markets was 173% and 216%, respectively, which was a big risk for investors. By the end of 2013, the risk premium level had fallen to −71% and −64%, respectively, and the characteristics of the stock market downturn and stock investment value emerged.

From the perspective of the price-earnings ratio index, the price-earnings ratio of A shares calculated by the weighted average of the total share capital at the end of December 2013 was about 12 times lower than that of the S&P 500 in the US stock market. From the perspective of the international comparison of the P/E ratio, the P/E ratio of Chinese (mainland) stocks has been much higher than that of the US and Hong Kong (China) markets in the past. However, by the end of 2012, it had been lower than that of the US market and only slightly higher than that of Hong Kong (China) market. From the comparison of the major stock markets in the world, we can find that the P/E ratio of the stock markets in New York, London, South Korea, Singapore, and Thailand fluctuated below 20 times most of the time before 1996, while the P/E ratio of the stock markets in Tokyo and Taiwan (China) was relatively high, mainly because there was a delayed process to digest the bubble accumulated by the excessive market speculation in the late 1980s. In 1992, the Tokyo stock market traded at a low average of 13.2 times, 23.5 times lower than Taiwan's average of 36.7 times earnings. However, by 1994, Tokyo's average P/E jumped to the top, reaching 79.5 times, up 66.3 from 1992 and 66.8 times higher than New York's average P/E of 12.7. Since then, the average P/E ratio of the Tokyo stock market has continued to rise, reaching 85.55 times in 1996. Between 1992 and 1999, the average P/E ratio of the Tokyo stock market not only far exceeded the average P/E ratio of major stock markets in the world during the same period, but also kept first place in the world stock market P/E ratio and further widened the gap with the stock market at a lower P/E level.

However, due to the wide variation of listed companies in different markets, risk premiums in different markets are also different, and due to other factors, the P/E ratio cannot be simply compared. However, the comparison at least suggests that the level of stock prices in the Chinese market is relatively low. Because China's economic growth rate is relatively fast, the economic growth rate is higher, and the actual P/E ratio is generally higher to be more reasonable.

Around the world, the average P/E ratio of the stock market is influenced by a number of factors, the most important of which are the economic potential of the market's location and market interest rates. The experience of mature stock markets is that the P/E ratio moves up and down within an investment range depending on a number of factors. This is because a higher P/E ratio means higher investment risk and lower investment value, indicating a more speculative atmosphere in the market and a larger bubble component. Therefore, the overall high P/E ratio will be difficult to sustain for a long time, and any excessive speculation will inevitably be punished by the law of the market, and the stock price will inevitably return to the reasonable value center. This is true in Japan, Taiwan (China), and other emerging markets. At the same time, we must also recognize that we cannot use a static view to set the standard for the stock market P/E ratio.

Therefore, from 2013 to 2014, China's stock market was at a low level, which had a high investment value from both vertical and horizontal comparisons. Since the bear market of China's stock market lasted for several years after 2008, the severe downturn in stock prices has become an adverse factor in economic growth, because the direct impact of the market downturn is the destruction of the financing function of the stock market, and then the crisis of resource allocation and the play of the function of "barometer." Therefore, the government should support China's stock market and take some active policies to promote the stock market to return to its intrinsic value.

6.5.3 *Government Regulatory Behaviors to Prevent Stock Market Risks*

The goal of securities regulation is to create a "fair, just, and open" market trading environment, which is a sign of the healthy development of the stock market. In order to effectively deal with the problems caused by the failure of the stock market, protect the interests of investors, maintain the safety and stability of the stock market, promote the development of the securities market, and thus promote the sustainable, stable, and coordinated development of the economy and society, we must organically integrate various regulatory resources including the government, market self-regulatory organizations, and social forces, and reasonably design the securities regulatory system to solve the question of who should supervise the securities market and how.

1. Basic Requirements of Stock Market Supervision

After more than 20 years of development in securities regulation, our stock market has made great achievements. However, there is still a long way to go for the improvement and development of the regulatory system. In fact, the market of developed countries is the same. Moreover, China's securities market is an emerging market with a history of only more than 20 years. There are inevitably problems, and the supervision of the securities market is an eternal theme. At present, China's stock market regulation should be improved in the following three aspects.

First, from a macro perspective, the government's goal of developing the stock market should be shifted from helping state-owned enterprises raise low-cost funds at this stage to maintaining the consistency of interests between enterprises and investors, effectively allocating resources, improving the financial structure, reducing financial risks and promoting the upgrading of China's industrial structure. As a bridge and link between financiers and investors, the stock market connects the supply and demand of funds directly and closely, which makes this direct financing method have an extraordinary effect compared with traditional indirect financing with banks as the main body. With the deepening of economic system reform and financial market, the government should fully realize the deep functions of the stock market and give full play to the superiority of the stock market as a production factor market in the allocation of resources. The stock market has a more direct allocation effect than the commodity market in terms of resource allocation. Its open bidding trading mode makes its cost lower. The powerful evaluation, selection, and supervision mechanism also optimizes the allocation of capital resources. With the establishment of the modern enterprise system, acquisition, merger, property rights transfer, and transaction have become the new growth points of China's stock market, which provides a good opportunity and a broad stage for the shaping of the stock market resource allocation mechanism and the play of the resource allocation function. Through the innovation of the operation mode of "backdoor listing" and "reverse merger," it can promote the reasonable flow of capital at the lowest cost and the fastest speed, promote the optimal allocation of stock assets to the maximum extent, realize the effective reorganization of the stock of assets, and truly realize the separation of government and enterprise, and finally promote and realize the advanced industrial structure.

Second, the government should gradually improve and perfect the self-regulatory rules of the securities exchange market and grant it enough authority to enhance its ability to fight against risks. Although our stock exchange has established basic rules and regulations on the basis of referring to foreign experience and summarizing our own experience and lessons, the rules for the settlement of market disputes, the rules for the prevention and treatment of large financial risks, and the rules for the substantial supervision and management of market participants have not been completely established. Therefore, the government should establish and improve the self-regulatory rules and regulations of the stock exchange, so as to carry out comprehensive and multi-angle management of securities brokerages, listed companies, insider trading, and acquisitions and mergers. On the whole, our security market is still a closed domestic market and is not a fully open trading market. Therefore, the government should open the securities market in a planned way according to the needs of our economic development, so as to introduce the successful experience of the international securities market and accelerate the standardized development of our securities market.

Third, the government should establish and improve the scientific market supervision system. The supervision system of the securities market should combine the supervision of the regulatory body with the self-discipline of the market participants and establish a scientific and effective supervision system of the securities market. In terms of market regulation, the government should promote and maintain the openness, fairness, and justice of the market and punish favoritism and irregularities by establishing an adequate information disclosure system, so as to improve investors' confidence in the market. In addition, the government should also strengthen efforts to regulate the intermediary institutions in the securities market, so that accounting firms, law firms, and asset appraisal agencies can really play their due role as intermediaries.

2. International Comparison of Stock Market Regulation

In the mature stock market, the main task of government supervision is to remove the obstacles that the market economy system described by Western economics cannot overcome, such as monopoly and manipulation, internal problems caused by information failure, and so on. Compared with emerging markets, regulators in countries such as the United States and the United Kingdom generally view their regulatory functions less from a "development" perspective, considering such issues as achieving the amount of capital to be raised in securities markets and keeping an eye on and maintaining a certain level and volatility in stock indexes. More often, these problems are left to the market itself, which relies on the "invisible hand" to regulate itself.

The emerging securities market is different. If the regulatory functions of the governments of developed countries are generally called "normative" functions, the governments of new countries also have a "development" function in addition to "normative" functions, which are given priority by the government. Any emerging markets, without exception, need to solve more serious "standardization" problems caused by the above-mentioned monopoly, manipulation, and incomplete information. However, when we give richer and deeper meaning to the failures of emerging securities markets and reveal the special reasons behind them, government regulators in emerging markets need to assume more varied and complex responsibilities than those in mature markets in this sense. This "development" function has two meanings. First, it refers to the government's institutional innovation and cultivation of the securities market. At the same time, it "actively" creates a macroeconomic environment to ensure the development of the securities market. The second is that the government "consciously" pays more attention to other social and economic aspects related to the securities market. Therefore, the selection of a supervision system for emerging securities markets faces more stringent constraints.

The inevitability of the failure of the securities market and the objective needs of the economic society for the function of the securities market determine the necessity of supervision. Due to the failure of the securities market, the government should actively intervene in the securities market. However, in dealing with the relationship between the government and the securities market, the government essentially needs to realize the balance between the market failure and the government failure and calculate the cost between the government's laissez-faire and the government intervention.

Due to the differences between the regulatory decision-making framework and the regulatory system of Western developed countries, "institutional loopholes" and a large number of "strong administrative" institutional arrangements that are unavoidable in the early stage of the construction of emerging markets facilitate the breeding and spread of rent-seeking behaviors. Among them, the most typical is the management system of "quota issuance." Under this kind of institutional arrangement with obvious planning color, it is precisely because the supply elasticity of the "listing quota" is insufficient that the supply cannot be increased without limit, thus generating the excess rent income and the corresponding rent-seeking behaviors of local enterprises and local governments. On the one hand, this kind of rent-seeking causes the unproductive loss of economic resources. On the other hand, it distorts the optimization mechanism of resource allocation in the securities market and seriously damages the improvement of efficiency and the embodiment of fairness.

Whether emerging market countries should adopt a certain securities supervision system or a combination of several supervision systems actually depends on a country's government regulators' target positioning of various effect indicators under certain historical conditions, as well as the cost needed to implement these supervision systems. In a certain historical stage and specific national conditions, a government will determine its goal expectation of the effects brought by the implementation of a certain regulatory system due to the objective limitations and subjective considerations of the level and structure of economic development, social politics and culture, financial system, social and economic development and reform strategy, legal construction and humanistic concept. In this way, the optimal choice of securities supervision system lies in the pursuit of the lowest total implementation cost of the supervision system on the premise of satisfying a government's established goals or preferences for various indicators under certain historical conditions.

Under different historical conditions, the choice of securities supervision system is subject to the different emphasis of government objectives. For example, at the beginning of an emerging market, it often adopts a substantive review system and good management of listed enterprises. One reason is that investors' irrationality and lack of knowledge and intelligence in emerging markets are far more serious than those in mature markets, so the government attaches a higher value to the index of "investor rationality and cultivation." In this historical condition, the effect value of the substantive audit system on the index is large, so the regulator must choose this system to meet the target value of the index. The difference in the target orientation of the government supervisors in different countries determines the choice of the core of the relevant securities supervision system. In Western mature markets, the core of the securities legal system is to protect the interests of investors, and regulators do not directly intervene in the amount of capital formation and industrial composition, while the supervision of emerging countries is quite different.

The key to the success or failure of securities regulation lies in the proper government design. Some problems may indeed be caused by regulatory failure or government failure, but this should not be the reason for deregulation, but the government's regulation design and implementation problems, so what needs to be done is not to reduce or deny regulation but to adjust and improve regulation. As some scholars have argued, it is important that government interventions are well designed, with appropriate regulatory objectives, principles, and scope, and carefully implemented. This is one of the conclusions of our economic analysis of the regulatory nature of emerging markets.

The biggest feature and advantage of the securities regulatory system of the United States is it gives full play to the respective advantages of various regulatory resources such as government regulation, market self-discipline, and social supervision, and strives to find a balance between government regulation and market mechanism. It ensures the prudent, steady, and safe operation of securities market players through necessary regulation, realizing the stability of the entire financial system, protecting the interests of investors and the public, and promoting the innovation ability and efficiency of the securities industry through regulation. Before the stock market crash of 1929, the United States federal government did not establish a strong securities regulator. After the crisis, the United States federal government and Congress adopted a series of measures to strengthen the supervision of the securities market. One of them was the establishment of the Federal Securities and Exchange Commission (SEC) according to the Securities Exchange Act of 1934. As a national securities regulator, the SEC implemented comprehensive and unified management of the securities market, thus creating a securities supervision model of centralized and unified supervision by the government. This model has been copied by many countries.

3. Analysis and Evaluation of China's Stock Market Supervision

(1) Supervision mode of China's securities market
At present, the securities market of our country implements a centralized and unified supervision system, namely government supervision as the leading, centralized

supervision and market self-regulation of the combination of the market regulatory framework. a) Regulatory body. The main body of securities supervision in our country, CSRC, will establish a centralized and unified securities futures supervision system. According to the regulations, all parts of the country will set up supervisory agencies and implement vertical management, strengthen the supervision of the securities futures industry, improve the quality of information disclosure, resolve securities and futures market risks, and maintain market stability. However, in reality, there are diversified phenomena among Chinese regulatory bodies, and the relationship between the departments in charge is complicated and discordant. b) Self-discipline organization. Self-discipline organization is an indispensable part of the capital market supervision system. There are two forms of self-discipline organization: social supervision organization and industry self-discipline. Social supervision organizations include intermediary services in the securities industry, such as certified public accountants and accounting firms, lawyers and law firms, auditors, and audit firms. After the CSRC confirms their qualification to engage in securities-related business, examine and approve the financial reports, asset evaluation reports, prospectus, and legal opinions of securities issuing enterprises according to national laws and regulations, implement social supervision, and assume corresponding responsibilities. Industry self-discipline includes two aspects: one is the stock exchange field self-discipline. The stock exchange supervises the trading of its members in the stock exchange and also plays an important role in the supervision of listed companies and members of securities brokerages. The second is the self-discipline of OTC trading. Securities Association of China is a national self-regulatory organization for the securities industry, which was established with the approval of the People's Bank of China, granted qualification by the China Securities Regulatory Commission, and approved and registered by the Ministry of Civil Affairs. It regulates over-the-counter securities transactions and ensures their fairness and standardization by formulating and implementing industry-wide self-regulatory systems. c) Regulatory system. Before 1998, the Chinese securities market and supervision were carried out through a series of administrative regulations, including nationwide administrative regulations and local regulations. In 1998, the *Securities Law of the People's Republic of China* was passed by the National People's Congress, marking that our country's securities market governing by law had entered a new stage. The *Securities Law* and *Company Law* are the legal basis of the supervision of the securities market in our country, and other securities administration laws and regulations make up the regulatory system of the securities market in our country.

(2) The main problems of supervising the system of Chinese securities market
First, the functions of securities regulators need to be strengthened urgently. At present, insiders generally believe that the main reason for the weak supervision of Chinese securities market lies in the inadequate regulatory powers of CSRC, and even calls for

proper direct "judicial intervention." In fact, according to relevant provisions, the China Securities Regulatory Commission has the right to investigate and take evidence, the right to inquire, the right to consult and copy relevant materials, the right to inquire, the right to apply for freezing, and other specific regulatory powers. These powers are actually very close to the power of the United States Federal Securities and Exchange Administration Commission. If relevant laws and regulations are effectively implemented, strong supervision over the securities market can be formed. The power of "judicial intervention" is not needed to improve work efficiency. In fact, the main reason for the inefficiency of our securities market supervision comes from the supervision system itself. The main problem of our securities supervision system is that the supervision is divided into functions and regions, affecting the supervision policy's efficiency.

Second, the securities market supervision law needs to be improved. The related laws of securities supervision are not perfect, which brings some difficulties in governing the market according to the law. Although the *Securities Law* has come into effect, there are still some imperfections. In addition, the *Company Law* related to the *Securities Law* also has the problem of weak operability. For example, the *Securities Law* prohibits market manipulation, insider trading, and defrauding customers. Violators will be fined, warned, and disqualified, and those who commit crimes will be sentenced according to law. There is no provision for civil compensation for investors' losses. Although our country, like other civil law countries, has a civil law, namely, *General Principles of the Civil Law*, it has a general regulation on damage compensation. However, it lacks the corresponding regulation to the special nature of securities disputes. However, the *Securities Law* puts the emphasis of legal liability on administrative punishment and criminal liability and only makes some brief and weak provisions on civil compensation. In fact, in mature foreign markets, whether listed companies disclose false information or intermediaries break the law, they will not only be punished by the regulators, but also investors can sue them for compensation. However, in our country, most of the listed companies and intermediaries only have administrative penalties after violating the law, and investors cannot recover their losses and become the biggest victims. It can be said that the existing laws in our country are rather weak in protecting the interests of investors who have suffered losses due to fraud.

Third, the level of securities supervision needs to be improved. The government often uses policy means to regulate the stock market, which turns the stock market into a policy market and information market, and the government becomes the biggest "banker" in the securities market. Some management policies are not scientific and rational, do not conform to international practices, and even aggravate the market's instability. In addition, the policy also lacks rationality regarding the illegal funds in the market.

Fourth, the regulation of listed companies needs to be strengthened. Listed companies are the cornerstone of the stock market. However, the listed companies in China's stock market tend to have excellent performance in the first year, even in the second year, and ST in the third year. The huge amount of money swallowed in the stock market soon evaporated without a trace, and investors' rights and interests became a luxury. The financing channels of listed companies have been continuously broadened, from rights issues and additional issues to convertible bonds; listed companies have diversified their direct financing methods, the threshold of refinancing has been lowered, and the financing capacity and scale of financing have been rapidly improved. Because financing does not need to pay costs, "raising money for the sake of raising money" has become the guiding ideology of listed companies, and the operating conditions of enterprises have not been improved. At the same time, due to the weak supervision, the fund operation of listed companies is quite random; the phenomenon of idle funds raised by listed companies is very serious.

Fifth, self-discipline management in name only. First of all, the industry's self-discipline function is not strong. At present, except for the two stock exchanges, which belong to a kind of industry self-regulatory organization to some extent, exercising part of supervision over its member institutions and listed companies on the floor, the securities industry association, as a non-governmental association of the industry, is still in a very weak position. However, due to the lack of legal mechanisms corresponding to the rights and responsibilities of the stock exchange, the performance is too much in pursuit of profit and neglects its due supervision function. At the same time, due to the fierce competition and lack of unity and coordination, the stock exchange cannot effectively perform the responsibility of protecting the interests of investors. In the execution of arbitration and punishment functions, there is a tendency to favor its members. Secondly, social supervision organizations do not play their due role. Among them, the most prominent problem belongs to certified public accountants and accounting firms. Generally speaking, the practice level of Chinese securities-qualified firms is low, mainly caused by the following two problems: first, the accounting statements audited by certified public accountants are distorted, including accounting errors and non-disclosure of information as required. In order to whitewash the accounting statements, many listed companies falsely increase profits, falsely increase assets, or falsely reduce liabilities in various ways. However, the firm either fails to find out in the audit process or still confirms the discovery and publishes inappropriate audit opinions. In terms of the disclosure of major events of listed companies, some major related transactions, major contingencies, non-recurring profit and loss items, etc., are not fully disclosed. The firm does not propose to the company during the audit process, nor does it disclose in the audit report, and issues inappropriate audit opinions. Second, accounting firms do not carry out audit business in accordance with the requirements of independent auditing standards and other craft norms. For example, many important accounting statements do not carry out necessary audit procedures and are confirmed without sufficient and appropriate audit evidence. The types of audit opinions issued by audit reports are improper, the audit projects lack quality control, the necessary review work is not in place, the preparation of audit working papers is not standardized, and the management is not rigorous. Some of them do not even practice in accordance with the requirements of independent auditing standards, and the overall quality and level of practice are obviously low. They do not have the professional competence required by securities-qualified firms.

4. The Future Trend of China's Stock Market Regulation

Securities market regulation aims to protect investors, ensure a fair, efficient, and transparent market, and reduce systemic risks. The construction of China's securities market supervision system should focus on the realization of the above goals. After China enters the WTO, it is objectively required that the supervision system of China's securities market should be in line with international practices as soon as possible. On the basis of fully considering the development status of China's securities market, we should draw lessons from the supervision experience of other countries and improve the supervision system of China's securities market. On the whole, the goal pattern of our securities market supervision is: based on establishing a set of perfect securities supervision laws, under the centralized and unified supervision of a single securities regulator, giving full play to the role of self-regulatory organizations, forming a regulatory system of government supervision and market self-regulation to coordinate the operation of their responsibilities. Specific aspects are as follows:

(1) Gradually improve and refine the laws on securities market supervision, so as to form a consistent legal system with strong operability. In particular, a civil compensation system should be established as soon as possible. The implementation of the civil compensation system can enable the majority of investors to protect their interests through the exercise of civil litigation and participate in the regulation of the market, but also ease the regulatory pressure of the CSRC. Faced with the prospect of civil claims, securities fraudsters weigh the costs of breaking the law and are faced with the prospect of high civil claims and administrative fines, as well as the prospect of protracted litigation; fraud can surely be curtailed to some extent.

(2) Realize the centralized and unified supervision of our securities market. In this respect, we can learn from the supervision mode of foreign developed securities markets. Information provided by the World Bank indicates that most countries have only one main securities regulator, as a single regulator would provide the most practical solution for the development of securities markets. For example, the SEC is the highest administrative organ of securities regulation in the United States. It is the three economic management departments parallel with the Federal Reserve and the Treasury Department. It has legislative, law enforcement, and quasi-judicial powers, independently exercises comprehensive supervision over the securities market, and integrates all management powers of the securities market. Under the premise of being

accountable to the Congress, carry out efficient supervision. In view of this, with the development of our securities market, diversified management should be replaced by a single regulator, so as to realize the centralized and unified management of our securities market. Only in this way can we improve the supervision efficiency of the securities market.

(3) Deepen the concept of market economic freedom and reduce government intervention in the market. The basic function of the securities market is to optimize the allocation of resources; that is, the economic subject with clear property rights decides the price through sufficient competition, and realizes the optimal allocation of resources under the guidance of price. Therefore, the foothold of government regulation should be to maintain the "three public" principles of the market, namely openness, fairness, and justice, instead of introducing some policies from time to time to affect the normal market operation for the so-called risk control. The government's direct participation in the market increases the uncertainty of the market. In fact, it increases the risk of the market. It also hurts the confidence of market participants. Therefore, the government's supervision concept of the securities market should be transferred from controlling risks to revealing risks. If risks can be fully disclosed through regulation, risk control will naturally become the conscious reaction and action of market participants such as investors, listed companies, and intermediaries. As a matter of fact, the government uses administrative methods to regulate some indicators in the market, which essentially shows some problems in the transformation of government functions that should be paid full attention to. It is important for governments to put in place institutions that ensure that markets work fairly and efficiently. At the same time, state-owned shareholders should act in accordance with the law and not use the authority and power of the government to participate in the affairs of listed companies. On the contrary, the state's management of the securities market should not be considered from the standpoint of shareholders but from the standpoint of the public. Only in this way can it be conducive to the healthy development of the securities market.

(4) Strengthen self-discipline management in the supervision of China's securities market. Self-discipline management has its rationality: a) The spontaneity of self-discipline management. Without an orderly market, market participants cannot maximize their profits. Therefore, driven by the interest mechanism, the participants in the securities market have the internal motivation to maintain the market order spontaneously. b) The irreplaceability of self-discipline management. It is difficult for the government to regulate the grey area of the securities market. The credit standards of the securities practitioners and the mutual restraint between the peers can restrain them, so as to maintain the normal market order. c) Self-discipline management is a kind of expert management. d) The efficiency of self-discipline management is higher. There are no complicated rules and regulations in self-discipline management, and it is easy to operate, but it needs certain conditions to play its role. From the perspective of law,

the self-regulatory body must be recognized and authorized by law and support its rules and regulations, in order to have a binding force on the object of its regulation. From the perspective of the interests of the constrained, only when the objects of regulation accept the self-discipline rules can bring them long-term interests, and the violation of the self-discipline rules will bring them loss of interests, can they have the motivation of self-discipline and mutual supervision. In general, self-regulation is a method of low cost and high efficiency in the long run, so we should strengthen the self-regulation mechanism of our securities regulation.

CHAPTER 7

Research on the Matching Cycle between the Stock Market and Economic Growth Based on Market Efficient Cycle Theory

The deviation between the share price index, which reflects changes in the stock market, and the GDP growth rate, which reflects changes in economic growth, is only a temporary phenomenon. Over a long enough period, the two must match each other. The matching cycle of the stock market and economic growth is the efficient cycle of the market. The matching cycle between the stock market and economic growth reflects the relationship between the stock market and economic growth. In fact, it is common for them to deviate at a certain point or time period. But there is no long-term deviation or permanent deviation. According to the long-run equilibrium theory, it is inevitable to find a period of time to make the two match, that is, the matching cycle between the stock market and economic growth. The shorter the matching cycle between the stock market and economic growth, the higher the efficiency of the stock market to discover value or reflect economic growth. Otherwise, it gets worse. In other words, the shorter the matching period, the healthier the development of the stock market, the clearer the response of the stock market to economic growth, and the more coordinated the development of the two. The main reason why traditional studies analyze whether the two deviate and come to different conclusions is the selection of sample data for empirical studies. To put it simply, the stock market is changing every day, so we cannot demand that it also has a strong correlation with economic growth. This chapter focuses on how long the matching between the two is in the time period, to find out how long the matching between the two, that is, to study the matching period of the two. From the point of view of long-run equilibrium, there must be a time period long enough for the two to match.

7.1 The Question of the Matching Cycle between the Stock Market and Economic Growth Proposed

On the relationship between economic growth and the stock market, there are a lot of research results in the theoretical circle, and the conclusions are no more than two kinds: one is the empirical research evidence of a strong correlation between the two, and the other is the empirical research evidence of their deviation. Here, we think that they must match over a long period of time. A large number of empirical studies in the theoretical circle hold that the deviation between the stock market and economic growth is mainly due to the results brought by the sample interval of empirical tests. The key to our study of this problem is not to test whether the two deviate, but to find out the time period when the two are matching.

The relationship between the stock market and economic growth is embodied in the relationship between the stock price index change reflecting the change of the stock market and the GDP growth rate reflecting the economic growth. The meaning of the matching cycle between the stock market and economic growth is expressed as follows: The change rate of the stock price index, which reflects the range of stock changes, and the GDP growth rate, which reflects the economic growth index, do not match each other at any time point or in a specific time period. There must be a long enough time period for the two to have a strong correlation or mutual matching, and this time period is defined as the matching cycle between the stock market and economic growth. While stock prices rise and fall all the time, economic growth rates change much more slowly. In other words, in the short term, it is normal for the stock market to deviate from economic growth at a certain time point or within a specific period of time, and the shorter the time period, the more irregular the correlation between the two is, which is a normal feature. However, in the long run, the two will match each other, and the formation of long-term equilibrium is inevitable. From the matching relation of the two, the shorter the matching cycle, the stronger the reflection function of the stock market on economic growth, and the better the stock market can play the role of economic "barometer." The longer the matching period is, the longer the deviation time is, and the poorer the stock market reflects the economic growth.

The stock price may lag behind the economic growth index for a period of time and exceed the economic growth index for a certain period of time. Still, in the long run, the stock price index and economic growth should match each other; that is to say, the stock market and economic growth should be highly correlated, and the stock market can reflect various information on economic development. The factors that affect the stock price will work together. In different economic entities (countries or regions), the matching time period of the two is different. When empirical researchers choose different time periods to test the two, they definitely come to different conclusions. Because the price index cannot be consistent with economic growth at any time, they test the conclusion that the two deviate from each other. If they match each other at every point in time, the market has reached an absolutely efficient state, which is Fama's efficient market. However, the fluctuation of the stock market has strong randomness, while the economic development indicators do not change at any time. Compared with the stock market, the economic development indicators have a certain stability; that is to say, the stock market cannot have a high correlation with the economic growth indicators every day, and it is impossible for the stock market to deviate from economic growth in a long period of time. In particular, it is not scientific to test the correlation between the data of the Chinese stock market and economic growth for several years. It is only 20 years since the establishment of China's stock market in 1990, and there are only a few listed companies at the beginning and then dozens of listed companies, which is very weak in the representation of the whole Chinese economy. Therefore, testing the long-term correlation between the two is bound to have more serious limitations.

What determines the rise and fall of the stock market is the growth in the performance of listed companies, and the performance of many listed companies ultimately determines the growth of the entire national economy. However, the changes of the two will not always keep pace with each other. The stock market has its own independent operation, which is not an honest reflection of economic growth indicators. Economic growth or recession determines whether the stock market goes up or down. Conversely, the bulls and bears of the stock market can provide sufficient financing opportunities for economic development and, in a sense, can determine economic growth. The stock price index and economic growth should match each other; that is to say, the stock market and economic growth should be highly correlated. The stock market can reflect various information on economic development, and the various factors affecting the stock price work together. It is just that the matching time period of the two is different in different countries. Empirical researchers would definitely come to different conclusions when choosing different time periods to test the two. In fact, it is impossible for the stock market to deviate from economic growth for a long time. If the above result occurs, it will mean that investors have been irrational for a long time, and arbitrage behavior does not exist, which must be contradictory to reality. The shorter the matching cycle between the stock market and economic growth, the stronger the effectiveness of the stock market.

In the research on the relationship between economic growth and the stock market, a lot of evidence shows that the rise and fall of the stock market is a period of time ahead of economic growth. Scholars summarize it as "the stock market is the 'barometer' of economic growth." From this economic phenomenon, we can conclude that the stock market also plays an important role in economic growth. We cannot simply conclude that the stock market is determined by economic growth, and the two should complement each other. When the economy is in recession, the stock market will be the first to start rising, promoting economic growth or restraining the economic recession. It has a driving effect on the economy, because the rising stock market will increase the financing opportunities of listed companies and increase investors' income, expanding investment demand and consumption demand; expanding demand means promoting economic growth. On the contrary, when the economy is overheating, if the stock market is the first to fall, it will inhibit the overheating of the economy. In fact, the recession wouldn't have been as bad, or the Great Depression wouldn't have been as bad, if the stock market hadn't crashed in the first place in 1929.

According to the general equilibrium theory of economics and the arbitrage theory of finance, the matching cycle of the stock market and economic growth proposed in this chapter will be theoretically deduced.

First, according to general equilibrium theory and arbitrage theory, when the stock market is in an unbalanced state, the stock price is lower or higher than its intrinsic value. From the perspective of the stock market as a whole, if the growth of the stock return rate lags behind the growth of the macroeconomy, the stock price is undervalued on the whole, and in the long run, the stock price will rise. On the other hand, if the growth of stock returns exceeds the growth of the macroeconomy, stock prices are generally overvalued, and in the long run, stock prices will fall. Its theoretical basis is arbitrage theory. When the price of a stock is lower than or higher than its intrinsic value, rational arbitrageurs will automatically correct the pricing deviation of the market at a certain point through arbitrage behavior, so that the price of a stock tends to its intrinsic value.

Secondly, according to behavioral finance theory, arbitrageurs should be rational market actors in a general sense. The arbitrage behavior will make the stock price return to the intrinsic value and form a matching cycle between the stock market and economic growth in the long run. However, if the arbitrageurs are irrational, although the irrational investment behavior may cause the stock price to deviate further from the intrinsic value, the random trader behaviors will cancel each other out. Each trader may not be rational, and their trading behaviors will tend to be average rational when combined. In the long run, the stock market plays the basic function of price discovery and makes stock price return to intrinsic value.

According to general equilibrium theory and arbitrage theory, we use market efficient cycle theory to analyze and study here. Market efficient cycle means that there must be a long enough time cycle in the stock market, so that the stock price can fully reflect all the information affecting the stock price in this period, and then the stock market is an efficient market. In the long run, stock markets and economic growth must match each other. It is impossible for the market to fully reflect all information at every time point. According to the market efficient cycle theory, the market is efficient in a period of time; that is, the average price of the market in a certain period of time fully reflects all information in a period of time, which means the market is efficient. The reaction of the stock market to information is a process rather than a quick realization. Gao Hongzhen and Lin Jiayong (2005) believed that market information transmission and price response were conditional and needed time. In the real securities market, due to the imperfect rationality of investors, information transmission and price response could not be completed immediately.

The stock market can reflect various information on economic development, and various factors affecting the stock price will work together. In different economic entities (countries or regions), the matching time period of the two is different. Empirical researchers definitely reach different conclusions when choosing different time periods to test the two. Because stock price indexes cannot always keep pace with economic growth, some empirical studies conclude that the two deviate from each other. If they match each other at every point in time, the market is absolutely efficient, which is what Fama calls the efficient market. But in fact, such perfectly efficient markets are not realistic. Among the two variables of the stock market and economic growth, the fluctuation of the stock market has a strong randomness, and the economic growth index does not change as frequently. Compared with the stock market, it has a certain stability; that is to say, at least the stock market cannot have a high correlation with the economic growth index at every moment. Nor can stock markets deviate from economic growth for very long periods of time. The operation of the stock market has its own independence and is not an honest reflection of economic growth indicators.

There is no doubt that stock price changes are random at a certain point in time, but in the long run, the stability of stock price fluctuations will appear strong. From the perspective of behavioral finance, the investor behavior that determines the stock market changes has a great impact on the market and directly determines the stock price trend. In the short run, investors can be irrational or even impulsive. In the long run, the average rationality will be formed. Under the behavior of arbitrage, the average behavior of the whole market will become rational, and the stock price will return to the intrinsic value, realizing that the stock price reflects the performance changes of listed companies and then making the whole stock market reflect the changes of the macroeconomy. Finally, we find that the deviation between the change rate of the stock price index reflecting the change in the stock market and the change rate of GDP reflecting economic growth is only a temporary phenomenon. In a long enough period of time, the two must match each other.

Therefore, for a long period of time, irrational behavior and market inefficiency will be spontaneously corrected under the action of the market mechanism. Although the corrected behavior is not properly realized at any point in time, there is also a deviation phenomenon, which is manifested that the stock price may be higher or lower than its intrinsic value, but in the long run, the security deviating from its intrinsic value will return to its intrinsic value. The stock market rises or falls when the economy booms or busts. Conversely, bull and bear markets in the stock market can provide sufficient or insufficient financing opportunities for economic development and can influence or even determine economic growth in a certain sense.

To sum up, the meaning of the matching cycle between the stock market and economic growth is expressed as follows: the stock price index reflecting the range of stock changes and the GDP growth rate reflecting the economic growth index do not match each other at any time point or in a specific period of time. However, there must be a long enough period for the two to have a strong correlation or mutual matching, and this period is defined as the matching cycle between the stock market and economic growth.

7.2 Review of Research on Correlation between Stock Market and Economic Growth

The deviation between the rate of change of the stock price index, which reflects changes in the stock market, and the rate of change of GDP, which reflects economic growth, is only a temporary phenomenon, and they must match each other over a long enough period of time. Theoretically, the two should not deviate. The stock market trend may have a strong randomness in a short period of time. In the long run, the stock market changes ultimately depend on the basic factors of economic growth. The return on investment in stocks ultimately depends on the performance of listed companies, which jointly affects and decides the whole macroeconomic trend. Therefore, the stock market and the macroeconomy should complement and match each other. However, a large number of empirical research results prove that the stock market deviates from economic growth. We believe that one of the important reasons for such a result is the selection of sample space. It is a normal phenomenon that the trend of the stock market and economic growth deviate from each other at a certain point or within a certain period of time. A large number of empirical studies have concluded that the deviation between the stock market and economic growth should scientifically be the deviation within a certain sample interval, and it cannot be considered as an eternal deviation. If we choose a long enough sample space in the mature stock market, the change in the stock market and economic growth will converge, and there must be a matching cycle. To take a simple example, the stock market changes and even fluctuates daily, while the economic growth indicators are very stable and cannot fluctuate daily. We cannot deny that the stock market has become a "barometer" of macroeconomic changes with a short period of deviation. The key to studying this problem is not to test whether the two deviate, but to find out the time period when they are matching.

There must be a long enough period between the stock market and economic growth to be highly correlated and well-matched. It's not surprising that the two deviate at one point or over a certain period of time. But there is no long time or permanent deviation. The shorter the matching cycle is, the stronger the stock market reflects the economic growth, and the better the stock market can be an economic "barometer." The longer the matching cycle is, the longer the deviation between the two, and the worse the reflection function of the stock market on economic growth, unable to play its role in promoting economic growth or even producing adverse side effects. In other words, the shorter the matching period between the two, the healthier the development of the stock market, and the clearer the stock market reflects the economic growth. Therefore, we believe that there must be a long time period for stock prices to fully reflect all the information in that time period. The stock market will reflect the changes of the whole macroeconomy over a long period of time, rather than reflect the changes of the macroeconomy at any time point or any time period.

On the relationship between economic growth and the stock market, there are a lot of research results in the theoretical circle, and the conclusions are no more than two kinds: one is the empirical research evidence of the strong correlation between the two, and the other is the empirical research evidence of their deviation. Theoretically, there must be a strong correlation between the stock market and economic growth. Levine and Zervo (1998) used the overall index proposed by Asli Demirguc-Kunt and Levine to empirically test the temporal and sectional data of 42 sample countries. The results show a strong correlation between the overall development of the stock market and long-term economic growth. Wu et al. (2010), based on the panel data of 13 countries of the European Union from 1976 to 2005, studied the dynamic impact of finance on economic growth and found that there is a long-term equilibrium relationship between bank development, stock market development, and economic development. Stock market value and liquidity have a positive long-term impact on economic development. However, the liquidity of the stock market in the short term on the impact of economic growth is uncertain and even negative. Tachiwou (2010) adopted the ECM model to analyze the relationship between the development of the stock market and the economic growth of the West African Monetary Union from 1995 to 2006 and proved that the development of the stock market of the West African Monetary Union had a great positive impact on economic growth from both long-term and short-term aspects. Jose and Pablo (1995) found that the development of financial markets and economic development had an obvious positive correlation in the large-sample multi-country model. Nazir (2010) et al. analyzed the relationship between the stock market and economic growth in Pakistan with the data from 1986 to 2008 and found a strong relationship between the two, and believed that economic growth could be promoted by stimulating the development of the stock market. Arusha (2010) used the model of Mankiw, Romer, and Weil (1992) to analyze the data of 35 developing countries and found that the development of the stock market has a very significant positive correlation with economic growth. The continuous development of the stock market plays a great role in promoting the economy. Adamopoulos (2010) used the VEC model, selected the data of the German market from 1965 to 2007, and conducted the Johansen cointegration test and Granger test based on the unit root test on the long-term relationship between the stock market and economic growth. The test results show that stock market development is the Granger cause of economic growth in the German market. Nicholas (2000) used the autoregressive distribution lag model to test the South African market from 1971 to 2007. By comparing the market value, exchange value, and turnover with real GDP, he found that economic development was the Granger cause of the stock market as a whole. Abu (2009) conducted a Granger causality test on GDP and stock market value of Nigeria between 1985 and 2006, and believed that there was a Granger causality relationship between the two. The development of the stock market plays a strong role in promoting economic growth. Salisu and Ajide (2010) used the Granger test to test the relationship between the stock market and economic development in Nigeria from 1970 to 2004. Finally, they concluded that there was a great correlation between the development of the real economy and the development of the stock market. At the same time, the development of the stock market can effectively promote the development of the economy. Zhuo Jialiang (2009) studied the relationship between the development of the Indian stock market and economic growth from 1980 to 2008 and found that the Indian stock market was positively correlated with the growth of the national economy.

Chinese scholars have studied a lot about the relationship between China's capital market and economic growth. Jin Xiaobin et al. (2000) believed that the development of China's capital market is not only related to economic growth, but also related to the continuous transformation of the economic system. They believed that with the gradual expansion of the scale of the capital market, the capital market would attract more and more savings, and its contribution to economic growth would gradually increase. It is suggested that adjusting the ownership structure of listed companies and giving play to the inspection and supervision function of legal person shares and tradable shares can improve the efficiency of the capital market. Tan Ruyong (1999) used the ordinary least squares method (OLS) to conduct linear regression on the relationship between financial intermediation, stock market, and economic growth in China, respectively, and found that financial intermediation and economic growth had a strong positive correlation, while stock market development and economic growth had an insignificant negative correlation, which meant that the development of financial intermediation would promote economic growth. The contribution of the stock market to economic growth was not significant. Subsequently, Cao Fengqi et al. (2003) included medium and long-term credit, bond issuance, and stock market funds into the model according to the Cobb-Douglas function and conducted empirical analysis. They found that medium and long-term credit significantly promoted economic growth, while bond financing and stock market development had little effect on economic growth. Liu Jinquan (2004) believed that virtual and real economies interact and influence each other. Still, the virtual economy has a significant "spillover effect" on the real economy and a significant feedback influence on the virtual economy. In the long run, real and virtual economies have a positive relationship of mutual promotion. Wang Aijian and Chen Jie (2004) believed that speculation psychology and independent movement law of virtual capital were common in the virtual economy market, and the development of the virtual economy and real economy often deviated from each other. When the excessive expansion of the virtual economy leads to an excessive imbalance between the virtual economy and the real economy, a bubble economy might be formed, and an economic crisis would be triggered.

Many empirical studies have also found that the correlation between the stock market and economic growth is not strong or even deviates. Wang Jun (2002) first analyzed the internal law of capital market development and economic growth theoretically, revealed the three mechanisms of capital market influence economic growth, and then empirically studied the role and contribution of the development of the stock market to economic growth since the reform and opening up. The results show that the role and contribution of the development of Chinese stock market to economic growth is very weak or even a negative one. Liang Qi and Teng Jianzhou (2005) used multiple VAR models to study the relationship between stock market development, bank development, and economic growth from 1991 to 2004. They found that there was a relationship between economic growth and stock market development in the model system by over-identifying the conditional cointegration vector analysis. The weak exogenous test shows no causal relationship between the development of the stock market and economic growth, which means that the development of the stock market does not promote and lead to economic growth. Wu Zhiwen and Zhou Jianjun (2005) used the data from 2001 to 2004, and the empirical results showed a comprehensive but not partial deviation between China's stock market and the macroeconomy. The stock market was neither a "barometer" of the state-owned economy nor a "barometer" of the non-state-owned economy, and the objective existence of deviation between the stock market and the economy could not be questioned. Sun Xiaochong et al. (2005) analyzed the relationship between listed companies and the national economy as well as the relationship between stock prices and corporate performance from the perspective of the internal operating efficiency of the Chinese stock market. The research results show that the Chinese stock index is divorced from the economic fundamentals to a certain extent. Cao Yuanfang (2008) made an empirical analysis of the relationship between Chinese real economy and the virtual economy based on the monthly data of 1998–2008 by applying the cointegration test, Granger causality test, impulse response, and variance decomposition. The research showed that Chinese real and virtual economies deviated from each other. There is no long-term stable cointegration relationship between the virtual economy and the real economy, and they do not become Granger. The real economy is not the basis for the development of the virtual economy. Tan Zhiqiang (2009) empirically tested the relationship between China's economic growth and the development of the stock market by using the quarterly data from 2001 to 2007 and found no strong correlation between China's economic growth and the stock market. Du Jiang and Shen Shaobo (2010) used the data of Chinese stock market from 1992 to 2008, adopted trend analysis, cointegration analysis, and causality test, and conducted an empirical test on whether there was a deviation between the stock market and the real economy. The research results showed a deviation between the stock market and the real economy in China. It is necessary to maintain economic, financial, and capital market stability by promoting the steady and rapid development of enterprises and effectively solving the deviation between virtual and real economies.

From this research literature, we find that the empirical results with a large sample space basically draw the conclusion that the stock market has a strong correlation with economic growth, while those with a small sample space are easy to draw the conclusion that the stock market deviates from economic growth. At the same time, the latter basically uses the data of China's stock market for research, indicating that the phenomenon that China's stock market and economic growth deviate is relatively serious.

Further studies believe that the stock market cannot always promote economic development, which is related to the degree of economic development of a country, the degree of economic system perfection, and the degree of the stock market itself. Harris (1997) made a distinction between developed countries and developing countries. He believed that there was a positive relationship between the stock market and economic growth in developed countries, but in developing countries, the relationship between the two was very weak.

7.3 Selection of Empirical Test Methods

The stock market data is divided into two parts for the analysis of the relationship between the stock market and the economic growth matching cycle. The first part is sampled from foreign countries. They are the Dow Jones Index (DJIA), the S&P Index (S&P), the FTSE-100 in Europe, the DAX in Frankfurt, the CAC40 in Paris, and the Nikkei 225 (NKY225). These indexes are highly influential and representative stock price indexes in the global market. The other part of the sample from China is the Shanghai Composite Index. China's stock market has a relatively short history, and the stock price index has a short traceability history. However, the Shanghai Composite Index has the longest published time and the strongest representation of domestic listed enterprises among the domestic stock index data. So, choose this index to test the matching cycle of economic growth and stock market development.

According to the experience of relevant research at home and abroad, the alternative indicator of economic growth in this study is the data of industrial added value, representing each country's monthly GDP growth. Although the representation of industrial added value data is not comprehensive, it is still an important standard to measure the overall macroeconomic situation of a country.

Due to the late establishment of Chinese stock market, the domestic and foreign research data were selected from December 1991 to December 2013 as research samples in order to maintain the consistency of data. Two empirical testing methods are used to analyze and test the matching cycle between the stock market and economic growth: the thermal optimal path method and the cross-spectrum analysis method.

The thermal optimal path method is a financial physics method, which is a model to judge the lead-lag relationship between two-time series. Sornette and Zhou (2005) used this method to study the lead-and-lag relationship between the federal government funds rate and the yields of various short-term and long-term Treasury bonds from October 2000 to September 2003. They found a chain of effects from the stock market to the Fed, from short-term to long-term returns. Using the thermal optimal path method, Guo Kun, Zhou Wexing, and Cheng Siwei (2012) tested the dynamic lead-lag relationship between China's stock index and GDP. The results showed no significant lead-lag relationship between China's Shanghai Composite Index and GDP before 2002, and from 2002 to 2006, the Shanghai Composite Index led GDP for about two quarters. After 2006, the relationship between the lead and lag became increasingly obvious, and the role of the barometer of the Chinese stock market became increasingly obvious. Dong Jichang et al. (2012) analyzed the real estate price index and the consumer price index from 2000 to 2011 by using the thermal optimal path method. They found that there was a close relationship between the real estate price and inflation, and inflation information was included in the real estate price. The relation between real estate price and inflation is always closely related to change.

As a nonparametric estimation method, the core of the thermal optimal path is to find the best match between two time series, that is, a reflection satisfying certain conditions. Thermal optimal path is very effective for the study of such problems. Compared with a parametric estimation based on linear relationship, the nonparametric estimation method is more effective for non-single factor linear relationships between virtual and real economies and more complex multi-factor nonlinear relationships.

Spectral analysis methods have a long history. In the study of economic time series, they are widely used to determine the fixed length period of economic variables. Martin and Albrecht (2009) made a spectral analysis of the relationship between the stock market cycle and the economic cycle in Germany before World War I. The economic variables used were the capital market volatility index and GDP change rate, and the result was that the capital market basically presented an efficient state under the assumption of the economic cycle and had a close correlation with the stock market. Huang Huaji and Ding Wei (2009) analyzed the economic cycle and the stock market by using the cross-spectrum analysis method. They concluded that, in the long run, there is a lead-lag relationship between the stock market and the economic cycle. The stock market is about 16 months ahead of the economic cycle, but in the short run, the stock market lags the economic cycle by two months. In addition, the Granger test showed that there is no causal relationship between stock market fluctuations and economic fluctuations in the short term, which explains the phenomenon of stock lagging behind economic growth in the short term.

Different from the time domain analysis method, frequency domain analysis or the spectrum analysis method can be divided into single spectrum analysis and cross-spectrum analysis. Single spectrum analysis is the basis of cross-spectrum analysis. Single spectrum analysis is generally used to analyze the periodic fluctuation of the time series of a single economic variable. The single spectrum analysis is carried out to eliminate the trend factor of the time series through the transformation method and obtain the cyclic factor (generally stationary time series). Whether it is single spectrum analysis or cross-spectrum analysis, the time series of economic variables is required to be stable. Then, the cycle characteristics of economic time series are analyzed according to the spectrum density function obtained. Cross-spectrum analysis is a spectral analysis method for two economic time series. For spectrum technology, one sequence and two sequences decompose a time series into a series of fixed-length periodic frequencies. Cross-spectrum analysis is usually used to evaluate the wavelength correlation of a group of economic indicators and to analyze the leading and lagging relationship of economic indicators.

7.3.1 Thermal Optimal Path Method

Thermal optimal path is a non-parameter estimation method, which is mainly used to study the lead and lag relationship between two-time series. This method was first proposed by Sornette and Zhou (2005), who pointed out that to determine the nonlinear lead-lag relationship between two-time series $X(t_1)$ and $Y(t_2)$, in essence, is to find the best match between two time series, that is to say, is to determine a reflection $t_2 = \phi(t_1)$ between two time series that satisfies certain conditions.

According to the research of Zhou Weixing (2007), the basic idea of the thermal optimal path method is to convert traditional economic problems into classical probability transfer model in statistical physics by introducing the distance matrix between two time series and using partition function for recursive operation, so as to obtain the dynamic lead-lag relationship between the two sequences.

For two stationary time series $\{X(t_1) : t_1 = 1, 2, \cdots, N_1\}$ and $\{Y(t_2) : t_1 = 1, 2, \cdots, N_2\}$, it is assumed that $N_1 = N_2 = N$. In order to make the two time series $X(t_1)$ and $Y(t_2)$ comparable, it is necessary to normalize them. Here, $X(t_1)$ and $Y(t_2)$ are used to represent the time series that have been normalized.

The thermal optimal path method first needs to define a distance matrix whose elements are:

$$\varepsilon\left(t_1,t_2\right)=\left|X\left(t_1\right)-Y\left(t_2\right)\right| \tag{7-1}$$

Where the value of $\left|X\left(t_1\right)-Y\left(t_2\right)\right|$ defines the distance between time series X at time t_1 and time series Y at time t_2. When the time series Y is equal to X, and a domain value is introduced to define the distance matrix $E_{X,Y}$ as a 0–1 binary matrix, the famous recurrence graph for studying nonlinear time series dynamics is obtained. When Y is not equal to X, a binary matrix defined by a field value is called a cross-recurrence graph, and its recurrence graph is a generalization when applied to two functions.

For a simple model $Y(t)=X(t-k)$, where $k>0$ and it is a constant, then when $t_2=t_1+k$, $\varepsilon\left(t_1,t_2\right)=0$, the general matrix is non-0 for the other combinations of (t_1,t_2).

1. Optimal Path at Zero Temperature

Finding the optimal path L from $(t_1=1,t_2=1)$ to $(t_1=N,t_2=N)$ of the distance matrix $E_{X,Y}$ is equal to finding a relatively smooth reflection $t_1\to t_2=\phi\left(t_1\right)$, such that the total energy along the path is the lowest, namely:

$$\min_{(t_1,\phi(t_1)\in L)}\int_L\varepsilon\left(t_1,\phi\left(t_1\right)\right) \tag{7-2}$$

This optimization problem has been studied a lot in statistical physics. Sometimes, the optimal path L is also referred to as a random qualitative polymer, and the distance matrix $E_{X,Y}$ is treated accordingly as an energy landscape.

A classical solution with polynomial time complexity is the transfer matrix method. For convenience, transform the original frame (t_1,t_2) into (x,t), and get:

$$\begin{cases} t_1=1+(t-x)/2 \\ t_2=1+(t+x)/2 \end{cases} \tag{7-3}$$

Thus, origin $(t_1=1,t_2=1)$ is converted to $(x=0,t=0)$. Figure 7-1 shows the iterative format of coordinate transformation and transfer matrix method.

For a given node (x,t), its potential energy is $\varepsilon(x,t)$, and let $E(x,t)$ be the sum of the energies of the optimal path L from the starting point to (x,t). The optimal path is determined by the transfer matrix method through the following equation:

$$E(x,t)=\varepsilon(x,t)+min\left[E(x-1,t),E(x+1,t),E(x,t-2)\right] \tag{7-4}$$

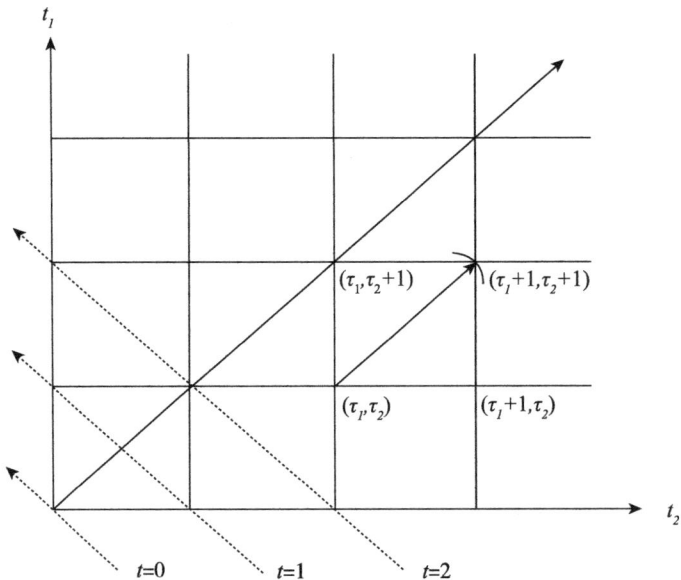

Figure 7-1 Iterative Format of Transfer Matrix Method for Rotation of Coordinate System (t_1, t_2) to Coordinate System (x, t)

This equation requires that the path with the lowest energy to node (x,t) must be preceded by $(x-1,t-1)$, $(x+1,t-1)$, or $(x,t-2)$. Thus, determining the optimal path to node (x,t) is equivalent to determining the former nodes of each node.

Let the starting point of the path be the original node, and determine the previous node with the lowest energy of each node in a top-down, left-to-right order. Thus, the optimal path and its corresponding energy are determined when the starting and ending points are determined. After the dependence of x with respect to t is determined, the local lag time is determined by $\tau = x(t)$.

For the time series with relatively high information noise, the obtained function $\tau(t)$ has high precision, but for the time series with relatively low information noise, the optimal path obtained is very sensitive to specific noise and will greatly deviate from the real path. In order to solve this problem, statisticians introduce temperature perception and estimate local lag time by thermal average.

2. Optimal Path at Finite Temperature

The optimal path method for determining finite temperature is called the thermal optimal path method. The thermal optimal path method allows the thermal stimulation of the condensed (i.e., the temperature is 0, $T=0$) energy landscape at a certain temperature, causing the oriented polymer to vibrate within a certain range so that the path with higher energy can exist with a certain probability. The probability of choosing path C with a total energy (the sum of the energies at each node) of E_c is proportional to the

Boltzmann factor $exp(-E_c/T)$, where temperature T determines the degree of allowed pulsation. When the temperature approaches 0 ($T\rightarrow 0$), the probability of choosing the path with energy slightly higher than the lowest energy also tends to be 0. In this case, the thermal optimal path is the optimal path with zero temperature. This is because, first of all, increasing temperature reduces the path sensitivity caused by specific noise. Second, too high a temperature will give the path with high energy a greater probability, making the energy landscape irrelevant and losing all information about the lead-lag structure. Therefore, it is important to select an appropriate temperature to determine a more accurate thermal optimal path. The thermal optimum path can be obtained by averaging the heat of different paths.

The recipe function of the qualitative node (x, t) is the sum of the probabilities of any feasible path (i.e., oriented polymer) C between the origin $(0, 0)$ and the end point (x, t):

$$G(x,t) = \sum_c e^{-E_c/T} \tag{7-5}$$

The total partition function at time t is:

$$G(t) = \sum_x G(x,t) \tag{7-6}$$

Local lag time $\tau(t)$ is the mean transverse thermal pulsation, namely the average leading (lagging) order $\langle x\ (t)\rangle$, which can be calculated by Equation 7-6:

$$\langle x\ (t)\rangle = \sum_x xG(x,t)/\ G(t) \tag{7-7}$$

$G(x,t)/G(t)$ in the equation can be seen as the probability of time t passing through the path of position x, so Equation 7-7 actually defines $\langle x\rangle$ as the thermal average position at time t, and gives an estimate of the local time lag, namely $\tau(t) = \langle x\rangle$. That is, in a quenched random energy field, the polymer oscillates randomly near its equilibrium position due to random thermal fluctuations. As the temperature T goes to zero, $G(x,t)/G(t)$ becomes a Dirac function $\delta\ [x - x_{DP}(t)]$, where $x_{DP}(t)$ is the globally optimal path at zero temperature. That is, when $T\rightarrow 0$, equation $\langle x\rangle = x_{DP}(t)$. When the temperature T is non-0, the optimal thermal average $\langle x\ (t)\rangle$ takes into account all feasible paths, and its variance is:

$$\sigma_x^2 = \sum_x (x - \langle x\ (t)\rangle)^2 G(x,t)/\ G(t) \tag{7-8}$$

Variance σ_x^2 is a measure of the uncertainty of the thermal optimal path, so the error estimates of two time-series lead-lag structures are given.

The determination of thermal optimal evaluation and its variance needs to first determine the partition function $G(x,t)$ at different time t and position x. According to the idea of the transfer matrix method and combined with the definition of the partition function, the recursive calculation equation of the partition function can be obtained:

$$G(x,t) = [G(x-1,t-1) + G(x+1,t-1) + G(x,t-2)]e^{-\varepsilon(x,t)/T} \tag{7-9}$$

In Equation 7-9, as the allowable temperature, the greater the T, the greater the probability of deviation from the absolute minimum energy point. In practical operation, too small T is easy to cause an overfitting phenomenon, while too large T can easily cause information loss. Moreover, the partition function values corresponding to different positions x at each time t need to be determined during the operation. Each iteration only involves three layers of time t, $t-1$ and $t-2$. Therefore, after one iteration, the partition function can be normalized and divided by $G(t)$ at each layer, so as to ensure that the partition function value will not overflow when t is large.

7.3.2 Cross Spectrum Analysis Method

1. Basic Forms of Spectrum Analysis

Under certain conditions, deterministic periodic functions can be regarded as the superposition of some sine and cosine functions. The spectrum analysis method aims to find out the periodic components of the time series and then describe them by the superposition of cosine (or sine) functions of different frequencies. For trigonometric functions:

$$y(t) = A\cos(2\pi\lambda_0 t + \phi) \tag{7-10}$$

It represents a simple wave cycle, where t is the time-independent variable and ϕ is the phase. The trajectory of $y(t)$ is a constant amplitude periodic pattern with amplitude $|A|$ and frequency λ_0. The phase ϕ is only related to the selected start time and does not affect the wave itself. Throwing a phase difference, the periodic function depends entirely on the amplitude $|A|$ or A^2. The frequency is the independent variable of the function, and the amplitude or intensity of the frequency component is the function value. A^2 is called the spectrum density of the function $y(t)$. For the spectrum density, there is a very obvious salient point at the frequency of the original periodic component.

The principle of spectrum analysis is to find the cycle or cycle structure in the data through spectrum technology, decompose the time series into a serial frequency function through the Fourier transform at a given moment, and then calculate the regression coefficient through the least square method.

Spectrum analysis requires the time series to be stationary. For stationary time series y_t, its expectation $E(y_t) = \mu$, the k order autocovariance is:

$$E\left(y_t - \mu\right)\left(y_{t-k} - \mu\right) = y_k \tag{7-11}$$

The Fourier transform of the autocovariance function is the spectrum density. After applying the Fourier transform to Equation 7-11, we can get:

$$S_y(\omega) = \frac{1}{2\pi} \sum_{k=-\infty}^{\infty} y_k e^{-i\omega k} \tag{7-12}$$

Where $\omega = \frac{2\pi}{T}$, according to Euler's equation, $e^{-i\omega k} = \cos(\omega k) - i \cdot \sin(\omega k)$, substituted into Equation 7-12, can be obtained:

$$S_y(\omega) = \frac{1}{2\pi} \sum_{k=-\infty}^{\infty} y_k \left[\cos(\omega k) - i \cdot \sin(\omega k)\right] \tag{7-13}$$

Based on the characteristics of the covariance stationary process, $y_k = y_{-k}$, and trigonometric function correlation, the above equation can be obtained:

$$S_y(\omega) = \frac{1}{2\pi} [y_0 + 2 \sum_{km-\infty}^{\infty} y_k \cos(\omega k)] \tag{7-14}$$

Let $\{\phi_t\}$ be the sample of time series $\{y_t\}$, and given n sample observations, the autocovariance can be calculated using the following equation:

$$y_t = \frac{1}{n} \sum_{t=1}^{n-k} \left(\phi_t - \mu\right)\left(\phi_{t+k} - \mu\right) \tag{7-15}$$

Where $k = 0, 1, 2..., n$, the spectrum density function is thus transformed into:

$$S_y(\omega) = \frac{1}{2\pi} [y_0 + 2 \sum_{k=1}^{n} y_k \cos(\omega k)] \tag{7-16}$$

According to the autocovariance function of samples, the larger k is, the fewer the sum terms of Equation 7-16 will be. For example, when $k = n-1$, $y_{n-1} = \frac{1}{n} \sum_{t=1}^{1} (y_t - \mu)(y_{t+k} - \mu) = \frac{1}{n}(y_1 - \mu)(y_{n-1} - \mu)$, samples are only y_1 and y_{n-1}, which may lead to a large error. Therefore, by adding a lag window λ_k, the spectrum density function is transformed from Equation 7-12 to:

$$S_y(\omega) = \frac{1}{2\pi} \sum_{k=0}^{M} \lambda_k y_k e^{-i\omega k} \tag{7-17}$$

After sorting out:

$$S_y(\omega) = \frac{1}{2\pi} [\lambda_0 y_0 + 2 \sum_{k=1}^{M} \lambda_k y_k \cos(\omega k)] \tag{7-18}$$

Where M represents the cut-off point, there are many options for the lag term, and the most commonly used one is the Tukey-Hamming window. The expression is as follows:

$$\lambda_k = \begin{cases} \frac{1}{2}\left[1+\cos\left(\frac{\pi k}{M}\right)\right], & |k| \leq M \\ 0, & |k| > M \end{cases} \tag{7-19}$$

M is called the truncation point or window parameter, and the size of M value affects the selection of the lag window. To select a lag window, the truncation point M should be selected first. In general theory, when $N \to \infty$, $M \to \infty$ and $M/N \to 0$ are required. In practice, there are several methods to obtain M value according to N: (1) A relatively large M will contain almost all sample data, leading to a large selection of k value. At this time, there will be more curve peaks and many false peaks. (2) A small M will lead to a small k selection, resulting in a large spectrum value, and the map will be too smooth because of too few samples included. (3) For general time series, the truncation point is between $\left[2\sqrt{n}, 3\sqrt{n}\right]$ (n is autocovariance).

2. Cross Spectrum Analysis

After spectrum analysis, the analysis used to evaluate the correlation degree of a group of economic indicators is called cross-spectrum analysis. For two time series $\{X\}$ and $\{Y\}$, the autocorrelation coefficient and cross-covariance are shown as follows:

$$R_x(k) = \frac{1}{N}\sum_{t=1}^{N-k}\left(x_t - \bar{x}\right)\left(x_{t+k} - \bar{x}\right), k = 0,\ 1,\ 2, \cdots, M \tag{7-20}$$

$$R_{xy}(k) = \frac{1}{N}\sum_{t=1}^{N-k}\left(x_t - \bar{x}\right)\left(y_{t+k} - \bar{y}\right), k = 0,\ 1,\ 2, \cdots, M \tag{7-21}$$

$$R_{yx}(k) = \frac{1}{N}\sum_{t=1}^{N-k}\left(x_{t+k} - \bar{x}\right)\left(y_t - \bar{y}\right), k = 0,\ 1,\ 2, \cdots, M \tag{7-22}$$

Where, $\bar{x} = \frac{1}{n}\sum_{t=1}^{n} x_t$, $\bar{y} = \frac{1}{n}\sum_{t=1}^{n} y_t$, $s_x = \sqrt{\frac{1}{n}\sum_{t=1}^{n}\left(x_t - \bar{x}\right)^2}$, $s_y = \sqrt{\frac{1}{n}\sum_{t=1}^{n}\left(y_t - \bar{y}\right)^2}$.

Therefore, the spectrum functions of each sequence can be obtained as follows:

$$s_x(f) = R_x(0) + 2\sum_{k=1}^{M} w(k) \cdot R_x(k) \cdot \cos(\pi f k) \tag{7-23}$$

Oblique spectrum (Equation 7-24), orthogonal spectrum (Equation 7-25), cross-spectrum (Equation 7-26), and coherent spectrum (Equation 7-27) are obtained:

$$ch(f) = R(0) + \sum_{k=1}^{M} w(k) \cdot [R_{xy}(k) + R_{yx}(k)] \cdot \cos(\pi f k) \tag{7-24}$$

$$qh(f) = \sum_{k=1}^{M} w(k) \cdot [R_{xy}(k) - R_{yx}(k)] \cdot \sin(\pi f k) \tag{7-25}$$

$$S_{xy}(f) = ch(f) + i \cdot qh(f) \tag{7-26}$$

$$C_{xy}(f) = \frac{S_{xy}(f)}{S_x(f) \cdot S_y(f)} = \frac{ch(f) + i \cdot qh(f)}{S_x(f) \cdot S_y(f)} \tag{7-27}$$

The closer the value of the coherence spectrum to 1, the stronger the correlation between the two time series. In the test of the matching period, consistency and phase can be used to measure the time difference between the leading index and synchronous index and the matching period length.

There has been a long history of research on the causal relationship between two time series. In economic and financial problems, the non-parameter estimation method is more suitable to determine whether two economic variables are correlated and whether one economic variable affects another economic variable and what kind of influence relationship exists. As a non-parameter estimation method, the core of the thermal optimal path method is to find the best match between two time series, that is, a reflection meeting specific conditions at a certain temperature, which is used to solve the matching cycle problem. The study of the thermal optimal path method is very suitable and effective.

Although the core of thermal optimal path and cross-spectrum analysis is to determine the lead-lag relationship of a set of time series data, their emphases are different. The thermal optimal path through the calculation of the thermal average position, the leading lag order at different time points of the two time series can be obtained, while the cross-spectrum analysis regards a group of time series as the period or frequency component without correlation, analyze the periodic changes of each component, and analyze the main wave characteristics of the time series from the perspective of frequency domain structure. Therefore, in the study of the time series problem, the spectrum method has the advantages that the time domain analysis method does not have.

The selection of the thermal optimal path method and cross-spectrum analysis method for the empirical test of the matching cycle is based on the maturity and perfection of the two methods by predecessors on the one hand and the representative significance of these two methods for the research of the stock market and cycle issues on the other hand. Both methods test the lead-lag and matching cycle. Only when both methods reach a positive conclusion can the research conclusion be considered credible.

7.4 Empirical Test of the Matching Cycle between the US Stock Market and Economic Growth

7.4.1 *Data Selection and Processing*
The data samples chosen here are the Dow Jones Index, the S&P Index, and monthly US GDP data from December 1991 to December 2013.

The Dow Jones Index is the longest-running stock price index in the world. The Dow Jones Index we chose is the Dow Jones Industrial Average (DJIA, the Dow Jones indexes mentioned below are the Dow Jones Industrial Average Index), one of the most widely used worldwide, most influential share price indices. The Dow Jones Industrial Average Index consists of 30 representative large industrial and commercial companies, which is an average reflection of the price level of the overall industrial and commercial stocks in the United States. With the development of the economy, the Dow Jones Industrial Average Index has been growing, and its role has become increasingly prominent. Today, the Dow Jones Index is no longer a simple financial indicator but a representative of the world's financial culture.

The Dow Jones Index is important for three reasons. First, it is representative of the companies selected. The Dow Jones Index consists of only 30 stocks. These 30 stocks are representative of companies in the United States, which are basically the largest companies with the most important impact in each industry. Changes in the stock prices of these companies are followed by global stock markets, and their fluctuations often have a significant impact on global stock markets. In order to maintain its representative status, the Dow Jones Index compilation company (Dow Jones & Company) always pays close attention to the performance changes of the companies in the index. It adjusts the companies included in the index at any time according to various indicators, eliminates the unrepresentative companies, and introduces dynamic and more representative new company stocks. The Dow Jones Index has changed its 30 stocks of industrial and commercial companies 30 times since its inception, although the number of companies it contains has remained the same. Secondly, the representation of data. The *Wall Street Journal*, as the world's most influential newspaper media in financial circles, has been the news carrier announcing the Dow Jones stock price average index. The newspaper always keeps reporting the changes in the Dow Jones Index every trading day. It reports the changes in the index every half hour, among which the percentage change rate of sampled stocks, the average index, the transaction amount of each sampled stock, and other indicators are calculated and reported once every hour, and the average index of stock prices after stock splitting is corrected at any time. Third, the representativeness of the Dow Jones Index is also related to the continuity of its data. Since its first release, the Dow Jones Index has never been missing. Its historical data can be used to compare stock quotations and economic development in different periods, and it is the main reference for observing market dynamics and engaging in stock investment. It is also one of the most sensitive stock price indexes reflecting the changes in the American stock market.

The S&P 500 Index, created and maintained by S&P, has been tracking the US stock market since 1957. It looks at 500 companies listed on the US stock market. The 500 companies have multiple trades on the New York Stock Exchange and NASDAQ. The S&P contains almost all the 500 most traded stocks in the United States. After the Dow Jones Industrial Average, the S&P is now the second-largest share price index in the country. It includes more companies, reflects market changes more comprehensively, and spreads risk more widely than the Dow Jones Industrial Average. In terms of the calculation method, the S&P Index adopts the market capitalization weighting method, which focuses more on the reflection of the actual importance of the company's stock in the stock market compared with the price weighting of the Dow Jones Index.

In order to more comprehensively reflect the relationship between the stock price index and economic growth in the United States, we test the relationship between the Dow Jones Index and the S&P Index and economic growth respectively. The empirical research of the stock market in this paper uses the monthly return data of the stock market price index. Since the monthly return should use the closing data of the stock price index on the last trading day of each month, the randomness is strong. There may be abnormal fluctuations. In order to eliminate the influence of abnormal fluctuations of the closing data of the last trading day, the average closing data of the month (the average value of the closing data of the week after summing up) is taken for analysis.

Here, the monthly GDP data of the US is selected for research. However, since most GDP data published by various countries are annual GDP and quarterly GDP total, industrial added value is selected to represent monthly GDP data of other countries based on empirical test experience and general empirical analysis method.

1. High-Pass Decomposition

In 1980, Hodrick and Prescott first proposed the high-pass method and used this method to analyze the post-war economic conditions of the United States. In the later development, this method is widely used to analyze the trend decomposition of macroeconomic data.

The idea of the high-pass method is basically equivalent to the minimization of variance of time series wave, and the spectrum analysis method of time series is its theoretical basis. As a method to analyze time series in state space, high-pass can be approximated as a high-pass Filter. The purpose of HP filtering of time series is to separate the high-frequency component from the low-frequency component in all components of different frequencies, remove the low-frequency component (that is, remove the long-term trend item), and measure the short-term random fluctuation item. The mathematical expression of the principle of the method is as follows.

Let time series $\{Y_t\}$ and $Y_t = \{y_1, y_2, \cdots, y_n\}$ exist, where n is the sample size, and trend factor is $G = \{g_1, g_2, \cdots, g_n\}$, where n is the sample size.

HP filter turns y_t ($t=1, 2..., n$) to decompose:

$$y_t = g_t + c_t \tag{7-28}$$

Where, g_t and c_t are unobservable. For time series $\{Y_t\}$, the unobservable part of the trend G is defined as the solution of the minimization problem of Equation 7-29:

$$min\left\{ \sum_{t=1}^{n} (y_t - g_t)^2 + \lambda \sum_{t=1}^{n} [B(L)g_t]^2 \right\} \tag{7-29}$$

Where, $B(L)$ is the delay operator polynomial:

$$B(L) = \left(L^{-1} - 1\right) - (1 - L) \tag{7-30}$$

By replacing Equation 7-29 with Equation 7-30, the HP filtering problem is converted into the loss function value of Equation 7-31 to obtain the minimum problem.

$$min\left\{ \sum_{t=1}^{n} (y_t - g_t)^2 + \lambda \sum_{t=1}^{n} [(g_{t+1} - g_t) - (g_t - g_{t-1})]^2 \right\} \tag{7-31}$$

Take the first-order derivative of y_t in Equation 7-31, set the derivative to 0, and get:

$$g_1 : c_1 = \lambda\,(g_1 - 2g_2 + 3g_3)$$

$$g_2 : c_2 = \lambda\,(-2g_1 + 5g_2 - 4g_3 + g_4)$$

$$\cdots$$

$$g_t : c_t = \lambda\,(2g_{t-2} - 4g_{t-1} + 6g_t - 4g_{t+1} + g_4)$$

$$\cdots$$

$$g_{n-1} : c_{n-1} = \lambda\,(g_{n-3} - 4g_{n-2} + 5g_{n-1} - 2g_n)$$

$$g_n : c_n = \lambda\,(g_{n-2} - 2g_{n-1} + g_n) \tag{7-32}$$

The matrix form is $c = \lambda F g$, and F is the coefficient matrix of matrix $T \times T$, as shown in Equation 7-33.

$$F = \begin{pmatrix}
1 & -2 & 3 & 0 & & & & & \cdots & 0 \\
-2 & 5 & -4 & 1 & 0 & & & & \cdots & 0 \\
1 & -4 & 6 & -4 & 1 & 0 & & & \cdots & 0 \\
0 & 1 & -4 & 6 & -4 & 1 & 0 & & \cdots & 0 \\
\vdots & \vdots & \vdots & \vdots & \vdots & \vdots & \vdots & & \ddots & \vdots \\
0 & \cdots & 0 & 1 & -4 & 6 & 4 & 1 & 0 & \\
0 & \cdots & & & 0 & 1 & -4 & 6 & 4 & 1 \\
0 & \cdots & & & & 0 & 1 & -4 & 5 & -2 \\
0 & \cdots & & & & & 0 & 1 & -2 & 1
\end{pmatrix} \qquad (7\text{-}33)$$

Through the above calculation, it can be obtained:

$$y - g = \lambda F g \qquad (7\text{-}34)$$

Arrangement Equation 7-34 gives:

$$g = (\lambda F + I)^{-1} y \qquad (7\text{-}35)$$

In matrix F, the sum of all column elements is zero; according to $c = \lambda F g$, the sum of its short-term fluctuations is zero. So $\sum_{t=1}^{n} c_t = 0$, $\lambda \sum_{t=1}^{n} [B(L) \cdot g_t]^2$ adjusts for the change in trend. The bigger λ is, the bigger $\lambda \sum_{t=1}^{n} [B(L) \cdot g_t]^2$ is. That is to say, different modes of random fluctuation and different degrees of smoothness are determined by the λ value.

When $\lambda = 0$, g_t and y_t are equal, and the sequence Y is the tendency to satisfy the minimization problem. When λ is not 0, the larger its value is, the smoother the estimated trend will be. The process of $\lambda \to \infty$, that is, the estimated trend is close to the linear function, then the HP filtering problem is reduced to the trend that can be estimated by the least square method.

From the perspective of statistical significance, any non-stationary time series is the combination of countless non-stationary trend components and stationary periodic components, so λ can be arbitrarily valued. However, the value of λ determines the tradeoff choice between the tracking degree of the trend element to the actual sequence and the smoothness of the trend.

γ_1^2 is used to represent the standard deviation of the trend component in the time series, γ_2^2 is used to represent the standard deviation of the periodic component, and the optimal value of λ is $\lambda = \gamma_1^2 / \gamma_2^2$. Generally speaking, the value of λ can be set in three ways: $\lambda = 100$ for annual data, $\lambda = 1600$ for quarterly data, and $\lambda = 14400$ for monthly data.

In the empirical study, in order to eliminate the influence of long-term trends on the research conclusion, we decompose three time series of US GDP data, Dow Jones Index, and S&P Index by HP filtering after logarithm, and obtain their Trend component and Cycle component. Where, *djia* represents the Dow Jones Industrial Average, *sp* represents the S&P Index, and *usgdp* represents US GDP data. Figure 7-2 to Figure 7-4 shows the HP filtering decomposition results of each time series.

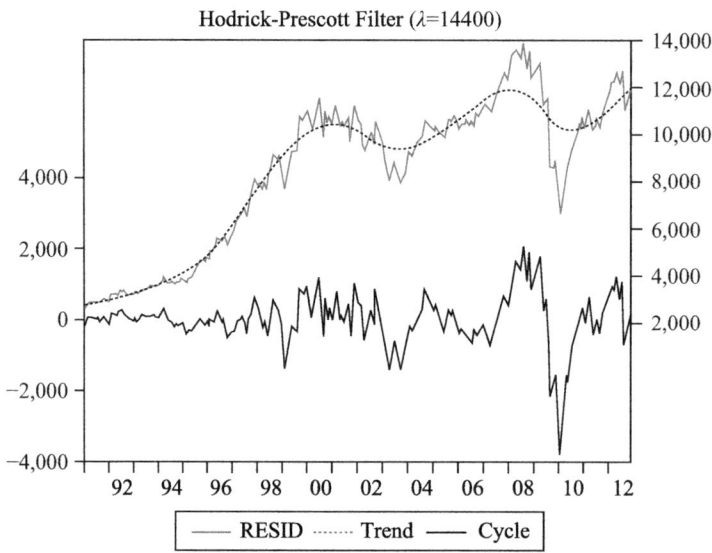

Figure 7-2 Decomposition Result of Dow Jones Index HP Filtering

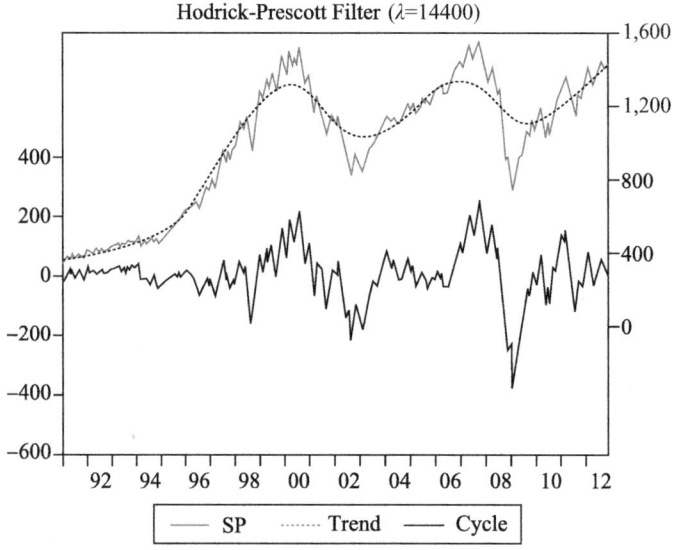

Figure 7-3 Decomposition Result of S&P Index HP Filtering

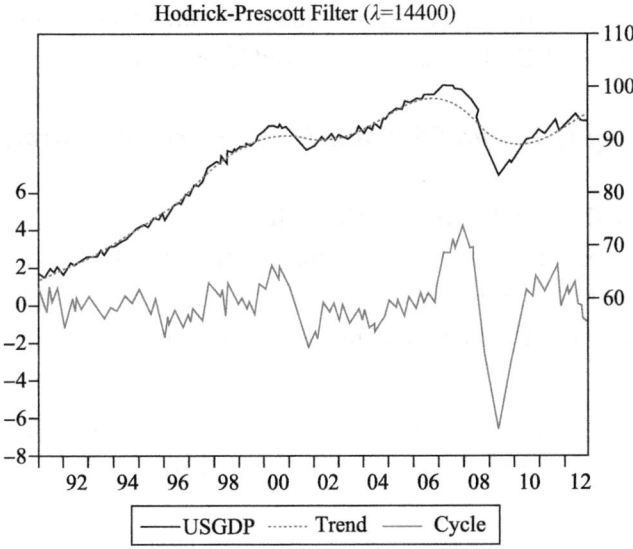

Figure 7-4 Decomposition Result of US GDP HP Filtering

2. Results of ADF Test

After HP filtering decomposition, the ADF test is conducted on the original data, trend data, and periodic data, respectively, where *djia* represents the original sequence of the Dow Jones Index, and *cdjia* represents the sequence of periodic components of the Dow Jones Index. *sp* represents the original sequence of the S&P Index, and *csp* represents its periodic component sequence; *usgdp* represents the original series of US GDP data, and *cusgdp* represents the series of cyclical components of US GDP data. The ADF test results are shown in Table 7-1.

Table 7-1 ADF Test Results

Variable		ADF	1% Level	5% Level	10% Level
djia	djia	−1.544	−3.455	−2.872	−2.573
	cdjia	−4.877	−3.455	−2.872	−2.573
sp	sp	−1.505	−3.455	−2.872	−2.573
	csp	−4.209	−3.455	−2.872	−2.573
usgdp	usgdp	−2.205	−3.455	−2.872	−2.573
	cusgdp	−5.287	−3.455	−2.872	−2.573

According to the ADF test, it can be seen that the original sequences of the US GDP data, Dow Jones Index, and S&P Index are all non-stationary sequences. In contrast, the periodic component sequences after trend conversion (HP filtering decomposition) are stationary. In view of this, here, the periodic component sequence of the Dow Jones Index, S&P Index, and US GDP data are selected for analysis.

7.4.2 Cycle Test of DJIA and S&P Matching US Economic Growth

1. Test Results of Thermal Optimal Path Method

Before the operation of the thermal optimal path method, the data should first be standardized, and then the distance matrix of the time series can be calculated. The distance matrix cd of the US GDP and Dow Jones index is:

$$
c_d = \begin{pmatrix}
0.43 & 0.24 & 0.25 & 0.24 & 0.31 & 0.11 & 0.18 & 0.31 \\
0.53 & 0.34 & 0.35 & 0.34 & 0.41 & 0.21 & 0.28 & 0.41 \\
0.09 & 0.1 & 0.09 & 0.1 & 0.03 & 0.23 & 0.16 & 0.03 \\
0.16 & 0.03 & 0.02 & 0.03 & 0.04 & 0.16 & 0.09 & 0.04 \\
0.16 & 0.03 & 0.02 & 0.03 & 0.04 & 0.16 & 0.09 & 0.04 \\
0.19 & 0.13 & 0.01 & 0.16 & 0.07 & 0.13 & 0.06 & 0.07 \\
0.4 & 0.21 & 0.22 & 0.21 & 0.28 & 0.08 & 0.15 & 0.28 \\
0.1 & 0.09 & 0.08 & 0.09 & 0.02 & 0.22 & 0.15 & 0.02 \\
0.34 & 0.15 & 0.16 & 0.15 & 0.22 & 0.02 & 0.09 & 0.22 \\
0.34 & 0.15 & 0.16 & 0.15 & 0.22 & 0.02 & 0.09 & 0.22 \\
0.13 & 0.06 & 0.05 & 0.06 & 0.01 & 0.19 & 0.12 & 0.01 \\
0.25 & 0.06 & 0.07 & 0.06 & 0.13 & 0.07 & 0.35 & 0.13 \\
0.25 & 0.06 & 0.07 & 0.06 & 0.13 & 0.07 & 0.29 & 0.13 \\
0.22 & 0.03 & 0.04 & 0.03 & 0.1 & 0.1 & 0.03 & 0.1 \\
0.28 & 0.09 & 0.1 & 0.09 & 0.16 & 0.04 & 0.03 & 0.16 \\
0.28 & 0.09 & 0.1 & 0.09 & 0.16 & 0.04 & 0.03 & 0.16 \\
0.28 & 0.09 & 0.1 & 0.09 & 0.16 & 0.04 & 0.03 & 0.16 \\
0.37 & 0.18 & 0.19 & 0.18 & 0.25 & 0.05 & 0.12 & 0.25 \\
0.31 & 0.12 & 0.13 & 0.12 & 0.19 & 0.01 & 0.06 & 0.19 \\
0.19 & 0 & 0.01 & 0.15 & 0.07 & 0.13 & 0.06 & 0.07 \\
 & & & \vdots & & &
\end{pmatrix} \cdots
$$

The distance matrix cs between US GDP and Dow Jones index is:

$$c_s = \begin{pmatrix}
0.22 & 0.29 & 0.26 & 0.22 & 0.24 & 0.14 & 0.27 & 0.18 \\
0.32 & 0.39 & 0.36 & 0.32 & 0.34 & 0.24 & 0.37 & 0.28 \\
0.12 & 0.05 & 0.08 & 0.12 & 0.1 & 0.2 & 0.07 & 0.16 \\
0.05 & 0.02 & 0.01 & 0.05 & 0.03 & 0.13 & 0 & 0.09 \\
0.05 & 0.02 & 0.01 & 0.05 & 0.03 & 0.13 & 0 & 0.09 \\
0.02 & 0.05 & 0.02 & 0.02 & 0 & 0.1 & 0.03 & 0.06 \\
0.19 & 0.26 & 0.23 & 0.19 & 0.21 & 0.11 & 0.24 & 0.15 \\
0.11 & 0.04 & 0.07 & 0.11 & 0.09 & 0.19 & 0.06 & 0.15 \\
0.13 & 0.2 & 0.17 & 0.13 & 0.15 & 0.05 & 0.18 & 0.09 \\
0.13 & 0.2 & 0.17 & 0.13 & 0.15 & 0.05 & 0.18 & 0.09 \\
0.08 & 0.01 & 0.04 & 0.08 & 0.06 & 0.16 & 0.03 & 0.12 \\
0.04 & 0.11 & 0.08 & 0.04 & 0.06 & 0.04 & 0.09 & 0 \\
0.04 & 0.11 & 0.08 & 0.04 & 0.06 & 0.04 & 0.09 & 0.15 \\
0.01 & 0.08 & 0.05 & 0.01 & 0.03 & 0.07 & 0.06 & 0.03 \\
0.07 & 0.14 & 0.11 & 0.07 & 0.09 & 0.01 & 0.12 & 0.03 \\
0.07 & 0.14 & 0.11 & 0.07 & 0.09 & 0.01 & 0.12 & 0.03 \\
0.07 & 0.14 & 0.11 & 0.07 & 0.09 & 0.01 & 0.12 & 0.03 \\
0.16 & 0.23 & 0.2 & 0.16 & 0.18 & 0.08 & 0.21 & 0.12 \\
0.1 & 0.17 & 0.14 & 0.1 & 0.12 & 0.02 & 0.15 & 0.06 \\
0.02 & 0.05 & 0.02 & 0.02 & 0 & 0.1 & 0.03 & 0.06 \\
0.16 & 0.23 & 0.2 & 0.16 & 0.18 & 0.08 & 0.21 & 0.12 \\
0.02 & 0.05 & 0.02 & 0.02 & 0 & 0.1 & 0.03 & 0.06 \\
& & & \vdots & & &
\end{pmatrix} \cdots$$

Figure 7-5 and Figure 7-6 show the topographic map of the distance matrix between industrial added value and the Dow Jones Index and between industrial added value and the S&P index of the United States.

Based on the distance matrix, the position of the sequence at each thermal average point can be calculated. When the thermal average point is positive, it can be considered that the change in the stock price index is ahead of the change in the macroeconomy. When the thermal average point is negative, it is believed that the change in the stock price index lags behind the change in the macroeconomy. Before calculating the average thermal position, according to the recursive equation, it can be found that there are obvious changes in the lag order for different T values. Some T values are shown in Table 7-2.

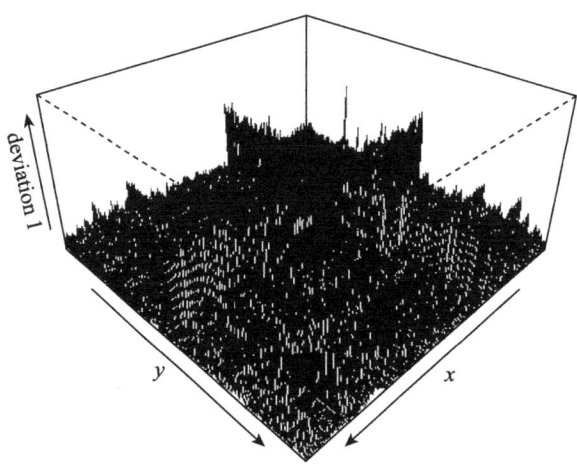

Figure 7-5 Energy Topographic Map of US GDP and Dow
Jones Index from December 1991 to December 2013

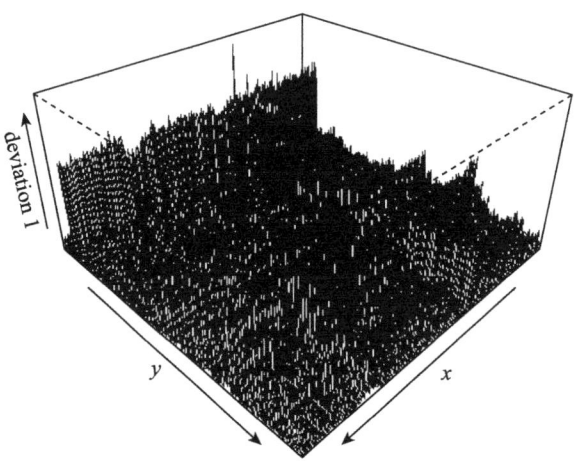

Figure 7-6 Energy Topographic Map of US GDP and S&P
Index from December 1991 to December 2013

Table 7-2 Dow Jones Index, GDPT Value and Lag Order Table (Take the Integer after the Score)

	1993	1995	1997	1999	2000	2005	2008	2010	2013
$T=2$	6	4	5	9	5	4	3	6	11
$T=5$	2	3	2	3	4	2	2	5	9
$T=10$	-1	-2	-3	2	3	5	4	5	6
$T=20$	1	-1	-1	1	1	3	4	6	7

The larger the T value is, the more stable the selection result of the lag order will be. However, no matter how T is valued, the changing trend of the lag order is the same. Considering the general characteristics of the T value and thermal optimal path comprehensively, it is concluded that the leading (lag order) when $T=5$ is more accurate.

According to the results of the thermal optimal path analysis, it can be concluded that from December 1991 to December 2008, the fluctuation of the Dow Jones Index almost kept pace with the economic growth. Still, there was a slight lead, with an average lead period of about 2.5 months. After 2008, the Dow Jones Index's lead over US GDP has become more pronounced. The barometer played a significant role, leading for about seven months. After analyzing the S&P Index, it is found that, like the Dow Jones Index, the S&P Index has always been a leading indicator of industrial added value within the sample range. Before 2005, the average leading industrial added value was 3.5 months. After 2005, the leading industrial added value was more significant, with an average leading industrial added value of 6 months.

It can be seen that both the S&P 500 and the Dow Jones Index are closely related to the growth of the US economy, and their fluctuations are ahead of economic growth. The S&P has moved more in tandem with economic growth and led for a shorter period of time than the Dow Jones Index.

2. Cross-Spectrum Analysis Results

(1) Time domain analysis
In order to explain the data from different perspectives, before the frequency domain analysis, we first carried out the basic time domain analysis of the data. Since the time series data used are all stationary series of order 0, the Granger causality test can be carried out on the construction of the VAR model.

A. ESTABLISH VAR MODEL
To establish VAR model, the lag order of the model should be selected. The test results of lag order between *cdjia* and *cusgdp, csp* and *cusgdp* are shown in Tables 7-3 and 7-4.

Table 7-3 Lag Order Table of VAR Model of *cdjia* and *cusgdp*

Lag	LogL	LR	FPE	AIC	SC	HQ
0	361.64	NA	0.00	−2.98	−2.95*	−2.97*
1	363.49	3.65	0.00	−2.97	−2.88	−2.93
2	370.85	14.42	0.00	−2.99	−2.85	−2.94

(Continued)

Lag	LogL	LR	FPE	AIC	SC	HQ
3	376.15	10.28	0.00	−3.01	−2.80	−2.92
4	379.08	5.64	0.00	−3.00	−2.74	−2.89
5	380.89	3.46	0.00	−2.98	−2.66	−2.85
6	382.09	2.27	0.00	−2.96	−2.58	−2.80
7	388.48	11.98	0.00	−2.97	−2.54	−2.80
8	397.25	16.31	0.00	−3.01	−2.52	−2.82
9	399.47	4.09	0.00	−3.00	−2.45	−2.78
10	405.80	11.54	0.00	−3.02	−2.41	−2.77
11	416.75	19.82	0.00016*	−3.08*	−2.41	−2.81
12	417.33	1.04	0.00	−3.05	−2.33	−2.76
13	422.98	10.04	0.00	−3.06	−2.28	−2.75
14	424.05	1.89	0.00	−3.04	−2.20	−2.70
15	424.50	0.77	0.00	−3.01	−2.11	−2.65
16	430.01	9.51	0.00	−3.02	−2.07	−2.64
17	433.59	6.12	0.00	−3.02	−2.01	−2.61
18	435.87	3.86	0.00	−3.00	−1.93	−2.57
19	437.40	2.58	0.00	−2.98	−1.85	−2.53
20	439.70	3.80	0.00	−2.97	−1.78	−2.49
21	440.97	2.10	0.00	−2.95	−1.70	−2.44
22	448.67	12.53*	0.00	−2.98	−1.68	−2.45
23	450.17	2.41	0.00	−2.96	−1.60	−2.41
24	452.75	4.11	0.00	−2.94	−1.53	−2.37

Table 7-4 Lag Order Table of VAR Model of *csp* and *cusgdp*

Lag	LogL	LR	FPE	AIC	SC	HQ
0	430.23	NA	0.00	−3.55	−3.52*	−3.54*
1	434.06	7.57	0.00	−3.55	−3.47	−3.52
2	441.10	13.78	0.00	−3.58	−3.43	−3.52

(Continued)

Lag	LogL	LR	FPE	AIC	SC	HQ
3	446.56	10.61	0.00	−3.59	−3.39	−3.51
4	454.03	14.38	0.00	−3.62	−3.36	−3.51
5	458.57	8.66	0.00	−3.62	−3.30	−3.49
6	459.23	1.24	0.00	−3.60	−3.22	−3.44
7	463.48	7.99	0.00	−3.60	−3.16	−3.42
8	466.54	5.69	0.00	−3.59	−3.10	−3.39
9	473.37	12.58	0.00	−3.61	−3.06	−3.39
10	475.02	3.01	0.00	−3.59	−2.99	−3.35
11	483.10	14.61*	9.12e-05*	−3.63*	−2.96	−3.36
12	483.89	1.42	0.00	−3.60	−2.88	−3.31
13	486.51	4.65	0.00	−3.59	−2.81	−3.27
14	487.73	2.15	0.00	−3.57	−2.73	−3.23
15	489.38	2.87	0.00	−3.55	−2.65	−3.19
16	491.58	3.79	0.00	−3.53	−2.58	−3.15
17	492.53	1.62	0.00	−3.51	−2.49	−3.10
18	493.64	1.87	0.00	−3.48	−2.41	−3.05
19	494.97	2.24	0.00	−3.46	−2.33	−3.01
20	496.81	3.05	0.00	−3.44	−2.26	−2.96
21	498.23	2.32	0.00	−3.42	−2.18	−2.92
22	502.88	7.56	0.00	−3.43	−2.12	−2.90
23	508.64	9.28	0.00	−3.44	−2.08	−2.89
24	513.30	7.43	0.00	−3.45	−2.03	−2.88

According to the above results, the five criteria (LR, FPE, AIC, SC, HQ) were comprehensively considered. Finally, the lag order of *csp* and *cusgdp* was selected as 11, and the lag order of *cdjia* and *cusgdp* was selected as 11 (the larger lag order was related to the selection of monthly data for analysis. The lag order of general annual data is 1–3 orders, the lag order of quarterly data is 4–5 orders, and the lag order of monthly data is 11–13 orders.) According to the selected lag order, the VAR model is re-established for estimation, and the chart verification of the AR root of the estimated result is shown in Figure 7-7.

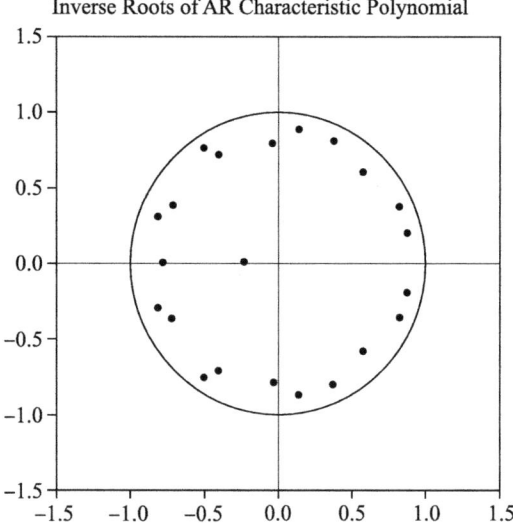

Figure 7-7 Verification of the AR Root

It can be seen from the above results that the reciprocal of all characteristic roots is within the range of unit circle; that is, the VAR model established according to *cdjia* and *cusgdp* is stable. We can run Granger causality tests. The VAR model of *csp* and *cusgdp* is re-established below. Figure 7-8 shows the chart verification results of AR root as shown in model estimation results.

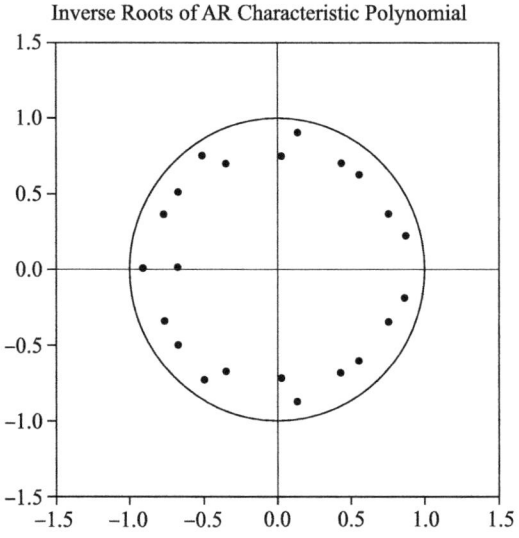

Figure 7-8 Verification of the AR Root

It can be seen from the above results that the reciprocal of all characteristic roots is within the range of unit circle; that is, the VAR model established according to *csp* and *cusgdp* is stable. We can run Granger causality tests. The VAR model estimation of the two sets of sequences shows that, for *cdjia* and *cusgdp*, the Dow Jones Index has a significant positive impact on the industrial added value when the lag period is 4. In contrast, the industrial added value has the biggest impact on the Dow Jones Index when the lag period is 11, and there is a hysteresis positive relationship between the two. For *csp* and *cusgdp*, the S&P Index has a significant positive impact on industrial added value when lagging one order, while the industrial added value has the greatest impact on the S&P Index when lagging three orders.

B. GRANGER CAUSALITY TEST

Due to the satisfaction of the sequence for stationarity, the Granger causality test was carried out on the periodic component sequence of the Dow Jones Index (*cdjia*) and the periodic component sequence of industrial value added (*cusgdp*), as well as the periodic component sequence of the S&P Index (*csp*) and the periodic component sequence of industrial value added (*cusgdp*). The test results are shown in Tables 7-5 and 7-6.

Table 7-5 Granger Causality Test Results (*cdjia* and *cusgdp*)

Null Hypothesis	*Obs*	*F*-Statistic	*Prob.*
cusgdp does not Granger Cause *cdjia*	240	0.98133	0.4704
cdjia does not Granger Cause *cusgdp*		2.86818	0.0007

Table 7-6 Granger Causality test results (*csp* and *cusgdp*)

Null Hypothesis	*Obs*	*F*-Statistic	*Prob.*
cusgdp does not Granger Cause *csp*	240	3.43007	0.0176
csp does not Granger Cause *cusgdp*		2.14741	0.0246

It can be seen from the above Granger test results that the time-domain analysis results are as follows: within the sample interval of this study, with 5% confidence, the Dow Jones Index is the Granger cause of industrial added value, but industrial added value is not the Granger cause of Dow Jones Index, and there is a single-directional Granger causality between industrial added value and Dow Jones Index. The industrial added value is the Granger cause of the S&P Index, and the S&P Index is also the Granger cause of the industrial added value. There is a single-directional Granger causality between the industrial added value and the S&P Index.

(2) Frequency domain analysis

A. SINGLE SPECTRUM ANALYSIS

Based on the time-domain analysis results, univariate and cross-spectrum analyses are used to measure the matching cycle between the Dow Jones Index, S&P Index, and US GDP, respectively. The first step is univariate spectrum analysis. In order to reduce the variance of the sample spectrum in the neighborhood of investigated spectrum values and smooth the sample spectrum, the Tukey-Hamming window was selected here. The window width was selected according to the number of samples, empirical experience, and the basic principle of the window width of Tukey-Hanning. After several operations, the window width was selected as 51. The following cross-spectrum analysis results are all the results after windows are added, as shown in Figure 7-9.

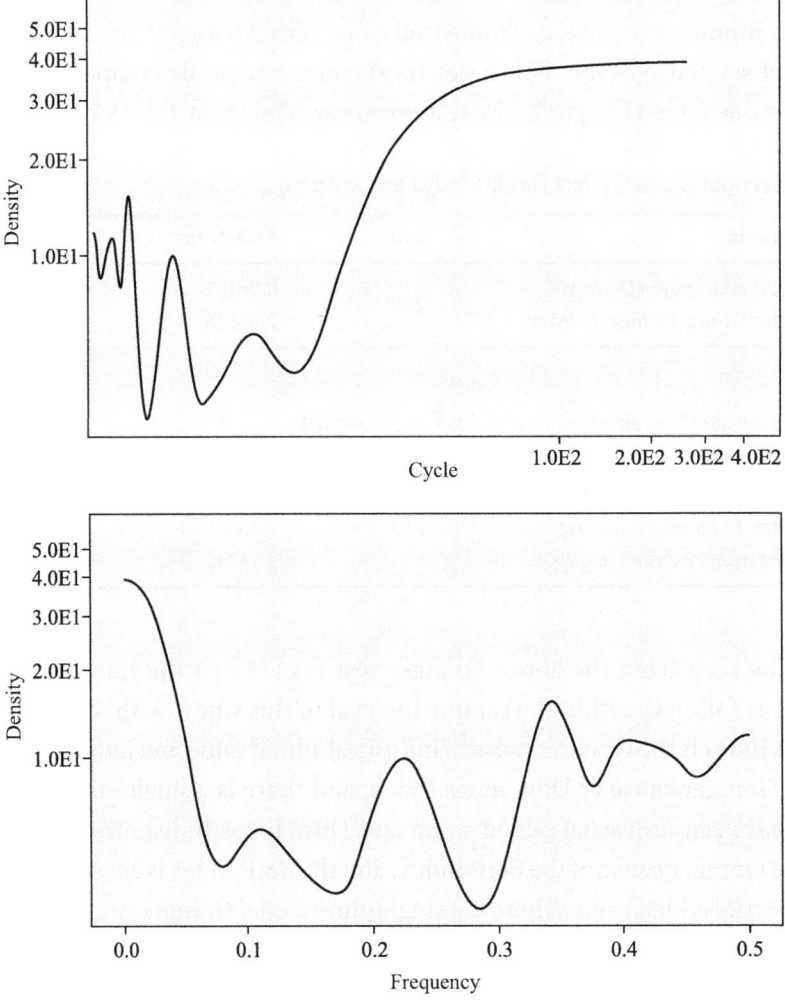

Figure 7-9 Spectrum Density of US GDP

As can be seen from Figure 7-9, the spectrum density curve of the cycle series of monthly industrial added value in the United States generated the main spectrum peak at the point of cycle 88, and the spectrum density was about 1.98. Combined with the spectrum density cycle data, it can be found that there was a macroeconomic fluctuation cycle of about 88 months (about 7.3 years) in the United States from January 1991 to December 2013. The spectrum density function of the Dow Jones Index and S&P Index is shown in Figures 7-10 and 7-11.

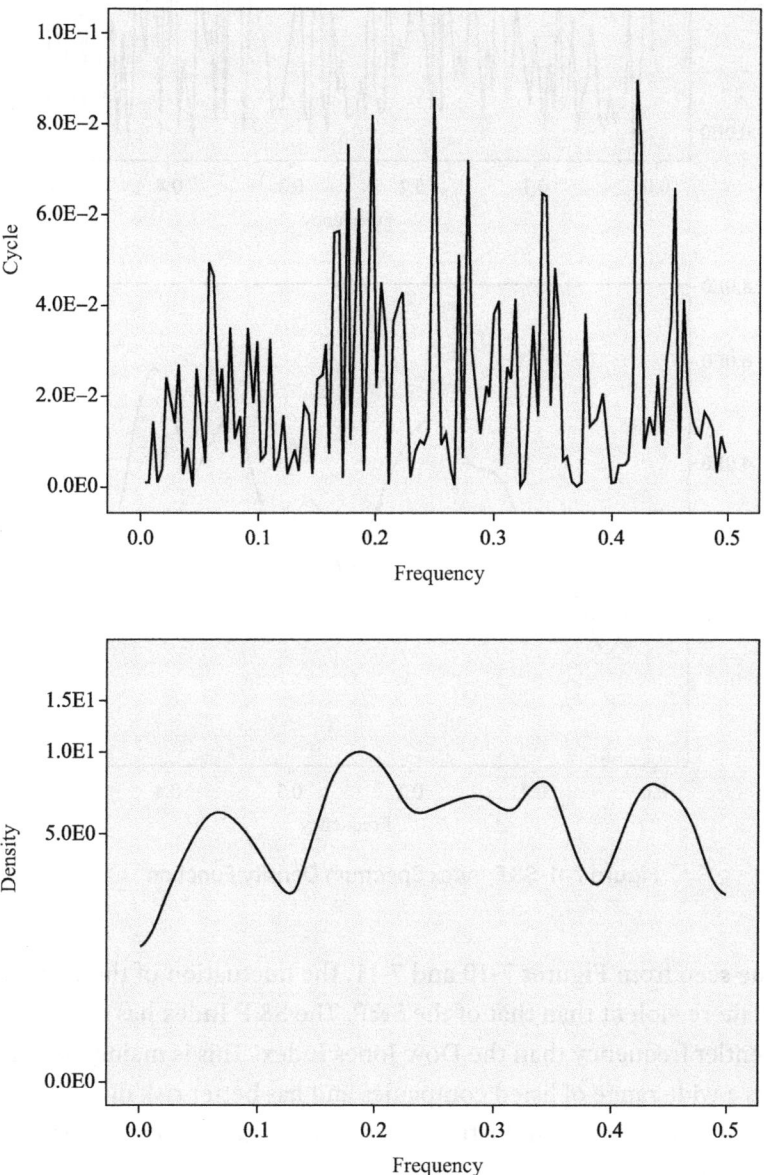

Figure 7-10 Cycle and Spectrum Density of the Dow Jones Index

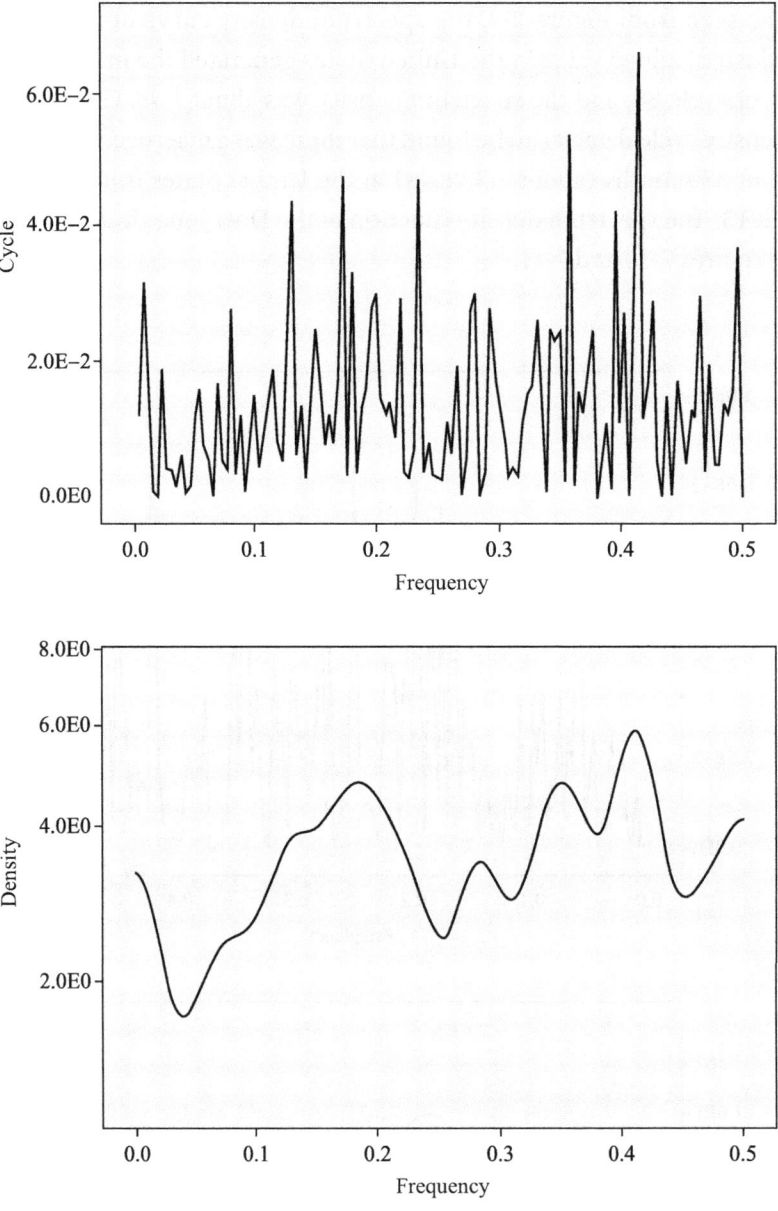

Figure 7-11 S&P Index Spectrum Density Function

As can be seen from Figures 7-10 and 7-11, the fluctuation of the Dow Jones Index is obviously more violent than that of the S&P. The S&P Index has a longer fluctuation cycle and gentler frequency than the Dow Jones Index. This is mainly because the S&P Index covers a wide range of listed companies and has better risk diversification ability, and its covered companies are industry leaders, able to maintain relatively stable returns to a certain extent.

B. CROSS-SPECTRUM ANALYSIS

For the general bivariate stationary time series $\{X_t\}$ and $\{Y_t\}$, the cross-spectrum density function $C_{xy}(\omega)$ is a complex function. If the real part and the imaginary part of it are set as $\alpha_{xy}(\omega)$ and $\beta_{xy}(\omega)$ respectively, then $\alpha_{xy}(\omega)$ reflects the correlation of the in-phase frequency components of the two time series, which is called Cospectrum. The imaginary part $\beta_{xy}(\omega)$ reflects the correlation of the dissimilar frequency components of two time series, which is called the Quadrature Spectrum. At this point, the cross-spectrum can be expressed as:

$$C_{xy} = S_{xy}(\omega) \cdot exp\left\{2\pi\phi_{xy}(\omega)\right\} \tag{7-36}$$

In Equation 7-36, $S_{xy}(\omega) = \sqrt{\alpha^2_{xy}(\omega) + \beta^2_{xy}(\omega)}$ is the square root of the sum of the square of the cospectrum and the square of the quadrature spectrum, representing the Cross-Amplitude Spectrum, which reflects the relationship between the amplitude spectrum of two serial frequency components. $\phi_{xy}(\omega)$ is the phase spectrum in the cross-spectrum density function, reflecting the phase difference of two time series cycles at each frequency point, that is, the time lag and lead relationship of two time series. Its mathematical expression is as follows:

$$\phi_{xy}(\omega) = arctan\left[-\beta_{xy}(\omega)/\alpha_{xy}(\omega)\right] \tag{7-37}$$

Table 7-7 shows the cross-spectrum analysis results of US GDP and Dow Jones Index.

Table 7-7 Cross Spectrum Analysis Results of US GDP and Dow Jones Index (Part)

Frequency (F)	Cycle Length (mp)	Cross Period (mv)	Quadrature Spectrum (os)	Phase Spectrum (ky)	Consistency (sd)
0	...	0	0	0	0.0006
0.0039	260	0.0097	−0.0251	−0.1319	0.0005
0.0423	23.6364	−0.0104	−1.2313	−1.0707	0.0245
0.0462	21.6667	0.0044	−0.8722	−0.8499	0.0189
0.05	20	0.0079	−0.4265	−0.4925	0.0132
0.0539	18.5714	0.0193	0.0439	0.0590	0.0106
0.0577	17.3333	−0.0070	0.4720	0.6576	0.0137
0.0923	10.8333	−0.0149	−1.1742	−2.4994	0.1829
0.0962	10.4	−0.0109	−1.4588	−2.3937	0.2199

(Continued)

Frequency (F)	Cycle Length (mp)	Cross Period (mv)	Quadrature Spectrum (os)	Phase Spectrum (ky)	Consistency (sd)
0.1	10	−0.0118	−1.6375	−2.3115	0.2399
0.1039	9.6296	−0.0032	−1.7152	−2.2396	0.2407
0.1077	9.2857	−0.0201	−1.7074	−2.1692	0.2261
0.1962	5.0980	−0.0478	−1.4806	−1.5867	0.0413
0.2	5	−0.0150	−1.4342	−1.3432	0.0369
0.2039	4.9057	−0.0026	−1.2811	−1.1105	0.0323
0.2077	4.8148	0.0406	−1.0277	−0.8685	0.0273
0.2115	4.7273	−0.0001	−0.6900	−0.5912	0.0226
0.2423	4.1270	0.0123	1.1259	0.9713	0.0485
0.2462	4.0625	0.0042	0.9893	0.9366	0.0436
0.25	4	0.0194	0.8103	0.8695	0.0362
0.2539	3.9394	0.0052	0.6217	0.7861	0.0276
0.2577	3.8806	−0.0017	0.4510	0.7130	0.0189
0.2615	3.8235	0.0176	0.3224	0.7089	0.0107
0.3885	2.5743	−0.0176	1.4110	2.3016	0.1115
0.3923	2.5490	0.0045	1.1499	2.4831	0.1028
0.3962	2.5243	−0.0147	0.9341	2.6473	0.1023
0.4	2.5	0.0040	0.7717	2.7715	0.1067
0.4039	2.4762	−0.0018	0.6617	2.8538	0.1124
0.4077	2.4528	−0.0011	0.5935	2.9041	0.1164
0.4615	2.1667	−0.0194	−2.6786	−1.9342	0.1425
0.4654	2.1488	−0.0150	−2.8938	−1.8153	0.1646
0.4692	2.1312	−0.0207	−3.0113	−1.6957	0.1815
0.4731	2.1138	−0.0048	−3.0168	−1.5664	0.1911
0.4962	2.0155	0.0022	−0.6564	−0.2926	0.1670
0.5	2	0.0171	0	0	0.1659

Each spectrum diagram is shown in Figure 7-12.

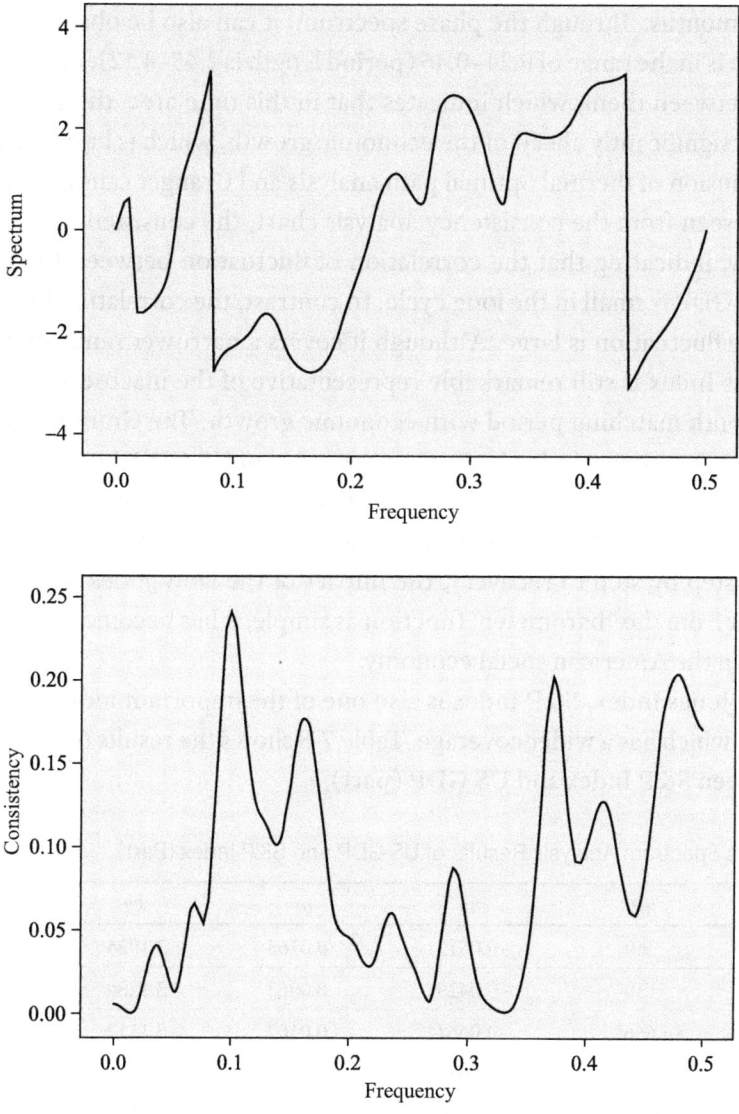

Figure 7-12 Phase Spectrum and Consistency of US GDP and Dow Jones Index

There is a strong correlation between US GDP and Dow Jones Index in the cycle length of 20, 10, 5, 4, 2.13, and 2. Considering the consistency, the matching cycle length of the two is finally determined to be 2.13 to 10 periods, with the strongest frequency of consistency being 0.106 and 0.24, respectively. That is, there is a matching period of about 2 to 10 months between US GDP and the Dow Jones Index, during which the correlation is strong.

The leading and lagging relationship between the two variables of US GDP and Dow Jones Index can be found through the calculation and analysis of the phase spectrum. The calculation results show that the Dow Jones Index leads the US economic growth index by about 2.07–3.11 months; that is, the US economy lags behind the Dow Jones

Index by 2–3 months. Through the phase spectrum, it can also be observed that when the fluctuation is in the range of 0.24–0.46 (period length is 2.45–4.12), there is a positive phase value between them, which indicates that in this time area, the growth of Dow Jones Index is significantly ahead of the economic growth, which is basically consistent with the conclusion of thermal optimal path analysis and Granger causality test.

As can be seen from the consistency analysis chart, the consistency is close to 0 at low frequency, indicating that the correlation of fluctuation between the Dow Jones Index and US GDP is small in the long cycle. In contrast, the correlation between short and mid-cycle fluctuation is large. Although it covers a narrower range of companies, the Dow Jones Index is still remarkably representative of the macroeconomy because of its 2–10-month matching period with economic growth. The Granger causality test proves that the Dow Jones Index is the Granger cause of US GDP. Looking back to the subprime crisis in 2007, the collapse of the US financial market began with the collapse of the Dow Jones Index, and after the crisis, the rising of the Dow Jones Index led the US economy step by step to recovery, the impact of the Dow Jones Index on the US economy is far from the "barometer" function as simple, it has become a very important factor affecting the American social economy.

Like Dow Jones Index, S&P Index is also one of the important indicators of the US stock market, which has a wider coverage. Table 7-8 shows the results of cross-spectrum analysis between S&P Index and US GDP (part).

Table 7-8 Cross Spectrum Analysis Results of US GDP and S&P Index (Part)

F	mp	mv	os	ky	sd
0.0039	260	−0.0512	0.0165	3.1026	0.7679
0.0077	130	−0.0429	0.0063	3.1230	0.6655
0.0115	86.6667	−0.0661	−0.0102	−3.1112	0.5235
0.0154	65	−0.0084	−0.0905	−2.7709	0.2877
0.0423	23.6364	−0.0060	−0.0122	−0.5609	0.0206
0.0462	21.6667	−0.0017	−0.0332	−0.8306	0.0771
0.05	20	0.0046	−0.0507	−1.8708	0.1086
0.0539	18.5714	0.0043	−0.0728	−1.7171	0.3892
0.0846	11.8182	−0.0027	−0.0295	−1.9795	0.0902
0.3885	2.5743	−0.0021	−0.0619	−2.7800	0.4751
0.3923	2.5490	0.0004	−0.0716	−2.7667	0.5475
0.3962	2.5243	−0.0707	−0.0278	−3.0240	0.6240
0.4	2.5	−0.0097	−0.0535	−2.9146	0.7405
0.4039	2.4762	−0.0356	−0.0997	−2.4106	0.1470
0.4077	2.4528	−0.0002	−0.1103	−1.0028	0.1456

(Continued)

F	mp	mv	os	ky	sd
0.4615	2.1667	−0.0249	−0.0553	−1.4027	0.0907
0.4654	2.1488	0.0148	−0.0044	−2.6745	0.0022
0.4692	2.1312	0.0051	−0.0134	−0.9289	0.0058
0.4731	2.1138	0.0013	−0.0237	−0.3791	0.1033
0.4769	2.0968	0.0088	0.0500	1.6022	0.0743
0.4808	2.08	−0.0001	0.0253	2.7900	0.1122
0.4962	2.0155	−0.0147	−0.0575	−2.7838	0.3056
0.5	2	0.0020	0	3.1416	0.2109

Figure 7-13 shows the cross-spectrum analysis of *cusgdp* and *csp*.

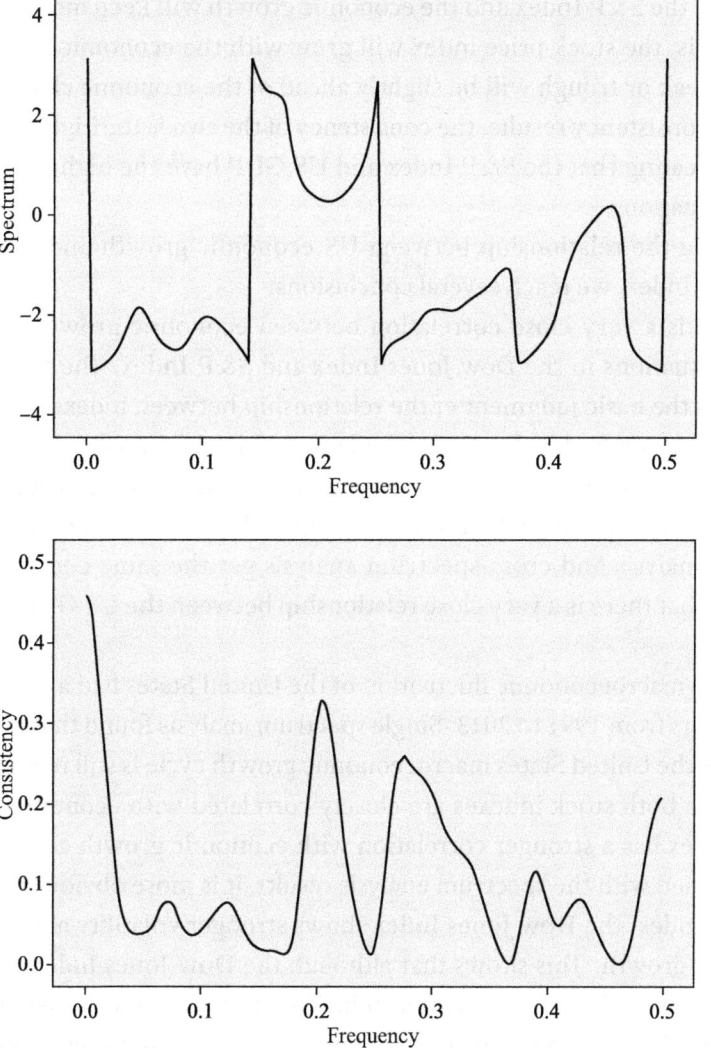

Figure 7-13 Phase Spectrum and Consistency of US GDP and S&P Index

According to Figure 7-13 and Table 7-10, it can be seen that there is a great correlation between US GDP and S&P Index at the points whose weekly length is 20, 10, 5, 4, and 2.5. By combining with the consistency test, it is found that the maximum correlation exists at the frequency of 2.5, followed by the frequency of 0.05. Therefore, it is determined that there is a 2.5–20 month matching period between US GDP and the S&P. Throughout the cycle, there is a strong correlation.

From the perspective of the main cycle, the phase spectrum value is positive only when the frequency is between 0.138–0.24. That is to say, the S&P Index has a positive impact on macroeconomic growth during a period of about 4–7 months, and this period is also the interval of high correlation between the two. When the phase spectrum reaches the maximum spectrum value (3.1026) at the lowest frequency, the leading angle of the S&P Index is close to π with the economic fluctuation, which indicates that in the long run, the S&P Index and the economic growth will keep moving in the same direction, that is, the stock price index will grow with the economic growth, and the arrival of the peak or trough will be slightly ahead of the economic change. As can be seen from the consistency results, the consistency of the two is the highest at the lowest frequency, indicating that the S&P Index and US GDP have the highest correlation in long-term fluctuations.

By analyzing the relationship between US economic growth and the Dow Jones Index and S&P Index, we reach several conclusions:

First, there is a very close correlation between economic growth in the United States and fluctuations in the Dow Jones Index and S&P Index. The thermal optimal path method is the basic judgment of the relationship between indexes, and the cross-spectrum analysis method is the exact calculation of the relationship between indexes. After verifying the relationship of the matching cycle between the US economic growth and Dow Jones Index and S&P Index, it is found that the two methods of thermal optimal path analysis and cross-spectrum analysis get the same conclusion, both of which believe that there is a very close relationship between the US GDP and the stock price index.

Second, the macroeconomic fluctuation of the United States had a fluctuation cycle of about 7.3 years from 1991 to 2013. Single spectrum analysis found that even in a short period of time, the United States macroeconomic growth cycle is still relatively obvious.

Third, while both stock indexes are closely correlated with economic growth, the Dow Jones Index has a stronger correlation with economic growth and a shorter lead period. Combined with the spectrum analysis results, it is more obvious that compared with the S&P Index, the Dow Jones Index shows stronger volatility and synchronicity with economic growth. This shows that although the Dow Jones Index covers a small range of company stocks, the company's ability to represent the macroeconomy is very strong, so it can show a significant and very close correlation with economic growth.

There is an inevitable correlation between the stock market and economic growth in theory. But in practice, the situation in the stock market deviates from economic growth frequently appears, and the function of the stock market "barometer" is increasingly questioned. Is it possible that stock markets have lost their original role in modern economic development and have become independent of macroeconomic growth? If the correlation still exists, is there a matching period of a certain length during which the stock market and economic growth are most closely correlated? This chapter tests these questions by analyzing US data.

American stock market has a long history, is large-scale, and has high maturity. In the analysis of the United States, in order to avoid the possibility of data mining, the empirical analysis is carried out by thermal optimal path and cross-spectrum analysis. The research focus of the thermal optimal path method is to find the lead-lag relationship of a set of time series through the method of statistical physics, and the cross-spectrum analysis method is to find the matching interval of the two sequences with the most correlation through the analysis of the frequency domain of time series. From two perspectives, these two methods use completely different research ideas to empirically test the relationship between the stock market and economic growth. The empirical result is that for each group of samples, the two methods have reached basically the same conclusion.

The test includes the two main stock price indexes in the United States, the Dow Jones Index and the S&P Index. The analysis of the thermal optimal path method found that the Dow Jones Index was ahead of the US economy by about four months, while the S&P Index was ahead by about 3.5 months. The monospectral analysis concludes that from December 1991 to December 2013, there was a fluctuation cycle of about 7.3 years in the United States macroeconomic fluctuation. This is a bit different from the period published by the NAER, mainly because of the difference in the sample. NAER looked at a longer time frame, covering 126 years from the 1860s to 2001. However, the sample time here is only more than 20 years. In the sample time we chose, the American economy has entered the recognized cycle stability stage. The cycle volatility has decreased significantly, so the macroeconomic cycle in this period has increased significantly compared with previous studies. The cross-spectrum analysis results show that there is a 2–10 month matching period between US GDP and the Dow Jones Index and a 2.5–20 month matching period with the S&P Index. At the same time, the fluctuation of the Dow Jones Index is significantly ahead of the fluctuation of economic growth indicators within the matching cycle, with a lead period of about 2–3 months, and the S&P Index also leads the economic growth indicators within the matching cycle of 4 to 7 months. Both indexes have a very good ability to reflect the American economy, confirming the speculation of the matching cycle theory.

7.5 Empirical Test of Matching Cycle between Japanese Stock Market and Economic Growth

7.5.1 Data Selection and Processing

In order to ensure the consistency of data, the data of the Nikkei 225 Index from December 1991 to December 2013 were also selected for the matching cycle test. Combined with empirical test experience and general empirical analysis methods, the industrial added value of Japan was chosen here to represent the monthly growth rate of GDP, analyzing its matching cycle with the Nikkei 225 Index.

1. HP Filtering Decomposition Result

In order to eliminate the influence of long-term trends on the research conclusion, we decompose the Nikkei Index data and the industrial added value data of Japan by HP filtering, respectively. The trend component and periodic component are obtained by HP filter decomposition. In HP filtering decomposition, *nky* represents the Nikkei 225 Index, and *vaj* represents Japan's industrial added value. Figures 7-14 and 7-15 show the HP filtering decomposition results of Japan's industrial added value and Nikkei 225 Index.

2. Results of the ADF Test

ADF test is conducted on the data, where *vaj* represents the original sequence of industrial added value in Japan, and *cvaj* represents the component cycle sequence of the smoothing index of industrial added value. *nky* represents the original sequence of the Nikkei 225 Index, and *cnky* represents the periodic sequence of the components of the Nikkei 225 Index. The ADF test results are shown in Table 7-9.

Table 7-9 ADF Test Results of Japan's Industrial Added Value and Nikkei 225 Index

		t-Statistic	1% Level	5% Level	10% Level
vaj	*vaj*	−3.7524	−3.4540	−2.8718	−2.5723
	cvaj	−6.3479	−3.4540	−2.8718	−2.5723
nky	*nky*	−2.2817	−3.4540	−2.8718	−2.5723
	cnky	−4.9689	−3.4540	−2.8718	−2.5723

Through the ADF test, it can be seen that the original time series of the monthly data of the Nikkei 225 Index is a non-stationary time series, but its periodic component time series after trend conversion is a stationary time series, while the original series of Japan's industrial added value is stationary series. However, in order to maintain the consistency of analysis data, the periodic component sequence of Japan's industrial added value after periodic conversion is still selected for the study. Therefore, both *cvaj* and *cnky*

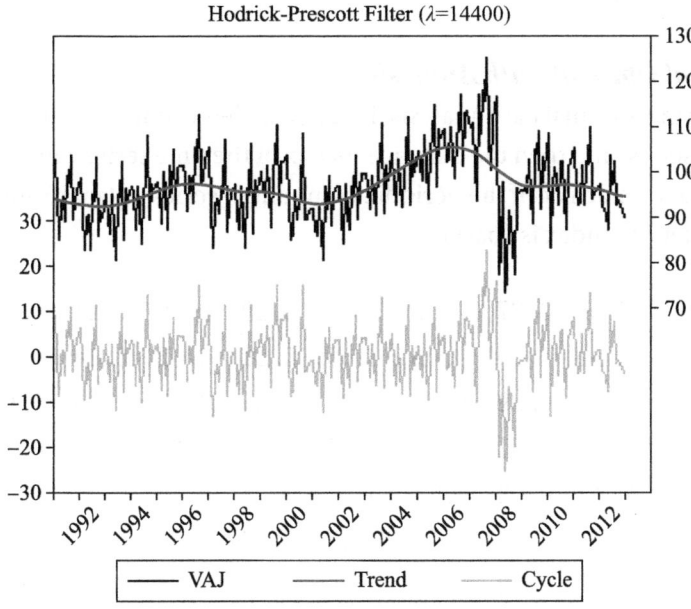

Figure 7-14 *vaj* Filtering Decomposition Result

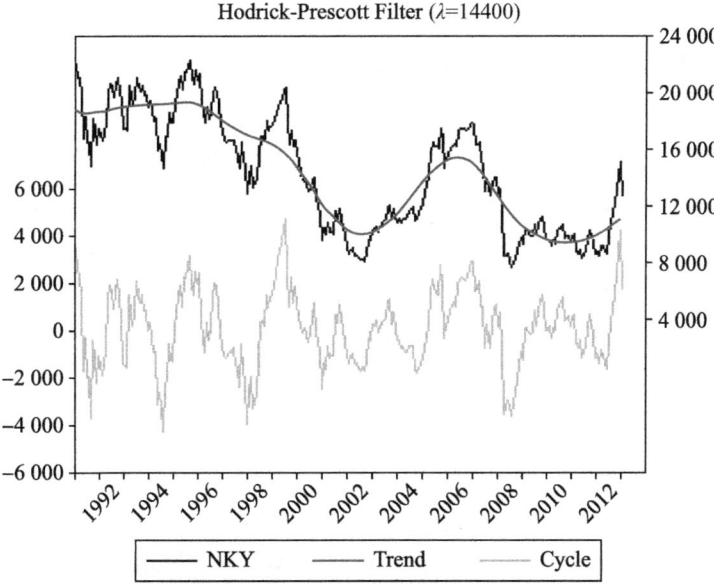

Figure 7-15 *nky* Filtering Decomposition Result

are stationary sequences, which can be selected for thermal optimal path analysis and cross-spectrum analysis.

7.5.2 Thermal Optimal Path Analysis

Before the thermal optimal path analysis, it has been determined that both *cvaj* and *cnky* are stationary series, and then the distance matrix of the time series can be calculated on them. The distance matrix c of the periodic component series of Japan's industrial added value and Nikkei 225 Index is (part):

$$c = \begin{bmatrix}
0.00 & 0.06 & 0.27 & 0.13 & 0.03 & 0.29 & 0.09 & 0.21 & 0.11 \\
0.61 & 0.14 & 0.20 & 0.06 & 0.05 & 0.21 & 0.02 & 0.14 & 0.19 \\
0.12 & 0.04 & 0.29 & 0.15 & 0.05 & 0.31 & 0.11 & 0.23 & 0.09 \\
0.40 & 0.18 & 0.51 & 0.38 & 0.27 & 0.53 & 0.34 & 0.46 & 0.13 \\
0.17 & 0.30 & 0.03 & 0.11 & 0.22 & 0.04 & 0.15 & 0.03 & 0.35 \\
0.59 & 0.04 & 0.38 & 0.24 & 0.13 & 0.39 & 0.20 & 0.32 & 0.01 \\
0.21 & 0.15 & 0.18 & 0.05 & 0.06 & 0.20 & 0.01 & 0.13 & 0.20 \\
0.61 & 0.07 & 0.40 & 0.26 & 0.16 & 0.42 & 0.22 & 0.34 & 0.02 \\
0.61 & 0.53 & 0.20 & 0.34 & 0.44 & 0.19 & 0.38 & 0.26 & 0.58 \\
0.15 & 0.08 & 0.25 & 0.12 & 0.01 & 0.27 & 0.08 & 0.20 & 0.13 \\
0.63 & 0.01 & 0.32 & 0.19 & 0.08 & 0.34 & 0.14 & 0.26 & 0.06 \\
0.38 & 0.28 & 0.05 & 0.09 & 0.19 & 0.07 & 0.13 & 0.01 & 0.33 \\
0.90 & 0.05 & 0.28 & 0.14 & 0.04 & 0.30 & 0.10 & 0.22 & 0.10 \\
0.56 & 0.19 & 0.14 & 0.00 & 0.10 & 0.16 & 0.04 & 0.08 & 0.24 \\
0.26 & 0.24 & 0.10 & 0.04 & 0.15 & 0.11 & 0.08 & 0.04 & 0.29 \\
0.08 & 0.36 & 0.02 & 0.16 & 0.27 & 0.01 & 0.20 & 0.08 & 0.41 \\
0.76 & 0.21 & 0.12 & 0.01 & 0.12 & 0.14 & 0.05 & 0.07 & 0.26 \\
0.36 & 0.13 & 0.20 & 0.06 & 0.04 & 0.21 & 0.02 & 0.14 & 0.18 \\
0.89 & 0.07 & 0.26 & 0.13 & 0.02 & 0.28 & 0.09 & 0.21 & 0.12 \\
& & & & \vdots
\end{bmatrix} \cdots$$

Figure 7-16 shows the topographic map of the distance matrix.

Based on the operation of the distance matrix, we can calculate the sequence position at each thermal average point. When the thermal average point is positive, it can be considered that the Nikkei 225 Index is ahead of Japan's industrial added value; when the thermal average point is negative, it can be considered that the Nikkei 225 Index is lagging behind Japan's industrial added value, that is, lagging behind macroeconomic growth.

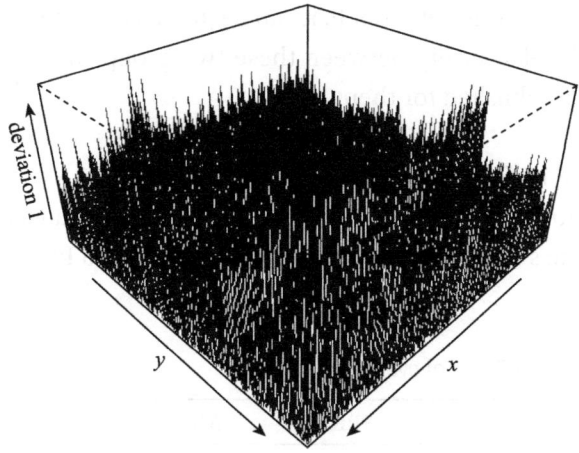

Figure 7-16 Distance Matrix of *cvaj* and *cnky*

Before calculating the average thermal position, T values need to be selected according to the recursive equation and lag order. Some T values are shown in Table 7-10.

Table 7-10 *T*-Values and Lag Orders of *cvaj* and *cnky*

	1993-12	1995-12	1997-12	1999-12	2000-12	2005-12	2008-12	2010-12	2013-12
$T=2$	0	2	−1	2	4	7	3	6	10
$T=5$	−1	1	−3	−2	0	3	5	4	2
$T=10$	−1	2	−1	0	2	3	7	9	10
$T=20$	−1	−3	−2	−1	0	1	2	1	2

When T increases, the selection result of the lag order tends to be stable. Still, no matter what T value obtains, the changing trend of the lag order is consistent, and considering the T value and the general characteristics of thermal optimal path analysis, it is finally considered that the leading (lagging) order at $T=5$ is more accurate. It can be seen from this that, through the results of thermal optimal path analysis, we believe that from December 1991 to December 2013, the volatility of Japan's Nikkei 225 Index was highly correlated with the macroeconomic volatility, and there was no obvious leading and lagging trend.

7.5.3 *Cross Spectrum Analysis*

1. Time Domain Analysis

In order to explain the data from different perspectives, before the frequency domain analysis, we first carried out the basic time domain analysis of the data. Since both *cvaj* and *cnky* are stable time series of order 0, it can be judged that there is a long-term stable cooperative growth relationship between these two groups of time series; that is, the VAR model can be established for them.

(1) Establishment of VAR model

To establish VAR model, the lag order of the model should be judged. The test results of the lag order of Japan's industrial added value and Nikkei 225 Index are shown in Table 7-11.

Table 7-11 VAR Models Lag Order of *cvaj* and *cnky*

LAG	LogL	LR	FPE	AIC	SC	HQ
0	284.5337	NA	0.000329	−2.344678	−2.315759	−2.333027
1	313.8413	57.88551	0.000266	−2.554699	−2.467941	−2.519746
2	333.2792	38.06923	0.000234	−2.682815	−2.538217	−2.624559
3	362.3744	56.50031	0.000190	−2.891074	−2.688638*	−2.809516
4	363.8148	2.773226	0.000194	−2.869833	−2.609557	−2.764972
5	369.0031	9.902938	0.000193	−2.879694	−2.561580	−2.751531
6	378.0931	17.19933	0.000185	−2.921934	−2.545981	−2.770470
7	384.6130	12.22811	0.000181	−2.942846	−2.509054	−2.768079
8	385.8956	2.384385	0.000185	−2.920296	−2.428665	−2.722227
9	393.1192	13.30820	0.000180	−2.947047	−2.397577	−2.725676
10	394.3049	2.164690	0.000184	−2.923692	−2.316383	−2.679018
11	419.4623	45.51300	0.000155	−3.099272	−2.434124	−2.831296*
12	421.8357	4.254366	0.000157	−3.085773	−2.362786	−2.794495
13	422.7813	1.679349	0.000161	−3.060426	−2.279600	−2.745845
14	435.8324	22.96136	0.000149	−3.135539	−2.296874	−2.797656
15	440.0703	7.385412	0.000149	−3.137513	−2.241009	−2.776328
16	441.8565	3.083272	0.000152	−3.119141	−2.164798	−2.734654
17	443.4818	2.778525	0.000155	−3.099434	−2.087252	−2.691645
18	448.1674	7.932421	0.000154	−3.105123	−2.035103	−2.674032
19	448.7631	0.998701	0.000159	−3.076872	−1.949013	−2.622479
20	453.9776	8.654817	0.000158	−3.086951	−1.901253	−2.609255
21	456.0674	3.433809	0.000160	−3.071099	−1.827561	−2.570101
22	457.7440	2.727038	0.000163	−3.051817	−1.750441	−2.527517
23	468.1072	16.68430	0.000155	−3.104624	−1.745408	−2.557021
24	477.2714	14.60188*	0.000149*	−3.147480*	−1.730426	−2.576575

According to the above results, considering the five criteria (LR, FPE, AIC, SC, HQ) comprehensively, the lag order of the VAR model of Japan's industrial added value and Nikkei 225 Index was selected as 24 order lag. The VAR model is re-established and estimated according to the selected lag order. The chart verification of the AR root of the estimated result is shown in Figure 7-17.

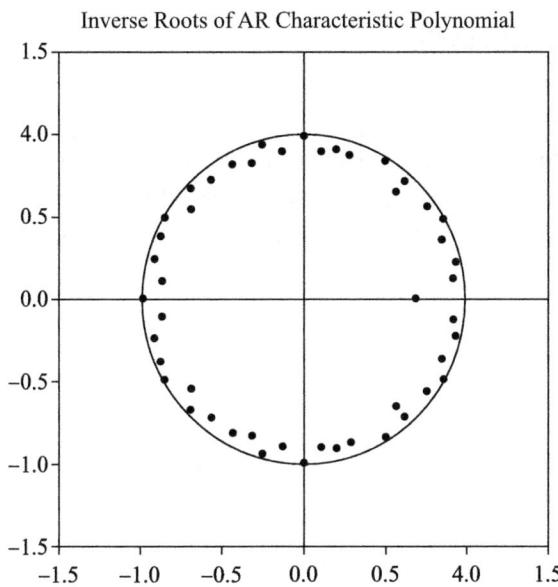

Figure 7-17 Diagram Verification of the AR Root of the Model

According to the above results, it can be seen that the reciprocal of all characteristic roots is within the range of a unit circle; that is, the VAR model established according to the cyclical series of Japan's industrial added value, and Nikkei 225 Index is stable. We can run Granger causality tests.

(2) Granger causality test
Since the sequence satisfies the stationarity, the Granger causality test is conducted on the periodic series of Japan's industrial added value and the periodic series of the Nikkei 225 Index, and the test results are shown in Table 7-12.

Table 7-12 Granger Causality Test Results (*cvaj* and *cnky*)

Null Hypothesis	Obs	F-Statistic	Prob.
CVAJ does not Granger Cause CNKY	241	1.2841	0.1788
CNKY does not Granger Cause CVAJ		1.7158	0.0249

   It can be seen from the above Granger causality test results that the time-domain analysis results of Japan's industrial added value and Nikkei 225 Index are: at the 5% confidence level within the sample interval of this study, Japan's industrial added value is not the Granger cause of the Nikkei 225 Index, but the Nikkei 225 Index is the Granger cause of Japan's industrial added value. There is a one-way Granger causality relationship between Japan's industrial added value and the Nikkei 225 Index.

2. Frequency Domain Analysis

(1) Single spectrum analysis

Based on the time-domain analysis results, the matching cycle between the Nikkei 225 Index and Japan's industrial added value is calculated by spectrum analysis and cross-spectrum analysis. Figure 7-18 shows the results of single spectrum analysis.

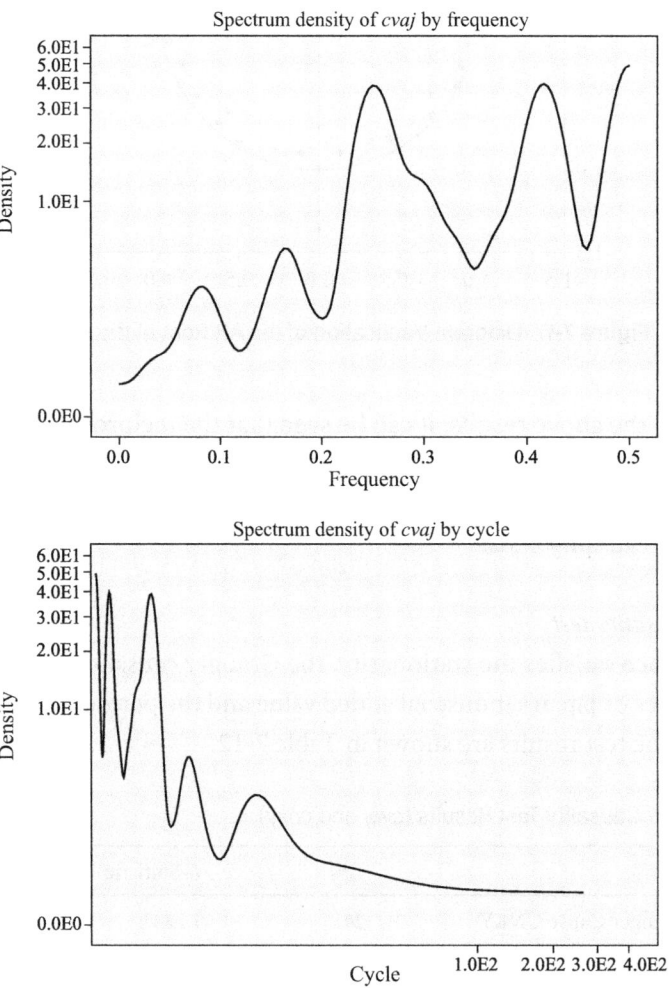

Figure 7-18 Single Spectrum Analysis of Japan's Industrial Added Value

According to Figure 7-18, combined with the single spectrum analysis results of Japan's industrial added value, it can be found that the effective fluctuation period of Japan's industrial added value cannot be observed during the sample period. This is related to the characteristics of Japan's economic development. Since Japan's economy was in stagnation or depression for a long time after 1991, the economic recovery process was always very slow. Therefore, there was no obvious macroeconomic cycle in the sample interval. The spectrum density and period of the Nikkei 225 Index are shown in Figure 7-19.

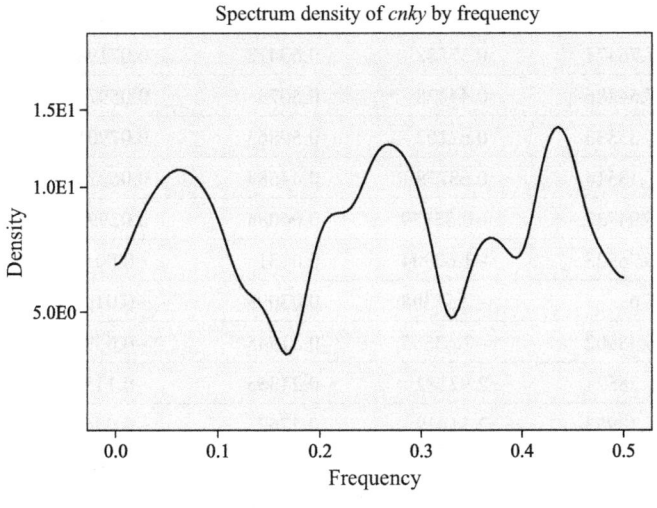

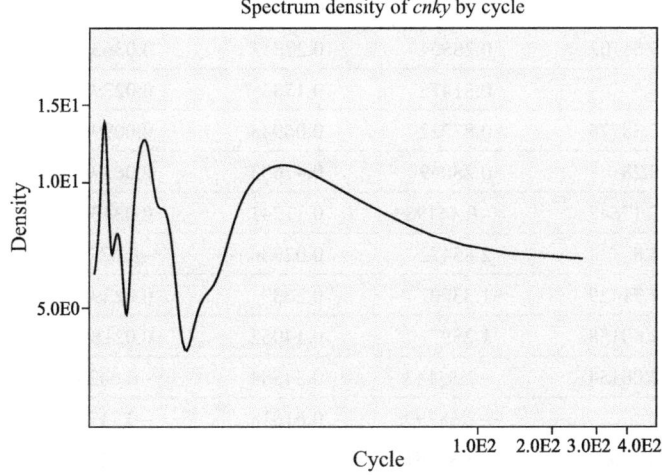

Figure 7-19 Single Spectrum Analysis of the Nikkei 225 Index

(2) Cross-spectrum analysis

Cross-spectrum analysis is the most important step in spectrum analysis and also the final step to determine the variable matching period. Table 7-13 shows some results of the cross-spectrum analysis of Japan's industrial added value and Nikkei 225 Index.

Table 7-13 Cross Spectrum Analysis Results of Japan's Industrial Added Value and Nikkei 225 Index (Part)

F	mp	mv	os	ky	sd
0.11742	8.51613	1.4845	0.08848	0.00186	0.02148
0.12121	8.25	0.85506	0.08385	0.01553	0.01785
0.125	8	0.51803	0.18474	0.03532	0.02013
0.12879	7.76471	0.57588	0.63472	0.07198	0.04674
0.13258	7.54286	0.44428	0.5074	0.05975	0.02844
0.13636	7.33333	0.62103	0.59863	0.07901	0.05653
0.14015	7.13514	0.63778	0.44584	0.06023	0.04464
0.14394	6.94737	−0.35579	0.06084	0.02999	−0.01114
0.14773	6.76923	−1.60904	0.0831	−0.00123	−0.03218
0.15152	6.6	−2.57308	0.03099	−0.01902	−0.01215
0.1553	6.43902	−2.63505	0.31948	−0.0591	−0.03279
0.15909	6.28571	2.92182	0.24355	−0.11387	0.02544
0.16288	6.13953	2.51439	0.2762	−0.08455	0.06129
0.16667	6	2.3366	0.25729	−0.06612	0.06876
0.17045	5.86667	2.37903	0.15525	−0.057	0.05445
0.17424	5.73913	2.00957	0.11075	−0.02707	0.05768
0.17803	5.61702	0.28504	0.22817	0.03633	0.01065
0.18182	5.5	0.51475	0.1583	0.02392	0.01353
0.18561	5.38776	0.87722	0.06943	0.00998	0.012
0.18939	5.28	0.28049	0.47633	0.06395	0.01842
0.19318	5.17647	−0.46198	0.11741	0.03436	−0.01711
0.20833	4.8	2.85472	0.02936	−0.02739	0.00808
0.21212	4.71429	1.33707	0.2639	0.02399	0.10078
0.21591	4.63158	1.2597	0.14052	0.02185	0.06796
0.24621	4.06154	−2.55143	0.54584	−0.64257	−0.43038
0.25	4	−2.58799	0.61518	−0.7172	−0.44328
0.25379	3.9403	−2.55761	0.74458	−0.72742	−0.48073
0.25758	3.88235	−2.54457	0.63154	−0.82593	−0.56144
0.26136	3.82609	−2.56697	0.58633	−0.2242	−0.14517
0.29924	3.34177	−2.6168	0.36039	−0.2376	−0.13755

(Continued)

F	mp	mv	os	ky	sd
0.30303	3.3	−2.13634	0.58402	−0.20202	−0.3183
0.30682	3.25926	−2.08745	0.64069	−0.13585	−0.23911
0.31061	3.21951	−2.08622	0.3298	−0.07311	−0.12905
0.31439	3.18072	−1.99143	0.34402	−0.06201	−0.13863
0.31818	3.14286	−1.7398	0.30273	−0.02236	−0.13104
0.32197	3.10588	−1.65833	0.10404	−0.00328	−0.03733
0.32576	3.06977	−1.95011	0.22322	−0.02609	−0.06545
0.32955	3.03448	−1.65814	0.14832	−0.00433	−0.04948
0.33333	3	−2.50849	0.31537	−0.0801	−0.05878

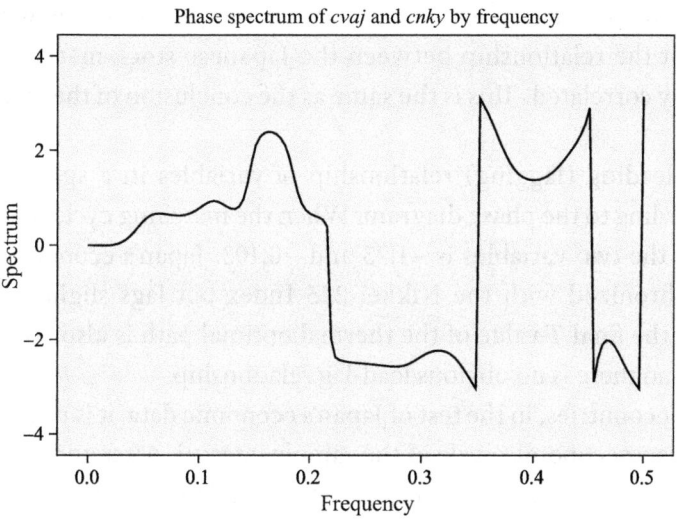

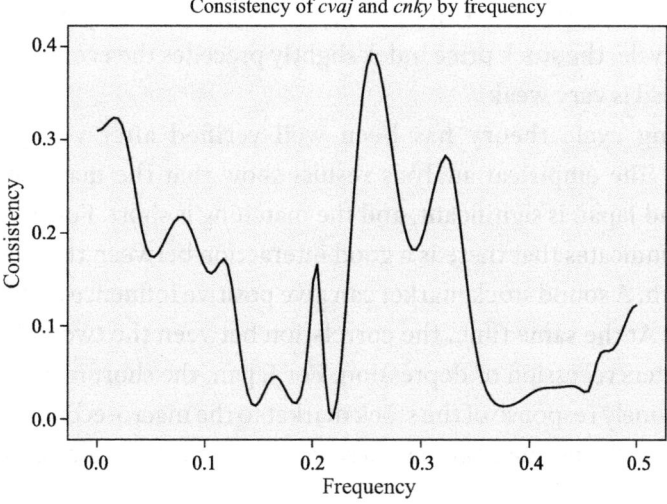

Figure 7-20 Cross Spectrum Analysis of Japan's Industrial Added Value and Nikkei 225 Index

Through the analysis of Table 7-13 and Figure 7-20, we can draw several conclusions after cross-spectrum analysis.

First, there is a matching cycle between the Nikkei 225 Index and Japan's economic growth, and the matching cycle may be eight months, four months, or 3.1 months long. At these three time points, the correlation is 0.185, 0.615, and 0.104, respectively. When the length is four months and 3.1 months, the correlation reaches the maximum correlation within the sample interval. Therefore, it can be considered that there was a matching period of about 3.1 months to 4 months between the Nikkei 225 Index and Japan's economic growth from December 1991 to December 2013.

Second, through cross-spectrum analysis, it can be observed that the matching cycle between Japan's economic growth and the Nikkei 225 Index exists, and the matching cycle is short; within the cycle range, the consistency of the two is 0.615, indicating that the correlation between the two is very obvious even within the cycle. This shows that the relationship between the Japanese stock market and economic growth is highly correlated. This is the same as the conclusion of thermal optimal path analysis.

Third, the leading (lagging) relationship of variables in a specific time can be measured according to the phase diagram. When the matching cycle is 3.1 to 4 months, the lag time of the two variables is −1.73 and −0.103. Japan's economic development is almost synchronized with the Nikkei 225 Index but lags slightly. The lag order determined by the final T-value of the thermal optimal path is also considered almost synchronous, and there is no obvious lead-lag relationship.

Unlike other countries, in the test of Japan's economic data, it is not found that there is an obvious macroeconomic cycle in the sample interval. After analyzing the thermal optimal path, it is found that the Japanese economy and the Nikkei 225 Index are almost in synchronization. The cross-spectrum analysis concludes that there is a matching cycle of about four months between the Nikkei 225 Index and Japan's macroeconomic growth. In the cycle, the stock price index slightly precedes the economic development index, but the lead is very weak.

The matching cycle theory has been well verified after verifying developed countries' data. The empirical analysis results show that the matching cycle of the United States and Japan is significant, and the matching is short. For the United States, this conclusion indicates that there is a good interaction between the stock market and economic growth. A sound stock market can give positive influence and feedback to the macroeconomy. At the same time, the correlation between the two will not end when the economy enters recession or depression. For Japan, the short matching cycle is not only due to the timely response of the stock market to the macro-economic information, but more importantly, because the Japanese economy has been almost stuck in a state of stagnation since the 1990s, and the stock market has been in a downturn for a long time. There is no significant fluctuation cycle in either of them, so the matching cycle is obvious.

7.6 Empirical Test of Matching Cycle between China's Stock Market and Economic Growth

7.6.1 Basic Data Processing

Shanghai Composite Index and China's industrial added value are selected for empirical analysis. China's industrial added value is the monthly GDP growth rate. In order to ensure the consistency of data, the data of the Shanghai Composite Index and industrial added value from December 1991 to December 2013 are also selected for the matching cycle test.

1. HP Filtering Decomposition Result

In order to eliminate the influence of long-term trends, it is necessary to decompose the SSE Index by HP filter to get its trend component and cycle component. Among them, *shz* represents the SSE Composite Index, and *vac* represents the industrial added value of our country. Figures 7-21 and 7-22 show the decomposition results of HP filtering.

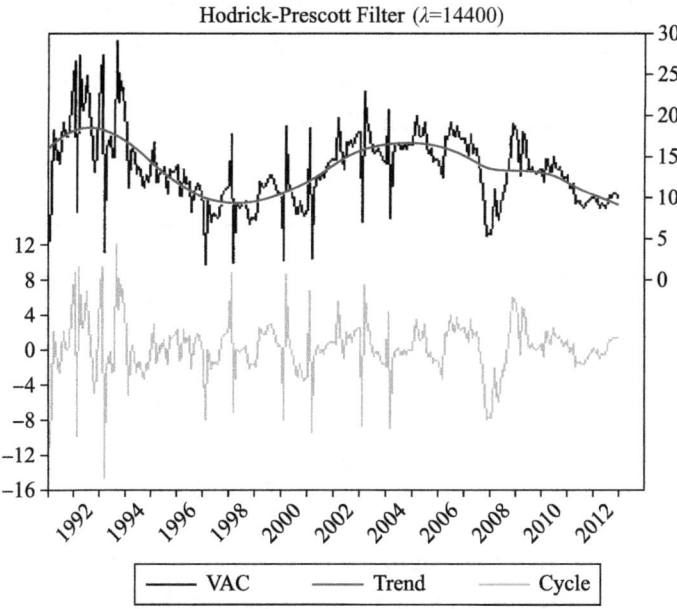

Figure 7-21 HP Filtering Decomposition Result of China's Industrial Added Value

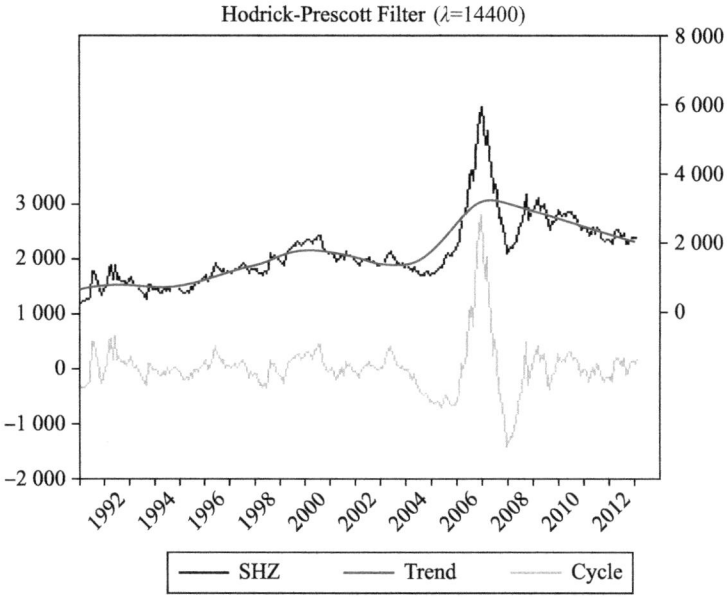

Figure 7-22 HP Filtering Decomposition Result of SSE Composite Index

2. Results of the ADF Test

Before other tests, the time series needs to be tested for stationarity. The stationarity test results are shown in Table 7-14, where *vac* represents the original sequence of China's industrial added value, and *cvac* represents the periodic component sequence of industrial added value; *shz* represents the original sequence of Shanghai Composite Index, and *cshz* represents the periodic component sequence of the Shanghai Composite Index. The ADF test results are shown in Table 7-14.

Table 7-14 ADF Test Results

		t-Statistic	1% Level	5% Level	10% Level
vac	*vac*	−2.1999	−3.4540	−2.8718	−2.5723
	cvac	−5.8014	−3.4540	−2.8718	−2.5723
shz	*shz*	−2.9679	−3.4540	−2.8718	−2.5723
	cshz	−13.6616	−3.4540	−2.8718	−2.5723

The ADF test shows that the original series of the time series of China's industrial added value and the time series of the Shanghai Composite Index are both non-stationary series, and the periodic component series after the periodic conversion are stationary time series. Therefore, the thermal optimal path analysis and cross-spectrum analysis can be carried out on the two periodic component series.

7.6.2 Thermal Optimal Path Analysis

After determining that both *cvac* and *cshz* are stationary series, the thermal optimal path analysis can be carried out, and then the distance matrix calculation of the time series can be carried out. The distance matrix *cz* of the periodic component series of China's industrial added value and Shanghai Composite index is (part):

$$c_z = \begin{pmatrix}
0.32 & 0.35 & 0.29 & 0.37 & 0.27 & 0.31 & 0.39 \\
0.26 & 0.29 & 0.23 & 0.31 & 0.21 & 0.37 & 0.33 \\
0.11 & 0.14 & 0.08 & 0.16 & 0.06 & 0.52 & 0.18 \\
0.11 & 0.14 & 0.08 & 0.16 & 0.06 & 0.52 & 0.18 \\
0.12 & 0.15 & 0.09 & 0.17 & 0.07 & 0.51 & 0.19 \\
0.17 & 0.2 & 0.14 & 0.22 & 0.12 & 0.46 & 0.24 \\
0.17 & 0.2 & 0.14 & 0.22 & 0.12 & 0.46 & 0.24 \\
0.11 & 0.14 & 0.08 & 0.16 & 0.06 & 0.52 & 0.18 \\
0.13 & 0.16 & 0.1 & 0.18 & 0.08 & 0.5 & 0.2 \\
0.15 & 0.18 & 0.12 & 0.2 & 0.1 & 0.48 & 0.22 \\
0.17 & 0.2 & 0.14 & 0.22 & 0.12 & 0.46 & 0.24 \\
0.18 & 0.21 & 0.15 & 0.23 & 0.13 & 0.45 & 0.25 \\
0.14 & 0.11 & 0.17 & 0.09 & 0.19 & 0.77 & 0.07 \\
0.41 & 0.44 & 0.38 & 0.46 & 0.36 & 0.22 & 0.48 \\
0.08 & 0.11 & 0.05 & 0.13 & 0.03 & 0.55 & 0.15 \\
0.13 & 0.16 & 0.1 & 0.18 & 0.08 & 0.5 & 0.2 \\
0.15 & 0.18 & 0.12 & 0.2 & 0.1 & 0.48 & 0.22 \\
0.16 & 0.19 & 0.13 & 0.21 & 0.11 & 0.47 & 0.23 \\
& & & \vdots & & &
\end{pmatrix} \cdots$$

Figure 7-23 shows the distance matrix of Shanghai Composite Index and China's industrial added value respectively.

Based on the operation of the distance matrix, we can calculate the sequence position at each thermal average point. When the thermal average point is positive, it can be considered that the Shanghai Composite Index is ahead of China's industrial added value; when the thermal average point is negative, it can be considered that the Shanghai Composite Index is behind China's industrial added value, that is, behind the macroeconomic growth.

Before calculating the average thermal position, *T* values need to be selected according to the recursive equation and lag order. Some *T* values are shown in Table 7-15.

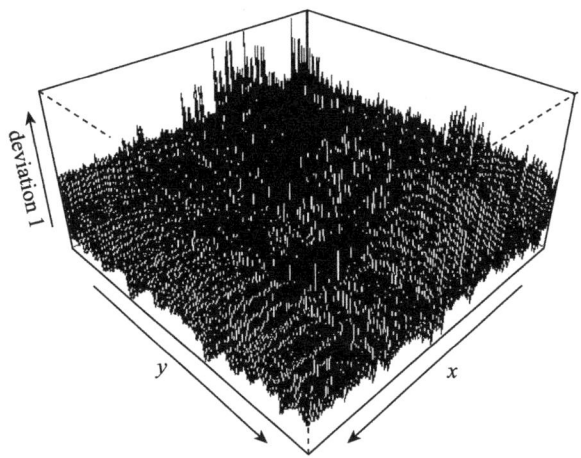

Figure 7-23 Energy Geomorphology of Shanghai Composite Index
and China's Industrial Added Value

Table 7-15 *T*-Values and Lag Orders of *cvac* and *cshz*

	1993-12	1995-12	1997-12	1999-12	2000-12	2005-12	2008-12	2010-12	2013-12
$T=2$	0	3	2	4	5	9	6	3	1
$T=5$	−1	3	4	1	3	5	4	9	6
$T=10$	−2	1	5	6	3	6	1	8	6
$T=20$	−1	−4	−2	1	5	3	4	6	4

As T increases, the result of choosing the lag order tends to be stable. Still, no matter what T value obtains, it is the trend of lag order being consistent, taking into account the T value case and the general characteristics of thermal optimal path analysis. Finally, it is considered that the leading (lagging) order at $T=5$ is more accurate.

It can be seen from the results of the thermal optimal path analysis that the volatility of the Shanghai Composite Index was ahead of the macroeconomic growth from December 1991 to December 1993, and the leading period was about one month. From December 1995 to December 2013, there was a strong correlation between the two fluctuations. The Shanghai Composite Index lagged behind the development of the macroeconomy for about six months; that is, the macroeconomy was ahead of the stock market for about six months. The stock market had no guiding effect on the macroeconomy, and it did not play its role as the "barometer" of the macroeconomy.

7.6.3 *Cross Spectrum Analysis*

1. Time Domain Analysis

In order to explain the data from different angles, the basic time domain analysis of the data is first carried out before the frequency domain analysis. According to the previous data processing results, it can be seen that *cvac* and *cshz* are 0-order stationary practical sequences, so the VAR model can be established for them, and the Granger causality test can be conducted.

(1) Establishment of VAR model

To establish VAR model, the lag order of the model should be judged. The lag order test results of China's industrial added value and Shanghai Composite Index are shown in Table 7-16.

Table 7-16 Lag Order of VAR Model of *cvac* and *cshz*

Lag	LogL	LR	FPE	AIC	SC	HQ
0	508.1414	NA	5.05e-05	−4.217845	−4.188840	−4.206158
1	545.6363	74.05229	3.82e-05	−4.496969	−4.409953	−4.461908
2	563.0762	34.15322	3.42e-05	−4.608968	−4.463942*	−4.550533
3	571.7210	16.78533	3.29e-05	−4.647675	−4.444638	−4.565866*
4	576.5815	9.356397	3.26e-05	−4.654846	−4.393798	−4.549662
5	578.9408	4.502360	3.31e-05	−4.641173	−4.322115	−4.512616
6	587.3952	15.99301	3.19e-05	−4.678294	−4.301224	−4.526362
7	589.7747	4.461517	3.23e-05	−4.664789	−4.229709	−4.489484
8	591.8208	3.802237	3.28e-05	−4.648506	−4.155416	−4.449827
9	597.1012	9.724743	3.25e-05	−4.659176	−4.108075	−4.437123
10	598.0909	1.806339	3.33e-05	−4.634091	−4.024979	−4.388664
11	601.0427	5.337806	3.36e-05	−4.625356	−3.958234	−4.356554
12	626.1087	44.90991	2.82e-05	−4.800906	−4.075773	−4.508730
13	628.6461	4.503834	2.86e-05	−4.788717	−4.005574	−4.473168
14	637.6353	15.80595	2.74e-05	−4.830294	−3.989139	−4.491370
15	640.5885	5.143487	2.77e-05	−4.821570	−3.922405	−4.459273

(Continued)

Lag	LogL	LR	FPE	AIC	SC	HQ
16	641.6388	1.811919	2.84e-05	−4.796990	−3.839815	−4.411318
17	648.7842	12.20669	2.77e-05	−4.823202	−3.808016	−4.414156
18	652.8185	6.824705	2.77e-05	−4.823488	−3.750291	−4.391068
19	654.4476	2.728756	2.83e-05	−4.803730	−3.672523	−4.347936
20	658.6559	6.978690	2.82e-05	−4.805466	−3.616248	−4.326298
21	661.8061	5.171528	2.85e-05	−4.798384	−3.551155	−4.295842
22	669.7154	12.85268	2.76e-05	−4.830962	−3.525722	−4.305045
23	682.3257	20.28163	2.57e-05	−4.902715	−3.539464	−4.353424
24	688.9059	10.47338*	2.52e-05*	−4.924216*	−3.502955	−4.351551

According to the above results, the five criteria (LR, FPE, AIC, SC, HQ) were comprehensively considered. Finally, the VAR model lag order of China's industrial added value, Shanghai Composite Index, and Shanghai A-share Index was selected as 24 order lag. The chart verification of the AR root of the estimated results is shown in Figure 7-24.

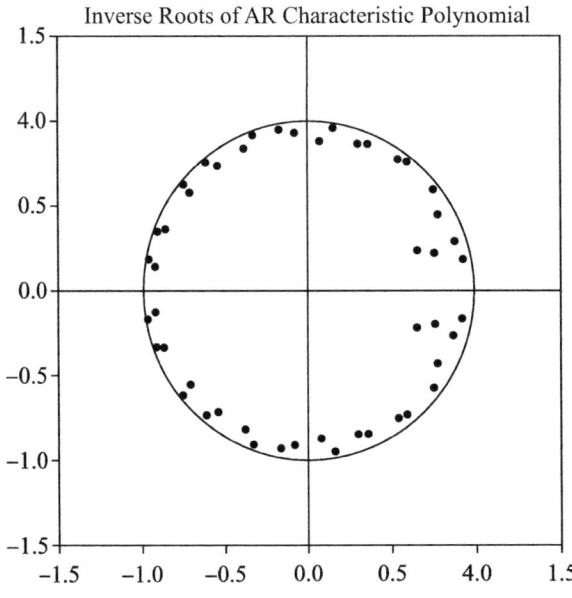

Figure 7-24 Diagram Verifying the AR Root of the Model

It can be seen from the above results that the reciprocal of all characteristic roots is within the range of a unit circle; that is, the VAR model established according to the cyclical series of China's industrial added value and the cyclical series of the Shanghai Composite Index is stable. We can run the Granger causality test.

(2) Granger causality test

Since the sequence satisfies the stationarity, the Granger causality test is conducted on the periodic series of China's industrial added value and the periodic series of the Shanghai Composite Index, and the specific test results are shown in Table 7-17.

Table 7-17 Granger Causality Test Results (*cvac* and *cshz*)

Null Hypothesis	*Obs*	*F*-Statistic	*Prob.*
cshz does not Granger Cause *cvac*	240	2.4362	0.0604
cvac does not Granger Cause *cshz*		1.0243	0.0004

It can be seen from the above Granger causality test results that the time-domain analysis results of China's industrial added value and Shanghai Composite Index are: At the 5% confidence level within the sample interval of this study, Shanghai Composite Index is not the Granger cause of China's industrial added value, but China's industrial added value is the Granger cause of Shanghai Composite Index. The changes in the Shanghai Composite Index cannot have an impact on industrial added value, while industrial added value will have an impact on the Shanghai Composite Index to some extent.

2. Frequency Domain Analysis

(1) Single spectrum analysis

Based on the time-domain analysis results, the matching cycle between the Shanghai Composite Index and China's industrial added value is calculated by spectrum analysis and cross-spectrum analysis. Firstly, a single spectrum analysis was conducted on the two variables respectively. The results of the single spectrum analysis are shown in Figure 7-25.

It can be seen from Figures 7-25 and 7-26 that there is a very obvious low-frequency fluctuation in China's industrial added value, and the contribution of each frequency cycle to the overall macroeconomic fluctuation can be clearly seen from the cycle chart. It can be inferred from the trend that there may be a longer cycle component; that is, China's industrial added value did not complete a long cycle fluctuation during the sample period. It can be seen from the density map that the fluctuations are mostly concentrated in the low-frequency region, which indicates that the fluctuations of China's industrial added value are mainly long-term fluctuations during the sample period. The fluctuation frequency of the Shanghai Composite Index is concentrated between 0 and 0.075, which means that the fluctuation energy of the Shanghai Composite Index is mainly contributed by the periodic fluctuation determined by the frequency within this range.

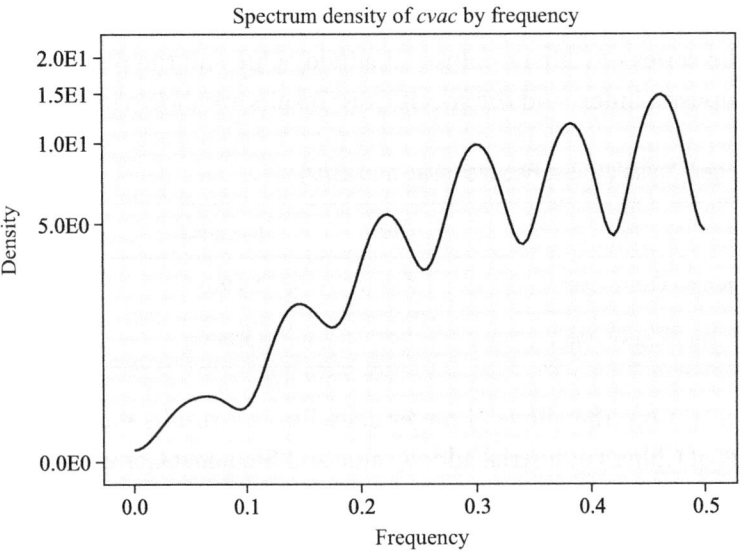

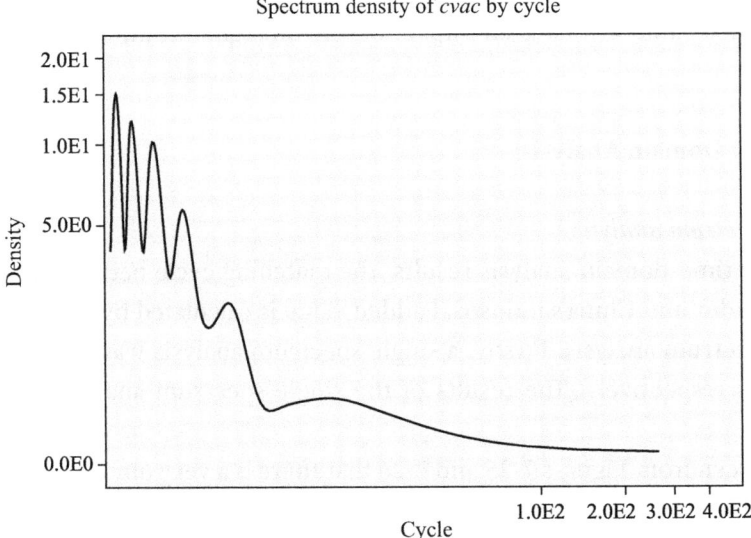

Figure 7-25 Single Spectrum Analysis of China's Industrial Added Value

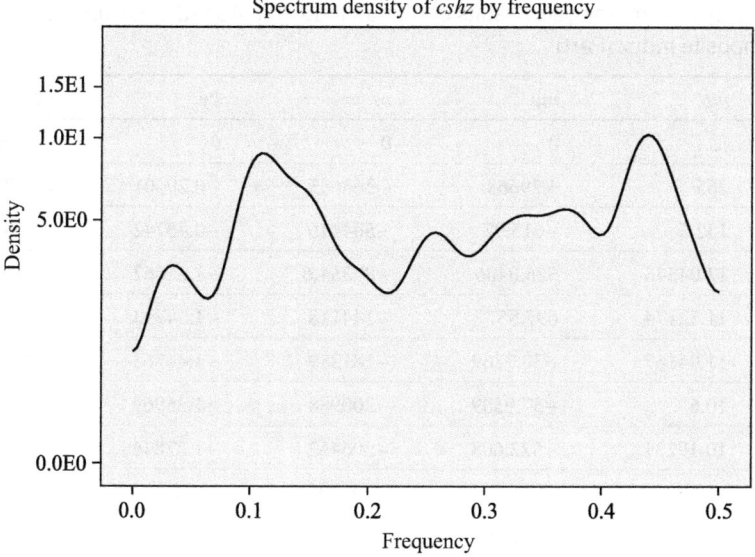

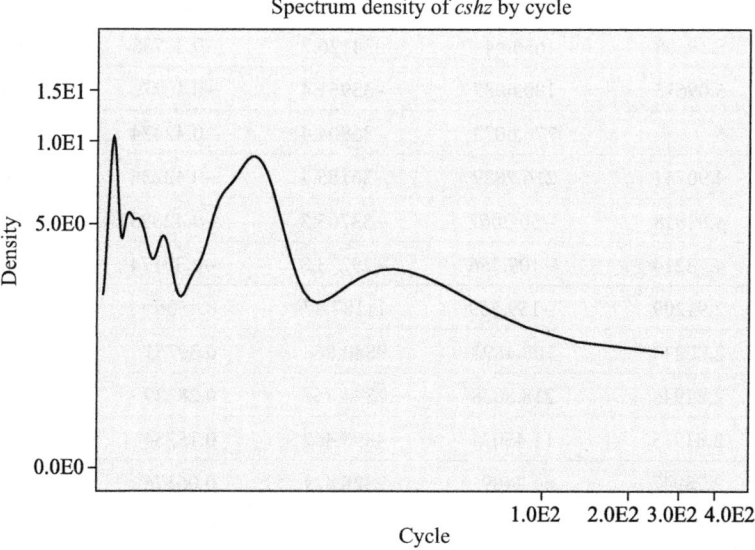

Figure 7-26 Single Spectrum Analysis of Shanghai Composite Index

(2) Cross spectrum analysis

As the core part of spectrum analysis, cross-spectrum analysis is also the final step to determine the variable matching period. Table 7-18 shows the cross-spectrum analysis results of China's industrial added value and Shanghai Composite Index. Figures 7-27 and 7-28 show the cross-spectrum analysis results.

Table 7-18 Cross Spectrum Analysis Results of China's Industrial Added Value and Shanghai
Composite Index (Part)

F	mp	mv	os	ky	sd
0	...	0	0	0	0.18019
0.00377	265	4.29668	−266655	−0.29601	0.20776
0.00755	132.5	−615.97	−504446	−0.45742	0.26861
0.08302	12.04545	526.0406	−87354.6	−1.51662	0.0416
0.08679	11.52174	697.8577	−144118	−1.54713	0.13013
0.09057	11.04167	−30.7769	−181289	−1.46763	0.20809
0.09434	10.6	−57.9589	−200988	−1.36969	0.24353
0.09811	10.19231	−522.608	−206462	−1.27846	0.24099
0.10189	9.81481	844.8053	−201508	−1.20475	0.21559
0.10566	9.46429	244.885	−189138	−1.15452	0.17919
0.18491	5.40816	61.25383	−29374	−0.36129	0.18789
0.18868	5.3	66.79249	−31734.9	−0.36941	0.1815
0.19245	5.19608	1656.44	−34126.7	−0.38738	0.16605
0.19623	5.09615	180.6087	−35961.4	−0.4077	0.14641
0.2	5	776.6073	−36804.4	−0.42474	0.12599
0.20377	4.90741	216.7889	−36185.4	−0.43236	0.1063
0.20755	4.81818	−30.2067	−33705.3	−0.42383	0.08785
0.21132	4.73214	−109.256	−29273.8	−0.39174	0.07187
0.3434	2.91209	−159.559	11187.47	0.4506	0.09517
0.34717	2.88043	100.4891	9840.868	0.39751	0.08709
0.35094	2.84946	218.8058	7574.151	0.28329	0.08529
0.35472	2.81915	11.45034	4893.442	0.15734	0.09215
0.35849	2.78947	64.0489	2328.421	0.06176	0.10635
0.38868	2.57282	−69.572	15438	0.20072	0.14229
0.39245	2.54808	−8.22608	18625.12	0.25899	0.12469
0.39623	2.52381	460.585	20719.31	0.32142	0.1033
0.4	2.5	6.70513	21378.18	0.38931	0.07943
0.40377	2.47664	267.0286	20501.99	0.47086	0.05436
0.40755	2.4537	−153.112	18035.06	0.58354	0.0307
0.41132	2.43119	229.0799	14116.49	0.80086	0.01193
0.48679	2.05426	338.2829	6510.718	0.19945	0.04674
0.49057	2.03846	177.6335	4900.694	0.16397	0.04696
0.49434	2.0229	−57.3484	2632.362	0.09465	0.04599

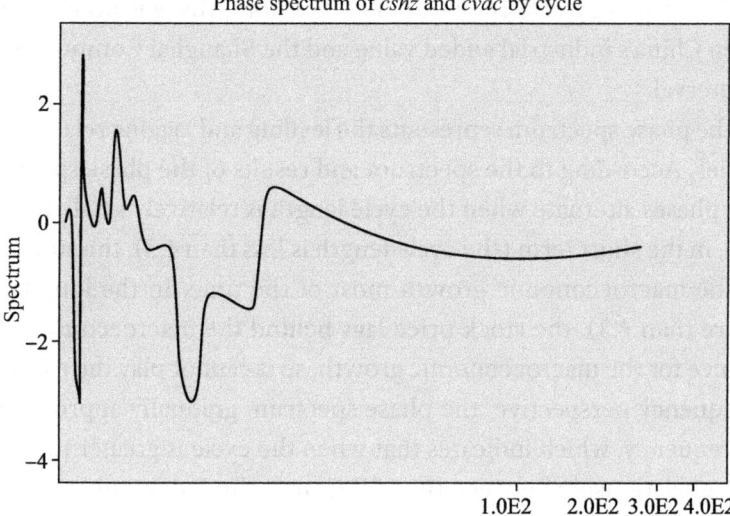

Figure 7-27 Phase Diagram of Cross Spectrum Analysis of China's Industrial Added Value and Shanghai Composite Index

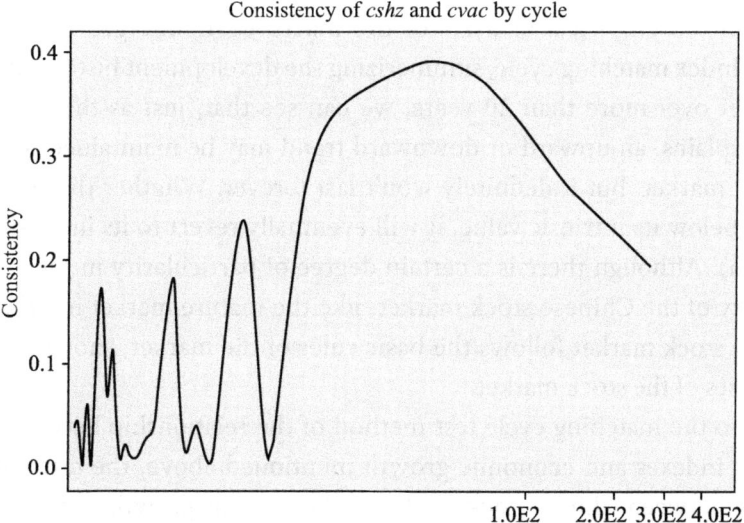

Figure 7-28 Consistency Chart of Cross Spectrum Analysis of China's Industrial Added Value and Shanghai Composite Index

Through the cross-spectrum analysis results of China's industrial added value and Shanghai Composite Index, the following conclusions can be drawn.

First, no matching period can be observed between China's industrial output and the Shanghai Composite Index within the sample interval. The results of cross-spectrum analysis show a great correlation between the two at the frequency of 0.49434, 0.39625, and 0.2. However, considering the consistent results, it is found that the maximum correlation between China's industrial added value and the Shanghai Composite Index is between the frequency of 0.1849–0.1735. Therefore, there is no effective matching cycle between China's industrial added value and the Shanghai Composite Index within the sample interval.

Second, the phase spectrum represents the leading and lagging relationship between two time series. According to the spectrum and results of the phase spectrum, positive and negative phases alternate when the cycle length is relatively small, mainly negative. That is to say, in the short term (the cycle length is less than 4.3), the stock market price is ahead of the macroeconomic growth most of the time. In the long run (the cycle length is more than 4.3), the stock price lags behind the macroeconomic growth and has no guidance for the macroeconomic growth, so it cannot play the role of barometer. From the frequency perspective, the phase spectrum gradually approaches 0 with the increase of frequency, which indicates that when the cycle is greater than four months, the leading-lag relationship between the SSE Composite Index and economic growth is gradually weak. This conclusion is consistent with the thermal optimal path; that is, the stock market leads to economic growth in the short term, while economic growth leads to stock market volatility in the long term. With the increase of time, the lead-lag of the two gradually weakened.

Based on the empirical analysis of the macro-economic growth and Shanghai Composite Index matching cycle, summarizing the development history of the Chinese stock market over more than 20 years, we can see that, just as the theory of mean reversion explains, an upward or downward trend may be maintained for a long time in the stock market, but it definitely won't last forever. Whether the price of a stock is above or below its intrinsic value, it will eventually revert to its intrinsic value (that is, the mean). Although there is a certain degree of particularity in the establishment and volatility of the Chinese stock market, like the mature market in other countries, the Chinese stock market follows the basic rules of the market, showing the inherent characteristics of the stock market.

Similar to the matching cycle test method of the relationship between the world's major stock indexes and economic growth mentioned above, the test method of the relationship between China's stock market and economic growth is still carried out by combining the thermal optimal path method and cross-spectrum analysis. After the test of the thermal optimal path method, it is believed that there is a leading lag period of about four months between China's stock market and economic growth within the sample interval. Macroeconomics precedes the stock market. Cross-spectrum analysis and Granger test both get the same conclusion. The two methods conclude that the stock price index of our country is not a leading indicator of macroeconomic growth in the long run, and there is no guidance for macroeconomic growth. Moreover, a matching cycle could not be observed between the macroeconomic growth and the stock price index from December 1991 to December 2013. However, this does not mean that there is no matching cycle between the two; the excessively long matching cycle could not be observed due to the limitation of the sample interval. It can also be seen from the empirical analysis results that although the stock market has a lag of about eight months on the macroeconomy in the long run, in the short run, the volatility of the stock market is ahead of the economic growth. With the shortening of the cycle length, the volatility of the two tends to be synchronous. In the short run, the stock price has an impact on the macroeconomy to some extent. According to the results of the thermal optimal path analysis, from December 1991 to December 1993, the stock price slightly outpaced the economic growth for about one month. Still, in the subsequent development, economic growth always outpaced the development of the stock market.

As can be seen from the result, our stock market is still not mature compared with the stock markets of developed countries. According to the matching cycle theory, the more developed and complete the stock market is, the closer the correlation is with the economy in which it is located, and there is a short matching cycle. For example, the matching cycle between the US and Dow Jones Index is only 2–10 months, that between the US and the S&P Index is only 2.5–20 months, and the matching cycle between the UK, Germany, and Japan is also within 25 months. However, there has been no significant matching period between China's economic growth and the stock market in the sample interval of more than 20 years, which indicates that China's stock market is still in the early development stage and has many problems. In order to transform into a mature market as soon as possible, China's stock market needs continuous and deep reform and improvement.

7.7 Conclusions and Implications

Through the empirical test, it is found that there is no obvious matching cycle between China's stock market and economic growth rate, indicating that China's stock market has not effectively reflected the changes in the macroeconomy. Although the development history of China's stock market is relatively short, only more than 20 years, it seems that certain reasons can be found to explain and illustrate. However, no matching period can be found in the development process of more than 20 years, which fully indicates that China's stock market has not played a good role as a "barometer" in the 20-year period and has not served the economic growth well. In the 13 years since 2000, the stock market has been in a bull market for three years and a bear market for ten years, which is very unusual for a fast-growing economy with an economic growth rate of more than 8%.

We analyze and explain the two aspects of stock market system construction and government regulation.

First, from the perspective of the long-term development of the stock market, it is a problem of system construction. The root cause of the long-term downturn of the stock market is still some problems in the construction of the market system. Only when the stock market system is mature can the stock market fully reflect the macroeconomy changes. Sun Guomao (2012) started with the transaction cost analysis theory of institutional economics and analyzed the serious deviation between China's stock market and economic operation. He believed that the lack of protection of investors' interests was the root cause of the sustained downturn of the stock market, and the alienation of regulators' behavior led to investors being at a disadvantage in the market game. The existing stock market system was difficult to reflect the "three principles" and could not adapt to the development of the market. Listed companies want only circle money, GEM market manufacture billionaires, investors become the last single buyer, and the market downturn can be imagined. From the point of view of system construction, reform the new share issue system and restrain the behavior of circle money. Separate issuance from listing, follow the steps of marketization of issuance first, then marketization of listing, and the two marketizations together will form a complete marketization model. After the issue does not necessarily list trading, it will enable investors to choose the primary market investment. After the company to be listed issues new shares, the uncertainty of whether it can be listed will enable investors to choose new shares rationally, which can not only enable the company with growth potential to get the support of direct financing, but also won't increase the pressure of the secondary market. At the same time, it will prevent the occurrence of the money circle phenomenon. Issuing and listing at the same time is the direct driving force of stock listing and becoming a money-making tool. This is because listing, at least to a certain extent, is a monopoly of resources, and the combined force of various factors leads to the smooth operation of the money circle with listing as the carrier. In a general sense, listing is to solve the liquidity problem of stocks that are not refundable securities. A prominent feature of China's stock market is that the direct purpose of listing is still to raise funds, and companies can easily get money as the motive for listing. After the issuance and listing are separated, the shares of enterprises can be issued as long as they meet the conditions, realizing the complete marketization of issuance, which is chosen by market investors. The newly issued shares do not necessarily need to be listed and circulated. The stock issue is just a means to raise funds, while the listed circulation is to solve the liquidity. Originally, stock issuing and stock listing are two separate and independent processes. The listing and issuing can be conducted separately and independently in time or combined and consecutively in time. The separation of issuance and listing can eliminate the false prosperity of the issuance market and restore the risks that should exist in the primary market.

Second, from the perspective of stock market failure to see the government regulation behavior. Government behavior plays an important role in preventing stock market risks and maintaining the healthy development of the stock market. The existence of the market failure phenomenon is an objective reality; the market is by no means omnipotent, and government regulation has become an important means to correct market failure. Simply denying the positive role of government behaviors in the stock market is certainly not advisable. The development history of the world stock market has proved that the development history of the stock market in both developed and developing countries has left a deep imprint on government behavior, which is one of the important factors determining the existence and development of the stock market. To completely deny government regulation is to avoid market failure, and the government is the only subject to correct market failure. The first driving force for the establishment of Chinese stocks is government behavior, which is quite different from the stock market spontaneously formed by the market in developed market economies in Europe and America. In more than ten years, we have completed a journey that took developed countries hundreds of years. Government behavior plays an irreplaceable role in the process of changing the stock market from scratch to great development. It can be believed that without the drive of government administrative measures, the successful emergence and gradual expansion of China's stock market would not have occurred. Although China's stock market has so many shortcomings, its rapid development is no doubt. Su Yuli et al. (2002) conducted an empirical study on the intervention behavior of the Hong Kong SAR government in 1998. They believed that the government behavior not only changed the downward trend of the stock market, but also reduced the range of price fluctuations, and the government played an important role in the healthy development of the stock market. Domestic scholars Zou Haoping, Tang Limin, and Yuan Guoliang (2000) used the game analysis method to build a dynamic game model of incomplete information between the government and investors, conducted empirical research on multiple interventions in China's stock market policies, and affirmed the positive effects of several major policies in China's stock market.

According to the theory of the matching cycle between the stock market and economic growth, the government should speed up the market-oriented construction of China's stock market and shorten the matching cycle between the stock market and economic growth as much as possible. Make the stock market truly become a "barometer" of macroeconomic movements to better provide financial support for economic growth. The mark of the government's regulation and control of the stock market is to shorten the matching cycle effectively. If the matching cycle is shortened, the regulation effect is positive. Otherwise, it is an unsuccessful regulation. If the matching cycle between the stock market and economic growth is too long, it will appear as a market failure, which needs to be corrected by the government behavior.

In order to make the stock market better serve economic growth, the government should improve the market's effectiveness and reduce the stock market's failure from the two aspects of improving the system and improving efficiency. The means of government behavior is to regulate and supervise the stock market. Solving these problems will make the stock market more relevant to economic growth and really become a factor in promoting economic development. The efficient market will definitely reflect the economic growth situation more accurately, and the shorter the matching cycle between the stock market and the economy and growth, the higher the effectiveness of the market. To achieve the above goals, we think we should start from two aspects: perfecting the stock market system and improving the market efficiency.

7.7.1 Main Problems Existing in Government Behaviors in China's Stock Market

In mature markets, governments that took market rescue were not uncommon. In 1987, when the stock market crashed in the United States, Federal Reserve Chairman Alan Greenspan tried to solve the problem by ordering banks to open the floodgates. After the September 11 attacks, the president of the United States made more than 20 speeches; the most direct content was to trust the American stock market and ordered securities dealers not to sell stocks. In 1997, the Hong Kong government used HK$100 billion to rescue the market and stabilize the city's financial system. These measures have worked well. However, different from the mature stock markets in foreign countries, China's stock market policies not only regulate the stock market but, more importantly, lead and determine the stock market's trend. Moreover, due to the influence of various factors, China's stock market policies have certain deficiencies, which are mainly reflected in the following aspects.

First, the policy focuses too much on the supply and demand of market funds while ignoring institutional construction and reform. Looking back at China's stock market policies over the past decade, the management has always focused on the supply and demand of funds. No matter the "three market rescue policies" in 1994, the admission of three types of enterprises to the market in 1999, or the vigorous development of institutional investors after 2003, they all made adjustments in the supply and demand of funds. This was very obvious in 2004 and 2005 when the market was extremely depressed, the number of fund issuances greatly increased, and the outside capital rushed to the stock market desperately. The capital in the stock market was not allowed to flee and even implied that institutional investors such as funds were not allowed to sell stocks. Led by the policy of blindly overemphasizing the supply of market funds, other policy measures rarely made substantial improvements, and there has been no substantial institutional reform and construction. As Wang Lianzhou, a famous economist and former deputy director of the Economic Law Office of the Financial and Economic Committee of the National People's Congress, pointed out, the Chinese stock market in nearly 15 years can be described as a "history of lost sheep." In the meantime, "expedient" policies frequently intervene in the stock market, and their value orientation is often different. Researchers have complained that it is impossible to see these so-called "policy markets." Market participants, market legislators, institutional investors, stock investors, scholars, and so on almost all come to the same conclusion: in more than a decade, in addition to the confusion around the stock index, technical tinkering, really called the construction of the stock market system is very rare. In helpless system reconstruction, China's stock market has been going through ups and downs for nearly 15 years, and the opportunity to reform again and again in the "expedient" is wasted. Since the reform of the non-tradable share structure started in 2006, the system has been thoroughly adjusted, and the stock market has gone out of the long-lost upward trend. It can be considered that the importance of system construction for the stock market is the top priority. The solution of non-tradable shares is not only of great significance to the perfection and development of China's stock market, but also of epoch-making significance to the perfection of China's market economic system.

Second, the management attaches too much importance to the rise and fall of the stock index and weakens the guidance of the investment concept. In the mature securities market, the securities supervision department is only responsible for supervision, regardless of the stock index. In China, the securities regulatory department should not only do a good job in supervision, but also "do a good job" in the stock index, not only be a good "gatekeeper," but also give play to the great power of the "visible hand." Whenever the stock market is in distress, the government will use various policy resources to support or rescue the market. Whenever the stock market is running at a high level, the government will use regulation and expansion as a means to "deflate the bubble." The management and investors of China's securities market are too concerned about, or even too sensitive to, the rise and fall of the stock index. The index can only rise but not fall. The continuous fall and plunge will cause panic among management and investors, which leads to a wrong consensus that China's stock market cannot fall. So, the management even directly targets the index when formulating relevant policies and measures. For example, before 2004, the rise of new shares on the day of listing was large, and the impact on the index was also large. Therefore, the management changed the previous day when the new shares were listed from not included in the index to the day when the new shares were listed. In the process of equity reform, due to the large decline of the stock price on the day of the implementation of the consideration, the management stipulated that the stock reform company should not include the consideration in the index on the day of the implementation of the consideration to avoid the negative impact on the index. This is unfavorable for improving the stock market and would inevitably lead to serious distortion of the stock index. In fact, the stock index has already had the problem of distortion and has become a major problem. This kind of expedient measure is not advisable.

Third, the policy issuance's timing and foresight are poor, often leading to significant adverse consequences. A typical example is the *Several Opinions on Promoting the Reform and Opening Up and Stable Development of the Capital Market*, issued in February 2004, which can be regarded as the most favorable policy in China's stock market history. However, since the two markets had already risen significantly when it was issued, at the same time, coupled with the expected impact of macro-control and non-tradable share reform, the stock index rose slightly. It fell all the way after a high period of sideways, and the decline was huge. If *Several Opinions on Promoting the Reform and Opening Up and Stable Development of the Capital Market* is issued in the market around 1,000 to 1,200 position, its effect will be very good. In the first half of 2004, the launch of the small and medium-sized enterprise board was also a big mistake, in the market just fell or fell in succession, is undoubtedly the bottom of the axe, funds immediately from the high board of the main board out, crazy speculation of small and medium-sized board and small and medium-sized board related varieties, the main board from now on into the medium and long term decline channel. However, the introduction of warrants in the reform of non-tradable shares is a big policy mistake. The superiority of the warrants trading mode has attracted a lot of funds from the A-share market, resulting in a significant adjustment of the A-share market due to serious loss of blood.

Fourth, the utilitarian tendency of policy control of the stock market is obvious. The government often intervenes in the operation of the stock market according to the "purpose" or "need" of the policy. In order to find the "legitimate" reason for the intervention of the market, it often makes a strong subjective evaluation of the operation of the stock market. For example, the skyrocketing stock market in 1996 and the May 19 stock market in 1999 were both caused by excessive speculation and high P/E ratios. Still, the government made completely opposite market evaluations for different policy purposes. Therefore, it seems that there is no objective criterion for whether the stock market is speculative excessively, and it all depends on the government's policy will. This inevitably gives the stock market a "hint" that the operation of the stock market is not determined by the market itself, but by the government's policy preferences. Therefore, a special "game" relationship and a "dependence" relationship between the market and the government are formed in the Chinese stock market. On the one hand, the market always keeps the vigilance of the policy and tries to figure out the intention of the policy. When it senses that the government intends to "suppress" the market, there will often be panic selling, resulting in plummeting stock prices. And when it senses that the government intends to "encourage" the market, it will form crazy speculation, resulting in skyrocketing stock prices. The stock market in 2000 is a case in point. On the other hand, the market has "policy dependence" on the government; especially when the stock market is in a downturn, the market will expect the government to "support the market" and "rescue the market." The longer the market downturn lasts, the stronger this policy expectation and dependence will be. The market even exerts pressure on the government through various channels, such as "appeal" and "urge" the government to take policy measures to boost the market. Once the favorable policies are introduced, the market will show another round of soaring prices.

Fifth, the regulation mode based on administrative means has produced special effects. In China's policy means system, financial means are relatively weak, while administrative means play a prominent role. Due to the segmentation of the financial system and to prevent the risk of the banking system, the central bank still does not allow credit funds to enter the stock market; the change of "margin ratio" cannot become an important means for the management to regulate the stock market. Therefore, the main feature of the management control method is that when the stock price index rises sharply, and the management wants the stock market to cool down, it will reiterate that credit funds are not allowed to flow into the stock market and punish the banking institutions that illegally invest credit funds into the stock market. On the contrary, when the stock market is in a downturn, the penalty cases for illegal funds will be significantly reduced, and the propaganda efforts to reiterate the ban will be significantly reduced. For a long period of time, the Chinese stock market has adjusted the scale of credit funds into the stock market, except for the money supply policy and interest rate policy, which is the administrative color of compulsory means and punishment measures. Administrative means have a greater effect on the stock price index, which breaks the normal circulation channels of stock market funds and peripheral funds and the original relatively stable scale, so that the peripheral funds suddenly withdraw or pour into the stock market on a large scale. Because the scale of China's stock market is relatively low relative to the scale of the national economy, the peripheral capital of the stock market is dozens of times the stock market stock. Therefore, on the one hand, the development potential of China's stock market is very large, and on the other hand, it also determines the great effect ability of policy regulation. This kind of energy is hard to find in mature stock markets.

The "policy market" features of China's stock market are the product of China's stock market under special historical conditions and the inevitable result of China's transition from a traditional planned economy to a market economy. It has played a certain role in the development of the stock market and has a positive significance in stabilizing it and protecting investors' interests. However, with the integration of the world economy and the development of China's economy and the stock market, the traditional regulation means of policy intervention in the stock market need to be thoroughly reformed, which is the inevitable requirement of the development of China's stock market. The principle and leading direction of reform should be to advance toward the goal of marketization, legalization, internationalization, and standardization. The core and starting point of reform is to protect the interests of investors to the maximum extent. The focus of policy formulation should be to improve the quality of listed companies. At the same time, the coordinated operation of relevant departments is also an important guarantee for the policy to play its role.

7.7.2 Improvement of Stock Market System Construction

The problems of China's stock market system mainly include the following aspects.

First, China's stock market has serious mechanism defects. The specific manifestations are the lack of market subjects with clear property rights relationships, the lack of market price formed through normal competition, and the lack of effective competition among market subjects formed through price. These defects are the root cause of the imperfect resource flow and dynamic combination mechanism in the Chinese stock market so as to form an effective resource allocation mechanism. The failure of the resource allocation mechanism in our stock market not only lies in that administrative power and administrative mechanism exclude or replace market competition and market mechanism to a certain extent, but also lies in the imperfect restraint mechanism and incentive mechanism of market and enterprise. In terms of restraint mechanisms, most listed companies in our country are reformed by state-owned enterprises. Because of the administrative mechanism's intervention and the lack of a market mechanism, the phenomenon of "transformation" generally does not exist in listed companies. For many listed companies, the change from state-owned enterprises to joint-stock listed companies, the most important changes are only two aspects: one aspect is "rebranding," that is, changing the name to a company limited by shares and establishing the corresponding organizational structure, the financial implementation of the joint-stock accounting standards, in the market according to the standard disclosure of enterprise information. Another aspect is "circle money," which can not only raise a huge amount of social funds at a high level of premium at the time of listing, but also get "cheap" funds from the market year after year without paying costs and returns as long as the qualification of rights offering is maintained. As for the interests of shareholders and returns to shareholders, they are put aside. Since state-owned shares are in the absolute holding position in most listed companies, and most of these state-owned shares are in the state of "false property rights" and "owner absence," which makes any administrative department, especially the original competent department of listed companies, can intervene in the enterprise as the representative of state-owned shares, but does not bear any responsibility for the consequences of such intervention. In the aspect of incentive mechanism, the imperfect phenomenon of incentive mechanism generally exists in Chinese listed companies. In developed market economy countries, listed companies generally implement the incentive system that combines the managers' immediate compensation (salary and annual bonus) and long-term compensation (stock options and restricted stock, etc.).

Practice shows that the property relation is the most core relation in the social economy, and the property rule is the most basic rule in the social economy. The interest relation and rule based on the clear property relation and the clear property rule are not only indispensable, but also have a huge reaction on the property relation and the property rule. If we can't see this point or can't effectively and orderly coordinate property relations and interest relations as well as property rules and interest rules, we can't establish an effective restraint mechanism and incentive mechanism, and the market cohesion and market competitiveness of listed companies will inevitably be weakened. On the governance structure of listed companies, most listed companies in

China are born out of traditional state-owned enterprises, and the original governance structure is difficult to eliminate in a short period of time. Due to the intervention of administrative mechanisms and the absence of market mechanisms, the phenomenon of "without transformation" is quite common in listed companies. In addition, the phenomenon of "insider control" in the process of reform leads to the fact that in listed companies, managers can either ignore the opinions of minority shareholders as representatives of state shares or ignore the will of the country as an "insider," which may damage the interests of minority shareholders as well as the interests of the country. In this situation, the listing of state-owned enterprises cannot effectively enhance the restriction of property rights and promote the real transformation of the enterprise management mechanism.

The practice has proved that the shareholding system has not played a due role in transforming the management mechanism and perfecting the governance structure of state-owned enterprises. However, China's stock market is only a place for state-owned enterprises to "circle money." It does not play the role of monitoring and survival of the fittest of listed companies. The "soft restraint" of state-owned enterprises and the "fatherism" of the government are further manifested and revealed in the stock market.

Second, the stock market regulation and the stock market rules defects. The Chinese stock market also has defective problems in market rules. Not only do many due laws and rules not have, but some of the existing laws also deviate from the basic principles of the market economy, becoming a variety of will "run-in" products and the result of the "platter." An important premise of the normal and effective stock market operation is that we must have a set of perfect and sound legal systems that reflect the essential requirements of the market economy and the inner rules of the capital market. But in our country, such legal systems have not been established yet. The 10-year journey of our capital market is the process of the fission of the old system and the birth pains of the new system. It is also the process of people's resistance to, indifference to, recognition, and understanding of the market economic system, market economic mechanism, and market economic culture. Therefore, the market rules formed in this process also bear the distinct imprint of The Times. It cannot master the essential requirements and internal rules of the market economy accurately, nor can it guide the operating practices of our capital market effectively. From the macroscopic point of view, regulating the stock market needs two most important laws, *Company Law* and *Securities Law*, and a series of corresponding relevant laws and regulations. However, our country's *Company Law* and *Securities Law* have obvious system defects. Take *Company Law* as an example; *Company Law*, which is currently in effect, has been drawn up since the late 1980s. After many iterations in the process of formulating the *Company Law*, it was officially implemented on July 1, 1994. When the *Company Law* was formulated, the socialist market economy theory had not been formally established, capital, capital market, and capital mechanism had not obtained legal status, and people did not have a clear understanding of the status and role of stocks, stock markets, and joint-stock companies. Under this background, the *Company Law* was actually the result of various wills and opinions. It has the characteristic of a deep system transition period. With the establishment of the theory of a socialist market economy and the production and development of the capital market, the incompatibility problem between *Company Law* and reality has become more and more prominent, and the problem of "law is not good to depend on" has become a big problem in the movement of the stock economy.

Reviewing the development course of China's stock market for more than 20 years, we can see that one of the biggest and most characteristic aspects of China's stock market is its typical "policy market" characteristics. This point runs through the whole development process of China's stock market. Although this feature tends to gradually weaken, the "policy market" will still exist and develop for a long time in the future due to the influence of many factors. The concentration of the "policy market" shows that policy has become the core and dominant force of the stock market operation. Policy determines the rise and fall of the stock market to a large extent and leads to the rise and fall of the stock index. As a result, investors become highly dependent on the policy and have serious policy after-effects. In the more than 20 years since the emergence of the stock market in China, the management has introduced hundreds of policies on the stock market, big or small, far or near, or up or down influence. Looking back on the history of China's stock market, it can be said that the rise and fall history was led by policy, and every rise or fall has a strong correlation with the policy.

7.7.3 *Improve Stock Market Efficiency*

The high efficiency of the stock market is a necessary condition for the full play of the market function and also an important sign to measure the maturity of the stock market. Generally, the efficiency of the stock market can be measured by its various functions, such as realizing the liquidity of assets, optimizing the allocation of funds, etc., which is embodied in the degree of saving transaction costs, the efficiency of information transmission, the accurate pricing of financial assets, and the use of capital raised. Therefore, the efficiency of our stock market can be discussed from three aspects: operational efficiency, information efficiency, and capital allocation efficiency.

First, the operational efficiency of the stock market. Operation efficiency refers to the trading efficiency of the stock market, which refers to whether the stock market can complete transactions for traders in the shortest time and with the lowest transaction costs. It reflects the efficiency of the organization and service functions of the stock market. This efficiency actually affects the liquidity of the stock market. When the transaction speed of the market is too slow, and the transaction cost is too high, it will affect the enthusiasm of traders to enter the market, reduce the number of transactions, and affect the stock price. Currently, the main defects in the operation efficiency of the Chinese stock market are as follows: (1) Trading commission pricing is too high. According to China's current regulations, the securities dealers charge the traders 0.35% of the transaction amount as a trade commission. Although the securities dealers have a certain autonomy, the small and medium-sized investors generally must bear this expense. The ratio is obviously high compared with foreign countries, which increases the transaction cost for traders and provides living space for the securities dealers with inferior service quality and low efficiency. It reduces the efficiency of the entire intermediary organization. (2) Full margin system leads to higher opportunity costs. What our country implements is the trading system of full margin. The transaction process is the order of transaction: first capital, last transaction, and then settlement. Traders can only trade if they have funds or securities equal to the transaction amount. Traders are not allowed to borrow or sell securities from securities dealers. This does reduce the risk of the stock market, but it also increases the opportunity cost of trading stocks. Because investors have to deposit the margin in the securities dealer's account before trading, the opportunity cost of the margin itself is lost for traders, and the implementation of the full margin system increases the opportunity cost. (3) The lack of a market maker system makes it difficult to ensure the continuity of market transactions. At present, our stock market adopts a computer automation trading system, implements entrust instruction drive mode, and has the characteristics of openness, justice, and fairness. The disadvantage is that the stock price fluctuates greatly, and sometimes it is impossible to transact because of the big difference between the buying and selling prices, which reduces the transaction efficiency and leads to the lack of continuity of the transaction. Market maker systems can make up for the shortcomings of the order-driven model and maintain the continuity of trading and market stability. When the price difference between buyers and sellers is too large, and the market is temporarily unbalanced, market makers have an obligation to use their own capital to buy the stocks they are responsible for at a slightly higher price and sell the stocks at a slightly lower price, so as to smooth the trading, which is conducive to improving the trading speed and market operation efficiency.

Second, the information efficiency of the stock market. Information efficiency refers to whether the market price of a stock can react quickly and timely to relevant information. Fama divided the information in the stock market into three categories: historical, public, and internal information, and defined three different levels of market efficiency: weak, semi-strong, and strong efficiency. Weak efficiency is the lowest efficiency of the stock market. In such markets, past trends in share prices have no bearing on the future direction of prices. Stock price changes are relatively independent; each price rise or fall has nothing to do with the previous price change. It is impossible for investors to "beat the market" by technical analysis to find out the law of stock price changes. Semi-strong efficiency means that not only historical data is invalid for judging future stock price changes, but also all the latest publicly published information (such as financial reports, announcements, policies, and new management regulations of listed companies) is useless for judging future stock price trends. Because in such efficient market conditions, all publicly published information that can affect the price of a stock is immediately reflected in the price. Strong efficiency is the highest degree of efficiency in the stock market. In this kind of market, all information, historical information, published information, and inside information does not affect the stock price forecast, and no information can be used to generate excess returns. At present, the theory circle generally believes that our country's stock market basically reaches weak efficiency.

Third, the capital allocation efficiency in the stock market. The efficiency of capital allocation means that the stock market has the mechanism of allocating funds to the enterprises that are most likely to use the funds effectively. Capital allocation is an important function of the stock market. However, the current control system on listing quotas and issuing prices seriously reduces the efficiency of capital allocation in the market. China's stock issuance is the total quota issued by the China Securities Regulatory Commission, the highest decision-making body of the Chinese stock market, and then distributed to all provinces and cities, administrative departments directly under the State Council, and major national companies. This equalitarian quota allocation method leads to the overall quality of listed companies is not high. Due to unbalanced economic development in various regions and departments, there are great differences in the number of enterprises, industrial structure, and enterprise size that meet the requirements for listing. The average distribution of listing quotas by departments and regions inevitably leads to some qualified enterprises being unable to list. In contrast, some unqualified enterprises become listed companies due to sufficient quotas in their industries. This also provides opportunities for administrative departments to set up rent. To achieve the purpose of listing, some enterprises often take unreasonable ways to seek rent. Whether they can get listed depends not on their business performance but on their public relations ability. In order to get listed, companies often produce false financial reports and are shielded by local governments. What's more, in order to seek their own interests, some local governments have the idea of using the funds in the stock market to revive troubled enterprises and deliberately select companies with poor performance to go public. In this way, the industrial and regional structures of listed companies are unreasonable, the overall efficiency is poor, and the funds cannot flow to industry and enterprise with good efficiency. Besides, the pricing model of our primary market is not conducive to the improvement of the efficiency of capital allocation. The issue price in China's primary market is not formed by free market bidding but calculated through the established equation, that is, the issue price of new shares = P/E ratio profit per share after tax. Among them, the P/E ratio is calculated based on the region and industry average of the company, and the after-tax profit is inferred based on the company's previous operating results. An issue price calculated in this way, which is not in line with market expectations of stock prices, is certainly unreasonable. Moreover, the stock issuance price in our country is often far lower than the actual value, causing great risk-free interest differences in the primary and secondary markets, transferring the risk of the primary market to the secondary market. However, this part of the interest difference originally belonged to the funds obtained by enterprises issuing stock and transferring property rights of state-owned enterprises, which should be used for production. Still, now it is in the form of interest difference. It is obtained by arbitrageurs depending on their own financial strength or luck, which encourages speculation. In order to obtain such benefits, hundreds of billions of arbitrageurs wander in the primary market, forming a large amount of idle funds.

Fourth, strategies to improve the efficiency of the stock market. The non-standardization of the stock market is the obvious defect of the stock market. Since China's stock market emerged and developed in the transition from a planned economy to a market economy and was dominated by administrative departments and administrative powers, it had obvious "congenital deficiency" from the day it was born and could not operate in a standardized way. This is mainly manifested in three aspects: (1) The listing process is not standardized. Originally, the stock issue and listing should be the result of market competition, but in our country, the administrative departments allocated quotas according to the administrative regions' cut blocks, screening through the administrative levels. Since the *Company Law* of China has a relatively low listing condition for listed companies—they must make a profit in the first three years of listing. Still, there is no specific and mandatory specification for making a profit, which leaves a huge space for the administrative department to exercise administrative power, greatly increasing the arbitrariness of administrative selection and greatly reducing the quality of listed companies. (2) The ownership structure is not standardized. The principle of equity equality is the most basic principle of the stock economy. For a joint-stock company, no matter where the capital comes from, it is necessary to take off the cloak of the original owner when it enters the company. The difference in investor status is only meaningful outside the company, and within the company, all shareholders are in the same position, with equal rights and corresponding obligations. However, in our country, the planned economy way of thinking is introduced into the company. It not only divides the company's stock into state, legal, and individual shares, but also most of the state-owned share stocks are divided according to the value of the stock, while the social public shares are purchased at a high premium. When the company allots or issues additional shares, the state-owned shares can give up the allotment or subscription but can share a high proportion of premium income, thus greatly eroding the legitimate rights and interests of the public shareholders. However, inside the company, the state-owned shareholders who discount shares at a low price control the decision-making power of the company and exclude the rights and interests of the public shareholders. The inequity of subscription price and equity exercise process leads to the deformed development of the shareholding structure and governance structure of joint-stock companies. The disorder and randomness of the decision-making process of state-owned shareholders, which is the dominant position, is also one of the reasons why the collusion between makers and listed companies can prevail in the market at present. (3) The operation process is not standard. This is not only reflected in the fact that listed companies do not operate according to market requirements, but also in the fact that listed companies collude with accounting firms, law firms, and even securities companies to publish false information and carry out insider trading and related transactions. If the "packaging" of listed companies before going public is to obtain the financing right of the stock market by issuing shares, then, after going public, the operation goal of many listed companies is to maintain the rights issue and the listed status. In recent years, it can be said that in order to protect rights and equity, some listed companies have exhausted the calculation of the authorities, frequent asset reorganization, and a large number of related transactions. As a result, listed companies gain money while investors' interests are abandoned. The "internal injury" caused by this non-standard operation to the market is extremely serious. If we are not determined to carry out a radical cure, it will inevitably damage investors' confidence in the market.

The improvement of efficiency is very important for the healthy development of the stock market. Specific to do the following aspects: (1) Perfect the stock market trading system. This requires the reform of the trading commission system. The current single commission rate set by the state has been changed to be determined independently by securities firms, which is conducive to competition and merger among securities firms, improving trading efficiency and reducing market transaction costs. The next step should be to reform the trading settlement system. While strengthening the risk supervision of the securities market, the trading margin should be gradually reduced, and the trading mode of "trading first, capital later, settlement later" should be implemented to reduce the opportunity cost of trading. In addition, when conditions are mature, the existing trading mode driven by orders should be perfected and supplemented, and the market maker system should be established to ensure the continuity of trading. (2) Improve the information system. In the final analysis, the stock market is an information market, which requires the market to standardize a series of information systems according to the principles of effectiveness, timeliness, and adequacy of information disclosure, such as information disclosure system, registered accounting audit system, securities credit rating system, news supervision system, and corresponding punishment system. (3) Improve the stock listing and pricing mechanism. Currently, many enterprises have listing requirements, but it is difficult to meet the conditions because of the market size. To take quota control of listing is necessary, in line with the objective reality. However, for the long-term purpose of ensuring the overall quality of listed companies and improving market efficiency, we should provide listing opportunities for those high-quality enterprises with sound systems, excellent benefits, scientific management, and advanced technology through the formulation and implementation of normative and scientific listed company standards, and gradually improve the internal quality of listed companies. At the same time, we can adopt the online adjustable and balanced bidding mode to determine the reasonable issue price and balance the risks in the primary and secondary markets through market competition. This will help balance market supply and demand, guide rational investment, and effectively protect the interests of small and medium-sized investors and the state.

Fifth, an effective stock market must have the function of optimizing resource allocation. The core point is to restore the nature of capital to improve the function of optimizing resource allocation of Chinese stock market. It must be observed that the nature of capital is chasing profit, the mechanism of capital generating, capital combining, capital competition, and capital multiplication is not perfect, and the mechanism of capital personalization is not formed, which is not only the direct result of low marketization degree of our stock market, but also the deep reason of the low resource allocation efficiency of our stock market. Therefore, it is necessary to strengthen the institutional innovation of the stock market so that it can become an efficient stock market that can optimize the allocation of resources as soon as possible.

Sixth, an efficient stock market must be a fair market. Equity is the foundation of the stock market, the prerequisite for attracting social funds, and the fundamental guarantee of sustainable development of the stock market. Starting from the present situation of our country, to reflect the fair principle of the market, the most important thing is to introduce the market mechanism and competition mechanism comprehensively, because for a market economy, only market and market competition are the fairest, the government's function is mainly to guarantee the improvement of market mechanism and the orderly conduct of market competition. In this regard, three aspects should be emphasized: (1) The market must have fair entry rules. Fair entry rules mean that enterprises and individuals should have equal opportunities and conditions to enter the primary and secondary stock markets. (2) The market must have equal rights and obligations. The market economy is an economy in which rights and obligations are relative. The rights of one party are the obligations of the other party at the same time. At present, in our country's stock market, the inclination of rights and obligations is very serious. This is not only manifested between the government and enterprise—the government has right but not duty, the enterprise has duty but not right, but also between the listed company and investors and between the state-owned, legal, and individual shareholders. In the stock issuing market, there is serious price discrimination between state-owned and public share shareholders. In the stock circulation market, state-owned shares cannot flow, and a large amount of precipitation, the problem will be greatly improved after the solution of the problem of share structure. Unequal rights and obligations not only form the distorted ownership structure, but also form the distorted stock price due to the distorted supply and demand relationship, thus artificially increasing the price risk of the stock market. Equity rights and obligations not only mean that the inherent contradictions of state-owned shares and legal shares in the stock market in our country must be resolved, but also mean that the risk pricing function of the stock market must be restored and the protection function of investors of all kinds, especially small and medium-sized investors must be strengthened, so that all participants in the market can make investment choices in a fair and just environment. (3) The market must have a fair legal environment. In this regard, it is necessary to establish a scientific legal system and abolish the planned economy of legislating on the basis of ownership. It is necessary to set up a legal system to protect investors, especially small and medium investors, introduce the cumulative voting system, the voting rights collection system, and the litigation and compensation system for directors and managers, listed companies, exchanges, and regulatory agencies, so as to greatly improve the fairness and justice of the stock market.

Seventh, an efficient stock market must be a transparent market. The stock market is expected to differ. Some people are bullish, and some people are bearish; bullish will buy, and bearish will sell, thus forming the market relationship between buying and selling and supply and demand. The ups and downs of the market and stocks result from various factors in the market. Theoretically speaking, any investor cannot fully grasp all the factors of market changes, but can only observe as many variables in the stock market and according to the changes of various factors in the market to make investment decisions. Therefore, the transparency of the market objectively determines the scientific degree of investors' decision-making. The more complete, faster, and fairer the information provided by the market, the stronger the guiding function of the market, the higher the credibility of the market, and the more effective the resource allocation function will be. On the contrary, because the market itself has an "invisible hand" at work, if there is not a complete, rapid, fair, and transparent information disclosure system, then investors will be like in the clouds, not only becoming the market makers "dumb" object but also having a reverse effect on the optimal allocation of resources. Here, we should emphasize three aspects: First, transparent information must be true. If the information is untrue, the more transparent it is, the more negative it will be. The financial situation of listed companies, related transactions of listed companies, and investment behavior of listed companies are all important matters affecting the company's operation, and investors have a comprehensive right to know about these aspects. Second, true information must have a unified and single channel of transmission. In this respect, the most important thing is to prevent insider trading, so we must emphasize the duty of loyalty, duty of care, and duty of non-competition of directors. Third, the demand for information transparency is not only for listed companies, but also for government departments. The "dark box" operation of the regulation department to formulate the stock market policy is the taboo of market regulation and also one of the reasons for the fluctuation of the stock market. With the acceleration of the marketization process of the Chinese stock market, the marketization problem of government behavior has become a more and more prominent contradiction. In this respect, it should start from the internal requirements of developing the stock market, improving the efficiency of stock market resources allocation, establishing the market economy system to adjust the government's own behavior pattern and behavior mechanism, and thus create a more suitable macro environment for the healthy development of the stock market.

Eighth, an efficient stock market must be an orderly market. Market orderliness and efficiency are two closely related aspects. Without the orderly operation of the market, we cannot talk about its effective operation. Similarly, the efficient operation of the market will create space and conditions for the market to pursue a higher degree of orderly operation. For our stock market, this kind of orderly should be the organic unity of main body, behavior, and supervision orders. First of all, as far as the main body order is concerned, the most important thing is to standardize all kinds of market entities, especially the internal structure of listed companies. In this respect, it is necessary to solve the common administrative tendency and the "insider" control problem of listed companies in our country, establish the perfect corporate governance structure through the balance of the property and interest relations, the property and interest rules, and gradually improve the company's restraint mechanism and incentive mechanism. It is necessary to stress in particular that, along with the class of shares in the Chinese stock market, that is the solution to the problem of dividing the stock of the listed company into state-owned shares, legal shares, and social public shares, the stock of listed company has become a fully circulated stock. When establishing the corporate governance structure of the company, on the one hand, it is necessary to open the door for individual shareholding, especially the listing of the company whose sponsors are individuals. On the other hand, it is also necessary to encourage the managers, scientific and technological personnel, and even employees of the listed company to hold the company's stocks through the option system and allow these stocks to be listed and circulated after meeting certain conditions, so as to find a practical way to establish the constraint mechanism and incentive mechanism. The realization of the "sufficient interest rate" in economics enables listed companies to use other people's money like their own, thus improving the operation efficiency of enterprises and even the market. Secondly, in terms of behavior order, it is necessary not only to formulate perfect rules for the whole process of entering the market, engaging in market activities, and exiting the market of joint stock companies, but also to perfect the management of the intermediary behavior, the financing behavior of listed companies, the guarantee behavior and the trading behavior of the secondary stock market, so as to meet the internal requirements of the market economy. Here, it needs to be emphasized that the formulation of the rules of conduct of the market economy is not to specify what enterprises must do but more to focus on what they are not allowed to do; only in this way, our listed companies can have their own characteristics, and the enterprise operation mode can be colorful. Currently, China implements a unified formatting mode for the articles of association of joint-stock companies. The differences in the articles of association are limited to the place of registration, the total amount of the articles of association, and the number of the board of directors and the board of supervisors. This kind of formalized article of association is not conducive to the construction of the corporate governance structure. It must be pointed out that the articles of association are the fundamental law of corporate autonomy. The pattern of the articles of association leads to the fact that each company is not "autonomous" but "governed by the public," and the company's independent will and interests become a mere formality. It must also be pointed out that an important difference between planned economy legislation and market economy legislation is that the former is more of a mandatory norm, that is, to stipulate what enterprises and individuals must do, while the latter is more of a contractual norm, that is, on the basis of stipulating what enterprises and individuals must not do, leaving broad space for self-agreement for enterprises and individuals. The uniformity and patternization of Chinese articles of association are outstanding manifestations of the *Company Law*'s emphasis on mandatory norms, which is the concentrated reflection of the legislative principle of the planned economy on the penetration of the market economy. Thirdly, in terms of regulatory order, the first thing is to clearly position the behaviors of individuals, enterprises, the market, and the government under the condition of the market economy. Then, there is the need to clarify the government's regulatory function. That is to say, government regulatory departments should not only regulate the market and restrict the behavior of market subjects but also restrict themselves, so that the regulatory behavior meets the requirements of relevant national laws and regulations and avoids the occurrence of various "offside" phenomena. At the same time, it is necessary to give full play to the self-discipline function of the securities industry association and the social supervision function of intermediary agencies and news media, so as to gradually form an all-round and three-dimensional supervision network and play a strong guarantee role for the reasonable and effective operation of the stock market.

CHAPTER 8

Research on Information Transmission Efficiency and Insider Trading Based on Market Efficient Cycle Theory

From the perspective of efficient cycle theory, information asymmetry and insider trading in the stock market are short-term phenomena. In the long run, the efficient market cycle requires the stock market to fully reflect all public information and insider information in a long enough period of time. Therefore, the market efficient cycle theory holds that insider trading only exists in the short term. Cracking down on insider trading in the short term will improve the market effectiveness, shorten the market efficient cycle, and improve the fairness and efficiency of market information transmission. According to the connotation of the efficient market hypothesis, insider trading is the study of the information transmission efficiency corresponding to the strong efficient market; that is, the market which reflects not only public information but also insider information is defined as the strong efficient market.

Information asymmetry and insider trading are concomitant phenomena. This chapter takes insider trading as the research object and conducts empirical research directly on the information transmission efficiency of strong efficient markets. If there is inside information in the market, there is an effective period for the market to reflect the information. In the long run, insider information must be fully reflected in stock prices; that is, there must be an effective cycle in the market. The most direct source of insider trading in the stock market is information asymmetry. Information asymmetry refers to the asymmetry in quantity and quality of the information possessed by two parties in a market transaction. Information asymmetry is the main reason for the abnormal fluctuation of stock prices, destroying the basic principles of openness, fairness, and justice. The direct consequence of information asymmetry is moral hazard and adverse selection in the stock market. Moral hazard refers to the behavior in which one party in a market transaction cannot observe the information controlled by the other party, and the latter deliberately fails to report or fabricates false information to deceive others. Adverse selection refers to the situation in which inferior goods drive out superior goods when one party cannot observe the important characteristics of the other party in market transactions.

Information asymmetry is directly manifested as insider trading, which can only occur under the condition of information asymmetry. It can be said that insider trading is the direct consequence of information asymmetry. This chapter divides information asymmetry into macro and micro information asymmetry. Macro-information asymmetry means that when the government management department makes information that has a significant impact on the stock price, the quantity and quality of the information obtained by market entities (including investors, listed companies, and securities intermediaries) are not equal, and the resulting insider trading is macro insider trading. Micro-information asymmetry refers to the information owned by listed companies that has a significant impact on the stock price. The quantity and quality of information obtained by market entities (including investors, listed companies, and securities intermediaries) are not equal, and the resulting insider trading is micro-insider trading. Severe information asymmetry and insider trading destroy the functions of the securities market, such as raising funds and allocating resources, make the market ineffective, and lead to the failure of the stock market.

This chapter believes that micro information asymmetry cannot be eliminated, which is a common problem faced by the stock markets in the world. The government should try its best to prevent information asymmetry and insider trading and establish an early warning system to identify them, but the degree of strictness can be moderately relaxed, and a certain degree of information asymmetry will promote market liquidity. Macro information asymmetry should be absolutely prohibited, because it involves the fairness of the government's regulation and supervision of the securities market. When the government formulates or announces the information that has an impact on the securities market, it must ensure the information symmetry of all securities participants.

8.1 Review of Information Asymmetry and Insider Trading

8.1.1 Information Asymmetry and Insider Trading Theory

The problem of market failure caused by information asymmetry has been in public economics for a long time. Many economists, such as Jevons and Walras, have put forward the necessity of information asymmetry and government intervention. Boadway and Wildasin (1984) proposed to restrict the transaction by the "contingent contract" between the two parties to correct the information asymmetry between the two sides of the transaction brought by inequality. Information asymmetry is a big problem that troubles the security market of all countries. George A. Akerlof, Michael A. Spence, and Joseph E. Stiglitz, winners of the 2001 Nobel Prize in Economics, have made important contributions to "using asymmetric information for market analysis." Many scholars believe that information asymmetry is the main cause of abnormal stock price fluctuations. Dai Yuanchen (2001) and Wu Jinglian (2001) believed that the main cause of abnormal stock price fluctuations was the manipulation of stock prices by institutions with asymmetric information in China's stock market. Information and the formation of asset prices are inseparable, because investors can only form investment decisions based on the information they have mastered. The influence of information acquisition on the asset pricing model is very important. In theory, in an efficient market, all information should be accurately and timely transmitted to all investors; that is, information has the characteristics of homogeneity. However, in practice, not all investors can get all the information in a timely and fair way. The differences of investors will also lead to different understanding and acceptance degrees of information, resulting in the phenomenon of non-homogeneity of information, that is, asymmetric information. Information asymmetry is an existing problem in almost all markets, but the degree of asymmetry differs. Information asymmetry is an important field of economics research in recent years, and the research of asset pricing under the condition of information asymmetry is an important branch of asset pricing research. Direct research on the relationship between information and asset pricing theory includes Grossman's (1980) rational expectations equilibrium model, Hellwig's (1980) discussion on the existence of rational expectations equilibrium model in the competitive market with asymmetric information, and a series of subsequent extension studies. They use investors' judgment of asset prices as a measure of information to form the equilibrium pricing model when the market is in equilibrium (that is, when supply and demand reach equilibrium). In addition, since information itself is difficult to describe quantitatively, the study of information transmission and the formation of asset equilibrium prices can also start from the volatility of asset prices and study the influence of information on the formation of asset prices by studying the changes in investors' trading behaviors caused by information (usually described by the volatility of asset prices or changes in trading volume). Representative articles in this field include Bollerslev et al. (1992), Barclay et al. (1990), and Ederington et al. (1993).

Direct studies on the relationship between information acquisition and asset equilibrium price are limited, mainly focusing on the impact of noise trading on asset pricing, such as De Long et al. (1990) and Daniel et al. (1998).

8.1.2 Research That Advocates Banning Insider Trading

Those who advocate banning insider trading hold that insider trading violates the principle of fairness, damages investors' interests, and harms the healthy development of the securities market, because serious insider trading will make the securities market lose investors' trust and eventually lead to market contraction. If insider trading and information asymmetry go unpunished, it will cause moral hazard for major shareholders and senior management of the company, which is not conducive to the healthy and long-term development of the company.

After considering the cost of information collection, Fishman and Hagerty (1992) proposed that insider trading would lead to more inefficient security prices. Bhattacharya and Daouk (2002) proved that insider trading leads to reverse operation and reduces the market information efficiency. Bhattacharya and Spiegel (1991) pointed out that when the market is imperfect and insider trading occurs, the efficiency of the market will be greatly reduced, leading to the collapse of the whole market. Kabir and Vermaelen (1996) conducted an empirical analysis of the stock market in Amsterdam, the Netherlands. They tested the influence of insider trading on stock prices by examining the stock liquidity two months before the publication of the annual report. They concluded that there was insider trading in the market and supported the government to restrict it. Bhattacharya and Daouk (2002) and Du and Wei (2003) conducted extensive international comparative studies on insider trading. From the perspective of the cost of equity, the former believed that the prosecution of insider trading would lead to an increase in stock prices and a decrease in the cost of equity. This reflected from one side the price drop caused by insider trading. The latter took a different approach to measuring the extent of insider trading, arguing that insider trading leads to increased volatility in securities prices and undermines the effectiveness of markets.

8.1.3 Research against Banning Insider Trading

The reasons for opposing the idea of banning insider trading are as follows: first, from a micro point of view, insider trading is a reward for entrepreneurs, which will promote entrepreneurs' innovation to a certain extent. Second, from the macro and micro levels, insider trading can slow down the volatility of securities prices, because if insider trading is allowed, internal insiders will slowly buy or sell securities, so that when the information is released, securities prices have risen or fallen to the due level, so as not to cause excessive volatility of securities prices. Third, the cost of banning insider trading is large, but the effect is not great, and the identification of insider trading is difficult.

Manove (1989) believed that insider trading could reflect securities prices more quickly and make securities prices closer to the actual situation of listed companies. Therefore, the information efficiency of securities prices could be improved to a certain extent, and insider trading could reduce the volatility of securities prices and market risks; Manne and Henry (1966) in the *Insider Trading and Stock Market* put forward against the ban on insider trading, from the microcosmic point of view, he believed that insider trading is the reward to entrepreneurs, banning insider trading is costly and ineffective and should not be banned. Leland (1992) made a deeper study of insider trading based on a rational expectation model. He believed that insider trading would increase the average price of securities, while the volatility of securities prices would also increase under normal circumstances. Although it is not certain that overall welfare changes will reflect insider trading, Leland argues that insider trading, if banned, should be modest. Repullo (1999) further extended Leland's model, and the results showed that when the insider is risk-averse and there are multiple insiders, the conclusion is consistent with Leland's (1992). However, if the insider is risk-neutral or the physical investment is earlier than the securities trading, the insider trading has no impact on the average price of the securities, but it can make prices more volatile.

Based on the work of Leland (1992), Repullo (1999), and Madhavan (1992), Shi Yongdong and Jiang Xianfeng (2004) studied the influence of insider trading on security prices under the order-driven mechanism. They found that when the uncertainty caused by noise trading was very small, insider trading could not change the average stock price of security. However, it can increase price volatility, and the conclusion is that insider bans should be treated differently. They argue that "if insider trading can increase the volatility (as measured by variance) of securities prices without increasing their prices, then insider trading should undoubtedly be prohibited. Insider trading should not be banned if it increases the price of shares without increasing the volatility of security prices. But when insider trading increases both the price of a security and the volatility of that price, it becomes a very complicated question whether insider trading should be banned."

8.1.4 *Domestic Research on Insider Trading*

Chinese stock market started relatively late, and domestic insider trading research mainly focuses on the legal system. From the perspective of economics, the research on insider trading started in the 1990s and is still in the initial stage of development. The research directions mainly focus on whether insider trading will obtain excess returns, the influence of insider trading on stock price, stock market liquidity, stock market risk, etc.

1. Research on the Legal Aspect of Insider Trading

Before 2000, Chinese scholars mainly studied and analyzed insider trading from a legal perspective. *Economic Analysis and Legal Mechanism of Insider Trading* by Qi Wenyuan and Jin Zegang analyzed the punishment mechanism of insider trading from the perspective of legal regulation. He Shaoqi (2000) made a comparative study of the relevant laws and regulations of insider trading in other countries, combined with the actual situation of our country's insider trading. He provided suggestions for the establishment of laws and regulations on insider trading. Gu Xiaorong (1998) also studied insider trading from legal and institutional aspects. Since 2000, the research on insider trading in economics has gradually developed.

2. Research on the Influence of Insider Trading on Market Effectiveness

Tang Qiming and Zhang Xuegong (2006) modified the non-competitive model of Michael and Kathleen (1992) to study the impact of insider trading on the effectiveness of securities prices based on the actual situation of China's securities market. The research proved that insider trading reduces the effectiveness of securities prices and proposed that the key to its regulation is to promote the uniform distribution of information among market participants. Shi Yongdong and Jiang Xianfeng (2004), using the same sample as Wang Guipu (2002), found that insider trading generally aggravated the information asymmetry in the trading process and damaged the fairness of the market.

3. Research on the Existence of Insider Trading before and after the Event

Zhang Xin and Zhu Hongmei (2003) used the event study method to study the asset reorganization events of listed companies. They found that the stock price and trading volume fluctuated abnormally during asset reorganization, and there were insider trading behaviors. Huang Yuhai (2003) demonstrated the ubiquity of insider trading by choosing two major events from 1998 to 2002, namely the high proportion of stock delivery, capital transfer, and control transfer of Shanghai-listed companies. He Jia and He Jibao (2001) analyzed the stock prices and turnover rates before and after five types of major news reports from 1999 to 2000, indicating that there were serious insider trading and stock price manipulation in China's securities market.

4. Research on Whether Insider Trading Can Obtain Excess Returns

Shi Yongdong and Jiang Xianfeng (2004) studied the influence of insider trading on information asymmetry based on the LMSW (2002) method. They used PPD (potential probabilistic disgorgement) to measure whether insider trading has excess returns. Wang Chunfeng et al.(2003) applied the event study method and came to the conclusion that insider trading can obtain exceptional returns based on the simple market model and the GARCH-modified market model. Tang Qiming and Zhang Xuegong (2006) put forward the EGARCH-modified model based on control securities and drew the conclusion that insider traders and followers had significant extraordinary returns, which was consistent with the above research results.

5. Research on Insider Trading Strategies

Tang Qiming and Zhang Xuegong (2005) conducted a causal analysis of the price and trading volume of China's stock market in the presence of insider trading through the non-linear causal test conducted by Taylor. They found that insider trading stocks had a single causal relationship from returns to trading volume, which further confirmed that insider traders affected stock prices through information transmission at a low cost and manipulated market trading to obtain profits. Wang Guipu et al. (2004) made a comparative analysis of insider trading and manipulation in China's securities market from 1993 to 2000. They concluded that pure market manipulation based on inside information had an unusually significant market reaction, and the information content was much greater than that of pure insider trading.

6. Research on the Identification of Insider Trading Behavior

Zhang Zongxin and Shen Zhengyang (2006) identified the behavior of insider information manipulation through the Logistic discriminant model and the decision tree model, and the prediction accuracy of 75% was achieved in the judgment of insider trading on the second day after the information announcement, which provided technical tools for the supervision of insider manipulation with securities regulatory departments. Zhang Zongxin (2007) introduced the neural network data mining method into the manipulation screening of insider trading behavior, improved the Logistic model and decision tree model, and achieved a prediction accuracy of 95.5% for the identification of insider trading behavior.

7. Research on Insider Trading Supervision

By comparing with foreign insider trading supervision, Zhang Zongxin and Yang Huaijie (2006) found that there was a big gap between Chinese securities supervision and the West in the definition of insider information, insider trading body, and insider trading behavior. Zhu Weihua (2007) analyzed and compared the effectiveness and efficiency of the supervision of insider trading and found that the supervision of insider trading could not achieve the expected effect from the perspective of vertical comparative analysis. From the horizontal comparative analysis, the supervision of internal trading is conducive to reducing the probability of insider trading. Jiang Huadong (2010) found that under the supervision of insider trading, the investment strategies of market investors would change. The profits obtained by insiders through insider trading by using insider information were not only related to the supervision of insider trading but also to the volatility of stock prices, the liquidity of the market, and other factors. The stricter supervision of insider trading in the market, the more volatile the share price, the more accurate the information available to outsiders, and lower market volatility will reduce the additional income for insider traders.

To sum up, in the early stage of the study on insider trading in the domestic economic circle, scholars mainly analyzed the advantages and disadvantages of insider trading by constructing theoretical models. Later, the event study method was gradually accepted. At present, domestic scholars mainly use the event study method to study insider trading, and the research direction is mainly to analyze whether insider trading exists in the security market and whether insider trading can obtain excess returns and its influence on the security market. However, there is little research on the supervision of insider trading and its impact on stock prices and trading volume. In addition, these studies mainly focus on the micro level, that is, the insider trading caused by the micro information asymmetry, while there is little research on the insider trading caused by the macro information asymmetry. Here, we learn from previous research methods and use the event study method and GARCH model to study the insider trading behavior caused by macro and micro information asymmetry.

8.1.5 *Measurement of Information Asymmetry and Insider Trading*

How to measure or identify information asymmetry and insider trading is not an easy task. Llorente et al. (2001) proposed a method to measure the information asymmetry in the transaction process (LMSW method), which provides a useful reference for this purpose. Llorente et al. (2001) believe that if price and trading volume show a high positive autocorrelation, then most of the transactions should be based on private information; that is, the transaction process has a serious degree of asymmetry. This is supported by the results of their empirical study using data from the US market. Grishchenko et al. (2002) evaluated the information asymmetry of 19 emerging stock markets, including Russia, by combining the LMSW method and the basic ideas of event studies. They found that trading based on private information is common in emerging markets, and the trading degree of private information has a positive relationship with the prohibition degree of insider trading and the protection degree of shareholders in various countries and a negative relationship with national risk.

The empirical research on information asymmetry and insider trading in China is short. Wang Guipu (2002) studied market manipulation based on inside information, measured the information content in the process of insider trading, and established the discrimination system for insider trading. He Jia and He Jibao (2002) mainly studied price changes before and after major events to judge information asymmetry and insider trading. They believed that insider trading existed in China's stock market, and within a certain range, information asymmetry and insider trading were serious. This chapter uses the abnormal fluctuation method of trading volume and price to judge whether there is insider trading and makes an empirical study on it.

8.2 Theoretical Research on Information Asymmetry and Insider Trading

The stock market information asymmetry discussed here is mainly caused by information manipulators, including two aspects: one is to hide the existing real information. The second is to create false information, including macro and micro levels.

8.2.1 Macro and Micro Analysis of Information Asymmetry and Insider Trading

By dividing information asymmetry and insider trading into macro and micro levels, we can clearly see that the macro level should be absolutely prohibited. In contrast, the micro level should be moderately prohibited, which has a certain progressive significance for solving the theoretical debate on whether to eliminate information asymmetry and prohibit insider trading.

(1) Macro information asymmetry and insider trading are relative to the systemic risk of the whole market, while micro information asymmetry and insider trading are relative to the non-systemic risk of individual securities in the market.

(2) Macro information asymmetry and insider trading should be absolutely prohibited, because it directly leads to the information asymmetry of all participants in the securities market and destroys the fair trading of the market. From the macro level, all market participants should share macro information. On the micro level, information asymmetry and insider trading will, to a certain extent, enhance the enthusiasm of companies for mergers, reorganization, and other innovations; this is because the senior managers of listed companies are generally the major shareholders of the company, and innovation will bring direct economic benefits to them. The government management department cannot require the company managers to disclose all the information about the company's development to the public. There is much information that should belong to the company's business secrets. It is not realistic or necessary to completely eliminate micro-information asymmetry and insider trading. Of course, the public information that should be published should also become the shared information of all market participants. From the perspective of fair trade, the information asymmetry at the macro level is more unfair than the information asymmetry at the micro level.

(3) As the manager, the government department should make the information of all the active subjects of the market symmetrical when formulating or implementing the policy information that has a significant impact on securities prices, and there should be no macroscopic insider trading. Severe micro information asymmetry and insider trading supervision are the responsibilities of the government management department, as a regulatory department should never create information asymmetry and insider trading.

(4) Information asymmetry and insider trading can promote market liquidity to some extent (under the condition of poor market liquidity). But even with this function, we also oppose macro information asymmetry. From the micro level, market liquidity is a basic premise to maintain the existence of the market. To maintain this liquidity, there must be two trading parties with inconsistent judgment on the future of the transaction, namely rational market investors with accurate information and the opposite market irrational investors guided by wrong information, namely "noise traders." The proper amount of noise traders have a basic lubricating effect on maintaining market liquidity. In a sense, the market depends on this asymmetric information environment to maintain its existence, but it must be based on the necessary "degree" as the premise. Information asymmetry and insider trading will lead to securities price manipulation, banking behavior, and loss of interests of small and medium investors; investors will lose market confidence, leading to market collapse. Therefore, monitoring and supervising different degrees of information asymmetry and insider trading has become the main task of government management departments.

8.2.2 Cause and Performance of Chinese Stock Market Information Asymmetry and Insider Trading

1. The Reasons for Information Asymmetry and Insider Trading
First, from a purely macro perspective, China's financial system has problems such as soft budget constraints, imperfect systems, and lagging legislation and law enforcement. Financial activities that should be carried out under the environment of policy information symmetry are often due to some market entities, especially banks, securities companies, and listed companies, who have learned the policy trend in advance through improper channels, making the nature of transactions become transactions under asymmetric information conditions, at this time, the party with information advantage can use the time difference of major information disclosure to manipulate the market, conduct insider trading, and transfer the risk to the other party in the market transaction (mainly the small and medium-sized investors in the information disadvantage), so that they can bear additional losses. The government management department has repeatedly improved the information disclosure system, which is an important measure to solve the macro information asymmetry.

Second, an imperfect economic reality full of complicated information makes collecting and obtaining information cost. Meanwhile, there are differences in time and space in the transmission of information. These two factors make investors pay time and money costs to obtain information first, which leads to the difference in the amount of information obtained by investors with different strengths.

Third, insider trading constitutes the artificial information asymmetry factor in market operation. Traders use insider information to obtain information faster than ordinary investors in advance and disclose the information after a certain period of time, so as to obtain abnormal excess profits from abnormal fluctuations in security prices. From this point of view, institutional investors have more information advantages than small and medium investors and often become one of the main participants in insider trading.

Fourth, in order to achieve the purpose of listing, the packaging or even camouflage of listed companies is a major cause of information asymmetry. Listed companies seeking to raise funds by issuing shares obviously know more about the investment, investment risk, and income of the raised funds than investors, who can only know the internal information of the issuing company through external channels such as published financial reports of listed companies. Even if securities investors have strong collection abilities, they cannot fully understand listed companies' real types and strategic intentions by spending huge collection costs. In terms of information possession, listed companies have an obvious comparative advantage.

2. The Performance of China's Stock Market Information Asymmetry

First, there is a serious asymmetry of information between issuers and investors. In order to realize the high price of stock issuance, retention of rights offering, listing qualification, and so on, many companies, with the cooperation of intermediaries, make false packaging, manipulate profits, deceive investors and regulatory authorities, hype up achievements, intentionally cover up problems, and cause major misunderstanding among investors; the amount of public information is not sufficient, the time is not timely, there is a large number of information curtain. There is a serious information asymmetry between issuers and investors. As the seller of securities and the source of market information, the issuer has the most real understanding of its own operating financial status, credit ability, actual profit level, and other information affecting the quality of securities, and the almost complete information in the primary market transactions. However, the information that investors possess as securities buyers mainly comes from various publicly available materials and reports. In China, this information, in its authenticity, accuracy, completeness, timeliness, and other aspects, is not enough to enable investors to judge the value of securities correctly. First of all, the public information contains false elements. In order to obtain the listing qualification, realize the qualification of issuing shares at a high price, and retain the qualification of the rights offering, many companies, with the cooperation of intermediaries, use virtual packaging, manipulating profits and deceiving investors and regulatory authorities. Secondly, public information has a serious misleading tendency. This is reflected in the fact that the issuer and relevant intermediary institutions publicize their achievements, understate the risks, and take risks lightly in the information disclosure process, leading to a major misunderstanding of the financial situation, credit capacity, and future development prospects of the issuer by investors. Finally, the public information is insufficient in quantity and not timely in time, and there is a large amount of information black screen. A large amount of information has not been disclosed or timely disclosed by the issuer, and deception and delay in disclosure of information are quite common.

Second, there is serious information asymmetry between institutional and individual investors. Institutional investors are closely linked to issuers and work together to manipulate stock prices. In the securities market, it is common for institutional investors to hide and monopolize information or even provide false information to the market. The information asymmetry between institutional investors and individual investors is manifested in two aspects: First, institutional investors are closely related to issuers due to their large holdings. Some institutions can directly participate in the internal operation and management decisions of issuers, and some institutions, such as securities companies, have provided securities underwriting, mergers and acquisitions, credit evaluation, and other related services for issuers. Therefore, they are in a better position than the general public investors to understand the true operating financial information of the issuer. Second, institutional investors have strong financial strength and sufficient ability to pay the cost of information collection. In contrast, individual investors usually give up collecting relevant information, especially inside information, because they cannot afford the search cost or the search cost may exceed their income. Third, in the securities market, the more information traders have, the more advantageous they are. Therefore, as the dominant party to obtain information, institutional investors will try to hide, monopolize information, or provide false information to the market, inevitably hindering individual investors from obtaining effective information. In our country, most of the information individual investors learn is outdated and invalid. Most institutional investors process information better than individuals. The information is not always clear at a glance. The processing and understanding of information require the receiver to have certain real connotations to make a correct interpretation. In this respect, institutional investors have certain advantages over individual investors.

Third, there is information asymmetry between governments and issuers. The government is the regulator and is the only subject to reduce or eliminate information asymmetry. In order to achieve the purpose of listing, securities issuers use false packaging and other methods to achieve the purpose of listing, which not only deceive investors but also deceive the government supervision department. The government should use its special position to correct this. However, it will cause the phenomenon of macro information asymmetry in the process of study and implementation of corrective measures.

8.2.3 *Analysis of Influencing Factors of Information Symmetry in Stock Market*

We divide all investors in the stock market into information manipulators and information recipients. The former may manipulate market information to cause information asymmetry and gain excess returns, while the latter can only passively receive information.

The meanings of symbols are as follows:

I—The total income of a market investor under a certain information

B—All non-excess returns of all investors in the market

r—The percentage of revenue received by the information recipient in revenue B, or the percentage of revenue lost by the information operator due to the publication of information in revenue B, that is, loss rate, and $r<1$

y—The undetected actual income of the holder of asymmetric information

z—The actual income of the holder of asymmetric information after being found out

p—The probability that the asymmetric information holder manipulates the information to be discovered

h—Penalty rate for holders of asymmetric information, $h=$ penalty amount $/I\text{-}B$ $(h>1)$

We propose the following hypothesis.

Firstly, the holder of asymmetric information rationally pursues the maximization of expected utility.

Secondly, the utility of holders of asymmetric information depends on the expected income, and they are risk avoiders.

Thirdly, analyze the first information.

First, we construct the income of the holders of asymmetric information under two conditions: undetected and detected.

$$y = I - rB \tag{8-1}$$

$$z = I - rB - h(I - B) \tag{8-2}$$

Then, its utility maximization can be written as:

$$maxEU(B) = (1 - p)U(y) + pU(z) \tag{8-3}$$

The conditions for maximization of this equation, namely first-order conditions and second-order conditions, are:

$$\frac{dEU}{dB} = (1 - p)U'_{(y)}(-r) + pU'_{(z)}(-r+h) = 0$$

$$\implies -r(1-p)U'_{(y)} - (r-h)pU'_{(z)} = 0 \tag{8-4}$$

$$\frac{d^2EU}{dB^2} = r^2(1-p)U''_{(y)} + p(r-h)^2U''_{(z)} \tag{8-5}$$

According to the risk avoidance hypothesis, $U''(y) < 0$, $U''(z) < 0$, Therefore, Equation 8-4 is less than zero, and we can see that the utility maximization constraint of the holder of asymmetric information is: $B^* = B^*(p, h, r, I)$.

For further analysis, complete differentiation of the left end K of Equation 8-4 is obtained:

$$dK = \frac{\partial K}{\partial p}dp + \frac{\partial K}{\partial h}dh + \frac{\partial K}{\partial r}dr + \frac{\partial K}{\partial I}dI + \frac{\partial K}{\partial B}dB = 0$$

$$\implies \frac{\partial K}{\partial B}dB = -\frac{\partial K}{\partial p}dp - \frac{\partial K}{\partial h}dh - \frac{\partial K}{\partial r}dr - \frac{\partial K}{\partial I}dI \qquad (8\text{-}6)$$

Variables B are independent of p, h, r, and I, and they have the following relation:

$$\frac{dB}{dp} = -\frac{\partial K/\partial p}{\partial K/\partial B} \qquad (8\text{-}7)$$

$$\frac{dB}{dh} = -\frac{\partial K/\partial h}{\partial K/\partial B} \qquad (8\text{-}8)$$

$$\frac{dK}{dr} = -\frac{\partial K/\partial r}{\partial K/\partial B} \qquad (8\text{-}9)$$

$$\frac{dK}{dI} = -\frac{\partial K/\partial I}{\partial K/\partial B} \qquad (8\text{-}10)$$

Due to $\partial K/\partial B = d^2 EU/dB^2 < 0$, we only need to prove the molecular symbols of Equations 8-7, 8-8, 8-9, and 8-10 above to prove the relationship between these variables. The asymmetric information holder was found to be affected by probability p:

$$\frac{\partial K}{\partial p} = rU'_{(y)} - (r - h)U'_{(z)} \qquad (8\text{-}11)$$

$U'(y) > 0$, $U'(z) > 0$, $h > r$, thus the Equation 8-11 sign is plus, and the Equation 8-7 sign is plus. Therefore, it can be proved that the higher the probability of being detected will make the asymmetric information holder's behavior more restrained; that is, the more real information is published, and the less false information is produced.

The asymmetric information holder is found after the penalty rate h effect:

$$\frac{\partial K}{\partial h} = pU'_{(z)} - (r - h)U''_{(z)}[-(I - B)]$$

$$= pU'_{(z)} + (r - h)(I - B)U''_{(z)} \qquad (8\text{-}12)$$

Where, $U'(z) > 0$, $U''(z) < 0$, $h>r$, $I>B$, so the sign of Equation 8-12 is plus, and the sign of Equation 8-8 is also plus. Therefore, it can be proved that the heavier the punishment for asymmetric information holders, the more restrained their behavior, that is, the more real information is published, and the less false information is produced.

Asymmetric information holder loss rate r influence:

$$\frac{\partial K}{\partial r} = (1-p)U'_{(y)} - r(1-p)U''_{(y)}(-B) - pU'_{(z)} - p(r-h)U''_{(z)}(-B)$$

$$= -\left[pU'_{(z)} + (1-p)U'_{(y)}\right] + B\left[(r-h)pU''_{(z)} + r(1-p)U''_{(y)}\right] \tag{8-13}$$

Due to $U'(z) > 0, U''(z) < 0, h>r$, the former sign is negative, and the latter sign needs further proof. We use Arrow-Pratt's absolute risk aversion measure: $R_A(y) = -\frac{U''_{(y)}}{U'_{(y)}}$, $R_A(z) = -\frac{U''_{(z)}}{U'_{(z)}}$, the latter term of Equation 8-13 is processed as follows:

$$B\left[-(r-h)pU'_{(z)}R_A(z) - r(1-p)U'_{(y)}R_A(y)\right] \tag{8-14}$$

It can be obtained from Equation 8-3:

$$-(r-h)pU'_{(z)} = r(1-p)U'_{(y)} \tag{8-15}$$

Let's say that's equal to M, and we plug in Equation 8-14:

$$MB\left[R_A(z) - R_A(y)\right] \tag{8-16}$$

If the absolute risk avoidance degree decreases, this is, $R_A(z) > R_A(y)$, then Equation 8-16 is greater than zero, and the sign of Equation 8-13 is uncertain, as is the sign of Equation 8-9. That is to say, the impact of asymmetric information holder loss rate on information asymmetry is uncertain. If the absolute risk avoidance degree increases, this is, $R_A(z) < R_A(y)$, Equation 8-16 is less than zero, Equation 8-13 is less than zero, and Equation 8-9 is also less than zero. It can be concluded that under the condition of increasing absolute risk avoidance, the loss rate and published information change inversely; that is, the higher the loss rate, the less published information, and the more real information hidden or false information produced, the more serious the information asymmetry is.

The effect of asymmetric information holder income I:

$$\frac{\partial K}{\partial I} = -(1-p)U''_{(y)} - (r-h)pU''_{(z)}(1-h) \tag{8-17}$$

If $U''_{(y)} < 0$, then the former term is greater than zero, and $U''_{(z)} < 0, h{>}1, h{<}r$, then the latter term is greater than zero. Thus, the sign for Equation 8-17 is plus, and the sign for Equation 8-10 is plus. However, this does not mean that the increase in income will be accompanied by the increase in income of the holders of asymmetric information will converge their behavior (i.e., the holders of asymmetric information are satisfied). Here, unlike in the case discussed earlier, the *dK/dI* notation cannot determine the degree of information asymmetry. We must consider the ratio of the loss of income of the holder of asymmetric information due to the publication of true information or the creation of false information to the total income of the holder of asymmetric information. We use Arrow-Pratt's absolute risk aversion index to process Equation 8-17 as follows:

$$\frac{\partial K}{\partial I} = r(1-p)U'_{(y)}R_A(y) + p(r-h)(1-h)U'_{(z)}R_A(z) \qquad (8\text{-}18)$$

Substituting Equation 8-15 into Equation 8-18 gives:

$$\frac{\partial K}{\partial I} = M\left[R_A(y) - (1-h)R_A(z)\right] = M\left\{hR_A(z) - [R_A(z) - R_A(y)]\right\} \qquad (8\text{-}19)$$

From Equation 8-5:

$$\frac{\partial K}{\partial B} = -r(1-p)U'_{(y)}R_A(y) + p(1-h)(r-h)U'_{(z)}R_A(z)$$

$$= -M\left\{hR_A(z) - r[R_A(z) - R_A(y)]\right\} \qquad (8\text{-}20)$$

From Equations 8-10, 8-19, and 8-20:

$$\frac{dK}{dI} = -\frac{\partial K/\partial I}{\partial K/\partial B} = \frac{hR_A(z) - [R_A(z) - R_A(y)]}{hR_A(z) - r[R_A(z) - R_A(y)]} \qquad (8\text{-}21)$$

If the absolute risk avoidance degree increases, i.e., $R_A(z) < R_A(y)$, the relationship between the income of the holder of asymmetric information and the information asymmetry is uncertain. If the absolute risk avoidance degree decreases, i.e., $R_A(z) > R_A(y)$, $dK/dI{<}1$ can be deduced, indicating that as the information brings more income to the operator, the holder of asymmetric information will hide more true information or create more false information, and the more serious the information asymmetry is.

8.3 Empirical Study on Information Asymmetry and Insider Trading

8.3.1 *The Empirical Analysis Method of Macroscopic Information Asymmetry and Insider Trading*

Macro information asymmetry refers to the phenomenon of information asymmetry when the government announces information that has an important impact on the stock price. This is a very important government behavior. When the government administrative department releases information that has a significant impact on the stock market, all investors must be allowed to obtain the information at the same time, so that each participant in the stock market has an equal opportunity to make investment and financing decisions. At present, there are not many individual studies on macro insider trading in domestic and foreign literature. From the actual development of China's stock market, the phenomenon of macro information asymmetry and insider trading is real. This is an absolutely prohibited phenomenon of insider trading, because it is different from the micro information asymmetry and insider trading. It is the government management department that directly destroys the fairness of the market. The following is an empirical study on macro information asymmetry and insider trading using Chinese stock data.

1. Sample Selection

Macro information asymmetry and insider trading have been introduced in detail in the previous part. The so-called macro information asymmetry mainly refers to the difference in the quantity and quality of information obtained by investors, listed companies, and other market entities when government management departments formulate and publish policies that have a significant impact on securities prices. And this leads to abnormal fluctuations in the securities market. Here, when investigating the insider trading behavior caused by macro-information asymmetry, we choose the policy events that have a great influence on the securities market formulated by Chinese government management departments. By examining the market reaction conditions of several selected macro-information announcements that have a great influence on the market, we use the event study method to calculate the cumulative abnormal return. Combined with the volume index to analyze the macro information asymmetry and insider trading of our securities market. The specific test methods will be introduced and explained in detail below.

Here, in the selection of macro-information samples, we first refer to a large amount of literature on securities market volatility and find that among the factors leading to securities market volatility, the government management department can adjust or control the main deposit and loan benchmark interest rates of financial institutions, deposit reserve ratio, stamp duty, personal income tax, etc. In addition, the monetary policy formulated by the People's Bank of China, the decision of the administrative department on securities reduction, the reform of non-tradable shares, and the reform of the capital market will also lead to the volatility of the securities market. By referring to relevant literature and combining with the policies made by Chinese government management departments in recent years that have had a significant impact on securities prices, as well as the data recorded on major events in the securities market, the research samples of macro information asymmetry and insider trading selected by us can be obtained by final statistical summary, as shown in Table 8-1.

Table 8-1 Macro Information Asymmetry and Insider Trading Research Sample

Time	Major Event
2002.06.24	The State Council has issued a notice to stop selling state shares through the domestic securities market.
2004.01.31	The State Council issued *Several Opinions on Promoting the Reform and Opening Up and Steady Growth of the Capital Market*, namely "Nine Policies of State Department."
2005.01.23	The Ministry of Finance lowered the stamp duty on securities (stock) transactions from 0.2% to 0.1%.
2005.04.29	China Securities Regulatory Commission issued the *Notice on Issues Related to the Pilot of Share-Trading Reform of Listed Companies*, announcing the start of the pilot work of non-tradable share reform.
2007.03.18	The People's Bank of China decided to raise the benchmark deposit and lending rates of financial institutions by 0.27 percentage points from Thursday.
2007.05.30	The Finance Ministry has decided to raise the stamp duty on stock transactions from the current 0.1% to 0.3%.
2008.10.09	Individual income tax will be temporarily exempted from interest earned by individual investors on securities trading settlement funds in the securities market.
2008.11.17	The People's Bank of China released the *Report on the Implementation of China's Monetary Policy in the Third Quarter of 2008*.
2010.05.02	The People's Bank of China raised the RMB deposit reserve ratio by 0.5 percentage points to 17%.
2012.07.05	The RMB deposit and lending rates of financial institutions were lowered, with the one-year deposit rate cut by 0.25% and the one-year lending rate cut by 0.31%.

Macro information asymmetry and the insider trading caused by it should be studied here. As we all know, in the security market, the most active trading, the most mature market, and the most sensitive and rapid response to information asymmetry belong to stock trading. Besides, the stock is the main form of security in our stock market, and the related data is also the most accessible and accurate. Therefore, in the analysis of insider trading in the securities market, relevant data on stocks are used for empirical research. By analyzing the stock market reflection of the sample occurrence point, we judge whether the release of macro information will cause insider trading in the stock market. If it causes insider trading in the securities market, the government departments have leaked the policy contents when formulating relevant policies and regulations. Macro information asymmetry is an extremely serious phenomenon. In principle, macro information asymmetry should be absolutely prohibited, because all participants should share macro information. However, macro information asymmetry directly leads to the information asymmetry of all participants in the securities market and undermines the fairness principle of market transactions.

2. Inspection Method

There are many methods to test insider trading behavior in the securities market, among which the event study method is more commonly used, and the theory is perfect and mature. Combined with the relevant content of literature review, it is found that scholars mostly adopt the event study method for insider trading research, and the differences in the research are the selection and calculation methods of characteristic index variables. Therefore, the event study method is also used to study insider trading behavior caused by information asymmetry. This method was first proposed by Dolley in 1933 to study the effect of stock splits on stock price changes. The event study method used by the current research field is the improvement and supplement of the event study method proposed by Ball and Brown (1968) in order to study the information content of surplus. Fama (1969) used the event study method to study the effect of stock dividends. Since then, the event study method has been applied worldwide to test the changes in security prices before and after the event and the reaction degree of prices to information disclosure.

The event study method is a widely used empirical analysis method in financial market research. Mainly through the securities (or financial) market data to determine and analyze the impact of a specific economic event on the value of listed companies and then analyze the impact on the securities market or financial market. The rationale for this approach is based on the efficient market hypothesis, which assumes that markets are rational and that the price of stocks already reflects all known public information. Then, when related economic events occur, rational investors will react rationally to the new information, that is, to choose short selling or buying stocks. In this case, the impact of the related event will be immediately reflected in the security price, resulting in abnormal price fluctuation and abnormal return.

The basic idea of the event research study is to set the time period during which the event exerts influence as the event window, calculate the daily abnormal rate of return (the difference between the actual rate of return and the expected rate of return without the event) and the cumulative abnormal rate of return during the event window, and measure the significance degree of the event influence with the statistical test of these two indicators. When we apply the event study method here, economic events are the announcement of macro information (macroeconomic events) summarized above, and the measurement indicators adopted are the cumulative abnormal return rate and cumulative abnormal trading volume of stocks.

(1) Define events and estimated duration
The time point when the event occurs is the date macro information is published (or the first trading day after it if the time point is a non-trading day) and is marked as 0, which is the event window. If the market has reacted in advance three trading days before the information is disclosed, that is, there are obvious abnormal fluctuations, we believe there is a possibility that the information is leaked in advance.

The estimation window refers to a period of time before the event occurs. Variable indicators during this period are used to estimate the yield and trading volume indicators that should be available on the event day under normal circumstances. Here, the changes in market trading prices and turnover before and after the public disclosure of macro information are used to infer whether the information is leaked in advance. The 120 days before the occurrence of the event (the days before and after mentioned in the paper refer to the trading days before and after the occurrence of the event) are selected as the estimation period and compared with the indicators of the window period. Sometimes, when conducting research, the time period after the occurrence of an event may be used for measurement, that is, the rear window.

The relationships between the estimation window, event window, and rear window are shown in the figure below.

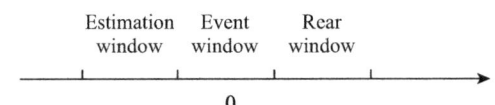

Figure 8-1 Relationships between Estimation Window,
Event Window, and Rear Window

(2) Determine sample data
After defining the study events and periods, we need to determine the sample data to be analyzed. Based on the insider trading caused by macro information asymmetry to be studied here, the stock price changes of domestic listed companies can be selected for research. The listed companies in Shanghai Stock Exchange, Shenzhen Stock Exchange, and all listed companies including them are selected as sample data. There will be specific selection methods and objects in the empirical part below, which will not be repeated here.

(3) Calculate cumulative abnormal returns and trading volumes
The core of the event study method is to calculate the abnormal rate of return during the event period, that is, the difference between the actual return during the event period

and the estimated normal rate of return if the studied event did not occur. Mark R_t as the stock yield on day t, $\bar{R}$ represents the average return of 120 trading days before the event, UR_t represents the abnormal return of the stock on day t, GUR_t represents the cumulative abnormal return of stocks. Q_t represents stock turnover on day t, $\bar{Q}$ represents the average trading volume of the 120 days before the event, UQ_t represents the abnormal volume of shares on day t, GUQ_t represents the cumulative abnormal volume of the stock.

The equation for calculating the abnormal rate of return is:

$$UR_t = R_t - \bar{R} \tag{8-22}$$

The equation for calculating the cumulative abnormal rate of return is:

$$GUR_t = \sum_{t=-3}^{-1} UR_t \tag{8-23}$$

The equation for calculating abnormal volume is:

$$UQ_t = Q_t - \bar{Q} \tag{8-24}$$

The equation for calculating cumulative abnormal volume is:

$$GUQ_t = \sum_{t=-3}^{-1} UQ_t \tag{8-25}$$

(4) Statistical test

In the third step, the cumulative abnormal rate of return and the cumulative abnormal volume of stocks on day t are obtained through calculation. Therefore, the cumulative abnormal rate ratio of return and the cumulative abnormal volume ratio can be constructed, and on this basis, the existence of insider trading in the securities market can be further judged. Further calculation results in the cumulative anomalous returns GUQ_{-t} (or cumulative abnormal volume GUQ_{-t}) for the three days before the event under study, and the cumulative abnormal yield GUQ_{-t} (or cumulative abnormal volume GUQ_t) over the three trading days following the event, compare the two and you get the cumulative abnormal return ratio $PGUR$, $PGUR_t = GUR_{-t}/GUR_t$ (or the cumulative abnormal volume ratio $PGUQ_t = GUQ_{-t}/GUQ_t$). If the absolute value of $PGUR$ (or $PGUQ$) is greater than 1, it indicates that the reaction degree of the stock market before the announcement date is greater than that after the announcement date, which indicates the existence of information leakage and can further confirm the existence of insider trading.

At this point, it is necessary to conduct a significance test for the cumulative abnormal return ratio of $PGUR$ greater than 1. If the test results accept the original hypothesis that the cumulative abnormal return ratio is greater than 1, it indicates the existence of insider trading caused by macro information asymmetry. Conversely, indicates that although the macro information of our country has a certain degree of leakage, the resulting insider trading is not significant. There are many ways to test whether a variable is greater than 1. As there are not many sample data of macro information selected here, T test method is selected in this paper for the accuracy of the test. $PGUR_t$ follows a normal distribution of $N(1, \sigma)$, σ is the population variance, the original hypothesis is: $PGUR_t$ is greater than 1, the test statistic is: $T = \dfrac{\overline{PGUR} - 1}{S/\sqrt{n-1}}$, following the t-distribution with $n-1$ degrees of freedom, Where, $S^2 = \frac{1}{n-2} \sum\limits_{i=1}^{n} (PGUR_i - 1)^2$ is the sample variance, and n is the sample number. If the calculated $PGUR$ is less than 1, the original hypothesis cannot be rejected; that is, the existence of macro information asymmetry leads to insider trading. Similarly, it can test whether $PGUQ$ is greater than 1, and the method is the same as the test method of cumulative abnormal return rate ratio.

8.3.2 An Empirical Analysis Method of Micro Information Asymmetry and Insider Trading

1. Sample Selection

Micro information asymmetry refers to the difference in the quantity and quality of information obtained by investors, listed companies, and other market entities when the listed companies make strategic trends, investment and financing decisions, and other major events. Insider trading caused by micro information asymmetry is more common than that caused by macro information asymmetry, and its influence is less than macro information. It belongs to the non-systemic risk of individual securities in the market, and a certain degree of micro insider trading will enhance the enthusiasm for corporate restructuring, mergers, and other innovations. In view of the micro information asymmetry, it mostly occurs in mergers and acquisitions or asset acquisition of listed companies. Therefore, when we select the data samples of insider trading caused by micro-information asymmetry, we mainly include these two situations.

The sample space of our research on insider trading caused by micro-information asymmetry is 20 representative listed companies that had asset acquisition or merger and reorganization from 2000 to 2012 and were punished or sentenced by the China Securities Regulatory Commission and judicial system in accordance with laws and regulations related to insider trading and market manipulation. Then, we analyze whether insider trading will generate excess returns and the changes in stock market volatility and liquidity caused by insider trading. In the empirical analysis of this paper, the specific company data selected will be introduced in detail below.

2. Define the Time Window for Insider Trading

The three stages of estimation window, event window, and rear window are introduced in the research on insider trading caused by macro information asymmetry. Similar to what is introduced above, the primary task of the research on micro information asymmetry and insider trading behavior is to determine the estimation window and event window. During the estimation window, the yield rate and other indicators of the sample are normal, so it is mainly used to estimate the normal return of the sample when the research event occurs. That is, the data of this period is used to measure the parameters of the normal return model, so as to estimate the normal return. The event window is used to examine whether the stock price has an obvious abnormal reflection of the selected events due to the occurrence of micro information asymmetry.

For the reference of relevant literature, when defining the event window of insider trading, the time disclosure date is set as day 0 (if the day is not a trading day, the first trading day thereafter is set as day 0), the event window is defined as the first ten days from the information disclosure date to the last ten days from the information disclosure date $(-10, 10)$, and the estimation window is the first 120 days from the event window $(-130, -10)$.

The relationship between the estimation window and the event window is as follows:

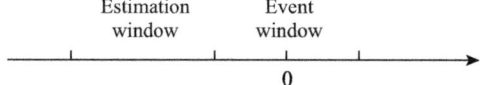

Figure 8-2 The Relationship between Estimation
Window and Event Window

3. Inspection Method

When examining insider trading caused by micro information asymmetry, we mainly use three index variables, namely, the characteristic index of yield, the characteristic index of volatility, and the characteristic index of liquidity. Among them, the characteristic index of return, as the most commonly used variable with a perfect theory and the most accurate test results, is the main indicator variable we use when detecting insider trading caused by microscopic information asymmetry. In order to further determine the accuracy of using the characteristic index variable of return, we further test the micro information asymmetry and insider trading by using volatility index variables and liquidity index variables. These three indicator variables measure micro information asymmetry and insider trading in the following ways.

(1) The measure of yield characteristic index

The core of this research method is the calculation of the abnormal rate of return. The abnormal rate of return is the difference between the actual rate of return during the event and the estimated normal rate of return if the event did not occur.

A. ESTIMATED NORMAL RATE OF RETURN

The rate of return is the return that an investor gets when he or she goes long and short on a stock in the security market. The equation for calculating returns of individual stocks and market indexes is as follows:

$$R_{it} = (P_{it} - P_{i,\,t-1})/P_{i,\,t-1} \tag{8-26}$$

Where, R_{it} is the yield of the ith stock on trading day t, P_{it} is the closing price of stock i on trading day t, and $P_{i,\,t-1}$ is the closing price of stock i on trading day $t-1$. Here, when we calculate the market return rate, the closing price of individual stocks is replaced by the Shanghai A-Share Closing Index and Shenzhen A-Share Closing Index of that day respectively, and the return rate of stocks on the date with the exclusion rights is corrected.

The first 120 days of the event window are selected as the estimation window to calculate normal stock return. The coefficient of stock system risk β can be calculated based on the regression analysis of characteristic stocks. The normal rate of return of stocks can be obtained with the capital asset pricing model (CAPM). Therefore, in order to calculate the normal rate of return of stocks, the ordinary least square (OLS) is first used for regression to calculate the systemic risk of stocks.

The market model of stock return rate is:

$$R_{it} = \alpha_i + \beta_i R_{im} + \varepsilon_{it} \tag{8-27}$$

Where, R_{it} represents the return rate of the ith stock on trading day t, R_{im} represents the market return rate on trading day t, β_i represents the systemic risk of the ith stock, and ε_{it} is the random error term.

The coefficient β of each stock can be obtained by regression analysis of the daily return rate of each stock to the market profitability using the above model. Then, the capital asset pricing model (CAPM) is used to calculate the normal rate of return. The CAPM model is a classic model that presents the relationship between stock returns and systemic risks. A detailed introduction of its assumptions and models can be found in the book *Investments (7th Edition)* (Bodie et al.). The equation of the CAPM model is:

$$E(R_{it}) = R_f + \beta_i (R_m - R_f) \tag{8-28}$$

Where, $E(R_{it})$ is the normal rate of return of the ith stock, R_f is the risk-free rate of interest, usually calculated by the one-year deposit rate of banks, R_m is the market return rate, β_i is the systemic risk of the ith stock, the normal rate of return of the stock can be obtained by this model.

B. CALCULATION OF CUMULATIVE ABNORMAL RATE OF RETURN

The abnormal rate of return refers to the difference between the actual rate of return during the event period and the expected normal rate of return if the event does not occur. The equation for calculating the daily abnormal rate of return UR_{it} is:

$$UR_{it} = R_{it} - E(R_{it}) \tag{8-29}$$

Where, the actual rate of return during the event R_{it} is the original known data, and the expected normal rate of return if the event does not occur is $E(R_{it})$. The calculation method has been introduced above, from which the daily abnormal rate of return of stocks can be obtained. For research, the cumulative abnormal return rate of the stock is further calculated. The equation for calculating the cumulative abnormal return rate GUR_{it} is:

$$GUR_{it} = \sum_{t=-10}^{10} UR_{it} \tag{8-30}$$

C. STATISTICAL TEST

After the corresponding calculation, we can get the daily abnormal return rate UR_{it} and cumulative abnormal return rate GUR_{it} of stocks. Next, statistical tests are conducted to determine whether the event studied at a certain significance level (such as 5%) has an impact on the stock's return rate.

• *Significance test of one-day abnormal return rate*

First, the original hypothesis $H_0 : UR_{it} = 0$, micro information has no significant impact on the stock price; $H_1 : UR_{it} \neq 0$, micro information has a significant impact on stock price.

Second, test statistics are constructed. According to the assumption of the model, the abnormal rate of return UR_{it} follows the normal distribution $N(0, \sigma_i^2)$, where the estimated value of σ_i, is: $S = \widehat{\sigma_i} = \sqrt{\frac{\sum UR_{it}^2}{N-1}}$. That is, the variance of the sample population is unknown, so the T statistic is selected to test the original hypothesis; that is, the test statistic is: $T = \frac{UR_{it}}{S/\sqrt{N-1}} = \frac{UR_{it}}{\widehat{\sigma_i}}$.

Finally, the statistical T-value is calculated and compared with the T-value of a predetermined confidence level α (5%) (which can be obtained by looking up the table). When $T > t_{\alpha/2}$, the original hypothesis H_0 is rejected, indicating that the new information has an important impact on the stock price, and the abnormal return rate of the stock is significantly not 0. At that time, microscopic information leakage leads to information asymmetry. Otherwise, the original hypothesis H_0 is accepted, indicating that the new information has no significant impact on the stock price.

• Significance test of cumulative abnormal return rate

The original hypothesis $H_0 : GUR_{it} = 0$, micro information has no significant influence on stock price; $H_1 : GUR_{it} \neq 0$, micro information has a great influence on stock price.

According to the hypothesis of the model, the known abnormal rate of return UR_t obeys normal distribution $N(0, \sigma_i^2)$, since the sum of normal distribution variables still obeys normal distribution, the mean value is the sum of the mean value of the original normal distribution, and the variance is the sum of the variance of the original normal distribution. Therefore, the cumulative abnormal rate of return GUR_{it} also follows the normal distribution $N(0, \frac{(T_2 - T_1 + 1)\sum \delta_i^2}{N-2})$, where T_1 and T_2 are the time starting points of the cumulative abnormal rate of return, and δ_i is the unknown variable. Then, the statistical test quantity T can be constructed to test whether the cumulative abnormal rate of return is greater than zero, that is, to judge whether the micro information has a significant impact on the stock price. Significance test of the same one-day abnormal rate of return, construct the T statistic; at this time, $T = \frac{GUR_{it}}{S/N}$, S is the variance estimate value of the cumulative abnormal return rate sample, $S^2 = \frac{(T_2 - T_1 + 1)\sum \delta_i^2}{N-2}$, therefore, $T = \frac{GUR_{it}}{S/N} = \frac{GUR_{it}}{\sqrt{(T_2 - T_1 + 1)\sum \delta_i^2/(N-2)}}$, where the estimated value of δ_i has been estimated in the significance test of one-day abnormal returns, which can be directly applied here.

We can judge the influence of information on stock price by testing whether the cumulative abnormal return rate is significantly greater than zero. If for a certain confidence level α (5%), when $T > t_{\alpha/2}$, we reject hypothesis H_0 and accept hypothesis H_1. It means that the new information has an important impact on the stock price, and the cumulative abnormal return rate of the stock is significantly not 0. In this case, micro information leakage leads to information asymmetry.

In order to further determine whether insider trading exists, a significance test should be conducted on the cumulative abnormal return ratio at this time. The ratio of cumulative abnormal return here is the ratio of cumulative abnormal return rate before and after the occurrence of the event. The accounting method of this index and the significance test method of whether it is greater than 1 have been explained and introduced in detail in the test of insider trading caused by macro information asymmetry, so it will not be repeated here. Different from macro information asymmetry leading to insider trading, the investigation time of micro information asymmetry and insider trading is from ten days before the occurrence of the event to 10 days after. The other methods and principles, as well as the steps of the calculation test, are the same as the test of insider trading caused by macro information asymmetry.

(2) The measure of the characteristic index of volatility

In the method of testing the micro information asymmetry and insider trading, besides the abnormal return rate, the degree of volatility and liquidity of the stock can also be measured. First of all, the characteristic index of volatility is introduced. Yield and variance are two basic characteristics of stock volatility. When micro information asymmetry exists in the security market and leads to insider trading, abnormal changes in stock price will certainly occur in the event period. When the stock price changes abnormally, its own variance will also change abnormally. Volatility is to determine the volatility characteristics of the stock price by measuring the variation degree of variance, so as to find out whether the inside information has an impact on the stock volatility, that is, the information is leaked in advance.

Here, the generalized autoregressive conditional heteroskedasticity (GARCH) model is used to fit the volatility of sample stocks. The assumption of classical regression requires that the random error term must obey the assumption of homoscedasticity, but in reality, the random error term often shows some volatility. In this case, the classical regression model cannot be used for simulation, but the autoregressive conditional heteroskedasticity (ARCH) model or GARCH model can be used for testing. The GARCH model is an extended form of the ARCH model. If the order q of random error term lag is large in the ARCH model, the GARCH model should be considered for description. The Lagrange multiplier method (LM test) is the most commonly used method for testing GARCH and ARCH models. We believe that when there is no event, the stock fluctuations are stable, and there is no ARCH effect. Therefore, ARCH can be used to test whether there are abnormal fluctuations in the variance of the stock during the event period, so as to determine whether the inside information has an impact on the stock, that is, whether the information is leaked in advance.

The ARCH model can be expressed as:

$$\delta_{it}^2 = \alpha_0 + \alpha_1 \mu_{it-1}^2 + \cdots + \alpha_q \mu_{it-q}^2 + \eta_{it} \tag{8-31}$$

The expression of the GARCH model is:

$$\delta_{it}^2 = \alpha_0 + \alpha_1 \mu_{it-1}^2 + \cdots + \alpha_q \mu_{it-q}^2 + \beta_1 \delta_{it-1}^2 + \beta_p \delta_{it-p}^2 \tag{8-32}$$

Whether a model can be fitted by GARCH, the LM test of the ARCH effect can be used first. If the q value of the auxiliary regression equation (Equation 8-31) of the LM test is large (such as $q>7$), the test is still significant; that is, there is a high-order ARCH (q) effect in the residual sequence, GARCH (p, q) model should be considered. Generally, the GARCH (1,1) model can describe a large amount of financial time series data. The conditional volatility δ_{it}^2 obtained from the above equation represents the volatility of stock i. If there is abnormal volatility in the event research window, it means that inside information impacts the volatility of stock; that is, information is leaked in advance.

Here, we plan to build the GARCH model as follows:

$$R_{i,t} = \alpha + \beta R_{i,t-1} + \varepsilon_{i,t}$$

$$\sigma_{i,t}^2 = a_0 + a_1 \varepsilon_{i,t-1}^2 + a_2 \sigma_{i,t-1}^2 \tag{8-33}$$

Where, $\varepsilon_{i,t}$ follows $N(0, \sigma^2)$, and conditional variance $\sigma_{i,t}^2$ represents the volatility of the i stock in period t. After the regression of the above GARCH model, we can judge whether there is insider trading from the situation of $\sigma_{i,t}^2$: if the conditional variance $\sigma_{i,t}^2$ changes significantly before the information is published, it indicates that there is insider trading.

(3) Measurement of liquidity characteristic indicators
Liquidity refers to the exchange degree of stock in a certain period of time. The higher the degree of exchange, the stronger the stock liquidity. Generally speaking, when the market is in a stable stage, and there is no insider trading, the market has a greater impact on this index of stocks. If information asymmetry and insider trading occur in the market, the impact of the market on this stock index is much smaller than that in the stable period. The main reason is that when there is information asymmetry in the market, the main factor affecting the stock liquidity index will become the influence of inside information on the stock. Therefore, the relationship between stock turnover and market turnover calculated by using the estimation period is compared with the relationship between the two in the event period. If the correlation between the two in the estimation period is significantly greater than the latter, it indicates that the phenomenon of information leakage and insider trading occurred in the event period. The main indexes are the influence of the regression coefficient and the influence of the decision coefficient.

For the liquidity characteristic index, we choose the volume index, denoting it as $V_{i,t}$, then the regression model is as follows:

$$V_{it} = \alpha_{0i} + \alpha_{1i} V_{mt} + \varepsilon_{it} \tag{8-34}$$

V_{it} is the daily turnover of stocks, V_{mt} is the daily turnover of the market, and ε_{it} is the random error term. The test period is the change of abnormal stock trading volume in the ten trading days before the official announcement of the information. The period of the reference regression equation is 120 trading days before the official release of information. If the regression coefficient and decision coefficient of the event occurrence period are obviously smaller than the coefficient and decision coefficient of the estimation period, it indicates that the information is leaked and there is insider trading.

The optimal variable to measure the liquidity index is the turnover rate. However, since the turnover rate index of all stocks is not easy to obtain, trading volume is used to replace the turnover rate here. This is the existence of the deficiency in the liquidity index test.

8.3.3 *The Empirical Test of Macro Information Asymmetry and Insider Trading*

1. Data Source

Macro information asymmetry is a systemic risk to the securities market, so it has an impact on every stock. Therefore, when selecting the stock data, the best method is to select the stock data, including all the companies listed on the Shanghai Stock Exchange and Shenzhen Stock Exchange. However, the total number of listed companies on the Shanghai and Shenzhen stock exchanges is so large that data collection, collation, and analysis are inconvenient. Therefore, we use the market index to measure. Generally speaking, the Chinese stock market index refers to the SSE Composite Index of the Shanghai Stock Exchange and the Shenzhen Component Stock Index of the Shenzhen Stock Exchange. Although the calculation methods of the two are different, they represent the stock market conditions of the Shanghai and Shenzhen stock exchanges respectively. They can replace the trends and characteristics of all the stocks of the Shanghai and Shenzhen stock exchanges to a certain extent. Therefore, the Shanghai Composite Index and Shenzhen Component Stock Index are selected as the corresponding sample data to analyze the macro information asymmetry and insider trading in this book. Since the CSI 300 Index is based on December 31, 2004, and the sample points in this book date back to June 2002, for data uniformity, the CSI 300 Index is not used as the analytical data in this book.

Ten samples (i.e., ten macro events that have a significant impact on the securities market) are selected here. In each sample, the Shanghai Composite Index and Shenzhen Component Stock Index are used as the data to measure information asymmetry and insider trading. The relevant index data of the market index here comes from the data of the CSMAR database from 2001 to 2011, the data of the Shanghai Composite Index of the Shanghai Stock Exchange in 2012, and the data of the Shenzhen Component Stock Index in 2012. The estimated period of the index in the data is 120 trading days before the event.

2. Empirical Test and Result Analysis

The event study method is used here, following the steps of the event study method described above. The known event period is three days before the release of macro information, and the estimated period is 120 trading days before the event period. Using the obtained sample data, the cumulative abnormal rate of return is calculated first. According to the calculation method of related indexes above, the cumulative abnormal return rate and cumulative abnormal return rate ratio of the Shanghai Composite Index and Shenzhen Component Stock Index corresponding to each sample can be obtained. The cumulative abnormal rate of return and cumulative abnormal rate of return ratio of 10 samples are summarized as shown in Table 8-2.

Table 8-2 Cumulative Abnormal Return Rate (Ratio)

Sample Number	Shenzhen Component Stock Index			Shanghai Composite Index		
	Cumulative abnormal return rate in the 3 days prior to the event	Cumulative abnormal return rate on the 3 days after the event	Cumulative abnormal return rate ratio	Cumulative abnormal return rate in the 3 days prior to the event	Cumulative abnormal return rate on the 3 days after the event	Cumulative abnormal return rate ratio
1	3.659	−0.332	−11.021	2.512	0.960	2.618
2	−0.387	1.252	−0.309	−0.503	3.400	−0.148
3	1.901	−0.556	−3.420	1.672	−1.512	−1.106
4	1.349	−4.469	−0.302	1.658	−2.519	−0.658
5	−1.902	−1.639	1.160	−1.981	−1.045	1.896
6	0.766	−10.212	−0.075	1.556	−9.990	−0.156
7	0.803	−1.507	−0.533	−1.073	−0.126	8.503
8	11.471	2.624	4.372	9.722	1.741	5.584
9	−0.728	−3.636	0.200	−0.845	−1.570	0.538
10	−0.825	0.591	−1.397	−0.794	−1.340	0.593

In order to more clearly analyze the trend characteristics of the cumulative abnormal return rate of the two indexes of ten samples before and after the event, the line chart of cumulative abnormal return rate can be obtained from the table of cumulative abnormal return rate.

From Table 8-2 and Figure 8-3, the following conclusions can be made: (1) Both the Shenzhen Composite Index and the Shanghai Composite Index showed significant fluctuations in the cumulative abnormal returns for the three days before and after the event, indicating that macro information did have a significant impact on the securities market. (2) The cumulative abnormal return rates of the Shenzhen Component Stock Index and the Shanghai Composite Index show a consistent trend before or after the event, indicating that macro information is a systematic factor affecting the market, and thus has a consistent impact on all securities. This trend can be further determined by combining the cumulative abnormal return rate line chart in Figure 8-3. (3) By observing the above table and combining it with the line chart of cumulative abnormal return rates, it can be seen that the cumulative abnormal returns of the two indexes before the event

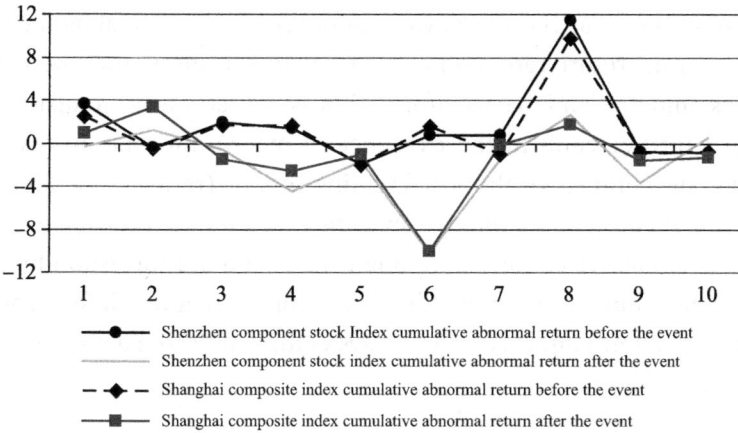

Figure 8-3 Line Chart of Cumulative Abnormal Return Rate

of sample 8 (*Report on the Implementation of China's Monetary Policy in the Third Quarter of 2008* released by the People's Bank of China on November 17, 2008) had the most significant fluctuations, which were much more prominent than those after the event. It indicates that the macro information of sample 8 has the most serious information leakage among all samples. (4) At the time point of sample 6 (on May 30, 2007, the Ministry of Finance decided to raise the stamp tax rate of securities (stock) trading from the current 0.1% to 0.3%), the cumulative abnormal return rate volatility after the event was significantly greater than that before the event. It shows that sample 6 has a significant impact on the stock market, and it is preliminarily determined that there is no information leakage problem. (5) It can be seen from the table that the absolute value of the cumulative abnormal return rate ratio of the two indexes in samples 1, 3, 5, and 8 are all greater than 1, indicating that there is information leakage in samples 1, 3, 5, and 8 no matter in the Shanghai Stock Exchange or the Shenzhen Stock Exchange. In sample 7, only the cumulative abnormal return rate ratio of the Shanghai Composite Index is greater than 1, indicating that certain information leakage occurs in sample 7 in the Shanghai Stock Exchange. In sample 10, certain information leakage occurred only in the Shenzhen Stock Exchange.

Among the ten samples, there are six samples in at least one of the Shanghai Composite Index or Shenzhen Component Stock Index, and the cumulative abnormal return ratio is greater than 1. It indicates that the reaction degree of the stock market caused by the event before the announcement date is greater than that of the stock market after the announcement date, indicating the existence of information leakage, which can further confirm the existence of insider trading. At this time, we need to have the significance test of the cumulative abnormal return rate ratio greater than 1. The original hypothesis is that $H_0 > 1$, and the Shanghai Composite Index and Shenzhen Component Stock Index are used in this paper, so the number of test samples becomes $10 \times 2 = 20$. At this point, SPSS is used for testing, and $T=1.822$ is obtained, which is greater than the significant level of 5%. Therefore, we cannot reject the original hypothesis that the cumulative abnormal return rate ratio is greater than 1. It shows that there exists macro information asymmetry, and macro information asymmetry leads to insider trading.

In order to further confirm the existence of macro information asymmetry and insider trading, the cumulative abnormal trading volume (ratio) was analyzed. With the same calculation method of cumulative abnormal return rate (ratio), we can obtain the corresponding cumulative abnormal trading volume and the corresponding cumulative abnormal trading volume ratio of the Shenzhen Component Stock Index and Shanghai Composite Index of ten samples on three days before and three days after the event, as shown in the table below.

Table 8-3 Cumulative Abnormal Volume (Ratio)

Sample Number	Shenzhen Component Stock Index			Shanghai Composite Index		
	Three days before the event	Three days after the event	Cumulative abnormal volume ratio	Three days before the event	Three days after the event	Cumulative abnormal volume ratio
1	426,092.78	429,260.11	0.99	−371,156.76	652,592.89	−0.57
2	228,770.19	387,159.73	0.59	282,032.10	569,120.17	0.50
3	−15,121.88	−29,057.27	0.52	−46,826.66	−62,583.82	0.75
4	64,937.83	−16,190.62	−4.01	63,598.94	−36,177.82	−1.76
5	644,844.01	555,240.49	1.16	−204,023,681.81	−204,314,687.73	1.00
6	819,912.64	470,166.46	1.74	1,724,753.99	1,164,793.83	1.48
7	−106,939.01	−63,593.42	1.68	−65,154.14	36,381.81	−1.79
8	2,239,905.23	1,221,655.62	1.83	1,564,151.17	2,553,839.64	0.61
9	−352,210.20	−385,513.90	0.91	−853,453.35	−671,574.70	1.27
10	−206,683.95	−167,402.60	1.23	−731,942.83	−427,038.03	1.71

To observe the fluctuations of the cumulative abnormal volume ratio more clearly, the line chart of the cumulative abnormal volume ratio can be shown in Figure 8-4.

From Table 8-3 and Figure 8-4, the following conclusions can be made: (1) The fluctuation range of trading volume is obviously greater than that of the return rate, especially that of the Shenzhen Stock Exchange. This is because a small piece of information may lead to a huge change in stock trading volume, so the sensitivity of trading volume to information is better than the yield index. However, there is little difference in stock turnover before and after the same sample event; that is, the change range of the cumulative abnormal turnover ratio is smaller than that of the cumulative abnormal return rate ratio. (2) Different from the yield index, the trading volume in

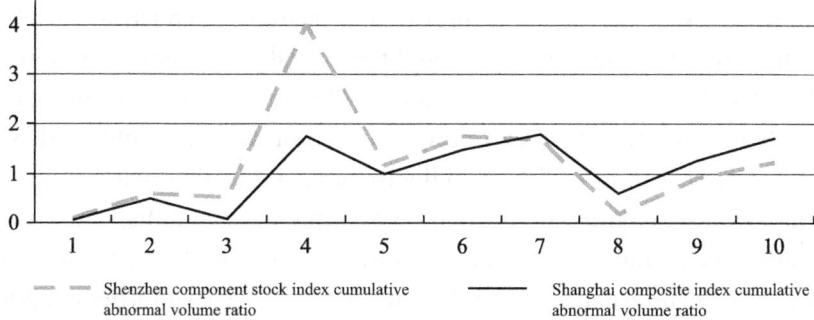

Figure 8-4 Line Chart of Cumulative Abnormal Volume Ratio

the two indexes is significantly different. For example, in sample 1, the trading volume of the Shenzhen Component Stock Index was positive before the event, while that of the Shanghai Composite Index was negative before the event. This is due to the inconsistencies in the stocks contained on the Shanghai and Shenzhen Stock Exchanges. (3) It can be seen from Figure 8-4 that the cumulative abnormal turnover ratio of most samples is greater than 1, indicating that the stock market reaction degree caused by the event before the announcement date is greater than that after the announcement date, which indicates the existence of information leakage and can confirm the existence of insider trading. (4) The absolute value of the cumulative abnormal volume ratio of samples 4, 5, 6, 7, and 10 are all greater than 1, indicating that there is information leakage in both the Shenzhen Stock Exchange and the Shanghai Stock Exchange of these five samples. However, in sample 9, only the cumulative abnormal volume ratio in the Shanghai Composite Index is greater than 1, indicating that information leakage occurs in the stock exchange to a certain extent.

Among the ten samples, there are seven samples in at least one of the Shanghai Composite Index or Shenzhen Component Stock Index, and the cumulative abnormal volume ratio is greater than 1. It indicates that the reaction degree of the stock market caused by the event before the announcement date is greater than that of the stock market after the announcement date, indicating the existence of information leakage, which can further confirm the existence of insider trading. At this time, we need to have the significance test of the cumulative turnover ratio greater than 1. The original hypothesis is that $H_0 > 1$, and the Shanghai Composite Index and Shenzhen Component Stock Index are used in this paper, so the number of test samples becomes $10 \times 2 = 20$. At this point, SPSS is used for testing, and $T=1.73$ is obtained, which is greater than the significant level of 5%. Therefore, we cannot reject the original hypothesis that the cumulative abnormal volume ratio is greater than 1. It shows that there exists macro information asymmetry, and macro information asymmetry leads to insider trading. Further proved that information leakage and insider trading phenomena exist when the macro policy is announced.

The empirical test results of macro information asymmetry and insider trading show that the cumulative abnormal return rate and the cumulative abnormal trading volume of both the Shanghai Composite Index and the Shenzhen Component Stock Index both show obvious fluctuations before the macro information is published. Yield and trading volume appear to have abnormal fluctuations, indicating that information may be leaked in advance, and macro information asymmetry is an indisputable fact. From the information leaks, most of the abnormal fluctuations of the stock index occurred three days before the information was released. Once the macro information is leaked, it would lead to the formation of insider trading, which will affect the fairness of securities market trading. Therefore, the government should strengthen the secrecy of macro information and do a good job in secrecy, so as to avoid the phenomenon of macro information disclosure and insider trading.

8.3.4 Micro Information Asymmetry and Insider Trading

1. Data Source

Micro information asymmetry mostly occurs in the period of asset reorganization, expansion or merger, and acquisition of listed companies, and micro information is a non-systematic influencing factor, which will not affect the volatility of the entire securities market but will affect the stock volatility of related companies. Therefore, when selecting microdata, this chapter takes the historical data punished and sentenced by CSRC and the judicial system in accordance with insider trading and market manipulation laws and regulations from 2000 to 2012 as the overall sample. It selects 20 representative companies with asset acquisition, share capital expansion, reorganization, and merger as the target samples for our investigation. The information on these 20 sample enterprises comes from the official website of the China Securities Regulatory Commission, which is summarized as follows:

Table 8-4 Micro Information Asymmetry and Insider Trading Sample Data

Sample Number	Company Name	Stock Code	Time	Event
1	Yuefuhua	000507	2007.06.14	Foreign equity investment dividend of Yuefuhua wholly-owned subsidiary
2	Bright Furniture	000587	2008.01.2	Bright Furniture and the Great Wall Harbin office restructured.
3	Sihuan Pharmaceutical	000605	2007.03.14	Tianjin Teda Investment Holding Co., Ltd. acquired Sihuan Pharmaceutical Co., Ltd.
4	Tungsten in ST	000657	2009.11.16	Construction Engineering Group reorganized tungsten in ST.

(Continued)

Sample Number	Company Name	Stock Code	Time	Event
5	Leading Technology	000669	2009.12.11	China Oil Jinhong Natural Gas Transmission Co. Ltd. and Lead Technology restructured.
6	Zhongshan Public Utility	000685	2007.08.20	The merger of major shareholder Zhongshan Group and the acquisition of assets through the private placement of assets.
7	Jieli Shares	000996	2007.05.16	Jie Li shares acquired in Liaoning metaphase.
8	Ningxia Hengli	600165	2010.09.28	Xinri Investment in Ningxia Hengli restructured.
9	Gree Real Estate	600185	2007.12.13	Zhuhai Gree Group to Gree Real Estate backdoor listing.
10	Chuang Hing Real Estate	600193	2007.05.24	Cooperated with Shanghai Zhenlong Real Estate Company for refinancing and asset injection.
11	Tongwei Stock	600438	2008.07.22	Private placement.
12	Hangxiao Steel Structure	600477	2007.03.15	Signed a residential project contract in Angola with China International Fund Co., Ltd.
13	Keda Electric	600499	2010.04.29	Foshan Henglitai Machinery Co., Ltd. acquired Keda Mechanical and Electrical.
14	Gaochun Ceramics	600562	2009.05.22	Asset reorganization with China Electronics Technology Group Corporation.
15	ST Yellow Sea	600579	2008.01.14	China National Chemical Corporation reorganized ST Yellow Sea.
16	ST Industrial	600603	2008.06.27	Jiangsu Yinzhou Real Estate Group reorganized ST Industrial.
17	Sanai Rich	600636	2008.07.03	Sanaifu is Shanghai Huayi (Group) company backdoor.
18	Deheng of Liaoyuan	600699	2008.06.17	Bailui Trust Limited Liability Company restructured Liaoyuan Deheng.
19	Xinchao Industry	600777	2010.05.17	The relevant institution intended to acquire trendy industry.
20	ST Construction Machine	600984	2007.03.26	Merger and reorganization with Shaanxi Coal Chemical Industry Group Co., Ltd.

The above specific insider trading cases can be referred to the administrative punishment section of the official website of the China Securities Regulatory Commission, and the article will not be described here. According to the definition requirements of the window period of the event study method, the date of information release in the company report is selected as the event day, and the event estimation period is selected as point 0 of the event window period. If the date on which the event is published is not a trading day, the first trading day after that is taken as the event window period. The data corresponding to specific indicators of the samples are all from the CSMAR database, in which the risk-free interest rate is calculated by the one-year deposit rate.

2. Empirical Test and Result Analysis

In the empirical study on micro information asymmetry and insider trading, this paper mainly adopts three methods to test: the characteristic indicators of return rate, volatility, and liquidity, among which the characteristic indicator of return rate is the main test, and the other two tests are auxiliary verification. The three empirical tests and results will be analyzed below.

(1) The test of yield characteristic index

According to the principles and steps of the rate of return characteristic indicators described above, we first determine the daily rate of return of each stock:

$$R_{it} = (P_{it} - P_{i,t-1})/P_{i,t-1} \tag{8-35}$$

The estimation window taken here is the first 120 days of the event window, and the event window is the first ten days to the last ten days of the information release date. The corresponding daily rate of return of each stock can be calculated according to the above method. Then, the closing price of each stock is replaced by the closing index of Shanghai A-Share or Shenzhen A-Share to calculate the market rate of return R_{mt}. The market model using stock yield is: $R_{it} = \alpha_i + \beta_i R_{im} + \varepsilon_{it}$. The system risk coefficient β_i corresponding to each stock can be obtained, as shown in Table 8-5.

Table 8-5 Summary of Systemic Risk Coefficient β_i

Sample	1	2	3	4	5	6	7	8	9	10
Coefficient	1.1153	0.3549	1.269	0.9248	0.8745	1.0724	0.8507	1.1556	1.4606	0.8955
Sample	11	12	13	14	15	16	17	18	19	20
Coefficient	1.2426	0.8218	0.8605	1.0092	0.6899	0.6886	1.1144	0.4842	1.2043	0.7327

β_i is an indicator to measure the systemic risk of a stock. The larger β_i is, the higher the systemic risk of the stock of the sample company is, and investors require a higher return rate when buying. β_i corresponding to each sample is obtained by regression, and the normal rate of return corresponding to each sample stock is calculated by the CAPM model. The period from 130 days before the event to ten days before the event is selected as the estimation period, and the average value of the normal rate of return corresponding to the sample stock is calculated during the estimation period. Then, the average value is used to determine the abnormal rate of return of the sample stock during the event occurrence period (the ten days before the event announcement date to the ten days after the event announcement date).

Thus, the abnormal return rate of each sample stock in the event period can be obtained. Since each sample contains 21 sample points and 20 samples in total, the information on abnormal return rate contains 420 abnormal return points. Due to the large amount of information, the attached table is no longer displayed here. It can be seen from the line chart of the abnormal return rates of samples that the abnormal return rates of 20 samples all showed obvious fluctuations in the event period, and the fluctuations were relatively severe. Therefore, we preliminarily determined that there was information leakage in these 20 samples.

Figures 8-5, 8-6, 8-7, 8-8 show the line of abnormal return rates:

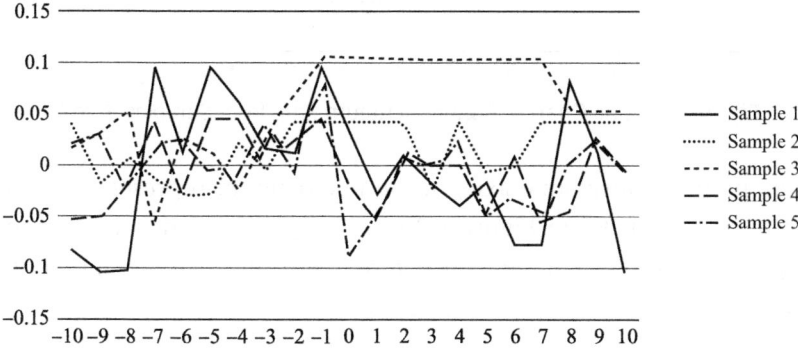

Figure 8-5 Line Chart of Abnormal Return Rate from Samples 1 to 5

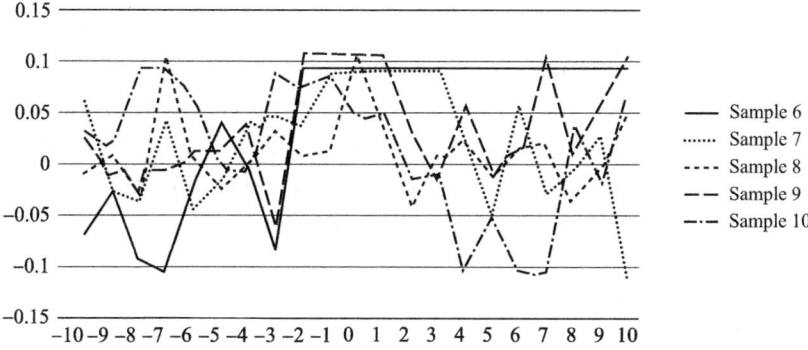

Figure 8-6 Line Chart of Abnormal Return Rate from Samples 6 to 10

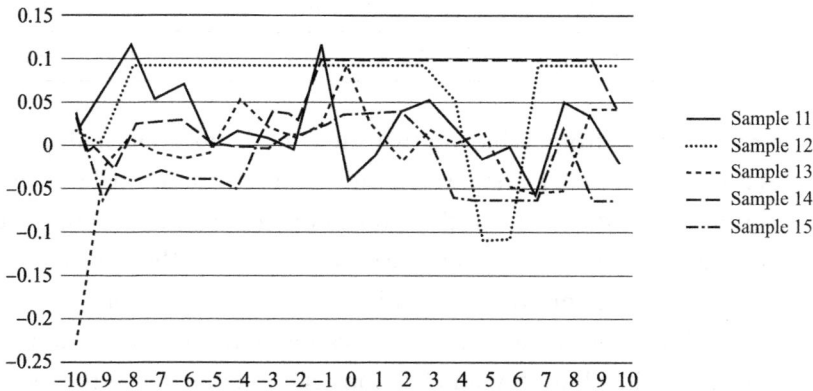

Figure 8-7 Line Chart of Abnormal Return Rate from Samples 11 to 15

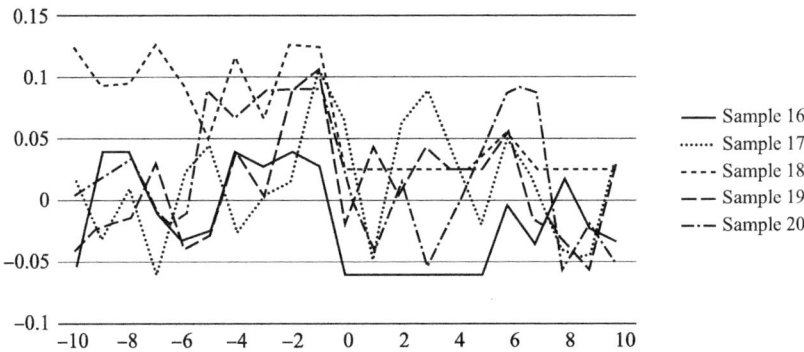

Figure 8-8 Line Chart of Abnormal Return Rate from Samples 16 to 20

The time point 0 (horizontal axis) in the line diagram represents the occurrence time point of the event. From Figure 8-3 to Figure 8-6, it is not difficult to find that the abnormal return rates of 20 samples before the occurrence time point of the event all showed obvious and violent fluctuations. After the occurrence time point, the abnormal return rates of some samples remained at a certain level, such as samples 4, 6, and 14. It shows that the abnormal return rates of the three samples are maintained at a characteristic level after the occurrence of microscopic events. The other samples showed abnormal and violent fluctuations either before or after the event time point, so we can preliminarily determine the existence of information disclosure and insider trading in these 20 listed companies. In order to further determine the existence of micro information disclosure and insider trading, the cumulative abnormal return rate equation $GUR_{it} = \sum UR_{it}$ is used to obtain the cumulative abnormal return rate of each sample stock in the event period, as shown in Table 8-6.

Table 8-6 Table of Cumulative Abnormal Return Rates of Samples

Sample	1	2	3	4	5	6	7	8	9	10
GUR	−0.326	−0.326	−0.170	−0.169	−0.108	0.005	0.126	0.162	0.195	0.209
Sample	11	12	13	14	15	16	17	18	19	20
GUR	0.334	0.336	0.381	0.514	0.543	0.575	0.859	1.115	1.178	1.386

It can be roughly seen from Table 8-6 that the cumulative abnormal rate of return of all samples is basically not 0, among which the cumulative abnormal rate of return of sample 6 is closest to 0, indicating that the return rate fluctuation of Zhongshan Public before the information publication date is the least significant. The information leakage phenomenon is relatively light. The cumulative abnormal return rates of samples 18, 19, and 20 are all above 1, obviously not 0, indicating that the information leakage of Liaoyuan Deheng, Xinchao Industry, and ST Construction Machine is the most serious, and the phenomenon of insider trading is the most prominent. In order to further verify the existence of micro information asymmetry and insider trading at the sampled points, the significance test is adopted below to verify the significance of one-day abnormal returns and cumulative abnormal returns.

First of all, the null hypothesis for the significance test of the one-day abnormal return rate is: $H_0 : UR_{it} = 0$; that is, micro information has no significant impact on stock prices. At this time, the sample data tested is the abnormal returns of 20 stocks within 21 days, 420 data in total. The t value obtained by direct T-test operation with SPSS is 6.272, while the t standard value at a 5% significance level is about $1.73 < t$. Therefore, the rejection of the original hypothesis indicates the existence of micro information asymmetry and insider trading. This indicates that the information of the 20 listed companies we selected was leaked in advance when they were carrying out asset reorganization or mergers and acquisitions, and there was insider trading.

Secondly, the significance of cumulative abnormal returns is tested. The null hypothesis is $H_0 : GUR_{it} = 0$, and the micro information has no significant impact on the stock price. At this time, the sample data for testing is the cumulative abnormal return rate of 20 samples in the corresponding event period, with a total of 20 data. Similarly, the T value obtained by using SPSS for T-test is 3.809, while the standard t value at the 5% significance level is $1.73 < t$. Therefore, the null hypothesis is rejected. Namely, the existence of micro information asymmetry and insider trading is consistent with the test results of the one-day abnormal return rate.

(2) The test of the characteristic index of volatility
The fluctuation of the stock return rate is a time-varying variable. When the return rate fluctuates significantly, it is because the market has been affected by some information. If the rate of return shows an obvious change before the release of information, it indicates the existence of inside information; if it shows an obvious change after the release of information, it indicates that there is no inside information phenomenon.

Take the 20 stocks selected above as a whole and examine their yield fluctuations during the event period. After estimating the GARCH model, conditional variance sequence in the event period can be obtained. See Figure 8-9 for specific conditional variance:

It can be clearly observed from Figure 8-7 that from the first three days to the first ten days of the information release date, the rate of return fluctuated in a relatively stable range, while from the first two days before the information release date, the rate of return fluctuated significantly, which indicates that the market had received certain information shocks before the official release of the information. This information was released in advance and should be made public on day 0.

It can be clearly found from the test results of volatility characteristic indicators that there is an obvious micro inside information phenomenon in the Chinese stock market, and the specific information early release period is roughly two days.

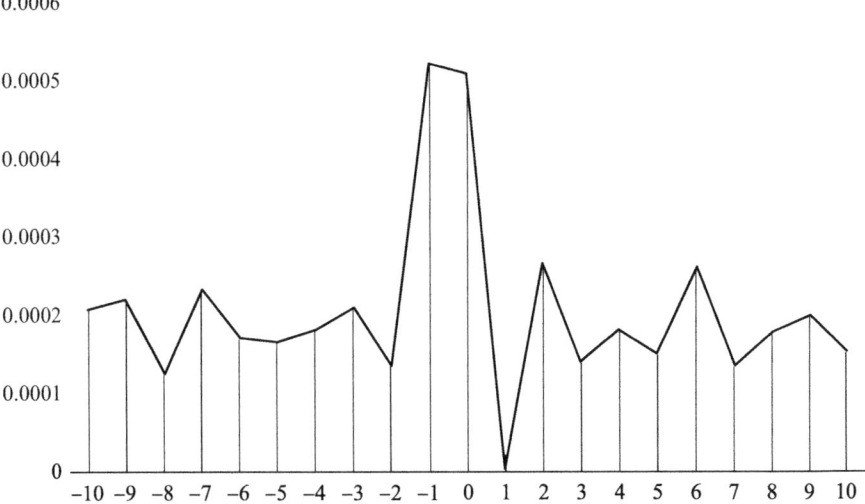

Figure 8-9 Yield Volatility during the Event Period

(3) The test of the characteristic index of liquidity

As the theoretical basis of the test of liquidity characteristic index is relatively immature among the three test methods, this method is only briefly analyzed and taken as an auxiliary test method for the first two methods. The corresponding trading volume and market turnover of 120 days before the event periods of 20 samples were used for regression, and the results were compared with the trading volume and market turnover of 20 samples in event periods. The regression model is $V_{it} = \alpha_{0i} + \alpha_{1i}V_{mt} + \varepsilon_{it}$. After eliminating heteroscedasticity and autocorrelation, the final result is shown in Table 8-7.

Table 8-7 Estimation Period Regression Results and Event Period Regression Results

Variable	Estimation Period Regression Results			Event Period Regression Results		
	Coefficient	t-value	p-value	Coefficient	t-value	p-value
C	1,070,140	151.1065	0.000	6,3267,52	56.2831	0.000
VM	4.1116	661.822	0.000	1.47098	26.4087	0.000
R-Squared	0.9946	...	...	0.6253	...	...
Adjusted R-Squared	0.9946	...	...	0.6244	...	...

From the regression results, we can draw the following conclusions: (1) The daily market turnover has a significant impact on the daily stock turnover in both the estimation period and the event period, indicating that market factors do have a significant impact on stock trading. In addition, the market influence coefficient of the estimation period was significantly greater than that of the event period (4.116>1.47098), indicating that information leakage and insider trading did exist in the event period, thus reducing the influence of market factors on stock trading volume in the event period. (2) From the perspective of the decision coefficient, the decision coefficient of the estimation period is 0.995, while that of the event period is 0.625. That is, 99% of the turnover changes of each share in the estimation period can be described by the market turnover, and the stock turnover is consistent with the market turnover. During the event period, 62% of the turnover of each share can be described by the market turnover. At this time, there is an obvious inconsistency between the stock turnover and the market turnover. It was further confirmed that the micro information was leaked during the event period and caused the phenomenon of insider trading, which resulted in the trend that the trading volume of stocks in the event period was significantly different from the overall market trading volume.

The three test results all show that information asymmetry and insider trading do exist in the selected 20 listed companies. The information was leaked at least ten days before publication, resulting in unusual fluctuations in the stock market. Micro information asymmetry and insider trading phenomenon have become indisputable facts. In addition, in the test of insider trading, it was found that none of the 20 listed companies showed that there was no insider trading in the sample. This shows that in China's securities market, due to the imperfection of the legal system, inadequate management and supervision, and the lack of awareness of internal insiders, when China's listed companies make major changes, the information about the changes will always be disclosed in various ways in advance, and insider trading will be triggered. A certain degree of micro insider trading can promote the activity of the securities market. Still, when it becomes a common phenomenon, it will affect the fairness of investor trading to a large extent and the reasonable and orderly development of the securities market. Therefore, the government should strengthen the supervision and punishment of the phenomenon of microcosmic information asymmetry and insider trading and effectively reduce the phenomenon of microcosmic information asymmetry and insider trading.

8.4   Conclusion and Enlightenment

The stock market is very active. The characteristics of the market determine that the stock market is most prone to information asymmetry. It is difficult for us to completely eliminate the information asymmetry in the stock market. Generally speaking, we can only reduce the degree of information asymmetry, control it within a range, and make the stock market develop healthily and orderly. The following describes how to reduce information asymmetry and insider trading from four aspects: information disclosure, information supervision, regulation of intermediary services, and establishment of credit system.

First, to analyze the generation of asymmetric information, the main reason is that the information cannot be timely and completely transmitted to investors, so the information disclosure mechanism is the most important and effective means to weaken the information asymmetry in the stock market. Specifically speaking, information disclosure has the following requirements: (1) The authenticity of information disclosure. The authenticity of information disclosure is the most fundamental requirement for accounting information disclosure. Information disclosure can play its role only when it is based on objective facts and accurately reflects the operating and financial status of the company. Information distortion will harm the interests of owners and creditors, the public, the country, and the company itself. (2) Timeliness of information disclosure. The time value of information is the core of information value. The invalid information cannot be called information in a strict sense. The timeliness of information requires that information must be disclosed in a timely manner. Periodic reports should be disclosed in accordance with the specified time, and interim reports should be disclosed in a timely manner, so as to prevent misdirection caused by untimely information and harm to information users. (3) Fairness of information disclosure. The fairness of information disclosure means that the information disclosed by the company should be notarized by social notary agencies or organizations, such as accounting statement information, asset evaluation information, etc., should be examined and appraised by accounting firms. The fairness of information disclosure guarantees the authenticity and legitimacy of information. (4) Integrity of information disclosure. The integrity of information disclosure refers to the information released by the company, which must meet the requirements of various information reports in terms of content, without missing or omitting items or intentionally avoiding some of the company's weaknesses. The integrity of information disclosure is very important for the correct analysis of the company's situation. Otherwise, incorrect analysis results will be generated.

Second, to strengthen the supervision of listed companies, take the supervision of listed companies as the focus of government and legal supervision. The requirement of information disclosure itself cannot guarantee its implementation in the securities market, which needs the information supervision of securities. Information supervision should aim at improving information disclosure and establishing a dynamic information disclosure mechanism. Improve the relevant laws and regulations of information disclosure, establish and improve a set of laws and regulations with the *Securities Law* as the core, including accounting standards, learn from foreign experience, and establish a set of information disclosure standards in line with foreign countries. In addition, it is necessary to establish and improve the organizational structure system of securities supervision and establish a set of securities supervision organization systems, including the state securities supervision department, the market trading organization department, the industry, the intermediary organization, and the investor interest protection organization. In addition, a punishment system should be established to raise the cost of trust-breaking and severely punish the institutions and personnel that create false trust-breaking, so as to raise the cost of trust-breaking and even bring them to justice.

Third, intermediary organizations should be independent, fair, and not falsified accounts to standardize the intermediary service market. In order to achieve this, we must strengthen the self-discipline of intermediary organizations and strengthen external supervision, including the supervision of the government and public opinion.

Fourth, we should establish a credit culture, including moral norms, codes of conduct, personal ethics, and legal systems. This is the basis for the honesty and trustworthiness of market players and an important condition for the orderly operation of a market economy.

Although micro information asymmetry can promote market liquidity under certain conditions, it does not become a reason to indulge in micro insider trading. It is still the main task of government management departments to reduce information asymmetry and insider trading as much as possible.

CHAPTER 9

Asymmetric Mean Reversion Based on Market Efficient Cycle Theory and the Formation Mechanism of Financial Crisis

No matter in economic theory or economic practice, the financial crisis is a worldwide problem. It can be imagined that the theory and method to solve the financial crisis must be no less than the historical significance of the Keynesian revolution. The research on the theory of financial crisis should follow the following thoughts: first of all, can the financial crisis be completely eliminated? If it can be completely eliminated without side effects on economic development, we can imagine the greatness of this theory. Secondly, if the financial crisis cannot be completely eliminated, it is necessary to study how to prevent and reduce the losses caused by the crisis. This discussion also has strong application value. Throughout world economic development, the birth of Keynesianism and the implementation of Roosevelt's New Deal have been a great revolution in economic theory and practice. The great crisis, like 1929 to 1933, has indeed disappeared or at least eased a lot. In solving the economic crisis, Keynes's theory undoubtedly has a milestone significance in the history of economic development. Generally speaking, the way to solve the economic crisis is marked by government macro-control and fiscal and financial means aimed at stimulating effective demand. However, using fiscal and financial means to solve the economic crisis has also brought financial crisis. In recent decades, the crisis in the economic field has basically manifested itself as the financial crisis. From the perspective of the development of economic theory, it is self-evident that the exploration and research on the means to solve the financial crisis will be of great importance. The reason is that the number one economic problem facing the world today is the continuous occurrence of financial crises, which are more and more frequent. It continues to impact economic stability and even social stability. Scholars in the field of economic theory have studied and discussed the causes of the formation of the financial crisis, the formation mechanism, and the countermeasures to solve the financial crisis, which seems to occupy a lot of space, but the final functional effect is still limited. Here, the asymmetric mean reversion theory is used to explore and study the formation mechanism of the financial crisis. In view of the fact that the stock market, known as the "barometer," has fully reflected the overall macroeconomic situation, this paper chooses the stock market as an example for empirical research. On the basis of this analysis, the paper puts forward the three-step theory of the government to prevent and control the financial crisis before and after the event.

9.1 Asymmetric Mean Reversion and Stock Market Bubble Burst

9.1.1 *The Rapid Mean Reversion of Asset Bubbles Is Directly Manifested as Financial Crisis*

The accumulation of asset bubbles is the fundamental cause of financial crises, but the accumulation of bubbles is not necessarily manifested as a financial crisis; even the vast majority of asset bubbles do not eventually form a financial crisis. According to the theory of no-arbitrage pricing, the market has the basic function of price discovery: the mean value is the intrinsic value of assets, and the reversion of the mean value is an inevitable trend. Asymmetric mean reversion (the asymmetric feature of asset price reversion to intrinsic value) is the main cause of the financial crisis. If the bursting process of the asset bubble is rapid, that is, asset prices quickly revert to the mean, it will form a financial crisis. The direct cause of mean reversion is the accumulation of asset bubbles to a certain extent. In essence, the financial crisis is the phenomenon of rapid reversion of mean value after the accumulation of asset bubbles to a certain extent. Generally, there would be no financial crisis without the accumulation of bubbles. If bubbles accumulate to a certain extent, the reversion to intrinsic value is slow and does not lead to a financial crisis. The most likely outcome of asset prices being too high (that is, the bubble is too big) is a rapid or slow decline. When asset prices deviate too much from the intrinsic value, a certain event with the nature of the fuse may rapidly reverse asset prices. If it is accompanied by the debt chain break after the price collapse, it is easy to cause a chain reaction and directly lead to the outbreak of financial crises. The accumulation of economic bubbles and their accompanying catalysts, such as financial liberalization, runaway financial "innovation," and the resulting excessive consumption and excessive speculation, eventually lead to the bursting of financial bubbles and damage to the real economy.

The main manifestation of the financial crisis is the rapid decline of asset prices, including currency and debt crises, causing company and bank crises. The currency crisis refers to the sharp fluctuation of the exchange rate, which means that a country's currency is faced with large-scale selling pressure in the foreign exchange market, resulting in the sharp depreciation of that currency. The debt crisis is due to the sharp decline of asset prices (such as stocks), which increases the investment risk of investors and increases losses faster than expected, resulting in the debt crisis. Company crisis refers to the failure of the main body of economic activities to pay the principal and interest of matured debts, including private sector and government debts. The above three crises are the performance and result of the debt chain fracture. The debt chain fracture will also cause market participants to lose confidence in the banking system, and individuals and companies will withdraw deposits from the banking system in large amounts to form a run and form a banking crisis. Basically, the direct cause of the debt chain fracture is the sharp fluctuation of asset prices.

From the history of economic development in various countries, the pursuit of economic growth and the implementation of the expansionary macro policies that adapt to it are almost doomed to form an asset bubble. There are only two ways to solve the bubble: one is to burst it quickly, and the other is to eliminate it slowly. The former is the financial crisis, and the latter is the economic soft landing. From the reality of world economic development, the asset bubble has become a phenomenon that both developed and developing countries that have made great progress in economic development must face. Since the 1980s, many financial crises have occurred. Black Monday in 1987 was the accumulation of the stock market bubble. The US financial crisis in 2000 was the accumulation of a bubble in Internet stocks. The US subprime mortgage crisis in 2007 was the accumulation of the real estate bubble. The Japanese financial crisis in 1989 was caused by the accumulation of stocks and the real estate bubble. The Southeast Asian financial crisis led by Thailand in 1997 resulted from the overvaluation of the currency and the adherence to the fixed exchange rate system. In essence, it was the accumulation of the money printing bubble. An important manifestation of the financial crisis is the sharp decline of stock prices in a short period of time. Taking the American Internet bubble in 2000 as an example, the NASDAQ Index has dropped by nearly 70% in a year and a half since 2000. The sharp fluctuation of stock prices is not only an important manifestation of the financial crisis, but also the cause of the financial crisis. Understanding why stock prices plummeted provides insight into the causes of the financial crisis.

In recent decades, the global economy has grown rapidly for many years in a row. This growth should be attributed to the successful implementation of monetary policy. However, it is the unprecedented good situation of the global economy that provides the possibility for the growth of systemic risks. Low-interest rates and overly optimistic expectations for the future have pushed up the prices of stocks and real estate, and the pursuit of high returns has constantly led to the emergence of various high-risk assets. However, the regulatory measures of the central banks of various countries often contribute to the excessive inflation of asset prices. The process of asset bubble accumulation may be very long, and the process of reversion may be very fast. A rapid reversion may lead to the full outbreak of the financial crisis.

As the "barometer" of the macroeconomy, the stock market plays an important role in the national economic system. Today, with the gradual formation of the world financial integration pattern, the fluctuations of the stock market in any country will have an impact on the financial industry and the real economy of other countries. Throughout the several large-scale financial crises in the capitalist world, there is no doubt that they will have a chain impact on the world financial system, resulting in widespread economic depression.

The history of several major economic depressions since the 1980s, including the famous Black Monday in 1987, the stock market disaster that led to the collapse of the Japanese economy in 1989, and the bursting of the US Internet stock bubble in 2000, has a similar reason. That is, the stock market trend deviates from its fundamental market level, resulting in a large bubble. Once the bubble bursts, the stock price falls too fast, which leads to the rupture of the capital chain, and then a series of chain reactions are caused. It should be said that the fluctuation of the price of financial assets deviating from its basic value was the internal cause of most financial crises.

Before that, scholars analyzed the formation mechanism of the financial crisis mainly from the aspects of the national macroeconomic policy, the pursuit of the false high in the stock market, and people's speculative psychology, and analyzed the formation and impact of the financial crisis. At the same time, there were few articles on the causes of the crisis from the perspective of mean reversion. Mean value reversion, as the name implies, means that the return on securities assets will fluctuate around the market level. Its fluctuation is mainly due to the fact that the market always goes through a process of digesting information, which makes the actual return of securities assets not always consistent with the actual value, and always has a reverse correction when it deviates from its intrinsic value, so as to reverse to its intrinsic value. Black (1988)'s research analyzes the causes of the stock market crash in 1987 and the continuous process of the crisis from the perspective of mean reversion and introduces the psychological factors of the adjustment of reversion expectations. After that, Hillebrand (2002) deepened Black's theory and put forward the theory of the "mean reversion illusion" of people before and after the financial crisis, and examined the similarities and differences of the mean reversion process before and after the crisis in detail. The subsequent asymmetric mean reversion model, the ANST-GARCH model, which tested the return on securities assets, provided the feasibility for the asymmetric test of the financial crisis.

We selected four representative stock indexes in the world, namely the S&P 500, NASDAQ Composite Index, Nikkei Stock Average, and FTSE 100. We selected their daily data from April 1984 to the end of 2012 for nearly 30 years as the research object. First of all, we analyze its growth and the fluctuation rules before and after the financial crisis from the graph, and then use the ANST-GARCH model to test its asymmetric mean reversion for nearly 30 years and come to the conclusion that the four stock price indexes tested will cause people to overreact when experiencing negative market shocks, and in the case of negative shocks, the volatility of the stock market is significantly more severe than the case of positive shocks. The following conclusions can be drawn from the previous graph analysis: First, the asymmetric mean reversion of securities assets is intrinsically related to financial crisis: financial crisis is a special form of mean reversion. Second, the intensification of the stock market volatility has an inevitable connection with the occurrence of a financial crisis. Third, world financial integration has led to the transmission mechanism of the financial crisis.

We can draw two conclusions from the research of market efficient cycle theory: one is that the existence of market efficient cycles is inevitable, but some stock market efficient cycles are longer; some stock market efficient cycles are shorter. The shorter the effective cycle is, the more fully the stock market responds to economic growth. Another conclusion is that since the existence of market efficient cycles is inevitable, mean reversion is inevitable, but the time length and speed of mean reversion are random. In terms of the length of the regression period, there are cases where the regression period is longer and cases where it is shorter. In terms of restore speed, there are cases where the restore is faster and cases where the restore is slower. A rapid reversion would cause stock prices to plummet in a short period of time, leading directly to the financial crisis. Therefore, from the perspective of the market efficient cycle, stock prices should be prevented from rising too much and forming stock market bubbles to avoid the occurrence of the financial crisis. Bubbles are the most significant manifestation of stock prices deviating from the mean. Because the main form of a financial crisis is a collapse in asset prices, there is little room for a collapse in asset prices without a bubble that is seriously off the mean. A bubble means that the stock market price seriously exceeds the actual value of the stock.

9.1.2 The World Stock Market Crashes Are All Rapid Bursts after the Accumulation of Bubbles

1. The Mississippi Stock Market Crash in France
The Mississippi stock market crash in France in 1720 and the South Sea Stock Market crash in England were the earliest stock market crashes since the establishment of the world stock market. The immediate cause of the crash was the excessive speculation in the market that led to the collapse of the Mississippi company's stock. In 1710, France had

a fiscal deficit of nearly 100 million lithium and a national debt of nearly 3 billion lithium. However, in that year, the fiscal revenue was only 69 million lithium, and the expenditure was 147 million lithium. The fiscal revenue was not beyond the expenses, and the French government and various departments were almost paralyzed. In order to get out of the country's financial crisis, the French government authorized John Law to set up a private bank with a capital of about 6 million lithium. In 1717, the French government allowed taxes to be paid on paper money issued by John Law's private bank. The following year, the French government changed John Law's private bank into a national bank, gave it the power to issue banknotes, and chartered law to establish the Mississippi Company and the General Tax Office. Thus, John Law controlled the exclusive right to issue paper money in France, the monopoly on the North American trade, the agency of indirect taxes, and the three accompanying monopolies—the National Bank, the Mississippi Company, and the Tax Office. In 1718, the Mississippi Company planned to issue 200 million shares at a price of 500 lithium each to exploit the Louisiana gold mine. John Law used various promotional methods to create an atmosphere of social buying and allowed holders of government bonds to use their bonds to buy stocks. With bonds trading at less than half their face value, most bondholders are desperate to swap their bonds for shares, and there has been a stampede. The market speculation became increasingly intense, and the money poured in like a flood all over Europe. In July 1719, the share price of the Mississippi Company reached 5,000 lithium; in August, it rose to 10,000 lithium; in October, it rose to 21,000 lithium, and at its peak, it reached 31,000 lithium. The price increase was 62 times the issue price, and it set the highest record for the world stock market to soar for a considerable period of time. In July 1720, the speculative frenzy was finally coming to an end. Many investors began to worry about the high price of the stock. People who had made money wanted to convert their shares into paper money. The investors began to sell a large number of Mississippi shares, and the share price fell rapidly. In order to prop up the stock price, John Law even issued paper money in large quantities to absorb the stock sold by investors. As a result, the stock price of the Mississippi company collapsed and created the world's highest stock market record, which still stands today with a drop of 99% at a time. The selling frenzy quickly turned into a run on the bank, leading to the collapse of French banks. Countless paper money instantly turned into waste paper, and the French economy fell into a long depression.

2. The South Sea Stock Market Crash

The South Sea stock market crash in England is a major stock market crash in the world stock market history after the Mississippi stock market crash in France in 1720, and its impact is more far-reaching than the Mississippi stock market crash in France. In 1711, the South Sea Company was established. In order to show its strong economic strength, the company subscribed for 10 million pounds of government bonds with huge sums of money, thus obtaining the credit of the government and the public. In return, the government guaranteed a 6% interest payment on the converted bonds and an exemption from indirect taxes. In addition, the South Sea Company acquired trade privileges between Britain and the east coast of the American continent and all trade rights between Britain and the west coast of the American continent. However, the South Sea Company had no experience in commodity trading and management, and its operating profit was very small. To change this, the South Sea Company bribed government officials to speed up the process of commercialism. The British public and speculators also wanted the South Sea Company to counter the French Mississippi Company, which stopped the flow of money. In 1720, South Sea Company decided to raise its reputation by providing funds for all the national debt of up to 31 million pounds, which was not only welcomed by the British government, but also catered to many speculators. On January 1, 1720, the South Sea Stock Index rose sharply. The South Sea Company used fraudulent means to create false prosperity, with the share rising from 130 pounds to 300 pounds. On April 12, the South Sea Company issued new shares at a price of 300 pounds per share. In May, South Sea Company issued new shares of 400 pounds per share. On June 15, the South Sea Company issued new shares again in the form of a cash payment of 10%. At this time, the share price of the South Sea Company has risen to 800 pounds. On July 1, 1720, the South Sea Stock Index rose to 950 points and reached 1050 points, 7.08 times higher than the initial issue price of 130 pounds. The stock boom of the South Sea Company has produced a huge demonstration effect. The promoters of some enterprises also started to set up companies and put a large number of new shares in the stock market. As a result, a large number of new companies appeared as quickly as "blowing bubbles." In July 1720, in order to protect the interests of South Sea Company and maintain its monopoly position, the British government promulgated the "No Bubble Company Act," suspended the listing of some "Bubble Company" shares, and dissolved some companies. In August 1720, some directors and senior staff of South Sea Company realized that the stock price of South Sea Company was completely decoupled from the company's unproductive operating performance, so they sold their shares in large quantities. After discovering the truth about South Sea Company, investors were crazier to sell their shares, and the shares of South Sea Company plummeted all the way, with a decline of 78.04%. Affected by this, the stock of the Bank of England fell from 227 points on September 1 to 135 points on October 14. The entire British stock market collapsed completely, with a large number of banks and companies going bankrupt. In the next more than a century, the stocks of the British market almost disappeared.

3. The World Stock Market Crashes of 1929 and 1987

The world stock market crash of 1929 originated in the United States. In 1920–1921, there was an economic crisis in the United States. Since then, the US economy has bottomed out and started to pick up. In 1923, the US stock market took off and climbed steadily to 1928. The market value of US equities rose 78% from $27 billion to $48 billion, an annual increase of 13%. During this period, the US stock market was basically in a slow bull trend, and the stock market and the US economy continued to grow roughly. Stimulated by the stock market boom, the famous American economist Irving Fisher put forward a famous view in 1929: "The stock market has reached a plateau like a permanent plateau." The mood of joy and peace that prevailed in the United States greatly stimulated the ambitions of Wall Street speculators, who turned what was once a prosperous stock exchange into a kind of crazy speculation. Many investors rushed into the market, and the United States appeared in an unprecedented national stock craze. Against this backdrop, the US stock market soared, with the Dow Jones Index reaching 452 points in early September 1929, more than doubling from the beginning of the year, and 5.95 times higher than the lowest point in 1921. Stock prices far exceeded their real value, and stock market risks were on the verge of breaking out. While the stock market soared, the US economy, which had been growing for seven years, began to show signs of fatigue in the second half of 1929, with industrial production shrinking. On September 5, 1929, when Roger Babson, an American financier, predicted that "a market crash was coming sooner or later," and the saying was quoted on the Dow Jones automated financial news recorder, the market did indeed change abruptly, with wild rises in stock indices replaced by sharp falls. On Black Monday, October 21, 1929, when the US stock market opened like a burst torrent, more than 16 million shares changed hands on the New York Stock Exchange, which was the largest turnover in the history of the exchange. On the 24th, despite the president of the United States issuing a "stable economy" news speech, the New York stock market was still pressured by the 13 million shares sold. On the 28th, the New York Stock Market, which was on the verge of collapse, plunged by 12.82%, and stock owners were eager to sell their shares regardless of the price. By July 1932, the Dow Jones Index had fallen to 58 points, 89% lower than the peak of 452 points in September 1929, and the market value had lost 82.3%. The stock price of the famous General Electric Company dropped from $396 to $8 at the lowest. The American stock market entered a 5-year long bear market. Not only has the US economy been paralyzed, but it has also triggered a global economic crisis lasting for four years. It was not until 1954, after 25 years, that the Dow Jones Index returned to its peak of 452 points in 1929.

The 1987 world stock market crash also originated in the United States. Ronald Reagan was elected President of the United States in 1980. In 1982, the United States economy recovered, and the inflation rate fell. The United States and even the entire Western economy entered a sustained growth period. Under the dual guidance of higher interest rates in the United States and sustained economic growth in the United States, a large amount of international hot money flowed into the United States, prompting a sharp rise in share prices. The Dow Jones Index rose from 776.92 in 1982 to 1,955.57 in 1986 and rose to 2,722.40 on August 25, 1987, up 2.5 times from the lowest point in 1982. The stock markets of all Western countries entered an unprecedented comprehensive bull market.

Although the US economy continued growing, many hidden dangers remained. In 1986, the United States had a fiscal deficit of $221 billion, a foreign trade deficit of $156.2 billion and a foreign debt of $263.6 billion. The United States has become the world's largest debtor. In order to attract foreign funds and make up for the shortage of domestic funds, the United States maintains a high-interest rate. On October 19, 1987, the stock market crash broke out. On that day, the Dow Jones Index plunged 508.32 points, a decline of 22.62%. The market value lost $500 billion in one day, surpassing the record of 12.82% crash on October 28, 1929, which triggered the economic crisis. The collapse of the US stock market triggered a worldwide stock market crash. On October 19, the Financial Times Index fell 183.70 points, the Nikkei Index in Japan fell 620 points on October 19, and the Hang Seng Index in Hong Kong fell 420 points on October 19, both of which set the highest daily decline record in the history of the world stock market at that time. The whole Western stock market fell into a panic crash. In the whole of October, the stock market crash caused a loss of 1,792 billion dollars in the market value of the world's major stock markets, which is 5.30 times the direct and indirect economic loss of 338 billion dollars in World War I.

4. Regional Stock Market Crash

The 1997 financial crisis and stock market crash in Southeast Asia is a typical example of the regional stock market crash in the world. Before 1997, Southeast Asian countries and regions had been one of the regions with the fastest economic growth in the world for 20 years. At the same time or after the rapid economic growth, these countries and regions also had problems such as excessively loose bank lending, increasing non-performing assets, increasing external debt, excessive financial liberalization, etc., which laid the root for the financial crisis and stock market crash in Southeast Asia. In February 1997, the Thai baht exchange rate fluctuated as a result of the stagnant Thai real estate market and severe cash flow problems in Thai financial institutions. In May, Thai investors dumped the baht and bought dollars as the central bank sought to stabilize the exchange rate. To no avail, it sold $4 billion to buy the Thai baht. Southeast Asia's financial crisis erupted on July 2 when the Thai government was forced to unpeg the baht from the dollar and move to a floating exchange rate system, with the exchange rate of Thai baht falling by 20% on the day.

Affected by this, the local currencies of the Philippines, Indonesia, and Malaysia also depreciated rapidly. Apart from the Hong Kong dollar, the currencies of almost all other countries and regions with open financial markets have depreciated to varying degrees. The Indonesian rupiah depreciated by more than 70%, the Thai baht by more than 50%, the Korean won, the Malaysian ringgit, and the Philippine peso by 30%–40%, and the Japanese yen by 17% from the beginning of 1997. The stock market of these Southeast Asian countries and regions fell no less than the extent of currency depreciation. As of December 31, 1997, almost all the stock markets in the southeastern countries and regions had suffered from the financial crisis, with a decline of about 20%–60%. The further spread of the financial crisis in Southeast Asia has led to a sharp decline in other global stock markets, including the United States stock market. In November, Sanyo Securities Company, Hokkaido Colony Bank, and Yamaichi Securities Company went bankrupt or closed down in Japan. On January 12, 1998, Hong Kong Peregrine Investments Holdings Limited, which is engaged in a huge investment business in Indonesia, announced its liquidation. On the same day, the Hang Seng Index of Hong Kong plunged 773.58 points, the Singapore Index fell 102.88 points, the Taiwan Weighted Index fell 362 points, and the Nikkei Index fell 330.66 points. It was not until the end of January that the worsening trend of the financial crisis and stock market crash in Southeast Asia was initially stopped. From July 1997 to January 1998, the financial crisis and stock market crash in Southeast Asia experienced more than eight months. The financial turmoil caused by currency devaluation is the direct trigger of the outbreak of the Southeast Asian stock market crash, which has exacerbated the further devaluation of the currency, thus pushing the Southeast Asian financial crisis into the abyss.

5. Japan Stock Market Crash

Japan is one of the countries with the most frequent stock market crashes in the world. From the end of World War II to 1997, in the past 50 years, Japan had seven stock market crashes, including three since the 1980s, the most serious of which was the bubble economy-type stock market crash in 1991–1992. The Japanese called the extraordinary economic boom that began in December 1986 "the booming situation of the Heisei Period." After this boom, Japan's per capita GNP at that time exceeded that of the United States, Germany, France, and the United Kingdom. The proportion of Japan's GNP in the world also increased from 6.4% in 1970 to 13.7% in 1990. The net external assets reached 383 billion dollars in 1991, ranking first in the world. With the support of "economic prosperity," the Japanese stock market rose almost unilaterally from 1986 to 1987. The Nikkei Index rose from 13,113 points in December 1985 to 26,000 points in September 1987, up nearly 1 time. In October 1987, a worldwide stock market crash broke out. Japan not only failed to learn from the collapse of the US stock market, but also immediately recovered. At the end of 1988, the Nikkei Index broke through 30,000 points. On December 19, 1989, the Nikkei Index of Japan reached a new high of 38,915 points, more than three times higher than the lowest point in 1985. The market value of Japanese stocks reached 630 trillion yen, 1.6 times the GNP of that year. In the face of Japan's economic prosperity and the soaring stock market, Japanese citizens have invested in the stock market. However, Japan's economic prosperity implied a huge bubble economy. In the early 1980s, Japan implemented financial liberalization and the loose ultra-low interest rate policies. In the situation of economic boom and increasing income, the Japanese had more bank deposits transferred to the stock market and real estate and had no hesitation in borrowing from banks for speculation. In order to expand their business share and market share, banks actively encouraged people to speculate on land, real estate, and stocks, thus raising the prices of land, real estate, and stocks to an alarming level. However, a bubble economy could not last. In 1989, the Japanese government raised the official interest rate five times, and the Japanese stock market began to fluctuate sharply. In 1990, when the Gulf War broke out, Japan, which was completely dependent on oil imports, fell into extreme panic, and its share price fell sharply. Although the Japanese stock market rebounded after the end of the Gulf War, it could not change the downward trend from then on, falling to 14304 points on August 18, 1992 (the lowest point dropped to 7,607 points in April 2003), with a cumulative decline of 63.24%. Since then, the Japanese economy has plunged into a deep economic crisis and still cannot recover after more than ten years. By the end of 2013, the Nikkei Index was only at more than 10,000 points, which was still far from the historical peak.

9.2 Theoretical Analysis of the Formation of Asymmetric Mean Reversion and Financial Crisis

9.2.1 Overview

The traditional interpretation of mean reversion in finance is the "time-varying rational expectation hypothesis," that is to say, there is a positive correlation between security risk and expected rate of return, and investors will change their risk preference due to the change of investment environment, thus leading to the expected rate of return reverting to the mean. That is to say, investors' rational adjustment of stock price prompts stock price to reverse to its intrinsic value. Later, Fama and French expanded on the theory by arguing that stock prices diverge from intrinsic value, making them more volatile, and investors demand compensation for risk, and that such compensation tends to bring prices closer to the mean.

Another explanation is the "overreaction hypothesis" proposed by the behavioral finance school. Its basic content is that when people face good and bad news, they tend to have blind confidence in an upward or downward trend as the trend continues, so they will chase up or sell down in large numbers, which will promote the stock market and cause excessive ups and downs in the stock market. This creates huge volatility in the stock market. In recent years, economists have found plenty of evidence to support this claim. Through the research on mean reversion, people found that in addition to the above basic features, mean reversion also has another feature—asymmetry. Since people are generally risk-averse in the stock market, that is to say, the bad news is more likely to cause greater volatility in the stock market, so in the case of positive or negative shocks in the stock market, the mean reversion process of the stock market presents different characteristics: after the negative impact of the market, the rate of stock reverse to the mean is obviously faster than the impact of the good news. That is to say, people generally overreact to the negative news and underreact to the good news, which can also be seen from the stronger volatility caused by the negative news. Therefore, from the perspective of asymmetric mean reversion, people's pessimism in the face of bad news is just an overreaction in the face of negative news. The "overreaction hypothesis" is obviously more convincing to explain today's stock price changes.

As a barometer of the macroeconomy, the stock market plays an important role in measuring the situation of the real economy. Generally speaking, the level of the real economy market can be regarded as the intrinsic value of stocks. Therefore, the good and bad of the national economy can be directly reflected in the stock market, and the ups and downs of the stock value can also reflect some information about the company, industry, and even the national policy. The two influence each other. However, since the stock market is a trading market with speculative factors, the stock price is also mixed with many human factors, such as the change of people's expectation factors, insider trading, manipulation of stock prices by institutional investors, etc., which greatly weakens the role of the "barometer" of the stock market. These factors lead to abnormal volatility in the stock market. The stock price deviates too much from the intrinsic value, thus breeding the hidden danger of financial crises.

The US stock market crash in 1929 was a typical financial crisis caused by the stock market crash. The stock market bubble burst quickly, resulting in the crisis. At that time, Americans rushed to invest in the stock market, hoping to get rich overnight, so as to ignore the intrinsic value of their stocks. The rising stock price also caused its price to deviate too much from its intrinsic value. It seriously violated the law of value and eventually led to the failure of stock prices, the collapse of the bubble, the collapse of people's confidence, and the race to sell their stocks, so that the stock market plummeted all the way and nearly collapsed. The collapse of the stock market also had a profound impact on the national economy. Investors rushed to the bank and ran on their deposits due to the substantial decline in wealth. It led to the collapse of banks on a large scale, which announced the break of the capital chain of most of the real economy. Then, the real economy announced bankruptcy, and workers had to face the fate of unemployment, and the American economy entered a long winter. It can be said that the stock market and the real economy complement each other, and the continuous rise of the stock market is good for the country's development. However, the US government allowed the stock market to rise endlessly. It failed to take effective measures to rescue the market when it was facing a collapse, which has to be called the mismanagement of the national management. When the stock market fluctuates abnormally, the government can be used to conduct macro-control on the economy or introduce some favorable and negative policies to control the volatility of the stock market and moderate and slow down its growth. Only in this way can the economy truly achieve a soft landing and minimize the damage of the stock market bubble bursting.

Looking back at the American subprime crisis from 2007, it was mainly caused by the frequent innovation of modern financial instruments and the lack of effective supervision and correct rating, which was manifested as the frequent trading of financial derivatives and the interlocked capital chain. Once the initial capital could not be guaranteed, the capital chain would be completely broken, and investment companies would go bankrupt one after another. Then, the national economy suffered, and the performance in the stock market was due to the flight of funds and lack of confidence, so the stock market showed an overall decline from October 2007 to March 2009 in a year and a half, the Dow Jones Index, S&P 500, NASDAQ Index and so on have shrunk by about 55%, can be said to be hit hard. However, because the US government issued a series of rescue measures and macro-control measures, the US entity enterprises did not suffer the worst result, so the stock market recovered its vitality in a short time. In the following three years, the US stock market began to grow steadily, and at the end of 2012, it was close to the state before the subprime crisis. The subprime crisis in the United States did not result in the large-scale depression of the stock market crisis in 1929, which was not only due to the correct regulation and control policies of the United States government, but also related to its unique world economic dominance. However, the influence of the financial crisis continues to expand due to the inextricable relationship between the economic development of the United States and other countries, which is directly reflected in the Chinese stock market, namely the Shanghai Composite Index, which fell from the peak of 6124 points to 1664 points in just one year. I believe that the impact of the subprime crisis is one of the reasons. But the more important reason is that the Chinese stock market deviated far from its intrinsic value when the stock price index reached its peak in 2007. The bubble burst and reversing to its intrinsic value is the inevitable result. However, after this round of stock market bubble burst, the Chinese stock market did not improve much in the past two years, and the Shanghai Composite Index was basically hovering within 2,000–3,000 points. The development of the financial industry entered a cold winter.

To sum up, the violent volatility of the stock market is inseparable from the formation of the financial crisis. Such stock market volatility that violates the law of value is harmful to the development of the financial industry.

9.2.2 The Formation of Asymmetric Mean Reversion and Financial Crisis

First, if investors behave rationally, security prices do not deviate from their intrinsic value. However, such an idealized situation is difficult to exist in reality. The imperfect rational investment of investors causes securities prices to deviate from the mean. However, as mentioned in the mean reversion theory above, investors tend to be "average rational" in the long term, and deviation from the mean will revert to the mean. Then, the reversion from the mean should be symmetrical or irregular if the investor's risk preference is neutral. However, in the face of good and bad news, people's risk preferences and expectations of reversion are time-varying, which results in the asymmetry of the mean reversion process. Generally speaking, due to people's risk aversion, the mean reversion process will show that bad news has a greater impact than good news. People overreact to the bad news, and their expectations for the market are lower again and again, resulting in the process of falling the price of securities assets becoming more intense. Once the process has a certain scale, it can easily cause the capital chain fracture. Today, with the prosperity and development of financial derivatives, the capital chain fracture often causes a series of chain reactions, resulting in extremely bad effects—this is one of the major reasons for the financial crisis.

Second, the fundamental cause of the financial crisis is the expansion and long-term accumulation of stock market bubbles. Generally, after a period of stable development of the national economy, with good macro fundamentals, investors become more tolerant of risk in the stock market and adopt optimistic expectations for the stock market, which promotes the rise of the stock market. Bubbles occur in the stock market, and some rational investors lock in the risks by taking hedging strategies (such as using put options) and have no fear of the false prosperity of the stock market, thus causing the expansion of the stock market bubble, and the excessive deviation of stock prices from their intrinsic value also fosters the occurrence of financial crises: In the long run, mean reversion is inevitable. The deviation of the stock price from intrinsic value will bring the stock price back to its mean as market participants return to rationality. Normal slow reversion will not have a big impact on the stock market, but the continuously inflated stock price can easily cause the speed of mean reversion to be too fast; that is, the endpoint of reversion is consistent with the normal mean reversion. There was only a quick correction after it deviated from the normal reversion trajectory. Still, due to the large amplitude and strength of the correction, it caused severe shocks in the securities market and the subsequent financial crisis.

To sum up, the accumulation of asset bubbles leads to the asymmetric reversion of securities asset returns, which plays an important role in the financial crisis.

Several representative financial crises in the capitalist world, such as the crash of the American stock market in 1929, the crash of the American stock market in 1987, the bursting of the Japanese stock market bubble in 1989, and the bursting of the American Internet bubble in 2000, are all typical irrational expansion of asset bubbles, which caused panic selling after the bursting of bubbles. The process of the financial crisis in which the stock market shrank greatly is consistent with the discussion in the first two paragraphs. However, the sharp decline of the stock market caused by the devaluation of the Mexican currency in 1994, the Asian financial crisis caused by the devaluation of the Thai baht in 1997, and the capital outflow caused by the fiscal crisis in Brazil in 1999 were not caused by the bursting of the stock market bubble. After the crisis was transmitted to the stock market, it also caused a large shrinkage. In the process, due to the deterioration of the macroeconomic environment, people's expectations on the market level decreased, and the mean reversion expectations of the stock market also made corresponding negative adjustments, thus worsening the crisis.

By comparison, we can find that the stock markets of developed countries tend to be more speculative due to their strong economic strength. When good news occurs in their stock markets, there is often a high degree of chasing in the stock market, resulting in false prosperity. Then, the mean reversion process—the rapid decline of prices leads to the financial crisis. Several classic examples of economic depression caused by the expansion and bursting of asset bubbles all appear here. On the road to economic development, developing countries often rely on external forces, such as foreign loans, foreign capital inflow, and import and export, to pursue rapid development. Excessive reliance on external forces makes its economy too dependent on foreign capital, and its exchange rate, foreign exchange reserves, and foreign exchange surplus deficit are prone to great fluctuations under the influence of international economic conditions. At the same time, its stock market fluctuations are also greatly affected by foreign capital. Therefore, the stock market of developing countries is more vulnerable than developed countries. Recessions that follow financial crises tend to last longer.

9.2.3 Review of Foreign Research

The previous foreign research on the characteristics of mean reversion of securities assets began in the 1980s, and its unique characteristics of price around value were deepened, resulting in investment theories such as reverse investment strategy. Later, Black (1988) applied the mean reversion theory for the first time to explain stock market shocks and financial crises. More than a decade later, Hillebrand (2004) drew on Black's views and expounded on the occurrence mechanism of the financial crisis from the perspective of asset bubble expansion and expected changes in investors' mean reversion. Later, the GARCH model describing the volatility of financial assets began to attract people's attention. As a further development of the model, the ANST-GARCH model has its advantages in describing the asymmetric mean reversion of financial assets, and its unique mean and volatility two-way asymmetric mean reversion test also opens a new way to study stock market volatility and crisis. The following is its development sequence:

De Bondt and Thaler (1985) clarified that most stocks with good and poor performance in the history of the subsequent trend are completely different. They divided 35 stocks listed on the NYSE into "winners" and "losers" groups. During the study period, the "loser portfolio" had an annual yield of about 8% higher than the "winner portfolio," which means that the "loser portfolio" had a significantly more optimistic upside and trend. For stocks, chasing the upside and selling the downside may not be as effective as "ultra-low buying" and "ultra-high selling." It is also a wise choice for people to invest in undervalued stocks. The well-known god of stocks, Buffett, is a loyal supporter of this investment theory. This also provides the basis for the later "Contrary Investment

Strategy": ranking according to the stock return in the past period, mainly investing in the stocks with poor performance and selling the stocks with good performance, thus seeking excess profits.

Fama and French (1988) and Poterba and Summers (1988) studied the NYSE market in the United States, and their empirical results showed that there was indeed a mean reversion of stock returns. Kim, Nelson, and Startz (1991) tested the mean reversion of the stock market before and after World War II. Through the analysis of empirical results, they found that the stock market before World War II had obvious features of mean reversion, but the empirical results after World War II showed mean aversion. Balvers and Gilliland (2000) tested the mean reversion for the stock returns data of 18 convincing countries from 1969 to 1996, and the result showed that there were features of mean reversion.

Campbell and Shiller (1987) established the "Fed Model," the main content of which is that the surplus yield of stocks is related to the nominal yield of 10-year government bonds. Through research and analysis, the nominal yield of government bonds presents the characteristics of volatility. Assuming that the earnings yield on equities is the nominal yield on 10-year government bonds and plotting the two in the same coordinate, the earnings yield (equivalent to the P/E ratio) will show the same volatile characteristics as the yield on 10-year government bonds. This model also assumes that the stock price series is non-stationary, and the earnings per share series is also assumed to be two non-stationary series, which have cointegration. After that, the P/E ratio, as a linear combination of two cointegration variables, will be similar to all stationary series, and it is expected that the P/E ratio will show the trend of mean reversion.

The American stock market crash in 1987 was a typical example of a crisis caused by rapid correction of mean reversion. Black (1988) and Hillebrand (2004) et al. made a thorough explanation of the occurrence of this crisis. They analyzed the formation mechanism of financial crises from the perspective of mean reversion for the first time.

Shiller (1987) pointed out that October 19, 1987, was the biggest single-day drop in the history of the United States, which was in line with the two-day drop on October 28–29, 1929. His research looked at the reasons for the remarkable change in the economic environment in 1987: first, the most commonly cited and persuasive argument, the insurance portfolio strategy in financial markets, which had grown rapidly before the crisis and was the biggest contributor to it. The second is the mechanism by which the crisis worsens: the "knock-on effect," in which an initial sell-off by an insurance portfolio strategist causes prices to fall, leading to a deeper fall in prices, creating a chain reaction. Other factors, such as futures trading strategies at the time, were not the main cause of the crisis, but were one of the factors that accelerated and deepened the recession.

Fama and French (1988) pointed out that slow mean reversion of the security market may lead to negative autocorrelation of return rate. This autocorrelation has a strong explanatory power in the market validity test of long-term returns. The authors chose the securities data of the United States from 1926 to 1985 as empirical data. They obtained the following results. The high negative autocorrelation of returns over one year indicates that the predictability of price changes caused by mean reversion largely depends on the variance of returns in 3–5 years. For a small company's portfolio, 40% of the forecast change depends on the variance of earnings over three to five years, and for a large company, this drops to 25%.

Fischer Black (1988) is a loyal supporter of the idea of mean reversion of stock return rate. He believed that the wrong estimation of mean reversion expectation would lead to the collapse of the stock market. He also explained the decline of the American stock market in 1987 from the perspective of people's risk preferences and mean reversion expectations. He believed that during the stock market crash in 1987, investors' preferences changed before the crisis—their investment philosophy also changed before and during the crisis. Before the crisis, investors' preferences became more and more volatile (with the increase in asset size, they became more risk-prone). Similarly, before the crisis, investors' estimation of the mean reversion became slower than the actual situation, intensifying their estimation bias. From this point of view, the main triggering factor of the crisis is that investors suddenly realize that the degree of reversion to the real average is higher than expected. This understanding led them to reduce their estimate of the expected return on the securities market. The stock price then fell to the expected return enough to make investors willing to hold the existing common securities. At the same time, the continued crisis reduced investors' willingness to hold securities at a given expected rate of return, which further reduced the equilibrium level of the market.

Mitchell and Netter (1989) discussed the "pull the trigger" of the 1987 stock market crash, that is, the anti-takeover clause issued by the Ways and Means Committee of the US House of Representatives on October 13, 1987, and approved on October 15, 1987, which caused several times of more than 10% declines in the stock market in October. This arguably triggered the October 19 crash. Its provisions included restrictions on corporate takeovers, leveraged buyouts, and recapitalizations and imposed restrictions on other hostile takeovers.

In his article "1929 Stock Market Boom and Bust," White (1990) discussed the similarities and differences between 1987 and 1929 stock market crashes in detail and qualitatively proved that fundamental factors and stock market bubbles played an important role in the two crises.

Jacklin, Kleidon, and Pfleiderer (1992) used the multi-period framework proposed by Glostn and Milgrom (1985) to study the market collapse in 1987. The analysis showed that if the market's prior belief underestimated the degree of dynamic hedging strategy (such as an insurance portfolio), then the price would deviate from the fundamentals. The emergence of an insurance portfolio makes people misjudge the market, and the impact of negative information is underestimated. As a result, as time goes by, once the balance is broken by external forces, the errors of the insurance portfolio are corrected, and the stock market shocks will follow.

Hillebrand (2004) made a brief summary of the previous theories and empirically tested the stock price index data, proving Black's point of view was correct quantitatively for the first time. The author selected the daily data of S&P 50 from January 4, 1982, to December 30, 1991, with a total of 2,563 measured values, and used the model of stock return to conduct theoretical empirical research. Using the data before and after the 1987 stock market crash, the model found that the mean reversion phenomenon in the ten months before the 1987 crisis was much lower than that in 1982–1986, which supported the "mean reversion illusion" argument. After the crisis, the mean reversion phenomenon began to intensify; that is to say, the "illusion of mean reversion" was corrected at this time. This phenomenon can be attributed to the disclosure of people's hedge "insurance portfolio." But that was not enough. More importantly, people expected a sharper reversion to the mean that is inferred from basic market information. In the case of further simulation of this model, the result of data analysis was that the probability of the stock market falling significantly by 20% or more is more than 7%. After correction, the probability of the stock market falling can even reach 40%. In the cause of the subsequent financial crisis, the author elaborated that when the a priori reversion speed is expected to be fast, market participants can make hedging strategies against the fast reversion, but when the hedge position is non-public information, the so-called "illusion of mean reversion" will occur. The market was divided into two groups of investors: A and B. Group B first made a hedging strategy (such as combining put options) after anticipating the information of rapid reversion, but at this time, there was no sign of rapid reversion in the market, so group A investors also adjusted the reversion expectation to slow speed, that is to say, the mean reversion trend was underestimated at this time, so that the market continued to rise. As time went by, a large amount of hedging behavior of group B investors was known, and the "illusion of mean reversion" of group A investors was corrected, resulting in a selling boom, a large number of asset bubbles burst, and the crisis formed. The security price process at this time did not clearly reflect the real a priori expectation of mean reversion. The end of the trajectory it followed seemed to be consistent with normal mean reversion, with a quick correction after the deviation. Still, because of the large magnitude and intensity of the correction, the securities market has been hit hard.

In recent years, many foreign analysis methods of stock market volatility research have been related to the GARCH model. Nam, Pyun, and Avard (2002) used the ANST-GARCH model to convincingly test the same feature—the asymmetry in the conditional mean and variance equations. They used the monthly data of the American stock market from January 1926 to December 1997 for empirical test. They tested the asymmetric process in the mean reversion process through the asymmetric nonlinear GARCH model; that is, the mean reversion speed of the negative rate of return is faster than that of the positive rate of return, while the continuity of the positive rate of return is more lasting. This means that the hypothesis of time-varying expectations is not valid here, and the empirical results are consistent with the overreaction hypothesis. They then used three ANST-GARCH models to examine different asymmetries. These models included different asymmetric terms and tested the relationship between the asymmetric reversion of the stock market and the hypothesis of time-varying rational expectations. This hypothesis theory holds that stock volatility and expected return change in a positive way, and the change of expected return rate leads to the mean reversion of stock return rate, and the mean reversion process comes from people's rational adjustment of stock return rate. However, from the point of view of this hypothesis, the positive and negative returns of the stock market should theoretically be equal in the long run; that is, the impact of positive and negative news should cancel each other out in the long run, and the positive and negative reversion process of stock returns should be symmetrical. The result of the ANST-GARCH model this time was that the mean reversion speed of negative returns was faster than that of positive returns. It was inconsistent with the results of the time-varying expectation hypothesis, which led to the failure to verify the time-varying expectation hypothesis again. The conclusion expounded by the ANST-GARCH model that people overreact in the face of negative information is also consistent with the fact that people's lack of confidence during the actual financial crisis led to the collapse of stock prices, thus creating space for the study of the occurrence mechanism of the financial crisis.

With the gradual formation of the pattern of world financial integration, the research on stock market volatility has gradually explored the linkage effect of stock markets between countries.

Karunanakaye, Valadkhani, and O'Brien (2010) discussed the volatility of the world stock markets and the interaction between the stock markets under the subprime crises in detail. They used the MVECH and ADF models to explore the stock market volatility of the United States, the United Kingdom, Australia, and Singapore, as well as the cross-volatility spillover effect among the stock markets of the four countries, which also has some reference for our research.

9.2.4 Review of Domestic Research

Domestic research on mean reversion and volatility of securities assets was a little later than overseas research. Since 2000, domestic researchers have begun a study on the effectiveness of domestic and foreign stock markets and have successively proved the weak effectiveness and mean reversion characteristics of the stock market in our country. However, due to the late start of the stock market in our country, the scale is relatively small, and due to its powerful macro-control, there has been no huge stock market crash, so there are few analyses on the correlation between mean reversion and financial crisis. However, in recent years, the country has been gradually closely connected with the world financial system, and the aftershocks of the foreign financial crisis have clearly had an impact on China, so some scholars have started to study similar issues. The following is a summary of the specific literature content.

Wei Weixian and Kang Zhaofeng (2001) selected samples of 100 A-shares listed and traded on the Shanghai Stock Exchange before 1994. They conducted an empirical analysis based on their weekly returns, equity ownership, non-frozen share capital in each year, book assets of stocks, and other indicators, and analyzed the above weekly data of stocks from 1994 to 2000. By analyzing the cumulative weekly return rate of the stock portfolio, it is concluded that the return rate of the stock listed on the Shanghai Stock Exchange has a general inertia and has a relatively obvious mean reversion feature, and using the mean reversion principle to formulate the investment strategy of the Shanghai stock market can get good investment fruits.

Ma Hongchao (2001) analyzed from the perspective of the stock market volatility and yield and concluded that not only the stocks listed on the Shanghai Stock Exchange have the trend of mean reversion, but also the stocks listed on the Shenzhen Stock Exchange have the characteristic of mean reversion. He analyzed the volatility and trend of the four representative indexes in the Shanghai and Shenzhen Stock Exchange in terms of their monthly excess returns from 1990 to 2000. The results showed that the volatility of the Chinese stock market was strong, while the Shenzhen Composite Index fluctuated more violently because the stock stability of its listed companies was different from that of the Shanghai market. The analysis of the monthly excess return rate showed that only a small part of the return of Chinese investors is optimistic, and there is a positive correlation at high frequency and a negative correlation at low frequency. All these characteristics have the characteristics of asymmetric mean reversion. The reason may be that ordinary investors are easily affected by the information affecting the stock price with a unique "herd effect," and the market maker makes use of these weaknesses of ordinary investors to carry out a reverse impact, which results in the mean reversion in the Chinese market.

Huang Yong, Feng Yitao, and Chen Jinquan (2002) carried out a specific analysis of the stock index of the United States. By analyzing the price/earnings ratio trend of the S&P 500 Index from 1871 to 2001, they drew the corresponding chart and concluded that it had the feature of mean reversion. It had a time-span reversion cycle: over the 100-plus years, its P/E ratio has ranged from 5 to 45, with an average of 15.8. Among the yield values in these periods, there were four obvious highs, and after these highs, the stock market experienced a decline after the peak, thus completing a process of mean reversion. Through these reversion graphs and their moving averages, it could be concluded that the American stock market had obvious periodicity. It was 1891–1936, 1937–1977, and then it didn't complete the full cycle until 2001. The cycle length was about 40 to 45 years, the range of fluctuation was 4 to 13, and the time interval through the 10-year moving average was 17 to 24 years. The United States experienced an obvious cycle of mean reversion, but this method could not be applied to China (at least at that time). The author used this method to analyze China's stock market but could not get corresponding results. The reason was that China's stock market had just started in the 1990s, and a clear investment system and correct investment concept had not been formed. Therefore, it did not form a complete cycle of volatility, and the results were reasonable.

Ma Xide and Zheng Zhenlong (2006) used the least square method to make an empirical analysis of a single stock—Shenzhen Development A-share. They obtained the mean reversion characteristics of stock returns through its stock prices for 13 years from 1991 to 2004. The concrete empirical results can be expressed as follows. First of all, the β-coefficient of a single stock follows the mean reversion process, especially in the long-term process. Its value will fluctuate around its mean value, and the mean value of its volatility is determined by the enterprise's environment, internal factors, and scale. This conclusion is consistent with the traditional capital asset pricing model. However, when the company has an unexpected event, or the environment deteriorates suddenly, its β will fluctuate greatly in a short period of time, which is contrary to the traditional capital asset pricing model. Secondly, β is predictable, that is, the approximate value of β can be predicted accurately: $\bar{\beta}$ can be roughly calculated with GLS, and then the recent β_t can be calculated with the traditional capital asset pricing model, and the latter phase β_{t+1} can be inferred with its reversion speed. Therefore, the capital asset pricing model is of relatively useful value in the process of estimating β. And with the continuous expansion of the variety and number of security portfolio, the calculation of β will be more accurate and timelier.

Song Yuchen and Kou Junsheng (2005) selected A and B shares of the Shanghai Stock Exchange and Shenzhen Stock Exchange respectively. They conducted empirical tests on their monthly returns during the 14 years from 1990 to 2004 by using the methods of autocorrelation and variance ratio test. The results showed that among the four stock indexes tested, only the Shanghai Composite Index showed mean reversion. At the same time, other Shanghai Composite B Index, Shenzhen Component Index, and Shenzhen Component B Index did not have mean reversion, but showed random walk or mean aversion. Zhao Zhenquan, Su Zhi, and Ding Zhiguo (2005) analyzed several representative stock price indexes in the world and China by using the ANST-GARCH model, and roughly determined two asymmetrical trends of stock return rate through analysis: The asymmetry of fluctuations and the asymmetry of the reversion speed once again confirmed the correctness of the "overreaction hypothesis" of behavioral finance. The empirical results show two problems. First, when the price of securities falls due to negative shocks, it is often accompanied by greater fluctuations, which is contrary to the content of the "time-varying rational expectations hypothesis." Second, in the process of mean reversion, the negative impact causes the mean reversion speed of the stock return rate to be different from the positive impact, which also coincides with the "overreaction hypothesis" emphasized by behavioral finance, but deviates from the "time-varying rational expectation hypothesis." Li Jia and Wang Xiao (2009) tested the effectiveness of China's stock market by using the variance ratio test method proposed by Lo and Mackinlay in 1988. By testing the data of China's Shanghai-Shenzhen 300 Index and fund Jinxin from April 8, 2005, to November 29, 2007, and from November 26, 1999, to November 29, 2007, respectively, it was concluded that China's securities market presented a random walk with no predictability in the short term, while in the long term, it presented a trend of mean reversion, our stock market still cannot be effective in a long term. Wang Mingming (2010) used the GARCH model to study the stock volatility of the Shanghai and Shenzhen stock markets during the financial crisis. The selected period was more than 1,000 data from April 1, 2005, to October 31, 2009, and the research object was the highly representative stock in the two markets. The daily return rate of its stock was analyzed, and the conclusion was as follows. First of all, for ordinary A-shares, the impact of the outbreak of the financial crisis on the volatility of the stock market will gradually weaken over time; that is to say, the financial crisis has no obvious long-term impact on the stability of the stock market, the market's ability to digest information is gradually increasing, and its effectiveness is gradually increasing. Secondly, for the small and medium-sized boards, the outbreak of the financial crisis has greatly impacted its volatility. The continuity of volatility is prolonged, the existing risks in the market and the asymmetry of information are further deepened, and the time and ability of the market to digest information are not as good as before the outbreak of the crisis, which deserves our attention.

Song Yuchen (2012) elaborated on the methods to solve the differences between traditional and behavioral finance. He answered the question of whether the market is efficient, which has been debated for a long time in the academic circle, namely the theory of mean reversion, and proposed the reversion cycle. He believed that the "rational man hypothesis" and the "time efficiency of the market" proposed by standard finance did not exist in reality. However, it is not as untraceable as what behavioral finance scholars said. It should be said that irrational behaviors of investors will cancel each other out with the passing of time and the expansion of investor teams, thus forming an "average rationality." The market will have a process of digesting information, so there will be an intrinsic value in the market. The price fluctuates up and down around value to achieve a dynamic balance, which is also the best explanation for the divergence between traditional and behavioral finance. Then, the author selected the Dow Jones Index, S&P 500 Index, NASDAQ Index, and other representative stock indexes for empirical tests and reached the conclusion that the stock market has the feature of mean reversion. And it found that the reversion cycle is generally less than four months.

It should be said that in today's increasingly updated financial environment, both traditional standard finance theory and emerging behavioral finance theory have certain shortcomings in describing the operation law of financial markets. However, the emergence of mean reversion theory has given new vitality to securities pricing, and its description of stock return rate and volatility has opened a new chapter for the study of finance. Through the study of the mean reversion characteristics of the financial market, the operating law of the securities market can be described clearly. However, practice is always the only standard to test the truth. Theories applicable to today may become invalid tomorrow due to changes in some factors. The next research is to constantly introduce new ideas to adapt to the changes in the rhythm of the times.

9.3 Empirical Model Selection

ANST-GARCH is derived from the ARCH model and GARCH model. The ARCH model (autoregressive conditional heteroskedasticity model) is made by Engle (1982) and Bollerslev (1986). This model takes all available information as conditions and uses some form of autoregression to describe variance variation. Available information at different moments is different for time series, and the corresponding conditional variance is different. You can plot the conditional variance over time. The GARCH model, called the generalized ARCH model, is an extension of the ARCH model and was developed by Bollerslev (1986). It is a special case of the ARCH model. GARCH (p, q) is expressed as Equation 9-1:

$$\sigma_t^2 = \omega + \sum_{i=1}^{p} \alpha_i \varepsilon_{t-1}^2 + \sum_{i=1}^{q} \beta_i \sigma_{t-1}^2 \tag{9-1}$$

It is widely used to forecast the returns and risks of financial assets. In fact, the ARCH model is only applicable to the short-term autocorrelation process of the heteroscedasticity function. Compared with the ARCH model, the GARCH model can better reflect the long-term memory properties of actual data. Although the GARCH model can provide a general description of the volatility of the security market, it cannot accurately capture the asymmetry of the impact of positive and negative market shocks on the volatility of the security rate of return. Therefore, people begin to transform GARCH.

After that, many GARCH models describing the conditional mean and double asymmetry of the variance equation of stock mean reversion emerged, including the adjusted GARCH model proposed by Glosten (1993), Gonzalez-Rivera (1998), et al., the SVSARCH model proposed by Fornari and Mele (1997), and the ARCH model of Markov fluctuation transformation (MSVARCH) proposed by Turner et al. (1989) and Hamilton and Susmel (1994).

9.3.1 Standard ANST-GARCH Model

Nam and Anderson (2002) first added a smooth transition parameter to the GARCH model and proposed the ANST-GARCH model. The basic equation is as follows:

$$R_t = I_0 + [I_1 + I_2 F(\varepsilon_{t-1})] R_{t-1} + \varepsilon_t \qquad (9\text{-}2)$$

$$h_t = a_0 + a_1 \varepsilon_{t-1}^2 + a_2 h_{t-1} + [b_0 + b_1 \varepsilon_{t-1}^2 + b_2 h_{t-1}] F(\varepsilon_{t-1}) \qquad (9\text{-}3)$$

Among them, $F(\varepsilon_{t-1}) = 1/\{1 + exp[-\gamma(\varepsilon_{t-1})]\}$ represents an endogenous regime switching function, whose value fluctuates between 0 and 1; ε_t and ε_{t-1} represent the market information impact at time t and $t-1$; R_t and R_{t-1} represent the stock (stock index) yield of period t and period $t-1$ respectively; h_t is the variance equation, its parameters determine how the concentration of volatility changes from the past to the present, which is determined by the magnitude and characteristics of the past information shocks that interfere with the rate of return.

Compared with the ordinary GARCH model, the ANST-GARCH model has an additional endogenous regime switching function $F(\varepsilon_{t-1})$, whose value depends on the value of ε_{t-1} impacted by market information in the last period. Generally speaking, if the market experiences a negative impact, $\varepsilon_{t-1} < 0$, $F(\varepsilon_{t-1})$ will be closer to 0 as the absolute value of ε_{t-1} increases. When the market experiences a positive impact, $\varepsilon_{t-1} > 0$, the value of $F(\varepsilon_{t-1})$ becomes more and more close to 1 as the absolute value of ε_{t-1} increases. It is worth noting that γ here represents the unknown endogenous regime switching control parameter.

First, for Equation 9-2, the time-varying sequence correlation of the equation is controlled by $I_1 + I_2 F(\varepsilon_{t-1})$, and since $F(\varepsilon_{t-1})$ is between 0 and 1, its variation range is also between I_1 and $I_1 + I_2$. Consider two extreme situations: when the market is affected by a considerable negative shock, resulting in $F(\varepsilon_{t-1}) = 0$, the sequence correlation is described by I_1; on the contrary, if $F(\varepsilon_{t-1}) = 1$ is caused by a positive shock of the same degree, the sequence correlation is described by $I_1 + I_2$. It is worth noting that due to the need for an asymmetric response, the persistence of volatility follows that the negative shock impact of the return rate is always greater than that of the positive shock. Therefore, the parameters of the mean equation $I_1 < 0$ and $I_2 > 0$ are required, which indicates that the return rate is negatively (positively) sequentially correlated with the negative (positive) shocks that occurred before. $I_1 < 0$ and $I_2 > 0$ also indicate that the mean reversion trend of negative shocks of return rate is stronger than that of positive shocks, which further confirms the asymmetry of return rate reversion. Here I_0 is not significant in the analysis.

The second asymmetry of the model is the asymmetry of volatility persistence. It can be seen from Equation 9-3 that the volatility persistence of the model is determined by a series of parameters $a_1 + b_1 F(\varepsilon_{t-1}) + a_2 + b_2 F(\varepsilon_{t-1})$. When the market is affected by a considerable negative impact, is caused $F(\varepsilon_{t-1}) = 0$, and the sequence correlation is described by $(a_1 + a_2)$. If $F(\varepsilon_{t-1}) = 1$ is caused by a significant positive shock, the sequence correlation is described by $(a_1 + a_2) + (b_1 + b_2)$. However, the asymmetric volatility requires $(a_1 + a_2)$ to be larger than $(a_1 + a_2) + (b_1 + b_2)$, so $(b_1 + b_2) < 0$

becomes the key to producing asymmetric volatility when the yield suffers positive and negative shocks. Under the condition of $(b_1 + b_2) < 0$, the continuity of current volatility to negative shocks is better than that of positive shocks of the same degree. When the market experiences negative shocks, $0 < F(\varepsilon_{t-1}) < 0.5$, the current volatility can be called "high volatility sustained regime"; conversely, when the market experiences a positive shock, the $0.5 < F(\varepsilon_{t-1}) < 1$, the current volatility can be called "low volatility sustained regime"; when $\varepsilon_{t-1} = 0$, $F(\varepsilon_{t-1}) = 0.5$ means that the current volatility is in the center of the high and low volatility regime. Here, the endogenous regime switching control parameter γ controls the conversion between wave regimes. With the increase of γ, the wave regime conversion speed also increases gradually.

9.3.2 The Adjusted ANST-GARCH Model

After some modification, this equation is the same as the asymmetric GARCH model introduced before. For example, if the values of parameter b_1 and b_2 of Equation 9-3 are set to 0, it becomes the Gonzalez-Rivera model. Similarly, when the conditions of this model are changed and the endogenous regime switching control parameter γ is set to infinity, as long as $\varepsilon_{t-1} \geq 0$, corresponding $F(\varepsilon_{t-1}) = 1$, $\varepsilon_{t-1} < 0$, corresponding $F(\varepsilon_{t-1}) = 0$, and the values of parameter b_1 and b_2 of Equation 9-3 are set to 0, was Glosten et al.'s adjusted GARCH (1,1) model.

Later, considering that the time variability of the expected rate of return is partly due to the adaptation problem considering the changes of market fluctuations, a new ANST-GARCH-M model was developed to test the asymmetric reversion in order to verify the time-varying rational expectation hypothesis:

$$R_t = I_0 + [I_1 + I_2 F(\varepsilon_{t-1})]R_{t-1} + \delta\sqrt{h_t} + \varepsilon_t \qquad (9\text{-}4)$$

$$h_t = a_0 + a_1\varepsilon_{t-1}^2 + a_2 h_{t-1} + [b_0 + b_1\varepsilon_{t-1}^2 + b_2 h_{t-1}]F(\varepsilon_{t-1}) \qquad (9\text{-}5)$$

δ here represents the risk premium ratio of volatility and measures the impact of future volatility on the expected rate of return. Therefore, when $I_2 > 0$ and $\delta \neq 0$ is adopted, it can be determined that there is no relationship between the asymmetric mean reversion of the equation and the time-varying rational expectation hypothesis.

A key question to highlight is whether equity markets need a higher risk premium when they are known to be able to measure higher negative volatility in the future. The answer to this question plays a key role in the study of the asymmetric reversion of short-term returns.

Under the time-varying rational expectations hypothesis, a positive correlation between future volatility and risk premium means that investors need an additional risk premium to cover excessive volatility due to negative shocks in the future. This theory has since been disproved by the behavior of investors. The conventional way of doing business is that there should be a positive relationship between future volatility and risk premium—but this is questionable. The following model illustrates the relationship between excess volatility expected in the future and risk premium in the same period.

$$R_t = I_0 + I_4 F\left(\varepsilon_{t-1}\right) + \left[I_1 + I_2 F\left(\varepsilon_{t-1}\right)\right]\sqrt{h_t} + \varepsilon_t \qquad (9\text{-}6)$$

$$h_t = a_0 + a_1\varepsilon_{t-1}^2 + a_2 h_{t-1} + \left[b_0 + b_1\varepsilon_{t-1}^2 + b_2 h_{t-1}\right] F\left(\varepsilon_{t-1}\right) \qquad (9\text{-}7)$$

When the market suffers a negative shock, $F(\varepsilon_{t-1}) = 0$, its risk premium parameter is I_1, and volatility persistence is determined by $(a_1 + a_2)$; when the market suffers a positive shock, $F(\varepsilon_{t-1}) = 1$, its risk premium parameter is $(I_1 + I_2)$, and volatility persistence is determined by $(a_1 + a_2) + (b_1 + b_2)$. According to traditional theories about future volatility and risk premium, leverage must be consistent with $I_1 > (I_1 + I_2)$ or $I_2 < 0$. At this point, $I_1 < 0$ implies a negative correlation between future volatility and risk premium. In other words, when $I_1 < 0$ is applied, investors actually reduce the risk premium by acquiring information about negative yield shocks—even though the expected future volatility will be greater.

Finally, people are interested in the relationship between the asymmetric mean reversion part of expected short-term returns and investors' mispricing behavior. In order to clarify the relationship, the following equation is introduced:

$$R_t = I_0 + I_4 F\left(\varepsilon_{t-1}\right) + \left[I_5 + I_6 F\left(\varepsilon_{t-1}\right)\right]R_{t-1} + \left[I_1 + I_2 F\left(\varepsilon_{t-1}\right)\right]\sqrt{h_t} + \varepsilon_t \qquad (9\text{-}8)$$

$$h_t = a_0 + a_1\varepsilon_{t-1}^2 + a_2 h_{t-1} + \left[b_0 + b_1\varepsilon_{t-1}^2 + b_2 h_{t-1}\right] F\left(\varepsilon_{t-1}\right) \qquad (9\text{-}9)$$

Since the previous negative (or positive) shocks affecting the yield $F(\varepsilon_{t-1}) = 0$ (or 1), the sequential correlation is determined by I_5 (or $I_5 + I_6$), and $I_1 > I_1 + I_2$ determines the relationship between future volatility and risk premium, and a high/low volatility persistence associated with the interpretation of a conditional variance process.

If an asymmetric mean reversion model is the result of mispricing caused by investors' overreaction, I_5 and I_1 should be inversely correlated, and $I_6 > 0$, $I_2 > 0$ is shown in Equation 9-8. This means that investors reduce the risk premium due to their unwarranted optimism about expected adverse returns, thus causing current stock prices to rise. This is consistent with the fact that negative shocks affecting yields revert to the mean faster than positive shocks of the same degree.

9.4 Data Selection and Empirical Research

9.4.1 Empirical Data Selection

Here, we select four representative and persuasive stock price indexes in the world, namely the S&P 500, NASDAQ Composite Index, Nikkei Stock Average, and FTSE 100, and choose their daily data from April 1984 to the end of 2012 as the research object. The main reason is that at the beginning of the 1980s, the development of stock markets in various countries was relatively stable, and many high-tech enterprises emerged in the 1980s, and the degree of world financial integration began to become more and more obvious. The impact of financial market fluctuations in various countries on other countries is also deepening. Therefore, the study of the financial crisis in this period and the mean reversion phenomenon of the stock market has a strong guiding significance for reality. We take the logarithmic rate of return of four stock indexes as the research object to study the volatility and reversion of the four stock indexes during this period. Word 2007, Eviews 7.2, and Rats 8 are used as auxiliary software for analysis.

Let's start with these stock price indexes.

1. S&P 500

As the giant of the world economy, the trend of the United States stock market has become the wind vane of the world stock market. Therefore, we first choose the two stock price indexes with relatively large influence and representation in the United States as the research object to analyze.

The S&P 500 Index includes the stocks of 500 listed companies in the United States as its component. These companies are listed on major stock exchanges in the United States. Its index includes more companies and covers a wider range, which can better reflect the development level of the overall stock market in the United States. Therefore, the S&P is a more comprehensive comparison with the Dow.

The S&P 500 Index is compiled by S&P. Since 1957, it has consisted of 425 industrial stocks, 15 railroad stocks, and 60 utility stocks. A change occurred in 1976, when the number of industrial stocks was reduced by 25 and 40 financial stocks were added, while the number of railroad and utility stocks was adjusted to 20 and 40. It takes 1941–1942 as the base period, and the base number is 10 points. The numerator is the sum of the price of each stock multiplied by the number of shares issued, and the numerator is the sum of the stock price of the base period multiplied by the number of shares issued, which is expressed as the percentage after dividing. It is calculated using the weighted average method. Due to the professionalism of the S&P company in securities rating, the accuracy of its S&P 500 Index has a long guarantee. Its coverage is relatively wide, and it can flexibly adjust the price changes caused by the subscription of new shares, share dividends, and stock splits, so it has better continuity than other indexes. It is widely accepted by stock market investors and is the ideal stock index futures contract target.

2. NASDAQ Composite Index

The US Internet bubble burst in 2000, as it became known, dealt a big blow to the NASDAQ. The reason for this phenomenon is that the composition of the NASDAQ Index is mostly related to high-tech growth enterprises. Therefore, this stock price index is chosen as a research object here.

The NASDAQ Composite Index is based on the companies covered by the automatic quotation system established by the National Association of Dealers of the United States. It is different from the S&P 500 in that it covers not only the listed companies in the United States, but also all the foreign listed companies in its trading market, taking their common stocks as the valuation basis, which was first established in 1968.

The NASDAQ market covers a wide range, has been the world's largest stock exchange market, has more than 5,200 listed companies representing 55 countries and regions, and has more than 260,000 network terminals. Therefore, it belongs to the innovation and technology of the emerging force in the financial industry. And it has developed new indices to keep innovators ahead of the curve.

The NASDAQ Index is based on 100, which mainly describes the stock price index of companies listed on the NASDAQ Stock Exchange Market. It covers almost all high-tech industries, such as software and computer, telecommunications, biotechnology, retail and wholesale trade, etc. It is mainly composed of hundreds of the fastest developing advanced technology, telecommunications, and biological companies in the United States, including such household high-tech names as Microsoft, Intel, AOL, and Yahoo, thus becoming the synonym of the "new economy" in the United States. Companies such as Microsoft have emerged as household names. The NASDAQ Composite Index has become one of the most representative composite indexes.

3. Nikkei Stock Average

Japan's economy ushered in a prosperous period after World War II, gradually becoming a significant economy in the world and entering the ranks of developed countries early. Its stock market is also the most representative in Asia. The bursting of Japan's stock market bubble in 1989 was a financial crisis with far-reaching influence, which caused a major blow to its stock market and economic development. It was also one of the crises worth thought and vigilance. Therefore, we chose the commonly used Nikkei Stock Average to analyze the Japanese stock market, hoping to sum up some common things.

The Nikkei Index is commonly referred to as the Nikkei Stock Average. It was first published in 1979, reflecting the changes in the stock prices of listed companies on the Tokyo Stock Exchange, Japan. It was drawn and published by the Nihon Keizai Shimbun. It was once very popular in 1989 and soared to nearly 39,000 points, but then experienced a decline in the stock market and began a 14-year-long bear market. Because this index has a long duration in Asia and has a strong contrast, it is a good choice to observe and consider the long-term and short-term behavior and change trends of the Japanese stock market.

The Nikkei Stock Average sampled a wide range of stocks from manufacturing, construction, transportation, power and gas, warehousing, aquaculture, mining, real estate, finance and services, etc. In addition, the most convincing listed companies in each industry are selected as the index components. What is more convincing is that the composition and proportion of the components will also change with market changes. Therefore, it is also one of the most convincing stock price indexes in Japan and even Asia.

4. FTSE 100

London and New York have always been the most important financial centers in the world, and their foreign exchange transactions also occupy a large proportion of the world. Therefore, the London stock market shocks will have a great impact on the outside world, and its FTSE 100 is one of the most influential stock indexes in the world.

The FTSE 100 Index (or the FTSE 100 Index of share prices) is short for FTSE 100. It was first created in early 1984 to describe the shares of the 100 largest companies listed on the London Stock Exchange and quickly became one of the most influential share price indices in Europe, representing the UK macro fundamentals.

The FTSE 100 is compiled by the powerful index compiler FTSE. The composition of the index changes every three months. Since its inception in 1984, the index has been compiled with a handpicked selection of 100 listed companies from nine countries representing the European economy. The other two are France's CAC-40 Index and Germany's DAX Index, with BP, Royal Dutch Shell, HSBC, Vodafone, Royal Bank of Scotland and GlaxoSmithKline among the largest companies. In addition to Britain, the countries involved also include Germany, France, Italy, Finland, Switzerland, Sweden, the Netherlands, and Spain, which are European economic powers, so it has a good effect on describing the dynamic and development trend of the European stock market.

9.4.2 Empirical Analysis and Test

First of all, the stationarity test and graph analysis of the above four stock price index returns are carried out to give a general description of their trends and volatility. Then, the ANST-GARCH model is estimated to verify the asymmetry of their mean reversion. A general summary is made of their volatility rules and performance during the financial crisis.

1. Index and Its Return Stability Test and Graph Analysis

This paper selects the data of four stock price indexes from early April 1984 to the end of 2012, carries out logarithm first-order difference, and obtains the daily return rate of stock price indexes, namely $R_t = ln(P_t/P_{t-1})$. The data source is Yahoo Finance in the

United States. Firstly, statistical description and stationarity analysis are carried out, and an ADF test is used. Table 9-1 lists the descriptive statistics and variance ratio test results of each index:

Table 9-1 Four Stock Price Index Yield Statistics and Variance Ratio Test Results

	S&P 500	NASDAQ C	Nikkei 225	FTSE 100
Sample Number	7,249	7,249	7,068	7,261
Mean Value	0.0302%	0.0343%	−0.0009%	0.2300%
Maximum Value	10.96%	13.25%	13.23%	9.38%
Minimum Value	−22.90%	−12.04%	−16.14%	−13.03%
Standard Deviation	1.1743	1.4309	1.4577	1.1248
Kurtosis	27.795	7.944	8.444	8.297
Skewness	−1.274	−0.231	−0.274	−0.376
ADF Tests the t Value	−64.6456	−61.7879	−62.8629	−39.6158
1% Threshold	−3.4311	−3.4311	−3.4311	−3.4311
p Value	0.0001	0.0001	0.0001	0.0000

From the perspective of the returns of the four stock price indexes, the distribution of the phenomenon of peak and thick tail exists in varying degrees, which is consistent with the characteristics of traditional stock price index returns. The S&P 500 Index is more obvious; its peak is significantly skewed to the left, while the other three stock price indexes are similar. In addition, from the results of the ADF stationarity test, the T-value of the four stock price indexes is significantly far less than its 1% critical value; that is to say, under the significance level of 1%, the daily returns of the four stock price indexes are stable time series.

The following graph analyzes the stock price index and its daily yield.

First, let's look at the S&P 500 Index.

Looking at the chart of the S&P 500, the index experienced three more significant financial crises between 1984 and 2012.

The first time: On "Black Friday" and "Black Monday" on October 16 and October 19, 1987, the global stock market plunged under the lead of the Dow Jones Industrial Average Index in New York. This was a stock market plunge caused by the bursting of the stock market bubble, and the direct impact was that the economies of various countries suffered serious setbacks. In the late 1980s, the Great Recession followed. As can be seen from Figure 9-1, there was a sharp drop in the index on that day, and correspondingly, the yield in Figure 9-2 obviously reached the minimum value of −22.9% in the whole observation period.

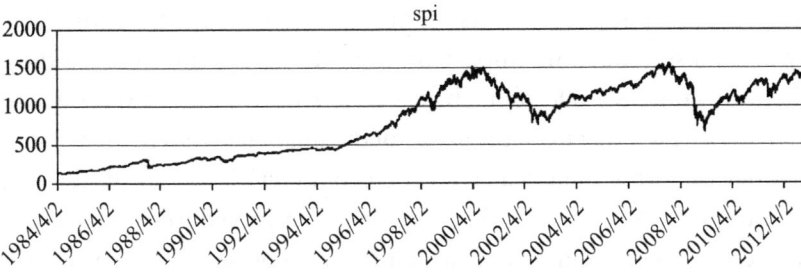

Figure 9-1 S&P 500 Trend

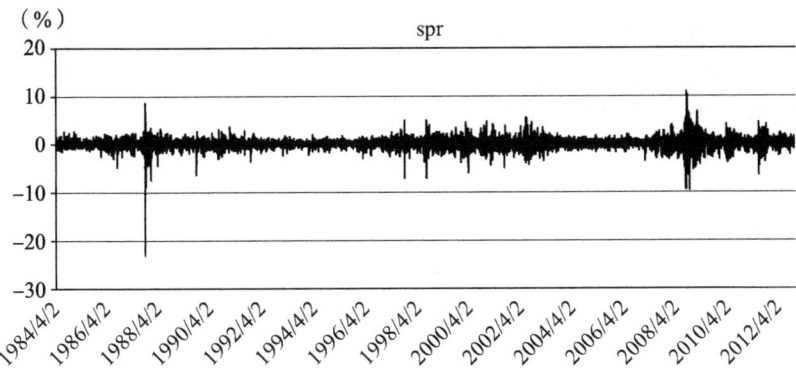

Figure 9-2 S&P 500 Daily Return (%)

The second time: After the economic recession in the late 1980s, the United States ushered in rapid economic development in the 1990s with the rise of high-tech industry, the change in the financial system, and the benefits brought by the integration of the world economy. However, with the rising heat of the technology industry, the Internet stock market bubble began to accumulate and began to burst on March 10, 2000. The NASDAQ index, which was dominated by high-tech stocks, suffered a heavy fall, caused a series of chain reactions, and affected the stock markets of other industries. As can be seen from Figure 9-1, the S&P 500 dropped from 1,300 points at the end of 2,000 to 800 points in July 2002, a decrease of nearly 40% in a year and a half. It can also be seen from Figure 9-2 that the return rate of the stock index fluctuates greatly during this period, and the negative return rate is obviously more dominant.

The third time: After the US economy walked out of the pain of the bursting of the Internet economic bubble, it experienced a period of steady development from 2002 to 2007. However, with the outbreak of the subprime crisis in 2007, the US stock market fell from the peak to the bottom again. The S&P Index fell from more than 1,500 points in the middle of 2007 to less than 700 points in March 2009. The decline of more than 50% in less than two years can be said to be another heavy blow to the American economy. As we can see from Figure 9-2, the daily return of the stock index also showed increased volatility during this period.

Other crises, such as the 1997 Asian financial crisis and the 2010 wave of global unemployment, also had some impact on the S&P 500. Still, because they caused a strong rebound in the S&P 500 after a brief decline, they did not have much impact and can be temporarily excluded from the scope of the financial crisis in the US stock market.

Throughout the three financial crises, before the crisis occurred, the stock market had an obvious peak. At that time, the stock price continued to rise sharply, which also foreshadowed the huge decline later, which can also be seen as the process of bubble formation. By observing the volatility chart of the stock price index return rate, it can be seen that the return fluctuated less during the two intervals between the three crises. The economy was also growing slowly, and the volatility of stock index yields had increased sharply during the crisis.

Here's the chart of the NASDAQ.

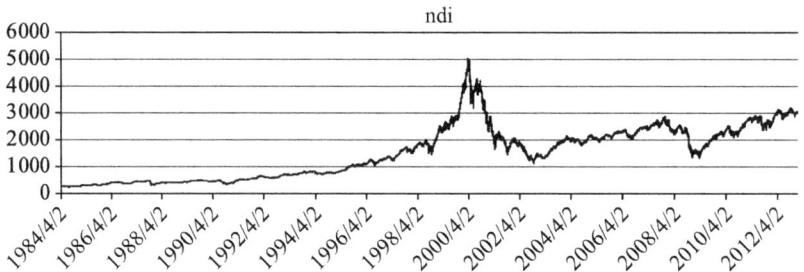

Figure 9-3 NASDAQ Composite Index Trend

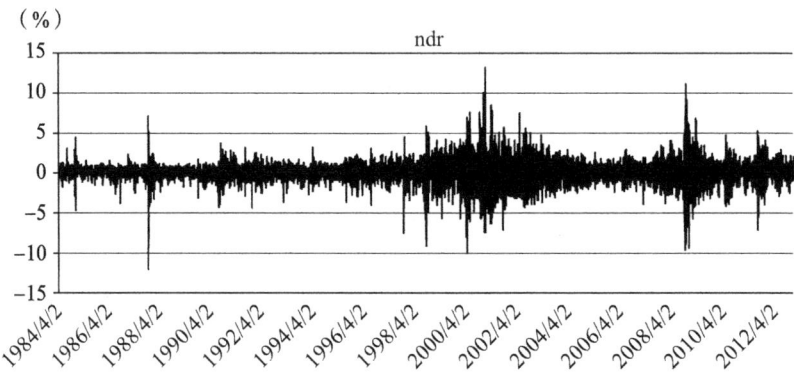

Figure 9-4 NASDAQ Composite Index Daily Return (%)

According to the two charts, the NASDAQ has also been through three bigger financial crises. There are similarities between the NASDAQ and the S&P 500, which describe the share prices of American companies. However, since the NASDAQ Composite Index consists mostly of high-tech companies, the bursting of the Internet bubble in 2000 was the most influential of the three crises.

In 1987, within ten days of the crisis "Black Friday" and "Black Monday," the NASDAQ Index fell from 406 points to 292 points, but it recovered in the following year and did not have a big impact. This was mainly due to the fact that, at that time, the American technology enterprises did not form a scale and had a strong ability to recover after a short-term blow. Moreover, the index value was not large, and it was not easy to form a large-scale plunge. The most important reason is that at that time, high-tech stocks just started, and their stock prices did not contain much bubble, so when the stock price fell below its intrinsic value, it was easy to rise again with people's rational investment.

The bursting of the Internet bubble in 2000 had a profound impact on the NASDAQ Index. As can be seen from Figure 9-3, it reached the highest point of 5132.52 on March 10, 2000. The bubble began to burst on March 10 and fell from 5,038 to 4,879 as soon as the market opened on March 13, and only six days later, NASDAQ lost nearly 900 points, falling from 5,050 on March 10 to 4,580 on March 15. Then the bubble burst and spread to 2001. The NASDAQ bottomed out on September 21 of that year, falling to 1,423, down more than 70% from its peak. In the next few years, the NASDAQ has not broken the 3,000 points, which can be said to have caused a devastating blow to the development of high-tech industries. As can be seen from Figure 9-4, the volatility of the NASDAQ yield during this crisis was greater, and the time span was longer compared with the other two crises.

The subprime crisis in 2007 started from the break of the real estate capital chain, but the impact of this crisis was comprehensive. The NASDAQ Index, which has just improved, was also affected by this crisis, from 2,800 points in October 2007 to 1,300 points in November 2008, halved in a year's time. As can be seen from its yield volatility chart, volatility in yields during this period has also been obvious. Still, it was smaller than the previous Internet bubble burst.

From the perspective of the NASDAQ Composite Index, the volatility size and impact degree caused by the three financial crises are slightly different from that of the S&P Index. Still, both of them have the same volatility rule: before the crisis, the stock market had an obvious and rapid rise, which can also be seen as the process of bubble accumulation, and the volatility of the return rate showed aggregation, that is, the volatility increased significantly during the crisis.

Next up: Nikkei Stock Average.

As can be seen from Figure 9-5, the Japanese stock market was obviously different from the American stock market in that the ups and downs of the American stock market were relatively average, and the stock price index always experienced a cycle of stable development—upturn—decline—stable development. However, after the Nikkei Stock Average experienced a big peak in 1990, the stock market bubble burst, resulting in the depression of the Japanese economy for nearly ten years. The economy recovered occasionally but never recovered, and by the end of 2012, its share price index was less than a quarter of its 1990 peak.

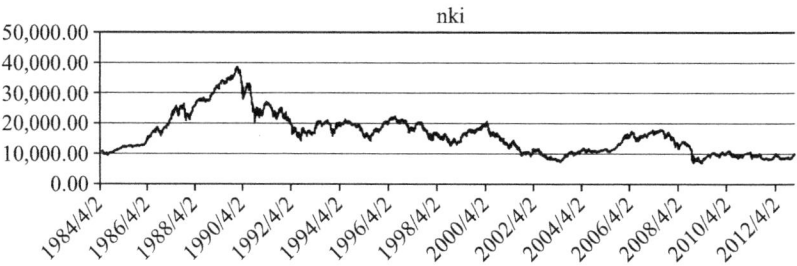

Figure 9-5 Nikkei Stock Average Trend

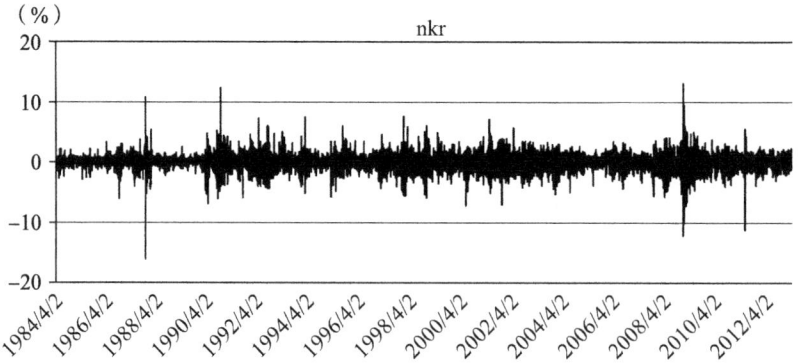

Figure 9-6 Nikkei Stock Average Daily Return (%)

After 1990, Japan's economy was always affected by another wave when it had a slight recovery, so Japan's economy never picked up. Here is a detailed look at the process:

After experiencing the bursting of the stock market bubble in 1990, the Japanese stock market was affected by the bursting of the Internet bubble in the United States in 2000, and its stock price index went through two stages of decline. The first one was from the highest 20,327 points in April 2000 to 10,153.33 points in September 2001, and after a short rebound, the second round of declines began in June 2002 and reached a low of 7,604, back to its lowest point since the mid-1980s, a drop of 62%.

After experiencing a brief uptick from 2002 to 2007, the Japanese stock market was successively affected by the subprime crisis in 2007, and the world unemployment wave in 2009, which kept hovering below 10,000 points, which can be described by saying that the house is leaking, but the rain falls overnight.

From the perspective of stock market volatility (see Figure 9-6), the yield of the Nikkei Stock Average was little affected by the 1987 stock market "Black Monday," and its sharp fluctuations were calmed in a very short time. Subsequently, the Japanese stock market began to fluctuate smoothly from 1987 to 1990, and the index also reached its peak. Later, with the bursting of the stock market bubble, the stock market began a period of turbulence. However, it is difficult to find a clear dividing line of volatility in the figure after that. That is to say, from 1990 until now, the Japanese stock market has always been in great volatility.

A final analysis of the FTSE 100.

Figure 9-7 FTSE 100 Trend

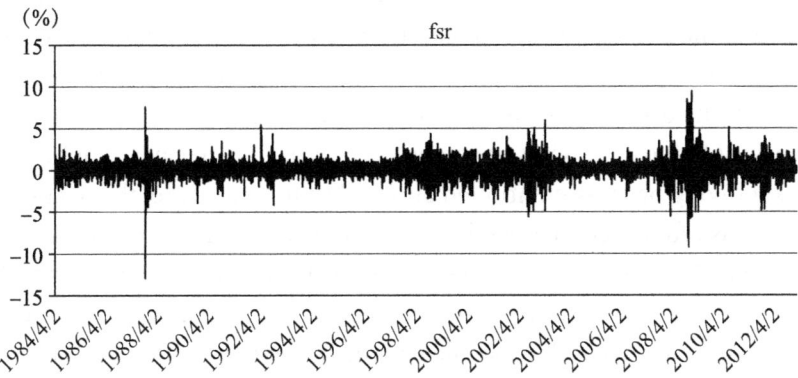

Figure 9-8 FTSE 100 Daily Return (%)

By comparing Figures 9-2 and 9-8, it can be seen that the fluctuation of the FTSE 100 in London is very similar to the trend and fluctuation of the S&P 500 in the United States. This is mainly because the fluctuation of the United States, as the bellwether of the world stock market, has a great impact on the European stock market. Just as the saying goes, "When Wall Street coughs, the world stock market will catch a cold."

Therefore, it can be seen from Figure 9-8 that the fluctuation aggregation of the three crises and the two periods of stable development intermingled with them. In other words, under the influence of the United States, the European stock price index also produced three relatively large financial crises: The only difference between "Black Friday" in 1987, the Internet bubble bust in 2000, and the subprime crisis in 2007 is that the S&P was already near its peak at the end of 2012 and was not much affected by the wave of global unemployment in 2010. The European stock index did not rise sharply with the rise of the US stock index because of the unemployment wave in 2012 and the impact of the sovereign debt crisis not long ago.

From the above analysis, we summarize some characteristics of stock market volatility in the period of economic development:

First, before every financial crisis occurs, the stock market has a sharp rise and produces an obvious peak, and there are obvious traces of manipulation by market makers. Generally speaking, there will be a large selling behavior of several financial giants on that day, and the bullish and bearish forces in the market will produce a zigzag on that day and form the volume before the sharp fall. It can also be seen as the process of accumulation and expansion of bubbles before the collapse of the stock market, such as the Japanese economic bubble in 1989 and the Internet bubble in the United States in 2000. When the bubble expanded rapidly, the stock market would often reach an unprecedented peak. Still, because it deviated too much from the intrinsic value, the force of reversion to the mean was too strong. That caused the stock market to plunge, which in turn caused the economy to plummet.

Second, generally speaking, the volatility degree of the stock index return rate will vary with the economic environment change. In a period of stable economic development, the volatility of the stock index return rate is generally small, which can be regarded as a period of healthy economic development. However, as the stock market continues to rise, the accumulation of bubbles becomes larger. It is easy to cause a bubble burst—the stock market diving process mentioned above. At the same time, the occurrence of the financial crisis is often accompanied by large fluctuations in the return rate of the stock price index, which generally results in stock market setbacks and the economy entering a depression period. In the study period, the frequency of financial crises is usually once every 5–10 years. How to prolong stable economic development and restrain the sharp fluctuation of stock yield is a difficult problem to be solved to prevent financial crises.

Third, from the perspective of the mutual influence of the four stock indexes, the fluctuation of the United States stock market, due to its dominant position in the economy, can often directly affect other countries. The three major financial crises of the United States have caused direct impacts on the stock markets of other countries, and the shock degree is no less than the source. However, the Asian financial crisis in 1997 had little impact on American stock indexes.

2. ANST-GARCH Model Estimation

Next, we carry out ANST-GARCH model estimation for the four stock price indexes, which is mainly characterized by its ability to describe the double asymmetry of the mean and variance of time series. As mentioned before, the ANST-GARCH model has several basic and changing forms, and we mainly choose the following model:

$$Y_t = \beta_0 + [\beta_1 + \beta_2 \cdot F(\varepsilon_{t-1})] \cdot Y_{t-1} + \varepsilon_t \tag{9-10}$$

$$h_t = a_0 + a_1 \cdot \varepsilon_{t-1}^2 + a_2 \cdot h_{t-1} + (b_0 + b_1 \cdot \varepsilon_{t-1}^2 + b_2 \cdot h_{t-1}) \cdot F(\varepsilon_{t-1}) \tag{9-11}$$

Where, $F(\varepsilon_{t-1}) = 1/\{1 + exp[-\gamma(\varepsilon_{t-1})]\}$ represents an endogenous regime switching function, and γ here describes the regime-switching speed, which becomes faster with the increase of γ, and slower on the contrary; ε_t and ε_{t-1} represent the market information impact at time t and $t-1$. It is worth noting that $\varepsilon_t < 0$ here represents the negative impact of market information, while $\varepsilon_t > 0$ stands for bullish news. R_t and R_{t-1} represent the stock (stock index) returns of t period and $t-1$ period respectively; h_t is the variance equation.

When the ANST-GARCH model is used for empirical estimation, if parameter $\beta_2 \neq 0$ and it is significant, then the mean is asymmetrical. If parameter $b_1 + b_2 \neq 0$ and it is significant, then the variance is asymmetrical.

Using ratsv8 as auxiliary software, the ANST-GARCH model was used to estimate the returns of four stock price indexes, and the results are shown in Table 9-2.

Table 9-2 Four Stock Price Index Models Estimate Results

Serial Number	Coefficient	S&P 500 Coefficient Value	NASDAQ C Coefficient Value	Nikkei 225 Coefficient Value	FTSE 100 Coefficient Value
1	β_0	0.0002*	0.0004***	0.0001	0.0002**
2	β_1	−8.6639***	−5.8050**	2.2347***	−3.2503***
3	β_2	17.3337***	11.8209**	4.5072***	6.5354***
4	γ	0.2786***	0.3054***	0.4761***	0.2039***
5	a_0	0.0059***	0.0040***	0.0056***	−0.0004***
6	a_1	3.6414***	0.8244***	2.2007***	6.6345***
7	a_2	6.5001***	4.0346***	3.3646***	67.2564***
8	b_0	−0.0118***	−0.0079***	0.0112***	0.0008***
9	b_1	−7.1263***	−1.4317***	4.1464***	13.1255***
10	b_2	−11.1986***	−6.3095***	−5.0216***	−132.6734***

Note: *, **, and *** represent significance levels of 10%, 5% and 1%, respectively.

It can be seen from Table 9-2 that the fluctuation rules of the four stock price indexes are relatively similar.

As can be seen from each parameter, the key parameter β_2 controlling mean reversion of the stock return rate and $b_1 + b_2$ are significantly not 0 at the 5% confidence level, so the mean and variance equations of the four stock price indexes are asymmetrical.

In terms of the parameters β_1 and β_2, they control the time-varying sequence correlation of the equation, and since the value of $F(\varepsilon_{t-1})$ is between 0 and 1, its variation range is also between β_1 and $\beta_1 + \beta_2$. In other words, when the market is affected by a fairly large negative shock, resulting in $F(\varepsilon_{t-1}) = 0$, the sequence correlation is described by β_1, whereas if a positive shock of the same magnitude causes $F(\varepsilon_{t-1}) = 1$, the sequence correlation is described by $\beta_1 + \beta_2$. The parameters $\beta_1 < 0$ and $\beta_1 + \beta_2 > 0$ indicate that the response caused by positive and negative market shocks is asymmetric, and the sustainability of its volatility follows that the negative impact of the return rate is always greater than that of the positive impact. It can also be said that the previous negative shocks and the return rate of the stock index are negatively sequentially correlated; that is, they are inverted. On the contrary, the positive impact and the return rate of the stock price index are positively sequentially correlated, showing the characteristics of inertia. $\beta_1 < 0$ and $\beta_2 > 0$ also predict that the mean reversion trend of reverse shocks of return rate was stronger than that of positive shocks, further confirming the asymmetry of return rate reversion.

Therefore, a conclusion can be drawn from the study of the first equation, that is, in the several stock price indexes studied for nearly 30 years, people overreact to the shock of bad news and underreact to the good news.

By comparing the β_1 and $\beta_1 + \beta_2$ values of the four stock price indexes, it can be found that the reaction speed to bearish and bullish news is S&P 500 > NASDAQ C > FTSE 100 > Nikkei Stock Average. In other words, the American stock market reacts most quickly to the market news, followed by the European stock market. Japan's stock market is more sluggish.

Then, several parameters of the second equation of the model are used to explore the volatility persistence of the stock return rate. First, the volatility persistence of the model is determined by a series of parameters $a_1 + b_1 F(\varepsilon_{t-1}) + a_2 + b_2 F(\varepsilon_{t-1})$. When the market is affected by a considerable negative shock, $F(\varepsilon_{t-1}) = 0$ is caused, and the serial correlation is described by $(a_1 + a_2)$. If $F(\varepsilon_{t-1}) = 1$ is caused by a positive shock of the same degree, the sequence correlation is described by $(a_1 + a_2) + (b_1 + b_2)$. From the obtained results, it can be found that the $(a_1 + a_2)$ of several groups of parameters is obviously larger than $(a_1 + a_2) + (b_1 + b_2)$. It can also be said that the result of $(b_1 + b_2) < 0$ is obtained from several parameters of equation 2, proving that the fluctuation of return rate under positive and negative shocks is asymmetrical. Under the condition of $(b_1 + b_2) < 0$, negative shocks cause more volatility in stock returns than positive shocks; that is to say, the unexpected decline of securities leads to investors' lack of confidence, which leads to increased volatility in the stock market.

Therefore, it can be concluded from the study of the second equation that, in several stock price indexes studied in nearly 30 years, people tend to overestimate risks in the face of negative news shocks, resulting in increased volatility of the stock market, thus producing obvious uneven fluctuations in the volatility curve of the stock price index yield. The results suggest that people overreact to bad news.

9.5 Conclusion and Enlightenment

Four representative stock indexes in the world are selected above, and the graph analysis and asymmetric reversion analysis are carried out on the stock price indexes and their returns during 1984–2012. Combining the empirical results of the two, the following conclusions can be drawn.

First, the asymmetric mean reversion of securities assets is intrinsically related to financial crises.

Due to the speculative and anticipatory factors of securities investment, the rise and fall of the stock market cannot fully reflect all the information that should be included—it takes a certain time to digest the market information, so the stock price should fluctuate around its intrinsic value. With the increase of its deviation from the intrinsic value, its reversion power will increase accordingly.

It can be inferred from the conclusion of asymmetric reversion of the rate of return mentioned above that, after the steady development of the economy (positive impact on the market), due to the trust in the macroeconomic environment, investors will have a kind of inertia towards the upward growth of the stock market, thus promoting the stock bubble. Moreover, market speculators will cause the stock price to deviate too much from the intrinsic value. Once the bubble bursts, a stock market crash is inevitable, resulting in the break of investors' capital chain. At this time, after the negative information impact of the market occupies a high level, the conclusion from the above is that people will overreact to the decline of the stock market in the face of the negative information impact, thus lowering the expectation of the stock market and making the stock market fall below the normal level. It can be known from previous studies that the end of the trajectory it follows also seems to be consistent with normal mean reversion, but there is a quick correction after the deviation. However, the large magnitude and strength of the correction caused a big crash in the stock market. After the crisis gradually subsides and the positive market impact appears again, a new round of the stock market cycle begins. The graph observation of nearly 30 years shows that the general stock market cycle is 5–10 years. Therefore, the financial crisis is a necessary part of the development of the stock market, and it can also be attributed to the stock market crash caused by the financial crisis as a special case of the asymmetric mean reversion of the stock market.

Second, the intensification of stock market volatility is inextricably linked to the occurrence of the financial crisis.

By looking at the charts of the four stock price indexes, it can be seen that the volatility of the stock price index returns is much larger during the financial crisis than during the period of stable economic development, while the volatility of the stock price index returns is also small during the period of stable economic development, showing a clear aggregation of volatility, which is also in line with the conclusions drawn from the model estimation later on. Negative shocks often cause more volatility in stock returns than positive shocks. That is to say, the unexpected decline of securities leads to the lack of investor confidence, which leads to the intensification of the volatility of the stock market. In contrast, the positive impact of securities generally does not cause the sharp volatility of the stock market.

Therefore, it can be said that the increased volatility of the stock market is a dangerous signal. Generally, the increased volatility indicates the occurrence of a potential financial crisis. The stock market is also faced with the risk of decline, which can be well reflected in the Nikkei Stock Average: Since 1990, the yield of the stock price index in Japan has fluctuated sharply, and its stock market has also experienced a long-term slump. Until 2012, its stock price index has fallen to the bottom, even less than a quarter of the peak.

Third, global financial integration has created a transmission mechanism for financial crises.

From the previous comparison between the S&P 500 and the FTSE 100, they have very similar trends and volatility charts. The main reason is that with the gradual opening up of the world financial environment, the capital liquidity barriers of various countries are gradually reduced, the interactivity of the stock markets of various countries is gradually strengthened, and the pattern of world financial integration has gradually formed. Thus, stock market volatility in any country can directly affect the financial environment in other countries.

Among them, due to its transcendent world economic hegemonic position, the financial crisis in the United States can always cause seismic effects, thus having a great impact on the stock markets of all countries in the world. As can be seen from the previous article, the typical three financial crises in the United States had a bad impact on the stock markets of Europe and Japan. However, when looking at the financial crises in other countries, for example, the Japanese stock market crash in 1989 and the Asia stock market crash in 1997, had limited influence on the United States, which also reflected the dependence on the world on the American economy.

The above three points are the characteristics of the financial crisis and asymmetric mean reversion in the stock markets of various countries in recent years. However, the current stock market in China has just experienced several years of the bear market. From the perspective of its past development, China's stock market is still in a relatively early stage, with many problems such as the unreasonable composition of investors, low quality of small and medium investors, institutional investors' grasp of the market, and other unstable factors, so we put forward several feasible suggestions based on the characteristics of the financial crisis in Europe, America, and Japan and the situation of China's stock market.

First of all, in view of the tendency of financial crisis to break out every once in a while, the country should not blindly pursue the high growth of the economy and the stock market, but should try to reduce the degree of bubbles in the stock market and make its fluctuations stable on the basis of stable development. What we should do is establish a more complete monitoring and warning mechanism in the stock market. Since there are many standards to measure a certain stock, such as price-earnings ratio and price-to-book ratio, when the price-earnings ratio and other indicators of a certain stock or a certain industry stock exceed certain standards, it is possible to try to control the continuous rise of its price, such as changing the limit range of trading limits, limiting trading volume, curbing speculation or releasing bad news in the market, so as to control the expansion degree of the bubble. Make it as close to its intrinsic value as possible. In view of the different speeds of the stock market to digest the information, the use of multiple short news to control the stock market trend should follow the principle of moderation.

Secondly, the proportion of retail investors is relatively high in China's stock market compared with other countries' mature stock markets, so it is prone to the so-called "herding effect." Moreover, its widely believed investment philosophy of chasing up and killing down is likely to play a role in adding fuel to the flame when the stock boom is formed, thus contributing to the bubble's expansion in the stock market. Once the bad news overwhelms the rise at this time, the stock market bubble will burst, and people's general overreaction to negative shocks will cause the stock price to continue to decline. At this time, the financial crisis is inevitable. The solution to this problem is to advocate a healthy concept of value investment, vigorously promote knowledge education of the stock market, strictly and regularly conduct financial knowledge tests for investors with assets exceeding a certain number, and restrict the manipulation of the stock market by institutional investors.

Thirdly, as the stock market continues to rise and there are signs of the bubble bursting, the country should take effective actions as soon as possible to slow down the bubble bursting of the stock market and realize the slow regression of the mean reversion process, so as to make the economy "soft landing." Take the US subprime crisis in 2007 as an example. When the crisis occurred, the US government and titans from all walks of life began to rescue the market one after another. However, they underestimated the severity of the crisis, and as a result, the crisis spread to the stock market due to the policy lag. When the US stock market fell continuously, the plunging trend was difficult to restrain, thus forming a disastrous stock market crisis. Our country's polity determines that macro-control and the policy can be implemented quickly, which makes the restrain of the stock market's sharp rise and plunge easier.

Finally, in the prevention of financial crisis and the recovery after the crisis, the most important thing is to rely on the overall economic fundamental strength of the country. As mentioned above, the unique world economic dominance of the United States enables its domestic crisis to be easily transmitted to other stock markets. After the financial crisis, the recovery ability of the United States stock market is also obvious to all. After the real economy has developed to a certain extent, financial innovation in the United States has developed by leaps and bounds. The subprime crisis is the inevitable product of financial innovation to a certain extent. However, after the crisis, the recovery of the American economy depends on the rescue of the real economy. Hence, financial innovation divorced from the intrinsic value is more prone to problems. The lesson of the American stock market is that we should learn from it and further develop our real economy, achieve sustained and steady economic development, and further consolidate the status of the largest creditor country to the United States. On the other hand, we should vigorously develop the virtual economy and improve and strengthen the supervision of the stock market, so that the Chinese stock market can realize international integration as soon as possible, achieving the dual development of real and virtual economy, so as to really eliminate the potential financial crisis invisible.

CHAPTER 10

Research on Stock Long-Term Investment Strategy Based on Market Efficient Cycle Theory

Studying investment strategies from the perspective of the efficient cycle of the market will certainly help long-term investment. In the long run, when the stock deviates from the intrinsic value, it must return to the intrinsic value, but the return cycle is random. The efficient cycle of the market shows that timing is very important in a long-term investment strategy. Those who stick to long-term investments when the stock market or a particular stock is relatively depressed will benefit the most. At the same time, from the development of financial investment theory, a large number of empirical research results have confirmed that long-term returns are more predictable than short-term returns. This chapter will study the stock investment strategy from the perspective of long-term investment based on the market efficient cycle theory. The 2013 Nobel Prize in Economics was awarded to Eugene Fama of the United States, Lars Peter Hansen of the University of Chicago, and Robert Shiller of the United States. The Royal Swedish Academy of Sciences said the three economists laid the foundation for the current understanding of asset values. There are few ways to accurately predict the direction of stock and bond markets in the coming days or weeks. However, it is possible to predict prices beyond three years through research.

10.1 Overview of Long-Term Investment Strategy

Based on the theoretical research and empirical analysis of the market efficient cycle and mean reversion in the previous chapters, we can draw the conclusion that deviation from the mean has the inevitability of regression, and the further deviation from the mean, the greater the probability of regression to the mean. This theory provides us with an important basis for long-term investment. The specific method is the application of an inversion strategy in stock market investment. In a general sense, the further the stock return deviates below the mean, the greater the probability that the stock will rise, and the further the stock return deviates above the mean, the greater the probability that the stock will fall. The formulation of the reversal strategy should refer to the mean deviation rate. The further the deviation from the mean, the greater the probability of successful implementation of the reversal strategy. In extreme cases where the deviation from the mean is too far away, the reversal strategy will form investment opportunities close to risk-free arbitrage, which is what Buffett said about taking advantage of the market's stupidity to benefit himself. Buffett believes that the most basic strategy of value investment is to take advantage of the divergence between the stock price and the enterprise value and buy the stock at a much discount price lower than the intrinsic value of the stock. To make an excess profit by selling the stock at or above its value after it has risen. If there is an efficient cycle in the market, the mean value is the intrinsic value; that is, the market automatically corrects its pricing deviation, and the market must have the basic function of long-term price discovery. Buffett thinks the stock market is a voting machine in the short run, but it must be a weighing machine in the long run. The stock market tends to align with the broader economy in the long run. However, as the stock market is a voting machine, the process and way of this tendency changes are very variable and can even vary widely. Therefore, the stock market becomes difficult to grasp and predict.

10.1.1 Long-Term Yield Is Rational Target for Investors

The goal of investment is to achieve good returns. The fundamental measure of an investment variety and investment strategy is to measure its long-term returns rather than short-term speculative returns. According to the basic rules of probability and statistics, the ultimate expected rate of return of speculation is zero. Speculation in stocks, futures, gold, foreign exchange, and so on must not be worth the loss. In the previous research, we conducted empirical tests on China's Shanghai Composite Index, America's Dow Jones Industrial Index, NASDAQ Index, S&P 500 Index, Britain's FTSE 100 Index, Germany's DAX Index, and Japan's Nikkei 225 Index. The results show that they all have the characteristics of mean reversion, but the time period of regression is different. This also provides an important basis for investors to implement the reversal strategy.

The long-term investment strategy is based on the result that the probability of the stock market running in the future is higher, and the probability of the stock market rising after a long period of decline is higher. The stock market has a high probability of falling after a long period of rise. In general, the short-term random walk of the stock market, the long-term mean reversion, and the long-term investment are far more predictable than the short-term. Everything will always return to normal; in other words, the probability of returning to normal and close to normal will be far greater than the probability of abnormal or extreme circumstances. Making investment decisions based on such expectations is the application of mean reversion and market efficient cycle theory. This is similar to the philosophical principle that prosperity leads to decline, and adversity leads to prosperity. Good things will turn to bad when they reach the extreme, and vice versa; bad things will turn to good when they reach the extreme. Stocks tend to fall when they rise too much and rise when they fall too much.

Being a successful investor is easy in theory but difficult in practice. It is easy in theory because investors can eventually bypass their own forecasting ability, buy and hold a portfolio, and conduct empirical tests. There is no psychological difficulty between holding and not holding. The hypothesis of the theory is long-term holding, and the ultimate test is the yield rate of long-term holding. Investing is difficult because most people try to beat the market quickly rather than stick to a long-term investment strategy. Long-term stock returns will be more stable than short-term returns, and long-term predictability is better than short-term predictability, which has been proved by empirical research in behavioral finance. If you choose between stocks and bonds, as a general rule of thumb, the proportion of stocks and bonds in a portfolio depends on different economic conditions. Historically, stocks in a long-term portfolio should account for a higher percentage of your portfolio. High inflation will devalue the currency and is a long-term phenomenon, and holding bonds must be full of long-term risks. However, if we can hold stocks for up to 20 years or more, empirical studies have found that stocks offer higher returns and lower risk than bonds.

Long-term investments can do wonders of compound interest. When Einstein helped a friend, the friend wanted to repay him, saying, "I will help you to buy some stocks." Einstein didn't know how to manage money and let his friends buy it. Many years later, when his friend was dying, he asked Einstein to take a look at his stock. Einstein opened his stock account and saw that the amount of money had grown to the astronomical amount it seemed at the time. Einstein exclaimed: "Compound interest is the greatest human invention, the most powerful force in the universe, and the world's eighth wonder." The way of trading is simple. You won't make money if you don't buy stocks in the upward trend. You will lose money if you don't sell stocks in the downward trend. Using the right method, wealth is like a snowball. Those who can master the objective law in the stock market and persevere in the systematic operation are likely to achieve great success! Buffett is great not because he has a great title and great wealth gained in the stock market, but because he created the miracle of compound interest of funds with the method of value investment, which lasted for his whole life.

10.1.2 Choose Undervalued Investments

One of the main criteria for selecting undervalued investments is the price-earnings ratio of stocks, which is an important indicator to measure whether stocks are reasonably priced and determine the stock market bubble. China's stock market has been around for just over 20 years. After summary, we find that the long-term strategy has a better chance of success when we choose the investment cycle based on the average P/E ratio and the arithmetic average stock price.

The historical average price-earnings ratio of the Chinese stock market is below 20 times, and the arithmetic average price of the stock price is below 7 yuan or so, which corresponds to the relative bottom of the market.

(1) In 1994, the average price-earnings ratio of 325 points was 10.65 times, and the average stock price was only 4.24 yuan.

(2) In 1996, the price-earnings ratio of 512 points was 19.44 times, and the average stock price was 6.17 yuan.

(3) In 2005, the price-earnings ratio of 998 points was 15.42 times, and the average share price was 4.77 yuan.

The historical average price-earnings ratio of the Chinese stock market is above 50 times, and the arithmetic average price of the stock is above about 15 yuan, which corresponds to the relative top of the big bull market.

(1) The average P/E ratio of 1,510 points in 1997 was 59.64 times, and the average stock price was 15.16 yuan.

(2) The average P/E ratio of 1,756 points in 1999 was 63.08 times, and the average stock price was 14.1 yuan.

(3) The average P/E ratio of 2,245 points in 2001 was 66.16 times, and the average stock price was 17.51 yuan.

(4) In 2007, the average P/E ratio of 6,124 points in the Shanghai market was 69 times, and the average stock price was 20.16 yuan.

Looking back at the historical price-earnings ratio of China's stock market, the price-earnings ratio in 1996 was very low, only between 10 and 20 times, which left a huge space for the stock market to rise in 1996 and 1997. From 1996 to 1999, P/E ratios fluctuated between 30 and 50 times, and from mid-2000 to mid-2001, P/E ratios hovered around 60 times. But the excessive P/E ratio eventually returned to its intrinsic reasonable level, leading to a sharp correction from the second half of 2001 to 2005. On June 6, 2005, the Shanghai Stock Index hit a low of 998 points, and P/E ratios were 14.7 times. In 2007, the Chinese stock market experienced a three-year rally, and the Shanghai stock market reached 69 times, which peaked at 6,124 points. This has become the main reason and force for the drop to 1,664 points in 2008.

The "reasonable P/E ratio" is a quantifiable measure. In the modern stock market, we calculate the value by the share price. According to capital asset pricing theory, the average return rate of the stock market should be equal to the risk-free rate plus the total risk return of the market. For the mature securities market, the reasonable P/E ratio should be the reciprocal of the average market return level. Usually, the one-year bank interest rate is regarded as the average market return level. Jeremy Siegel's research found that in more than 30 years, from 1970 to 2001, the annual return of major stock markets in Europe and America was not much different: the UK was 11.97%, the United States 11.59%, Japan 11.12%, Germany 10.88%. The Japanese stock market peaked near 40,000 points in 1989 and has yet to reach a record high. If you look at annual returns up to 1989, Japanese stocks have outperformed those of other countries by a wide margin, but if you extend them to 2001, they are roughly in line, a kind of mean reversion of returns.

Using market efficient cycle and mean reversion theories is an important basis for making long-term investment decisions. In the long run, the risk of the stock market will be low. In particular, the longer you hold the stock, the lower the risk and the higher the average return.

10.2 Random Walk of Short-Term Trend and Mean Regression of Long-Term Yield

Short-term stock movements are intrinsically random. What is randomness? For example, if a coin flip lands heads or tails, it is random and unpredictable. It has nothing to do with whether the forecaster is experienced or skilled. Similarly, trying to predict whether the stock market will rise or fall tomorrow is impossible because, like flipping a coin, the result is a random event. Due to the randomness of the stock market in nature, it brings great difficulties to judgment and prediction and generates many problems that have to be paid attention to. Any analysis and prediction tools and methods cannot be 100% accurate. It is just luck that some analysts are able to accurately predict short-term trends. It is impossible for everyone to fail. If everyone fails, it is not a random event but an inevitable event. Plus, stocks can only move up or down on a daily basis, so the analyst has a 50% chance of getting it wrong and a 50% chance of getting it right. And the chances of getting it right several times in a row are 0.5 to the power, getting smaller and smaller.

The random walk theory states that there are thousands of smart people in the stock market, each of whom knows how to analyze, and that the data flowing into the market is open for all to see; there is no secret. Therefore, the market price of a stock already reflects all the information that determines the intrinsic value of the stock. The so-called intrinsic value is measured by the value of assets per share, price-earnings ratio, dividend ratio, and other basic factors. The current market price of stocks essentially represents the views of millions of smart people, constituting a reasonable price. Market prices move up and down around intrinsic value at random and without any track to follow. The volatility is due to the random emergence of new economic and political news and other influencers, which randomly flow into the market. New information causes basic analysts to revalue the stock and make trading policies, resulting in new changes in the stock. Because the news is untraceable, comes out of the blue, and no one can predict it in advance, the idea of stock speculation does not work. Since all stock prices in the market have reflected their fundamental value, this value is fairly determined by the buyer and seller, and it will not change unless unexpected news such as wars, acquisitions, mergers, interest rate hikes and cuts, and oil wars, good or bad news. But you don't know if the news is going to be good or bad next time. Stocks don't have a memory system. The rise and fall of one day do not mean the rise and fall of the next day, and there is no correlation between the rise and fall of one day and another. Since stock prices have no memory system, trying to use stock price fluctuations to find a principle to beat the market to win excess profits is not worth the loss. Since stock prices rise and fall irregularly in the short term, we can't predict where the stock market will go tomorrow. No one is a winner or a loser.

Among the countless studies, three, in particular, support the random walk theory:

(1) If you look at stocks in the S&P Index over a long period of time, you can see that the percentage of stocks that go up or down sharply (up four or five times or down 99%) is very small. Most stocks go up or down 10 to 30%. There is a phenomenon of normal distribution in statistics; that is, the larger the rise or fall, the smaller the proportion, and there is no single trend in stock prices. Buying shares depends on whether you are lucky or not, and there is an equal chance of buying a rising or falling stock.

(2) In another experiment, a US senator threw darts at a financial newspaper and picked out a portfolio of 20 stocks. The random portfolio performed about as well as the stock market as a whole, not worse than the experts' recommendations and even better than some of them.

(3) Some people have studied the performance of unit funds and found that the best performance this year is likely to be the worst next year, and some funds that were disappointing in previous years may come out on top this year. There is no trace; the fund you buy depends on your luck. The investment technique is not practical because the stock market has no memory, and everyone just chances.

Mean regression indicates that long-term investment is predictable. Many great and successful long-term investors basically choose to buy at a low price and hold the stock for five years or more or even for life. The stock price tends to rise steadily, achieve amazing returns, and realize the dream of wealth in life. For more than a century, despite many recessions and stock market crises, the general trend of stock prices has continued to rise, and the historical data is sufficient to justify the correctness of investing in the long term.

Next, we use Chinese stock market data to test the mean regression. We selected 50 stocks in the CSI 300 Index that have been listed for a long time to conduct a mean regression test. Monthly returns of these stocks from the month of listing to the end of 2013 were selected for empirical analysis in the sample space. The KSS test proposed by Kapetanios et al.(2003) was used in Chapter 4, and the model was as follows:

$$y_t = \alpha y_{t-p} + \beta y_{t-p} y_{t-1}^2 \qquad (10\text{-}1)$$

p was taken as 1, 3, 6, 12, 24, and 48 months, respectively, and substituted into Equation 10-1 for testing. The statistics of test results are shown in Table 10-1.

Table 10-1 Individual Stock Inspection Statistical Table (Unit: Month)

Name of Stock	Regression Cycle	Name of Stock	Regression Cycle	Name of Stock	Regression Cycle
1. Oriental Pearl	48	18. Construction and Development Shares	null	35. Aseng Group	24
2. Conch Cement	6	19. Zhejiang Pharmaceutical	48	36. Deep Speed	6
3. Shanghai Pudong Development Bank	24	20. Capital Share	12	37. Entrepreneurial Environmental Protection	6, 24
4. Zoomlion	48	21. Public Use	1	38. Guangzhou Shipping International	1, 24
5. Wanhua Chemical	null	22. Jiangxi Copper	1, 6	39. China Glass Fiber	null
6. Lujiazui	1, 3, 48	23. Cosco Shipping	48	40. Aerospace Electronics	1, 3
7. Gemdale Group	null	24. Foton Motor	6, 12	41. Aerospace Machinery	3, 6, 12, 48
8. Tongfang Shares	1	25. Dongfeng Motor	24	42. Yutong Bus	null

(Continued)

Name of Stock	Regression Cycle	Name of Stock	Regression Cycle	Name of Stock	Regression Cycle
9. Baosteel	12	26. China Southern Airlines	24	43. Xingang	1
10. Kangmei Pharmaceutical	null	27. Tielong Logistics	48	44. Mass Transportation	1
11. Masteel	1	28. China International Trade	1	45. Swellfun	12, 48
12. China Grand Energy	null	29. Beijing Construction	6	46. SIPG	1, 12
13. Shanxi Fenjiu	3	30. Anyang Iron and Steel	24	47. Dalian Holdings	24
14. Huaneng International	1, 6	31. Shanghai Mechanical and Electrical Machinery	1, 3	48. Pudong Jinqiao	48
15. Youngor	null	32. Jisco Hongxing	24	49. Xinhuangpu	12
16. Gehua Cable	1	33. Nanshan Aluminum	1	50. Xining Special Steel	3, 12
17. Zhang Jiang Gao Ke	null	34. Entertainment Stock	24		

It can be seen that 41 of the 50 stocks have the characteristics of linear or nonlinear mean regression in different lag periods. At the same time, only 9 of the 50 stocks have no mean value regression feature in the monthly return rate within 48 months. The remaining 41 stocks have a mean value regression during the period. The shortest mean value regression cycle is only one month, so the predictability of long-term investment is relatively strong.

10.3 Basic Idea of Long-Term Investment Strategy

For long-term investment, the stock yield in bonds, gold, and other investment varieties is the highest. The conclusions of Liu Xibiao (2012) are very enlightening to us. He used some statistical data from the American capital market to analyze the characteristics of stock investment, hoping that the historical experience reflected in the statistical data would bring some useful enlightenment to investors' long-term investments. He looked at the stock markets of six developed countries in the 20th century. He observed that the average real rate of return on equity investment in different countries after deducting the inflation rate is positive, and the gap between them is very small. Between 1926 and 2005, the average return of world stocks was 9.85%, and that of American stocks was 10.17%, both higher than the returns of bonds, 5.77% and 5.38%. He believes that from the perspective of long-term investment, the stock is one of the best tools to resist inflation. Long-term investment yield in the stock significantly exceeds the bond yield, and the return on investment in small-cap stocks is significantly higher than in large-cap stocks.

According to the historical trend of the Dow Jones Index in the United States, it stood at 800.36 on December 31, 1969, exceeded 1,000 in March 1981, closed at 1,258 at the end of 1983, and rose to more than 17,000 in 2014. In 1987, the Hang Seng Index fell to 1,894 points. After 20 years, it hit a record high of 31,958 points in 2007, an appreciation of nearly 17 times in 20 years. Share prices are bound to move randomly in the short term, especially now that derivatives can dominate the market and booms and busts seem inevitable. In addition, the information is more developed than ever before, and the market spreads the information that determines the trend of the stock market very fast. The effective period of the market is shortened, and the efficiency of the market is gradually improved. Investors will quickly grasp the information and make investment decisions, although investor sentiment can influence or dominate short-term movements and make short-term movements more uncertain. However, the history of stock markets, especially in Europe and America, tells us that the bull market cycle is much longer than the bear. The rising stock market reflects the continued growth of the capitalist society's economic system, and the profits of the best companies will increase over time. Among them, if you can select some outstanding listed companies, the stock price will rise, the dividend will also increase, and you will absolutely enjoy attractive returns from the long-term investment. Long-term investors will choose to sell their stocks for a long time. Most of the time, it is based on the fact that the value of the stocks has reached their goal or the total amount of money is enough to make them retire early, the cost of their children's education, or the purchase of a home.

By accumulating outstanding stocks over the years and sticking to your investment goals, you can reduce trading fees and taxes and enjoy long-term returns. In other words, investors are definitely not holding for the sake of holding, understanding that they are investing in quality companies and sharing in the fruits of economic growth.

Long-term investment should be prepared for the following points: long-term investment should endure the psychological torture brought by sharp fluctuations in the stock price during the investment period, should endure the book profit has been made and then be reduced by the pain of stage. In the course of the market, long-term investors should give up many other assured investment opportunities and have to endure the temptation and stimulation of other stocks rising. Long-term investors must hold on to their shares for a long time and withstand all the noise in the market. In an upward band, while other investors enjoy the joy of winning, long-term investors may suffer periodic losses, making more people abandon their previous efforts. When the market is extremely depressed or crazy, long-term investors need to keep a clear head and always abide by the long-term investment strategy. The success of long-term investment is the goal everyone yearns for, but few people can achieve the hardships during this period. In short, long-term investors should not stare at the stock market every day and must have a strong tolerance and detachment.

In the world of securities investment, there are all sorts of investment strategies, and there are "masters" of different investment styles to learn from. Take the United States, the most developed and mature securities market, as an example. The five investment masters, known as the Wall Street "dream team," have their own investment strategies, and the other masters also have their own. However, it is almost certain that they all adhere to long-term investment and value investment strategies, and none of them rely on short-term speculation to achieve success.

10.3.1 Graham's Investment Philosophy

Benjamin Graham (1894–1976), known as the "Godfather of Wall Street" and "Father of Value Investment," is a famous security investment theorist and analyst. Graham is the author of three books: *Security Analysis*, *The Interpretation of Financial Statements*, and *The Intelligent Investor*. Graham's core investment ideas include the penny stock principle, the Mr. Market principle, and the margin of safety principle. Buffett believes that Graham's investment ideas will always be the cornerstone of rational investment.

Graham believes that the "intrinsic value" of stocks is the fundamental value of stock investment. His theory is mainly reflected in the research on value investment. He believes that investment is a behavior that can be expected to break even and have a satisfactory return through careful analysis. Behavior that does not meet these conditions is called speculation. He defined "careful analysis" as "the careful study of the facts and the attempt to reach a conclusion based on mature principles and right logic." He describes analysis as a three-step process: description, judgment, and selection. In the description stage, the analyst gathers and articulates all the salient facts. In the evaluation stage, the analyst is concerned about the quality of information, focusing on whether the obtained information objectively reflects the facts. In the selection stage, the analyst determines whether the security under investigation has investment value. Therefore, it is suggested that investors' energies should be better spent on detecting whether individual securities are undervalued rather than on the price level of the whole market.

Graham was the first scholar to emphasize the "intrinsic value" of stocks. Graham believes that the difference between the intrinsic value of stocks and the market price is a normal phenomenon in the market. The market price of a stock will often deviate from its intrinsic value, and when such deviation occurs, the market will naturally correct it. In practice, investors are often faced with the tendency for the market price of a stock returns slowly to its value. The process of this return may be short or long. The speed of this return depends on the adjustment of the market. In this process of regression, investors may also face certain risks. If they want to avoid these risks, investors must adopt the following methods: First, investors should invest and analyze stocks in an environment that is unlikely to change greatly. Second, investors should pick some stocks that attract the most attention or interest in the market. Third, investors should adjust their investment behavior according to the overall changes in the market. If the market behavior tends to be stable, investors should choose relatively "cheap" stocks; if the market fluctuates violently, investors should tend to be cautious. Graham argued that the intrinsic value of a stock could have an approximation or range rather than an exact value like its market price. The goal of investors in security analysis is not to obtain the exact intrinsic value of stocks, but to compare the intrinsic value with the market price and analyze whether the intrinsic value is sufficient relative to the market price. Although Graham thought it was not necessary to measure the intrinsic value of stocks, he still proposed a calculation method of intrinsic value. He believed that the intrinsic value of stocks should be measured by the expected average return of stocks in the next few years and a capitalization rate; that is, the intrinsic value is equal to the ratio of the expected average return of stocks to the capitalization rate in the next few years. This pricing method is similar to our current price-earnings ratio pricing method. As for capitalization rate, Graham believes that it is comprehensively determined by the company's management, balance sheet status, dividend change record, current stock interest rate, general long-term background, corporate characteristics, and other factors.

In addition, Graham also put forward the concept of "the overall value of stocks," holding that the overall value of stocks requires investors to have the mentality of buying the whole company when buying stocks; that is to say, investors should judge the value of stocks from the perspective of the controlling shareholders of the company and determine speculation and investment. Graham also distinguishes between the concepts of investing and speculation: investing is the practice of not using margin and often choosing safe securities with a steady income. On the other hand, speculation refers to the use of margins and the selection of risky securities that are intended to make capital gains and can be changed quickly. Investment is the acquisition of long-term income, while typical speculation is the pure pursuit of capital appreciation. Graham argues that this division is neither scientific nor accurate and misses the fundamental difference between investing and speculation. In some cases, low-quality bonds with a steady income are not good investment vehicles, while high-quality preferred or common stocks may be. Even without margin, buying speculative securities is a long way from investing. Graham believes that the fundamental difference between speculators and investors lies in their attitude towards stock price movements. Speculators aim to get capital gains, while investors are interested in holding stocks. The continuous fluctuations of the market just provide investors with the opportunity to buy undervalued stocks at a cheap price. Graham's investment concept emphasized the importance of the purchase price of stocks, which was the basis of his later important idea of "margin of safety." Graham mentioned in his classic book *Security Analysis* that the investment value of a stock is closely related to its price. A stock may have good investment value at a certain price, while it may become a tool for speculation at other prices. This is the basic idea of Graham's long-term investment, portfolio investment, and control investment.

Graham believes that long-term investment should be adhered to, but he believes that long-term investment is not simple. It must be held for a long time when the stock has investment value or is lower than the intrinsic value, which includes value judgment and band operation. In fact, the "long term" of his long-term investment is relatively long term (the scholars think it is about three years). Since Graham believes in long-term investment, he basically rejects the role of technical analysis and expresses skepticism about various economic policies and trends. He believes that the focus of securities analysis is to evaluate the value of stocks, while market analysis is only to forecast the trend of the market, which can only serve as a supplement to securities analysis. Security analysis and market analysis are two distinct categories. Graham also believes that investors get income in two ways: timing and price. The so-called timing is committed to predicting the market trend, buying the stock when the market is predicted to rise, selling the stock when the market is predicted to fall, value investors should buy the stock when the price is lower than the reasonable price, and sell the stock when the price is more than the reasonable price. Both of these ways can make investors profit. Thus, Graham praised investors who hold stocks for a long time in order to get a fixed dividend, as well as investors who take advantage of market price fluctuations. His dominant idea was that "only long-term patience will yield considerable gains."

"Margin of safety" is the core idea in Graham's investment thought. The so-called "margin of safety" means that there is a certain gap between the purchase price and the intrinsic value of the stock investors want to invest in. The lower the purchase price is than the intrinsic value, the smaller the risk of holding the stock and the greater the margin of safety. The thought of "margin of safety" emphasizes the control of risk, which contains the concept of risk premium in modern securities portfolio theory. Investors need to guarantee their investment fruits between the intrinsic value of stocks and the market price. Stock prices eventually return to value; the wider the gap, the higher the return for investors. He even thinks that the volatility of stocks, which is the variance in modern portfolio theory, is not the risk of stocks, and the decline is not the risk of stocks, but the intrinsic value of stocks is the benchmark to judge the risk of stocks.

10.3.2 Fisher's Investment Strategy

Philips Fisher (1907–2004) was regarded by Wall Street as the "father of growth stocks investing," a stock quality analyst. Fisher's famous book *Common Stocks and Uncommon Profits and Other Writings* received a welcome from the majority of investors in the

Wall Street, and received a high evaluation. Fisher's core investment philosophy is mainly embodied in finding and buying truly outstanding companies with growth stock characteristics and mastering the buying timing and selling reasons of stocks. Fisher's growth stock investment practice is also very successful.

Fisher said investors should focus on companies that allow them to gain the most with the least cost and risk. These are so-called "growth stocks." He put forward 15 points to choose growth stocks. He believes that if a company can meet a considerable number of points, it has a relatively high investment value and can be called a "growth stock." These 15 points roughly revolve around the following four areas: First, the company's market conditions and competitiveness. Whether the company's turnover can grow significantly in a few years and whether it has superior sales channels are the basic conditions to judge whether a company is worth studying. The growth prospects of turnover first depend on the growth of demand, and the management level of the company must also be maintained at a high level. In many cases, the analysis of enterprise sales ability is often ignored, and the vast majority of analysts are only content to rely on some rough indicators to analyze enterprise sales ability. Fisher believed that these ratios were too crude to be a basis for judging the value of an investment. To understand a firm's true marketing ability, one had to make hard and detailed investigations of its competitors and customers. The second is the company's level of research and development. Fisher believed that the most fundamental guarantee of a company's financial soundness lies in its ability to continuously develop new product lines that can guarantee considerable profits, which directly depends on the level of R&D activities. There are two most important aspects to observing R&D activities: on the one hand, the economic benefits of R&D activities. On the other hand, the attitude of the company's top management toward research and development activities is whether they can recognize the growth limits of the current market and plan for a rainy day. The third is the company's cost and revenue situation. How does the company's cost control level? What is the profit level, and what effective measures have been taken to maintain or improve the profit level? Is there a long-term profit outlook? Fisher attached great importance to the long-term profitability of enterprises. He has also been pursuing companies whose net profit margin continues to be higher than the industry average. He clearly pointed out: "Investing in companies with low-profit margins will never achieve the highest long-term profits." He believed that companies with low-profit margins are too weak in financial health and weak in resistance to shocks and are most likely to fall first in the economic downturn. The fourth and most important point is the management level of the company. How about the company's personnel relationship and the relationship within the management team? Does the management have enough depth? In the foreseeable future, will the company continue to issue shares to raise funds, and will the interests of existing shareholders be greatly damaged by the expected growth? Is the integrity attitude of the management beyond doubt?

10.3.3 Peter Lynch's Investment Strategy

Peter Lynch, born in 1944, is widely regarded as a "genius stock picker" and "the world's most legendary fund manager" in the investment community. He has published three books: *One Up on Wall Street*, *Beating the Street*, and *Learn to Earn*. Peter Lynch's most famous stock-picking strategy is the "Tenbagger" strategy, and he has come up with 13 rules for picking stocks. During his 13 years as a fund manager, he increased investors' assets by 29 times and achieved an investment legend with an average annual compound interest rate of 29%.

Although Peter Lynch focused on the fundamentals of stock selection and relentlessly eliminated the weak companies, some of his basic principles are of great practical value in screening and discrimination. He believes that finding a good company is only half the success of our investment strategy. How to buy at a reasonable price is the other half of success. Peter Lynch paid the most attention to the company's profitability and asset evaluation when evaluating the value of stocks. Profit evaluation focuses on the enterprise's ability to obtain income in the future. The higher the expected income, the greater the value of the company. The enhancement of profitability means the rise of the stock price. Asset evaluation is very instructive in determining the process of a company's asset restructuring.

Peter Lynch attaches great importance to the analysis of the P/E ratio. He believes that the company's potential profitability is the basis for determining the company's value. Sometimes, the market expectation is so advanced that the stock value is overestimated with an expectation that is too high, and the P/E ratio can help you check whether there is a bubble in the stock price. Generally speaking, stocks with high growth are allowed to have higher P/E ratios, while stocks with poor growth are allowed to have lower P/E ratios. How does the P/E ratio compare vertically with its historical average? By studying the performance of the P/E ratio over a long period of time, we should have a basic ability to judge the normal level of the index. This knowledge can help us avoid those stocks whose prices are overestimated or timely and warn us whether it is time to sell these stocks or continue to hold them. Suppose a company is satisfactory in all aspects, but we should still avoid it if the price is too high. Our next step is to screen companies whose current P/E ratio is lower than the average of the past five years. This principle is relatively strict. In addition to reviewing the current value level of the company, it also requires a positive growth of its performance in five years. Then, we should study how the P/E ratio compares with the industry average, which can help us understand whether the company's stock price is undervalued compared with the whole industry, or at least help us find out whether the price of this stock is different. Is the company's poor growth the reason for the difference? Or is the value of the stock ignored? Lynch believes that the ideal is to find companies that are ignored by the market and have a certain share in an industry with strong monopolies and high barriers to entry. Then, we can find out the companies whose P/E ratio is lower than the average of the whole industry from these screening results, which is our ultimate goal.

Maintaining a reasonable price as growth is the final tip of stock picking, choosing stocks with P/E ratios below the company's historical and the industry's average. Here, we can see how Peter Lynch finds the balance between value and growth. One useful measure is to compare a company's P/E ratio to its PEG. The P/E ratio is considered to be more attractive when it is half of the historical PEG, and it is not good if the ratio is higher than 2. In addition to PEG, he also takes into account the dividend yield. This adjustment recognizes the compensation value of dividends to investors' earnings by dividing the P/E ratio by the sum of PEG and dividend yield.

10.3.4 Buffett's Investment Strategy

Born in 1930 in Omaha, Nebraska, Warren Buffett is currently the Chairman of the Board of Berkshire Hathaway Inc. He became the world's richest man in 2007 with a fortune of $62 billion, and his personal wealth exceeded $58 billion in 2013, ranking him second in the world. Buffett is considered the world's greatest investor. Take Buffett as an example; the so-called use of market mispricing is the use of the market efficient cycle and mean regression principle.

Buffett's strategic investment idea is formed from the sublimation of actual combat and guides his investment behavior in practice. The core of the concept is to invest for a long time and hold companies and stocks with substantial value (excellent performance). This strategic investment concept of near-zero risk not only fully understands and grasps the market, but also stays away from the market, and then overcomes the market.

In the spring and summer of 1973, Buffett paid $10.6 million for a 12% stake in the *Washington Post*, becoming the paper's second-largest shareholder and launching a fortune that rose more than 100 times over the years. Buffett bought the *Washington Post* based on its brand awareness, influence, circulation, revenue, net profit, etc. In the two years after Buffett became the second largest shareholder of the *Washington Post*, the company's stock price actually continued to decline, and his total investment fell from $10.6 million in 1973 to $8 million by the end of 1974, and remained below Buffett's acquisition cost until 1976. But these huge "losses" did not shake or affect his faith, determination, and patience in firmly valuing the *Washington Post*. The *Washington Post* went public in 1971 at $6.50 a share. After a stock split, it rose to $770 a share in 2007, an average annual growth rate of about 16%. The value of Buffett's investment in the *Washington Post* has ballooned to an incredible $1 billion, a gain of at least 100 times. One of the main reasons Buffett was willing to pay this price was that it came at a time when most family-owned newspapers had just gone through a spate of sales, and prices were falling. He was sober and early to recognize the value of the *Washington Post*, which was undervalued by the market at the time.

Buffett's strategic investment philosophy can be roughly subdivided into five investment logics, ten investment essentials, eight stock selection criteria, and two investment methods. First of all, the five investment logics are as follows: First, I become an excellent investor by treating myself as an enterprise operator, and I become an excellent business operator by treating myself as an enterprise investor. Second, the real value of an enterprise is more important than the price of the stock market. Third, lifelong pursuit of enterprises of a specific industry. Fourth, what ultimately determines a company's share price is its real value. Fifth, there is no time to offload the best companies. Secondly, the ten investment essentials are as follows: (1) Use the market to invest regularly. Clear investment decision behavior should not be affected by external factors and change at will. (2) The purchase price is one of the factors that determines the rate of return. Securities strategic investment should eliminate all kinds of market interference and influence factors and only pay attention to what stocks to buy and the purchase price. (3) The compound growth of profits, transaction costs, and avoidance of tax burden benefit investors infinitely. (4) Relative to the annual profit income of the enterprise, it pays more attention to the investment income in the next 5–10 years. (5) Invest only in businesses with high certainty of future earnings. (6) Inflation is an investor's worst enemy. (7) The investment concepts of value and growth types are similar. Value is the discounted present value of the future cash flow of an investment, while growth is just a forecasting process used to determine the value. (8) The financial success of an investor is in direct proportion to his knowledge of the business in which he invests. (9) The investment function of the "margin of safety" is to cushion the possible price risk and obtain a relatively high rate of return on equity. (10) It is foolish to own a stock and expect it to go up next week. Thirdly, the eight investment criteria refer to the following: (1) Must be a high-performing company in a particular industry. (2) The business of the enterprise is simple and easy to understand, and the prospect is promising. (3) Have a stable business history. (4) Financial soundness. (5) High operating efficiency and good earnings. (6) Managers are rational and loyal and always take shareholders' interests as the first priority. (7) Low capital expenditure and abundant free cash flow. (8) Reasonable price. Finally, there are two types of investment: long-term holding (for some companies, even for life) and short-term arbitrage (when the market overestimates the price of holding stocks, you can also consider it).

Buffett's strategic investment concept was formed in the United States, which has more than 100 years of history in the securities market. His investment income made him the most successful securities investor in the United States in the 20th century, and he was called the God of stocks. However, through more than 100 years of legal supervision and its own competition norms, the American securities market has formed the securities market with investment as the main body. It is precisely because of such a market that the investment intensifier Buffett and Buffett's strategic investment concept came into being.

Therefore, to learn and draw on Buffett's strategic investment thought and methods, we should not simply imitate or copy, nor have a partial and one-sided understanding. Instead, we should have a comprehensive, profound, and rational understanding of the real market and its current situation. At the same time, we should have our own unique and effective choice of various information and methods of the market. On this premise, we learn, draw on, absorb, and digest Buffett's strategic investment concept and effectively integrate Buffett's method into investment practice to form our own investment strategy.

The first time Buffett ran into a big bull market, he decided to get out of stocks. In 1968, trading in American stocks reached a frenzy. In May 1969, fearing that he would be caught lamenting misery and losing his profits, Buffett finally took the unusual step of announcing the dissolution of his private equity fund. He announced his withdrawal at the height of the bull market: "I can't adapt to this market environment, and I don't want to hurt my performance by trying to play a game I don't understand." Buffett's decision turned out to be a brilliant one. By May 1970, the average stock on the stock exchange was 50% lower than at the beginning of 1969.

The second time Buffett ran into a big bull market, he chose to sell most of his stocks. In 1972, the US stock market had another big bull market, and stock prices rose sharply. At that time, almost all investment funds concentrated on a group of growth stocks with large market value and prominent corporate reputations, such as Xerox, Kodak, Polaroid, Avon, and Texas Instruments, which were called "beautiful 50 shares," with an average price-earnings ratio of 80 times astronomical.

In early October 1974, when the Dow Jones Index plunged from 1,000 to 580, almost every stock in the United States was trading at a single-digit P/E ratio, a rarity on Wall Street. No one wanted to hold on to stocks, and everyone was selling. In the midst of the pessimism of the market, Buffett cheered loudly. He said in an interview with the reporter of *Forbes*: "I feel like a very lecherous young man who has come to the country of daughters. It is time to invest."

At the 1999 annual meeting, Buffett was attacked by shareholders, and almost every newspaper said his investment strategy was outdated, but Buffett remained unmoved. Buffett made his views on the big bull market clear as early as Berkshire's 1986 annual report: "There is nothing more exhilarating than participating in a bull market in which the returns to shareholders become completely disconnected from the company's slow growth. However, unfortunately, it is absolutely impossible for stock prices to outstrip the value of companies indefinitely. In fact, because stockholders buy and sell so frequently and they bear the cost of managing their investments, their aggregate investment returns are bound to underperform the performance of the listed companies they own over a long period of time. If American companies as a whole are earning about 12% a year on equity, investors are bound to end up with much lower returns. Bull markets can darken mathematical laws, but they cannot be abolished." The results proved that Buffett was right. In 2000, 2001, and 2003, the US stock market fell by 9.1%, 11.9%, and 22.1%, a total decline of more than half, while Buffett's performance rose by more than 30% in the same period.

From the trend characteristics of China's stock market, years of experience tell us that in order to really make money from the stock market, we must be based on long-term investment. And for the current Chinese stock market, this return is very high. Long-term investment cycles are often closely related to macroeconomic cycles. When there are many problems in the economy, people are panicking, and the government continues to introduce measures to stimulate the economy, it is often the best time for long-term investment in the stock market. "It's only when the tide goes out that you find out who's been swimming naked, and it's only then that you find out what the really good companies are," Warren Buffett says. As government stimulus measures continue to roll out and sentiment improves, the stock market quietly rises until it fizzles out in a frenzy, when it is time to sell for the long term. A bull market bear market cycle in China's stock market is generally in three to four years. Even the long bear market, from 2000 to 2005, was about five years. If an investor had the misfortune to buy the stock at 2,245 in 2000 and hold it until the peak of 6,124 in 2007, the market return would have averaged 272.78% over a seven-year period, not taking into account possible covering over the past six years, equivalent to 15.41% compound interest income.

From the results of securities investment theory and empirical research, short-term behavior should be defined as speculation, and long-term behavior should be defined as investment. Investing has a much higher probability of success than speculation. Being long-term oriented and rational is a prerequisite, and perhaps the path, to successful investing.

10.4 Behavioral Finance Explanation of Long-Term Investment Psychology

The concept of long-term investment is easy to be accepted by investors, and the implementation of long-term investment behavior is actually a test of investor psychology. Long-term investment strategies are not unacceptable. The key is that the implementation of long-term investors' strategies requires many specific steps, especially the psychological test of investors, even long-term psychological torture. However, there are plenty of facts to suggest that so many investors actively buy stocks even when the market is down, sell what they get, and do it repeatedly. It is hard to hold shares for long. For them, owning shares can be really depressing. After rising, share prices can fall rapidly, moving up and down, alternating between profit and loss. This is a psychological test for every investor; most investors simply cannot stand the pressure. Some investors find it difficult to resist the current profits when the stock price rises sharply for a while.

Lack of patience, persistence, and shortsightedness are human's greatest weaknesses. When the investment is occasionally successful, most people are overconfident and think that they can predict the future trend. This not only shows innocence, but also is almost doomed to failure.

10.4.1 Why Only a Few People Make Money in the Stock Market?

The success of only a few people in the stock market can be reasonably explained by the psychological characteristics of investors. Only a few people succeed in the stock market. Statistics show that less than 10% of investors actually make money after each run. Even in a big market, no matter how high the market rises, it is always the few who get to keep their profits once the market ends. It can be said that a bull market will trap a group of investors, and a bear market will eliminate a group of investors. This is an iron rule of the stock market. To become a successful investor, you should study how to become one of the few. The following ideas may help you a lot.

It is generally believed that the behavior of investors can be divided into investment and speculation. In defining the concepts of investment and speculation, investment and rationality, speculation and irrationality are always mentioned in the same breath. In fact, it is difficult to strictly distinguish between investment and speculation, because any kind of investment behavior has risks to varying degrees. Still, some risks are larger, and some risks are smaller. When the probability of success is larger, speculation should be considered as "rational speculation." Charlie Munger, Buffett's partner, said, "When the probability of success is high, make a big bet." There is no return without risk, there is no great success without high risk, and the criterion of whether to take risks is the probability of success. It has been proved by hundreds of years of investment practice that only a few people make money in the stock market. The reasons can be summarized as follows:

(1) From the timing of entry. A lot of facts show that many investors, especially small and medium investors, basically enter the market when they see others making money; that is when the market is very profitable, at least in the middle or even the end of the bull market. However, it is highly unlikely that a rising bull market will be caught up as soon as a new investor enters the market. Because in the short term, even the end of the bull market has not changed the upward trend of the stock market, the chances of making money in the market far outweigh the chances of losing money. They made money as soon as they entered the market cautiously. By human nature, with the appearance of the profit effect, investors will gradually expand their investment scale, and finally, when the bull market ends and the stock market falls, they will lose a lot. In fact, this route is the investment career of many small and medium investors. One conclusion we can draw from this is that a bull market will trap a group of small and medium investors. On the contrary, from the perspective of human nature, what most people can't do is to buy stocks when others lose money very seriously and to invest in the market when others

lose money. One thing is certain, that is, it is cheaper than others. But few people can do this, so only a few make money in the stock market.

(2) Most people are wrong in the stock market. People influenced by a custom, a belief, or a value tend to be collectively irrational, and it is not surprising that most people make the same mistake. This weakness of human nature is most obvious in the stock market. Since the stock market is a place of speculation, there should be a small probability that most people make money. If most people make money, the stock market will no longer exist, because it does not have the function of supporting all investors. From the perspective of human nature, no one will leave the stock market for making money but for losing money. Ordinary people cannot leave the stock market when they make money, and this is due to people's dissatisfaction. Here is a parable to illustrate. Once upon a time, a shepherd led a goat and rode a donkey into the city to go to market. Three swindlers knew about it and tried to trick him. While the shepherd was dozing on the donkey's back, the first swindler took the bell off the goat's neck, tied it to the donkey's tail, and led it away. When the shepherd looked back, he saw that the goat was missing and was busy looking for it. Then, the second swindler approached and asked him eagerly what he was looking for. The shepherd said the goat had been stolen and asked if he had seen it. The swindler pointed casually and said that he saw a man holding a goat who had just passed through the woods. It must be that man. Run after him. The shepherd rushed to chase the goat and left the donkey in the care of the "kind man." When he returned empty-handed, the donkey and "kind man" had disappeared. The shepherd was so sad that he cried as he went. When he came to a pool, he found a man sitting by the pool, crying more than he did. The shepherd was very strange: Is there anyone unlucky than me? He asked the man why he was crying. The man told the shepherd that he had taken two bags of gold coins to the city to buy something and had rested his feet by the water and washed his face, but he had accidentally dropped the bags into the water. The shepherd said, "Then go down and get it." The man said that he could not swim. If the shepherd brought them up, he would give him 20 gold coins. The shepherd was overjoyed and thought: "This is great. Although the goat and donkey were lost, there may be 20 gold coins in hand here. There is still more money to make up for the loss." He quickly stripped off his clothes and jumped into the water. When he climbed out of the water naked and empty-handed, his clothes and dry food were gone, and only a little money was still in his pocket. These are the basic mentality of stock investors and the root cause of serious losses. This shepherd can be defined as an ordinary person.

(3) Most people do not have the basic quality of investment success. To put it bluntly, investing in the stock market is also a profession. It is impossible for everyone to have investment knowledge. If everyone knows it, it will not be called science. Will anyone work if everyone makes money when investing in the stock market? Buffett has a famous saying, "When you play poker, there is always one person who will be unlucky. If you

look around and can't see who will be unlucky, it is you." If you want to be a successful stock investor, that is to say, you want to be a winner in a game where a few people make money, why? Just as an athlete can participate in the Olympic Games because he can run fast, when we want to become a few successful people, we should have the basic quality of success. On this premise, the lucky investors can become moneymakers. When an investor holds funds to invest in the stock market, he must ask himself, why? Why would you succeed? Why do others fail? Graham viewed the market fluctuation in this way: "Intrinsic value is one of the two major factors that affect the stock market price; the other factor is speculative. The interaction of value factor and speculative factor makes the stock market price fluctuate around the intrinsic value of the stock, and the value factor can only partially affect the market price." The intrinsic value will rise with the development of listed companies. This part of the change will be very slow, and the impact on the stock price will be long. The speculative part will fluctuate quickly and is a "zero-sum game," that is, the profit of the moneymaker is based on the loss of the moneymaker. Just like gambling, it is impossible for all gamblers to win money, and of course, it is impossible for all gamblers to lose money. Of course, you must have good luck on the premise of having a certain quality; otherwise, you will not succeed. In fact, there are not many investment experts in the market, but often excellent investors are in charge of large-scale funds and become the main force of market making, which is more likely to cause large areas of retail investors to be covered, making most people join the ranks of losers.

(4) Investors are vulnerable to the influence of the market atmosphere, and most people make mistakes under the influence of the herd effect. Buffett said, "Fear when others are greedy, and be greedy when others are afraid." Ordinary people can only say but can't do it, and those who can do this will undoubtedly become a few successful people. What most of us can do is to be greedy when others are greedy and to be afraid when others are afraid. In fact, the market tends to be bullish at the end of the bull market in the stock market. It is not easy to leave the stock market calmly in this atmosphere. Those who can leave and endure the long wait will become one of the few moneymakers. On the contrary, when the stock market is in a depression, few people can have a strong investment interest, and most people will not invest boldly and learn to be greedy at this time. In the spring of 1966, when the stock market in the United States was bullish, Buffett was restless. Although his stocks were soaring, he found it difficult to find cheap stocks that met his standards. Although the rampant speculation in the stock market has brought windfall profits to speculators, Buffett is unimpressed, arguing that the price of stocks should be based on corporate growth, not speculation. In May 1968, with the stock market booming, Buffett informed his partners that he was retiring. Between 1970 and 1974, the US stock market plunged without any sign of life, and sustained inflation and low growth pushed the US economy into a period of "stagflation." However, the once-frustrated Buffett secretly exulted. Because he saw the money coming in—he found

too many cheap stocks, and Buffett was confident when everyone else was losing faith in the stock market. That's Buffett.

(5) A careful study of the flow of market funds will reveal that the stock market is actually a container of liquid funds. Like a container of water, the more water is poured into it, the higher the water level will be. Similarly, when the stock market is a completely fixed capacity market, that is, no new companies are listed, and the stock-listed companies do not increase capital and expand shares, the more capital flows into the stock market, the higher the market value of the stock. In this case, it is bound to produce an all-win situation for most people in the market to make money. When the capacity of the market continues to expand, new shares continue to be listed, and listed companies also expand their shares and increase their capital. The funds flowing into the market continue to flow into listed companies, resulting in very limited funds to promote the rise of the stock market, so it is very difficult for the market to achieve a win-win situation, and can only maintain a volatile trend at most. When the market capacity continues to expand and the source of capital inflow is blocked, there is no need for any reason; the market will fall rapidly, and the market price level will drop rapidly, which often leads to a situation of losing all. Finally, we find that the volatility of the stock market does not bring the greatest benefits to investors but provides a blood transfusion machine for listed companies. Since the establishment of the Chinese stock market, the market capacity has been expanding, the number of listed companies has been increasing, and the market value has also been growing, resulting in the vast majority of funds flowing into the market flowing into the entity listed companies through capacity and share expansion. In addition, the maintenance of the huge capital market service system also needs to intercept a considerable portion of market funds. In this way, there is very little money left for investors to earn through market games. Therefore, in this market environment, it is completely understandable that a few people make money and most people lose money, and there is a sufficient reason for its existence.

10.4.2 The Mental Strategy of The Long-Term Investor

The Intelligent Investor has been the stock market bible since it was first published in 1949. Up to now, this book has always been the number one sales volume of Amazon Bookstore's public investment books, affecting a number of investors in the world and making a number of millionaires. What is written in the book: Be a patient investor, willing to wait until the price of the enterprise becomes attractive before buying stocks. No matter Wall Street or anywhere else, there is no sure and easy way to get rich. These are all things that a mature investor must understand. Graham has brought education and inspiration to people around the world, and his value investment philosophy has benefited many investors.

He tells the lemming-investing fable of an oil prospector who is about to enter heaven when St. Peter stops him and gives him the very bad news: "You do deserve to enter heaven, but the space allotted to oil men is full, and I can't fit you in." The oil prospector listened, thought for a moment, and then made a request to St. Peter: "May I go in and speak to the people who live in heaven?" St. Peter granted his request. The oil prospector shouted to the people in heaven, "Oil has been found in hell!" As soon as the words fell, all the people in heaven rushed to hell. St. Peter was so surprised to see this that he invited the oil prospector to live in heaven. But the oil prospector hesitated for a moment and said, "No, I think I'll go to hell with those people."

This parable warns investors against blindly following the crowd and tells people that it is actually very difficult to conquer oneself. In many cases, the drastic changes that often occur in the stock market are caused by investors blindly following the trend, rather than by the changes in the companies' earnings. As soon as a rumor appears in the stock market, many investors quickly and blindly buy or sell stocks based on the rumor before it is proven. Following the rumor overrides rational thinking. This leads to wild swings in stock prices and often causes mediocre performance for these investors.

Peter Lynch, who used to host cocktail parties at his home for a while, discovered a curious pattern in the stock market cycle, which typically has four stages.

Stage 1: When asked at the reception what he does for a living, Peter Lynch replied, "I manage mutual funds." The person would nod politely, then turn away; if he didn't, he would quickly change the topic. After a while, he might talk to a dentist near him about congestion in the gums. The stock market is likely to rise when ten people would rather talk to a dentist than the guy who runs a mutual fund.

Stage 2: After Peter Lynch revealed his occupation to the chat-up guest, the guest may have a longer conversation with him about stock risk, etc. By this time, the stock market was already higher than it had been in the first stage, but no one was paying attention.

Stage 3: The stock market has gone up so much that most cocktail-goers ignored the dentist, and the evening revolved around Peter Lynch. People kept pulling him aside to ask him what stocks to buy, and the people at the party talked enthusiastically about what had happened in the stock market.

Stage 4: At the party, people gathered around Peter Lynch again. This time, they advised him on which stocks to buy and recommended several stocks. A few days later, Peter Lynch read in the newspapers that the stocks they recommended had already gone up, that the stock market had peaked, and that the decline was coming.

Whether it's Warren Buffett's "Be fearful when others are greedy, be greedy when others are fearful" or Peter Lynch's cocktail theory, there are plenty of times when investing should be a little more reverse thinking.

Reverse thinking corresponds to herd mentality. When a few people are bullish in the stock market, the market will not change qualitatively. When most people are bullish, the market will change qualitatively. So will the bear market. The stock price keeps falling, and the pessimism pervades the whole market. For some people with reverse thinking, it is the best time to invest. Buffett has a maxim: When people rush in, you should be careful. When people are afraid, you should try to be interested in it.

Whether it is so-called investment or speculation, the real motivation for people to invest in stocks is to obtain high ultimate profit returns. In both mature and emerging markets, a bit of reverse thinking is in order. For example, China's A-share market has experienced several years of the big bear market. During this period, problems such as share trading put the entire market in a state of panic. Many stocks have a large amount of funds to buy and hold when they are tens of yuan, but when they fall to the zero price at the peak of the stock price, the daily trading volume is scarce, and there is a lack of bold buying holders. This is exactly the best portrayal of why the stock market long-term losses more than win, buy up, not buy down; the herd effect in the stock market fluctuations over the years made countless investors lose their money. Since the inception of A-shares, those who have dared to buy in times of panic selling have proved to be the most stable and profitable.

Reverse thinking is manifested in the following aspects of the stock market:

(1) Extreme things must reverse: when everything reaches its limit, it will turn in the opposite direction. This is the general law of development and change of everything. When the overwhelming majority is bullish, the market can peak, and when the overwhelming majority is bearish, the market changes.

(2) Minority becomes majority: In a bear market, when the stock price falls to the bottom of the area, most people have already left, the main money has also left, most people believe that the market will continue to fall, the result is that the market will slowly strengthen.

(3) Majority becomes minority: In a bull market, when stock prices have climbed to the peak, so to speak, there is the vast majority of people who are bullish and believe that stock prices will rise. When all the people who want to buy stocks have bought them, who do they sell them to? What else can drive the stock market up?

It should be noted that when using reverse thinking, investors need to have a strong will and confidence in self-judgment and can stick to their choice to the end; otherwise, they are bound to lose more than ordinary people.

Finally, reverse thinking doesn't always work; sometimes, the opposite is the right thing to do. Reverse thinking is just a way of thinking, not a forecasting system. That is to say, we must pay attention to timing when using reverse thinking, and timing is often difficult to master. Proverbs such as "bull market tops out" and "bear market bottoms out" illustrate that even if stock prices are absolutely overvalued or undervalued, we should never assume that a turn is imminent. More often, we know the general trend is going to change, but we don't know when.

10.4.3 Long-Term Investment Psychology Strategy Summary

According to the author's summary, the relationship between stock investment and psychology is very close. The main body of stock investment is people, and people's behavior will be affected by their psychological activities. Therefore, any investment behavior is undoubtedly affected by the psychology of investors. Investors' confidence will increase with the rise of stock price and decrease with the decline of stock price.

Investors who really achieve great success have to follow these principles:

First, stick to a long-term investment strategy. Long-term compounding returns are huge. The annual compound growth rate of the Shanghai Composite Index reached 14.19% from the start of statistics to 2,115 points at the end of 2013. The famous investment master Buffett's average annual return of 23.5% is not very high in the eyes of many domestic investors. Still, the reason why he became one of the world's richest people lies in the compound growth lasting more than 30 years. According to the fund investment equation, when the expected annual rate of return is 15%, if 500 yuan is invested in the fund investment every month, the cumulative investment cost will be 180,000 yuan for 360 consecutive months, and the income will be 3.46 million yuan after the expiration. The worst way to maximize compound interest is to change hands frequently. Buffett likens investing to a snowball. All an investor has to do is find a wet snow (looking for an investment with higher compound interest) and a slope long enough (to compound interest over a long period of time) to roll out a huge snowball (to make a huge investment return).

Second, to have a good investment mentality, we must first overcome our own to beat the stock market. The first step to becoming a successful investor. Don't stare at the stock market all day long and pay less attention to the rise and fall of the stock market, especially those who are not trained enough and are excited and want to buy and sell when they see the stock market rise. We should gradually train ourselves to operate only according to the expected plan, so that we can see the rise of the stock without being anxious and see the rise of the stock without being excited; that is, we can stay in the midst of many rising stocks without moving, which is the noble realm. In the case that it is not in line with its own plan and market strategy, it is necessary to have no desire for those stocks that are rising, such as the rise of individual stocks in each rebound during the fall of the bear market. The real ability to see the rise without desire is the sign that investors really enter the "highest level of success." If no matter how refined investors are, they still can't change the mentality of being excited when the stock market rises and wanting to buy when the stock market rises, then the chances of success will become more and more distant, and it will become inevitable that they will eventually be eliminated by the market. To become a successful investor, the first thing to study is not how to defeat the market but how to defeat yourself first.

Third, oppose excessive trading and speculation. The market-oriented behavior of excessive trading will make investors believe that he is using his judgment, but it is only a guess. The investors thought he was speculating, but in fact, he was gambling. Once the market situation becomes so uncertain that it is impossible to make an accurate judgment on the future direction, people should stay away from the market, which is very important to maintain the objectivity of investors. If we only make investment decisions based on some paradoxical facts, then our confidence in this decision is not strong. Therefore, we are extremely vulnerable to the impact of even a little bad news or unexpected price fluctuations and hurriedly stop an investment. Excessive trading will damage investors' insight. This insight can be regarded as an ability to look forward to and grasp the future. In a bull market, most stocks will rise, just as all ships will rise with the tide. In a bear market, most stocks will fall most of the time. However, the rise or fall is usually carried out through trend operation. In the process of rising, there will be a backlash; in the downward trend, there will often be a rebound. In fact, speculation is a zero-sum game. The success of speculation should be attributed to luck. The patronage of luck cannot be a regular phenomenon.

Fourth, grasp the timing of buying and selling. Once the investment decision is made after rational judgment, it is necessary to stick to the investment discipline and life discipline and get rid of the impact and influence caused by the market atmosphere and emotions. Only when we defeat ourselves can we defeat the stock market. When the stock market rises, we should sell bravely to reduce risks. When the stock market is in a downturn, we should buy bravely and wait for success.

APPENDIX

Empirical Test of Mean Regression of Monthly Returns of 50 Individual Stocks

Stock Name and Code	Period / Coefficient	1	3	6	12	24	48
Oriental Pearl (600832)	α	−0.0062	−0.1026	−0.0886	0.0763	−0.0322	0.0646
	p value	0.9390	0.1864	0.1996	0.2908	0.6714	0.3785
	β	0.4462	1.4373	−3.0365	3.2771	−2.5457	−3.0535
	p value	0.3043	0.3898	0.2151	0.1261	0.1891	0.0611
Conch Cement (600585)	α	0.1694	0.2210	−0.1729	−0.0446	−0.2477	0.0687
	p value	0.1899	0.0210	0.0956	0.6570	0.0131	0.5789
	β	−2.2680	−4.6433	2.5724	−2.1789	5.8575	−0.0507
	p value	0.0871	0.0699	0.1708	0.3709	0.0023	0.9907
Shanghai Pudong Development Bank (600000)	α	0.2394	−0.0291	−0.0787	−0.1274	0.0533	−0.0843
	p value	0.0335	0.7388	0.3878	0.1412	0.5674	0.3906
	β	−1.2455	3.3563	−0.8901	−0.4311	−7.1225	6.7327
	p value	0.4067	0.1578	0.6990	0.8135	0.0249	0.1038
Zoomlion (000157)	α	0.1114	0.0200	−0.1028	0.0757	0.0652	0.0045
	p value	0.3587	0.8483	0.2534	0.3984	0.4733	0.9577
	β	0.4210	1.3327	0.7396	−1.7819	−3.3248	−7.8383
	p value	0.6523	0.5653	0.7199	0.4672	0.2904	0.0711
Wanhua Chemical (600309)	α	0.2256	−0.0287	0.0625	−0.0426	−0.0187	0.0736
	p value	0.0549	0.7587	0.5304	0.6730	0.8557	0.5314
	β	−2.9114	−1.0504	−0.5251	−1.9755	0.9836	−2.2867
	p value	0.0502	0.6619	0.8369	0.4825	0.7368	0.6701
Lujiazui (600663)	α	−0.1540	0.1219	0.0755	−0.0032	0.0205	−0.1608
	p value	0.0511	0.1114	0.2933	0.9638	0.7371	0.0064
	β	0.1905	−2.5502	−1.9961	2.5495	−0.5231	−0.0100
	p value	0.1704	0.0393	0.1250	0.2468	0.5701	0.9742
Gemdale Group (600383)	α	0.0625	−0.0134	−0.1260	−0.0486	0.0369	−0.0766
	p value	0.6188	0.8992	0.1995	0.6225	0.7135	0.4576
	β	1.4474	2.0367	3.2417	−2.8883	1.7794	8.4471
	p value	0.2712	0.3512	0.0382	0.1161	0.4023	0.0259

(Continued)

Stock Name and Code	Period / Coefficient	1	3	6	12	24	48
Tongfang Shares (600100)	α	0.0988	−0.0160	−0.0489	−0.0289	−0.0121	0.0007
	p value	0.2512	0.8379	0.5340	0.6935	0.8541	0.9930
	β	−0.5452	1.5571	−0.1791	0.5740	1.5441	−3.2193
	p value	0.0725	0.3473	0.9220	0.6080	0.0458	0.4723
Baosteel (600019)	α	−0.0012	−0.0107	−0.0482	−0.1666	−0.1015	−0.0015
	p value	0.9921	0.9005	0.6249	0.0555	0.2625	0.9872
	β	−0.6343	−2.1303	−0.7947	2.1278	0.2754	8.6600
	p value	0.5823	0.2794	0.7986	0.2390	0.8610	0.0631
Kangmei Pharmaceutical (600518)	α	0.0304	−0.0005	−0.1506	−0.0224	−0.0933	−0.0095
	p value	0.8137	0.9959	0.1077	0.8128	0.3893	0.9308
	β	−0.3422	2.2460	3.7972	9.2418	4.2333	−4.4176
	p value	0.8878	0.4212	0.2238	0.0241	0.3507	0.5530
Masteel (600808)	α	−0.0327	−0.0008	−0.0839	0.0022	0.0185	−0.0963
	p value	0.6683	0.9911	0.1594	0.9739	0.7626	0.1279
	β	−0.3358	1.4328	1.7794	1.0553	−2.7635	0.0006
	p value	0.0725	0.0592	0.0438	0.5634	0.1947	0.9998
China Grand Energy (600256)	α	0.1534	0.0352	−0.1877	−0.0751	0.1350	−0.0380
	p value	0.2143	0.7179	0.0601	0.4535	0.2418	0.7442
	β	−0.6737	−0.9844	6.0224	2.6699	−4.3218	−4.7330
	p value	0.7028	0.7165	0.0109	0.3643	0.2689	0.2129
Shanxi Fenjiu (600809)	α	−0.0481	0.0651	−0.0604	−0.0142	−0.0410	0.0222
	p value	0.5459	0.3507	0.4008	0.8371	0.4891	0.7314
	β	0.1512	−1.5090	1.5588	1.4775	−2.1159	−0.4135
	p value	0.5803	0.0480	0.2651	0.4320	0.4645	0.9068
Huaneng International (600011)	α	−0.2325	0.0342	−0.2619	−0.0594	−0.0412	0.0020
	p value	0.0540	0.7355	0.0090	0.5632	0.6573	0.9851
	β	1.1393	−0.1876	2.6460	1.0903	−2.3860	2.3336
	p value	0.4975	0.9481	0.3335	0.6860	0.4035	0.7131
Youngor (600177)	α	0.0398	0.0546	−0.0494	−0.1811	−0.0024	−0.0434
	p value	0.6862	0.4903	0.5368	0.0305	0.9767	0.6270
	β	0.4328	1.6478	0.2730	1.8713	−0.7918	2.0867
	p value	0.5136	0.2389	0.9069	0.0124	0.6959	0.4468
Gehua Cable (600037)	α	0.1946	−0.0393	0.0175	0.0382	−0.0131	0.0093
	p value	0.1563	0.7107	0.8667	0.7156	0.9030	0.9401
	β	−6.8425	1.1976	−3.0579	0.0078	−7.7605	−2.5899
	p value	0.0353	0.7618	0.4326	0.9987	0.1159	0.6465

(Continued)

Stock Name and Code	Period Coefficient	1	3	6	12	24	48
Zhang Jiang Gao Ke (600895)	α	−0.0017	−0.0722	−0.0337	−0.0286	−0.0247	−0.1432
	p value	0.9846	0.3310	0.6790	0.7064	0.7502	0.0697
	β	−0.2884	2.8949	1.7577	2.3087	−0.0558	6.2858
	p value	0.5958	0.1119	0.5500	0.4011	0.9768	0.0383
Construction and Development Shares (600153)	α	0.4162	0.0192	−0.2398	0.0734	0.0395	0.0814
	p value	0.0001	0.8276	0.0067	0.3908	0.6565	0.3903
	β	−5.6290	1.8989	7.5613	−0.7551	3.8186	−3.8205
	p value	0.0002	0.4659	0.0323	0.7847	0.3124	0.4725
Zhejiang Pharmaceutical (600216)	α	−0.0917	−0.0376	−0.1024	−0.0279	0.0002	−0.0199
	p value	0.4589	0.6994	0.2545	0.7608	0.9980	0.8418
	β	−0.1032	0.9436	0.1431	−1.1705	−0.7374	−6.9786
	p value	0.9388	0.5591	0.9358	0.5095	0.7234	0.0741
Capital Share (600008)	α	−0.0107	−0.0232	−0.0953	−0.0459	0.0663	−0.0419
	p value	0.9235	0.8050	0.2914	0.6237	0.5144	0.6894
	β	−0.8495	−0.6176	−0.6938	−5.4488	1.7467	12.8308
	p value	0.4637	0.6780	0.7216	0.0796	0.6725	0.0761
Public Use (600635)	α	−0.1474	0.0541	−0.0508	−0.0150	−0.0547	0.0012
	p value	0.0553	0.4033	0.4665	0.8172	0.3881	0.9834
	β	0.2116	−0.4882	−0.6898	0.8761	1.5902	−1.1637
	p value	0.1398	0.3751	0.6923	0.1618	0.1907	0.4766
Jiangxi Copper Industry (600362)	α	0.1740	0.0648	−0.1827	−0.1309	−0.1286	−0.0549
	p value	0.1853	0.4951	0.0709	0.1728	0.2149	0.6130
	β	−1.8340	−1.2433	0.9580	0.0456	1.1404	0.2797
	p value	0.0740	0.3693	0.5035	0.9703	0.4731	0.9119
Cosco Shipping (600428)	α	0.1089	0.0123	0.0465	−0.0652	−0.1030	0.0934
	p value	0.3114	0.8895	0.6450	0.4782	0.2922	0.4287
	β	−1.0948	−1.1260	−0.7425	0.8583	0.2537	−9.5300
	p value	0.1403	0.4366	0.7965	0.6518	0.8911	0.0651
Foton Motor (600166)	α	0.1389	0.0851	−0.2564	0.1144	−0.1226	−0.0571
	p value	0.2026	0.3268	0.0022	0.1606	0.1638	0.5288
	β	−0.0654	0.6206	1.4405	−4.7305	2.0403	4.0965
	p value	0.9561	0.7241	0.4972	0.0089	0.3358	0.1555
Dongfeng Motor (600006)	α	0.0385	0.0123	−0.2715	0.0993	0.0917	−0.0611
	p value	0.7748	0.9044	0.0065	0.3305	0.3456	0.5782
	β	1.8663	1.8651	7.1278	−0.8005	−7.3172	−1.0499
	p value	0.5180	0.6064	0.0583	0.8375	0.0854	0.8583

(Continued)

Stock Name and Code	Period Coefficient	1	3	6	12	24	48
China Southern Airlines (600029)	α	0.0095	0.2464	−0.0772	−0.1131	0.0027	0.0388
	p value	0.9463	0.0211	0.4823	0.2820	0.9809	0.7499
	β	1.1489	−0.9923	1.0621	1.7406	−4.8009	−4.5368
	p value	0.3896	0.6307	0.5051	0.3373	0.0850	0.4141
Tielong Logistics (600125)	α	0.0094	−0.1239	−0.0933	−0.0197	0.0521	−0.1514
	p value	0.9332	0.1437	0.3022	0.8100	0.5517	0.0968
	β	0.1289	11.4110	2.4829	1.6009	−0.6920	5.7133
	p value	0.9442	0.0064	0.4512	0.5555	0.8463	0.1818
China International Trade (600007)	α	0.1271	0.0910	0.0431	0.1041	−0.0140	−0.1976
	p value	0.2095	0.3107	0.6063	0.2037	0.8686	0.0284
	β	−3.5504	−3.0550	−2.6775	−5.6630	−0.5717	9.6508
	p value	0.0020	0.2587	0.2212	0.1996	0.1343	0.0235
Beijing Construction (600266)	α	−0.0669	0.0303	−0.2135	−0.1243	−0.0737	−0.1127
	p value	0.5401	0.7254	0.0112	0.1772	0.4465	0.2969
	β	1.0736	−0.7770	4.7314	3.4506	2.8615	2.5394
	p value	0.3523	0.7072	0.0067	0.1599	0.2342	0.4098
Anyang Iron and Steel (600569)	α	0.2437	0.1120	−0.0537	−0.0607	−0.0029	−0.0020
	p value	0.0437	0.2188	0.6022	0.5168	0.9754	0.9853
	β	−2.1187	−0.0820	−0.6789	1.8771	−6.7389	1.1725
	p value	0.0332	0.9653	0.8613	0.2905	0.0399	0.7932
Shanghai Mechanical and Electrical Machinery (600835)	α	−0.1459	0.0969	0.0402	0.0270	−0.0925	0.1084
	p value	0.0707	0.1671	0.5558	0.6893	0.1594	0.1401
	β	0.2246	−2.0012	−0.1101	−0.3681	5.3583	−4.0288
	p value	0.4672	0.0493	0.9351	0.7711	0.0012	0.2113
Jisco Hongxing (600307)	α	0.0938	0.0470	−0.1469	−0.1565	−0.1728	0.0477
	p value	0.4866	0.6299	0.1312	0.1231	0.0896	0.8023
	β	−0.9234	−0.6771	1.8147	−0.3797	0.9971	−2.4839
	p value	0.3274	0.4988	0.1472	0.7317	0.5037	0.5429
Nanshan Aluminum (600219)	α	0.1940	0.0505	−0.0484	−0.1004	0.0611	−0.0441
	p value	0.1099	0.5635	0.6256	0.2771	0.5067	0.6583
	β	−2.7060	−0.8810	0.3622	1.4698	−4.4607	−4.6021
	p value	0.0172	0.6322	0.8326	0.3360	0.1158	0.1406
Entertainment Stock (600770)	α	−0.0912	−0.0358	−0.0104	0.0551	−0.1380	0.0457
	p value	0.3905	0.6469	0.9017	0.4919	0.0928	0.5663
	β	0.7567	−0.3113	−0.4628	−0.9651	1.8161	0.2121
	p value	0.3072	0.7474	0.6682	0.5032	0.3087	0.9045

(Continued)

Stock Name and Code	Period / Coefficient	1	3	6	12	24	48
Aseng Group (600108)	α	0.0931	0.0033	−0.1885	0.1845	0.1199	0.1880
	p value	0.3276	0.9664	0.0114	0.0204	0.1364	0.0478
	β	−0.2184	1.4791	2.2583	1.2707	−3.8685	−14.3171
	p value	0.6398	0.0072	0.0099	0.1930	0.0473	0.0036
Deep Speed (600548)	α	−0.0508	0.0099	−0.0890	−0.0496	−0.1336	0.0143
	p value	0.6978	0.9269	0.3500	0.6319	0.1868	0.8873
	β	−1.4350	−2.5494	−6.4395	2.3680	2.6020	−4.8794
	p value	0.4133	0.4005	0.0294	0.3382	0.4053	0.2385
Entrepreneurial Environmental Protection (600874)	α	0.0225	−0.0703	0.0149	0.0395	0.0309	−0.0749
	p value	0.8217	0.3431	0.8449	0.5850	0.6839	0.3326
	β	−0.3780	0.1665	−3.2902	−0.3303	−7.9929	4.0125
	p value	0.6981	0.9036	0.0897	0.8928	0.0083	0.2638
Guangzhou Shipping International (600685)	α	0.0216	0.0780	−0.0764	−0.1990	−0.1442	−0.0168
	p value	0.7774	0.2498	0.2589	0.0049	0.0366	0.8063
	β	−0.3069	0.8378	1.2021	2.9526	1.6671	−3.0201
	p value	0.0775	0.1720	0.0853	0.0472	0.4755	0.2195
China Glass Fiber (600176)	α	0.0869	−0.0526	−0.1629	−0.1216	0.0330	−0.0025
	p value	0.4471	0.5333	0.0644	0.1808	0.7369	0.9823
	β	−1.1324	1.7279	6.2229	0.4731	−3.4667	−2.7799
	p value	0.4935	0.4465	0.0217	0.8642	0.2953	0.5584
Aerospace Electronics (600879)	α	0.0503	0.1082	−0.1113	−0.0418	−0.0812	−0.0006
	p value	0.5454	0.1538	0.1434	0.5874	0.2739	0.9938
	β	−0.8130	−3.0033	1.8731	−1.9184	1.8658	0.5796
	p value	0.0386	0.0706	0.2251	0.4029	0.1410	0.7898
Aerospace Machinery (600151)	α	−0.1747	0.0553	0.0749	0.0979	−0.0883	−0.0059
	p value	0.0865	0.4995	0.3749	0.2208	0.3174	0.9453
	β	1.1516	−1.5610	−1.9298	−4.8007	1.0088	−4.4322
	p value	0.0370	0.0774	0.0279	0.0073	0.5876	0.0045
Yutong Bus (600066)	α	0.0843	−0.0058	−0.0225	0.2183	0.0566	0.1076
	p value	0.3760	0.9416	0.6767	0.0050	0.4978	0.1877
	β	−0.1373	5.3983	−0.6665	−4.7387	1.9697	0.3153
	p value	0.8634	0.1136	0.8297	0.0653	0.5369	0.9440
Xingang (600782)	α	0.1258	0.1206	−0.0366	0.1019	0.0657	0.0099
	p value	0.2433	0.1729	0.6660	0.2225	0.4342	0.9012
	β	−1.3647	−2.1608	0.0459	−0.1186	−0.0329	1.9662
	p value	0.0984	0.1360	0.9716	0.9299	0.9841	0.3834

(Continued)

Stock Name and Code	Period / Coefficient	1	3	6	12	24	48
Mass Transportation (600611)	α	−0.1747	0.0855	−0.0295	0.0072	−0.0739	−0.0752
	p value	0.0477	0.2282	0.6548	0.9051	0.2198	0.1634
	β	0.2833	0.2045	−0.1900	0.3678	−0.2834	2.8679
	p value	0.1290	0.6785	0.4385	0.6907	0.6639	0.0658
Swellfun (600779)	α	0.0958	0.0203	−0.0513	0.0083	−0.1265	−0.1488
	p value	0.2642	0.7862	0.4888	0.9116	0.1098	0.0598
	β	−0.4023	−2.4188	−0.2274	−2.9319	2.6617	4.9504
	p value	0.2256	0.3139	0.8729	0.0643	0.0986	0.1229
SIPG (600018)	α	0.0729	0.1889	−0.1298	0.0102	0.1221	−0.0405
	p value	0.5205	0.0671	0.1070	0.8979	0.1804	0.7154
	β	−0.1242	−3.0138	0.4513	−1.1650	−2.2554	−1.8854
	p value	0.0978	0.0127	0.0339	0.0724	0.3770	0.7904
Dalian Holdings (600747)	α	0.1482	−0.0779	−0.0718	0.1223	0.0648	−0.0603
	p value	0.0971	0.2996	0.3192	0.1123	0.3681	0.4063
	β	−0.7566	1.5348	2.0106	−1.0935	−1.7958	2.4130
	p value	0.0799	0.0261	0.0065	0.4162	0.0798	0.1990
Pudong Jinqiao (600639)	α	−0.1246	−0.0942	0.0129	0.0951	0.0108	−0.1448
	p value	0.1378	0.1963	0.8657	0.2134	0.8895	0.0867
	β	0.2185	0.2032	−0.7133	−2.9408	1.8087	0.2731
	p value	0.5971	0.8496	0.6737	0.1866	0.2540	0.9221
Xinhuangpu (600638)	α	−0.0867	0.0157	−0.0321	0.0445	−0.0327	−0.1011
	p value	0.2549	0.8061	0.6589	0.5032	0.6182	0.1122
	β	0.0132	−0.4270	−0.4157	−6.0635	0.8772	3.5822
	p value	0.9335	0.5131	0.8827	0.0007	0.6388	0.0106
Xining Special Steel (600117)	α	0.0591	0.0483	−0.2181	0.0141	−0.1061	−0.0471
	p value	0.5699	0.5418	0.0108	0.8614	0.2147	0.5880
	β	−0.8982	−2.6045	2.9752	−2.3820	−1.0889	0.0178
	p value	0.1993	0.0018	0.0273	0.0385	0.5184	0.9952

References

Chinese References

Cai, Chuijun, and Li Cunxiu. 2004. "An Empirical Study on the Cross Market Price Volume Information Transmission between Taiwan Stock Index and Index Futures—Price Discovery and Price Volume Relationship." *China Management Review*, no. 7.

Cao, Fengqi. 2003. *China's Capital Market Development Strategy*. Peking University Press.

Cao, Honghui. 2002. "An Analysis of the Overreaction of the Stock Market to the Reduction of State-Owned Shares." *Journal of Central University of Finance and Economics*, no. 3.

Cao, Yuanfang. 2008. "The Deviation between the Real Economy and the Virtual Economy in China—An Empirical Study Based on Data from 1998 to 2008." *Comparison of Economic and Social Systems*, no. 6.

Cen, Jian. 2011. "Reflections and Policy Suggestions on the Reform of the IPO System." *New Finance*, no. 1.

Chen, Dongqi. 1999. *Theory of New Government Intervention*. Capital University of Business and Economics Press.

Chen, Ling. 2004. "How to Improve China's Securities Regulatory System from the Perspective of Public Choice Theory." *Enterprise Economy*, no. 7.

Chen, Shoudong. 2008. *Securities Investment Theory and Analysis*. Science Press.

Cheng, Siwei. 2003. *Diagnosis and Treatment: Revealing China's Stock Market*. Economic Science Press.

Dai, Yuanchen. 2001. "The Formation Mechanism of Stock Market Foam and the Deep Thinking Triggered by the Great Debate." *Economic Research*, no. 4.

Ding, Zhiguo, and Su Zhi. 2005. "Investor Sentiment, Intrinsic Value Estimation and Securities Price Volatility—Market Sentiment Index Hypothesis." *Management World*, no. 2.

Dong, Jichang, Yu Yong, Lin Rui, and Li Xiuting. 2012. "Empirical Study on the Impact of Real Estate Price Fluctuation on Inflation in China." *Modern Management Science*, no. 7.

Du, Jiang, and Shen Shaobo. 2010. "Analysis of the Correlation between China's Stock Market and the Real Economy." *Qiusuo*, no. 5.

Fan, Gang. 1998. "The Role of the Government in Economic Development." *Economic Daily*, September 28.

Fang, Kuangnan, and Cai Zhenzhong. 2012. "Research on the Price Discovery Function of China's Stock Index Futures." *Statistical Research*, no. 5.

Franz, X. 1993. *Efficiency: Theory, Argument, and Application.* Shanghai Translation Publishing House, 1993.

Fu, Yan, and Deng Zixin. 2012. "On the Legal Path to Deepen the Reform of China's IPO System." *Securities Market Guide*, no. 5.

Gao, Hongzhen, and Lin Jiayong. 2005. "Experimental Research on Asymmetric Information Capital Market." *Economic Research*, no. 2.

Gu, Xiaorong. 1998. *Securities Crimes and Securities Violations.* China Prosecutorial Publishing House.

Guo, Kun, Zhou Weixing, and Cheng Siwei. 2012. "The Economic Barometer Role of China's Stock Market." *Journal of Management Science*, no. 1.

Han, Bing, and Yan Bing. 2004. "Empirical Analysis of China's Stock Market Dynamics and Reasonable P/E Ratio." *Journal of Shanghai University of Finance and Economics*, no. 12.

Han, Zhiguo. 2003. "China Needs a Positive Stock Market Policy." *Shanghai Securities News*, September 9.

He, Chengying, Zhang Longbin, and Chen Wei. 2011. "Research on the Price Discovery Ability of CSI 300 Index Futures Based on High Frequency Data." *Research on Quantitative Economy, Technical Economy*, no. 5.

He, Jia, He Jibao, and Liu Shengjun. 2001. "Information Disclosure of Major Events in China's Stock Market and Changes in Stock Prices." *Research Report of Shenzhen Stock Exchange*, SZZYZ No. 0044.

He, Qiang. 2003. *Research on the Interaction of China's Economic Cycle, Policy Cycle, and Stock Market Cycle.* Law Press.

He, Shaoqi. 2000. *A Legal Perspective of Securities Investment Funds.* People's Court Press.

Hu, Jinyan. 2002. "Empirical Analysis of Policy Effects, Efficiency, and Policy Market." *Economic Theory and Economic Management*, no. 8.

Huang, Huaji, and Ding Wei. 2009. "Spectral Analysis of the Interaction between China's Stock Market and Economic Cycle." *Industrial Economy Research*, no. 6.

Huang, Yong, Feng Yitao, and Chen Jinquan. 2002. "Fluctuation of P/E Ratio, Mean Reversion—A Comparison from the Chinese and American Stock Markets." *Securities Market Guide*, no. 3.

Huang, Yuhai. 2003. "Empirical Study on Insider Trading in China's Securities Market." PhD diss., Fudan University.

Jia, Li. 2006. "Analysis on the System Defects of the Stock Issuance Approval System." *Productivity Research*, no. 3.

Jiang, Huadong, and Qiao Xiaonan. 2010. "Insider Trading Supervision, Investor Trading Strategy, and Market Benefit Distribution." *Financial Research*, no. 5.

Jin, Xiaobin, Yuan Guoliang, Zheng Jianghuai, and Hu Zhiqian. 2000. "Macro Mechanism and Micro Basis of China's Stock Market Promoting Economic Growth: Hypothesis and Inspection." *Research Report of Haitong Securities Co., Ltd.*

Li, Jia, and Wang Xiao. 2010. "Empirical Study on the Efficiency of China's Stock Market—Test Method Based on Variance Ratio." *Economic Jingwei*, no. 1.

Li, Honggang, and Fu Qian. 2002. "Analysis of the Reasonable Range of China's Stock P/E Ratio." *Reform*, no. 2.

Li, Yuankui. 2005. "Excessive Intervention and Moderate Exit: Analysis of Government Behavior in China's Securities Market." *Shanghai Finance*, no. 7.

Li, Zhilin. 2002. "The Biggest Defect of Policy Market and Chinese Stock Market." *Yuehai Information Daily*, December 2.

Liang, Qi, and Teng Jianzhou. 2005. "Stock Market, Banking and Economic Growth: Empirical Analysis of China." *Financial Research*, no. 10.

Liu, Li, and Chen Xingzhu. 2001. "Research on China's Stock Market Overreaction." *Research Journal of Guanghua School of Management, Peking University*.

Liu, Jinquan. 2004. "The Econometric Test of the Association between the Virtual Economy and the Real Economy." *China Social Sciences*, no. 4.

Liu, Xibiao. 2012. "Enlightenment of Statistical Data on Long-Term Investment in Stocks." *Finance and Accounting (Financial Management Edition)*, no. 2.

Liu, Yufei. 2002. *Contemporary Western Finance*. Peking University Press. 1st ed., July.

Liu, Yuzhen, Liu Weiqi, and Xie Zhengneng. 1990. "Research on Overreaction of Taiwan Stock Market." *Science Development Monthly*, no. 19.

Lu, Kequn. 2002. "'A Well-Off Society in an All-Round Way' Must Vigorously Develop the Capital Market." *China Securities Journal*, December 10.

Lü, Jihong, and Zhao Zhenquan. 2000. "Volatility, Policy Intervention and Market Effect of China's Stock Market." In *Collection of Research on Frontier Theory of China's Capital Market*. Social Science Literature Press.

Ma, Hongchao. 2001. "Empirical Research on Speculation in China's Stock Market." *Financial Research*, no. 3.

Ma, Xide, and Zheng Zhenlong. 2006. "The Mean Regression Process of Beta Coefficient." *Industrial Technology and Economy*, no. 1.

Mills, Terence C. 2002. *Econometric Model of Financial Time Series*. Translated by Yu Zhuojing. Economic Science Press. 2nd ed.

Qi, Guanghua. 2003. "On Policy Failure in China's Securities Market Regulation." *Journal of Beijing Institute of Administration*, no. 1.

Qian, Kangning, and Jiang Jianrong. 2012. "International Comparison of Stock Issuance System and Its Reference to China." *Shanghai Finance*, no. 2.

Qiao, Guiming, and Zhan Yubo. 2002. "Game Analysis of the Behavior of the Government and Investors in China's Stock Market." *Financial Research*, no. 12.

Shen, Xiaoping. 2004. "Optimizing Stock Market Policies to Solve Stock Market Failure." *Journal of Central University of Finance and Economics*, no. 1.

———. 2004. "Review of China's Stock Market Macro-Control Views." *Economic Research Reference*, no. 87.

Shen, Yifeng, and Wu Shinong. 1999. "Is China's Securities Market Overreacting?" *Economic Research*, no. 2.

Shi, Yongdong, and Jiang Xianfeng. 2004. "Insider Trading, Stock Price Fluctuation and Information Asymmetry." *World Economy*, no. 12.

Shriver, Andre. 2003. *Not an Effective Market—Introduction to Behavioral Finance*. China Renmin University Press.

Song, Ling, and Zhang Ling. 2002. "Empirical Test of China's Securities Market Overreaction." *Journal of Hunan University (Social Science Edition)*, no. 5.

Song, Yuchen. 2012. "Defects and Solutions of Modern Financial Theory." *Social Sciences*, no. 2.

Song, Yuchen. 2006. "Stock Market Failure and the Choice of Government Behavior." PhD diss., Jilin University.

Song, Yuchen, and Kou Junsheng. 2005. "Empirical Test of Mean Regression in Shanghai and Shenzhen Stock Markets." *Financial Research*, no. 12.

Su, Zhi, and Chen Yanglong. 2012. "Research on the Efficiency of Price Discovery of Stock Index Futures Based on Morlet Wavelet Time Frequency Cross Correlation." *Research on Quantitative Economy, Technology and Economy*, no. 6.

Sun, Guomao. 2012. "Analysis of the Reasons for the Deviation between China's Stock Market and Economic Operation." *Theoretical Journal*, no. 2.

Sun, Xiaochong, Gao Feng, Ma Jingyun, and Cui Wenqian. 2005. "Is the Shanghai Composite Index Divorced from the Chinese Economy—Also on How to Improve the Shanghai Composite Index." *Financial Research*, no. 10.

Tan, Ruyong. 1999. "Empirical Study on the Relationship between China's Financial Development and Economic Growth." *Economic Research*, no. 10.

Tan, Weimin. 2001. "The Stock Market Downturn Urgently Needs Regulation." *Market News*, October 20.

Tan, Zhiqiang. 2009. "Retesting the Relationship between China's Economic Growth and the Development of the Stock Market: 2001–2007." *World Economic Situation*, no. 1.

Tang, Qiming, and Zhang Xuegong. 2005. "Analysis of the Causal Relationship between Volume and Price of China's Stock Market Based on Insider Trading." *Research on Quantitative Economy, Technical Economy*, no. 6.

———. 2006. "Determination of Excess Return on Insider Trading—A New Method and Others." *Quantitative Economics in the 21st Century* (Volume 7).

Tu, Renmeng. 2012. "Institutional Design Deviation and Reform of China's Stock Market." *Wuhan Finance*, no. 6.

Wan, Ming. 2002. "Rational Thinking on the Position of the Government in the Current Stock Market." *Journal of Zhongnan University of Economics and Law*, no. 5.

Wang, Aijian, and Chen Jie. 2006. "Research on the Scale Appropriateness of China's Virtual Economy." *Finance and Trade Economy*, no. 8.

Wang, Baishi, and Jiang Yinglai. 2008. *50 Required Investment Classics*. Beijing University of Technology Press.

Wang, Chunfeng, Jiang Xianglin, and Li Gang. 2003. "Volatility Estimation of China's Stock Market Based on Random Volatility Model." *Journal of Management Science*, no. 4.

Wang, Chunfeng, Li Shuangcheng, and Kang Li. 2003. "Empirical Study on the Overreaction of China's Stock Market and the 'Policy Market' Phenomenon." *Journal of Northwest University of Agriculture and Forestry Science and Technology (Social Science Edition)*, no. 7.

Wang, Guipu. 2002. "Research on the Information Content of Insider Trading in China's Securities Market." PhD diss., Xi'an Jiaotong University.

Wang, Guipu, Chi Renyong, and Chen Weizhong. 2004. "Information Content of Insider Trading in China's Securities Market and Comparison with Market Manipulation." *China Management Science*, no. 4.

Wang, Guogang. 2002. "Some Problems in the Current Capital Market." *Xiangcai Securities Research*, no. 1–2.

———. 2004. "Reform Plan Mechanism to Safeguard Investors' Rights and Interests." *Economic Information Daily*, January 29.

Wang, Jun. 2002. "Theoretical and Empirical Research on the Relationship between Capital Market Development and Economic Growth." *Economic Review*, no. 6.

Wang, Kaiguo. 2002. "Solving the Ten Difficulties in China's Securities Market." *Outlook Weekly*, December 10.

Wei, Weixian, and Kang Chaofeng. 2001. "Empirical Analysis of Price Volume Relationship in Shanghai Stock Market." *Forecast*, no. 6.

Wu, Ge, and Liao Jun. 2003. "'Failure' in the Securities Market: A Comparison between China and the United States." *Financial Research*, no. 5.

Wu, Jinglian. 2001. "My Views on the Securities Market." *21st Century Economic Report*, February 12.

———. 2001. "My Views on the Securities Market." *China Economic Times*, March 8.

———. 2001. *Ten Years of Stories on the Stock Market*. Shanghai Far East Press.

Wu, Mingli. 2001. "Distribution and Analysis of P/E Ratio Structure of China's Stock Market." *Research on Quantitative Economy and Technological Economy*, no. 5.

Wu, Shinong, Xu Nianxing, Cai Haihong, and Chen Weigang. 2002. "The Formation Mechanism and Measurement of Stock Market Foam." *Financial Science*, no. 4.

Wu, Weimin. 2002. "Reduction of State Owned Shares and Policy Regulation of the Stock Market." *International Financial News*, February 22.

Wu, Xiaoqiu. 1995. "China's Stock Market and Its Macro-Control Issues." *Journal of Renmin University of China*, no. 3.

Wu, Zhiwen, and Zhou Jianjun. 2005. "The Debate on the Existence of 'Stock and Economic Deviation' and Its Verification." *Financial Research*, no. 3.

Xia, Wanjun. 2004. "Game Analysis of Securities Regulation." *Journal of Anhui Normal University of Technology*, no. 2.

Xiao, Hui, Bao Jianping, and Wu Chongfeng. 2006. "Research on the Price Discovery Process of Stock Index and Stock Index Futures." *Journal of Systems Engineering*, no. 8.

Xie, Baisan. 2003. "Whether the Stock Market Can Get Rid of the Downturn Depends on Four Major Events." *Nanfang Daily*, August 18.

Xie, Zhiyu. 2001. *Economic Game Theory*. Fudan University Press. 2nd ed.

Xu, Hongyuan. 2002. "The Government Should Intervene in the Weak and Sharp Decline of the Stock Market." *Securities Guide*, February 1.

Xu, Junhua. 2001. "Empirical Study on the Impact of Macro Policies on China's Stock Market." *Economic Research*, no. 9.

Xu, Junhua, and Li Qiya. "Empirical Study on the Impact of Macro Policies on China's Stock Market." *Economic Research*, no. 9.

Yao, Feng, and Shi Ningzhong. 2003. "Econometric Analysis of Japanese Economic Development and Sino-Japanese Trade." *Journal of Management Science*, no. 4.

Yao, Feng. 2003. "Econometric Models and Methods of Dynamic Economic System Analysis." *Journal of Management Science*, no. 2.

Yi, Xianrong. 2007. "Analysis of the Basic System of China's Stock Market." *Journal of the Party School of the CPC Central Committee*, no. 8.

———. 2004. "The Domestic Stock Market Should Not Fall into the Policy Market Quagmire." *China Economic Times*, February 6.

You, Daming, and Zhou Wei. 2002. "Game Analysis of Securities Regulation." *Journal of Central South University of Technology*, no. 12.

Zeng, Xin. 2003. *Research on Moral Hazard in China's Securities Market*. Southwestern University of Finance and Economics Press.

Zeng, Yang. 2012. "On the Relationship between Public Offering and Listing." *Nanjing Social Sciences*, no. 6.

Zhang, Renji, Zhu Ping, and Wang Huaifang. 1998. "Empirical Test of Shanghai Stock Market Overreaction." *Economic Research*, no. 5.

Zhang, Rui. 2003. "Defects and Correction of Capital Market." *China Industrial and Commercial Times*, February 8.

Zhang, Xin, and Zhu Hongmei. 2003. "Economic Analysis of Insider Trading." *Economics (Quarterly)*, no. 3.

Zhang, Zongxin, and Shen Zhengyang. 2007. "Insider Manipulation, Market Reaction and Behavior Recognition." *Financial Research*, no. 6.

Zhang, Zongxin, and Yang Huaijie. 2006. "International Comparison of Insider Trading Regulation and Its Implications for China." *Contemporary Economic Research*, no. 8.

Zhao, Wenguang. n.d. "The Market Expects One Positive and Two Stable." [EB/OL] http://finance.sina.com.cn/stock/ychd/20050317/16231438847.shtml.

Zhao, Wenguang, and Qi Jianhong. 2003. "How Shareholders Understand the Relationship between 'Policy Market' and 'Market Market.'" *China Economic Times*, February 10.

Zhao, Xisan, and Zhao Bao. 2004. "To Curb Violations, 'Heavy Punishment' Is not a Long-Term Solution—On the Supervision of Securities Regulators." *Journal of Zhengzhou Institute of Technology*, no. 1.

Zhao, Xijun. 2000. *On Securities Regulation*. China Renmin University Press.

Zhao, Yulong. 1998. "Information Content of Accounting Earnings Disclosure—Empirical Evidence from Shanghai Stock Market." *Economic Research*, no. 7.

Zhao, Zhenquan, Ding Zhiguo, and Su Zhi. 2005. "Research on Asymmetry of Overreaction in China's Securities Market." *Journal of Social Sciences of Jilin University*, no. 7.

Zheng, Shunyan. 2002. *Research on Localization of Insider Trading Regulation*. Peking University Press.

Zhou, Weixing. 2007. *Introduction to Financial Physics*. Shanghai University of Finance and Economics Press.

Zhou, Xiaochuan. 2002. "Organizational Structure of China's Capital Market." Speech at the International Seminar on the "Year of China's Capital," December 5.

Zhou, Xiaohua, Zhao Weike, and Liu Xing. 2006. "Comparative Study on IPO Pricing Efficiency under China's Stock Issuance Approval System and Approval System." *Management World*, no. 11.

Zhou, Zhengqing. 2003. "Taking Effective Measures to Activate the Stock Market." *Shanghai Securities News*, April 21.

Zhu, Hongjun, and Qian Youwen. 2010. "The Riddle of High IPO Underpricing in China: 'Pricing Efficiency View' or 'Rent Distribution View'?" *Management World*, no. 6.

Zhu, Weihua. 2007. "Summary of Research on Insider Trading Regulation and Regulatory Dilemma." *Securities Market Guide*, no. 9.

Zhuo, Jialiang. 2009. "Empirical Research on India's Stock Market and Economic Growth." *World Economic Situation*, no. 1.

Zou, Haoping, Tang Limin, and Yuan Guoliang. 2000. "The Impact of Policy Factors on China's Stock Market: Game Analysis between the Government and Stock Market Investors." *World Economy*, no. 11.

English References

Agrawal, A., J. Jaffe, and G. Mandelker. 1992. "The Post-Merger Performance of Acquiring Firms: A Re-examination of an Anomaly." *Journal of Finance* 47, no. 4: 1605–1621.

Allen, B. 1982. "Strict Rational Expectations Equilibria with Diffuseness." *Journal of Economic Theory* 27, no. 1: 20–46.

Allen, F., and G. Gorton. 1993. "Churning Bubbles." *Review of Economic Studies* 60, no. 205: 813–836.

Alonso, A., and G. Rubio. 1990. "Overreaction in the Spanish Equity Market." *Journal of Banking and Finance* 14, no. 3: 469–481.

Andreou, E., N. Pittis, and A. Spanos. 2001. "On Modelling Speculative Prices: The Empirical Literature." *Journal of Economic Surveys* 15, no. 2: 187–220.

Antonios, A. 2010. "Stock Market and Economic Growth: An Empirical Analysis for Germany." *Business and Economics Journal* 4: 1–12.

Arthur, W., S. Durlauf, and D. Lane. 1997. *The Economy as an Evolving Complex System II*. Reading, MA: Addison-Wesley.

Asquith, P., R. Bruner, and D. Mullins. 1983. "The Gains to Bidding Firms from Merger." *Journal of Financial Economics* 11, no. 1–4: 121–139.

Atkins A., and E. Dyl. 1990. "Price Reversals, Bid-Ask Spreads, and Market Efficiency." *Journal of Financial and Quantitative Analysis* 25, no. 4: 535–547.

Bachelier, L. 1900. *Théorie de la speculation*. Paris: Gauthier-Villars.

Bacon, D., and D. Watts. 1971. "Estimating the Transition between Two Intersecting Straight Lines." *Biometrika* 58, no. 3: 525–534.

Ball, R. 1978. "Anomalies in Relationships between Securities' Yields and Yield-Surrogates." *Journal of Financial Economics* 6, no. 2–3: 103–126.

Ball, R., and P. Brown. 1968. "An Empirical Evaluation of Accounting Income Numbers." *Journal of Accounting Research* 6, no. 2: 159–178.

Ball, R., and S. Kothari. 1989. "Nonstationary Expected Returns: Implications for Tests of Market Efficiency and Serial Correlation in Returns." *Journal of Financial Economics* 25, no. 1: 51–74.

Balvers, R., Y. Wu, and E. Gilliland. 2000. "Mean Reversion across National Stock Markets and Parametric Contrarian Investment Strategies." *Journal of Finance* 55, no. 2: 745–772.

Banz, R. 1981. "The Relationship between Return and Market Value of Common Stocks." *Journal of Financial Economics* 9, no. 1: 3–18.

Barberis, N., and A. Shleifer. 1998. "A Model of Investor Sentiment." *Journal of Financial Economics* 49, no. 3: 307–343.

Barclay, M., R. Litzenberger, and J. Warner. 1990. "Private Information, Trading Volume and Stock-Return Variances." *Review of Financial Studies* 3, no. 2: 233–253.

Beechey, M., D. Gruen, and J. Vickery. 2000. *The Efficient Market Hypothesis: A Survey*. Reserve Bank of Australia, Economic Research Department.

Bekaert, G., and R. Hodrick. 1992. "Characterizing Predictable Components in Excess Returns on Equity and Foreign Exchange Markets." *Journal of Finance* 47, no. 2: 467–509.

Bernard, V., and J. Thomas. 1990. "Evidence that Stock Prices Do Not Fully Reflect the Implications of Current Earnings for Future Earnings." *Journal of Accounting and Economics* 13, no. 4: 305–340.

———. 1989. "Post-Earnings-Announcement Drift: Delayed Price Response or Risk Premium?" *Journal of Accounting Research* 27: 1–36.

Bernstein, L. 1991. "Opting Out of the Legal System: Extralegal Contractual Relations in the Diamond Industry." *The Journal of Legal Studies* 21, no. 1: 115–157.

Bhattacharya, U., and H. Daouk. 2002. "The World Price of Insider Trading." *Journal of Finance* 57, no. 1: 75–108.

Bhattacharya, U., and M. Spiegel. 1991. "Insiders, Outsiders and Market Breakdowns." *Review of Financial Studies* 4, no. 2: 255–282.

Black, F. 1988. *An Equilibrium Model of the Crash*. NBER Macroeconomics Annual, MIT Press, Cambridge, Massachusetts, 269–275.

Black, F., and M. Scholes. 1973. "The Pricing of Options and Corporate Liabilities." *Journal of Political Economy* 81, no. 3: 637–654.

Black, F., M. Jensen, and M. Scholes. 1972. "The Capital Asset Pricing Model: Some Empirical Tests." In *Studies in the Theory of Capital Markets*. New York: Praeger.

Blanchard, O., and M. Watson. 1982. "Bubbles, Rational Expectation, and Financial Markets." In *Working Paper*. National Bureau of Economic Research.

Boadway, R., and D. Wildasin. 1984. *Public Sector Economics*. Little, Brown and Company.

Bollerslev, T. 1986. "Generalized Autoregressive Conditional Heteroskedasticity." *Journal of Econometrics* 31, no. 3: 307–327.

Bollerslev, T., R. Chou, and K. Kroner. 1992. "ARCH Modeling in Finance: A Review of the Theory and Empirical Evidence." *Journal of Econometrics* 52, no. 1–2: 5–59.

Boswijk, H., C. Hommes, and S. Manzan. 2007. "Behavioral Heterogeneity in Stock Prices." *Journal of Economic Dynamics and Control* 31, no. 6: 1938–1970.

Bowman, R., and D. Iverson. 1998. "Short-Run Overreaction in the New Zealand Stock Market." *Pacific Basin Finance Journal* 6, no. 5: 475–491.

Buffett, W. 1986. "The Chairman's Letter to the Shareholders of Berkshine Hathaway Inc."

———. 1988. "The Chairman's Letter to the Shareholders of Berkshine Hathaway Inc."

———. 1996. "The Chairman's Letter to the Shareholders of Berkshine Hathaway Inc."

Campbell, J., A. Lo, A. MacKinlay, and R. Whitelaw. 1998. "The Econometrics of Financial Markets." *Macroeconomic Dynamics* 2, no. 4: 559–562.

Campell, J., and R. Shiller. 1987. "Cointegration and Tests of the Present Value Models." *Journal of Political Economy* 95: 1062–1088.

Chan, K. 1988. "On the Contrarian Investment Strategy." *Journal of Business* 61, no. 2: 147–163.

Chan, K., and H. Tong. 1986. "On Estimating Thresholds in Autoregressive Models." *Journal of Time Series Analysis* 7, no. 3: 179–190.

Chan, K., K. Chan, and G. Karolyi. 1991. "Intraday Volatility in the Stock Index and Stock Index Futures Markets." *Review of Financial Studies* 4, no. 4: 657–684.

Chan, L., N. Jegadeesh, and J. Lakonishok. 1996. "Momentum Strategies." *Journal of Finance* 51, no. 5: 1681–1713.

Chaudhuri, K., and Y. Wu. 2003. "Random Walk Vversus Breaking Trend in Stock Prices: Evidence from Emerging Markets." *Journal of Banking and Finance* 27, no. 4: 75–92.

Chen, S., and H. Kim. 2011. "Nonlinear Mean Reversion across National Stock Markets: Evidence from Emerging Asian Markets." *International Economic Journal* 25, no. 2: 239–250.

Chopra, N., J. Lakonishok, and J. Ritter. 1992. "Measuring Abnormal Performance: Do Stocks Overreact?" *Journal of Financial Economics* 31, no. 2: 235–268.

Chu, Q., W. Hsieh, and Y. Tse. 1999. "Price Discovery on the S&P 500 Index Markets: An Analysis of Spot Index, Index Futures, and SPDRs." *International Review of Financial Analysis* 8, no. 1: 21–34.

Conrad, J., and G. Kaul. 1993. "Long-Term Market Overreaction or Biases in Computed Returns?" *Journal of Finance* 48, no. 1: 39–63.

———. 1988. "Time-Variation in Expected Returns." *Journal of Business* 61, no. 4: 409–425.

Cooray, A. 2012. "Migrant Remittances, Financial Sector Development and the Government Ownership of Banks: Evidence from a Group of Non-OECD Economies." *Journal of International Financial Markets, Institutions and Money* 22, no. 4: 936–957.

Cox, J., and S. Ross. 1976. "The Valuation of Options for Alternative Stochastic Processes." *Journal of Financial Economics* 3, no. 1–2: 145–166.

Cusatis, P., J. Miles, and J. Woolridge. 1993. "Restructuring through Spinoffs: The Stock Market Evidence." *Journal of Finance* 33, no. 3: 293–311.

Da Costa, Newton Jr. 1994. "Overreaction in the Brazilian Stock Market." *Journal of Banking and Finance* 18, no. 4: 633–642.

Daniel, K., D. Hirshleifer, and A. Subrahmanyam. 1998. "Investor Psychology and Security Market under-and Overreactions." *Journal of Finance* 53, no. 6: 1839–1885.

De Bondt, W., and R. Thaler. 1985. "Does the Stock Market Overreact?" *Journal of Finance* 40, no. 3: 793–805.

———. 1987. "Further Evidence on Investor Overreaction and Stock Market Seasonality." *Journal of Finance* 42, no. 3: 557–581.

De Gregorio, J., and P. Guidotti. 1995. "Financial Development and Economic Growth." *World Development* 23, no. 3: 433–448.

De Long, J., A. Shleifer, L. Summers, and R. Waldmann. 1990. "Noise Trader Risk in Financial Markets." *Journal of Political Economy* 98, no. 4: 703–738.

Demsetz, H. 1968. "The Cost of Transaction." *Quarterly Journal of Economics* 82, no. 1: 33–53.

Desai, H., and P. Jain. 1997. "Long-Run Common Stock Returns Following Stock Splits and Reverse Splits." *Journal of Business* 70, no. 3: 409_433.

Dharan, B., and D. Ikenberry. 1995. "The Long-Run Negative Drift of Post-Listing Stock Returns." *Journal of Finance* 50, no. 5: 1547–1574.

Dimson, E. 1979. "Risk Measurement When Shares Are Subject to Infrequent Trading." *Journal of Financial Economics* 7, no. 2: 197–226.

Dimson, E., and M. Mussavian. 1998. "A Brief History of Market Efficiency." *European Financial Management* 4, no. 1: 91–103.

Dow, J., and G. Gorton. 1997. "Stock Market Efficiency and Economic Efficiency: Is There a Connection?" *Journal of Finance* 52, no. 3: 1087–1129.

Ederington, L., and J. Lee. 1993. "How Markets Process Information: News Releases and Volatility." *Journal of Finance* 48, no. 4: 1161–1191.

Efron, B. 1979. "Bootstrap Methods: Another Look at the Jackknife." *The Annals of Statistics* 7, no. 1: 1–26.

Engle, R. 1982. "Autoregressive Conditional Heteroscedasticity with Estimates of the Variance of United Kingdom Inflation." *Econometrica* 50, no. 4: 987–1007.

Eun, C., and S. Shim. 1989. "International Transmission of Stock Market Movements." *Journal of Financial and Quantitative Analysis* 24, no. 2: 241–256.

Fama, E. 1965. "The Behavior of Stock-Market Prices." *Journal of Business* 38, no. 1: 34–105.

———. 1970. "Efficient Capital Markets: A Review of Theory and Empirical Work." *Journal of Finance* 25, no. 2: 383–417.

———. 1991. "Efficient Capital Markets II." *Journal of Finance* 46, no. 5: 1575–1617.

———. 1976. "Forward Rates as Predictors of Future Spot Rates." *Journal of Financial Economics* 3, no. 4: 361–377.

———. 1976. "Inflation Uncertainty and Expected Returns on Treasury Bills." *Journal of Political Economy* 84, no. 3: 427–448.

———. 1998. "Market Efficiency, Long-Term Returns and Behavioral Finance." *Journal of Financial Economics* 49, no. 3: 283–306.

———. 1969. *Risk and the Evaluation of Pension Fund Portfolio Performance.* Park Ridge, III: Bank Administration Institute.

Fama, E., and K. French. 1993. "Common Risk Factors in the Returns on Stock and Bonds." *Journal of Financial Economics* 33, no. 1: 3–56.

———. 1992. "The Cross-Section of Expected Stock Returns." *Journal of Finance* 47, no. 2: 427–465

———. 1996. "Multifactor Explanations of Asset Pricing Anomalies." *Journal of Finance* 51, no. 1: 55–84.

———. 1988. "Permanent and Temporary Components of Stock Prices." *Journal of Political Economy* 96, no. 21: 246–273.

Farmer, J., and A. Lo. 1999. "Frontiers of Finance: Evolution and Efficient Markets." *Proceedings of the National Academy of Sciences* 96, no. 18: 9991–9992.

Fisher, K., and M. Statman. 1999. "A Behavioral Framework for Time Diversification." *Financial Analysts Journal* 55, no. 3: 88–97.

Fishman, M., and K. Hagerty. 1992. "Insider Trading and the Efficiency of Stock Prices." *The Rand Journal of Economics* 23, no. 1: 106–122.

Fornari, F., and A. Mele. 1997. "Weak Convergence and Distributional Assumptions for a General Class of Nonlinear ARCH Models." *Econometric Reviews* 16, no. 2: 205–227.

French, K., and R. Roll. 1986. "Stock Return Variances: The Arrival of Information and the Reaction of Traders." *Journal of Financial Economics* 17, no. 1: 5–26.

French, K., G. Schwert, and R. Stambaugh. 1987. "Expected Stock Returns and Volatility." *Journal of Financial Economics* 19, no. 1: 3–29.

Frino, A., and A. West. 2003. "The Impact of Transaction Costs on Price Discovery: Evidence from Cross-Listed Stock Index Futures Contracts." *Pacific-Basin Finance Journal* 11, no. 2: 139–151.

Fudenberg, D., and J. Tirole. 1991. *Game Theory. Cambridge: MIT Press.*

Fuller, R., L. Huberts, and M. Levinson. 1993. "Return to E/P Strategies, Higgledy-Piggledy Growth, Analysts' Forecast Errors, and Omitted Risk Factors." *Journal of Portfolio Management* 19, no. 2: 13–24.

Fung, A., and K. Lam. 2004. "Overreaction of Index Futures in Hong Kong." *Journal of Empirical Finance* 11, no. 3: 331–351.

Garbade, K., and W. Silber. 1983. "Price Movement and Price Discovery in Futures and Cash Markets." *The Review of Economics and Statistics* 65, no. 2: 289–297.

Glosten, L., and P. Milgrom. 1985. "Bid, Ask and Transaction Prices in a Specialist Market with Heterogeneously Informed Traders." *Journal of Financial Economics* 14, no. 1: 71–100.

Glosten, L., R. Jagannathan, and D. Runkle. 1993. "On the Relation between the Expected Value and the Volatility of the Nominal Excess Return on Stocks." *Journal of Finance* 48, no. 5: 1779–1801.

González-Rivera, G. 1998. "Smooth-Transition GARCH Models." *Studies in Nonlinear Dynamics and Econometrics* 3, no. 2: 61–78.

Goodhart, C., P. Hartmann, and D. Llewellyn. 1998. *Financial Regulation: Why, How, and Where Now?* London: Routledge and Bank of England.

Grishchenko, V., L. Litov, and J. Mei. 2002. *Measuring Private Information Trading in Emerging Markets.* SSRN Working Paper.

Gropp, J. 2004. "Mean Reversion of Industry Stock Returns in the US, 1926–1998." *Journal of Empirical Finance* 11, no. 4: 537–551.

Grossman, S. 1978. "Further Results on the Informational Efficiency of Competitive Stock Markets." *Journal of Economic Theory* 18, no. 1: 81–101.

———. 1976. "On the Efficiency of Competitive Stock Markets Where Trades Have Diverse Information." *Journal of Finance* 31, no. 2: 573–585.

Grossman, S., and J. Stiglitz. 1980. "On the Impossibility of Informationally Efficient Markets." *American Economics Review* 70, no. 3: 393–408.

Grossman, S., and O. Hart. 1988. "One Share-One Vote and the Market for Corporate Control." *Journal of Financial Economics* 20, no. 1–2: 175–202.

Guimaraes, R., B. Kingsman, and S. Taylor. 1989. *A Reappraisal of the Efficiency of Financial Markets.* Springer-Verlag GmbH.

Hamilton, J., and R. Susmel. 1994. "Autoregressive Conditional Heteroskedasticity and Changes in Regime." *Journal of Econometrics* 64, no. 1–2: 307–333.

Harris, L., and E. Gurel. 1986. "Price and Volume Effects Associated with Changes in the S&P 500 List: New Evidence for the Existence of Price Pressures." *Journal of Finance* 41, no. 4: 815–829.

Harris, R. 1997. "Stock Markets and Development: A Re-assessment." *European Economic Review* 41, no. 1: 139–146.

Harrison, J., and D. Kreps. 1979. "Martingales and Arbitrage in Multiperiod Securities Markets." *Journal of Economic Theory* 20, no. 3: 381–408.

Harsanyi, J. 1968. "Games with Incomplete Information Played by 'Bayesian' Players." *Management Science* 14, no. 5: 320–334.

Haugen, R. 1996. "Finance from a New Perspective." *Financial Management* 25, no. 1: 86–97.

Hellwig, M. 1980. "On the Aggregation of Information in Competitive Markets." *Journal of Economic Theory* 26, no. 3: 477–498.

Hillebrand, E. 2002. *A Mean-Reversion Theory of Stock-Market Crashes.* Stanford University, Working Paper.

Hodrick, R., and E. Prescott. 1997. "Postwar US Business Cycles: An Empirical Investigation." *Journal of Money, Credit and Banking* 29, no. 1: 1–16.

Hong, H., and J. Stein. 1999. "A Unified Theory of Underreaction, Momentum Trading and Overreaction in Asset Markets." *Journal of Finance* 54, no. 6: 2143–2184.

Huang, R., and H. Stoll. 1994. "Market Microstructure and Stock Return Predictions." *Review of Financial Studies* 7, no. 1: 179–213.

Ikenberry, D., and J. Lakonishok. 1993. "Corporate Governance through the Proxy Contest: Evidence and Implications." *Journal of Business* 66, no. 3: 405–435.

Ikenberry, D., G. Rankine, and E. Stice. 1996. "What Do Stock Splits Really Signal?" *Journal of Financial and Quantitative Analysis* 31, no. 3: 357–375.

Ikenberry, D., J. Lakonishok, and T. Vermaelen. 1995. "Market Underreaction to Open Market Share Repurchases." *Journal of Financial Economics* 39, no. 2: 181–208.

Jacklin, C., A. Kleidon, and P. Pfeiderer. 1992. "Underestimation of Portfolio Insurance and the Crash of October 1987." *Review of Financial Studies* 5, no. 1: 35–63.

Jackson, M. 1991. "Equilibrium, Price Formation, and the Value of Private Information." *Review of Financial Studies* 4, no. 1: 1–16.

Jegadeesh, N., and S. Titman. 2001. "Profitability of Momentum Strategies: An Evaluation of Alternative Explanations." *Journal of Finance* 56, no. 2: 699–720.

———. 1993. "Returns to Buying Winners and Selling Losers: Implications for Stock Market Efficiency." *Journal of Finance* 48, no. 1: 65–91.

Jegadeesh, N. 1990. "Evidence of Predictable Behavior of Security Returns." *Journal of Finance* 45, no. 3: 881–898.

———. 1991. "Seasonality in Stock Price Mean Reversion: Evidence from the US and the UK." *Journal of Finance* 46, no. 4: 1427–1444.

Jensen, M. 1968. "The Performance of Mutual Funds in the Period 1945–1964." *Journal of Finance* 23, no. 2: 389–416.

Jorge V., T. Salvador, and A. Julián. 2005. "STAR and ANN Models: Forecasting Performance on the Spanish 'Ibex-35' Stock Index." *Journal of Empirical Finance* 12, no. 3: 490–509.

Joshua, T., and W. David. 1999. "Price Discovery and Causality in the Australian Share Price Index Futures Market." *Australian Journal of Management* 24, no. 2: 97–113.

Julan, D., and W. Shang-Jin. 2004. "Does Insider Trading Raise Market Volatility?" *The Economic Journal* 114, no. 498: 916–942.

Kabir, R., and T. Vermaelen. 1996. "Insider Trading Restrictions and the Stock Market: Evidence from the Amsterdam Stock Exchange." *European Economic Review* 40, no. 8: 1591–1603.

Kahneman, D., and A. Tversky. 1979. "Prospect Theory: An Analysis of Decision under Risk." *Econometrica* 47, no. 2: 263–292.

Kapetanios, G., Y. Shin, and A. Snell. 2003. "Testing for a Unit Root in the Nonlinear STAR Framework." *Journal of Econometrics* 112, no. 2: 359–379.

Karunanayake, I., A. Valadkhani, and M. O'Brien. 2010. "Financial Crises and International Stock Market Volatility Transmission." *Australian Economic Papers* 49, no. 3: 209–221.

Kendall, M., and A. Hill. 1953. "The Analysis of Economics Time Series, Part I: Prices." *Journal of the Royal Statistical Society* 116, no. 1: 11–34.

Khandani, A., and A. Lo. 2011. "What Happened to the Quants in August 2007? Evidence from Factors and Transactions Data." *Journal of Financial Markets* 14, no. 1: 1–46.

Kim, M., C. Nelson, and R. Startz. 1991. "Mean Reversion in Stock Prices? A Reappraisal of the Empirical Evidence." *Review of Economic Studies* 58, no. 3: 515–528.

Krueger, A. 1974. "The Political Economy of the Rent-Seeking Society." *American Economic Review* 64, no. 3: 291–303.

Kryzanowski, L., and H. Zhang. 1992. "The Contrarian Investment Strategy Does Not Work in Canadian Market." *Journal of Financial and Quantitative Analysis* 27, no. 3: 383–395.

Laffont, J., and E. Maskin. 1990. "The Efficient Market Hypothesis and Insider Trading on the Stock Market." *Journal of Political Economy* 98, no. 1: 70–93.

Lakonishok, J., and T. Vermaelen. 1990. "Anomalous Price Behavior around Repurchase Tender Offers." *Journal of Finance* 45, no. 2: 455–477.

Lakonishok, J., A. Shleifer, and R. Vishny. 1994. "Contrarian Investment, Extrapolation, and Risk." *Journal of Finance* 49, no. 5: 1541–1578.

Lehman, B. 1990. "Fads, Martingales and Market Efficiency." *Quarterly Journal of Economics* 105, no. 1: 1–28.

Leland, H. 1992. "Insider Trading: Should It Be Prohibited?" *Journal of Political Economy* 10, no. 4: 859–887.

LeRoy, S. 1989. "Efficient Capital Markets and Martingales." *Journal of Economic Literature* 27, no. 4: 1583–1621.

LeRoy, S., and R. Porter. 1981. "The Present-Value Relation: Tests Based on Implied Variance Bounds." *Econometrica* 49, no. 3: 555–574.

Levine, R., and S. Zervos. 1998. "Stock Markets, Banks and Economic Growth." *American Economic Review* 88, no. 3: 537–558.

Lewellen, J., and J. Shanken. 2002. "Learning, Asset-Pricing Tests and Market Efficiency." *Journal of Finance* 57, no. 3: 1113–1145.

Lihara, Y., K. Kato, and T. Tokunaga. 1996. "Intraday Return Dynamics between the Cash and the Futures Markets in Japan." *Journal of Futures Markets* 16, no. 2: 147–162.

Lim, K., and V., Liew. 2007. "Nonlinear Mean Reversion in Stock Prices: Evidence from Asian Markets." *Applied Financial Economics Letters* 3, no. 1–3: 25–29.

Lintner, J. 1965. "The Valuation of Risk Assets and the Selection of Risky Investments in Stock Portfolios and Capital Budgets." *The Review of Economics and Statistics* 47, no. 1: 13–37.

Llorente, G., R. Michaely, G. Saar, and J. Wang. 2002. "Dynamic Volume-Return Relation of Individual Stocks." *Review of Financial Studies* 15, no. 4: 1005–1047.

Lo, A. 1997. *Market Efficiency: Stock Market Behaviour in Theory and Practice.* Edward Elgar Publishing.

Lo, A., and A. MacKinlay. 1999. *A Non-random Walk down Wall Street.* Princeton University Press.

———. 1989. "The Size and Power of the Variance Ratio Test in Finite Samples: A Monte Carlo Investigation." *Journal of Econometrics* 40, no. 2: 203–238.

———. 1988. "Stock Market Prices Do Not Follow Random Walks: Evidence from a Simple Specification Test." *Review of Financial Studies* 1, no. 1: 41–66.

Lo, A., and C. MacKinlay. "Data-Snooping Biases in Tests of Financial Asset Pricing Models." *Review of Financial Studies* 3, no. 3: 431–467.

Loughran, T., and J. Ritter. 1995. "The New Issues Puzzle." *Journal of Finance* 50, no. 1: 23–51.

Lucas, R. 1972. "Expectations and the Neutrality of Money." *Journal of Economic Theory* 4, no. 2: 103–124.

Luo, B., L. Sun, and R. Mweene. 2005. "The Evolvement and Relevant Factors of Price Discovery: A Case Study of Cross-Listed Stocks in China." *Expert Systems with Applications* 29, no. 2: 463–471.

Madhavan, A. 1992. "Trading Mechanisms in Securities Markets." *Journal of Finance* 47, no. 2: 607–641.

Madrigal, V., and S. Smith. 1995. "On Full Revealing Price When Markets Are Incomplete." *The American Economic Review* 85, no. 5.

Malkiel, B. 1992. *Efficient Market Hypothesis.* New Palgrave Dictionary of Money and Finance, Macmillan, London.

Malkiel, B. 2003. "The Efficient Market Hypothesis and Its Critics." *Journal of Economic Perspectives* 17, no. 1: 59–82.

Malkiel, B., and A. Saha. 2005. "Hedge Funds: Risk and Return." *Financial Analysts Journal* 61, no. 6: 80–88.

Malliaropulosa, D., and R. Priestley. 1999. "Mean Reversion in Southeast Asian Stock Markets." *Journal of Empirical Finance* 6, no. 4: 355–384.

Mandelbrot, B. 1966. "Forecasts of Future Prices, Unbiased Markets, and 'Martingale' Models." *Journal of Business* 39, no. 1: 242–255.

Manne, H. 1966. *Insider Trading and Stock Market.* New York: Free Press.

Manove, M. 1989. "The Harm from Insider Trading and Informed Speculation." *Quarterly Journal of Economics* 104, no. 4: 823–845.

Marsh, T., and R. Merton. 1986. "Dividend Variability and Variance Bounds Tests for the Rationality of Stock Market Prices." *The American Economic Review* 76, no. 3: 483–498.

Martin, U., and R. Albrecht. 2009. "Stock Markets and Business Cycle Comovement in Germany before World War I: Evidence from Spectral Analysis." *Journal of Macroeconomics* 31, no. 1: 35–57.

McCauley, J., K. Bassler, and G. Gunaratne. 2008. "Martingales, Detrending Data and the Efficient Market Hypothesis." *Physica* 387, no. 1: 202–216.

McQueen, G. 1992. "Long-Horizon Mean-Reverting Stock Prices Revisited." *Journal of Financial and Quantitative Analysis*, 27, no. 1: 1–18.

Metcalf, G., and B. Malkiel. 1994. "*The Wall Street Journal* Contests: The Experts, the Darts, and the Efficient Market Hypothesis." *Applied Financial Economics* 4, no. 5: 371–374.

Michaely, R., R. Thaler, and K. Womack. 1995. "Price Reactions to Dividend Initiations and Omissions: Overreaction or Drift?" *Journal of Finance* 50, no. 2: 573–608.

Milgrom, P., and N. Stokey. 1982. "Information, Trade, and Common Knowledge." *Journal of Economic Theory* 26, no. 1: 17–27.

Mitchell, M., and E. Stafford. 2000. "Managerial Decisions and Long-Term Stock Price Performance." *Journal of Business* 73, no. 3: 287–329.

Mitchell, M., and J. Netter. 1989. "Triggering the 1987 Stock Market Crash: Antitakeover Provisions in the Proposed House Ways and Means Tax Bill?" *Journal of Financial Economics* 24, no. 1: 37–68.

Mitchell, R., and L. Ricardo. 1998. *Evidence of Short-Term Price Reversals Following Large One-Day Movements in the Emerging Markets of Latin America and Asia*. Rider University, Working Paper.

Monoyios, M., and L. Sarno. 2002. "Mean Reversion in Stock Index Futures Markets: A Nonlinear Analysis." *Journal of Futures Markets* 22, no. 4: 285–314.

Mossin, J. 1966. "Equilibrium in a Capital Asset Market." *Econometrica* 34, no. 4: 768–783.

Nam, K., C. Pyun, and A. Arize. 2002. "Asymmetric Mean-Reversion and Contrarian Profits: ANST-GARCH Approach." *Journal of Empirical Finance* 9, no. 5: 563–588.

Nam, K., C. Pyun, and S. Avard. 2001. "Asymmetric Reverting Behavior of Short-Horizon Stock Returns: An Evidence of Stock Market Overreaction." *Journal of Banking and Finance* 25, no. 4: 807–824.

Nash, J. 1950. "Equilibrium Points in N-Person Games." *Proceedings of the National Academy of Sciences* 36, no. 1: 48–49.

Nazir, M., M. Nawaz, and U. Gilani. 2010. "Relationship between Economic Growth and Stock Market Development." *African Journal of Business Management* 4, no. 16: 3473–3479.

Neumann, J., and O. Morgenstern. 1944. *The Theory of Games and Economic Behavior*. Princeton University Press.

Nicholas, B., and S. Andrei. 1998. "A Model of Investor Sentiment." *Journal of Financial Economics* 49, no. 3: 307–343.

Niederhoffer, V., and M. Osborne. 1966. "Market Making and Reversal on the Stock Exchange." *Journal of the American Statistical Association* 61, no. 316: 897–916.

Nofsinger, J., and R. Sias. 1999. "Herding and Feedback Trading by Institutional and Individual Investors." *Journal of Finance* 54, no. 6: 2263–2295.

Nurudeen, A. 2009. "Does Stock Market Development Raise Economic Growth? Evidence from Nigeria." *The Review of Finance and Banking* 1, no. 1: 15–26.

Odhiambo, N. 1997. *Stock Market Development and Economic Growth in South Africa: An ARDL-Bounds Testing Approach.* SA Financial Sector Forum, Working Paper.

Osborne, M. 1977. *The Stock Market and Finance from a Physicist's Viewpoint.* Crossgar Press.

Pericli, A., and G. Koutmos. 1997. "Index Futures and Options and Stock Market Volatility." *Journal of Futures Markets* 17, no. 8: 957–974.

Poterba, J., and L. Summers. 1988. "Mean Reversion in Stock Prices: Evidence and Implications." *Journal of Financial Economics* 22, no. 1: 27–59.

———. 1986. "Reporting Errors and Labor Market Dynamics." *Econometrica* 54, no. 6: 1319–1338.

Radner, R. 1972. "Existence of Equilibrium of Plans, Prices and Price Expectations in a Sequence of Markets." *Econometrica* 40, no. 2: 289–303.

———. 1979. "Rational Expectations Equilibrium: Generic Existence and the Information Revealed by Prices." *Econometrica* 47, no. 3: 655–678.

Raymond, A., and J. Boyan. 1993. "Stock Markets and Development." *European Economic Review* 37, no. 2–3: 632–640.

Repullo, R. 1999. "Some Remarks on Leland's Model of Insider Trading." *Economica* 66, no. 3: 359–374.

Richardson, M., and J. Stock. 1989. "Drawing Inferences from Statistics Based on Multiyear Asset Returns." *Journal of Financial Economics* 25, no. 2: 323–348.

Richardson, M. 1993. "Temporary Components of Stock Prices: A Skeptics View." *Journal of Business and Economic Statistics* 11, no. 2: 199–207.

Ritter, J. 1991. "The Long-Run Performance of Initial Public Offerings." *Journal of Finance* 46, no. 1: 3–27.

Roberts, H. 1967. *Statistical Versus Clinical Prediction of the Stock Market.* Unpublished paper presented to the Seminar on the Analysis of Security Prices, University of Chicago.

Roberts, H. 1959. "Stock-Market Patterns and Financial Analysis: Methodological Suggestions." *Journal of Finance* 14, no. 1: 1–10.

Roll, R. 1984. "A Simple Implicit Measure of the Effective Bid-Ask Spread in an Efficient Market." *Journal of Finance* 39, no. 4: 1127–1139.

Ross, S. 1976. "The Arbitrage Theory of Capital Asset Pricing." *Journal of Economic Theory* 13, no. 3: 341–360.

Rouwenhorst, K. 1998. "International Momentum Strategies." *Journal of Finance* 53, no. 1: 267–284.

————. 1999. "Local Return Factors and Turnover in Emerging Stock Markets." *Journal of Finance* 54, no. 4: 1439–1464.

Rubinstein, M., and P. Stephens. 2001. "Rational Markets: Yes or No? The Affirmative Case." *Financial Analysts Journal* 57, no. 3: 15–29.

Salisu, A., and K. Ajide. 2010. "The Stock Market and Economic Growth in Nigeria: A Empirical Investigation." *Journal of Economic Theory* 4, no. 2: 65–70.

Samuelson, P. 1958. "An Exact Consumption-Loan Model of Interest with or without the Social Contrivance of Money." *Journal of Political Economy* 66, no. 6: 467–482.

————. 1965. "Proof That Properly Anticipated Prices Fluctuate Randomly." *Industrial Management Review* 6, no. 1: 41–49.

Scheiber, P., and R. Schwartz. 1986. "Price Discovery in Security Market." *Journal of Portfolio Management* 12, no. 4: 43–48.

Schwert, G. 2002. *Anomalies and Market Efficiency*. NBER *Working Papers*, No. 9277.

Selten, R. 1965. "Spieltheoretische Behandlung Eines Oligopolmodells Mit Nachfragetr Gheit." *Journal of Institutional and Theoretical Economics* 131, no. 2: 301–324.

Sentana, E., and S. Wadhwani. 1992. "Feedback Traders and Stock Return Autocorrelations: Evidence from a Century of Daily Data." *The Economic Journal* 102, no. 411: 415–425.

Shafer, G., and V. Vovk. 2001. *Probability and Finance: It's Only a Game*. Wiley & Sons.

Sharpe, W. 1964. "Capital Asset Prices: A Theory of Market Equilibrium under Conditions of Risk." *Journal of Finance* 19, no. 3: 425–442.

Shefrin, H., and M. Statman. 1994. "Behavioral Capital Asset Pricing Theory." *Journal of Financial and Quantitative Analysis* 29, no. 3: 323–349.

————. 2000. "Behavioral Portfolio Theory." *Journal of Financial and Quantitative Analysis* 35, no. 2: 127–151.

Shiller, R. 1981. "Do Stock Prices Move Too Much to Be Justified by Subsequent Changes in Dividends?" *The American Economic Review* 71, no. 3: 421–436.

————. 1987. *Investor Behavior in the October 1987 Stock Market Crash: Survey Evidence*. NBER Working Paper.

————. 2000. *Irrational exuberance*. Princeton University Press.

————. 1981. "The Use of Volatility Measures in Assessing Market Efficiency." *Journal of Finance* 36, no. 2: 291–304.

————. 1979. "The Volatility of Long-Term Interest Rates and Expectations Models of the Term Structure." *Journal of Political Economy* 87, no. 6: 1190–1219.

Shleifer, A. 2000. *Inefficient Markets: An Introduction to Behavioral Finance*. Oxford University Press.

Shleifer, A., and R. Vishny. 1986. "Large Shareholders and Corporate Control." *Journal of Political Economy* 94, no. 3: 461–488.

Sornette, D., and W. Zhou. 2005. "Non-parametric Determination of Real-Time Lag Structure between Two Time Series: The Optimal Thermal Causal Path & Close Curly Quote Method." *Quantitative Finance* 5, no. 6: 577–591.

Spies, D., and J. Affleck-Graves. 1995. "Underperformance in Long-Run Stock Returns Following Seasoned Equity Offerings." *Journal of Financial Economics* 38, no. 3: 243–267.

Stambaugh, R. 1986. *Bias in Regression with Lagged Stochastic Regressors*. University of Chicago, Working Paper.

Stiglitz, J., and A. Weiss. 1981. "Credit Rationing in Markets with Imperfect Information." *The American Economic Review* 71, no. 3: 393–410.

Su, Y., Y. Yip, and R. Wong. 2002. "The Impact of Government Intervention on Stock Returns Evidence from Hong Kong." *International Review of Economics and Finance* 11, no. 3: 277–297.

Summers, L. 1986. "Does the Stock Market Rationally Reflect Fundamental Values?" *Journal of Finance* 41, no. 3: 591–601.

Tachiwou, A. 2010. "Stock Market Development and Economic Growth: The Case of West African Monetary Union." *International Journal of Economics and Finance* 2, no. 3: 97–103.

Terasvirta, T., and H. Anderson. 1992. "Characterizing Nonlinearities in Business Cycles Using Smooth Transition Autoregressive Models." *Journal of Applied Econometrics* 12: S119–S136.

Thaler, R. 1980. "Toward a Positive Theory of Consumer Choice." *Journal of Economic Behavior and Organization* 1, no. 1: 39–60.

Timmermann, A., and C. Granger. 2004. "Efficient Market Hypothesis and Forecasting." *International Journal of Forecasting* 20, no. 1: 15–27.

Tirole, J. 1982. "On the Possibility of Speculation under Rational Expectations." *Econometrica* 50, no. 5: 1163–1181.

Tóth, B., and J. Kertész. 2006. "Increasing Market Efficiency: Evolution of Cross-Correlations of Stock Returns." *Physica* 360, no. 2: 505–515.

Turner, C., R. Startz, and C. Nelson. 1989. "A Markov Model of Heteroskedasticity, Risk, and Learning in the Stock Market." *Journal of Financial Economics* 25, no. 1: 3–22.

Vermanelen, T., and M. Verstringe. 1986. *Do Belgians Overreact?* University of Louvain, Belgiun, Working Paper, 1986.

Wahab, M., and M. Lashgari. 1993. "Price Dynamics and Error Correction in Stock Index and Stock Index Futures Markets—A Cointegration Approach: Introduction." *Journal of Futures Markets* 13, no. 7: 711–742.

West, K. 1988. "Bubbles, Fads, and Stock Price Volatility Tests: A Partial Evaluation." *Journal of Finance* 43, no. 3: 639–656.

White, E. 1990. "The Stock Market Boom and Crash of 1929 Revisited." *The Journal of Economic Perspectives* 4, no. 2: 67–83.

Wichern D., R. Miller, and D. Hsu. 1976. "Changes of Variance in First-Order Autoregressive Time Series Models—With an Application. *Journal of the Royal Statistical Society* 25, no. 3: 248–256.

Wu, J., H. Hou, and S. Cheng. 2010. "The Dynamic Impacts of Financial Institutions on Economic Growth: Evidence from the European Union." *Journal of Macroeconomics* 32, no. 3: 879–891.

Zarowin, P. 1989. "Does the Stock Market Overreact to Corporate Earning Information?" *Journal of Finance* 44, no. 5: 1385–1399.

Index

SONG YUCHEN, born in 1965, is a distinguished professor of finance and a recognized doctoral supervisor focusing on quantitative economics. He holds a prestigious position in the Department of Applied Finance at the School of Business and Management, Jilin University. Additionally, he is honored as a leading professor under the esteemed "Kuang Yaming Scholar Awards" at Jilin University, a recognition that underscores his substantial contributions to the field.

Professor Song has dedicated his academic career to the rigorous exploration of financial markets, investment theory, and asset pricing. His seminal work involves the innovative proposition and construction of the Market Efficient Cycle Theory, which seeks to amend the classical Fama Efficient Market Hypothesis. By applying this groundbreaking theory, he addresses the persistent dual divergence between financial investment theory and real-world investment practices. This divergence manifests as a disconnection between standard and behavioral finance and a schism between theoretical constructs and practical applications in finance.

In a direct response to traditional financial paradigms that advocate for "rational individuals" and "risk-free arbitrage," along with behavioral finance's notions of "bounded rationality" and "limited arbitrage," Professor Song introduces two revolutionary concepts: "long-term rationality" and "long-term risk-free arbitrage." He meticulously explores the practical applicability of the Market Efficient Cycle Theory from six diverse angles, thereby enhancing the depth and breadth of its real-world relevance.

As a prolific scholar, Professor Song is the esteemed author of *Market Efficient Cycle Theory: Construction, Empirical Study, and Application*, a significant work selected for inclusion in the 2014 National Library of Philosophy and Social Sciences. His scholarly prowess is further evidenced by his extensive publication record, with over 80 papers featured in reputable journals such as the *Journal of Financial Research* and the *Journal of Quantitative & Technological Economics*. Through his publications, Professor Song continues to shape the discourse in finance, bridging theoretical insights with practical implications to foster a deeper understanding of modern financial systems.

ZHANG CHAOHUI, born in 1973, is an esteemed Associate Professor, dedicated Doctoral Supervisor, and distinguished Postdoctoral Fellow in Quantitative Economics, primarily focusing on Information Management and E-commerce. His international academic pursuits include a tenure as a visiting scholar at the Terry College of Business, University of Georgia, USA (2010–2011) and a fellowship at the School of Business and Information Technology, Ontario Institute  of Technology, Canada (2019–2020). With a solid theoretical and methodological foundation, Professor Zhang's extensive experience in Management Science and E-commerce has positioned him as a seasoned educator and prolific researcher. His scholarly endeavors are reflected through over 20 publications in reputable journals such as *Sustainability*, *Studies in Science of Science*, and *Management Review*. Professor Zhang has led significant projects to leverage digital technology to transform and upgrade traditional industries in Jilin Province, notably developing and implementing a *Digital Entrepreneurship Ecosystem Model*. His work continually bridges the theoretical and practical divides in his field, fostering meaningful collaborations between academia, industry, and policy-making entities and significantly contributing to the evolving discourse in Information Management and E-commerce on national and international platforms.